W9-DBI-887

THE ART CIRCLE:

A Theory of Art

George Dickie

Haven Publications

THE ART CIRCLE
George Dickie
Copyright © 1984 by Haven Publications. Published in 1984.
ISBN #0-930586-29-8
Library of Congress Catalogue #83-083295
Printed in the United States of America. All rights reserved.
Published by Haven Publishing Corporation
G.P.O. Box 2046
New York, N.Y. 10001

For Monroe Beardsley
For Suzanne

CONTENTS

PREFACE

In Chapters I and VII of *Art and the Aesthetic* I advanced what I called "the institutional theory of art." In spite of its curious name, the theory attracted a great deal of attention—attention sufficient after a short time to leave the institutional theory a thing of shreds and pieces. *The Art Circle* is my attempt to pick up the pieces, rework them, and put them back together.

A great many people read all or part of the manuscript of this book at various stages of its development and gave me their comments. I thank them for their help.

My greatest debt is to Monroe Beardsley who read each chapter as it was written and provided me with invaluable comments and encouragement.

The following persons read the whole manuscript and gave me many useful suggestions: James Fletcher of George Mason University, Arthur Fine of the University of Illinois at Chicago Circle, Jeffrey Wieand of the University of Chicago, Suzanne Cunningham of Loyola University of Chicago, Marcia Eaton of the University of Minnesota, Peter Kivy of Rutgers University, James D. Carney of Arizona State University, Douglas Stalker of the University of Delaware, James C. Anderson of the University of Akron, and Mark Johnson of Southern Illinois University. I thank Robert Bouson of Loyola University of Chicago and Elmer Duncan of Baylor University for their comments on Chapter III and Carolyn Korsmeyer of S.U.N.Y. of Buffalo and Robert Schultz for their comments on Chapter VI.

I thank Kendall D'Andrade, Ernest Force, Michael Kelly, Benita Kitching, and Judy Walter who were members of my 1977 graduate seminar in aesthetics and who studied with me the many criticisms of *Art and the Aesthetic*.

I thank Peggy Brand, Bobbie Gene Christensen, Steve Kovalec, Vicki Limas, Alan Nelson, Richard Reed, and Donald Stahl who were members of my 1980 graduate seminar in aesthetics and who read and criticized an earlier version of *The Art Circle*. Special thanks are due Alan Nelson and Steve Kovalec for their exceptionally forceful and useful criticisms.

Time to write the first draft of this book during 1978–79 was made possible by a sabbatical leave granted by the University of Illinois and by a John Simon Guggenheim Fellowship.

George Dickie
Wilmette, Illinois

Degas

Chapter I   Introduction

Part I   The Philosophy of Art

Philosophizing about the nature of art begins, as so much in philosophy does, with Plato. Theorizing about art was never a primary concern for Plato but something done as a means to a larger and for him more important end. In *The Republic,* for example, Plato finds it necessary to say a little about art because he thinks art has dangerous effects on people, and he is there concerned with the organization of people in an ideal society. For the most part, philosophers until fairly recently have followed Plato's lead and have not made the philosophy of art the center of their attention. Both what little Plato did say about art and the philosophical method he used have had, however, long-lasting effects on philosophical thinking about art.

What Plato said about art is that it is imitation. This claim cannot be a definition of "art," since if it is treated as a definition, it *identifies* art with imitation, but not every imitation is art. Plato's claim is at best a partial definition, that is, a contention that imitation is a necessary condition of being art. If Plato had had a primary theoretical interest in art, perhaps he would have attempted to specify

3

a second condition or a set of further conditions which would distinguish those imitations which are art from those which are not. If he had made this specification, then we would have a Platonic theory of art.

What Plato was interested in doing in *The Republic* was to show how the nature of art justifies his severe attitude toward it and the strict controls he wanted to place on it. That a work of art is an imitation is, Plato claims, a kind of defect. A painting of a chair is less real than the chair it is a painting of, since it is at one remove from the chair. Furthermore, according to Plato, a chair is an object in the world of sense and undergoes constant change. The chair's Form, by contrast, is an object in the ideal realm and is eternal and unchanging. For Plato, a chair is thus less real than its Form. Plato speaks of physical objects (chairs and tables) as being *imitations* of the nonspatial, nontemporal Forms (Chairness and Tableness). Consequently, a painting of a chair or of anything else is twice removed from Platonic reality—the world of Forms; a painting is thus doubly defective. What Plato could have noted but did not is that works of art, like everything else in the world of sense, are directly related to the Forms. A work of art has to "imitate" the Form of Art and the Form of Imitation, since it is an instance of both art and imitation. Even if, however, a work of art has this more direct relation to the Forms (given Plato's theory), it would still have the more circuitous route to the Forms through what it represents in the world of sense. Plato, determined to find fault with art, would still no doubt regard the circuitous route through the world of sense as a defect for art. In addition to this metaphysical defect, there is another problem with art for Plato; he held that the creation and transmission of art inherently involves emotion and that this involvement produces dangerous effects in spectators. Plato has, therefore, two reasons to justify his severe attitude toward art and his advocacy of stringent controls for it.

The authority of Plato fixed the imitation theory of art in the minds of almost everyone as the correct account for more than 2000 years, or perhaps it was just the lack of interest in the philosophy of art that allowed such a clearly inadequate account to become the received view of the nature of art. The imitation theory of art, with all of its inadequacies as a theory, has then been around influencing thinking about art for a very long time. Even so, it is not clear that any philosopher has really held the imitation theory of art in a completely conscious way. The imitation theory of art has for a long time been "in the air" without being examined, defended, or even seriously thought about.

Plato's way of philosophizing about art (and other things) has had an even more pervasive and long-lasting influence than his view that art is imitation. Plato's way of drawing philosophical conclusions

4

has as its basis insight into the nature of the Forms. This insight takes two forms: a complete insight and an incomplete insight. Incomplete insight occurs when someone has sufficient insight into the nature of a Form to know that a proposed definition is inadequate. For example, the ability to see that a proposed definition of "justice" is faulty presupposes some insight into the nature of the Form of Justice, although not necessarily enough insight to give a correct definition of "justice." The ability to see that a counterexample to a definition is a counterexample and that, therefore, the definition is inadequate also involves at least this partial insight. Complete insight occurs when someone has sufficient insight into the nature of a Form to know that a proposed definition is adequate. For example, the ability to see that a proposed definition of "justice" is correct presupposes complete insight into the nature of the Form of Justice. What Plato's method supposedly yields when complete insight is achieved is knowledge of the real essence of a thing. Such knowledge, for example, presumes to be the foundation for Plato's account of a just society in *The Republic*.

Plato's method of seeking definitions which reveal essences by means of philosophical reflection became the method of many philosophers. When finally in the nineteenth century some philosophers began seriously to think about the nature of art, they did so by seeking a definition which catches the essence of art by means of philosophical reflection. The first theory to challenge the imitation theory was the expression theory of art. It is ironic that one of the things which Plato alleged to be an invariant feature of art and regarded as socially dangerous—its inherent connection with emotion—was seized upon by the expressionists as the essence of art. These nineteenth-century theorists held that the expression of emotion is the essence of art. Whether the expressionist theories succeed better than the imitation theory is not something with which I will concern myself here. I am here concerned with the persistence of a method. Once the hold of the imitation theory was broken in the nineteenth century, innumerable theories of the essence of art were brought forth. What seems to have happened when philosophers of art sought the essence of art is that they have simply taken a feature of art which was prominent or had seized the imagination at a particular historical time to be the essence of art. Thus have transient features of art been frozen into definitions and passed off as essences.

It is the discovery-of-the-essence-of-art-by-reflection method that first Paul Ziff and later Morris Weitz attacked in the 1950s.[1] They both urge us to look at the usages of the expressions "art" and "work of art" and to draw our conclusions about the definability of "art" or "work of art" on the basis of these linguistic data. The conclusions they draw are that there is no essence of art and, therefore, that no

5

definition of the traditional kind can be given of "art." As part of their conclusion they agree that there is no one condition or set of conditions which is necessary for something's being art; there is no essence which runs through every work of art.

The Ziff/Weitz challenge to the Platonic method of the earlier theorizing about art is important and enlightening. Their conclusions, however, that there is no necessary condition of art and, consequently, that there can be no definition of "art" in terms of necessary and sufficient conditions requires careful scrutiny. There may not be any Platonic essence which fixes and defines "art" and which can be discovered by philosophical reflection or intuition, but this does not mean that we cannot discover necessary and sufficient conditions of art by a careful attention to those human activities which are the arts. The institutional theory is an attempt to state such conditions for art.

The traditional theories of art are overly simple and too narrowly focused. The imitation theory focuses simply on subject matter, although it clearly implies a creator of the art. The expression theory is artist-centered. The imitation theory places the work of art within a two-place network between artist and subject matter. The expression theory places the work of art in a one-place relation to an artist. Subsequent theories of art place the work of art in similar simple networks of relations. The institutional theory attempts to place the work of art within a multi-placed network of much greater complexity than anything envisaged by the earlier theories. I turn now to a preliminary discussion of the institutional theory.

Part II   The Institutional Theory of Art

The version of the institutional theory of art which was worked out over a period of years and which was set forth most fully in Chapters I and VII of *Art and the Aesthetic* I now regard as mistaken in a great many of its details. I believe, however, that the institutional approach to the understanding of art is a viable one. By an institutional approach I mean the idea that works of art are art as a result of the position they occupy within an institutional framework or context. The institutional theory is, then, a kind of *contextual* theory. All, or almost all, of the traditional theories of art are, I shall suggest in Chapter IV, contextual theories of one kind or another. A pervasive difficulty of the traditional theories is that the contexts they imply are too "thin" to be sufficient. In this book I attempt to present a revised version of the institutional theory in which the defects of the earlier version are corrected and which provides a context "thick" enough to do the job. I realize the virtual impossibility of *proving* a positive philosophical thesis which is worked out in any detail at all. Still, I hope that the arguments and insights advanced in the book give enough support to make the institutional theory plausible enough to be taken seriously.

My realization of the need for revising the theory is largely the result of objections raised by its critics. The bulk of the changes are the result of consciously taking account of the criticisms of Monroe Beardsley, Timothy Binkley, Ted Cohen, James Fletcher, Peter Kivy, Colin Lyas, Robert Schultz, Kendall Walton and Jeffrey Wieand. Some of the changes are without doubt the result of the remarks of critics I have taken account of in a less conscious way. I am grateful to all of these critics.

7

Before indicating in a general way what the changes in the theory are to be, it will be useful first to have a summary statement of the old version of the institutional theory of art as it appeared in *Art and the Aesthetic* and then to note some misinterpretations of aspects of the earlier version some of which might well recur with the new version unless they are forestalled. Some of these misinterpretations are due to simple misreading, but many are probably due to the unclarity of my writing.

The summary statement of the old version can begin with the definition of "work of art" which was given in *Art and the Aesthetic*.

A work of art in the classificatory sense is (1) an artifact (2) a set of the aspects of which has had conferred upon it the status of candidate for appreciation by some person or persons acting on behalf of a certain social institution (the artworld).

First, the definition purports to be of a classificatory sense of "work of art," which is to be contrasted with an evaluative sense of the term. Some traditional theories build value into the notion of art. While I do not deny that "art" and "work of art" can be used in an evaluative way, I believe that there is a more basic, classificatory theory of art to be worked out.

Second, the first condition of art specified by the definition is artifactuality. As noted earlier, Ziff and Weitz deny that any condition is necessary for being art; they specifically deny that being an artifact is required for art. Their rejection of artifactuality seems to fly in the face of all (or virtually all) of the traditional theories of art as well as the ordinary view of people in general. The institutional theory attempts in this case to defend the ordinary view.

Third, the second condition of art specified by the definition is supposed to distinguish those artifacts which are works of art from the host of artifacts which are not art. Roughly, what this condition says is that works of art are those artifacts which have a set of properties which have acquired a certain status within a particular institutional framework called "the artworld." Further, it is claimed by the definition that this status is acquired by being conferred by someone and that it is conferred by someone acting on behalf of the artworld.

I now turn to misinterpretations of the older version of the institutional theory. A few readers misunderstood me to be using the expression "the artworld" to refer to the kind of chic cliques of the sort discussed by Tom Wolfe in *The Painted Word:* the powerful groups which have so much to say about which paintings get hung, which music gets performed, and the like. I, however, was not and am not at all concerned with the politics of success on the art scene but rather with the nature of art and the kind of context which is required for its creation. There is no basis at all for this misreading.

More readers mistakenly thought I conceived of the artworld as a formally organized body, perhaps of a kind which has meetings and requires a quorum to do business. My intent, however, was to give an account of the artworld as the broad, informal cultural practice that I conceive it to be. This misunderstanding was in large part due to my use of the expressions "conferred upon" and "acting on behalf of" in my definition of "work of art," phrases which so readily make one think of official bodies making and carrying out policy decisions. Also, many of the analogies I used involved formal organizations acting (a state, a university, and the like). It was the analogies perhaps which seduced me into using the misleading expressions and notions. A related misunderstanding of some readers is their conclusion that I thought that it is the artworld acting as a whole which makes art or at least that in some cases this happened. My intention was to claim that it is individual persons who typically make works of art or that in some cases it is groups of persons who make art, as for example when a group of people make a movie. My intent was to claim that the artworld as a whole is the background against which art is created. Again, it was my use of "conferred upon" and "acting on behalf of" which helps the misunderstanding along. It would have been far better for me to have written of artists working with the artworld as background rather than of artists acting on behalf of the artworld. It was some of Beardsley's remarks in his article, "Is Art Essentially Institutional?", which helped me come to see the confused mixture of formal and informal language in my account of the artworld. Also, in the definition I spoke of "some person or persons" acting on behalf of the artworld. Some readers apparently took the use of the plural "persons" to refer to the artworld as a whole and to mean that the artworld as a whole *creates* works of art or at least that the artworld as a whole has to *accept* an object before it can be an artwork. I intended "persons" to refer to groups of people who create works of art as typically happens when movies are made; I did not intend to refer to the artworld as a whole, and I certainly did not intend to claim that artworld *acceptance* is required for making art.

The final misinterpretation I want to comment on is one for which I unfortunately supplied maximum ammunition. In *Art and the Aesthetic* I sometimes wrote that art is a conferred status and sometimes that it is the status of candidate for appreciation which is conferred. Although I explicitly stated there that the talk of conferring the status of art is shorthand for talking about conferring the status of candidate for appreciation, this way of writing understandably misled some people. What may now complicate the situation even more is

9

that although I am now abandoning the notion of conferred status of candidate for appreciation entirely, I want in this book to maintain that being a work of art is a status. The view of art as a status which I now wish to defend, however, conceives of this status not as being conferred but as being achieved in another way.

In the remarks about this last misinterpretation I have noted a change which is to be made in the theory in this book, namely, the abandonment of the notion of conferred candidacy for appreciation. However, before going on to the general topic of changes which are to be made in the theory let me note a change which occurred in earlier accounts of the theory. The first formulation of the institutional definition of "work of art" read: "A work of art in the descriptive sense is 1) an artifact 2) upon which society or some sub-group of a society has conferred the status of candidate for appreciation." I soon realized that this formulation strongly suggests that it is some social group acting as a whole which creates art, a conclusion I had certainly not intended. Consequently, I modified the second condition to read "upon which some person or persons acting on behalf of a certain social institution (the artworld) has conferred the status of candidate for appreciation." In correcting this problem and using the expression "acting on behalf of," I unfortunately reinforced the already overly formal sounding expression "conferred the status . . . ," and thereby supplied further grounds for the second misinterpretation.

Let me now return to the topic of the new changes which are to be made in the theory. The first change to be noted is not so much a change in the theory as a change of view of the relation of the institutional theory to Arthur Danto's writings on the nature of art. From the very first reading of it I have regarded Danto's article, "The Artworld," as an important and stimulating piece of work. For a long time I regarded the institutional theory as a kind of straightforward development of Danto's conception of the artworld. With the publication of his "Artworks and Real Things" and "Transfiguration of the Commonplace," I came to realize that the two views are not as closely related as I had thought. In the two later articles Danto maintains that *aboutness* is a necessary condition for artworks; that is, he contends that a semantic dimension is required for being a work of art. In short, he maintains that a work of art must be about something. Thus, on Danto's view insofar as any institution is involved in the nature and creation of art, it is of a linguistic or semantic nature. By contrast, the institutional view as I have conceived of it holds that the relevant institution is art-specific, that is, that it is an institution or practice the specific function of which is the creation of art and which does not necessarily involve the category of language. The two views both use the expression "the artworld" but very different things are meant by it. What is common to Danto's view and the institutional theory is the contention that works of art are enmeshed in an essential framework or context of some considerable "thickness." Both theories specify rich contexts, but they differ widely as to the nature of the context. I should also note that I adopt Danto's "Visually-Indistinguishable-Objects Argument," the argument that if there are two visually indistinguishable objects and one is a work of art and the other is not, then there must be some context or framework in which the work of art is embedded which accounts for the different statuses of the two objects. This argument does not, of course, reveal the nature of the context.

What is certainly true is that Arthur Danto's "The Artworld" inspired the creation of the institutional theory of art.

Finally, I turn to the particular changes to be made in this book. In *Art and the Aesthetic* I devoted the bulk of my attention and space to the second condition of the definition, the condition which centers around conferring the status of candidate for appreciation, giving rather short shrift to the artifact condition. There were two reasons for this relative lack of attention. First, despite my attempt to refute the view of Weitz and others that artifactuality is not required for being a work of art, I regarded the artifactuality condition as being virtually self-evident. Consequently, my attempt at refutation was minimal. But it turns out that substantially more argument and comment is required to bring out what Weitz and others were attempting to do and to show why what seems false to some seems virtually self-evident to others. The second reason for devoting so little space to artifactuality was that it then seemed to me that all the really interesting things were embedded in the second condition. This second reason is mistaken.

One result of the unequal treatment of the two condition was that the impression was given that the conditions were not very closely related and that artifactuality was of lesser importance. In the new version of the theory, the whole approach is through the artifactuality condition, and although the new definition retains the two-part form, it will be evident that the two parts are intimately related.

Another result of my lack of attention to the first condition was my hasty conclusion that artifactuality is something which can be conferred as well as being achieved by work. I expressed some doubt about this conclusion in *Art and the Aesthetic*. It was suggested there that perhaps some other way should be found to solve the problems that "conferred artifactuality" was supposed to take care of, namely, the problem of how *Fountain* was to be understood as an artifact of Duchamp. It now seems to me that artifactuality is just not the sort of thing that can be conferred and that *Fountain* and its like must be construed as the artifacts of artists as the result of a kind of mimimal work on the part of those artists. The account of this mimimal kind of work may be controversial. An added benefit of this change is that the

11

mimimal work requirement acts as a limiting factor on the member-ship of the class of works of art, a factor which so many have pointed out is lacking in the old version. According to the new version, it is clear that not everything can become a work of art.

Earlier I mentioned that the notion of conferred candidacy for appreciation is dropped in the new version. The abandonment of this view is the result of two things. One thing is the acceptance of Beardsley's criticism that some of the language I was using to try to describe the various aspects of the artworld is too formal to fit the kind of institution I had in mind. Specifically, Beardsley's criticism is that the artworld as conceived in *Art and the Aesthetic* is not an institution of the kind which confers status. Another reason for abandoning conferred status of candidacy is the new emphasis on artifactuality. In the new version, it is the work done in creating an object against the background of the artworld which establishes that object as a work of art. Consequently, there is no need for the conferring of status of any kind, whether it be of candidacy for appreciation or artifactuality. The only kind of status even envisaged by the theory now is the status of being art which is achieved by the creative use of a medium. And by the way, it should perhaps be mentioned at this point that in speaking of the status of being art I do not wish to be taken to be suggesting that the object which enjoys this status is in any degree thereby valuable. Here, as before, the attempt is to give an account of the classificatory sense of "work of art."

The final change I wish to note here is a change of attitude toward the so-called problem of circularity. In *Art and the Aesthetic* I cheerfully admitted to the circularity involved in the one definition formulated there. In the new version, nothing is admitted, the circu-larity involved in the theory is flaunted. Moreover, in the new version, not one definition but a whole series of interlocking definitions is given. The justification for the interlockingness of the definitions is that the objects on which they focus constitute a complicated, inter-related system.

In the remainder of this introduction I shall discuss some of the presuppositions of the institutional theory of art. "Presupposition" may not be exactly the right word in some of the cases, but in any event, I shall be discussing matters which are foundational to the theory in one way or another.

The first assumption of the institutional theory is that a philosopher of art ought to take account of developments in the art-world. This does not mean that a philosopher must believe that every-thing an artist says is true or that everything an artist does has significance for the philosophy of art. There is, for example, no guarantee that everything an artist says is a work of art is in fact a work of art. A philosopher of art, however, must take seriously developments in the artworld, for the artworld is his primary domain and developments within it—especially radical ones—can be particularly revealing.

Secondly, I am assuming that the traditional theorists of art were right in the way they conceived of the domain of objects which they theorized about. Imitation theorists may be wrong in thinking that all works of art are imitations, but they were right in thinking that paintings, poems, plays, and the like are the things with which they should be concerned. Collingwood may have been wrong in thinking that works of art are located between the ears and that Shakespeare's plays are not works of art, but he was right in focusing on the correct domain, even if he referred to a part of that domain as "art falsely so-called." In brief, this assumption is that the theory of art is concerned with a certain kind of artifact. Since this presupposition has in recent times been challenged by Weitz and others, I find it expedient to say something by way of justification for this assumption.

A third assumption is that the theory of art is about a value-neutral, classificatory sense of "work of art." This means that something can be a work of art and be of no value, be of minimum value, be of maximum value, or be at some point on the scale between the last two. Being a work of art does not guarantee any value or any degree of value. Another way of putting this is that a theory of art should not have the result of making the expression "good art" redundant or the expression "bad art" self-contradictory. These two expressions are used to say important things and the theory of art ought to reflect this. In saying that the theory is about a value-neutral sense of "work of art," nothing other than what has just been indicated is intended.

That the classificatory-sense assumption is controversial derives from two sources. First, some uses of the expression "work of art" are laudatory, and some theorists have taken these uses to be basic. But there is a wider class of objects which contains the worthless, the indifferent, and the mediocre as well as the good and the excellent works. And since all of these works are art, it must be the wider class which is the basic domain for the philosophy of art. If someone wishes to theorize about the subclass of valuable works of art, fine, but that does not mean that it is the only set of objects worth attending to. The second reason that a classificatory theory has been controversial is that perhaps some have confused the activity of producing art with the works of art produced. The activity of producing art is of course a valuable activity. But all the products of a valuable activity need not be valuable, although of course a certain percentage would have to be. A classificatory theory deals with both the valuable and the worthless products. It is perhaps worth noting that the first theory of art—the imitation theory—is a classificatory theory. Of course, according to the evaluational account associated with the theory, being a good imitation makes for good art; but presumably to be a work of art it is sufficient (and necessary) simply to be an imitation.

The final assumption to be noted is that artmaking is something which almost everyone can do. It is not a highly specialized activity such as nuclear physics which is closed to those who lack a certain high degree of mathematical skill. Various primitive skills are required to make art, as well as the ability to understand the nature of the enterprise. Such skills and understanding are within the grasp of quite small children. Of course the creation of masterpieces requires skills of a kind which few can attain, but masterpieces constitute only a minute part of the class of artifacts with which the theory of art is concerned.

Chapter II   Danto and the Revival of Theory

In recent years Arthur Danto has aroused philosophers of art from their catatonic slumbers with a series of explosive but sometimes baffling articles: "The Artworld,"[1] "Artworks and Real Things,"[2] and "The Transfiguration of the Commonplace."[3] Despite their perplexing nature, these three papers more than any other single factor have been responsible for the revival of interest in the philosophy of art. In this chapter I shall attempt to provide a commentary on these three articles, trying to make clear what Danto is saying and trying to evaluate his argument and claims. In commenting on these articles, I take them to be an evolution of Danto's thought, so that if a conclusion or theme in an earlier article is abandoned, replaced, or rejected in a later article, I shall assume that the judgment of the later article is Danto's considered view. In addition to commenting on the articles, since I and other writers have associated Danto's views in the philosophy of art and my own institutional theory of art, I shall try to make clear the similarities and differences of the two positions.

Danto begins the first paper, "The Artworld," by talking about Socrates' conception of art—the view that art is an imitation of objects in the world of sense. He is also concerned with the view he attributes to Socrates that we already know what art is and that this knowledge guides our use of the word "art." I shall not concern myself with the question of whether these views are actually attributable to Socrates or Plato. Danto notes that the view that we know how to use "art" correctly and identify art correctly is shared with the most modern of anti-theorists of art such as Morris Weitz. Danto then flatly denies that we can always identify artworks, presumably having in mind such things as Duchamps' *Fountain* and other oddities. He then makes two

17

claims: 1) the epistemological claim that artistic theories help us tell artworks from nonartworks and 2) the ontological claim that artistic theories make art possible.

I shall consider the first claim first. Notice that this claim is that artistic theories *help* us identify artworks. This may leave open the possibility that we could on some occasions identify artworks without the use of an artistic theory, and perhaps we could always identify artworks without the use of an artistic theory. But how does an artistic theory help when it does help? Danto does not say how the imitation theory helped in the past, but it presumably helped by telling people that art is imitation. If they were faced with something which is not an imitation they knew it was not art, and if they were faced with something which was an imitation they knew it was art.[4] Then unusual things began to happen and artworks were produced that either were not very good as imitations or were not imitations at all. At the same time, what Danto calls "the Real Theory of Art" was invented—Art, the new theory says, is the creation of forms which are not imitations. The acceptance of this theory caused people to accept the new art. But how did (or does) the Real Theory help identify artworks? If faced with an object which is an imitation the new theory tells one that it may be art (although not because it is an imitation) and that may be some help.

Before the revolution, the Imitation Theory was presumably a big help with the identification of artworks—it explicitly ruled out things which are not imitations and ruled in those which were imitations. But after the revolution, the Real Theory of Art is not really much help. All it tautologically tells one when faced with an object is that it may or may not be art. Danto apparently realizes that the Real Theory is not of much help for the identification of artworks, for he launches into a discussion of what he calls the "is" of artistic identification which presumably will help one decide if an object is an artwork or not. The nature of this "is" is very obscure. The notion of the "is" of artistic identification was subjected to very hard criticism by William Kennick[5] and presumably because of this criticism (and perhaps other criticism) is not mentioned in Danto's two subsequent articles. I shall not concern myself with the "is" of artistic identification. It may be that the "is" of artistic identification is the same as identifying works of art by the use of an art theory. The epistemological problem of telling artworks from nonartworks by means of an artistic theory is not raised in the two later articles either.

I turn now to Danto's ontological claim that artistic theories make art possible. He defends this claim in a discussion of the question: why is Warhol's *Brillo Carton* a work of art and an ordinary Brillo carton not? After a discussion which amounts to assuring the reader that Warhol's carton is art and the ordinary carton is not,

Danto concludes, "What in the end makes the difference between a Brillo box and a work of art consisting of a Brillo Box is a certain theory of art. It is the theory that takes it up into the world of art . . ."[6] The theory in question is presumably the Real Theory, although he does not say so. He does not intend, however, to tie his claim solely to the Real Theory because a few lines later he writes, "It is the role of artistic theories, these days as always, to make the artworld, and art, possible."[7] But these remarks are not an argument in support of the second claim but are simply a restatement of the claim.

Danto begins the final section of "The Artworld" by saying that he will make some final remarks "about the theories that make artworks possible . . ."[8] He then talks about what he calls art-relevent predicate pairs such as representational-nonrepresentational, expressionist-nonexpressionist, and the like. Presumably, each art-relevant predicate pair is tied in some way to an art theory, since the talk about predicate pairs is supposed to show how artistic theories make art possible. Danto at this point contends that it is a necessary condition for being an artwork that at least one pair of art-relevant predicates be sensibly applicable to it. He also contends that one and only one of each of the art-relevant predicates will apply to an artwork, which means that if an object is an artwork, then it will be representational or nonrepresentational and expressionist or nonexpressionist, and so on. Danto then spends the rest of the article illustrating this second contention. He should, however, defend or at least discuss his first contention that having at least one pair of art-relevant predicates is a necessary condition for something's being an artwork. The only thing he says relevant to the contention about a necessary condition occurs at the very end of the article when he says that objects become artworks in virtue of having an art-relevant predicate applied to them. But this remark just repeats the original claim.

So in the end we are left with just the unsupported claim: artistic theories make art possible. But even if Danto has given no arguments, his claim might provide a valuable insight into the nature of art. He seems to be asserting that in some sense an art theory is a necessary condition for the creation of art, but what exactly does he mean? Does he mean that one must be consciously aware of an art theory and be able to state what the theory is in order to create a work of art? In the midst of his discussion of art theories making art possible, Danto notes, "It would, I should think, never have occurred to the painters of Lascaux that they were producing *art* on those [cave] walls. Not unless there were neolithic aestheticians."[9] Because of the context, I take Danto to be asserting that it would not have occurred to the painters of Lascaux that they were producing art because they were not producing art. The reason that the drawings cannot be art, he seems to be saying, is that there must not have been any aestheticians at the time. Since an aesthetician is a kind of person who consciously holds an art theory and can state what the theory is, I take Danto to be implying that the painters of Lascaux or any other persons must either be aestheticians and consciously hold an art theory or have an art theory told to them by an aesthetician so that they can consciously hold the theory in order to create works of art. If this is what Danto means by art theories making art possible, his claim must be false, because works of art must have been being created for a very long time before anyone consciously formulated any art theory. By the way, I do not wish to be understood to be saying that the painters of Lascaux were, *too*, producing art and, therefore, that Danto must be wrong because of this. No one knows enough of the activities of the painters of Lascaux to say one way or the other what it was they were doing. It seems safe enough, however, to say that artworks were being produced in more recent times long before art theories were being produced by aestheticians.

His remarks about neolithic aestheticians notwithstanding, someone might want to interpret Danto's remarks in a weaker sense to claim that an art theory's making art possible is simply the having of ideas either explicitly or implicitly about what counts as art in order to create art. This claim seems reasonable enough as a practical account of the basic conditions for the creation of art, but it would certainly be employing the weakest possible notion of having a theory. In this weak sense, everyone would have a theory about almost everything that he did: one would have a theory of gravity in throwing a ball; a theory of personality in dealing with people; and the like. If this weak sense of theory had been what Danto intended, surely he would have been able to say so in a clear and obvious way. In fact, what Danto does say about art theory and creating art, including his remark about the lack of neolithic aestheticians, makes it sound as if he has in mind much more than this minimal interpretation.

I conclude that in "The Artworld" neither the claim that artistic theories help us identify artworks nor the claim that artistic theories make art possible, understood as Danto seems to intend them, is established. Perhaps, one should not worry much about these two claims, for Danto does not raise them at all in the later articles. The theory that art theories make art possible seems to be replaced by another theory in the later articles; at the very least, Danto puts forth *another* account of what is necessary for art.

In his second article, "Artworks and Real Things," Danto is not directly concerned with the question of identifying artworks. Here he is primarily concerned to discover what it is that makes something a work of art, but, as just mentioned, he does not raise the notion that artistic theories make art possible.

Danto begins the second article, as before, with some remarks about the Platonic philosophy of art. The main point of these initial remarks seems to be that according to the imitation theory there is a "distance" between art and the reality it imitates. He ends the discussion by in effect asking—What happens to that "distance" when in the present day some artworks are visually indistinguishable from nonartworks (reality)? He is, I think, convinced that art "is at a distance" from reality. His concern then is this: Since we have (rightly) abandoned the imitation theory we do not have as yet a clear way to understand that "distance." The problem of the second article is to show how of two visually indistinguishable objects one can be an artwork (and stand at a "distance" from reality) and the other can be a nonartwork (a reality). Since the difference between the two objects is not visually discoverable, it must reside in the different backgrounds of the objects.

Danto conducts a thought experiment with four visually indistinguishable objects: a necktie painted uniformly blue by Picasso, a tie painted by a forger who copies the Picasso tie, a tie painted by a child to make his father's necktie attractive, and a tie painted blue by Cezanne. According to Danto, only Picasso's tie is an artwork and "stands at a distance from reality," the other three are simply real things (nonartworks). The latter three are simply ties which have had paint put on them. Why is this? Cezanne's tie is not an artwork because in his time the art community, which presumably included Cezanne, was not ready for it. Today's art community was ready for Picasso's tie. Whatever this readiness involves (and it is not very clear), according to Danto it is a background which enables Picasso to make a statement with his tie, and with the background missing Cezanne cannot make a statement with his tie. The forger's tie is just a quotation of the statement made by Picasso's tie, but a quotation of a statement is not a statement. The child's tie is not a statement because the child could not ". . . have sufficiently internalized the history and theory of art to make a statement . . . by means of a painted necktie."[10] (Later Danto seems to deny that a child can create a work of art of any kind, not just not create one with a painted tie.)[11] Since Picasso's tie is a statement, it is, according to Danto, a representation of reality. By being a statemental representation of reality, the tie is at a remove from reality but without being an imitation. Thus, what Danto takes to be a correct insight of the imitation theory (art is at a remove from reality) is satisfied by Picasso's tie without its being an imitation. Danto concludes the episode of the ties by saying that Picasso's tie is (i.e., would be if it existed) ". . . a statement in part about reality and art sufficiently penetrating to enable its own enfranchisement into the world of art."[12] It seems at this point that Danto is at least suggesting one of several theories of art. Given the just-quoted remark, he may be suggesting a sufficient condition of art:

1) if something is a) a statement and b) a sufficiently penetrating statement, then that is a sufficient condition for that thing to be an artwork. But perhaps he is suggesting only a necessary condition of art: 2) in order for something to be an artwork, it is necessary for that thing to be at some remove from reality (and being a statement is *one* way of being at some remove from reality, but there are or may be other ways). Or perhaps he is suggesting a more specific necessary condition of art: 3) in order for something to be an artwork, it is necessary for that thing to be at some remove from reality by being a statement.

Danto next introduces a discussion of what he calls "Found Drama," and it is here that one finds which of the three possibilities just mentioned is his actual view. A "Found Drama" consists of a playwright declaring "in the light of certain conventions" that an arbitrarily selected slice of the life of a particular family is an artwork. His treatment of "Found Drama" leads Danto to the conclusion that "artwork" is an ascription which is true of an object if certain defeating conditions do not hold. He then goes on to discuss two defeating conditions: being a fake and being the product of a nonartist. The case of fakes is virtually identical with the case of the copy of Picasso's tie; a fake cannot be an artwork because a fake does not make a statement, it only pretends to. The defeating condition of not being by an artist turns out to have the same source as fakes; the examples he gives—children, chimpanzees, and counterfeiters—turn out to be individuals who for one reason or another do not make statements by the products they produce. These remarks suggest that Danto is opting for a view which involves there being a certain necessary condition for art, but is not here concerned with sufficient conditions of art. The view could be formulated as follows: in order for something to be an artwork it is necessary for that thing to be a nonfake, and be the result of an artist and so on. Since each of the two defeating conditions Danto mentions turns on the notion of making a statement, perhaps all the defeating conditions do. If they all turn on making a statement, then the view just formulated reduces to 3) above. But perhaps there are defeating conditions which have a different source. Danto makes clear his intention by asserting that "art *is* a language of sorts, in the sense at least that an artwork says something, . . ."[13] Assuming that "says something" means "makes a statement," this assertion means that making a statement is, according to Danto, a necessary condition of art. This conclusion clearly means that Danto's position is 3) above, namely, in order for something to be an artwork, it is necessary for that thing to be at some remove from reality by being a statement.

In the brief concluding section of "Artworks and Real Things" Danto draws the paradoxical conclusion that in the present day art

22

and the philosophy of art have become the same thing! His reasons are 1) art has increasingly become ". . . its own (and only) subject . . ." and 2) the philosophy of art has as its subject art.[14] Perhaps it is true that art has increasingly taken itself for its subject (although it might not be very easy to say precisely what this means), but I doubt that this is as pervasively true as Danto suggests. But suppose that a work of art does take as its subject art, would this make it philosophy of art? As Colin Lyas notes, to conclude that two things (in this case art and the philosophy of art) are identical because they share a characteristic (in this case have art as subject) is to commit the fallacy of undistributed middle term.[15] Also, it is quite possible that when art takes itself as its own subject that art and philosophy of art address themselves to their subjects in different ways.

The third article, "The Transfiguration of the Commonplace," begins, as did the second article, with the consideration of two visually indistinguishable objects: a painting and an accidentally produced object which exactly resembles it. The problem again is to say why one is art and the other is not. Danto concludes these initial remarks by saying, "Something is an artwork, then, only relative to certain art-historical presuppositions. . . ."[16] This remark is reminiscent of the first article, "The Artworld," which talked of artistic theories and art history, but Danto does not follow up this lead and tell us what the art-historical presuppositions are and how they function to provide a background for art. What he does do is to pretty much reproduce the substance of "Artworks and Real Things." He is again essentially concerned to claim that all artworks have a particular necessary property. This article is an advance over the second mainly in that its aim and terms are more clearly specified.

Danto here gives for the first time a clear account of what he means by the term "reality" in the context of these three articles. Reality is characterized semantically. Language has a representative function. Reality is that which is "devoid of representationality."[17] Danto then advances his thesis about art: artworks ". . . are linguistic to the extent of admitting semantical assessment and in contrasting in the required essential way with reality."[18] More specifically he claims that artworks are *about* something. This is a bit of a change from the second article where it was claimed that artworks make statements. No explanation is given for the change. He does note for the first time that his thesis does not distinguish artworks from other means of "representation," and he does not propose (at least there) to make the distinction.[19] It is now clear that, even if Danto does not give a definition of "art," he has claimed that art is a species of language, that is, that "being linguistic" is a necessary condition of "art."

After a great deal of discussion of a variety of topics which touch on the central issue, Danto returns to his thesis at the end of his

23

article. He distinguishes the vehicle of a work of art (in the case of a painting presumably the line and colors), the denotation function or aboutness of an artwork, and the content of a work (what it denotes or is about). He asserts that "even the most abstract painting" has these features. Consider now some of the works of art which Danto has used to illustrate his theory. The *Polish Rider* and *La Tempesta* are traditional paintings which in a clear sense are about something. His hypothetical *Untitled* which is simply a square of primed canvas he claims is about art. Works such as *Untitled* may stand in line of descent from Duchamp's *Fountain* and may perhaps be said to be about art, that is, in some way not easy to explain they seem to be being used to indicate an attitude about art. Also, without giving an example, Danto has said that "even the most abstract painting" is about something.[20] This is, I think, true, because an *abstract* painting abstracts from something and is therefore about that something. But what of nonobjective painting? Such paintings have a historical connection with abstract paintings but are generally considered to have crossed the line which marks the loss of representation. Danto's hypothetical *Untitled* is of course a nonobjective painting which I have admitted may be about something, but what of more typical nonobjective paintings? For example, consider a design which consists of a number of interpenetrating triangular-shaped areas and is entitled *#23*. Is it about triangles? About art? Nothing in the painting or its title gives one any reason to think that it is about anything at all in any ordinary sense of "about." Perhaps Danto would deny that *#23* is an artwork, but there are many works of this type which are generally regarded as artworks. He may be making such a denial at the end of his article when he says of Jasper Johns' work that it collapses ". . . the distance between vehicle and content, making the properties of the thing shown coincident with the properties of the vehicle, and hence destroying the semantical space between reality and art. Needless to say, I regard all such attempts as logically foredoomed."[21] Logically foredoomed to what, Danto does not say but presumably to not being art. He is in a difficulty and when faced with works which are not representational (in his broad sense) he must say, apparently that they are not art. Thus, in the end we have the case of a philosopher trying to dictate to artists. Danto should have backed off from his semantic thesis instead of trying to dictate to artists and sought to explain the space (the difference) between art and reality (nonart) in some other way. It is worthwhile noting that even if Danto's view could be patched up so that it fits paintings, it does not seem possible that the great bulk of music could be shown to have a semantic dimension.

Let me sum up the content of the three articles before going on to compare the institutional theory of art as it has thus far been stated[22] with Danto's view. Assuming that the articles represent an

24

evolution of Danto's thought on art rather than a collection of his thoughts, a number of conclusions follow. The view that artistic theories make art possible seems to have been abandoned. The focus of the last two articles is the semantical nature of art; in the second article it takes the form of the claim that artworks make statements and in the third the form of the claim that artworks are about something. It seems that the statement thesis has been replaced by the aboutness thesis, so that in the end the positive theoretical content of the three essays comes down to the view that it is a necessary condition of being an artwork that it be about something. Danto alludes to the art-historical conditions which make it possible for an object to be about something, but he never tells us what they are. The aboutness thesis is not supported by arguments, but is presumably presented as an insight which when pointed out is obvious or at least plausible. While it is true that many artworks are about something (and that this may be an important thing about those works), it seems that some works are just not about anything. So *aboutness* cannot be a necessary condition of art. I conclude that Danto's claim about art is false. Even if, however, Danto's positive thesis about art is false, his indistinguishable-objects argument is a solid contribution to the philosophy of art. In fact, this argument, in showing art's dependence on a background, has furnished the basis for the revival of theorizing about art.

I shall now proceed to the comparison of Danto's view with the institutional theory as it was stated in *Art and the Aesthetic*. Formally, the two theories as proposed have different scopes. Danto is concerned only to specify *a* necessary condition of art; he explicitly says that he is not attempting to distinguish art from other modes of representation. (In this chapter, I am talking only about Danto's three articles. In his recent book, *The Transfiguration of the Commonplace*, Danto develops his views at great length and attempts to distinguish a second necessary condition of art.) The institutional theory of art is an explicit attempt to give the necessary and sufficient conditions of art.

The two views agree that "the background" of artworks plays an essential role in making those objects art. Danto makes the point about background in a striking way by focusing on visually indistinguishable objects, one of which is an artwork while the other is not. For Danto the background enables the object which is art to be about something. But he is not very helpful about what makes up the background. In "The Artworld" he really says no more about what makes art possible than that it is ". . . an atmosphere of artistic theory, a knowledge of the history of art: an artworld."[23] In "The Transfiguration of the Commonplace" he says only, "Something is an artwork, then, only relative to certain art-historical presuppositions , . . ."[24] Again this is all he has to say about the background which makes it possible for an object to be about something. In *Art and the Aesthetic* at least a sketchy account is given of what I thought the background to consist of. The background, according to the institutional theory, is a structure of persons fulfilling various roles and engaging in a practice which has developed through history. (This is a characterization of the artworld as it was described in the earlier book. In chapter V of this book, I will give what I hope is a fuller and more careful description of the artworld.) Within this structure, some persons serve to create objects for possible appreciation by themselves and others. On this view, there is no requirement that the objects created be about something, although many of them are.

The two theories also agree that, to use Danto's words, there is "a space" between art and something else, although the two kinds of things separated by "a space" are characterized differently by the two views. For Danto "the space" is between art which is representational and reality which in this context is that which is "devoid of representationality." "The space" is the difference between language and that to which it refers. For the institutional theory, "the space" is between art and nonart, the former being the set of objects which occupy positions in the structure which I have called "the artworld."

In "Artworks and Real Things" Danto claimed that fakes (forgeries, copies, and the like) cannot be artworks, giving as his reason that they are not statements. They are like quotations of statements which are not themselves statements. In *Art and the Aesthetic* I followed Danto's lead, concluding that fakes are not works of art. I now think that it was a mistake to have drawn this conclusion.[25] Danto's argument that they cannot be statements and, therefore, not art seems to me to be invalid, as it seems false that being a statement (or being about something) is a necessary condition of art. Of course, it might still be the case that fakes are not works of art for some other reason. But I see no reason why such works cannot satisfy all the requirements for being works of art in the classificatory sense: forgeries are works of art about whose creator we are or have been mistaken; copies are unimaginative or completely derivative works of art. These remarks may give the impression that I once thought that making a statement is a necessary condition of art and that that was the reason I thought fakes not to be works of art. I have never thought that making a statement is a necessary condition of art; I simply failed to understand Danto's argument.

In "Artworks and Real Things," Danto says, ". . . children, chimpanzees, counterfeiters: tracing an object to any of these defeats it as an artwork. . . ."[26] I have just made some suggestions about counterfeiters (forgers, copiers). About chimpanzees, I am inclined to agree with Danto, although he and I have different reasons for this conclusion. Chimpanzees can neither grasp the institutional framework of artworks (my view) nor make objects which are about something (Danto's view). I am of course talking about present and past chimpanzees. The training now being given some apes might make it possible for them to create art some day. I think Danto is wrong about children. Even if his own view is granted, I do not see why a child is incapable of making a statement with a painting or making an object which is about something, unless Danto means by a child an infant in arms or close to it. In any event, children can be and are taught the rudiments of artmaking at a very tender age, and the institutional theory has no difficulty in accomodating this fact. Children may for a long time lack the technique and control which is only possible with long training, practice, and more mature intellectual and physiological development, but they catch on to the general idea of artmaking nonetheless and can produce imaginative if primitive works of art of great charm.

I have adopted the name "the institutional theory of art" for my own view. There are reasons for saying that Danto's view is institutional in nature, although even if this is granted the two views are very different. In "The Transfiguration of the Commonplace," as already noted, Danto writes, "Something is an artwork, then, only relative to certain art-historical presuppositions, ..." and this remark has an institutional sound to it, but, also as noted, Danto tells us no more about these presuppositions. In the earlier "Artworks and Real Things" Danto had made the even more institutional sounding remark that "artwork" is an ascriptive term which attaches ". . . to objects in the light of certain conventions. . . ."[27] But instead of characterizing the conventions, Danto goes on to discuss what he takes to be some defeating conditions of art: being a fake and being of nonartistic provenance. As it turns out, these defeating conditions involve not being a statement or, as the third article would put it, not being about something. The conventions, therefore, must be conventions which are involved in making a statement or making something be about something. Indeed, Danto states that ". . . art *is* a language of sorts, in the sense at least that an artwork says something, ..."[28] Within Danto's theory the conventions involved in artmaking (insofar as we can infer anything about them) are very similar to the conventions generally involved in language use. Thus, insofar as one can tell, Danto's theory is institutional only in the sense that a language of sorts would be institutional. He does not try to tell us anything specifically about the institutional nature of art as art. At most, Danto tries to show the institutional nature of art as a language of sorts. The institutional theory is an attempt to sketch an account of the specific institutional structure within which works of art have their being. Whereas Danto sees art as a language of sorts, the institutional theory does not.

Chapter III   Art as Artifice

Philosophers of art may not know much about art, but they once knew that a work of art is an artifact, which is—as the dictionary tells us—"an object made by man, especially with a view to subsequent use." This fact about art was so evident to them that they did not bother to say that works of art are artifacts, although they clearly assumed that they were. It must have seemed such an obvious fact to them that they thought no one had to be told. Besides, these old-fashioned philosophers were more concerned with matters they took to be controversial, say, with whether art is an imitation or an expression of emotion or a symbol of human feeling. It should be clear that Danto's thoughts about art belong to this old school of art theorizing. However radical some of his ideas are, Danto is, I think, talking about artifacts. There is today, however, an influential group of philosophers of art who are convinced that a work of art need not be an artifact; they have developed a theory which yields a *new* conception of art. What brought about this radical challenge to our old conception of art?

In the first part of this chapter I will examine and evaluate the new conception of art, focusing on its conclusions about artifactuality. The view that I am calling "the new conception of art" is that of Morris Weitz[1] and those who follow him. The somewhat similar view of Paul Ziff[2] needs a rather different treatment and will require a separate discussion. In the last part of this chapter I will comment on what I now regard as the mistaken notion of conferred artifactuality set forth in *Art and the Aesthetic* and elsewhere.

The chief conclusion to be drawn in this chapter, contrary to the

29

new conception of art, is that art is artifactual. This conclusion is necessary for the development of the institutional theory of art but does not of course distinguish it from the traditional theories of art. The aim of this chapter is perhaps best thought of as a justification for the return to the traditional way of philosophizing about art, insofar as its underlying assumption is that works of art are artifacts. It should be made clear at this point that an artifact need not be a physical object. For example, a poem is not a physical object, but it is man-made and is, therefore, an artifact.

Philosophers have recently begun to take notice of how the expressions "art" and "work of art" are actually used and to draw conclusions from these linguistic facts. They have noticed that in ordinary speech "art" and "work of art" are sometimes applied to artifacts such as the *Mona Lisa* and the *Night Watch*, but that some-times these expressions are applied to nonartifacts such as sunsets and waterfalls. Many would regard the application of "work of art" or "art" to an object such as a sunset or a waterfall to be a metaphorical use of the expression, but the new conception of art, I shall try to show does not. Presumably, this usage has been occurring for a very long time and has nothing to do with recent developments in the artworld.[3]

In addition to this long-standing kind of usage, in recent times a more extraordinary kind of usage of "art" and "work of art" has occurred within the artworld and has also influenced philosophers. Some recent artists have claimed things which they themselves have not made in any obvious way as their art, in part because they have *called* the objects "art." For example, Duchamp declared that a urinal was *Fountain*, and it has been reported that Dali pointed at some rocks, said they were art, and claimed they were thereby art.

Philosophers of art such as Weitz and those who follow him have taken note of these uses of "art" and "work of art." These philosophers have also been influenced by the claims of Wittgenstein and others that at least some of our concepts are not governed by necessary and sufficient conditions. Such concepts have been charac-terized as being open, i.e., not "closed" by necessary and sufficient conditions. These philosophers of art have concluded that the concept of *art* (or *work of art*) is open because the wide variety of the uses of "art" (or "work of art") does not exhibit any common feature. If there is no common feature, then no feature can be necessary and no set of features can be necessary and sufficient for the use of the concept of *art*.

What picture of the concept of *art* do these philosophers of art give? According to the new concept of *art*, at any given time there will be a set of objects to which the word "art" can be correctly applied. The members of the class will be very diverse with no necessity for a

30

common feature. The criteria which the objects will have satisfied in order to be works of art will be a large disjunctive set. Although the members of the class of works of art have no common feature, there are resemblances such that every member resembles some other member. The class of works of art may be enlarged at any time. It may be done in this way: someone who is familiar with works of art notes that some object *A* which is not a work of art is similar in some respect to some work of art; he says that *A* is a work of art and *A* becomes a work of art. Such a new addition to the set of works of art may supply a new criterion, and if it does a new disjunct is tacked on to the set of criteria of *art*. On this view, the concept of *art* is constantly changing by adding to its criteria (or as some say, evolving). According to the new view, the concept of *art* is a kind of conceptual vortex which continually draws into itself new criteria. The bases for this adding of new criteria to the concept of *art* and new objects to the class of works of art are 1) noted similarity and 2) calling something "art." Noted similarity and calling something "art" are, for Weitz, sufficient for making that something art.

Traditional philosophers of art have been interested in only a small subset of the class of works of art as the new conception of art conceives of the class of works of art, namely, the subset of paintings, poems, plays, and the like. The traditional philosophers have tried to develop theories which capture the essential features of the works which occupy this subset. The new philosophers of art are claiming that the interest of the old philosophers of art is too narrow. It is wrong, they say, for a philosopher of art to focus attention only on this small subset of art; one ought to focus attention on the whole class of objects to which "art" and "work of art" can be meaningfully applied. All meaningful uses of "art" and "work of art" should function as the touchstone of the philosophy of art. It is the total set of such uses of these expressions which determines what the concept of *art* is and which objects are included in the class of works of art. The new conception of art may be more or less summed up by the following principle-like statement: Any meaningful use of the expression "art" or "work of art" marks the use of the concept of *art* and refers to an individual which is literally a member of the class of art objects.

Maurice Mandelbaum[4] in an early criticism of the new conception of *art* noted that Wittgenstein, who is Weitz's model, had not spoken simply of resemblance or similarity but rather of *family* resemblance. Mandelbaum pointed out that family resemblance is not simply a matter of resemblance, but rather it is resemblance among those who share a genetic relationship. Thus, family resemblance has a two-fold criterion: resemblance and genetic connection. Similarly, Mandelbaum maintains resemblance or similarity alone cannot be a criterion for either the concept *game* or the concept *art*. For if similarity alone were the criterion of *game* or *art*, then each concept would apply to practically everything, since everything resembles everything else. What Mandelbaum failed to notice was that for the new conception of *art* there is a two-fold criterion for art: similarity *plus* the use of the word "art." Thus, the new conception of *art* is more complicated than Mandelbaum thought, and it does try to limit the far-reaching inclusiveness of similarity alone by requiring the use of "art" or "work of art." The use of "art" or "work of art" does not provide a genetic connection of the kind enjoyed by members of a family; it is just the second factor in the new conception of *art*. Whether this particular two-fold criterion is adequate is of course another matter.

A close look at the new conception of art reveals some interesting consequences. One striking feature of the new conception is that it makes it impossible to use "art" or "work of art" metaphorically. Someone comes upon an object which is not a work of art and desires to call attention to it and praise it by calling it "a work of art" because of its similarities to some work of art. The person so calls the object, and it literally becomes a work of art. Thus, instead of applying "work of art" metaphorically, the person has created a work of art. The only objects to which "work of art" could be applied metaphorically are objects which the speaker thinks do not resemble a work of art, but in such cases there would be no point in using the term because there would be no basis for the metaphor.

A second interesting feature of the new conception is the way in which it makes it impossible for two people really to disagree over whether an object is a work of art. Suppose Arthur and Zachary attempt to disagree over whether a certain object is a work of art. Zachary says the object is not a work of art. Arthur replies that the object is a work of art. Since the object is bound to resemble some prior-established work of art and Arthur has called it a work of art, the object becomes a work of art, and Arthur wins. Next time, if Zachary persists in holding to the new conception, he will know not to try to take the negative side of such a question.

A third striking feature of the new conception is that, unless it is supplemented in some way, it requires an infinite regress of works of art which means that there could not be any works of art at all. On the new view, the members of the class of works of art will have in common as art-making features the resembling of some prior-established work of art and of having been called "art" or "work of art." It is the art-making requirement of resembling some prior-established work of art which causes the problem. For example, according to the new conception of art, today's sunset (Saturday's) could be a work of art in part because it resembles Friday's sunset which was a work of art. But why was Friday's sunset a work of art?

32

Because it resembled Thursday's sunset which was a work of art. And why was Thursday's sunset a work of art? Because it resembled a painting of a sunset which in turn resembled an earlier painting or an earlier sunset, and so on. The new conception has no way to block the regress, but if it could not be blocked there could be no works of art. The point of the regress argument is that if the new conception of art were all there is to the notion of art, it would have been impossible for there ever to have been any art at all. Since works of art exist, the new conception must be wrong. The new conception requires supplementing; it needs some way of showing how something can be a work of art independently of whether it resembles a prior-established work of art and how such a work of art can block the infinite regress. Such a "blocking" work of art might in fact resemble a prior-established work of art, but its *being* a work of art must not *depend* on its resembling a prior-established work of art. The new conception of art altered in the required way would be a "double" theory; it would have to have two ways in which something could come to art: 1) resembling a prior-established work of art and being called "art" and 2) some other way which is independent of the condition of resembling a prior-established work of art.

To sum up, the new concept of *art* has several interesting properties. In either its altered or unaltered form the new conception makes it impossible to use "art" or "work of art" metaphorically and impossible to disagree about whether an object is a work of art, and this seems to make the concept of *art* different from other concepts. But, of course, maybe it just is different. Furthermore, the new conception of art altered in the way required yields two very different subclasses of works of art.

Paul Ziff's version of the new conception of art differs from Weitz's in that calling something "art" plays no role. It also differs in speaking of *sufficient* similarity rather than simply of similarity. Ziff's view may be summed up as follows: something is a work of art if and only if it has enough characteristics which sufficiently resemble those features of a characteristic case which make the characteristic case a work of art. By "characteristic case" Ziff means a clear-cut case of a work of art, and he gives as an example of such a case Poussin's "The Rape of the Sabine Women." Ziff remarks that "No rules can be given to determine what is or is not a sufficient degree of similarity."[5] Presumably, one would be able to tell in given cases. (By the way, it is clear that artifactuality is not required by Ziff for a sufficient degree of similarity.)

Ziff's version of the new conception would not rule out the metaphorical use of "work of art." Things which are similar to works of art but not sufficiently similar to *be* works of art could be called "works of art" metaphorically; such usage would not turn those things into works of art. Also, on Ziff's view it is quite possible for people to disagree about whether something is a work of art. What they would have to debate about is whether the object is sufficiently similar to a characteristic work of art. There would be no ready way to settle such disputes, but they would be possible.

But if Ziff's version of the new conception allows for metaphorical use and disputes about whether something is a work of art, it must be altered in a way similar to the way in which Weitz's account requires altering. The fact that Ziff's view differs from Weitz's in that it specifies 1) *sufficient* similarity rather than just similarity and 2) similarity to a characteristic case of a work of art rather than just similarity to a work of art does not prevent it from generating an infinite regress. Unless there is also some way of becoming art in addition to being sufficiently similar to a characteristic case of a work of art, an infinite regress of characteristic cases is required. Despite their differences, Weitz's and Ziff's views each require two different ways of becoming art in order to block a regress. The two ways required by either view are not, however, merely two distinct ways of becoming art; they are necessarily related in that the similarity way of becoming art depends on the nonsimilarity way of becoming art. There could never be art of the similarity kind if there had not first been art of the nonsimilarity kind. Nonsimilarity art has a kind of priority which makes it primary; nonsimilarity art forms a *core* of the class of works of art as that class must be depicted when the details of Weitz's and Ziff's views are worked out.

The new conception of art in either of its versions does not attempt to give an account of the nonsimilarity core of art. Indeed, the whole thrust of the new conception is to suggest that similarity art is the complete story. Even so, both Weitz and Ziff say things which imply, although they are unaware of it, that nonsimilarity art is most plausibly identified with artifactual art. (By "artifactual art" I mean artifacts which are or were intended by their creators to be art.) Weitz writes, ". . . mostly when we describe something as a work of art, we do so under the conditions of there being present some sort of artifact, made by human skill, ingenuity, and imagination, which embodies in its sensuous, public medium—stone, wood, sounds, words, etc.— certain distinguishable elements and relations."[6] And when Ziff discusses the notion of a characteristic case of a work of art, he uses as his example Poussin's "The Rape of the Sabine Women." It would seem that, for Weitz, what we "mostly" have in mind and, for Ziff, what we "characteristically" have in mind when we speak of a work of art is a certain sort of artifact, that is, a work of art which is a work of art, not because of its resemblance to any other *object*, but because of the way in which it *came to be*. Of course, there is nothing in the new conception which *necessitates* that nonsimilarity art has to be artifac-

34

tual, but the ways in which both Weitz and Ziff develop their account strongly suggests artifactuality. Furthermore, I believe that its being artifactual is the only plausible way of conceiving of the nature of nonsimilarity art—the art which the new conception presupposes as the core of the class of works of art. I realize that I have not proven that artifactual art can be identified with nonsimilarity art. It is possible, for example, that at some time in the past that people just began calling a particular group of objects (say, a particular set of rocks) "works of art" and that this set of objects is the original nonsimilarity art. Any member of this set could block the regress, and, thus, there is an alternative to artifactual art for the role of regress-blocker. Artifactual art, however, seems to me to be a much more plausible candidate for nonsimilarity art, although I admit that I cannot prove the identity of nonsimilarity art and artifactual art.

The new conception of art in either of its versions is, then, a "double" theory, requiring two very different ways for something to become art. The class of works of art, on this view, consists of two very distinct subclasses: 1) the subclass of similarity art, each member of which is a member in virtue of its resemblance to such prior-established or characteristic work of art and 2) the subclass of artifactual art (nonsimilarity art), each member of which is a member in virtue of being an artifact. The subclass of artifactual art is the old familiar class of paintings, poems, musical pieces, and the like, which are crafted in various traditional ways.

Given the great internal cohesiveness of the subclass of artifactual art and the weak bond (similarity) which unites the diffuse subclass of similarity art to the subclass of artifactual art, why should the members of the two classes be thought to be literally things of the same type, i.e., literally works of art? Put otherwise, given these classes and their relation, why should we think that the new conception of art has given an accurate account of our conception of art? There is clearly an important relationship between what I have called "artifactual art" and "similarity art" (with the former having a certain kind of priority), but it does not follow from this that both are literally art. The kind of relationship which exists between artifactual art and similarity art seems more like the kind of relationship which typically holds between the class picked out by the literal uses of a word and the class picked out by the metaphorical uses of that word than it does like anything else.

The philosophy of art has traditionally been the task of theorizing about the essential nature of a class of artifacts: paintings, poems, plays, and the like. In view of the foregoing remarks, how seriously should one take the view of some philosophers of language that philosophers of art must abandon their traditional task as impossible because "art" and "work of art" can be meaningfully applied to nonartifacts as well as artifacts? I have tried to show above that there is some reason for thinking that artifactuality is a necessary condition for literal uses of "art" and "work of art." But even if it were the case that both artifactual art and similarity art are literally art, why should the philosopher of art abandon his traditional concern with what in effect is artifactual art? What I have here been calling "artifactual art" is the product of a certain kind of human activity: an activity of making. Similarity art is a result of another kind of human activity: roughly, the noticing of similarities. Surely these two activities are sufficiently different that a philosopher can focus theoretically on artifactual art and the activity of making it without bringing in similarity art; that is, he can do traditional philosophy of art. (Of course, one cannot focus theoretically on similarity art without bringing in artifactual art, because the former presupposes the latter.) If a philosopher of art desires, he might try to make whatever theoretical remarks there are to be made about similarity art also, and in so doing enter the wider sphere of the philosopher of language. Acting in the capacity of philosopher of language, he might even try to develop a comprehensive theory of artifactual art plus similarity act.

Is it enough to note that artifactual art can be distinguished from similarity art as the product of a different kind of activity? Does this difference alone justify focusing attention on artifactual art alone, as the traditional philosophers of art have unhesitatingly done? But it is not that the activities in question are merely different; they are so very different that it would just never occur to anyone to try to subsume the two activities and their products under the same theory, unless they were under the influence of powerful philosophical motives—motives which regard the use of words or similarities as determining concepts. But while usage or similarity may be a helpful indication as to what belongs where, the nature of the actual activities and their products (to which the words apply and between which the similarities obtain) must be taken into account as determinants of concepts. And the activity of making and the activity of noticing similarities are so different it does not seem possible that their respective products can be things of the same type. What justification could be given for forcing these products into the same category? Consider this example from Hume's *Treatise*. ". . . Let us suppose, that by the dropping of its seed, [a tree] produces a sapling below it, which springing up by degrees, at last overtops and destroys the parent tree: I ask, if in this instance there be wanting any relation, which is discoverable in parricide or ingratitude?"[7] Now someone might say of the still living tree, "That tree is a parricide," and it would be a perfectly reasonable thing to say. Does the meaningfulness of the statement mean that the tree is literally a parricide and that moral philosophers and law enforcement officers must concern themselves with the case? Presumably not, and

36

I do not see that there is any more reason why philosophers of art and art critics should concern themselves with similarity art.

The first question with which philosophers of art must deal is "What are the limits of *making?* " not "What are the limits of the use of 'art' and 'work of art'?" or "What are the limits of similarity?" I shall consider the problem of the limits of *making* in my remarks on conferred artifactuality at the end of this chapter.

In the foregoing the concept of art was the focus of attention; let me now shift emphasis a bit and talk about the closely related topic of the meaning of "art" or "work of art." In *Art and the Aesthetic* I spoke of "art" (or "work of art") as having more than one sense, and a number of people have objected to this way of speaking. I claimed that there is a classificatory sense, an evaluative sense, and a derivative sense. The classificatory sense was taken as being applicable to the class of objects which includes as typical members the *Mona Lisa,* Grandma Moses' paintings, drawings made by children in art classes, and so on. The evaluative sense was taken as being applicable to the class of objects which includes as typical members the Grand Canyon, a particular bit of broken-field running by a football player, Cezanne's *The Saint Victoire, Seen from the Quarry Called Bibemus,* and so on. The derivative sense was taken as being applicable to the class of objects which has as its members objects which are not members of the classificatory class but which resemble members of the classificatory class.

Whether or not speaking of a number of senses of "work of art" is the correct way of conceiving of this matter I am not sure. The original motivation for speaking of a variety of senses of "work of art" was an attempt to combat Weitz's view that "work of art" cannot be defined because the class of works of art is one whose members have no common feature. The implication of Weitz's view is, I believe, that it is pointless to speak of senses (or even a sense) of "work of art." Earlier an account of Weitz's conception of *art* or *work of art* was given. Recall now the general features of that description: the expression "art" (or "work of art") is used on a wide variety of occasions such that the objects to which the expression applies constitute a diverse set and the objects have no (defining) feature in common. One basis for something's being included in the set is resemblance to an already established work of art, but resemblance is not enough because many objects which are not art resemble works of art in some way. The application of the expression "art" or "work of art" also functions in resemblance cases in making something art. So on Weitz's view, resembling a prior-established work of art and being called "art" is sufficient for making something art. Weitz speaks of particular resemblances as crite*ria* of art, but for him this is really one complex crite*rion* of art: resembling prior-established art and being

37

called "art." Of course, traditional crafting (painting, sculpting, and so on) are also sufficient for making art. Thus, for Weitz the concept of *art* is the disjunctive pair of criteria: a) traditional crafting and b) resembling prior-established art and being called "art." Weitz's view can be illustrated with the following diagram in which "A_1," "A_2," etc., stand for works of art and the line around them indicates that they belong to a class.

Diagram I

The expression "art" (or "work of art")

applies to objects in virtue of the concept of *art* which is the disjunction pair of criteria *a* and *b*.

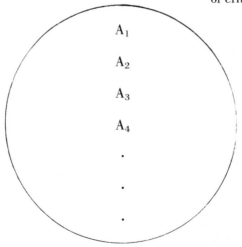

A_1

A_2

A_3

A_4

.

.

.

But this account of Weitz's view is not yet complete and does not bring out everything that is implicit in his view because he distin-

guishes between a descriptive use and an evaluative use of "art." I
take it that the descriptive and the evaluative uses of "art" are applicable to both traditionally crafted objects as well as the other members of the class of works of art; it is just that the descriptive use has
no evaluative content. The descriptive/evaluative distinction may be
represented in a diagram of the class of works of art by replacing A's
with D's (works to which the descriptive use of "art" applies) and E's
(works to which the evaluative use of "art" applies. The D's and E's
can then be separated into two subsets.

Diagram II

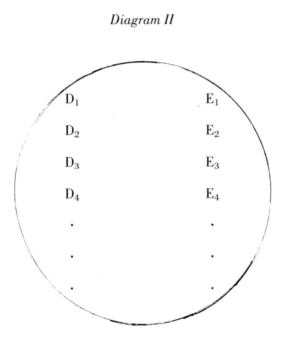

The class of works of art is now seen to have a certain structure
because according to Weitz the term "art" has distinctive *uses*.
Weitz's theory does not make anything of this structure. But the class
of works of art has more structure than the diagrams have yet revealed
because its members are admitted by a pair of disjunctive criteria:
traditional craftsmanship, and resembling prior-established art and
being called "art." This means that some D's are traditional crafted

39

works of art such as paintings and statues; I shall call these "descriptive art artifacts" or DA's for short. Some D's become art by resembling prior-established art and being called "art"; I shall call these "descriptive art nonartifacts" or DN's for short. Some descriptive art nonartifacts may be artifacts but not art artifacts because they are not crafted in traditional artistic ways. For example, a car might be a descriptive art nonartifact even though it is an artifact, because it is not crafted in traditional artistic ways. Some descriptive art nonartifacts might not be artifacts in any way. I expect that most descriptive art nonartifacts would be nonartifacts such as seashells and the like which happen to have characteristics which make them look like representations.

The descriptive use of "art" presumably involves no evaluation. The evaluative use of "art" is applicable to an object on the basis of resemblance to prior-established art which in some way is considered valuable *or* perhaps just because the object is thought valuable, so that whether an object to which the term is applied is crafted by traditional artistic means or not is irrelevant. Thus, one might use "art" evaluatively of a Rembrandt, a car, or a sunset. Consequently, the artifact/nonartifact distinction does not have to be used among the E's. The distinction under discussion can be represented as follows:

Diagram III

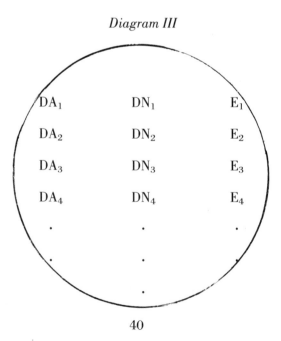

The class of descriptive art artifacts is identical with the class which I earlier called "artifactual art." Artifactual art also includes some E's of course, but it does so only because those E's are first descriptive art artifacts. One could divide the E's into two subclasses—representing those E's which are descriptive art artifacts and those which are descriptive art nonartifacts. One could even indicate by pairings that some artifactual art is valuable, for example—(DA_2, E_3). Further refinements are possible, but Diagram III is not intended to be a complete representation of the class of works of art as conceived by Weitz. Diagram III is sufficient for present purposes.

Now Weitz is quite uninterested in the structure that exists within the class of works of art. He focuses his entire attention on the fact that the members of the class do not have any interesting characteristics in common, and the conclusion he draws is that no definition of "art" or "work of art" is possible.

So far in this section of the chapter, following Weitz, I have been speaking of "the class of works of art." The class that Weitz is talking about might better be characterized as "the class of objects to which 'art' or 'work of art' can be meaningfully applied." Either expression may be applied for quite different reasons: because an object is a descriptive art artifact; because an object is a descriptive art nonartifact; or because an object is evaluative art. Putting the matter in this way enables us to see better the possibility that meaningfully applying "art" or "work of art" to an object does not necessarily mean that that object is literally a work of art. Putting the matter in this way also enables us to see better the possibility that there might be different literal senses of the expressions. It also helps us to focus on the structure within the class of objects in question. As was noted earlier, Weitz's conception does not allow for the metaphorical use of "art" or "work of art." But if we talk about the class of objects to which "art" or "work of art" applies, it makes it easier to see how some of the applications could be metaphorical.

How do the considerations of structure relate to questions of the literal and metaphorical applications of the terms? A metaphorical application in some way derives from a literal instance. The structure of the class of objects to which "art" and "work of art" applies furnishes the clue as to which applications are literal and which metaphorical. If we look at the way this class has been divided up, it is evident that the division is not an arbitrary one but one which reflects an important fact about how we understand an aspect of our world and an important linguistic parallel about our use of "art" and "work of art." Earlier it was argued that descriptive art artifacts (there called "artifactual art") have a certain kind of priority over similarity art (roughly, what I am now calling descriptive art nonartifacts) and that descriptive art artifacts constitute a core of the class of objects to

41

which "art" or "work of art" can be meaningfully applied. The priority and coreness of descriptive art artifacts is reflected in our usage of "art" and "work of art." On occasion when in thought or utterance we apply "art" (or "work of art") to a descriptive art artifact, we understand it to have a specific sense, and the sense is roughly "crafted in some traditional artistic way." Someone might object, "First you divide the class of objects up in a way that yields subclasses the members of which have certain things in common. Then you point out that the members of a particular subclass have in common a certain feature and take the linguistic counterpart of this feature as a sense which picks out that subclass. You built in your conclusion about a sense at the beginning." I want to maintain, however, that the division into the particular subclasses is not something that I did; it is something that one finds when one reflects carefully on our use of "art" (or "work of art") and the way in which we apply the word.

We can see how these divisions function if we reflect *on what we are doing* when we use "art" or "work of art" in different cases. Consider first the descriptive art artifact sense. Now we do not with much frequency *utter* "art" in the descriptive art artifact sense, although we frequently use it in our thought (by which I mean our understanding of the aspects of the world around us). When we walk into an art museum, we *recognize* that many of the objects in sight are works of art in the sense of their having been crafted in some traditional way. Occasionally we may relieve someone's puzzlement by *saying* of a pile of rocks on a museum floor, "It is a work of art." In this last case we are pointing out that the rocks have been crafted, not just dumped, although "traditional" takes further explaining in such cases. In general, what we are doing in using the descriptive art artifact sense of "art" or "work of art" is to locate a particular object within a certain framework.

Now suppose we say of a naturally occuring rock formation or a seashell either of which resembles a human face, "it is a work of art." Assuming that the term is not being used evaluatively, what we would probably be doing is bringing out or calling to someone's attention that the object in question has a resemblance to something else in somewhat the way that certain works of art (in the descriptive art artifact sense) do. Thus, although we use the same word in the cases just discussed, we use it in markedly different ways because we use it to do such different things.

Finally, suppose we say of a Rembrandt, a sunset, or a car, "It's a work of art," with emphasis on each word in the phrase "work of art" and with longer than usual time intervals before and after "of." The expression with such phrasing is characteristically used to praise. The basis for the evaluation might be different in different cases. In the case of the Rembrandt one might be saying that it is near the top of the class of descriptive art artifacts. In the case of the sunset one might be saying that it has qualities similar to the valuable qualities of some works of art in the descriptive art artifact sense. In the case of the car one might be saying that it is beautiful in appearance (as some descriptive art artifacts are) or that it is well-made (as some descriptive art artifacts are).

Whether in the cases of the evaluative use of "art" or "work of art" and the uses which pick out descriptive art nonartifacts there are distinct senses or metaphorical uses or some combination I am not sure. One thing that is meant by there being a distinct sense of a word is that there is a stable application of that word. Whether the evaluative use of "art" or "work of art" has the required stability I am not sure. That there is a distinct sense of "art" (or "work of art") in which the term means that an object has been crafted in a traditional artistic way seems evident. A spelling out of what is involved in crafting in a traditional artistic way will, I think, reveal the specific necessary and sufficient conditions of descriptive art artifacts, but I shall not go into that until later. It suffices for present purposes to say that crafting in a traditional artistic way is necessary and sufficient for an object's being a descriptive art artifact. And the descriptive art artifact sense is basic for the other uses in that in one way or another the descriptive art nonartifact uses and the evaluative uses are parasitic upon descriptive art artifacts. To say of some object that it is art in the descriptive art nonartifact "sense" is to say that the object resembles some prior-established work of art. The prior-established work may be a descriptive art artifact or another descriptive art nonartifact, but if it is another descriptive art nonartifact, as we saw earlier, the trail must lead ultimately back to a descriptive art artifact. To say of some object that it is art in the evaluative "sense" is to say that (if it is a descriptive art artifact) it is a very good descriptive art artifact or (if it is not a descriptive art artifact) it has qualities similar to the valuable qualities of some descriptive art artifact or the like. I am not claiming of course to have mapped out all the ways in which "art" or "work of art" can be used. There are endless uses of the terms. "Work of art" can, for example, be used perjoratively: one might say, "Her dress is a work of art," in a certain tone of voice and with a raising of the eyebrows to mean that the dress is awful because it is overly elaborate.

The thesis about "art" or "work of art" for which I am arguing can perhaps be made more plausible by taking note of a distinction about different kinds of words which Paul Ziff makes in *Semantic Analysis*.[8] Ziff distinguishes between words which have meaning but not *a* meaning in English and words which have both meaning and *a* meaning in English. He gives as an example of a word which has meaning but not *a* (particular) meaning "tiger." "Tiger" does not have *a* (particular) meaning because the word has no set of necessary and sufficient conditions. Conditions such as being striped and being four-legged which may be thought of as necessary can be missing from an individual and that individual can still be a tiger—for example, albino tigers and three-legged tigers. Ziff maintains that being feline is a necessary condition of being a tiger, but it is of course not sufficient. As an example of a word which has meaning and *a* (particular) meaning, he gives "brother," which in one of its senses means "male sibling." This sense of "brother" has necessary and sufficient conditions, namely, being male and being a sibling. Weitz's claim, in effect, is that "art" (or "work of art") is something like "tiger" as Ziff describes it, although not just like it because Weitz claims that there are no necessary conditions for "art." I believe that "art," like "brother" has *a* particular meaning in English—at least one distinct sense. I have also tried to show that this sense is basic and that the class of objects that it picks out is likewise basic.

In *Art and the Aesthetic*[9] and elsewhere I maintained that the artifacts which are art become so in two distinct ways: by being made (painted, sculpted, composed, and the like) or by having artifactuality conferred on them. I maintained that art such as the *Night Watch* is made, but that some works of art had artifactuality conferred on them. This second notion was an attempt to show how things such as unaltered driftwood hung on walls and the urinal Duchamp used fall within the limits of artifactuality of artists. I now believe it was a mistake to think that artifactuality can be conferred; it just is not the sort of thing that can be conferred: an artifact must be made in some way. My mistake was caused, at least in part, by my confounding two quite different things. I wrote of natural objects which become works of art although they are unaltered: "one way in which this might happen would be for someone to pick up a natural object, take it home, and hang it on the wall . . . Natural objects which become works of art in the classificatory sense are artifactualized without the use of tools—artifactuality is conferred on the object rather than worked on it."[10] I wrote of picking up and hanging on a wall and of conferring artifactuality as if they were one and the same thing; that is, I thought of picking up and hanging on a wall as a way of conferring artifactuality. But while conferring artifactuality is impossible (as it now seems), picking up and hanging on a wall is quite easy to do. Picking up and hanging and similar actions are ways of *achieving* (not conferring) artifactuality. Of course, it is not just the motion of lifting and affixing or the like which makes something an artifact, it is lifting and affixing or the like plus something else.

How are we to understand these actions which produce artifacts but which are not straightforward cases of making? Consider a series of cases in which a piece of driftwood plays a central role. In the first

44

case one picks up a piece of driftwood and moves it to another part of the beach merely to get it out of the way. In this case there is no inclination to think that the driftwood has become an artifact, it has just been moved from one place to another. In the second case one picks up a piece of driftwood and with a knife whittles a handle on one end and a point on the other with the intention of using it to spear flounders in the surf. In this case we have a clear case of an artifact, although a crude one; it is an object which has been altered (carved) to suit it to serve a purpose. It is an artifact, of course, even if it is never actually used as a spear or used in any way at all. This second case obviously satisfies the dictionary definition of "artifact": "An object made by man, especially with a view to subsequent use." In the first case, there is nothing in any sense which is made.

Now let us consider some cases which, so to speak, fall in between the first case and the second case. In considering these cases, the test will be to see if there is any sense in which something is made. Suppose one picks up a piece of driftwood and without altering it in any way digs a hole in the sand or brandishes it at a threatening dog. The driftwood has been *made* into a tool or a weapon by the use to which it is put. These cases differ from the driftwood-spear case in that the tool or weapon is not made prior to an intended use and the piece of wood is not altered in any way. But what exactly has been made if the piece of driftwood has not been altered? In the driftwood-spear case what is made is the complex object: the wood carved in a certain way for use as a spear. In the other two cases what has been made are also complex objects: the wood used as a digging tool and the wood used as a weapon. In neither case is the driftwood alone the artifact; the artifact is the driftwood manipulated and used in a certain way. For the purposes of the immediate discussion the driftwood alone (unaltered and unused) is a *simple* object and the driftwood altered or used is a *complex* object. The complex objects are complex because their original (simple) objects have undergone a change at the hands of an agent.[11] When anthropologists speak of unaltered stones found in conjunction with human or human-like fossils as artifacts, they have in mind the same notion of complex objects made by simple-objects-used which I have been discussing.[12]

Now suppose a piece of driftwood is picked up by someone who is familiar with the world of art and taken home and hung on a wall, unaltered, with the intention to display its characteristics as the characteristics of a painting are displayed. The driftwood is being used as an artistic medium and being displayed within the context of the artworld, and it thereby becomes part of a more complex object. The complex object—the-driftwood-used-as-an-artistic-medium—is an artifact of an artworld system. If a piece of driftwood were picked up and hung on a wall without any artistic context and just to get it out of the way (the wall being a convenient place to put it), there would be no reason to think that an artifact had been made; the driftwood would not have become part of a more complex object. The urinal Duchamp used to make *Fountain* is like the driftwood used as an artistic medium; it became an artifact of an artworld system. *Fountain* is the urinal used as it is, as an artistic medium. In saying that the driftwood and the urinal are used as an artistic medium, I am saying that they are used as pigments, marble, and the like are used when more conventional works of art are made. The urinal, unlike the driftwood, was of course an artifact to begin with, but at the beginning it was not Duchamp's artifact (of Duchamp's making). But Duchamp's use of the plumbing fixture within the artworld also made it into an artifact of that system. *Fountain* is thus a double artifact; it is an artifact of the artworld which is made from an artifact of the plumbing trade. Such a double artifact is not of course at all unusual; a painting is made of pigments which in turn are manufactured.

At the beginning of the paper I mentioned Dali's alleged claim that some rocks were art because he had pointed at them and said they were art. Is "pointing and calling" sufficient to make the rocks into artifactual art or are they simply similarity art? Are the rocks an object with which the philosopher of art must contend, i.e., an object such as the *Night Watch* or *Fountain,* or can the rocks be ignored? Put otherwise, is "pointing and calling" sufficient to create an artifact of the artworld? There does not seem to be any sense in which something is *made* by "pointing and calling." The rocks are not altered in any way by the "pointing and calling." Nor are the rocks used in any way similar to the way in which driftwood may be used to dig a hole in the sand or the like or the way in which Duchamp used the famous urinal. In the cases such as the unaltered driftwood digging tool and *Fountain* we seem to have come to the limit of artifactuality; the driftwood and *Fountain* are just barely artifacts. Between *Fountain* and the rocks Dali pointed at there is a gap, the gap which marks the dividing line between artifact and nonartifact.

In this chapter I have attempted to show that artifactuality is a necessary condition of art, or at the very least that it is a necessary condition of the art in which philosophers of art are interested. I have also made some attempt to clarify the notion of what it is to be an artifact. As noted at the beginning of the chapter, however, the institutional theory of art is not alone in holding to the necessity of artifactuality; this is the traditional view. More now needs to be said to distinguish the institutional theory from traditional theories of art. Specifically, what now needs to be shown is the institutional nature of art.

Chapter IV   The Institutional Nature of Art

Monroe Beardsley's incisive attack on the institutional theory provides a good point of departure for a discussion of the institutional nature of art.[1] Beardsley proposes as a contrast with the institutional conception of art and artist what he calls the "Romantic" conception of the artist—an artist working and producing art in isolation from any institutions. Of course, he does not think all artists work in such isolation, but if even one could Beardsley thinks that the institutional conception of art must be false. Beardsley characterizes the Romantic artist as follows.

> *Withdrawn into his ivory tower, shunning all contact with the business, governmental, educational, and other institutions of his society . . . he works away on his canvas, carves his stone, polishes the rhymes and meters of his precious lyric. . . . Of course, we cannot deny that the Romantic artist may be supplied electricity by an institution, that his paper or canvas has to be manufactured, that his very thoughts will be . . . to some extent 'moulded' by his acquired language and previous acculturation. But that is all beside the point, which is (on this account) that he can make a work of art, and validate it as such, by his own free originative power. And it is this claim that has in recent years been explicitly challenged by those who hold that art is . . . essentially institutional.[2]*

In a way, what I shall want to argue against Beardsley is that although an *artist* can withdraw *from contact* with various of the institutions of

49

society, he cannot withdraw *from* the institution of art because he carries it with him as Robinson Crusoe carried his Englishness with him throughout his stay on the island.

Beardsley does not argue in favor of the Romantic conception of art, rather he argues against several particular versions of the institutional view, finding them all inadequate. Consequently, everything Beardsley says may be true and the Romantic view false if an as yet unformulated version of the institutional theory or some other non-Romantic view is true.

Beardsley begins his attack on institutional theories by formulating two principles, either of which, he claims, states a sufficient condition for art's being essentially institutional.

1) *If the existence of some institution is included among the truth-conditions of "A is an artwork" then artworks are essentially institutional objects.*

2) *If the existence of some institution is included among the truth-conditions of "this artwork has property P," where P is a normal property of artworks, then artworks are essentially institutional objects.*[3]

Beardsley takes the second principle to apply to views such as the following: works of art belong to genres and belonging to a genre is an institutional property, hence, works of art are institutional. I shall ignore this principle and claims associated with it, because it does not concern the really basic issue of the institutionality of art.

Beardsley takes the first principle to be the principle of an institutional theory such as mine. There are several problems with Beardsley's claim. First, the name "A" in the antecedent of the first principle is ambiguous; it could refer to some particular object or to all the members of the class of artworks. It must be understood in the latter way, otherwise it lacks the generality to support the consequent which has the form of a universal generalization. I assume that Beardsley wishes "A" to be understood in this general way. Second, he has formulated the first principle in terms of a *sufficient* condition only, but my theory claims that institutionality is both necessary and sufficient. He states the first principle in this weaker form, presumably, because he wants to formulate two principles each of which is sufficient *and* because if institutionality could be shown not to be a sufficient, this would show it not to be necessary *and* sufficient. But even if Beardsley were to show that the first principle is false he would not have shown that institutionality is not a necessary condition of art. And, of course, he would have to show that institutionality is not necessary in order to show that the Romantic view is true. As noted earlier, Beardsley does not argue in a positive way for the Romantic view. Furthermore, he does not attempt to show that institutionality as such is not sufficient, but that particular theoretical accounts of institutionality have not been shown to be sufficient. Consequently, even if everything Beardsley says is true, he will not have shown that institutionality in some form is not sufficient.

In what follows I shall first note and accept some of the criticisms Beardsley makes of my theory, thus amending my conception of the institutional nature of art. Second, I shall focus on Beardsley's conception of the Romantic artist in order to use it as a foil in developing an account of the institutional nature of art.

Before beginning a discussion of the notion of the Romantic artist, it will be useful to consider a very important point which Beardsley makes. He distinguishes between what he calls "institution-types" and "institution-tokens." By "institution-type" he means a practice such as tool-making, storytelling, marriage, or the like. By "institution-token" he means an organization such as General Motors, Columbia Pictures, the Roman Catholic Church, or the like.[4] Institution-tokens execute the kind of activities specified under institution-types. Of course some institution-types (practices) can exist without institution-tokens (organizations).

Beardsley uses the institution-type/institution-token distinction to criticize an aspect of my theory. He cites the definition of "work of art" from *Art and the Aesthetic*; it runs as follows: "A work of art in the classificatory sense is (1) an artifact (2) a set of the aspects of which has had conferred upon it the status of candidate for appreciation by some person or persons acting on behalf of a certain social institution (the artworld)." Beardsley raises a number of questions about various elements of the definition, but at the moment I am concerned with only one. He notes that I characterize the institution of the artworld as an "established practice" which in his terminology makes it an institution-type. He points out that the definition contains expressions such as "conferred," "status," and "acting on behalf of" which typically have application within institution-tokens (the University of Illinois, the United States government, and the like). The difficulty as Beardsley sees it is that the artworld as I have conceived it is not an institution-token but a practice. Beardsley queries, ". . . does it make sense to speak of acting on behalf of a *practice?* Status-awarding authority can center in an institution-token, but practices, as such, seem to lack the requisite source of authority. Perhaps the artworld, as Dickie conceives it, could not confer status."[5]

Beardsley is, I think, completely right on this point. The formulation of the institutional theory which I have given is not coherent. The expressions in question from the definition are much too formal and appropriate only for groups of the kind Beardsley calls institution-tokens. These expressions led me to give inaccurate descriptions of the artworld and some of its functions. For example, I attempted to give accounts of how the conferring of the status of candidate for appreciation occurs in the artworld. It now seems clear that the activity of creating art does not involve conferring. If, however, the institutional theory as I formulated it earlier is not correct, it does not follow that some institutional theory cannot be formulated which is correct, nor does it follow that the Romantic view of art is true. Stated very generally and without elaboration, what I now mean by the institutional approach is the view that a work of art is art because of the position it occupies within a cultural practice, which is of course in Beardsley's terminology an institution-type.

Jeffrey Wieand has refined and extended Beardsley's remarks on institutions by distinguishing between Action-institutions and Person-institutions.[6] Action-institutions are types of acts such as promising and the like. These kinds of actions are governed by rules which those who participate in the activity understand. The tokens of an Action-institution are the particular performances of that type of action. Person-institutions are organizations which behave as quasi-persons or agents, as, for example, the Catholic Church and General Motors do. Typically, selected members of the organization act on behalf of it. Person-institutions can participate in Action-institutions, as when an organization promises to do something. Given Wieand's refinements, I now want to say that art-making is an Action-institution and does not involve any Person-institution in any essential way. Of course, many Person-institutions—museums, foundations, churches, and the like—have relations with art-making, but no particular Person-institution is essential to art-making.

Now that Beardsley's and Wieand's criticism has been accepted, let me return to Beardsley's Romantic conception of art and artist, which he takes to be the antithesis of the institutional view. A discussion of the Romantic view will be useful in stating the institutional view in more detail and making it plausible. Of course, Beardsley's description of the Romantic artist was stated with my earlier formulation of the institutional theory in mind, but this fact does not affect the conflict between the Romantic conception and the general institutional point of view. But what exactly do the two points of view disagree about? Beardsley is quite right that the fact that society supplies an artist electricity, canvas, paper, or the like is irrelevant to whether his art is Romantic or institutional in nature. But Beardsley also lumps in with these irrelevancies the fact that an artist's ". . . very thoughts will be . . . to some extent 'moulded' by his acquired language and previous acculturation." In this quickly passed-over idea about the molding of thoughts lies buried the issue which divides the Romantic and institutional theories. Being supplied some kinds of thoughts by one's society can be like being supplied electricity or canvas, but being supplied other kinds of thoughts is very different. The similarities and differences bear looking into.

If Beardsley is talking about the molding by the cultural environment of thoughts about, say, social justice, racial attitudes, sexual mores, governmental actions, human affection, and the like (the sorts of things which can be the subject matter of art), then the fact that an artist has such culturally derived thoughts when he creates art is irrelevant to whether his art is essentially institutional. And I do not think that anyone would have supposed that these kinds of thoughts are relevant. If, however, the culturally derived thoughts that an artist will have are not merely thoughts about subject matters of art but are thoughts about *art itself*, then things are different and there is good reason to think that the art he creates is essentially institutional. Of course, not every thought about something which is a work of art is relevant here. For example, a kind of thought about art I am *not* talking about here involves thoughts of objects which although in fact works of art are not known to the person having the thoughts to be works of art. A person's remembering or reflecting on an ancient artifact which he does not realize is a work of art is a case of a thought about art in one sense, but it is not a relevant case. A person's seeing and then thinking about *Fountain* in any way without knowing that it is a work of art is another example of a thought about art which is not a relevant case. Relevant thoughts about art are thoughts about objects which a person who has the thoughts knows to be art, thoughts about the activity of producing art, and the like. In short, relevant thoughts are thoughts that involve an understanding in some degree of the concept of art; they are, as noted just above, thoughts about *art itself*. If artists create works of art at least in part because of the thoughts of the relevant kind about art that they have derived from their language and acculturation, then a possibility is opened up that the existence of something which might be called the institution of art is a condition for their works being works of art.

The question now naturally arises: 1) how do the relevant thoughts about art function in an artist's experience and 2) what does it mean to say that these thoughts about art involve something which might be called the institution of art? In answering the first question it must be said that thoughts about art function in two ways. At one end of the range they might take the form of *conscious* thoughts about art itself as is no doubt frequently the case when dadaists, creators of happenings, and the like do their work. At this same end of the range are those who create art of a traditional kind and who at some time

53

during the creative process consciously view their work as falling under the category of art. At the other end of the range the thoughts about art are never consciously in mind at any time during the creative process, but the artists create what they do as a result of their previous exposure to examples of art, training in artistic techniques, or general background knowledge of art. The first question has now been answered; thoughts about art may function consciously or unconsciously, just as thoughts do in countless other domains. In answer to the second question it may be said that thoughts about art involve something which might be called the institution of art because the artists described employ those thoughts consciously or unconsciously as a framework within which they work. At the close of this chapter and in the next chapter I shall attempt to explain in more detail the nature of the framework.

Can art be created outside the kind of framework I have suggested? I believe that Beardsley thinks it can be and that this is the point of his notion of the Romantic artist. His description of the Romantic artist as he has put it, however, it is not an effective contrast to the institutional view because it is not clear what Beardsley means by saying that an artist's very thoughts will be to some extent molded by his acquired language and previous acculturation. Drawing now on what was just said about thoughts about art, his notion of the Romantic artist can be made to be an effective contrast by understanding the Romantic artist's "free originative power" to create works of art to be an ability to create works of art independently of the framework within which artists work, the framework which is typically acquired by having experienced examples of art, having had training in artistic techniques, having been given a background knowledge of art, and the like. Having sharpened up the conception of the Romantic artist, it is very difficult to imagine such a being existing in the world today. How could anyone over the age of two or three years escape knowledge of the basic elements of the framework? Grandma Moses and such primitive painters do not qualify as Romantic artists. They are not people totally ignorant of art; they are people who have a basic understanding of art, although they may be ignorant of many art techniques and the latest doings in advanced art circles. Thus, at the very least the occurrence of a Romantic artist seems highly implausible. Even so, despite the implausibility of such an event, it may seem logically possible that a Romantic artist could spring up. One *can* imagine a member of a primitive tribe which has no conception of art or a member of our own society who is so culturally isolated as to be completely ignorant of art. One can conceive of either of these individuals suddenly having and employing the kind of framework I have been discussing and as a result making a work of art with whatever materials are at hand. This thought experiment, however, obviously does not show that a work of art can be created independently of the framework being sketched, for it pictures art being created within the context of an art-specific framework. What this thought experiment *does show* is that it is logically possible for art together with its framework to have a Romantic occurrence. I have now distinguished between two things both of which Beardsley's view supports: 1) the occurrence of a Romantic artist and 2) the Romantic occurrence of the institution of art. That something of the magnitude of a full-blown institution will occur spontaneously is quite implausible. The present concern, however, is not with whether it is logically possible for the whole institution of art to spring into existence, it is the question of whether art can be created independently of a framework, i.e., whether there can be an occurrence of a Romantic artist. The question is whether one can create a work of art simply by the exercise of one's, to use Beardsley's phrase, "own free originative power." Beardsley's notion of a Romantic artist, as I have interpreted it, holds open the possibility that art-making in at least some cases could be totally a product of individual initiative, a process which could occur in a cultural vacuum. Suppose that a person totally ignorant of the concept of art (the member of a primitive tribe or the culturally isolated individual mentioned above, for example) and unacquainted with any representations were to fashion a representation of something out of clay. Without trying to diminish the significance of the creation of an unprecedented representation, such a creation would not be a work of art. While the creator of the representation would certainly recognize the object as a representation, he would not have any cognitive structures into which he could fit it so as to understand it as art. Someone might make the mistake of identifying art with representation (a deeply ingrained identification) and thereby conclude that the representation is art. Once this temptation is put aside, we can see that the creator of the representation cannot recognize his creation as art and that, therefore, it cannot be art. This case should not be confused with the case discussed earlier of the artist who creates art without consciously having a thought that he is creating art, for such a person could have the relevant thought. In the case in question, the person who creates the representation could not have the relevant thought or thoughts because he lacks the relevant cognitive structures. Art cannot exist in the contextless vacuum that Beardsley's view requires; it must exist in a cultural matrix, as the product of someone fulfilling a cultural role.[7]

It seems inconceivable then that there could ever have been a Romantic artist or that there could ever be one in the future. Now, although a Romantic artist, i.e., someone creating art without a framework, seems inconceivable, someone might think, however, that the institution of art itself must have had a "Romantic" beginning, for otherwise it could never have gotten started. The implausibility of the institution of art springing into existence with its inventor functioning as a Promethean art-giver (with framework thrown in) is something of an embarrassment to the Romantic explanation of art and its origins. Moreover, it is perfectly reasonable to suppose that art did not have the instantaneous beginning that the Romantic-origin thesis requires. Art may have emerged (and no doubt did emerge) in an evolutionary way out of the techniques originally associated with religious, magical, or other activities. In the beginning these techniques would have been no doubt minimal and their products (diagrams, chants, and the like) crude and in themselves uninteresting. With the passage of time the techniques would have become more polished and specialists have come to exist and their products would have come to have characteristics of some interest (to their creators and others) over and above the interest they had as elements in the religious or whatever other kind of activity in which they were embedded. At about this point it becomes meaningful to say that primitive art had begun to exist, although the people who had the art might not yet have had a word for its art.

To give a possible account of the beginnings of art which does not have a role for a Romantic origin does not of course show that there was in fact no Romantic origin(s). The implausibility, however, of some untutored person suddenly having and employing the kind of framework I have been discussing and thereby creating the institution of art at a single stroke just seems like too much to swallow. I want to emphasize again that the question of the Romantic origin of the institution of art is not the main issue which divides Beardsley and me. The fundamental issue is whether there could be a Romantic artist, i.e., a person who creates art independently of a framework.

There is, however, something about Beardsley's notion of the Romantic origin of the institution of art which should be taken account of. The Romantic originator as I have depicted him is a rather complex individual, and it is this complexity which makes his existence implausible. It is more plausible to think of what might be called Romantic proto-artists, i.e., persons whose actions initiate practices which over a period of time develop into something recognizable as an institution of art. I have in mind such actions as the use of a pigment to color a traditional object or a traditional representation, an action which enhances the object or representation. The sort of actions I am envisaging can be identified with "the polishing of techniques" and "the development of specialists" which I spoke of earlier. The cumulative effect of such acts of individual initiative in certain circumstances might ultimately be the creation of an institution of art. The kernel of truth in Beardsley's conception of a Roman-

56

tic originator can thus be incorporated into the institutional view without swallowing the whole conception.

It is possible, perhaps even probable, that Beardsley really intends "Romantic artist" to refer to the kind of individual I have just called "Romantic proto-artist." Understood in this way, a Romantic artist would be an individual who contrives an object because he likes one or more of its characteristics: representative, expressive, aesthetic, for example. According to Beardsley, the object so created would be a work of art. Beardsley's view would be, on this interpretation, that the first artifact which initiated the particular chain of events which resulted in an artworld system is itself a work of art. Now, I said earlier that the action of an individual such as Beardsley here conceives no doubt lies at the beginning of the development which resulted in a system within which works of art are created. The institutional view, however, is that it is further along in the chain of events envisaged that it becomes reasonable to say that there are works of art, namely, at a time when roles have become established with regard to the creation and "consumption" of such artifacts.

Having now attempted to deal with the challenge presented by the theory of the Romantic artist, I must face a radically different kind of opposition in Timothy Binkley's conception of art—a view which up to a certain point takes an institutional-like approach.

Binkley begins "Deciding About Art" by asserting that, as Duchamp demonstrated, ". . . in order to 'create' a work of art it is necessary only to *specify* what the artwork is."[8] Near the end of his article he makes the following statement which he insists is not a definition but ". . . a description of the current state of artistic institutions": "A work of art is a piece specified within artistic indexing conventions."[9] With his specification version of an institutional-like theory of art in hand, he proceeds to attack all traditional definitions of "art" at a stroke. His argument is that for every traditional definition of "art" there will be something which the definition excludes as not art. Binkley then *specifies* that the something which a traditional theory says is not art is a work of art. He claims that any traditional theory is thereby refuted.

My institutional theory of art, however, Binkley says is not defeated by this argument.[10] He has, nevertheless, a number of other arguments to direct against my view. As many others have done, Binkley attacks my notion of conferred artifactuality as inadequate. As I have already conceded on this point and his remarks raise no new questions, I will not comment on this matter. He also objects that the institutional theory is wrong in incorporating the notion of "candidacy for appreciation" into the definition of "art." I think Binkley is right that candidacy for appreciation does not have a place in the

57

definition of "work of art," but I shall not address this question until Chapter VI.

Binkley has a third objection to my version of the institutional theory. As noted, he agrees with the general institutional approach that something is art because of the place it occupies in the artworld, but he questions whether the ". . . notion of status conferral accurately designates how something achieves a place in the index of artworks."[11] I did not intend to claim, as this quotation would have it, that arthood itself is a conferred status but rather that a set of the aspects of an artifact (an artwork) is what has status conferred on it. The status that was supposedly conferred was candidacy for appreciation, not arthood. Unfortunately, several passages in my book give the impression that I thought that it is the status of art which is conferred. My intent was to claim that two conditions are required for art: 1) artifactuality and 2) status of candidacy for appreciation having been conferred on some aspects of the artifact by a member of the artworld. My claim was that status conferral is involved in artmaking, but that it is only part of the story. According to my earlier view, arthood was achieved as the result of two actions occurring within the context of the artworld: creating an artifact plus an act of conferral. In those cases in which "conferred artifactuality" was supposedly involved, according to the earlier view, arthood was allegedly achieved as the result of two different acts of conferral within the artworld context.

Binkley's basic criticism amounts to asking if the notion of conferral of status of art is different from the notion of specifying the status of art. For him specifying is the correct account of artmaking, and if conferral is different it is wrong. The two are different, he maintains, and therefore conferral is not the correct account of artmaking. Binkley offers some other acute criticisms of artmaking as status conferral, but since I did not claim that artmaking is a kind of status conferral, these criticisms are misdirected. In any event, I have already conceded in my discussion of Beardsley's article that the notion of status conferral does not play any kind of role in the creation of art. What remains to be seen is whether Binkley's specification version of the institutional view is adequate.

What exactly is it to specify something as art? Binkley writes that "Success at specifying is not a question of whether you're an artist, but rather of whether you know and can use existing specifying conventions, or else can establish new ones."[12] This remark tells us that specifying art involves the use of some convention or other. What are these conventions? An example he gives involves the actions of a traditional artist: "The mere fact that he used the artistic convention of painting on canvas assured that what he specified as the piece would be art."[13] In the event that it is not clear from this passage, the artistic convention of painting on canvas is identical with specifying art. Painting on canvas is one way of specifying as art; one can presumably also specify as art by painting on wood, chiseling on stone, and in a host of other ways. In addition to the traditional conventions of the kind listed in which a person performs an action with some materials, there is, according to Binkley, what I shall call "simple specification." Simple specification occurred, according to Binkley, when Robert Barry made a work of art by saying (specifying) that it is "all the things I know but of which I am not at the moment thinking—1:36 P.M.; 15 June 1969, New York." Thus, according to Binkley, all the things that Robert Barry knew but was not thinking of at the specified time became a work of art. I believe that Binkley also thinks that simple specification was used when Duchamp made *Fountain*. At the end of his article Binkley claims to make everything in the universe art by simple specification, thereby eliminating the problem of keeping track of which things in the universe are and which are not art. (Simple specification should not be confused with the specification which architects make or which sculptors sometimes make for works which others are to fabricate, or the like. This latter specification can be part of a process which produces a work of art, but simple specification is supposed to produce a work of art all by itself.)

That works of art are made by painting on canvas, chiseling on stone, and the like does not, I suppose, need defending, although there must be more to the story than that. One can, for example, paint on a canvas and not create a work of art, as when someone hired merely to prime canvases paints on a canvas. Binkley tells us that painting on a canvas *done as a convention* results in a work of art. But what exactly is involved in the convention? He mentions that cultural tradition and something's being intended for "artistic consumption" are involved, but that is all he says.[14] One wants to be told more, especially when simple specification is involved and the use of convention is all that is involved in artmaking.

Since we are not told more of the convention(s) used in artmaking, it will be useful to focus attention on Binkley's justification for saying that the Robert Barry "piece" and things of that type (which Binkley calls "Conceptual Art") are works of art. Binkley writes

> . . . I don't know what to say except that they are made (created, realized, or whatever) by people considered artists, they are treated by critics as art, they are talked about in books and journals having to do with art, they are exhibited in or otherwise connected with art galleries, and so on. Conceptual art, like all art, is situated within a cultural

tradition out of which it has developed. . . . The same critics who write about Picasso and Manet write about Duchamp and Barry.[15]

The first thing to note about this justification is that Binkley treats Duchamp's *Fountain* and Barry's "piece" as if they were of exactly the same type. They are, however, quite different: *Fountain,* to begin with, is a work of *visual* art (although I am not saying that what meets the eye is all there is to it) and Barry's "piece" is not.

Barry's piece is not even a kind of art in the way that *The Wasteland* is a poem or *War and Peace* is a novel either; it is, if Binkley is right, art which has transcended the need for a medium and, therefore, cannot be art of any particular kind. The *Mona Lisa* was crafted with paint and canvas as its media, The *Wasteland* and *War and Peace* with pen, ink, and words, and *Fountain* with a urinal used as an artistic medium. Barry's "piece," however, has no medium; it was not crafted with anything, it was just specified. The fact that Barry's "piece" is not physical is of no significance here, Binkley's "piece" which is the universe is certainly physical; it is just that neither *Thoughts* or *Universe* (if I may give them titles) can be said to have been crafted, as were the *Mona Lisa* and *Fountain* (although the crafting involved in creating *Fountain* is at an absolute minimum). *Fountain* is thus not, as Binkley thinks, a case of conceptual art, if conceptual art is art made by simple specification. Also, *Fountain* is an artifact of Duchamp's making, but *Thoughts* and *Universe* are not artifacts of anyone. This division puts *Fountain* on the side of the *Mona Lisa, The Wasteland,* and *War and Peace,* and thereby highlights important differences. We are still left with the question of how simple specification is supposed to create art.

Binkley's argument for Barry's *Thoughts* and its ilk being art, as we have seen, is that they are created by recognized artists, treated by critics as art, written about in art journals, and, finally, that they have developed out of a cultural tradition. Binkley is of course right when he says that a philosopher in constructing a philosophy of art should look to the actual practices of artists, the sayings of critics, and so on. It does not follow from this, however, that a philosopher must take seriously *everything* that the denizens of the artworld do; one may have to look beneath the surface of things a bit to find out what is really going on. First, not everything created by an artist (or a plumber) is necessarily a work of art (or a piece of plumbing). Similarly, just because something is treated as a thing of a certain type (art) by someone (art critics) does not necessarily mean that something is a thing of that kind. Binkley would perhaps agree with these remarks, but he would, I think, also reply that an artist working within the cultural tradition he is talking about can create art by simple specification because the artist intends to do so. Creating art by simple specification thus seems to come down to having an intention to make art plus saying that something is art. Is intending to do something and saying that it is accomplished enough to accomplish that thing? Sometimes it is, as Austin has taught us, as when, given certain antecedent conditions, the minister pronounces a couple husband and wife. But is the cultural tradition of making art so similar to the cultural tradition of making matrimony? Making art has had at its center working with a medium. Learning to be an artist has meant learning to work in some medium or other—paint, stone, words, tones. For hundreds of years thousands of people have been learning to use a medium and thereby to create art. Then one day Duchamp used a urinal as a medium in somewhat the way in which a sculptor uses a piece of stone and manages (just barely) to make a work of art. A new and surprising medium was thereby added to the arsenal of artists. Barry and others, impressed with Duchamp's feat, seem to have decided that if Duchamp can create art by working with such a medium as a urinal, they can create art with no medium at all. It will not do, I think, to say that Barry's unthought knowledge is his medium. Barry does not work his unthought knowledge nor does Binkley the universe, they just *refer* to these things in an unusual way. Duchamp at least caused the urinal to change place and to be displayed within the artworld framework. Duchamp did not do much by way of applied skill, but he at least did something with something. Barry and Binkley merely make a reference to something. Duchamp's and Barry's actions are similar in certain ways, but they are basically of an entirely different sort; Duchamp's action is an act of making, while Barry's is just an act of pointing at something. The gap which divides the two actions marks the difference between making art and just saying one is making art. Duchamp manages to remain within the cultural tradition which Binkley speaks of, but Barry in trying to (or pretending to) perpetuate that cultural tradition passed out of it completely. Some will no doubt wish to claim that with *Thoughts* Barry is trying to extend and succeeds in extending the cultural tradition in somewhat the way it was expanded when another actor was added to the Greek drama or when artists began to use acrylic paints. But what in the tradition is being extended by *Thoughts*? No new medium is being introduced or altered; in fact, Barry here abandons all media. (Incidentally, I am not drawing any conclusions about any of Barry's activities except *Thoughts*).

Binkley criticizes my ill-fated notion of conferred artifactuality by asking if christening is enough to make something into an artifact.

He thinks it is obvious that christening is not enough, and I think he is right.[16] It is also obvious that referring to something with whatever intention does not turn that thing into a work of art.

At this point it will be useful to take stock of the conclusions reached thus far in this chapter. Beardsley's notion of a Romantic artist, when its implications are made clear, has been seen to involve substantial difficulties. The failure of the Romantic artist approach shows that artists produce art only as a result of having experienced examples of art (knowing what they were), having been trained in artistic techniques, having a background knowledge of art, or something of the sort. In short, artists produce art as a result of being enmeshed in a complex historically developed framework. It is this sort of framework, I think, that Binkley has in mind when he speaks of cultural tradition and artmaking conventions. Binkley is, therefore, headed generally in the right direction. His version of the institutional view, however, involves several difficulties: 1) he thinks that artifactuality is not necessary for works of art, i.e., that simple specification is sufficient for creating art and 2) he explains virtually nothing about the nature of the conventions which are supposedly involved in artmaking.

What is now needed is for more to be said about the framework—more about why a framework is essential for an object's being art and more about the nature and details of the framework which is essential for an object's being art.

Since a substantial amount has really already been said about the question of why a framework is essential, I shall begin with it. The failure of the notion of the Romantic artist has shown the necessity for some kind of a framework for the creation of art. In addition to the argument revolving around the notion of a Romantic artist, there is another argument which, so far as I know, has its origin in Danto's "The Artworld" and is used in both of his succeeding articles. This argument focuses on visually indistinguishable objects, one of which is a work of art and one of which is not: Warhol's *Brillo Box* and an ordinary Brillo box, a can-opener which is a work of art and one which is not, the painting *The Polish Rider* and an accidentally produced object which looks just like it. To this list can be added *Fountain* and a urinal which is its twin but is not a work of art.

What each of these cases of pairs shows is that it is not the visible characteristics of an object alone which make it a work of art, since the work of art is visually indistinguishable from an object which is not a work of art. This fact shows that the object which is a work of art must be enmeshed in some sort of framework (not visible to the eye in the ways that the colors of the objects, for example, are) which is responsible for its being a work of art. This argument does not rule out the possibility that what makes one of the visually indistinguishable objects a work of art is the possession of a nonnatural (nonrelational) property. It seems impossible to defeat this mysterious view; however, since no one holds or takes this view seriously, I shall not concern myself with it. Incidentally, the Indistinguishable-Objects argument with minor adjustments applies outside the realm of visual objects.

In "The Artworld" the framework or context is used by Danto as an *explanation* of why one member of an indistinguishable pair can be a work of art and the other not. In the later articles, Danto uses the fact that one member of such a pair is a work of art and the other member is not as an *argument* for the *necessity* of a context. It is the argument which I am using here.

Some have had doubts about this argument when it makes use of the "Fountain" pair, because they maintain either that "Fountain" is not in fact a work of art or that it is unclear whether it is a work of art. Consequently, they feel that with the "Fountain" pair the argument never really gets started. Fortunately, the argument is not tied necessarily to the "Fountain" pair; either the actual case of the "Brillo Box" pair or the hypothetical case of "The Polish Rider" pair or some other hypothetical case is sufficient to get the argument off the ground. In addition, the argument can be modified so that it works for the "Fountain" pair even if "Fountain" is not a work of art. "Fountain" does not actually have to be a work of art to show the necessity of a context. It is sufficient that at some time some person mistakenly (although not insanely so) thought (or even could have thought) "Fountain" to be a work of art. The context within which "Fountain" apparently had a place would in this case explain the mistake. And, of course, many people have thought "Fountain" to be a work of art.

All of the traditional theories of art have, I think been committed to a framework of some sort but have not made it the focus of their theorizing. Consider, for example, the imitation theory. The view that art is imitation has implications in two directions: toward someone who creates the imitation and toward a subject matter. Thus, for the imitation theory a work of art exists within the framework of artist and subject matter, but it is not made clear by the theory whether the framework exists only for the creation of a given work of art at a specific time or whether the framework persists through time such that the *same* framework is the background for the creation of many works. Also, the theory does not make clear whether the framework itself may be the invention of a (Romantic) originator or whether the framework persists as an ongoing cultural matrix for particular artists. Consider another example. If, as Langer maintains, "Art is the creation of forms symbolic of human feeling,"[17] works of art would exist within a framework and one which would be rather similar to that of the imitation theory. "Creation of forms" points toward a creator, and "forms symbolic of human feeling" points toward a certain specific subject matter. Here the focus is so firmly aimed at the alleged subject matter of art (human feeling) that the rest of the framework which is presupposed for the creation of art is virtually ignored. Thus, as with the imitation theory, the nature of the framework is not explored. All of the traditional theories of art could, I think, be shown to presuppose a framework of some kind for the creation of art, although perhaps not in so straightforward and simple a manner as in the cases of the imitation theory and Langer's theory. The point of these remarks about traditional theories is to indicate that the notion of a framework which makes possible the creation of art has been present all along in theorizing about art but that it has not been developed.

Even Beardsley's theory allows for a *minimal* framework in that if a Romantic artist created a work of art, the work would stand in relation to the agent who created it. The theory presupposes, however, that if a Romantic artist created art, the framework itself would be invented or created anew with the creation of the work of art. An important difference between Beardsley's theory and traditional theories such as the imitation theory in this regard is that the latter theories leave it unclear as to whether the framework is sometimes created on the spot or whether they view it as a persisting thing, while in Beardsley's view when a Romantic artist creates art what little framework there is is also created on the spot. Of course Beardsley's view does not rule out the possibility that once a framework has been created it might become a part of the culture and persist through time as the matrix for the activity of artists. It is clear that something more than a minimal framework of the kind that Beardsley's theory presupposes is required for the creation of art; for one thing, a framework which persists through time is required. In drawing this conclusion, I have moved beyond the question of why a framework is essential for an object's being a work of art into the question of the nature of the framework which makes art possible—namely, I have concluded that such a framework must persist through time. What else can be said about the nature of the framework?

I shall take as a point of departure for developing an adequate framework the relatively simple kind of frameworks involved in the imitation theory and Langer's theory. The frameworks of these theories, as mentioned earlier, consist of an agent (an artist) and a subject matter. It should also be noted that these frameworks are ones which persist through time rather than ones which are created on the spot by the agent. In both cases the agent's imitative action can be seen as the fulfilling of a cultural role.

I shall begin my description of the framework by subtracting something: the description does not need to contain an account of a specific kind of subject matter or a subject matter of any kind. I take it that at this late date I do not have to refute the claims of the imitation theory, Langer's theory, and other traditional theories that some subject matter or other is a necessary feature of art. I have tried to show in Chapter II that Danto's more recent and more sophisticated claim that art is necessarily about something, which is a way of saying that art must have a subject matter, is false.

Something must also be said about Danto's view that "It is the role of artistic theories . . . to make the artworld, and art, possible," for if this claim is true, a place must be found within the framework for the functioning of artistic theories. Again, I have tried to show in Chapter II that Danto's contention about the role of artistic theories is false. Danto himself seems to have abandoned this view, which he never managed to make at all clear anyway in favor of his *aboutness* theory. So, there appears to be no reason to try to accommodate the functioning of artistic theories within the framework.

Only the role of the artist remains from the primitive framework of the traditional theories with which I started. Clearly this reduced conception is little more satisfactory as an explanation itself than was the primitive framework from which it was derived, but at least it leads in the right direction—in the direction of the artist and away from subject matter. In order to obtain an adequate account of the framework, as a first step it must be discovered what it is that makes it possible for someone to assume the role of artist.

Earlier in this chapter in opposing the notion of a Romantic artist, I made a suggestion about the framework within which art is created. I suggested that it is a framework which is typically acquired by a person's having previously experienced examples of art knowing that they are art, of having had training in artistic techniques, of having a background knowledge of art, or the like. This characterization, inadequate as it is, focuses on the artist and his knowledge or understanding of his role. Whenever art is created there is an artist who does it, but an artist also creates for a *public* of some sort. So, the framework also includes a role for a public to whom art is presented. Of course, a particular work of art does not have to be presented to a public in order to be art. The relations of a given work to a public are various. Many works of art have been created with the intention of presenting them to a public but for various reasons have never reached that public. A very large number of paintings, poems, and other kinds of works of art are experienced by only those persons who created them; for one reason or another, their creators do not want anyone else to experience their work. Art which is intended for a public, whether it reaches it or not, clearly presupposes a public. Even art not intended for public presentation presupposes a public, for not only is it possible to present it to a public (as sometimes happens), it is a thing of a type which has as a goal presentation to a public. The notion of a public hovers always in the background, even when a given artist refuses to present his work.

By a public I do not mean just a collection of people. The members of a public are such because they know how to fulfill a role. Being a member of a public requires knowledge and understanding similar in many respects to that required of an artist. The following are examples of what I have in mind. To be a member of the public of representational paintings one must be able to see that certain designs depict objects, although of course this ability is not sufficient. To be a member of the public of stage plays one must have a knowledge of what it is for someone to act a part, and so on. Many of the abilities and sensitivities involved in being a member of a public are of an ordinary, everyday sort (although not thereby simple or uncomplicated) but others are achieved only as the result of special training and development.

Compare now the framework as it has thus far been developed with the framework of the imitation theory and Langer's theory. In the latter two the work of art is suspended between artist and subject matter. Disregarding the question of whether subject matter is an essential factor, the frameworks of these two theories are very thin. Neither theory relates an artist to his past or his culture, although neither theory denies the relation. The relation, so far as the theories are concerned, is just irrelevant; an artist is just someone who makes something which resembles something else. The institutional theory sets works of art in a complex framework in which an artist in creating art fulfills a historically developed cultural role for a more or less prepared public. I speak of a more or less prepared public because artists sometimes surprise their publics. An audience at a traditional play, or museum-goers faced with traditional pictures will typically be well prepared to experience and appreciate what they confront. Persons faced with avant-garde art are frequently less well prepared, although if they realize that what they are confronting is art, they are thereby part of a public and are prepared in a general sort of way.

A frequent complaint against *Art and the Aesthetic* is that although it is there claimed that art-making is institutional, nothing is done to show how art-making is rule-governed. The assumption of this criticism is that rule-governedness distinguishes practices such as promising which are institutional from practices such as dog-walking which are not. The assumption and the criticism are well-taken. Ironically, in *Art and the Aesthetic* there is substantial explicit discussion of conventions or rules which govern the presentation of artworks[18] and the behavior of members of publics,[19] but no discussion of rules which govern art-*making*. Art-making rules are implicit in *Art*

66

and the Aesthetic's account of the creation of art, in that the account makes claims about the necessary conditions of art-making. To state a necessary condition for an activity is one way of stating a rule for engaging in that activity.[20] Unfortunately, I did nothing to call attention to the rule-governed nature of art-making. In addition and as already noted, my account confused action-institution language and person-institution language. This confusion in turn obscured the implications which the account has for the rules of art-making, which is action-institutional.

In Chapter III I claimed that being an artifact is a necessary condition for being a work of art. This claim implies one rule of art-making: if one wishes to make a work of art, one must do so by creating an artifact.[21] In the present chapter I have claimed that being a thing of a kind which is presented to an artworld public is a necessary condition for being a work of art. This claim implies another rule of art-making: If one wishes to make a work of art, one must do so by creating a thing of a kind which is presented to an artworld public. The two rules are jointly sufficient for making works of art. The rules may appear to be satisfied by things which are not works of art, but it must be remembered that the rules operate *within* a specific, historically developed, cultural domain. A discussion of how this domain is isolated is presented in the following chapter.

I earlier argued that a framework is essential for something's being art. I then set about to describe a framework for art, talking primarily about artists and publics. The question now naturally arises: "Why is the framework which is being described the one which is essential; might not there be some other framework which is the essential one?" "Subject matter" frameworks of the kind envisioned by the imitation theory, Langer's theory, or even Danto's "aboutness" theory are not, it is clear, viable frameworks. Danto's remarks in his first article about artistic theories and art history suggests some kind of theoretical and historical framework, but he never makes clear what he means. The framework which I have begun to describe owes something to Danto's suggestions about art history, although it is hard to pinpoint exactly the relationship; that is, I have stressed the historical dimension of the artist's and the public's role—what they have learned from the past. Still, the fact that some frameworks will not do and the fact that Danto's suggestions have been taken account of in my conception of the framework do not prove that my description is the correct one. It can be said for my view that it is a conception of a framework in which works of art are clearly embedded and that no other plausible framework is in the offing. It is to be hoped that with the detailed description of the artworld in the next chapter the essential relation of works of art to their artworld context will become even clearer. For lack of a more conclusive argument that my conception of art's essential framework is the right one, I shall have to rely on the description itself in this chapter and the next to function as an argument for the rightness of the conception. If my description of the essential framework is correct, or approximately so, then the description should evoke a "that's right" experience in the reader.

Chapter V   The Artworld

Thus far in discussing the institutional nature of art I have described art's essential framework. In doing so I have concentrated on the roles of artist and public, sketchily characterizing them in terms of what those who fulfill these roles know from the past about art, its creation, and the experience of it. It may be wise at this juncture to point out the obvious fact that creating art is an intentional activity; accidents, fortuitous and not, may occur *within* the creative process, but the overall activity is not accidental. I shall continue the discussion of artist and public roles, focusing on the relation between artist and public. In creating art an artist is always involved with a public, since the object he creates is of a kind to be presented to a public. The relationship is, then, one of creating an object of a kind which is presented. Actual presentation of the created object or even being intended by its maker for presentation cannot be required, because, as noted earlier, some works of art are never presented and some are not even intended by their makers for presentation to a public. What is to be emphasized here is that the created object is of a *kind* which is made for presentation. Consider some cases in which works of art are *not* presented. Some works are not presented by their creators because they consider them to be practice works, not worthy of presentation. Practice works are of a kind for presentation, other- wise it would be pointless to judge one unworthy of presentation. Some works of art are not presented because their creators are uncer- tain of their worth. Some works of art are not presented because their creators believe the works to be too revealing about themselves. One could go on. In these kinds of cases, there is what might be called a "double intention"; there is an intention to create a thing of a kind

71

which is presented, but there is also an intention not to actually present it. Artist and public in relation may be called, as I did on an earlier occasion, "the presentation group."[1] A presentation group is, in fact, the minimum framework for the creation of art.

The role of artist has two central aspects. First, there is the general aspect which is characteristic of all artists, namely, the awareness that what is created for presentation is art. Second, there is the wide variety of art techniques, of which the ability to use one in some degree, enables one to create art of a particular kind. When these two aspects are taken together the wide variety of things that artists do (paint, sculpt, write, compose, act, dance, and so on) are seen to be subsumed under the description "creating an object of a kind which is presented." The role of artist may be realized in various ways. The role may be filled by a single person as is typically the case with painters. Even with painters the role of artist may be internally complex in the sense that a number of persons may be involved, as when an assistant (or assistants) aids a master. In cases of this kind there is still a single role, but it is being fulfilled by several persons. By contrast, in the performing arts it is the rule that the artist role is in fact a multiplicity of cooperative roles. For example, in the theater, the artist role encompasses the roles of playwright, director, and actors. These various roles might in a particular case be played by a single person. In such a case there is still a variety of roles, but they are being fulfilled by a single person.

The role of a member of a public also has two central aspects. First, there is the general aspect which is characteristic of all members of art publics, namely, the awareness that what is presented to them is art. The second aspect of the role of a member of a public is the wide variety of abilities and sensitivities which enable one to perceive and understand the particular kind of art with which one is presented. Some sensitivities or their opposites may be of a specific physiological kind: deafness, tone deafness, ordinary tone hearing, perfect pitch; blindness, ordinary color vision, acute color sensitivity; and so on. Such sensitivities may be sharpened by training and experience; and they may be blunted by aging, accident, or other factors. Some abilities do not have a specific physiological base and depend in a fundamental way upon one's having acquired certain information— the ability to recognize, for example. Other abilities are of a more specific sort—the intellectual ability to comprehend a number of elements as members of a whole, for example. One could go on.

At the beginning of this chapter I spoke of artist and public in relation as "the presentation group." If, however, artists create and publics perceive and understand, there is a function which lies between them and brings them together. In *Art and the Aesthetic* I characterized this function as the task of "presenter"—stage managers and their personnel, museum directors and their personnel, and the like. (There is a sense in which actors, directors, and the like are presenters, but they also participate in the artist role as well.) Also, in the earlier book, I distinguished a number of conventions (there called "secondary conventions") which are involved in the presentation of works of art to publics. A list of such conventions would be very long because of the diversity of the arts, but it is worth noting a few. One convention of theater discussed at length in the earlier book is the "nonparticipation-by-spectator" convention which functions as a rule for directing the behavior of the members of an audience. It is this conventional rule which is bent by Peter Pan's request for applause to save Tinkerbell's life and by similar devices employed in other plays. Another kind of convention is used to direct the audience's attention, for example, the curtain going up and the lights going down. Still another kind of convention of theater is the concealing of the actions of stagehands. In classical Chinese theater, however, the stagehand convention is to have the property man on stage among the actors during the performance. The two differing theatrical conventions for dealing with the same problem—the manipulation of various theatrical elements—provide an interesting and instructive contrast. In the domain of painting, it is a convention to hang paintings with their "backs" to the wall. As noted in the earlier book, we might have had the convention of hanging paintings with their "fronts" to the wall. The two actual solutions for the employment of stagehands and the way we actually hang paintings together with a conceivably different way of hanging them brings out an essential feature of conventions. Any conventional way of doing something could have been done in a different way.[2] The failure to realize that things of the kind just mentioned are conventions can result in confused theory; for example, certain aesthetic-attitude theorists failed to see that the nonparticipation theater rule is a conventional rule and concluded that it is a rule derived from "aesthetic consciousness" and is written in stone. These attitude theorists are horrified by Peter Pan's request for momentary audience participation, because they think that the request violates a dictate of aesthetic consciousness. The request, however, merely amounts to the introduction of a new convention (which permits momentary audience participation) which small children, but not some aestheticians, catch on to right away.

The various arts employ many different conventions to do many different things, but there is no *primary* convention in the arts to which the above discussed conventions are secondary, as I claimed in *Art and the Aesthetic*. I wrote there of the primary convention of theater as ". . . the understanding shared by the actors and the audience that they are engaged in a certain kind of formal activity."[3]

73

Of painting I wrote, "The *display* of a painting is the public aspect of the primary convention of presentation."[4] The first thing to be remarked about these two statements is that the first fails to mention playwrights and the second fails to mention artists (painters), that is, the creators of works of art. These failures arose because the statements occurred within a discussion of the presentation of works of art to audiences, a context within which the creators of works of art do not ordinarily play a big role. Any description of what earlier I mistakenly called "the primary convention" must exhibit a role for playwrights, poets, painters, and the like.

If, however, there is no primary *convention*, there is a primary *something* within which the conventions of the kind already described have a place. What is primary is the understanding shared by all involved that they are engaged in an established activity or practice within which there is a variety of different roles: creator roles, presenter roles, and "consumer" roles. There are, as I indicated, certain conventions involved in the presenting of works of art, and there are, no doubt, conventions involved in the creating of works. The practice within which these conventions are used and observed, however, is not itself conventional. One of the reasons that the way in which stagehands are employed in traditional Western theater is conventional is that it could have been done differently, and the way in which the same task is done in classical Chinese theater clearly shows this. The practice of theater itself or painting itself, however, is not just one way of doing something which could be done in one or more other ways, although there are alternative ways of doing theater and of painting, that is, engaging in these activities using different conventions.

There are rules of very different kinds within the institution of art. There are conventional rules which derive from the various conventions employed in presenting and creating art. There are, however, the more basic rules which govern the engaging in an art activity, and these rules are not conventional. The artifact rule—if one wishes to make a work of art, one must do so by creating an artifact—is not a conventional rule, it states a condition for engaging in a certain kind of practice.

Put in a formal way, the art enterprise can be seen to be a complex of interrelated roles governed by conventional and nonconventional rules. At the end of the last chapter, I discussed the nonconventional rules involved in the creation of art. Here at the beginning of this chapter, I have discussed the conventional rules involved in the presenting and receiving of works of art together with the practice within which these conventional rules have a place.

In addition to the roles of artist, presenter, and public, which are essential for presentation, there are supplementary roles for assisting presentation which exist in a society of any complexity. Some of these roles are aimed at assisting an artist mount his work: producers, theater managers, museum directors, art dealers, and the like. Some of these roles are aimed at assisting a public locate, understand, interpret, or evaluate a work presented: newspaper reporters, critics, and the like. Some other roles revolve around the presented work at a greater distance: art historians, art theorists, and philosophers of art.

The artworld consists of the totality of roles just discussed with the roles of artist and public at its core. Described in a somewhat more structured way, the artworld consists of a set of individual artworld systems, each of which contains its own specific artist roles plus specific supplementary roles. For example, painting is one artworld system, theater is another, and so on.

There is an ambiguity inherent in the way I used the expression "the artworld" in *Art and the Aesthetic* which needs to be recognized and dealt with. I sometimes wrote there of the artworld as a system of roles, as I intend to be speaking of it here. I also wrote of "the core personnel of the artworld,"[5] and this way of speaking at least suggests that I was talking about a particular group of people involved in a person-institution. If I were to use the word "personnel" in characterizing the artworld in this book, I would want it to be understood in a metaphorical way to mean a person fulfilling a role in an *action*-institution. It is the roles I want to emphasize here and not the particular persons who play the roles. There is of course always a community of persons who fill the artworld roles and in a sense are the artworld (personnel) at a particular time, but this is another sense of "artworld."

What all of the artworld systems have in common is that each is a framework or a system for the creation of an artifact for presentation to a public.

Kendall Walton in a review of *Art and the Aesthetic* raises what appears to be a difficulty for the institutional approach as I have presented it. He notes that I give a nonexhaustive list of artworld systems—painting, sculpture, literature, and so on. He observes that there are many nonart systems for creating and presenting artifacts—religious activity, athletics, fashion shows, and the like. Walton then remarks that "we need a way of telling whether a given system not on the list is part of the artworld" and that I do not furnish a way of making this identification.[6]

Walton makes several suggestions as to how the perceived difficulty might be resolved. The line he thinks most promising is the following: "Perhaps the systems of the artworld are connected by causal/historical ties; perhaps the artworld consists of a limited number of protosystems, plus any other systems which developed historically from these in a certain manner."[7] But this line, even if worked out successfully, would still leave what many would perceive as a basic difficulty. Walton's suggested solution could presumably show, for example, that happenings belong to the artworld because they are descended from an artworld protosystem and that fashion shows do not because not so descended. In addition, his suggestion could show why nonartworld systems contemporaneous with the artworld protosystems are not part of the artworld, since they could not have descended from an artworld protosystem. The suggested solution, however, cannot show why a protosystem of the artworld, say, painting, belongs to the artworld.

Many would, I suspect, feel that an art theory should explain why a protosystem is a protosystem. These people would feel that unless such an explanation can be given there is an unacceptable arbitrariness about belonging to the artworld. It appears momentarily that Walton may be one of those troubled by the arbitrariness because, although he does not regard it as as promising as the suggestion of his just discussed, he makes another suggestion which, if successful, would resolve the "arbitrariness problem." He suggests, "It may be that the systems constituting the artworld are linked by crucial similarities, that what qualifies a given system for membership in the bundle is its possession of certain (nonrelational?) features in common with other members of the bundle."[8] An attempt to show the distinguishing crucial similarities of artworld systems would be, I think, a return to the traditional way of theorizing about art, a way which is foreign to the institutional approach. Walton does not really take his suggestion about "crucial similarities" seriously because he later claims that the class of works of art is a hodgepodge of exceedingly diverse items, saying that it is "hardly a natural class."[9] He makes clear that he also thinks the class of artworld systems is a hodgepodge. It is true that both the class of works of art and the class of artworld systems are hodgepodges, if what is meant by "hodgepodge" when it is applied to a class of objects is that the members of the class lack the "crucial similarities" sought by traditional theories. A central point of the institutional approach is that despite the "hodgepodge aspect" of the class of works of art (the lack on the part of its members of the "crucial similarities" sought by traditional theories), the class is unified by the fact that its members are members in virtue of their place within an artworld system.

The problem, however, with which Walton is primarily concerned—the hodgepodge aspect of the collection of artworld systems—remains. The class of works of art has a unity because each work of art is embedded in an artworld system, but what provides the unity which binds the systems themselves together? What Walton takes to be the most promising solution, as I have suggested, does not resolve the hodgepodge aspect of the class of protosystems. And, if the hodgepodge aspect of the protosystems cannot be resolved, there does not seem to be much point in trying to resolve the hodgepodge aspect of the systems "not on the list" by relating them to the protosystems. What has to be accepted is the "arbitrariness" of being an artworld system—the lack of a "crucial similarity" of the kind sought by traditional theories which would easily and obviously distinguish it from nonartworld systems. If there were such "crucial similarities" there would be no need for an institutional approach—the traditional approach would suffice.

Some may feel these results involve a vicious circularity, just as some felt that the definition of "work of art" in *Art and the Aesthetics* did. I acknowledged there that the definition was circular but argued that it was not viciously so because the circle it ran was large and contained a lot of information about the artworld. There is something to be said for this argument, but I now believe that more can and should be said about the "problem" of circularity.

Although circularity in definition and explanation is widely regarded as a grave logical fault, little or nothing seems to have been written which explores the question in any depth. No doubt the explanation for this lack is that most have thought it obvious why circularity is a fault. No doubt circularity is a fault in many cases where it occurs, but is it always a fault?

There is a philosophical ideal which underlies the noncircularity norm of definition, although it does not seem to have been articulated.[10] The ideal goes something like this. There are basic or primitive terms which are unanalyzable and, hence, undefinable. One can learn the meaning of these primitive terms only in some nonlinguistic way: sensory experience, rational intuition, or whatever. In characterizing the ideal, the primitive terms can be represented by small letters: a, b, c, and d. The basic terms can be used to define first-level definable terms which can be represented by capital letters: A, B, C, and D. There may be second-level terms $(M, N, O,$ and $P)$ which are defined in terms of first-level terms or a combination of primitive and first-level terms. There may be third-level terms which are defined by lower-level terms and so on and so on. According to the ideal, all definitions lead back to and depend on the primitive terms and the things they denote. The primitive terms are the foundations of knowledge. The ideal may not envisage a multiplicity of levels above the primitive level, but it does require a level of primitive terms and a level of defined terms.

Can this ideal of the nature of definition be realized? Has it even been attempted on any scale at all? Dictionaries, which are large-scale attempts at definition, make no attempt to isolate a set of primitive terms and are unashamedly circular. Perhaps, however, the ideal might be achieved on a more limited scale. Even if in a domain more limited than that of a dictionary, say, the language of physical objects, one could achieve a set of reductive definitions as envisaged by the ideal, it does not follow from this that such an achievement is possible for definition in any other domain.

There may be a more pragmatic ideal underlying the norm of noncircular definition, one which is a kind of shadow of the first epistemological ideal sketched just above. According to this view, words used to define other words are only primitive relative to the context in which the defining occurs. The functionally primitive terms can be defined in other contexts. On this view, epistemologically primitive terms do not have to turn up, although perhaps they might in some cases. Perhaps some sets of dictionary definitions realize the pragmatic ideal, in that although there are no epistemologically primitive terms upon which they ultimately rest, they constitute a series of definitions which contain no elements which circle back. For example, the word "saddler" is defined as "One who makes saddles," and "saddle" is defined as "A seat for a rider, to be used on the back of a horse or other animal." There does not seem to be any reason to think that the definition of "seat," "rider," "back," and so on will require the use of the words "saddler" or "saddle." Just as the possibility that some definitions might realize the epistemological ideal does not show that all definitions must, the fact that some definitions realize (or seem to realize) the pragmatic ideal does not show that all definitions must. In other words, the fact that some dictionary entries realize the pragmatic ideal does not mean that every term in the language can be made to do so. Bearing in mind these observations about the two ideals, the only way to show that a circular account of art is incorrect would be either to show that either of the ideals under the discussion can be or has been achieved quite generally or that a correct, noncircular account of art can be or has been given. Since neither of these two has been accomplished, the way is at least open for an exploration of a circular account of art.[11]

This very way of putting it will, I suppose, send logical shudders through many, but if art is the sort of thing I think it is, the only correct account of it would have to be a circular account.

Part of, or at least attached to, the ideal of noncircular definition is the view that the role of definition is to inform someone of the meaning of an expression one is ignorant of by means of words one already knows. It is true that one does sometimes look up the definition of a highfalutin word with which one is unfamiliar, say, a word such as "penultimate." More often than not, however, one looks up the definition of a word in order to see if one really knows what it means (and usually discovers that one does) or in order to see what the exact meaning of a word is, although one knows in a general way what the word means and has no trouble in using it correctly in a wide variety of contexts.

The definitions which philosophers have given of "work of art" do not function, nor are they really intended to function, as the dictionary definition of a pedantic word such as "penultimate" functions for most of us. (This is no doubt true of the other definitions which philosophers have given.) Virtually everyone, including even quite small children, has at least a partial understanding of the expression "work of art." Virtually everyone can recognize some things as works of art, knows how some works of art are made, and the like. Thus, virtually no one is in need of a definition of "work of art" in the way that many would be in need of a definition if they came upon an unfamiliar word such as, say, "penultimate." So a philosopher's definition of "work of art" does not and cannot function in the way a definition is supposed to function according to the ideal mentioned earlier—to inform someone of the meaning of an expression one is ignorant of by means of words one already knows. The reason it cannot so function is that anyone who has gotten to the point of reading documents on the philosophy of art will already know what the expression "work of art" means.

What philosophical definitions of "work of art" are really attempting to do is then to make clear to us in a self-conscious and explicit way what we already in some sense know. That philosopher's definitions have been so frequently misdirected testifies to the difficulty of saying precisely what we in some sense already know—a difficulty that Socrates tried to get Meno and his slave boy to appreciate. Definitions of terms such as "work of art" cannot inform us of something we are really ignorant of. Furthermore, the fear that some philosophers have of circularity in certain definitions is, I think, groundless. In any event, if a definition of "work of art" is circular, it may just be so because of the very nature of what the definition is about.

In what now follows I shall present an account of art which is clearly circular, or to put it in a better way, an account which reveals the *inflected* nature of art. By "inflected nature" I mean a nature the elements of which bend in on, presuppose, and support one another. In *Art and the Aesthetic* I attempted to define only "work of art," although I discussed the other aspects of the artworld, as I then conceived of them, in some detail. There, in defining, I focused on the "center" of what I am now calling art's essential framework—works of art themselves. I now think that each of the structural intersections of the framework requires definition, for the framework's center is not its only vital part. Consequently, I shall now, in effect, try to supply a small dictionary—a dictionary for the philosophy of art. This series of definitions is just a shorthand way of presenting in summary form the major conclusions of the previous chapters.

I shall begin with a definition of the term "artist," not because it has alphabetical priority over the other terms to be defined, but because the series of definitions seems to flow most easily from this particular source. Any of the structural intersections would, however, serve as a beginning point.

I) An artist is a person who participates with under-standing in the making of a work of art.

There is nothing controversial, or even surprising, about this definition, so matters are off to a smooth start. The definition in itself is not circular, although it does cry out for a definition of "work of art" which will come along shortly. The "understanding" clause in the definition is necessary to distinguish an artist (say, a playwright or a director) from someone such as a stage carpenter who builds various stage elements. What the artist understands is the general idea of art and the particular idea of the medium he is working with. To forestall misunderstanding, let me hasten to add that a stage carpenter or the like may very well understand the art of the stage but that such knowledge is just not required for the carrying out of the function which constitutes his participation in the artistic process. This definition of "artist" also makes it clear that art-making is an intentional activity; although elements of a work of art may have their origin in accidental occurrences which happen during the making of a work, a work as a whole is not accidental. Participating with under-standing implies that an artist is aware of what he is doing.

These remarks lead naturally to the definition of "work of art."

II) A work of art is an artifact of a kind created to be presented to an artworld public.

Being a work of art, thus, involves having a status or position within a structure which in a way is somewhat similar to the earlier view of *Art and the Aesthetic*. According to the present view, however, the status in no way results from a conferral but rather is achieved through working in a medium within the artworld framework. Let me note here, as I did earlier, that an object need never actually be presented to an artworld public in order to be a work of art. The definition speaks only of the creation of a *kind* of thing which is presented. To forestall one possible misunderstanding, in using the word "kind" here I am not talking about genres or even larger categories such as *painting, play, poem,* or the like. The kind specified by the definition is of a larger sort, namely, an artifact of a kind to be presented. The kind in question is, of course, not to be identified with the kind *work of art,* because the kind in question is only an aspect of a work of art.

To forestall another possible objection to the definition, let me acknowledge that there are artifacts which are created for presentation to the artworld publics which are not works of art: for example, playbills. Things such as playbills are, however, parasitic or secondary to works of art. Works of art are artifacts of a primary kind in this domain, and playbills and the like which are *dependent* on works of art are artifacts of a secondary kind within this domain. The word "artifact" in the definition should be understood to be referring to artifacts of the primary kind. The definition could be explicitly reformulated: A work of art is an artifact (primary) of a kind created to be presented to an artworld public.

In the discussion following the definition of "artist," I remarked that art-making is clearly an intentional activity. In a parallel way, the definition of "work of art" implies that such objects are intentional, i.e., are the product of an intentional activity. The definition of "works of art" leads on to the notions of *public* and *artworld.*

> *III) A public is a set of persons the members of which are prepared in some degree to understand an object which is presented to them.*

This definition is not only not circular in itself, it is stated in a general way and does not necessarily involve the artworld. Put otherwise, it is a formulation which characterizes all publics, not just those of the artworld. The definition of "public" is not formerly tied to the other definitions I am giving. Any actual public, however, will be necessarily tied to some particular system; for example, the artworld public is necessarily related to artists, works of art, and other things.

> *IV) The artworld is the totality of all artworld systems.*

At this point it may be worth emphasizing what is perhaps implicitly clear enough, namely, that the roles of artist and public and the structure of artworld systems are herein conceived of as things which persist through time and have a history. In short, the definitions characterize an ongoing cultural enterprise. This definition of "the artworld" certainly gives the appearance of being circular in itself, although this impression is at least counteracted by remembering that the expression "all artworld systems" is short for a list which includes literary system, theater system, painting system, and so on. The circularity in itself of the definition of "the artworld" may be real or apparent, but the circularity of the whole set of definitions becomes transparent with the definition of "artworld system."

> *V) An artworld system is a framework for the presentation of a work of art by an artist to an artworld public.*

The series of definitions has not led down strata after strata until bedrock is reached. The "final" definition, that of "artworld system," simply reaches back and employs all the previous focal terms: "artist," "work of art," "public," and "artworld." What is to be made of this blatant circularity? Conventional philosophical wisdom tells us to recoil in logical horror and to reject it as uninformative and worse. Beginning with the charge of uninformativeness, as noted earlier, in a basic sense we do not need to be informed about art—we already have a fundamental understanding of it. Conventional wisdom notwithstanding, there is a sense in which the definitions are informative; if they accurately reflect the nature of art and the relations which hold among the various elements of the artworld, then they do in a way inform us. These remarks may counter the charge of uninformativeness, but what of the charge of logical fault—the "worse" of the "uninformative and worse"? If, however, the definitions accurately mirror the inflected nature of the art enterprise, then they are not logically faulty.

I have done what I could to show, in this chapter and the one before that works of art are embedded in what I have called an *essential* framework. What the definitions I have given do, I believe, is to give the leanest possible description of that essential framework and the embedded works. What the definitions reveal, by eliminating distracting detail, is that art-making involves an intricate, co-relative structure which cannot be described in the straightforward, linear way that such activities as saddlemaking presumably can be described. In short, what the definitions reveal and thereby inform us of is the inflected nature of art. The definitions help us get clear about something with which we are already familiar but about whose nature we have not been sufficiently clear from a theoretical point of view. What the definitions describe and thus reveal is the complex of necessarily related elements which constitute the art-making enterprise.

Danto's "indistinguishable-pairs" argument and the failure of the Romantic-artist thesis show that works of art require a framework, but what shows that the framework has the inflected nature that the definitions picture it as having? Reflection on how we learn about art

82

will, I think, reveal in what sense and why an account of art must be circular. How, then, do we learn what it is that we know about art?

We do not learn about art from the theories or definitions of philosophers; their remarks would be unintelligible if we did not already know about art. We learn about art in different ways, but we invariably do so at a tender age. Children are frequently taught about art by being shown how to make works for display: "Now draw a nice picture to take home to your mother or to put up on the board." One may be introduced to art in a more abstract, lecture-like way: "These are pictures done by some men who lived a long time ago to be put up in churches." Art instruction such as the foregoing are typically preceded by remarks which prepare a child for it; for example, "This is the way we draw a face," which helps a child come to understand representation. I do not mean to suggest by my example that a knowledge of representation is necessary for the subsequent understanding of art, but it is almost always involved in the beginnings of teaching about art—at least with Western art.

These, then, are some of the ways that we learn about art. *What* is it that such instruction teaches? We learn that a complex of interrelated things is involved in the art-enterprise: artists (oneself, other children, men who lived a long time ago), works (the nice picture, pictures of religious figures), an artworld public (mother, the other children, the teacher, people who go into churches). We also learn that special places can be set aside for the display of works (the refrigerator door at home, the board at school, the walls of a church).

Considered more abstractly, what is it that such instruction teaches us? We are taught about agent, artifact, and public all at the same time, and this is no accident for the various artworld elements do not exist independently of one another. In learning about what a poem, a painting, or a play is, we cannot fail to learn that it is an object with a past—an object which results from a human action—and that it is an object with an intended future—an object which is of a kind which is presented. When we come to know that an object is a work of art, or even just see an object as a work of art (perhaps mistakenly), we fit it into a certain kind of cultural role—the kind of role I have been trying to describe in this and previous chapters.

Perhaps a good way to round out the account of the artworld would be to consider some of the implications of the speculations of the last chapter about the origins of art. There it was speculated that the art enterprise must have evolved out of a prior activity or activities as the cumulative effect of the innovations of what I called "Romantic proto-artists." At a certain point—perhaps a rather elongated point—a prior activity ceased to be merely a single activity and became a complex one—say, religious activity plus an art form. The participants themselves (in a certain way) and some of the other elements of

83

the prior activity metamorphosed into the kind of structure I have called "an artworld system." Given this account, one can see that the activity or role of artist, the conception of the product of this activity as a work of art, and the activity or role of public had to develop together, growing into the identifiable elements of a single integrated whole—an artworld system.

Artist, work of art, artworld, and artworld system are what I shall call "inflected concepts." I mean the expression "inflected concept" to designate a concept which is a member of a set of concepts which bend in on themselves, presupposing and supporting one another. No member of such a set can be understood apart from all the other concepts in the set. Consequently, in coming to understand a concept which is a member of such a set, one must in some degree come to understand all the other member concepts as well. There are, I suspect, other sets of inflected concepts: law, legislature, executive, and judiciary, for example. The domain of "cultural concepts" is perhaps rife with inflected sets. In any event, an account of the art enterprise requires the use of a nest of inflected concepts.

But isn't there more to be said about art? Even many of those who are in general agreement with the institutional approach may feel that there is more to the nature of art than my remarks allow. Certainly those who disagree with what I have said, but still think that art has an essential nature, will feel that there is more to that nature than the institutional theory claims. Beardsley, for example, clearly thinks that more ought to be said. In the concluding paragraph of "Is Art Essentially Institutional?" he remarks that the institutional approach fails to answer the question which has motivated the main tradition of Western philosophy of art. This tradition, which according to Beardsley is a kind of essentialism, has assumed ". . . that there is a function that is essential to human culture, and that appears in some guise in any society that has a culture, and that works of art fulfill, or at least aspire or purport to fulfill."[12] At the end of his concluding paragraph, he remarks that the institutional theory does not tell us ". . . whether there are basic and pervasive human needs that it is the peculiar role of art to serve."[13] Beardsley does not hazard a guess as to what this essential function is or what the basic human needs are, but his remarks certainly suggest that he thinks that works of art fulfill an essential function, i.e., one which must occur in any human culture, which is to satisfy or try to satisfy certain basic human needs. The kind of essentialism which Beardsley has in mind here is different from the essentialism which has characterized many traditional theories. The essential in the imitation theory is that which is necessary for an object to be a work of art, namely, being an imitation. Even if the imitation theory were an adequate theory of art, there would be no compelling reason to conclude that imitations are necessary for human culture or that they satisfy *basic* human needs. Parallel remarks go also for the theories of art as symbols of human feeling, art as significant form, and other traditional theories. I suspect that what Beardsley has in mind as occurring in every human culture, i.e., as essential, are created objects which satisfy a (basic) aesthetic need, say, a need for aesthetic experience. To sum up, the essentialism of traditional theories differs from that which I think Beardsley has in mind in the following way. For the traditional theories what is essential is a property which an object must have in order for the object to be a work of art—the property of being an imitation or of being a symbol of human feeling, or whatever. For Beardsley, it is works of art themselves which are essential—essential to society to serve some purpose. The theory Beardsley has in mind is a theory of what works of art do, not of what they are. Beardsley's implied theory is not then a theory of art in the traditional sense and, hence, not in competition with the imitation theory, Langer's theory, or the institutional theory.

If I understand what Beardsley is suggesting, a number of difficult details would have to be worked out for it to be made plausible. First, there is the empirical question as to whether every human culture has works of art. This empirical question would have to be answered whether works of art fulfill an aesthetic function, some other kind of function, or a combination of an aesthetic function and some other kind of function. Then there is the difficult conceptual question of saying what "aesthetic" means when an aesthetic need is spoken of. Finally, there is the problem of specifying what it means to say that a need satisfied by art is *basic*.

In response to the first implied claim, it is not clear to me that a human culture must have art. Beardsley might reply that my formulation is too strong because he has written only of what is essential for ". . . any society that has a culture. . . ." If this qualification is made, it must then be discovered what it takes for a society to have a culture in order to even begin to test the empirical question, which now becomes "Does every society with a culture have art?" When put in this qualified way, the question may have lost its empirical nature.

If the need which Beardsley has in mind is an aesthetic need, one is faced with the notoriously difficult task of saying what "aesthetic" means. Actually, Beardsley speaks of needs rather than of a single need, so that he may have in mind that there is an aesthetic need plus one or more other needs which ". . . it is the peculiar role of art to serve." Of course, the larger the number of needs specified, the more difficult it is to envisage its being the peculiar role of art to serve them. In any event, I rather doubt that a satisfactory account can be given of an aesthetic need or of a set of needs which art serves, assuming that either of these is what Beardsley has in mind.

85

Finally, what does it mean to say that the envisaged needs are *basic?* Are they like the need for air, water, and food, i.e., necessary for life? Or are they like the need for social structure which is necessary for there to be a human culture? If the answer to this last question is in the affirmative, then perhaps we are back to the first thesis, namely, that art is essential for a society with a culture. Beardsley's remarks ought not to be pressed too hard, for he intended them only to raise an issue and to indicate a direction. I have discussed his remarks at the length that I have, because they articulate a feeling that many have—that there must be more to art than the institutional theory allows or reveals.

The institutional theory, however, places virtually no restrictions on what art may do, it seeks only to catch its essential nature. The institutional nature of art does not prevent art from serving moral, political, romantic, expressive, aesthetic, or a host of other needs. So there is more to art than the institutional theory talks about, but there is no reason to think that the more is peculiar to art and, hence, an essential aspect of art.

Still, many, as I suspect Beardsley does, would like the notion of an aesthetic *something*—experience, appreciation, attitude, or the like—to be an aspect of the essential nature of art. While I do not think that this traditional conception of the aesthetic has a role to play as an essential aspect of art, it requires examination. In *Art and the Aesthetic* I attempted to incorporate a "neutrally" and untraditionally conceived idea of aesthetic object into the definition of "work of art." For reasons which I hope will become clear in the next chapter, I have not attempted in the preceding chapters to even discuss my untraditional notion of aesthetic object, much less to try to make it an essential aspect of art. I turn now in the final chapter to recent attempts to revive the aesthetic attitude and to a recent attempt to make the "aesthetic," conceived in a traditional way, a criterion of aesthetic object. The discussion of these topics leads in the direction of an institutional conception of aesthetic object.

Chapter VI   Aesthetic Object

In the preceeding chapters I have been attempting to respond to criticisms which are addressed to global aspects of the institutional theory of art. A number of articles have been aimed more narrowly at what might be called the institutional conception of aesthetic object. Since this conception necessarily relates to works of art, the general problem is that of the aesthetic objects of works of art, also known as the problem of aesthetic relevance.

In *Art and the Aesthetic* I accepted what I took to be Monroe Beardsley's meaning of "aesthetic object of a work of art," namely, "those properties of a work of art which are properly appreciated and/ or criticized." I did not, however, accept Beardsley's way of determining which features of a work of art belong to its aesthetic object. I argued that his *principle of perceptibility* could not, on the one hand, rule *out* nonaesthetic aspects of a work such as the perceptible property man of a classical Chinese play or the ink marks used to print a poem or, on the other hand, rule *in* such aesthetic aspects of works of art as the meaning of a poetic line or the invisible wires used to "fly" Peter Pan about the stage. I also argued that Beardsley's *principle of distinctness* could not be wielded without presupposing a great deal. The positive part of my remarks—the institutional conception of aesthetic object—amounted to trying to make explicit "the great deal" that Beardsley was presupposing. My criticism of Beardsley's view still seems to me to be satisfactory, and I refer the reader to the earlier account for its details.

Before beginning an examination of the four articles to be discussed in this chapter, it will be useful to discuss briefly the notion of aesthetic object and why it arises. In the last chapter I characterized works of art as artifacts of a certain sort. Such artifacts may have properties of two very different kinds; for example, a painting might be completely blue and red on its front and have a white back. Both the blue and the white would be in some sense properties of the artifact which is the work of art, but it is intuitively clear that the two color properties would be of a very different sort. The blue might be intense or garish and the white might be brilliant or pallid, that is, both the blue and the white might be, to use Sibley's terminology[1], "aesthetic qualities." Although the two would be aesthetic qualities of a single thing, there would be an important sense in which they would be aesthetic properties of two quite different things. In this case it would be a reasonable thing to comment on the intensity or garishness of the blue *in* the painting. It would be odd, however, to comment on the brilliance or pallidness of the white *in* the painting, but not odd to comment on the brilliance or pallidness of the color of the back of the painting. (It would, of course, be rather unusual to talk about the color of the back of a painting.) It is the difference between what is in the painting (or any other work of art) and the other properties of the painting (or any other work of art) which generates the problem of the aesthetic objects of works of art. Some theorists have discussed this question as a problem of distinguishing between a work of art as a physical object and as an aesthetic object, but putting it this way raises unnecessary philosophical questions and obscures the real nature of the problem. Other theorists have discussed the question as a problem of what can and what cannot be the object of the aesthetic attitude, but this approach involves grave difficulties. Here, as in *Art and the Aesthetic*, I shall understand the problem of the aesthetic objects of works of art to be the problem of which properties of works of art are properly appreciated and/or criticized. One would properly appreciate and/or criticize the blueness in the hypothetical painting described above. One could appreciate and/or criticize the whiteness of the back of the painting, but this would be "improper" in the sense that one would have lost contact with or strayed from the point of art appreciation and/or criticism.

From the above it is clear that the notion of aesthetic objects of works of art has no direct connection with aesthetic qualities as Sibley conceives of them; aesthetic qualities may occur as elements in the aesthetic objects of works of art, as "other" properties of works of art, or as properties of things which are not works of art.

Some theorists have maintained that the notion of the aesthetic object of a work of art is a superfluous notion, being just another name for what is really the work of art itself. This contention is, I think, merely a terminological matter, for the problem then becomes one of distinguishing those properties which make up real works of art from those which are merely properties of the vehicles which bear the works of art. The problem is the same whatever terminology is adopted.

The first attack on the institutional theory of aesthetic object which I will consider is that of Robert Schultz.[2] In the first part of his article Schultz defends my attempt to undermine the notion of aesthetic attitude against a recent attack, but in the last part of his article he assails my account of aesthetic object, arguing that it tacitly depends upon a conception of the aesthetic which is very similar to that of the aesthetic-attitude theory. Schultz has, however, misunderstood the nature of my theory of aesthetic object.

Schultz prefaces his criticism by making a distinction of something more than simple terminological significance which I wish to adopt—the distinction between an independent sense of the aesthetic and a dependent sense of the aesthetic. The independent sense is independent because it has no necessary connection to art. A sense of aesthetic which derives from the aesthetic attitude would be an independent sense because the aesthetic attitude can, so the theory says, be taken toward virtually anything—not just art. Aesthetic qualities of the Sibley kind would also fall into the independent category because they have no necessary connection to the notion of art. The aesthetic of aesthetic objects of works of art (as characterized just above) is obviously dependent because it has application only to works of art.

Whether the independent sense and dependent sense of the aesthetic have any real connection is a question which will be dealt with at a later point in this chapter. Nevertheless, it is and has been my intention to keep these two senses conceptually separate. Schultz argues that despite my attacks on aesthetic-attitude theory that in my formulation of the definition of "work of art" in *Art and the Aesthetic* and earlier formulations I make an independent sense of the aesthetic basic to the definition. Specifically, what he has in mind is the use of the notion of appreciation in the aesthetic object aspect of my definition of "work of art"; his contention is 1) that appreciation is the pivotal concept in my definition (*the* thing that makes an artifact a work of art) and 2) that appreciation introduces an independent sense of the aesthetic (which is contrary to my wishes).

One way to deal with Schultz's criticism would be to say that since the notion of appreciation no longer plays a role in the definition of "work of art" as I have formulated it in this book, there is no need to discuss it. However, because Schultz's criticism brings out some difficulties in the earlier version of the institutional theory of aesthetic object while at the same time misconceiving the "spirit" of the older version, it should be discussed. I shall discuss Schultz's criticism not so much to defend the earlier version as to try to set the record straight.

Schultz's argument runs as follows:

1) *"Dickie wants to define an art object as, roughly, an artifact which is a candidate for appreciation."*
2) *". . . appreciation is* irrelevant *to the proper treatment of Duchamp's urinal as an art object."*
3) *"For Dickie, the independent aesthetic is to be characterized in terms of appreciation. Dickie is very careful to point out that the sort of appreciation he is speaking of is ordinary appreciation, with no special qualifications."*
4) *"But then what is principally relevant for the arthood of an object is, finally, the object's being deemed a* candidate *for having this ordinary state [appreciation] directed toward it."*
5) *Since any artifact can be a candidate for appreciation, ". . . Dickie's account makes it fundamentally arbitrary . . . just which . . . objects are art objects."*

First conclusion: [Being a candidate for appreciation] ". . . is a very implausible solution to the problem of relevance for various modernist works."

Second conclusion: It is an absurd result that ". . . Sophocles' Oedipus Rex, a 200-year-old pine tree, Goedel's Theorem, and an act of kindness . . ." can all be works of art.[3]

First, what is right about Schultz's criticism? His second premise serves to help uncover an important problem. He is quite right, following Ted Cohen,[4] to call attention to the inadequacies of my account of appreciation. Schultz does this by claiming that appreciation is irrelevant to Duchamp's *Fountain*. Cohen had made a similar charge, maintaining that Duchamp's *Fountain* cannot be appreciated, hence, cannot be a candidate for appreciation. I had responded to Cohen in *Art and the Aesthetic* that *Fountain* has qualities—a shiny surface, oval shape, and the like—which are things of a type which can be appreciated. Schultz says that the appreciation of such qualities is irrelevant "to the proper treatment of Duchamp's urinal as an art object." Schultz thinks that Cohen is right when he says, "What significance we can find in "Fountain" we find not in the urinal but in Duchamp's gesture."[5] I acknowledged in *Art and the Aesthetic* that Cohen is right about the significance of *Fountain* as a gesture, but the conception of *appreciation* I adhered to there prevented me from realizing the full thrust of Cohen's point. In *Art and the Aesthetic* I defined "appreciation" as follows: "All that is meant by 'appreciation' . . . is . . . in experiencing the qualities of a thing one finds them worthy or valuable."[6] Defining "appreciation" with reference to *qualities* caused me to respond to Cohen by saying that *Fountain* has qualities which one can appreciate (shiny surface and the like), virtually ignoring its gesture significance. I should have defined "appreciation" as meaning "in experiencing a *characteristic* or the *characteristics* of a thing one finds it or them worthy or valuable." This definition, which does not limit features one can appreciate to *qualities*, allows the protest characteristic of *Fountain* to be appreciated.

The redefinition shows how, contrary to Schultz's second premise, appreciation can be relevant "to the proper treatment of Duchamp's urinal as an art object." The criticism made by Schultz's second premise is, however, justified given the way the earlier version of the theory was formulated.

Now, what is wrong with Schultz's criticism? I shall consider the second conclusion first. Schultz's conclusion that anything (*Oedipus Rex*, a 200-year-old pine tree, and so on) can be a work of art and that this is absurd is correct, but he gives the wrong reasons for drawing this conclusion. The definition I gave in *Art and the Aesthetic* goes as follows:

> *A work of art in the classificatory sense is (1) an artifact (2) a set of the aspects of which has had conferred upon it the status of candidate for appreciation by some person or persons acting on behalf of a certain social institution (the artworld).*

Schultz's highly abbreviated version of this definition defines a work of art as

> "*roughly, an artifact which is a candidate for appreciation.*"

This overly rough statement preserves the two-condition nature of the definition, but his subsequent argument entirely ignores the artifact condition, which is the real source of trouble—the gate which allows in everything. The artifact condition, plus my allowance of "conferred artifactuality" allows in potentially everything. I will not comment on this point, as it was sufficiently discussed in Chapter III. The argument Schultz gives for the second conclusion can be summarized as follows:

1) *Dickie's use of appreciation is that of an independent sense of the aesthetic.*

2) *Dickie employs this independent sense as a criterion of arthood.*

3) *Anything can be an object of an independent sense of the aesthetic (an assumption embedded in the notion of an independent aesthetic).*

Conclusion: for Dickie, anything can be a work of art.

In effect, Schultz focuses entirely on the second condition of my definition. His summary statement of the definition is, however, too abbreviated, because he fails to take account of the context in which candidacy for appreciation is embedded. If he had taken this context into account, he would not have been tempted to think appreciation is being employed as an independent sense of the aesthetic.

First, the appreciation condition was intended as one of two conditions, not as *the* condition of arthood. Second, the appreciation condition was specifically intended to deal with the problem of the aesthetic object of works of art, not to function as *the* condition of arthood. In what follows, I shall be talking of appreciation as it relates to the aesthetic object of works of art, although Schultz speaks simply (too simply) of appreciation as it relates to works of art (i.e., as the condition of arthood). I could not have intended that it is *appreciation* as such which makes something the aesthetic object of a work of art, because as I noted things other than works of art can be appreciated. Nor could I have intended that it is *candidacy* for appreciation as such which makes something the aesthetic object of a work of art, because as I noted things other than works of art can be candidates for appreciation. It is the clear intent and the spirit of the earlier version of the institutional theory of art to claim that what makes something the aesthetic object of a work of art is that it is a set of aspects which has had conferred upon it the status of candidate for appreciation *within the artworld*. Schultz simply ignores the whole artworld context; in fact, he does not even mention the question of the institutionality of art, except for a brief remark in a footnote of which he makes no use in his article.[7] The main point of the theory is to call attention to the complicated institutional structure within which works of art have their being. The appreciatability (the capacity to be appreciated) spoken of in the theory is of a highly dependent sort, i.e., dependent on the existence and functioning of the artworld. Schultz focuses on one element in the theory, ignoring its connections to the other elements.

Schultz's first conclusion is that being a candidate for appreciation ". . . is a very implausible solution to the problem of relevance for various modern works." This conclusion about "various modern works" is more or less a generalization of Schultz's second premise which is about only *Fountain*. An aspect of the conclusion is justified; the aspect which turns upon Cohen's insight that *Fountain's* gesture character is relevant.

Cohen's criticism can be accepted and accommodated by expanding the scope of *appreciation*, as I did earlier. The general thrust of Schultz's conclusion, however, is very misleading in that it assumes (an assumption derived from his inadequate summary of my definition of "work of art") that simply being a candidate for appreciation is intended as a solution to the problem of relevance. The institutional theory of *Art and the Aesthetic* attempted to solve the problem of relevance (the question of which aspects of a work of art belong to its aesthetic object) by claiming that the relevant aspects are those which are candidates for appreciation as determined by the various artworld practices and the conventions which cluster around the individual practices. Neither appreciatability nor candidacy for appreciation is supposed to determine anything about relevance according to the earlier version of the institutional theory.

The second criticism of the institutional theory of aesthetic object which I will discuss is that of Gary Iseminger.[8] In an important respect Iseminger's notion of the aesthetic objects of works of art closely resembles that of Beardsley. Iseminger opens his article by speaking of aesthetic relevance and agrees with me that not every property of a work of art is aesthetically relevant; or, in my terminology, not every property of a work of art is an element of the aesthetic object of that work. He notes that the color of the back of a painting is not aesthetically relevant, and he presumably agrees that the colors on the front of the painting are aesthetically relevant. He then correctly points out that on the view of *Art and the Aesthetic* ". . . a necessary condition of a property's being aesthetically relevant is that it has a certain status conferred on it in accordance with the conventions which govern . . . the artworld."[9] Of course, I have now abandoned any notion of *conferred* status, but it is the necessity of artworld conventions for aesthetic relevance with which Iseminger really wishes to take issue. Consequently, the revised theory must take account of his arguments.

In the midst of his initial remarks, however, he says something which is very strange and which, I think, underlies the whole disagreement. He says that there are ". . . aesthetically relevant properties of things which are not works of art,"[10] and he gives as an example the delicacy of a flower. But the way "aesthetic relevance" is used in the literature of aesthetics ties it necessarily to works of art and to speak of aesthetically relevant properties of natural objects such as flowers is just a confusion. Iseminger seems to accept that "aesthetic relevance" means "that which belongs to the aesthetic object of a work of art" when he notes that the color of the back of a painting is not aesthetically relevant. But if that is what "aesthetic relevance" means, then it has no application to natural objects. Iseminger has not, however, just made a slip of the pen, for several pages later he writes,

> . . . we may more easily see the point of the artworld's conferring the status of a work of art on something if we suppose . . . that aesthetic relevance exists prior to and independent of the artworld. Indeed, it seems almost a commonplace to note that aesthetic properties characterize natural objects and that aesthetic states of affairs (as I shall call them) exist independently of the institutions of the artworld. And this fact, if it is a fact, would provide a satisfying natural answer to the question of why an agent of the artworld might choose to confer the required status on, say, a piece of driftwood. He could do so, normally, because he noticed that it already exhibited certain aesthetically relevant properties."[11]

In this passage, Iseminger speaks first of aesthetic relevance, then of aesthetic properties, then of aesthetic states of affairs, and finally of aesthetically relevant properties. These remarks, together with his earlier remark that the delicacy of a flower is an aesthetically relevant property, suggest to me that he is confusing the aesthetically relevant (that which belongs to the aesthetic object of a work of art) with aesthetic qualities or properties of the Sibley kind. Who would deny that aesthetic qualities exist prior to and independent of the artworld (at least many do). However, aesthetic relevance cannot exist independently of art.

In any event, Iseminger proceeds to try to develop a notion of appreciation with which he intends to "mark off the domain of the aesthetic."[12] After making such qualifications as that which is appreciated is known noninferentially and that actual appreciation need not occur, he produces the following definition-like statement: ". . . aesthetic states of affairs are those which are capable of being appreciated, . . ."[13] There is nothing in Iseminger's account of marking the domain of the aesthetic which treats works of art differently from natural objects, a feature which seems to me to be a grave shortcoming but one which Iseminger clearly intends.

He illustrates the difference between his view and my account by showing what the different results are in a given case. He chooses the case of the property man in traditional Chinese theater. The Chinese property man, dressed unobtrusively in black, moves about the stage *during* the performance, changing scenery, holding a certain kind of flag in front of an actor who has been "killed" on stage as the actor walks off stage, and the like. I had argued, as noted earlier, against Beardsley's perceptibility criterion of aesthetic object that the Chinese property man is perceptible under the normal conditions for viewing such plays, but that the property man is clearly not part of the aesthetic objects of such plays. My argument was that the Chinese property man, although plainly visible, is excluded from the aesthetic objects of such plays, i.e., is made aesthetically irrelevant, by the conventions of such theater. The knowledgeable theater-goer knows the conventions and thereby knows enough to ignore the activities of the Chinese property man. My point was that the Chinese property man's actions are not part of the performance of the play as are the activities of the actors. Iseminger seems to understand my argument. Nevertheless, he says, "But it seems clear that, on my account [Iseminger's], these activities [those of the Chinese property man] . . . are appreciable by the audience and hence the performance as characterized by them is an aesthetic state of affairs. . . I am inclined to think that *to the extent that* his activities are appreciable by the audience they are an aspect of the performance. . . It is not as if a convention could, by itself, *prevent* his activities from being a part of the performance if he regularly upstaged the (other?) actors."[14] It is no doubt possible that the property man might do something that would be appreciated by the audience, but he could not thereby upstage the actors, only an actor can upstage another actor; a Chinese property man cannot be part of the performance, he could only intrude on the performance, as a stagehand of a Western stage production or someone from the audience might intrude. Given Iseminger's account, a member of the audience who happened to wander onstage and whose action could be appreciated would become part of the performance. Thus, for example, for him, there is always the possibility that *Hamlet* might acquire another character at any moment, say, a Mr. John Smith from the audience who for some odd reason joins the actors onstage. On his account, anything which can be appreciated might become part of the aesthetic object of *Hamlet* or that of Renoir's *Three Bathers* or that of any other work of art. I am not denying that the Chinese property man could not exhibit an aesthetic property; he might, for example, move in a graceful way. What I am denying is that his graceful movement is part of the performance of the play as is, say, the graceful movement of an actress who portrays a Chinese empress. Similarly, Mr. John Smith might speak with great dramatic effect when he intrudes upon the stage, but such behavior cannot turn him into an actor portraying a character in *Hamlet*, even if he wears Elizabethean garb and speaks in iambic pentameter. It is true that a Chinese property man has a kind of regular relation to classical Chinese plays that Mr. John Smith does not have to *Hamlet*, but my point is that they are both distinct from the actors and action of the play. A number of people have objected to my conclusions about the Chinese property man, and I do not want the point of the argument to be obscured by the details of an exotic example. If the Chinese property man is properly appreciated and/or criticized, then I am wrong in my example, but the distinction between the aesthetic-object properties of a work of art and its other properties remains. Whatever may be the case about the details of these or any other examples, the main focus at this point must be on Iseminger's use of appreciatability as the criterion of the aesthetic objects of works of art.

Iseminger's account of aesthetic objects of works of art has essentially the same kind of flaw as Beardsley's account. What can be appreciated (for Beardsley it was what can be perceived) is not powerful enough to separate the aesthetically relevant properties of art from the aesthetically irrelevant properties of art or to separate the aesthetically relevant properties of art from anything else in the immediate environment of the work of art. The theories of both Beardsley and Iseminger fail because neither takes into account the fact that works of art are cultural objects which are created within complex artworld practices. They both treat works of art as if they were natural objects such as orange trees and sunsets. Let us return to the example of the color of the back of the painting with which this discussion began. On Iseminger's account, the reason that the color of the back of the painting is not aesthetically relevant must be because it is turned to the wall and we cannot see it and, hence, cannot appreciate it. If for some, say, historical religious reason our practice were to hang paintings with their fronts to the wall and we were allowed to turn them around only briefly to look at them, on Iseminger's account the color of the back of the painting would presumably be an aesthetically relevant property of the painting.

Iseminger tries to make one sense of "aesthetic" (whose criterion is appreciatability) do double duty: 1) to pick out properties such as delicacy and gracefulness (which may be properties of works of art or natural objects) and 2) to separate the aesthetically relevant properties of a work of art from its aesthetically irrelevant ones. Appreciatability, however, just cannot do the second job of separating the various properties of works of art. The failure of Iseminger's argument suggests that the word "aesthetic" has more than one sense. It is not clear to me that appreciatability can do the first job either, i.e., the job of distinguishing aesthetic qualities (gracefulness) from nonaesthetic qualities (squarishness), but I am not concerned with that question here.

Iseminger's theory resembles some of the older aesthetic-attitude theories in an important respect. These theories assumed that if a property of an artwork is an object of the aesthetic attitude it is automatically determined that that property is aesthetically relevant, i.e., determined that that property is part of the proper object of appreciation and/or criticism. In presenting his version of aesthetic-attitude theory, Jerome Stolnitz speaks, for example, of compatibility with disinterested attention as being the criterion of aesthetic relevance. Both Iseminger and Stolnitz try to make a single sense of "aesthetic" do two quite different things, although they do not characterize the sense in the same way. Stolnitz notes that one result of using the criterion he does (a single criterion of "aesthetic") is that some important aspects of works of art—moral vision, for example—turn out not to be aesthetically relevant, i.e., not proper objects of appreciation and/or criticism.

Two recent aesthetic-attitude theorists, Robert McGregor and Carolyn Korsmeyer, while defending the attitude approach, have acknowledged that such things as an artwork's moral vision are proper objects of appreciation and/or criticism.[15] Consequently, they have concluded that the proper object of appreciation and/or criticism contains things which fall into two distinct classes—those things which are the object of an aesthetic attitude and other things (such as moral vision) which are not the object of an aesthetic attitude. McGregor's and Korsmeyer's conclusion concerning aesthetic relevance is a step in the right direction, although I think that their attempts to defend the notion of the aesthetic attitude are misguided.

McGregor, whose view I shall discuss first, distinguishes two separate and unrelated senses of the word "aesthetic": a *descriptive* sense of "aesthetic" which applies to the objects of the aesthetic attitude and a *commending* sense of "aesthetic" which applies to characteristics of artworks which are not the object of the aesthetic attitude. The distinction he makes between two senses of "aesthetic" is one which must be made and is, I believe, the important contribution of his article. His characterizing of the second sense as a commending one, however, is badly confused.[16] A property of a work of art which may be appreciated and/or criticized but one which McGregor takes *not* to be an object of an aesthetic attitude may be commendable, but it may not be; commending has no necessary connection to such properties. Consequently, McGregor's notion of a commending sense of "aesthetic" is of no help in working out a theory of aesthetic object as it applies to works of art. As will be seen later, Korsmeyer's handling of such things as moral vision is more promising.

But what of McGregor's descriptive sense of "aesthetic"? Is there an aesthetic attitude and must it be used as a partial basis for the notion of aesthetic object? McGregor contends that my arguments against the aesthetic attitude in "The Myth of the Aesthetic Attitude"[17] fail and that the aesthetic attitude correctly conceived provides a sound, although partial, basis for aesthetic relevance. Taking Stolnitz's theory as a typical aesthetic-attitude view, I had originally argued that Stolnitz's central notion was disinterested attention and that he was wrong in saying that there are two kinds of attention: interested attention and disinterested attention. McGregor agrees that attention is primitive and cannot be split up into different kinds, but he maintains that Stolnitz's use of "disinterested attention" is just a manner of speaking and not central to his theory.[18] In short, I had aimed at the wrong target. I think McGregor is wrong in his interpretation of Stolnitz's theory, but let us assume that he is right.

McGregor wants to focus on *perception* rather than attention, distinguishing aesthetic perception from nonaesthetic perception. He says perception involves "at least three components: (1) the motives, purposes, and interests of the observer; (2) attention; (3) the properties or aspects of the object attended to." He has already agreed that attention is primitive, hence, it cannot be used as a variable in distinguishing aesthetic and nonaesthetic perception. The properties of the object attended to cannot be a distinguishing variable because, according to aesthetic-attitude theory, any properties or objects can be the object of aesthetic perception. McGregor chooses the first of the three and argues that it is ". . . the motives, purposes, and especially the interests of the agents . . ." which distinguish aesthetic from nonaesthetic perception.

Consider McGregor's examples of aesthetic and nonaesthetic perception at work. Nine men are looking at an orange tree and each makes a statement which is indicative of his interest. The statements are

(1) It's a Valencia;
(2) A tree that bears that well would be good to invest in;
(3) The species was first introduced from Brazil;
(4) The leaves are pale—it needs iron;
(5) The shape is very elegant;
(6) The pale green leaves contrast nicely with the dark brown of the trunk;
(7) The articulation of the branches is interesting;
(8) Exquisite odor, isn't it?
(9) Notice how languidly the fruit hangs on the boughs.

Let us call the man who said, "It's a Valencia," "George" and the man who said, "The articulation of the branches is interesting," "Jerome." McGregor says that our intuitions tell us that Jerome is

100

perceiving aesthetically and that George is perceiving nonaesthetically. In general, the first four statements are supposed to indicate nonaesthetic perception and the last five aesthetic perception. Let us assume that George's interest is practical, i.e., in classification and that Jerome's is nonpractical. What does this show about their perceiving? McGregor is right that the perceivings of George and Jerome are different because one of the three aspects of perception is different in the two cases, namely, the interests of the perceivers. To mark the difference McGregor is free to call Jerome's perceiving aesthetic and George's perceiving nonaesthetic if he wants to. But what does making the distinction and giving it a name accomplish? Nothing prevents practical George from noticing the articulation of the branches even though he is interested in classifying, which shows that perceiving aesthetically is not *necessary* for perceiving aesthetic qualities. And, nothing insures that nonpractical Jerome will notice the articulation of the branches, which shows that perceiving aesthetically is not *sufficient* for perceiving aesthetic qualities. Moreover, nothing prevents nonpractical Jerome from noticing that the tree is a Valencia. "Being a Valencia" does not sound like something one would call an aesthetic characteristic, and "having branches which are interestingly articulated" does sound like something one would call an aesthetic characteristic. But neither characteristic is necessarily brought into focus or created by the perceiver's interest, nor is noticing either characteristic prevented by the perceiver's interest. *Either characteristic can be seen independently of the interest of the perceiver.* (I do not, of course, wish to deny that our interests guide our perceptions.) So calling Jerome's perceiving "aesthetic" does not provide a connecting theoretical link between "aesthetic perception" and "aesthetic qualities" such as elegance, green contrasting nicely with dark brown, interesting articulation of branches, exquisite odor, and languidly hanging fruit.[19] Notice that the five aesthetic qualities McGregor mentions are of the kind that Frank Sibley notes are the referents of terms which he says, "function only or predominately as aesthetic terms."[20] Sibley lists "graceful, delicate, dainty, handsome, comely, elegant, garish, dynamic, pretty," and others. Sibley further maintains that "there are many words which are seldom used as aesthetic terms at all . . ." He lists "red, noisy, brackish, clammy, square, docile, curved," and others. Sibley distinguishes between perceptual qualities which are aesthetic and perceptual qualities which are nonaesthetic. McGregor is apparently following Sibley to the extent that the aesthetic qualities of the orange tree he lists are all "Sibley aesthetic qualities."

If, as McGregor seems to want to have it, "aesthetic quality" refers to the sort of perceptual qualities which Sibley calls "aesthetic," then there is no connection between McGregor's characterization of aesthetic perception and aesthetic qualities. Aesthetic qualities so conceived are quite independent of perceiver's interests.

Korsmeyer, like McGregor, wishes to defend a limited aesthetic-attitude view, conceding that some of the characteristics of a work of art which can properly be appreciated and/or criticized are not linked to aesthetic perception. Unlike McGregor, however, she chooses not to use the term "aesthetic" to refer to these characteristics, preferring the term "artistic." Korsmeyer's handling of the distinction is more clear-headed than McGregor's in that she does not attach any value connotation to the "artistic" characteristics as he does to his commending sense of "aesthetic". As noted earlier, these two attitude theorists in making the distinction here under discussion make a move in the right direction. Korsmeyer has, I think, made the move in a firmer, better way, but, of course, she had the benefit of reading McGregor's paper.

Neither of these two attitude theorists, in these papers at least, is much interested in (to use Korsmeyer's term) the "artistic" characteristics of art, i.e., those which are not linked to "aesthetic perception." Both McGregor and Korsmeyer are primarily interested in salvaging what can be salvaged of the theory of aesthetic perception. I turn now to Korsmeyer's defense of the limited aesthetic-attitude theory.

Korsmeyer's description of aesthetic perception, although perhaps not stated in as detailed a manner as McGregor's, is essentially the same. Unlike McGregor, however, Korsmeyer not only gives examples of aesthetic qualities, she gives a definition of "aesthetic quality." Her view is, thus, more formally developed than McGregor's. Ironically, the greater development makes it easier to reveal the difficulty in the theory. Korsmeyer characterizes aesthetic perception in the following way: "aesthetic perception must mean a kind of awareness or attention during which practical ends of any sort are not of foremost interest."[21] For her, "aesthetic qualities must mean those which can be appreciated without regard for practical, moral, or theoretical relevance."[22] The two characterizations appear to be related in that the first refers to the submerging of "practical ends" and the second refers to the submerging of "practical, moral, and theoretical relevance." The connection is, however, more apparent than real.

Consider the hypothetical case of a painting in which the basic composition is squarish, the color combination is delicate, and the representational aspects of which convey a particular moral vision. Korsmeyer would concede that the painting's moral vision can be properly appreciated, although it would not be with regard to a practical (moral) end. It is also proper to appreciate the painting's delicacy, and this would be a case of aesthetic appreciation because the appreciation could be (and in this case by hypothesis is) without regard to any practical end. Presumably for Korsmeyer, a characteristic such as being square, unlike delicacy, could not be appreciated aesthetically because it would have to be appreciated with regard to some practical end. For the purposes of the argument, let us agree that Korsmeyer's account of aesthetic qualities and her distinction between the aesthetic and the artistic enable us to distinguish among: 1) an "artistic" characteristic (moral vision) which is not an "aesthetic" characteristic, 2) an aesthetic quality (delicacy), and 3) a nonaesthetic quality (being square). The difficulty is that both the nonaesthetic quality (being square) and the aesthetic quality (delicacy)—and perhaps even the moral vision—can be perceived without regard to any practical end. In other words, aesthetic *perception* as characterized by Korsmeyer has no theoretical bearing on or connection with the aesthetic/nonaesthetic distinction as it relates to perceived qualities. For Korsmeyer, it is really aesthetic appreciation (appreciation without regard for practical, moral, or theoretical relevance) which does the supposed work of distinguishing aesthetic from nonaesthetic perception. Her notion of aesthetic appreciation is, however, left undeveloped.

In summary, what is the situation? McGregor and Korsmeyer begin by admitting that perceiving aesthetically as they understand it is only of partial help in resolving the problem of aesthetic relevance as it is traditionally understood. They both assert, however, that there is some vital connection between aesthetic perception and aesthetic qualities. It turns out, however, that perceiving aesthetically (without regard to any practical end) guarantees nothing about the aesthetic qualities of perceived objects. Someone might still think that perceiving aesthetically would at least be generally conducive to experiencing the aesthetic qualities of perceived objects. On the contrary, I am inclined to think that persons with a practical end in mind might on occasion experience aesthetic qualities which persons without practical ends in mind might miss. For example, a person with the end in mind of writing a review (a critic) might well be more attentive than someone without a practical goal. Having a practical goal, of course, is no more a guarantee of perceptiveness than is not having a practical goal. In any event, aesthetic perception has been characterized by both McGregor and Korsmeyer, but it is so weak a notion that it does not yield the desired results with respect to perceptual qualities.

Whatever is to be said about aesthetic perception, Sibley's distinction between aesthetic qualities such as elegance and nonaesthetic qualities such as squareness seems to have an intuitive plausibility about it. In saying this, I do not endorse Sibley's controversial and perhaps untenable views on taste which in some sense is supposed to provide a foundation for the distinction. There seems no reason, however, to deny that there is a sense of "aesthetic" which refers to a certain kind of perceptual quality, although no one, including the aesthetic-attitude theorists, has succeeded in working out a theory which underlies the distinction between aesthetic qualities and nonaesthetic qualities.

Let me now turn to the question of aesthetic relevance. Even if aesthetic perception did work as McGregor and Korsmeyer want it to work, i.e., by providing a theoretical connection to aesthetic qualities, it would not, as some think it does, have a bearing on the question which is the focus of this chapter, namely, the question of which properties of a work of art constitute the work's aesthetic object and how this is determined. Suppose that aesthetic perception could isolate aesthetic qualities, even then aesthetic perception alone could not distinguish, for example, between the aesthetic qualities of a painting and the aesthetic qualities of the wall on which the painting hangs. Unlike some aesthetic-attitude theorists, neither McGregor nor Korsmeyer claims that aesthetic perception determines the properties which belong to the aesthetic objects of works of art. What they do claim, I think correctly, is that both aesthetic qualities and such properties as moral vision are legitimate focuses of criticism. They also claim, I think incorrectly, that because of aesthetic perception the properties which are the aesthetic qualities of a work of art and the properties which are not aesthetic qualities (i.e., moral vision) are of a radically different kind. For them, for example, a novel has, in effect, *two* kinds of objects of criticism: an object which has as elements such things as imagery, dramatic tension, and other aesthetic qualities (which are supposed to have a special relation to aesthetic perception) *and* an object which has as elements such things as the moral vision of the work, truths revealed about human nature, and the like. Since there are basic difficulties with the aesthetic-attitude theory, there seems no good reason to require that there be *two* different kind of objects, both of which are proper objects of art criticism. As an alternative to the approach of McGregor and Korsmeyer, consider the way in which Beardsley conceives of the aesthetic objects of works of art: for him aesthetic objects of works of art are simply the proper objects of appreciation and/or criticism. Adopting Beardsley's approach gives one object which may have as its elements a variety of different kinds: nonaesthetic qualities of the Sibley kind (redness, squareness, etc.), aesthetic qualities of the Sibley kind (delicacy, gracefulness, etc.), personal qualities of the kind noted by Colin Lyas (perceptiveness, sensitivity, etc.),[23] expressive qualities (sadness, happiness), as well as characteristics such as a moral vision and being revealing of certain aspects of human nature. Thus an art critic might say of the aesthetic object of a particular painting that its dominant color is red and its composition squarish, that the various shades of red and earth colors are delicately balanced, that its composition and colors have the expressive quality of sadness, and that the represented scene reveals a sinister aspect of human nature.

I have now admitted of two senses of "aesthetic": a sense which refers to aesthetic qualities and a sense which refers to aesthetic objects of works of art, i.e., all the properties of a work which are properly appreciated and/or criticized, including aesthetic qualities. I want to maintain that, although the term "aesthetic" appears in both of these expressions, the two senses have little or nothing in common. "Aesthetic quality" refers to a certain kind of perceptual quality which can be distinguished, although just what the basis for the distinction is is not clear. "Aesthetic object of a work of art" is what might be called a "collection expression" in that it refers to the properties of a work of art which may properly be appreciated and/or criticized, and, consequently, its collected elements may in a given instance include various aesthetic qualities, nonaesthetic qualities, personal qualities, expressive qualities, representational characteristics, moral characteristics, and so on.

What then is the solution to the problem of relevance—the problem of which properties of works of art are properly appreciated and/or criticized, and the problem of how this is determined? Beardsley, earlier aesthetic-attitude theorists such as Stolnitz, and Iseminger share the view that there is some general, clear-cut way to do this. Roughly, Beardsley claims the determination can be made by applying the criteria of perceptibility and distinctness.[24] The earlier aesthetic-attitude theorists thought that the properties of works of art which are properly appreciated and/or criticized are those properties which can be the object of the aesthetic attitude.[25] The more recent aesthetic-attitude accounts of McGregor and Korsmeyer do not really attempt to give a coherent view of how aesthetic objects are determined. Iseminger claims the determination of which properties are properly appreciated and/or criticized can be made by applying the criterion of appreciatability. None of these accounts is satisfactory. It may seem to some that a theory of a kind these theorists are seeking— an account of a general criterion (or criteria) which will determine which *kind* of properties of works of art are aesthetically relevant— can be worked out.

I am doubtful that a theory of *kinds* of properties can account for which properties of a work of art are aesthetically relevant and which are not—the problem is just not one of distinguishing kinds of properties. Works of art have perceptible properties which are relevant and perceptible properties which are not; they have properties which can

105

be appreciated and which are relevant and properties which can be appreciated and are not relevant. One can "aesthetically perceive" both relevant and nonrelevant properties of works of art.

The solution to the problem of aesthetic relevance is not a general one of the sort sought by these philosophers; the solution, I believe, will have to be a piecemeal affair, and the determination of the aesthetic-object properties of a particular work of art will have to derive from knowledge of the art form within which the particular work falls. The conventions used in presenting works of art give guidance of limited generality. For example, the fact that the stagehands in traditional Western theater are hidden backstage and the Chinese property man of classical Chinese theater is dressed unobtrusively in black are clues which guide us to exclude them as aesthetically irrelevant. But such guidance is of limited generality; nothing prevented or prevents, for example, a clever playwright of classical Chinese theater from writing a play in which the property man in some way becomes part of the performance of the play. Similarly, with regard to the color of the back of a painting, nothing prevents a painter from creating a work of visual art similar to a painting but which is painted on both sides of a piece of canvas. If Picasso can depict an object from two different perspectives on one side of a canvas, another artist could depict an object from one perspective on one side of a canvas and from another perspective on the other side of the canvas. Such two-sided paintings would require a new way of presenting, similar perhaps to that of sculptures which are to be viewed from more than one place.

As long as one is faced with traditional kinds of art, one can rely on the established conventions for guidance. When innovation occurs, one will be to a certain extent on one's own to figure out what is going on, although since the innovation will occur within some traditional form or other, there will be some minimum of guidance.

Epilogue: Reflections on the Philosophy of Art

As noted in Chapter I, both Plato's remark that art is imitation and his method of philosophizing have had a long-lasting effect on the philosophy of art. First, even when art theorists have rejected his idea that art is imitation, the example of Plato's remark that art is imitation has influenced them to think that the defining feature(s) of art can be discovered by focusing narrowly on works of art themselves. Second, his method of seeking timeless essences has influenced philosophers of art to think that the features of art they take to be defining features are validated as defining because they reflect the timeless essence of art.

When philosophers of art at last began to think seriously about the nature of art in the Nineteenth Century, they easily saw that Plato's remark that art is imitation is false. If, however, they refused to follow Plato's lead concerning the nature of the essence of art, in trying to find a replacement for imitation, they nevertheless focused on works of art in as equally narrow a way as Plato did. What followed was a succession of theories each with its candidate for the essence of art—the expression of emotion, the communication of emotion, significant form, forms symbolic of human feeling, and others. Each of these theories shares two large problems with the imitation theory.

First, each of the theorists is trying to discover the essence of art in some highly visible property which is of some obvious value. The search for the essence of art seems to have been thought of as a search similar to the search for gold nuggets—a search in which one peers closely at individual things. The essence of art was presumed to be "on exhibit" to be seen or heard, if one just looked or listened in a clear-headed and intent enough way. The difficulty is that the defining features of art are more complex and harder to apprehend than these theorists supposed.

The second difficulty is related to the first. While each of the easily-noted properties specified as the essence of art by the various theorists does characterize some works of art, none of the properties characterizes each of the things which are works of art. Consequently, none of these properties can be a necessary condition of art.

Ziff and Weitz, in concluding that the platonic method of seeking essences is inapplicable to the theory of art, nevertheless follow the example of Plato's remark about imitation and examine only easily-noted properties of works of art. Of course, at the time Ziff and Weitz were writing, the theories available for refutation were formulated in terms of easily-noted properties. Even in rejecting artifactuality, which *then* was a more or less easily-noted property, they follow Plato's example. (Given recent developments in art, it is not *now* so easy to tell that a given work of art is an artifact.) In any event, the institutional theory completely rejects the platonic example and purports to discover the defining conditions of art in not-so-easily-noted properties of art.

It is perhaps worth noting that the institutional theory in no way derogates or wishes to diminish the properties of obvious value that the earlier theorists have found in art; the institutional theory easily accommodates the representative, expressive, symbolic, formal, and such properties of art, but it rejects them as defining characteristics. There is nothing about the institutional theory which inhibits or restricts art in any way. Art has been the bearer of a myriad of things, ranging from those of the greatest importance to the trivial. The institutional theory allows the freedom for art which Weitz quite correctly is so anxious to preserve in his attack on traditional theories of art. There is a sense in which the institutional theory absorbs all of the earlier theories, each of which has caught a glimpse of something that art can do.

The first task of a theory of art is to focus on properties which all works of art share. As we have seen in the course of this book, in order to discover properties that works of art have in common, it is necessary to step back and view works of art in their larger setting rather than focus on them narrowly and individually. The institutional theory emphatically does not emulate the example of Plato's remark which presumes that the search is for an easily-noted property.

The institutional theory also abandons Plato's method of seeking timeless essences by means of philosophical intuition, a method perpetuated in the work of many philosophers of art. These later philosophers perhaps did not conceive of their procedures as involving the philosophical intuition of a Form (of Art) which abides in an ontologically distinct realm. They did, however, think that the definition of "art" which they formulated caught the timeless essence of art just as surely as a faithful Platonist thinks his definitions can reflect essences.

Ziff and Weitz attacked the essentialist method of these philosophers of art, arguing that there is nothing shared by the members of the class of works of art and that, consequently, the class can have no essence. For Ziff and Weitz the question of what the essence of art is just cannot arise because they believe that there is no property which works of art share.

We have seen, however, that works of art do share properties—artifactuality and being of a kind created to be presented to an art-world public—and that these properties are sufficient for defining "art." Are these properties the essence of art? I have not shown that these properties do not derive from the Form of Art. Perhaps they do constitute the essence of art, but the institutional theory makes no claim that they do. What the institutional theory does try to do is to describe the human practice of creating and consuming art. In giving the description of the art enterprise that I have, I spoke of the *essential* framework of art. In so speaking, I do not intend to make any claim about a timeless essence of art but mean to describe the conditions necessary for a particular activity or practice. The institutional theory conceives of this practice as one which has emerged in and through time, as a historical development. This conception contrasts with the view of the earlier philosophers of art who conceived of their theories as ahistorical reflections of the timeless essence of art.

Another way of showing the difference between the institutional theory and the theories of earlier philosophers of art is to note the way in which the definition of "art" is regarded by the theories. In the case of the earlier theories, since each conceives of its definition as embodying the essence of art, its definition serves as a *foundation* for the theory. The various conclusions which make up the theory are derived from this foundation. In the case of the institutional theory, the definition of "art" is not at all foundational. First, it is one among several interconnected definitions, no one of which is foundational. The definitions are, as I said, inflected—they mutually support one another. Second, the definition of "art" and the other institutional definitions are formulated at the end of the development of the theory in Chapter V, and logically this is where they belong. The theory attempts to describe the art enterprise and the definitions are the distillation of that description.

The institutional theory of art thus marks a sharp break with traditional theorizing about art. The content of the institutional theory and its central definitions are radically different from those of the traditional theories, and the institutional theory's method of arriving at its conclusions also contrasts sharply with that of the earlier theories.

FOOTNOTES

Chapter I
[1] Chapter III contains a lengthy account and criticism of Ziff's and Weitz's views.

Chapter II
[1] *Journal of Philosophy*, October 15, 1964, pp. 571–584. Reprinted in *Aesthetics: A Critical Anthology*, G. Dickie and R. Sclanfani, eds. (New York, 1977), pp. 22–35. All references are to page numbers in the anthology.

[2] *Theoria*, Parts 1–3, 1973, pp. 1–17. Reprinted in *Aesthetics: A Critical Anthology, op. cit.*, pp. 551–562. All references are to page numbers in the anthology.

[3] *The Journal of Aesthetics and Art Criticism*, Winter 1974, pp. 139–148.

[4] I am assuming here that for the Imitation Theory being an imitation is both necessary and sufficient to make something art. If being an imitation were only a necessary condition of arthood, then that would not be a theory of art but only one necessary truth about art or part of a theory of art. Perhaps, neither Socrates nor anyone else has held the Imitation Theory so understood, but the theory has been around in the sense that some have thought that Socrates and others held the view.

[5] An abstract of Kennick's unpublished paper appears in *The Journal of Philosophy*, October 15, 1964, pp. 585–7.

[6] *Op. cit.*, "The Artworld," p. 33.

[7] *Loc. cit.*

[8] *Loc. cit.*

[9] *Loc. cit.*

[10] *Op. cit.*, "Artworks and Real Things," p. 558.

[11] *Ibid.*, p. 561.

[12] *Ibid.*, p. 558.

[13] *Ibid.*, p. 561.

[14] *Ibid.*, p. 561–2.

[15] "Danto and Dickie on Art," in *Culture and Art*, Lars Aagaard-Mogensen, ed. (Atlantic Highlands, N.J., 1976), p. 181.

[16] *Op. cit.*, "The Transfiguration of the Commonplace," p. 140.

[17]*Ibid.*, p. 141.

[18]*Ibid.*, p. 142.

[19]*Loc. cit.*

[20]*Ibid.*, p. 148.

[21]*Loc. cit.*

[22]George Dickie, *Art and the Aesthetic* (Ithaca, New York, 1974), pp. 19–52.

[23]*Op. cit.*, p. 29.

[24]*Op. cit.*, p. 140.

[25]William Kennick, who read the manuscript of *Art and the Aesthetic*, warned me against concluding that fakes are not art. I should have accepted his advice then.

[26]*Op. cit.*, p. 561.

[27]*Ibid.*, p. 558.

[28]*Ibid.*, p. 561.

Chapter III

[1]"The Role of Theory in Aesthetics," *Journal of Aesthetics and Art Criticism*, 15 (1956), 27–35. Weitz has discussed his conception of art in numerous other places but there has been no real change in his views.

[2]"The Task of Defining a Work of Art," *Philosophical Review*, 62 (1953), 58–78.

[3]At this point I am using the expression "the artworld" in a loose and informal way. As the analysis proceeds, the expression will come to have a more specific meaning.

[4]"Family Resemblances and Generalization Concerning the Arts," *American Philosophical Quarterly*, 2 (1965), 219–228.

[5]*Op. cit.*, "The Task of Defining a Work of Art," p. 65.

[6]*Op. cit.*, "The Role of Theory in Aesthetics," p. 33.

[7]David Hume, *A Treatise of Human Nature*, edited by L. A. Selby-Bigge (Oxford, 1888), p. 467.

[8](Ithaca, 1960), p. 182 ff.

[9](Ithaca, 1974).

[10]*Ibid.*, p. 45.

[11]This analysis was suggested to me by some of Colin Lyas' remarks on a somewhat similar topic in his "Danto and Dickie on Art," in *Culture and Art*, Lars Aagaard-Mogensen, ed. (Atlantic Highlands, N.J., 1976), p. 170.

[12]I want to thank Peter Kivy for calling my attention to this point of anthropological usage.

Chapter IV

[1]"Is Art Essentially Institutional?" in *Culture and Art*, Lars Aagaard-Mogensen, ed. (Atlantic Highlands, N.J., 1976), pp. 194–209.

[2]*Ibid.*, p. 196.

[3]*Ibid.*, p. 197.

[4]In giving these examples of types and tokens I am not attempting to correlate the particular types and tokens in the two lists of examples. I am not, for example, saying that General Motors is the token of which tool-making is the type.

[5]*Op. cit.*, p. 202.

[6]Jeffrey Wieand, "Can There Be an Institutional Theory of Art?" *Journal of Aesthetics and Art Criticism*, 39 (1981), pp. 409–417.

[7]I elaborate this point at greater length later in this chapter.

[8]In *Culture and Art, ibid.*, p. 92.

[9]*Ibid.*, p. 107.

[10]*Ibid.*, p. 99.

[11] *Ibid.*, p. 102.

[12] *Ibid.*, p. 98.

[13] *Ibid.*, p. 106.

[14] *Ibid.*, p. 101.

[15] *Ibid.*, p. 95.

[16] *Ibid.*, p. 100.

[17] *Feeling and Form* (New York, 1953), p. 40.

[18] *Art and the Aesthetic*, pp. 173–181. In this discussion of the conventions and rules which govern the presentation of artworks, I distinguished between what I called "the primary convention" and "the secondary conventions." I still want to distinguish between two things here, but I now think what I called "the primary convention" is not in fact a convention; consequently, what I called "the secondary conventions," which are conventions, do not need to be designated as secondary. I shall discuss this whole matter in the next chapter.

[19] *Ibid.*, pp. 104–106.

[20] I am not claiming that a necessary condition as such invariably entails a rule. The relevant kind of necessary condition has to be a condition of something the occurrence of which could involve rule-following. For example, there are certain necessary conditions for making sulphuric acid, but none of these conditions entails a rule—producing an acid is a matter of following a physical procedure. On the other hand, the necessary conditions of promising constitute the rules of promising. The difference here is between operating with physical laws and observing conventions.

[21] It is this rule that Dadaists such as Duchamp play around with, seeing how close they can come to breaking it and still make a work of art.

Chapter V

[1] *Art and the Aesthetic* (Ithaca, N.Y., 1974), p. 36.

[2] See David Lewis' *Convention: A Philosophical Study* (Cambridge, Mass., 1969), pp. 213 for a detailed analysis of convention.

[3] *Op. cit.*, p. 174.

[4] *Ibid.*, p. 177.

[5] *Ibid.*, p. 35.

[6] *The Philosophical Review*, January 1977, p. 98. I have restated Walton's observation somewhat so that it applies to my new version of the institutional theory as well as the old.

[7] *Loc. cit.*

[8] *Loc. cit.*

[9] *Ibid.*, p. 100.

[10] My idea of such an ideal derives from a suggestion in a seminar paper by Kendall D'Andrade.

[11] One reader of an early version of the manuscript of this book asked if I would be willing to consider the possibility of a self-contradictory account of art, since I am so willing to consider a circular account. I hope it will become clear that circularity is not necessarily the logical fault that self-contradiction is.

[12] *In Culture and Art* (Atlantic Highlands, N.J., 1976), p. 209.

[13] *Loc. cit.*

Chapter VI

[1] "Aesthetic Concepts," in Joseph Margolis' (ed.) *Philosophy Looks at the Arts* (New York, 1962), pp. 63–87.

[2] "Does Aesthetics Have Anything to do with Art?" *The Journal of Aesthetics and Art Criticism*, Summer 1978, pp. 429–440.

[3] Schultz, *op. cit.*, p. 438.

[4] "The Possibility of Art: Remarks on a Proposal by Dickie," *Philosophical Review*, January 1973, pp. 69–82.

[5] *Ibid.*, p. 79.

[6] *Op. cit.*, pp. 40–1.

[7] Schultz, *op. cit.*, p. 440.

[8] "Appreciation, the Artworld, and the Aesthetic," in *Culture and Art*, Lars Aagaard-Mogensen, ed. (Atlantic Highlands, N.J., 1976), pp. 118–130.

[9] *Ibid.*, p. 119.

[10] *Loc. cit.*

[11] *Ibid.*, p. 121.

[12] *Ibid.*, p. 123.

[13] *Ibid.*, p. 125.

[14] *Ibid.*, pp. 126–7. Iseminger has apparently confused the adjective "appreciable" with the adjective "appreciatable." I take it that he means the latter in this quotation.

[15] Robert McGregor, "Art and the Aesthetic," *The Journal of Aesthetics and Art Criticism*, Summer 1974, pp. 549–559. Carolyn Korsmeyer, "On Distinguishing 'Aesthetic' from 'Artistic'," *The Journal of Aesthetic Education*, 1977, pp. 45–57.

[16] For a penetrating discussion of McGregor's second sense of "aesthetic," see Robert Schultz, "Does Aesthetics Have Anything to do with Art?" *The Journal of Aesthetics and Art Criticism*, Summer 1978, p. 430.

[17] *American Philosophical Quarterly*, January 1964, pp. 56–65. A more recent version of these arguments occurs in *Art and the Aesthetic*, pp. 113–134.

[18] McGregor, p. 555.

[19] In general, my criticism of McGregor follows the line worked out in Schultz's article, *Op. cit.*

[20] "Aesthetic Concepts," in Joseph Margolis' (ed.) *Philosophy Looks at the Arts* (New York, 1962), p. 64.

[21] Korsmeyer, *op. cit.*, p. 54. Korsmeyer's characterization of aesthetic perception is somewhat less careful than McGregor's in that her remarks seem to presuppose different kinds of attention. I shall not take up this point, as it has already been dealt with.

[22] *Loc. cit.*

[23] Colin Lyas, "Aesthetic and Personal Qualities," *Aristotelian Society Proceedings*, 1971–72, pp. 171–193.

[24] See *Art and the Aesthetic* pages 147–173 for a detailed discussion of Beardsley's view.

[25] See *Art and the Aesthetic* pages 90–146 for a detailed discussion of these theorists' views.

CREDITS

We wish to thank the Frick Collection for permission to use James Abbott MacNeil Whistler's *Miss Rosa Corder* for the front cover. We wish to thank the Metropolitan Museum of Art for permission to use the following: James Abbott MacNeil Whistler's *Bridge* (The Metropolitan Museum of Art, Harris Brisbane Dick Fund, 1917.); Edgar Hilarie Germaine Degas' *Study for a Portrait of Edouard Manet at the Races*, c. 1864. (The Metropolitan Museum of Art, Roger's Fund, 1918). We wish to thank the Guggenheim Museum for permission to use the following: Ron Davis' *Double Booth*. 1969, Gift, Leo Castelli; (Solomon R. Guggenheim Museum, New York, photo: Robert E. Mates); Salvador Dali's *Neptune in Center*. 1947 (Solomon R. Guggenheim Museum, New York, photo: Robert E. Mates); Jean Ipousteguy's *La Grande Regle*. 1968 (Solomon R. Guggenheim Museum, New York, photo: Robert E. Mates); Vasily Kandinsky's *The Mirror*. 1907 (Solomon R. Guggenheim Museum, New York, photo: Robert E. Mates); Paul Klee's *Fright of a Girl*. 1922 (Solomon R. Guggenheim Museum, New York, photo: Robert E. Mates).

DATE LOANED

MAR 4 1966			

DATE DUE

OCT 0 3 1994			

DEMCO 38-297

JOHN WAYNE:

Prophet of the American Way of Life

by
EMANUEL LEVY

The Scarecrow Press, Inc.
Metuchen, N.J., & London
1988

Library of Congress Cataloging-in-Publication Data

Levy, Emanuel, 1947-
    John Wayne : prophet of the American way of life /
by Emanuel Levy.
        p.   cm.
    Bibliography: p.
    Includes index.
    ISBN 0-8108-2054-4
    1. Wayne, John, 1907-1979.   2. Moving-picture actors
and actresses--United States--Biography.   3. Moving-
pictures--Social aspects--United States.   4. United
States--Civilization--20th century.   I. Title.
PN2287.W454L49   1988
791.43'028'0924--dc19   87-28410

TO NATHAN

CONTENTS

ACKNOWLEDGMENTS

It is usually hard to remember the specific date on which the idea for a book originated. This book is an exception, for the idea to write a book about John Wayne was born on June 11, 1979, the day of his death. The reaction to his death really shocked me: Why would a movie star get such media blitz, with the news of his death occupying the front pages of every newspaper? Could movie actors in other countries have acquired such extraordinary popularity? How special was Wayne's stardom in the contexts of Hollywood and American society at large? These were some of the questions, which my close friends later lumped together as "the importance of being Wayne," I set out to explore.

I began to collect systematic data on Wayne's career and life in 1980, not realizing then the amount of work involved. But I wanted to be comprehensive and thus examine the sociocultural significance of John Wayne, that is his range of activities as an actor, star, folk hero, ideologue and political figure, and cultural icon. The scope of the book further expanded when I decided to compare between Wayne and other major stars of his generation: Gary Cooper, Jimmy Stewart, Henry Fonda, Clark Gable, James Cagney, Humphrey Bogart, and Cary Grant. This book, however, is neither a biography of Wayne nor a chronological examination of his films. Rather, it provides a sociological view of the historical, cultural, and cinematic importance of John Wayne as an actor-auteur.

Many friends and colleagues have read and commented on earlier drafts of ths manuscript. I would like to thank especially Jeanine Basinger, Sigmund Diamond, Robert Kapsis, Rob Remley, John Ryan, and Bill Shepard for providing extremely useful and detailed comments. This book owes a intellectual debt to the writings of Andrew Sarris on the auteur theory (and on John Ford). I have attempted to apply some notions of auteurism to John Wayne as an actor-auteur, though I am aware that auteurism best describes the work of directors rather than producers, screenwriters, or actors. I have also learned a good deal from Allen Eyles's book about John Wayne, one of the best of its kind.

Finally, my students at Columbia University and other schools have contributed to this book by challenging my ideas about film and society in general and the Western in particular. Over the years, I have introduced many students to Wayne's best Westerns, particularly Stagecoach, Red River, and The Searchers, and subsequently derived great pleasure from hearing two frequent remarks: "I never used to like Westerns, but Stagecoach (or Red River) changed my mind about the genre," and "I never realized John Wayne could really act until I saw The Searchers." Such remarks make the teaching of film stimulating as well as rewarding.

I spent a most pleasant sabbatical at the University of New Hampshire, where I worked on the final draft of the manuscript. I would also like to thank my friend Eli Meron, whose gracious hospitality I enjoyed during my extensive trips to Los Angeles.

The collection of data took place in many libraries, and I would like to thank the personnel of the Margaret Herrick Library of the Academy of Motion Picture Arts and Sciences, the Lincoln Center Library for the Performing Arts, and the libraries of the American Film Institute, the Museum of Modern Art, the University of California at Los Angeles, and the University of Southern California. Mary Corliss and Terry Geesken of the Museum of Modern Art's Stills Archive provided great guidance in selecting pictures for this book.

Finally, I would like to stress that this book could not have been completed without the assistance and moral support of my friends Rob Remley and Nathan Waterman.

Emanuel Levy
New York City
August 1987

FOREWORD

Back in the supposedly swinging and revolutionary (at least
sexually) sixties, an impromptu parlor game in liberal salons
propounded the following question: If you were drowning in
a lake, who would you rather have as your potential rescuer
on the shore--John Wayne or Dustin Hoffman? The answer
was invariably John Wayne. That stalwart reactionary, that
proud non-reader of The New York Review of Books, would
jump into the water without thinking, whereas Dustin Hoffman, chockful of "moral" courage and good intentions, would
meditate on his mission through his Method acting training,
before plunging into the briny deep.

John Wayne has come to embody even for his ideological
foes the survival of certain vestigial virtues--bravery, loyalty, stoicism in the face of pain, loss, and even death--in a
world reduced to mealy-mouthed relativism. It is for me at
least, and, I suspect, for Emanuel Levy as well, always
Keat's negative capability time in the corral as far as Big
John is concerned. We, the author and I, do not settle our
arguments with fisticuffs of firearms. We do not ride across
the horizon in heroic silhouette, and our worldviews are considerably less Manichean than Mr. Wayne's. Yet there is
something in his career persona--for we have known him
only vicariously--that stirs our imaginations almost in spite
of ourselves.

This "something" is the subject of Emanuel Levy's very
insightful disquisition on all the mythological reverberations
of the movie star born Marion Michael Morrison, May 26, 1907,
in Winterset, Iowa, later billed in pulp Westerns as Duke
Morrison, and finally as John Wayne, though "Duke" stuck
to him as a sobriquet. The conventional box-office wisdom
was that Wayne appealed more to men than to women, though
two of the most perceptively appreciative essays on the Duke

ix

have been written by Molly Haskell and Joan Didion. By the time he had concluded his long, visibly heroic combat against cancer, we were compelled to confront what the motion picture medium had transformed into a veritable force of nature.

Unlike many of his stellar contemporaries, Wayne was far from an overnight sensation. From his walk-on in a Richard Barthelmess vehicle entitled Drop Kick (1927) to his grand entrance as the Ringo Kid in John Ford's Stagecoach (1939), Wayne toiled away in 65 movies, most of which were produced in poverty row for the boondocks and kiddie matinee audiences.

Having obtained his big chance with Raoul Walsh's super-Western The Big Trail, Wayne saw his opportunity for stardom sidetracked for almost a decade. His youth was gone by the time Ford dragged him off to Monument Valley for a second chance. His biographers have written that Wayne was on the screen for almost 50 years, but it would be a mistake to say that his iconic flame burned with equal brightness throughout that period. Ultimately, Wayne appeared in some of the best films ever made in Hollywood-- Stagecoach, The Long Voyage Home, They Were Expendable, Fort Apache, Red River, She Wore a Yellow Ribbon, The Quiet Man, The Searchers, The Wings of Eagles, Rio Bravo, The Man Who Shot Liberty Valance, El Dorado--and some of the worst--Tycoon, The Fighting Kentuckian, Big Jim McLain, The Conqueror, The Alamo, The Green Berets. But his overall reputation with the public depended less on the classics and the disasters than on a steady stream of routine but robust romances from the 1940's through the 1970's. I happened to have grown up on the John Wayne of Dark Command, Seven Sinners, The Shepherd of the Hills, Lady for a Night, Reap the Wild Wind, The Spoilers, Flying Tigers, In Old Oklahoma, Tall in the Saddle, and Angel and the Badman. I remember responding to him in a relatively uncomplicated way, though he seldom functioned as a conventional hero. He could be accursed or obsessed. In Wake of the Red Witch, he drowns at the bottom of the deep so that he can sail forever on the ghostly high seas with his dead sweetheart (Gail Russell). He dies also in Reap the Wild Wind, Sands of Iwo Jima, The Man Who Shot Liberty Valance, The Cowboys, and The Shootist--an unusually high number of fatalities for a supposedly optimistic genre figure. And on many other occasions the characters he played faced a twilight existence of loneliness and dependency.

An appreciation of the compleat John Wayne depends therefore on a perceptive familiarity with the varieties and paradoxes of his career. Wayne's most enduring image is that of the displaced loner vaguely uncomfortable with the very civilization he is helping to preserve. He is not a Wild Man of the West seeking ever new frontiers, but he wanders much of the time nonetheless. At his first appearance we usually sense a very private person with some wound, loss, or grievance from the past. At his best he is much closer to a tragic vision of life than to a comic one. Shortly before Wayne's death, Ralph Richardson remarked in an interview that the Duke projected the kind of mystery one associated with great acting. Jean-Luc Godard once observed that as much as he despised the reactionary politics of John Wayne, he could never help but be moved in John Ford's The Searchers by the emotional sweep of the awesomely avuncular gesture with which Wayne gathers up Natalie Wood, after having given every indication that he wished to kill her for defiling his sacred memories of a little girl accepting his medal as a token of his chivalric devotion to her mother. In this, his greatest film, Wayne acts out the mystery of what passes through the soul of Ethan Edwards in that fearsome moment when he discovers the mutilated bodies of his brother, his beloved sister-in-law, and his nephew. Surly, cryptic, almost menacing even before the slaughter, he is invested afterward with the implacability of a figure too much larger than life for any genre but the Western.

Still, the notion of John Wayne as a great actor sits strangely with most people. Wayne himself would have scoffed at the suggestion that he belonged in the same category with, say, Laurence Olivier, whom he greatly admired. Toward the end of his life Wayne acknowledged the high-brow veneration accorded him by serious cineastes here and abroad: "I was just the paint for the palettes of Ford and Hawks," he once remarked with rueful modesty. This may have been true at the time of Ford's Stagecoach (1939) and Hawks's Red River (1948), but by the time of Ford's The Man Who Shot Liberty Valance (1962), and Hawks's El Dorado (1967), they needed him more than he needed them. To a great extent he had become his own auteur.

There is another factor to be considered, however, in Wayne's apparent self-denigration as an actor. The supposed authenticity of his personality could have been compromised by the stigma of self-consciousness. Carole Lombard once noted disapprovingly that Gary Cooper had become "feminine" in his narcissistic absorption with his own looks. A noted ballet critic once spoke approvingly of the rollicking sensuality of Wayne's posterior wiggle. The suspicion that such a maneuver might have been contrived with the actor's full awareness of its effect could do much to destroy the Duke's credibility with the mass of moviegoers on five continents. Yet when we recall Wayne's long career on the screen, without any cultural preconceptions, we are reminded of a long dance across disconcertingly natural backgrounds. As with Buster Keaton and Alfred Hitchcock, the kinetic and dynamic qualities of the medium itself have coalesced with a determined talent to produce images of genius.

Many theater people still believe that the only truly "serious" acting is performed on a stage, and within this circle Wayne is, of course, artistically non-existent. Certainly, no one ever suggested that Wayne's acting range extended to Restoration fops and Elizabethan fools. (Dustin Hoffman got a big laugh at a Village Voice Off-Broadway "Obie" award ceremony several years back, with his imitation of Wayne's undertaking a stage performance of Hamlet in London.) But as Olivier himself has demonstrated on too many occasions, the assumption of an infinite range contains its own pitfalls. A trick accent, a beard, an eye patch, old-age make-up--these are the accoutrements of acting to many people. That is why the worst acting is so often mistaken for the best, particularly on the screen, where being transcends pretending, and just standing there can often be more effective than doing something.

Wayne was dismissed not only because he lacked the wide classical range of the great British actors, but also because he lacked the emotional depth of the great Method actors. Wayne was thus less than Olivier on one level, and less than Brando on another. Indeed, nothing could be more alien to Wayne's temperament and upbringing than the Freudian-Stanislavskian mix of the Method. Instead of reaching back into his past to dredge up the feelings that would bring his characters to life, Wayne followed a relatively Jungian process of building up a new persona into which he gradually grew. He had never been a real-life Western hero like Tom Mix, nor even a real-life cowboy like Gary Cooper, but rather, a druggist's son in pinched middle-class surroundings. From an early age he found a more satisfying existence on the movie screen, and he labored long and hard to paint himself on that magical canvas so that it would seem that he had always inhabited it. In the end, Wayne himself was just about all that was left of the Old West in our imagination.

As a star he lacked the curiously calculating little-boy-lost quality of a Gable or a Cooper, and his clumsy exasperation was often mistaken for bullying. From time to time in his career, he ventured into relatively straight boy-girl projects in order to broaden his appeal. The results seemed discouraging at first glance. Wayne clearly lacked finesse, subtlety, and patience, the indispensable tools of womanizing on the screen. Of his performance opposite Jean Arthur in A Lady Takes a Chance (1943), James Agee wrote: "... John Wayne suggests how sensational he might be in a sufficiently evil story about a Reno gigolo...." And on his playing opposite Claudette Colbert in Without Reservations (1946), Agee was similarly clear-eyed: "Messrs. Wayne and Defoe have kinds of hardness and conceit, in their relations with women, which are a good deal nearer the real thing than movies usually get."

Marlene Dietrich, his co-star and reported flame in Seven Sinners (1940), The Spoilers (1942), and Pittsburgh (1942), once complained in print that Wayne had never read a book in his life. And despite his having been married to three Spanish-speaking women, he never learned more than a few words of Spanish. "I guess I never listened to what they were saying," he once confessed candidly, but not without a trace of self-mockery. Yet warmth and devotion are amply present in his screen liaisons with Maureen O'Hara in The Quiet Man and The Wings of Eagles, with Angie Dickinson in Rio Bravo, and with Patricia Neal in In Harm's Way. Like Faulkner's hero in Knight's Gambit, he improved with age, and he learned before our eyes both how to feel and how to project a deep and abiding love.

The great virtue of Levy's study of Wayne is its avoidance of the cant that has traditionally inundated the subject when treated by the politically and artistically censorious. Without embracing all the ideological implications of Wayne's career, Levy has stood off at enough of a disinterested distance to compute the pluses and minuses clearly and coherently. He has provided a multi-layered context in which John Wayne can be fully appreciated, warts and all, once and for all.

Andrew Sarris

INTRODUCTION

John Wayne was the most popular and durable star in film history. He was described by critic Eric Bentley as "the most important American of our time." General Douglas Mac-Arthur once told Wayne: "You represent the American serviceman better than the American serviceman himself." Despite differences in political persuasion, Wayne was one of the favorite stars of former president Jimmy Carter, who eulogized him as "a national asset" and "a symbol of many of the most basic qualities that made America great." Carter elaborated, "In an age of few heroes, he was the genuine article."

John Wayne was much more than an actor or a movie star; he was a national legend, a symbol of the American Dream. This book is a critical examination of the person, the actor, the film star, the political figure, and the mythic legend. It describes Wayne's film work in terms of his life, and his life in terms of his movies. The book's major concern is to understand the sociocultural significance of "the phenomenon of John Wayne," by placing him and his movies in the broader contexts of the film industry and American culture at large. The interplay between Wayne and his times (the Depression, the World War II, the McCarthy era, the tumultuous decade of the 1960s) constitutes the focus of the book, attempting to understand the extraordinary durability of Wayne's stardom.

Wayne's lengthy career spanned fifty years, from 1926 to 1976. He entered the film industry at a strategically crucial time, the transition from silent to talking pictures, and went on to pursue a viable career for five decades. The duration and popularity of his career made Wayne a chief figure in the international film world. His death, in 1979, marked the end of an entire era in the American cinema. An understanding of his life and work therefore sheds light on the structural changes that took place in the film industry as well as in American society.

Throughout Wayne's life, there have been considerable controversies about his contribution to film art, his status as an actor and, of course, his politics. This book attempts to provide an objective, dispassionate evaluation of Wayne's film work by comparing him with other major stars of his generation, particularly those who had similar, distinctly American, screen images, such as Gary Cooper, Henry Fonda, and James Stewart. During his illustrious career, Wayne appeared in close to 200 motion pictures, though it is impossible to assess their exact number because of the many series of "B" Westerns he made. Nonetheless, it is beyond doubt that Wayne's film output outnumbered that of every star in Hollywood's history.

Wayne's screen career consisted of five distinct phases, in each of which he performed different functions in American film and culture. The first phase, from 1925 to 1930, saw his rise from a prop man to a leading man in The Big Trail. In the second, from 1930 to 1939, Wayne declined from a potential star to the actor of numerous "B" Westerns. This phase was followed by a whole decade, between 1939 and 1948, in which he continued to grow as an actor. The most crucial phase of his screen career took place between 1949 and 1969, during which he reached the stature of America's most popular movie star. In 1970, after winning the Oscar award for True Grit, Wayne began the fifth and final phase of his career, which lasted until his death in 1979. This final stage was marked by Wayne's new functions in the American cultural scene, shifting from a movie star to a national legend and genuine folk hero who expressed his views on various issues: film, politics, economics, and education.

This book describes Wayne's contribution to two distinctly American genres: Westerns and war movies. While he did not make as many war films as Westerns, the former played a considerable role in his career and contributed immensely to his screen image. The Wayne combat movies and the heroes he portrayed in them differ substantially from the war movies of other stars, most notably Gary Cooper, Humphrey Bogart, James Cagney, and Errol Flynn, who, like Wayne, were not drafted into the war effort and therefore could make such movies during World War II.

But Wayne's claim to film notoriety and his greatest pride as an actor was based on the numerous Westerners he portrayed. The book demonstrates in great detail the unique Western hero that Wayne created, characterized by specific and consistent themes. His intimate association with the Western movie resulted in an unprecedented phenomenon: his very name became synonymous with the genre. The Western became Wayne's defining genre, to which he was committed throughout his career, regardless of fads and fashions in the film industry and the genre's popularity with the public at large. Only one other star enjoyed such close affinity with an American film genre: Jimmy Cagney and the crime-gangster film. However, unlike Cagney, Wayne used the Western consciously as an ideological weapon through which he expressed his value system and commented on contemporary life in America. Wayne's contributions to the Western genre, in ideological values, aesthetic form, and other technical matters (stunt work and fighting techniques), resulted in the creation of a distinct category, "the John Wayne Western," which differed from the film oeuvre of other great Western stars such as Henry Fonda, Gary Cooper, and James Stewart.

At the center of the book is a detailed examination of Wayne's tight control over his screen career and public image. Of all American actors, Wayne came closest to the notion of "actor as auteur." Contrary to popular notion, however, Wayne's image did not emerge spontaneously but was a gradual and systematic fabrication, a product of careful and deliberate design. The steps in creating the Wayne screen persona, including a new screen name, the abortive attempt to make a singing cowboy out of him, and the distinctive elements of his image are singled out and illustrated. The methods used by Wayne to achieve and maintain such unprecedented control are also analyzed.

Throughout his career, there were controversies over his acting skills and acting abilities. Some critics considered him to be a screen "personality," and not much of an actor. John Wayne deals with his natural performance style and his range as an actor, by comparing him with two contemporaries, Clark Gable and Gary Cooper. It also focuses on Wayne's complex relationships with film critics, especially the New York intelligentsia, which often reviewed his politics instead of his films. The book also dwells on the actor's work with two distinguished directors, John Ford and Howard Hawks. John Ford was influential in launching and shaping Wayne's screen career and in pushing him to heights which he would never have reached without him. The Ford-Wayne relationship was unparalleled, in extent, intensity, and impact, by other teams of directors-actors, such as John Huston-Humphrey Bogart or Anthony Mann-James Stewart.

In the last decade of his life, Wayne became an influential public figure, a genuine media star, using all the mass media (radio, film, television, books, recordings, advertisement campaigns) to promote his view of the American way of life. The book discusses the equation between Wayne's screen heroics and his true grit offscreen after licking cancer, which he nicknamed the Big C. Indeed, his lifestyle was intimately connected with his screen image--the private and public aspects of his life supported and reinforced each other. What made him an important national figure was his articulation and exemplification of some basic American values, such as hard work, upward mobility, individual attainment, economic success, and ordinariness. The book shows that conservatism and traditionalism marked every aspect of his life, being eternally concerned with projecting a positive image of American culture, on screen and off.

Wayne was not the only movie star to get involved in politics but, once again, what was distinctive about his politics was his success in integrating his politics into his professional career. John Wayne demonstrates that, surprisingly, the star's controversial politics neither damaged his career nor affected his popularity. Wayne's political philosophy was defined in terms of his unabashed patriotism and anti-Communist obsession. However, the book describes the changes that took place in his politics, particularly the mellowing of his reactionary image in the last decade of his career, when he was rewarded with social acceptance by the American public as some kind of a sentimental patriarch.

The connecting thread of John Wayne: Prophet of the American Way of Life is a demonstration of Wayne's success in convincing the American public that his screen image and personal life were inseparable. The book shows that gradually Wayne began to believe in his own screen heroics, though he made sure to invest them with his personal politics. The star's most significant role was as a propagandist, using the screen as an ideological weapon to promote his political and sociological propaganda. The propaganda in Wayne's films increasingly became more conscious and blatant, using his notion of the American way of life as a criterion to condone everything that reinforced it and condemn everything that threatened it. The book shows that of all movie stars, Wayne was the greatest prophet of the American way of life, strongly committed to white, middle-class culture as a unifying force and instrument of assimilation in an otherwise pluralistic and divided America.

There have been other books on John Wayne, though most are either superficial biographies or illustrated and trivia books. There is one notable exception, Allen Eyles's John Wayne, which is a chronological discussion, film by film, of the star's work. However, no book has addressed itself to the specific concerns of John Wayne: Prophet of the American Way of Life. This book is neither a conventional biography nor a year-by-year examination of Wayne's individual achievements. It is a critical document of Wayne's roles and powers as an American folk hero. Using a sociohistorical perspective, John Wayne examines the actor as a creation of the mass media, in relation to film, dominant culture, and politics of American society over the last half century. The book aims at contributing to the understanding of film genres (war movies and Westerns), the power of movie stars, the film industry during its golden age, and American popular culture.

Based on extensive research conducted over the last four years, the book draws on a diversity of sources and materials. First and foremost are Wayne's numerous movies, many of which have been seen three or four times. Their screenplays along with their reviews in various newspapers and magazines were examined systematically. Almost every major interview given by Wayne, from the 1940s on, was read. The box-office popularity of his movies is based on careful statistical analysis of data provided by leading trade papers, such as Variety and The Hollywood Reporter. The book also benefits from hundreds of biographies, autobiographies, and interviews with film figures published in the last decade.

1. THE CAREER OF A SUPERSTAR

John Wayne was born as Marion Michael Morrison on
May 26, 1907, in Winterset, a small town in Iowa. His father,
Clyde L. Morrison, was a druggist of Scottish descent, and
his mother, Mary Margaret Brown, of pure Irish stock. The
Morrisons had two boys: Robert Emmet, the elder, and Marion Michael. When he was six, the family moved to Lancaster
in Southern California, where his father settled on a ranch;
afflicted with lung congestion, he needed a drier climate.
But his father was unsuccessful at ranching and, after a
year, moved the family to Glendale, a suburb of Los Angeles.
At first, Clyde worked as a pharmacist, then opened his own
drugstore.

In his childhood, Marion acquired the nickname Duke,
which stayed with him for the rest of his life. Glendale's
firemen, not knowing his name, started calling him Duke because he was always seen with his dog Duke, a big Airedale.
"I wasn't named for royalty," Wayne was glad to remind, "I
was named for a dog."[1] In 1921, he entered the Glendale
Union High School, where he excelled in football. A good
student, he graduated four years later with a high average.
His major ambition at the time was to pursue a naval career
and attend the U.S. Naval Academy at Annapolis. He applied
and was named an alternate, but the person who was first
choice took the appointment. This rejection was a bitter disappointment, leaving a lifelong scar.

Wayne's parents divorced while he was in high school.
Remaining with his mother, he continued to see his father
regularly. To round the family's meager income, he held an
assortment of jobs, one of which was to distribute handbills
at the local movie theater, for which he was able to see all
the movies free. He also worked as a delivery boy for local
stores and as a map plotter for the Bell Telephone Company.

Upon graduation from high school, in 1925, he received
a football scholarship from the University of Southern California (U.S.C.), where he became a star of the Trojans, its
great football team. When Howard Jones, the Trojans' coach,
heard that he needed a summer job, he promised to talk to
Tom Mix, the Western movie star. Jones assured Mix choice
seats for the games, in return for which the star promised
to employ Wayne and his friends, which he did. Wayne
started to work in the prop department of Fox Studios in the
summer of 1925. Until then he had never thought of becoming an actor. In high school, he had been unwillingly drafted
into a play, but this experience had left no impact on him.
If it were not for Tom Mix, the first movie star he had ever
met, he never would have chosen the movies as a career.
One day, Wayne saw Tom Mix drive up in a big, fancy car.
"It was right there and then," he recalled, "I told myself this
was a good business for me to be in."[2]

The careers of Wayne and other stars of his generation
exemplify some of the unique attributes of acting as a profession. In the first place, it is a democratic occupation, open
to all social classes and providing an important channel for
upward mobility. More significantly, acting is one of the most
readily entered (but also readily left) professions. Unlike
other occupations that require planning, because of the necessity for formal training and certification, acting does not require official education. Wayne first performed, then decided
to pursue an acting career. Furthermore, Wayne, like many
others, neither intended to become an actor nor made a deliberate or rational decision to pursue a film career. In many
ways, he became an actor by accident, as a result of circumstances, being "the right man in the right place at the right
time." What set him apart, however, was his determination to
carve his own career and be successful at it--despite the fact
that luck and situational contingencies played a crucial role
at its inception (chapter 5).

From Prop Man to Leading Man

The first movie in which Wayne worked as a stunt man
was Brown of Harvard (1926), directed by Jack Conway, for
which he was paid $7.50. He doubled for Francis X. Bushman
in the football scenes; his assignment was to run 100 yards
and let some guy tackle him. He then appeared in another

football picture, The Drop Kick (1927), cast as himself in a
number of football scenes played by the U.S.C. team.

But his major line of work in the late 1920s was as a
prop man at Fox, at a salary of $35 a week. His work in
Mother Machree (1928), a melodrama about the relationship
between a poor Irish mother (Belle Bennett) in America and
her son (Victor McLaglen), is important because of his meeting with its director, John Ford. This meeting was one of
the most important events of his life, for Ford had an immense influence on his career and on his life. It is doubtful that he would have become a popular actor or reached the
professional heights that he did without Ford. When he met
Ford, "I was going to U.S.C., studying to be a lawyer and
had no particular interest in the motion picture business--
working at Fox was just something to pay the bills at school.
I wasn't thinking about a future in the studios."[3] However,
going back to school after his summer job, he started to think
more seriously about his future: "The other kids who were
going to law school all had connections--fathers and uncles
who had law firms. I had none and began to realize that if
I went into law, I was going to spend ten years in the back
rooms writing briefs before I could get started." Ford was
a role model in more senses than one: "He was my mentor,
my ideal, and I made up my mind, I wanted to be like him."[4]
Wayne's parents had divorced a few years earlier, so Ford
also served as a father figure. Wayne recalled that he had
"no thought about becoming an actor," when he worked at
Fox. His ambition was to be a director like John Ford.

Wayne worked for Ford in various capacities. He was
a second assistant prop man in Four Sons; appeared in a bit
part as an Irish peasant boy watching a horse race in Hangman's House; and worked again as a prop man in The Black
Watch and Born Reckless. "Ford appreciated the fact," Wayne
said, "that I was more than just another prop man, that I
was trying to get an education."[5] Indeed, his ambition and
seriousness impressed the director, for he could see "there
was a boy who was working for something--not like most of
the other guys, just hanging around to pick up a few fast
bucks." Ford was also intrigued with Wayne's perpetual
challenge "to do everything better, and harder, and longer
than anyone else ... he was never afraid to work."[6]

Ford's Salute (1929) was an inexpensive action movie

about the football rivalry between the Army and the Navy.
He asked Wayne's help in recruiting football players, but
shooting began before the semester was over and Wayne had
to convince the university president to let the students appear in the movie. He did, however, a good public relations
job, stressing the rewards of such an experience: the travel
to Annapolis and Washington D.C., the learning of the country's political and military institutions, and, of course, the
money. Producer Sol Wurtzel offered each football player
$75 a week but Wayne, trying to impress him with his mod-
esty, suggested instead only $50. Then Wurtzel proceeded
to tell Wayne the bad news: "I forgot to mention to you,
Duke, that you're doing double duty on this picture. You're
propping it and playing football too. Congratulations! You
just screwed yourself out of twenty-five bucks a week!"[7]

Ironically, Wayne was cast in Salute as George O'Brien's
brother, a cadet at the Annapolis Academy, something he
could never achieve in his real life. The critical response
to the film was moderate, but Salute was very popular at the
box office. This picture is also important for marking the
beginning of a lifelong working association and friendship
with Ward Bond, another student at U.S.C., who went on
to become an actor, by accident, like Wayne.

Of the pictures that Wayne made at the time, only one,
Ford's Men Without Women (1930), was of any distinction,
providing the first collaboration between Ford, screen writer
Dudley Nichols, and cameraman Joseph H. August. It was
also the first time that Wayne's part was more than a walk-
on. As one of the 14 men whose submarine is trapped in
the ocean, he had a few lines to deliver, but the cameraman
awarded him a nice close-up--his first. Wayne recalled that
"on location, at Catalina, five big actors were supposed to
take a dive from a ship into the Pacific for an important shot.
Ford turned to me and said, 'Jump, Wayne.'" And because
all five refused to dive, "I dived five times for five different
guys in a long shot." Wayne believed that his courage impressed Ford and "he made me an actor from that day on."[8]

The other movies at Fox were below routine. In Words
and Music (1930), a musical set in college, Wayne received
his first billing (as Duke Morrison), though he did not have
much to do. But these years provided a unique opportunity
to learn every possible aspect of the production process:

"If the property department was a little low, I worked in the electric department. If the electric department was a little low, I got a job as an actor." Wayne treasured this knowledge which proved invaluable in the future, when he began to produce and direct movies himself. "In those days a boy without financial backing stood a chance of learning the business," he recalled, whereas "today, it is unionized and departmentalized; you can only learn one part of it."[9]

In the meantime, Wayne lost his football scholarship because of an injury, and decided not to return to school, lacking both money and interest. He became increasingly fascinated with the movie industry, though still had not made a clear commitment to acting as a career. "I went six or seven years fighting the idea I was an actor," he recalled, until "one day I suddenly realized time was flying by and I better start learning that part of the business."[10] Ford provided the necessary psychological encouragement, telling Wayne he was good at acting, but "as much as I wanted to believe the big director, I was ashamed to admit I was hipped on the idea of acting. That's why I started in with the props."[11] Wayne, like other male stars at the time, wanted to establish himself "in some substantial endeavor that was secure, profitable, and reasonably respectable."[12] Like Gable and Cooper, he had to convince himself that acting was a suitable profession for men, as it has always suffered-- particularly then--from the prevalent stigmas that it was easy, frivolous, unserious, and therefore inappropriate for men. Wayne admitted that it took him a long time to realize "this business is a damn fine business," and to become "proud of it."[13]

In 1930, Raoul Walsh was casting a big-budget Western, The Big Trail, and needed a rugged, handsome guy to play the lead. The part was first offered to Gary Cooper, who reportedly turned it down, and, besides, Paramount refused to lend him out to Fox. Ford suggested Wayne for the part and showed Walsh a clip from Men Without Women, upon which he decided to meet him. Walsh first met Wayne on the studio lot carrying an overstuffed chair into the property warehouse. His first impression was of a "tall young fellow," who "had wide shoulders to go with his height." Walsh watched Wayne "juggle a solid Louis XV sofa, as though it was made of feathers, and pick up another chair with his free hand."[14] Their first conversation was awkward, with Wayne telling the

veteran director that he wanted to get into pictures but "this
is as far as I've come." Asked what else he could do, Wayne
grinned, "I can play football." Impressed with his honesty
and naiveté, particularly "the tone of his voice and the way
he carried himself,"[15] Walsh told him to let his hair grow
and to come and see him in two weeks.

After watching his first screen test, Winfield Sheehan,
Fox's production chief, was surprised to learn that Wayne
had been on the studio's payroll. Wayne had two more tests
before landing the part; his second test was with voice, and
for the third he read some scenes from the screenplay. Walsh
decided to give him the starring role "partly because there
was something about the hang of his shoulders and that
shuffle, that I thought I could use in the picture, and partly because I had to find somebody immediately."[16] "To be a
cowboy star," Walsh held, "You've got to be six-foot-three
or over, you've got to have no hips, and a face that looks
right under a sombrero," and Wayne met these requirements,
especially in his masculine look and his "feeling of honesty,
of sincerity."[17]

In The Big Trail, the story of a pioneer trek along the
Oregon trail, Wayne plays Breck Coleman, the leader of the
wagon train seeking to avenge his friend's murder. Despite
a big budget, an unprecedented $2 million, location shooting,
good actors (Tyrone Power, Sr., and Marguerite Churchill),
and a big publicity campaign, the movie failed at the box
office. The Big Trail was released in two versions: the
conventional 35mm print size and the large 70mm print, called
"Fox Grandeur." One problem was that it was released during the Depression, in October 1930, and very few houses
could afford to buy the new expensive projector, particularly
since many had just recently wired their houses for sound,
which was very costly. The Big Trail was one of the two
major pictures produced in 70mm (King Vidor's Billy the Kid
at MGM was the other), but after a few showcase runs, it
was distributed in the standard 35mm gauge.

Wayne received top billing, though he was still an inexperienced actor. Contrary to popular notions, neither
Wayne nor the movie received unfavorable reviews. The
New York Times critic, for instance, wrote that Wayne "acquits himself with no little distinction. He performance is
pleasantly natural." The picture was described as "an

John Wayne and Marguerite Churchill in Raoul Walsh's The Big Trail (Fox, 1930), the film that failed to make him a star.

overwhelming task," "a monumental work," one "that is stim-
ulation in much the same way as that old silent film classic,
The Iron Horse, was in its time."[18] Indeed, in scope and
action, The Big Trail was one of the more impressive Westerns; its Indian battle scenes were later used to pad out
numerous cheaper Westerns. The Times critic felt, nonetheless, that the authenticity of detail and the sweep of action were let down by the standardized "B" plot. The Big
Trail turned out to be one of the few Wayne movies to have
lost money in the American film market, though it proved to
be a greater success in Europe.

From Leading Man to "B" Westerns

The second phase in Wayne's career lasted a decade,
from 1930 to 1939, when he received his breakthrough role
in Stagecoach. Most of his 1930s movies were "B" Westerns,
the bottom of the bill of double features. But this decade
was important for various reasons: Wayne became committed
to screen acting as a career, he became associated in the
public's mind with the Western genre, and some elements of
his screen persona began to take shape.

The Big Trail launched Wayne as a leading man, but
did not make him a star, which was disappointing, as he recalled: "I sure thought I'd set the world on fire."[19] After
this Western, he only made two more films for Fox, Girls
Demand Excitement and Three Girls Lost, considered by him
the worst in his career. Fox decided not to pick up his contract and subsequently his career plummeted. Another decade passed before the right movie and the right part put
him at the forefront of actors.

Wayne was signed by Columbia, then a minor and less
prestigious studio than Fox, for which he made four features,
all released in 1931. In these movies he played supporting
roles to Tim McCoy and Buck Jones, two of Columbia's most
popular cowboy stars. He was cast in roles similar to those
he had played in the 1920s, playing a West Point cadet in
Men Are Like That or a football player in Maker of Man.
And his fourth feature at Columbia, The Deceiver, had the
distinction of casting him as a corpse!

He also appeared in several serials produced by Mascot,

another Poverty Row Company. These serials had similar
narratives but different locales. In the first, Shadow of the
Eagle, as a member of a traveling carnival who is also a
courageous skywriter and pilot, he battles against a villain
(the Eagle) threatening a large corporation. And in Hurri-
cane Express, his Larry Baker is also a pilot, this time of
air transport, determined to track down the murderer of his
father, killed in a mysterious train wreck. Each of the Mascot serials consisted of twelve chapters, presented as the
lower half of a double feature. But despite low budgets
and routine action, they were quite profitable.

Much more important to his career were the Westerns
he made for Warners in 1932-33, such as The Big Stampede
and Haunted Gold, patterned after some of the silent Ken
Maynard movies. Produced by cartoon maker Leon Schlesin-
ger, they used basic plots and action material, adding a few
chasing scenes and fights. Wayne was asked to wear the
same clothes as Maynard and ride the same kind of horse--
for matching up purposes. In one of the better films,
Haunted Gold, Wayne's John Mason fights an outlaw gang
for an abandoned gold mine, in the course of which he discovers that "the Phantom" haunting the mine is no other
than his girl's father. In all his Warners Westerns his hero's
name was John, such as The Telegraph Trail, in which his
army scout, John Trent, volunteers to complete the stringing
of the telegraph wires across the plains, after his best friend
has been killed by the Indians.

Wayne also appeared in non-Westerns at Warners, but
they did not do much for his career, despite the fact that
he was cast against major stars and in big productions. In
Baby Face, for example, he had a small part, a bank's un-
dermanager, serving as a stepping stone to Barbara Stanwyck's career woman. And in The Life of Jimmy Dolan, a
popular film about the moral rehabilitation of a prizefighter
on a Utah farm, he played a bit part of a prizefighter opposite Douglas Fairbanks, Jr. and Loretta Young.

A series of Westerns at Monogram, another Poverty
Row Company, whose actors tended to be either at the beginning or, unfortunately, at the end of their careers, followed his work at Warners. The budget of these pictures
was small, less than $10,000, and they were most efficiently
shot, in three to five days. Wayne appeared in 16 such

movies, billed as Lone Star Productions, and released in
rapid succession between October 1933 and July 1935. Most
were routinely directed, and often written, by Robert North
Bradbury, though nicely photographed by Archie Stout, and
featuring the popular character actor George (Gabby) Hayes.
What made them attractive to the public was not their narratives, which, with the exception of The Trail Beyond (drawing on James Oliver Curwood's novel), were all based on
"original" screenplays, but the fact that they contained distinguished action and stunt work by Yakima Canutt.

In all of them, Wayne played variations of basically
one role. One typical story line cast him as a federal government undercover agent sent to help ranchers get water rights
(Riders of Destiny) or sent to round up a gang of counterfeiters (Paradise Canyon). Another recurrent role was that
of a man wrongly accused and/or wrongly convicted of crimes
he did not commit (Sagebrush Trail), but always released (or
escaping) from jail in time to seek the real villains. Revenge
of parents' or siblings' death was also at the center of many
pictures (West of the Divide, The Dawn Rider, and numerous others).

In 1935, Monogram and Lone Star Productions merged
to form the new Republic Pictures, with Wayne's Westward
Ho! as its first offering. Republic soon distinguished itself
in making serials, Western and non-Western, often used as
training ground for many actors; Lionel Barrymore and
George Montgomery, among others, began their careers in
serials. Wayne's movies had bigger budgets, $30,000 to
$40,000, more prestigious casts, and better directors and
cameramen--but their narratives were formulaic, similar to
his previous Westerns. In Lawless Range, for example, he
is an undercover government agent set to discover mysterious raids, and in The Lawless Nineties, he is sent to break
up a terrorizing gang.

However, Wayne was cast in some of Republic's
best serials, most notably The Three Mesquiteers, loosely
based on William Colt MacDonald's stories. They were
often inconsistent in period or locale, with some set in
the nineteenth century (Covered Wagon Days), whereas
others in the present, dealing with racketeers (Come on
Wagon), and even escaped Nazi spies (Valley of Hunted
Men). They were strong, however, in their production

values: fast action, excellent stunt work, sharp cinematography, and even good music scores. Ray Corrigan, Bob Livingstone, and Syd Saylor played the leads in the first film, but other actors took over when they dropped out. Max Terhune replaced Saylor, and Wayne assumed Livingstone's role in Pals of the Saddle and others; Wayne's role was given back to Livingstone after he left. Wayne made all together eight movies, all directed by George Sherman and released within a short period of time, from August 1938 to August 1939. He achieved some distinction in playing Stony Brook, usually acting independently of the other two and also having the visual prominence of a white outfit and the only white horse.

It is hard to say that his career improved with his move to Universal, his next studio, though his six action pictures there had bigger budgets, about $60,000, better supporting casts, and were shown in better movie houses, which meant that they were taken slightly more seriously by audiences and critics. Full of adventure, like his Republic Westerns, but set in contemporary times, they provided him with a diversity of roles. He played a U.S. Coast Guard commander, outfighting a band of seal poachers and smugglers in The Sea Spoilers, and a cameraman, covering the Spanish Civil War, then dispatched to North Africa to report on an anti-British uprising in I Cover the War.

Arthur Lubin, who directed five of Wayne's six Universal pictures, recalled: "We had six days to shoot. There was no time schedule, as there is today, where if you go late at night or start early in the morning, you have to pay more. In those days, you could shoot twenty-four hours a day."[20] Lubin had the reputation of "doing pictures quickly and bringing them in on schedule." The last of Wayne's Universal movies, Adventure's End (1937), was "very extravagant," according to Lubin, because "we were going to shoot in ten days," and "it was going to be a big picture," budgeted at $90,000. One of the prominent considerations for making pictures was "what sets are up these days that we can make pictures on, that won't cost us much money?" Adventure's End was made because "there was a boat on Universal lot, and they could use that."[21]

In the 1930s, Wayne appeared in no less than 67 movies, over one-third of his entire film output. At least seven

of his pictures were released every year and in some even
more. In 1933, for example, Wayne starred in 11 movies.
Of these 67 pictures, over half (37) were "B" Westerns, the
rest action or adventure vehicles. Thus, his appeal became
closely associated with the Western genre, an association
which continued for the rest of his life. Wayne also made
some sports movies but, unlike the Western and later the
war movies, he very seldom returned to this genre.

Working mostly for the Poverty Row Companies, he
made three serials (each consisting of 12 episodes) for Mascot, 16 for Monogram, and 12 for Republic. But he also appeared in nine pictures at Warners, six at Universal, six at
Columbia, three at Fox, and two at Paramount. Most of his
movies had small budgets and were shot in a few days. "I
went in and out of those films so fast," he recalled, "that
half of the time I didn't know their titles."[22] Nor did the
critics or audiences, for that matter. Their titles were unimportant because their plots were similar and their quality
undistinguished. How could moviegoers differentiate The
Telegraph Trail from The Desert Trail or The Oregon Trail?
And Ride Him, Cowboy, Riders of Destiny, and Randy Rides
Alone, not only had similar titles, but similar stories as well.

Wayne did not make much of an impression on the movie
critics. Most of his pictures, in fact, were ignored by them
and those reviewed often did not even mention his name. A
typical review of the 1930s was Variety's of The Sea Spoilers:
"Wayne acquits himself along routine lines. He fidgets a bit
in the love scenes and looks stalwart otherwise."[23] And reviewing I Cover the War, the New York World Telegram
wrote that the acting was amateurish and that John Wayne
and the others "try their best, but their best is none too
good."[24] Of his performance in Adventure's End, the Variety critic noted that the actor "founders in the lead role."[25]

The 1930s were undoubtedly the most difficult years in
Wayne's career, making one "quickie" Western after another,
often working in as many as six pictures at the same time.
In some, he worked in various capacities: handling props,
acting, and stunting. At times, he was so discouraged that
he considered alternative occupations to acting, such as
stock brokerage and real estate. "I was a happy-go-lucky
fellow in those days," he later described, "but after ten
years of quickie Westerns, I realized I was in a rut."[26]

Were it not for the need to support a large family, a wife
and four children, he would have quit. Ford's continuous
moral support was instrumental: "Every time I'd get discouraged, Jack would insist that I hang on, that he's yet to
find the right part and put me across." To encourage him,
he said, Ford "invited me down on the yacht and rehearsed
me in the lines of the cheap Westerns in which I was playing."[27]

But the "B" Westerns had a positive side as well, providing an opportunity to learn the business inside out. Wayne
threw himself into learning every aspect of film production,
which proved useful later on. He attributed what he called
his "analytic viewpoint" of movies to the fact that he had appeared in so many bad pictures, learning "to look for things
that could hurt actors." He never regretted "my background
of quickie Westerns," because they helped him acquire discipline and take long hours and hardships at work. At the
same time, he was the first to consider himself "lucky to
have survived the dozens of 'B' pictures," because "they've
killed many a fine actor."[28]

The Rise to Stardom

Wayne's breakthrough role in Stagecoach began a new
phase in his career, which lasted a decade. This phase was
transitional but extremely important, establishing him not so
much as an actor but as a screen persona. After a decade
as a "B" player at the Poverty Row Companies, Wayne graduated into "A" movies and "A" directors and became a respectable star. He appeared in 31 pictures, making on the
average three movies a year. World War II slowed down
movie production in Hollywood because many directors and
actors were enlisted into the Army. Wayne was not drafted
because of his age (34 when the United States entered the
war), a large family, and an ankle injury. Of the 31 pictures he made between 1939 and 1948, half were for Republic, where he was under contract, but he also worked for
other studios: five pictures at RKO, three at Universal,
and two each at MGM, United Artists, and Paramount. The
major achievement was that he was no longer associated with
second-rate studios.

The crucial point in his career was getting the part of

the Ringo Kid in Stagecoach, which he considered "the film
that started my career."[29] Ford took a big risk in casting
Wayne because he was then labeled a "B" Western actor.
Wayne himself had serious doubts as to whether he was able
to play the part convincingly. However, the timing of Ford's
offer could not have been better, "just about the time I was
ready to resign myself to being a run-of-the-mill actor for the
rest of my life."[30] His first scene was unforgettable: Wayne
appears on the screen suddenly, out of nowhere, and stops
the stagecoach. The passengers ask, "Who are you?" to
which he replies, "The Ringo Kid. That's what my friends
call me. But my real name's Henry." "Those three sen-
tences," Wayne believed, "were my passport to fame." He
also recalled that "everybody told Ford he was committing
suicide, risking a third rate bum like me in a million dollar
movie."[31] Indeed, asked what had distinguished his career
from that of other "B" actors, he was quick to reply, "John
Ford." Wayne worked with many excellent directors, but
none has had the pervasive influence of Ford.

Unfortunately, a month prior to Stagecoach, Wayne
had signed a long-term contract with Republic which committed him to six pictures. When Ford asked the heads of
Republic to borrow the actor, the studio was dubious; it
feared that playing the lead in a prestigious movie like
Stagecoach would spoil him for low-budget Westerns. Wayne,
however, took a leave of absence to work for Ford and promised to return to Republic, which he did.

The premiere of Stagecoach took place on February 2,
1939, at the Fox Westwood Theater in Los Angeles. Wayne
invited some of his employers from Republic, who came "but
never said a word to me." Finally, when he asked for their
opinion, their response was short: "If they want Westerns,
they'd better let us make them." Apparently, they were impressed with neither the picture nor him. The audience, by
contrast, "yelled and screamed and stood up and cheered.
I never saw anything like that."[32] Wayne scored critical
acclaim as the Ringo Kid; it was the first time that the critics acknowledged his presence and really praised his acting.
The New York Daily News reviewer represented many when
he wrote: "John Wayne is so good in the role of the outlaw
that one wonders why he has had to wait all this time since
The Big Trail for such another opportunity."[33]

Stagecoach pulled Wayne out of his rut and out of the "B" Westerns, but it did not make him an instant star. It certified, however, for the first time, his abilities as a prominent screen personality who could "carry" a film. After this picture, many studios wanted to hire him, but he kept his word and returned to Republic. This studio apparently regarded Wayne's popularity as a passing fad, for it continued to cast him in low-budget Westerns, which were sort of an anticlimax and a low point in his career. Nonetheless, Republic must have sensed the interest in Wayne, because it held back his pictures until the release of Stagecoach, to cash in on his recently-acquired popularity. Still, it took Republic another decade to recognize Wayne's star potential and cast him in better roles in bigger-budget pictures, such as Angel and the Badman.

The four Republic Westerns, directed by George Sherman, were released in rapid order in 1939: The Night Riders in April, Three Texas Steers in June, Wyoming Outlaw in July, and New Frontier in September. They were important because they provided Wayne continuous exposure to moviegoers at an extremely crucial time in his career. Republic was as its peak in the 1940s, producing some of the fastest-moving Westerns, especially those starring Wayne. He continued to play his popular hero, fighting against a gambler who evicted innocent landowners in The Night Riders, or saving innocent settlers from getting worthless land in New Frontier.

Wayne's range of roles in the 1940s was probably the widest he ever attempted. Half of his film output in this decade consisted of Westerns, but he also appeared in war films, comedies, and adventures. The war movies constituted a particularly important addition to his range, making five such pictures during the war, including Flying Tigers and Back to Bataan. His best work was again under director Ford, in two war movies: The Long Voyage Home, the story of a crew aboard a British tramp freighter, and They Were Expendable, a saga of the P-T boats. His heroic roles in the war movies became central to his screen image and contributed immensely to his box-office popularity. From the 1940s on, he became associated almost exclusively with two genres: Westerns and war movies.

The 1940s were also a notable decade because he started

to work with Hollywood's best filmmakers. Raoul Walsh directed him again in The Dark Command, a pre-Civil War adventure starring Claire Trevor. And The Shepherd of the Hills, his first movie at Paramount, was directed by Henry Hathaway, beginning a long collaboration between the two that culminated in their best joint effort, True Grit. Wayne also worked with Cecil B. De Mille in Reap the Wild Wind, an expensive sea adventure starring Ray Milland and Paulette Goddard, and with Frank Lloyd in The Spoilers, the fourth and best film version of the Alaska gold mines adventure.

That Wayne did not become a major box-office star after Stagecoach is evident for he continued to get second billing in most of his 1940s pictures. He was reteamed with Claire Trevor in two historical Westerns, Allegheny Uprising and Dark Command--in both she got top billing. In his three pictures opposite Marlene Dietrich at Universal, Seven Sinners, The Spoilers, and Pittsburgh, she was billed first. Moreover, Wayne supported many movies that were designed as vehicles for their female stars. Thus, he was cast against Joan Crawford in Reunion in France, Jean Arthur in A Lady Takes a Chance, and Claudette Colbert in Without Reservations. The crucial achievement, however, was that he was cast against first-rate players, a dramatic change from the second-rate casts of his previous movies.

The Making of a Superstar

Red River, made in 1946 but released in 1948, began the fourth phase in Wayne's career, which lasted until the late 1960s. These two decades were the most important in his career, featuring his best performances and making him the biggest box-office attraction in film history. He was extremely busy, with every studio in Hollywood seeking his services. From 1948 to 1969 he made no fewer than 45 movies, achieving an annual record of two to three pictures. The largest number of films (11) were produced and/or released through Warners. In 1952 he signed a comprehensive deal with this studio, which stipulated that he could produce films for Warners without starring in them. But in addition to Warners, he appeared in seven movies at Paramount, seven at United Artists, six ar RKO, five at Republic, four at Twentieth Century-Fox, and two at Universal. Committed to his two specialized and favorite genres, he made 18 Westerns and 11 war movies.

Wayne's portrayal of Thomas Dunson, the ruthless cattle baron in Red River, is considered to be one of his best performances and, next to Stagecoach, his most important vehicle. This movie marked a turning point in his career, featuring his first portrayal of a character role which was well beyond his age. Apparently it was Howard Hawks who told Wayne, "You're going to be an old man pretty soon and you ought to get used to it. You better start playing characters instead of that junk you've been playing."[34] True, until the late 1940s, he played for the most part young, handsome, and charming cowboys. Furthermore, Red River not only featured his richest work to date, but also convinced his detractors that he could act. Ford was so impressed with his portrayal that he cast him in his cavalry trilogy, Fort Apache, She Wore a Yellow Ribbon, and Rio Grande, providing him some of his most interesting parts.

Red River began a long and creative collaboration with Hawks who, next to Ford, exerted the greatest influence on his career. Hawks proceeded to direct him in three Westerns, regarded by some as a trilogy because of their similar thematic concerns. These were: Rio Bravo, opposite Dean Martin; El Dorado, opposite Robert Mitchum; and the lesser endeavor Rio Lobo, which surrounded Wayne with a mediocre cast. In addition to these Westerns, Hawks also used Wayne in the highly entertaining adventure Hatari! concerning a professional team of animal hunters, filmed on location in Tanganyika.

Wayne appeared for the first time on the poll of the ten most popular stars in the United States in 1949, following his performance in Sands of Iwo Jima, a war film that also won him his first Academy nomination as Best Actor. Wayne went on to become the biggest box-office draw in film history, not just in America. He remained on this popularity poll, the most accurate and most important in the industry, for an all-time record of 25 years, from 1949 to 1974. No other star, male or female, American or foreign, has been as popular as Wayne for so long a time--and consistently so.

The most creative years in his career were from the late 1940s to the late 1950s. His best work was once again under Ford, who directed him in two excellent Westerns, The Searchers and The Man Who Shot Liberty Valance. Ford also cast Wayne in the distinguished idyllic romance The Quiet Man, beautifully photographed in Ireland and

highly praised by the critics. This director was also responsible for making a team out of Wayne and Maureen
O'Hara, casting them together for the first time in Rio
Grande. O'Hara went on to become his most favorite and
most frequent screen lady.

In 1951, Wayne and Robert Fellows, a veteran producer
and former Paramount executive, formed an independent production company, the Wayne-Fellows Productions, which made
many of Wayne's films, including Big Jim McLain, Island in
the Sky, and The High and the Mighty. Later, Wayne established Batjac, his own production company, over which he
had complete control. Batjac was instrumental in bringing to
the screen projects that reflected Wayne's personal politics
that no other studio would have touched.

The 1950s marked Wayne's first significant use of the
film medium as an ideological weapon, with such blatantly
propagandistic vehicles as Big Jim McLain, an anti-
Communist movie, and The Alamo, officially the saga of
Texas's fight for freedom, but replete with allusions to contemporary democracy and patriotism. This trend continued
in the 1960s, culminating with the oversimplified The Green
Berets, the only pro-Vietnam movie at the time. Of all
projects, however, The Alamo was his most ambitious, politically and personally; he produced, directed, and starred
in it. It was his labor of love and conviction, investing in
it, as he said, his soul and his money. The failure of The
Alamo, both critically and commercially, was the biggest
disappointment of his career. His second directorial effort,
The Green Berets (co-directed with Ray Kellogg), was even
more propagandistic, but much less distinguished as a picture. Panned by all critics, it curiously turned out to be
more popular with audiences that The Alamo. A lesser movie
on all grounds, its commercial bonanza is still a mystery.

Wayne's political power went far beyond making pictures or being a movie star. He was proud to be a founding member, and later president, of the Motion Picture Alliance for the Preservation of American Ideals, an extremely
right-wing organization, which supported Senator Joseph
McCarthy and the investigations conducted by the House
Un-American Activities Committee. Wayne's anti-Communism
could be described as a lifelong and deep-rooted obsession,
of which he made no secret.

This era also saw the merger of his screen image and offscreen life to the point where the two aspects became one inseparable entity. Undoubtedly, no other actor in the American cinema has displayed such a complete blend (or confusion) between life on screen and off. What contributed to this integration was the display of his onscreen courage and true grit offscreen, when he survived three major operations, beginning with his 1964 successful bout with cancer and his subsequent miraculous recovery.

Wayne's increasing age, however, combined with the decline in American film production in the 1960s, slowed down his work. He made fewer movies and, like other stars, began to appear in cameo roles, most of which to disastrous effects. His worst cameo appearance was in George Stevens's The Greatest Story Ever Told, in which he was miscast as a Roman centurion! Two bit parts were somehow more successful: as Lt. Colonel Benjamin Vandervoort in the epic war movie The Longest Day, and as General Randolph in Cast a Giant Shadow, the biopicture of Colonel David Marcus (Kirk Douglas), who contributed to the formation of Israel's modern army. These cameo roles, however, were the exception, for unlike other major stars, forced to accept supporting roles as they aged, Wayne was always the leading man and center of his movies.

From a Superstar to a Legend

The fifth and last phase of Wayne's career began with True Grit, for which he was honored with an Oscar, and ended with his last picture, The Shootist, in 1976. In these seven years he made 12 movies, of which ten (and the first six in the 1970s) were Westerns. Most of his features, such as Chisum and Big Jake, were produced, by Batjac and released through Warners. Despite his age, his career was still viable and every major Hollywood studio was glad to employ him. Warners reportedly agreed to finance The Cowboys within 24 hours after the project was submitted to them, a clear indication of his firm standing at the box office.

Wayne's portrayal of Rooster Cogburn in True Grit was the climax of his professional career. His wonderful performance was unanimously praised, receiving both official recognition and the highest acting accolade, the Best Actor

Oscar from the Academy of Motion Picture Arts and Sciences.
But True Grit also represented, as one critic observed, "the
true climax of a great and well-beloved career, if not as an
actor then as an American institution."[35] "One can only
hope that when he does decide to hang up his boots (if not
his political guns!)," wrote another critic, "it will be with a
vehicle as sympathetic and felicitous as True Grit."[36] This
prophecy turned out to be true: The Shootist was a most
appropriate swan song, featuring Wayne in the mythic role
of an aging gunfighter dying of cancer! He could not have
appeared in a more autobiographic or reverential movie.

But there were some unfortunate projects as well,
such as his attempt (the last) to expand his range in two
crime thrillers: McQ and Brannigan. Prior to that, he had
never played a cop or a private eye, a genre which became
extremely popular in the 1960s, with Sean Connery's James
Bond movies, and in the 1970s with Clint Eastwood's Dirty
Harry pictures. "I felt like a bit of change myself," Wayne
said, "but I had to stick to action movies, of course, and
the tough cop thriller is where a lot of action is these
days."[37] The switch to crime pictures was not by choice,
however. In the 1970s, both Westerns and war movies declined in appeal, so the action-adventure was really his only
viable alternative. Unfortunately, both movies failed, critically and commercially. Comparisons with Steve McQueen
(Bullitt and others) and Clint Eastwood's vehicles were inevitable, and they were not to Wayne's advantage. Reviewing McQ, Nora Sayre represented many critics when she
wrote: "Surely Mr. Wayne should stick to Westerns; he's
simply too slow to play any kind of policeman."[38] And another critic went farther: "Out of the saddle and into the
Hornet," Wayne "is as stony-faced and over-aged as ever."[39]

But his 1970s Westerns did not fare much better, being tedious repetitions of his old formulaic films. Chisum
was a traditional, old-fashioned, and conservative Western,
which fictionalized as well as trivialized the real-life cattle
baron to suit the actor's persona. And Rio Lobo, the weakest Wayne-Hawks collaboration, was a feeble copy of their
previous achievements in Rio Bravo and El Dorado. As for
Rooster Cogburn, it stirred a lot of interest and publicity
for its casting of two legendary stars for the first time,
Wayne and Katharine Hepburn. But combining Wayne's role
in True Grit with elements of Hepburn's spinster missionary

John Wayne and Richard Attenborough (right) in Brannigan
(United Artists, 1975), one of Wayne's abortive attempts to
expand his range and go beyond the Western film.

in The African Queen, compounded with the fact that both
looked old and tired, made the film an embarrassing disappointment.

       In the 1970s, however, Wayne became much more than
a movie superstar. He came to be regarded an American
folk hero, with his offscreen activities and statements getting as much publicity--at times more--as his movies. His
political views, particularly his previously emotionally charged
battle against Communism, seemed to have mellowed, resulting
in his acceptance as some kind of national treasure by most
Americans, including his detractors. Wayne succeeded in
becoming a popular culture figure, an icon, using a variety
of mass media to promote his social propaganda, his version
of the American way of life. Thus, he began to appear
more frequently on television, in variety and talk shows, and
starred in his first television special, Swing Out, Sweet
Land, a sentimental and patriotic pastiche. His tremendous body of film work, especially his old movies, have been

shown almost regularly on the small screen. Wayne even recorded an album, and later a book, America, Why I Love
Her. In short, his visibility as a public figure was extra-
ordinarily prominent, particularly following his various commercial and advertisement campaigns.

In 1975 Wayne dropped out of favor as a movie star
and, for the first time in 25 years, he was not among the
top ten box-office stars in America. Insurance problems,
stemming from his declining health, made it more difficult
for studios to employ him and, more importantly, it was not
easy finding suitable roles for him. Characteristically though,
he did not consider retirement. During the production of
The Shootist, he liked to tease reporters, "Bull! It won't
be my last picture," reiterating his gusto for life, "Unless I
stop breathing, or people stop going to see my films, I'll be
making more of them."[40] Indeed, shortly before his death,
he was planning a new movie, a comedy titled Beau John.

But his health deteriorated rapidly: in March 1978,
he had bronchial pneumonia and underwent open-heart surgery to replace a defective mitral valve. And in January
1979, doctors discovered a low-grade malignant tumor in his
stomach, during a gall bladder operation. His cancerous
stomach was replaced with a new one, fashioned from parts
of his intestines. Wayne, of course, assured his family and
friends that he was fine and was going to resume his work
soon--but this time he was unfortunately wrong. His last
public appearance was appropriately on April 9, 1979, at the
annual Oscar ceremonies, when he presented the Best Picture
Award, which ironically was given to The Deer Hunter, a
powerful anti-Vietnam movie. Wayne's speech was the emotional high point of the evening and he was greeted with a
lengthy standing ovation.

John Wayne died on June 11, 1979; he was 72 years
old. He was buried three days later in a plot near his Newport Beach home in California. Wayne's death marked the
end of an entire era in American film. The media blitz that
his death precipitated, occupying the front pages of newspapers all over the world, was a clear testament to his popularity as a movie star and to his prominence as a national
legend. It is unlikely that there will ever be another American star of comparable popularity, durability, and power, in
and outside the film industry.

2. THE WAR HERO

John Wayne contributed extensively to two distinctly
American genres: the Western and the war film. Although
he did not make as many war movies as Westerns, the former
played an important role in his career and contributed immensely to his screen image and popularity.

Wayne was anxious to make war films because of a personal frustration: he was too young (seven) to take part in
World War I, and too old (34) to fight in World War II. But
in addition to age, he was draft-exempt for having family
commitments--he was married and had children--and an injury from playing football at the University of Southern California. Even the connections of John Ford, who during the
war was chief of the Field Photographic Branch at the OSS
with the rank of lieutenant commander in the Navy, did not
help to get him drafted.

Wayne's frustration grew when many stars of his generation were enlisted. Jimmy Stewart was the first big Hollywood star to enlist into military service, on March 21, 1941,
even before the United States joined the war. He went out
of his way to get drafted, much to the disappointment of the
industry. Deferred by the board for being underweight, Stewart had to put on ten pounds. His enlistment got tremendous publicity, especially the drastic pay cut he had to take.
The difference between his monthly military remuneration and
his Hollywood income amounted to 11,979 dollars.[1] Stewart
did not make any films for five years, during which he flew
missions over Germany as a bomber pilot, rising in rank
from private to colonel.

Many stars followed Stewart. Clark Gable enlisted into
the Air Force in 1942, after the death of his wife, actress
Carole Lombard, in an air-crash accident. He too achieved

23

the high rank of major for flying bombing missions over Germany. Henry Fonda was also enlisted into the Navy in 1942, serving as an assistant operations and air combat intelligence officer in the Pacific. All of these actors were singled out for their patriotic services. Gable received the Distinguished Flying Cross and Air Medal, and Fonda was awarded a Bronze Star and a presidential citation. Stewart retired from the Armed Services in 1968, as a brigadier general in the Air Force Reserve, the highest-ranking entertainer in the U.S. military.

Realizing that he could not take part in the "real" action, Wayne immersed himself in making flag-waving war pictures. What contributed to his interest in this genre was the fact that by 1941 most Hollywood stars had already made war movies, which was important to their careers as well as to the nation's morale. Robert Taylor made Flight Command, the story of Flight Squadron Eight, at MGM in 1940, and a year later, Ray Milland and William Holden appeared in I Wanted Wings; Tyrone Power in Yank in the R.A.F.; and Errol Flynn in Dive Bomber. Gary Cooper's performance in Sergeant York not only won him his first Oscar, but the film itself enjoyed extraordinary popularity as the top money-making picture of 1941, grossing $6 million in domestic rentals. [2]

Actors not drafted were used by their studios most efficiently, to make up for the shortage in male stars. James Cagney and Humphrey Bogart reached new heights of popularity at Warners during the war, and Spencer Tracy became MGM's biggest star and most employed actor; Clark Gable and Robert Taylor, the studio's other stars, were drafted. Errol Flynn also continued to do his heroics in adventure and costume pictures, though, ironically, he was classified 4F and was turned down by every branch of the Armed Forces because of a combination of a heart defect, recurrent malaria, and a measure of tuberculosis. This rejection hurt his ego and was concealed from the public for fear of bad publicity.

During World War II, the Western film declined in popularity. Historians estimate that about one-third of the films produced in Hollywood (500 out of 1,700) between 1942 and 1945 were about some aspect of the war: the battle or the home front. [3] Wayne, like other stars, had to switch from playing Westerners to playing soldiers.

Broadly defined, Wayne made 16 war pictures (about 10 percent of his film output) beginning with The Long Voyage Home and Three Faces West in 1940 all the way to The Green Berets in 1968. Most of these pictures, such as Sands of Iwo Jima and The Longest Day, dealt with World War II and with good reason: it was the last American war unanimously perceived as a "good" war for a noble cause. By contrast, Wayne did not make any movie about the Korean War, a revealing omission from his repertoire. However, he was the first filmmaker to treat the Vietnam War on the screen in The Green Berets, one of his most propagandistic pictures (see chapter 13). Other Wayne pictures, such as Pittsburgh, used the war as background, but were not typical genre movies.

Wayne's War Heroes

Wayne succeeded in establishing a coherent war hero, characterized by specific themes that recurred consistently in his pictures. The most important elements of his screen persona in the war genre were: the tough commander and patriotic role model, the man of action who wanted to fight and hated desk work, and the charismatic leader. But most important in his war movies was his attitude toward soldiers and his obsessive desire to make "real men" out of them. In many pictures there was a two-generational plot, contrasting Wayne's leader with his younger, inexperienced soldiers.

In Flying Tigers (1942) Wayne is cast as Jim Gordon, the squadron leader of the American volunteer group, fighting for China's freedom against the Japanese. This film is important because it introduced the generational conflict between Wayne and his soldiers, which later became a distinctive attribute of the "John Wayne movie." A competent leader but tough as nails on his men, he is contrasted with a new recruit, Woody Jason (John Carroll), who signs up because he needs the money to pay off a breach-of-promise suit. Jason does not make a secret out of his eagerness to get the $500 reward for every Japanese plane knocked down. Wayne despises him for his selfishness, especially after his failure to be at the base when needed; another flier takes over and finds his death. "I was a kid," Jason laments, "it took somebody to die to make a man out of me." But he begs for another chance and his heroics even save Wayne's life: bombing a Japanese supply train, his plane catches

fire but he pushes Wayne out, thus redeeming himself, paying for his errors with his life.

Wayne is a commander who nurtures his soldiers to
manhood by teaching them to accept military discipline. But
he is also a sensitive leader, aware of the anguish of sending
innocent soldiers out to die. In one scene, he regrets having
allowed a young soldier to fly on a deadly mission: "Should
have stayed in college where he came from. But he begged
me for a chance and I gave it to him!"

Sergeant John M. Stryker in Sands of Iwo Jima (1949)
is disliked by his men because of his ruthless training. His
major critic is a new recruit, Peter Conway (John Agar),
who hates Stryker's rigid discipline. (Stryker trains his
novices by ruthlessly bullying and whipping them into shape.)
The animosity between Stryker and Conway has other sources:
the former had served under Conway's father, who had been
killed in action in Guadalcanal. Conway, however, does not
share Stryker's respect for his father, because the latter
used to poke fun at him for being "too soft." In the film's
climax, Conway tells Stryker how he will bring up his new-
born son: "I won't insist he read the Marine Corps Manual.
Instead, I'll get him a set of Shakespeare. In short, I don't
want him to be a Sergeant John M. Stryker--I want him to
be intelligent, considerate, cultured, and a gentleman."

Later in the picture, Stryker saves Conway's life when
a live grenade falls at his feet while he dreamily reads a letter from his wife. But Conway gets the opportunity to save
Stryker's life and even apologizes for getting "out of line."
In this movie too, Wayne is the sensitive commander who does
not let it show, believing in hard discipline. After Stryker
is shot by a sniper, an unfinished letter is found on his body
in which he concedes of being a failure in many ways. At
the end, however, Conway becomes the fighter Stryker and
his father have always wanted him to be. Killing the Japanese sniper, he takes over the command and adopts Stryker's
style of leadership.

Flying Leathernecks (1951) made a deliberate attempt
to repeat the success of Sands of Iwo Jima and thus had a
similar plot. Wayne's Major Dan Kirby, commander of the
Marine fighting squadron in the South Pacific, is resented
by his men because they wanted executive officer Carl Griffin

A key scene in <u>Sands of Iwo Jima</u> (Republic, 1949), Wayne's best war movie which also catapulted him to box-office stardom.

(Robert Ryan), a more popular and amiable man, to get the command. They also dislike Kirby for his rugged ways and strict discipline. The film, however, makes it very clear that it is Kirby who is more suited for command, particularly under pressure. Griffin defends Kirby's tactics in front of the men but in private criticizes him, "No man is an island." When he takes over the command, however, he models his leadership after Kirby. Furthermore, as in other war pictures, the soldiers learn to respect and even like Kirby for the kind of leader he is.

In most of his war movies, Wayne's roughness is more of a façade. In <u>Flying Leathernecks</u>, Wayne is frustrated when he does not get mail from his family and he is the one to write letters of condolence to the victims' families. His leaders are by no means insensitive, especially when it comes

to respect for soldiers who have died in duty. In They
Were Expendable, he states firmly, "a serviceman is supposed to have a funeral--that's a tribute to the way he's
spent his life. Escort, firing squad, wrapped in the flag
he served under and died for." Wayne even recites poetry--
awkwardly--in honor of one of the casualties who "was always
quotin' verse."

     Producer Darryl F. Zanuck was determined to get Wayne
to play one of the cameo roles in The Longest Day (1962),
the epic reconstruction of D Day and the Allied invasion of
Normandy. "Since Wayne has taken care of the Alamo and
had never lost any historical battle," Zanuck reasoned,
"there is no reason why he should not take care of the
Omaha Beach."[4] Wayne was first considered for the part of
General Cota (later played by Robert Mitchum) but was cast
as Lieutenant Colonel Benjamin Vandervoort of the Eighty-
Second Airborne Division. His part was small but tailor-
made, and it included some of the picture's most memorable
episodes. A stern commander who broke his ankle while
landing in the town of St. Mere Eglise, Vandervoort continues to lead his men using his rifle as a crutch. Wayne's
portrayal contained all the familiar elements of previous war
movies, particularly his toughness; he is told on various occasions to ease up on his men as well as on himself. Proud
of his battalion, Vandervoort believes it is one of the best in
the whole army. But he is also the committed patriot who cannot stand the humiliation of seeing the body of an American
soldier hung up.

     The generation conflict between Wayne and his imma-
ture soldiers is most explicitly developed in Otto Preminger's
In Harm's Way (1965). Wayne's Captain Rockwell Torrey,
commander of a ship cruiser, is described by one of his officers as "all Navy." We also learn that Torrey's commitment
to his career resulted in a broken marriage. Moreover, he
believes that his wife's Bostonian origins have had a negative
influence on their son Jere (Brandon De Wilde), whom he has
not seen for 18 years. Jere is an opportunistic officer, preferring a "soft" job over a fighting assignment. Torrey is
ashamed of his son and their first meeting is bitter and awkward. Addressed by Jere as "Sir," he resents the manner
in which his son talks about the war, referring to it as "Mr.
Roosevelt's War." He also despises him for revealing a top
secret out of negligence. Later, when Jere is assigned to

John Wayne as Lt. Col. Benjamin Vandervoort in the blockbuster war film The Longest Day (Twentieth Century-Fox,
1962).

the same operation and is placed under Torrey's command,
he does not get any special treatment: "I'm not going to
act like a father now," states Torrey, "I threw that opportunity 18 years ago."

However, father and son become closer when Torrey
has to break the tragic news that his boy's girlfriend (Jill
Hayworth) has been raped (by Kirk Douglas) and committed
suicide. At the end, they are reunited when Jere models
himself after his father--but not before committing himself
to the war's ideals. Jere redeems himself, becoming a better soldier and dying heroically. Now Torrey can really
accept his son and be proud of him.

Wayne's paternal attitude toward the younger generation and his function as a sociological father extends beyond
his relationships with American soldiers. In two war films,

Back to Bataan and The Green Berets, he serves as role
model to Philippine and Vietnamese children, which critic
Joan Mellen sees as a testament to his imperialistic and
patronizing attitude toward smaller and weaker nations.

Wayne's Colonel Joseph Madden helps the Philippine
guerrillas fight the Japanese in Back to Bataan (1945), a
picture that was better but less popular than Bataan (1943),
starring Robert Taylor. Colonel Madden has a special relationship with Maximo (Ducky Louie), the Philippine kid who
adores him. When Maximo's father is killed, Madden is the
one to provide comfort, "war hurts everyone." In an earlier, quite touching scene, Madden commits him to the war effort by the symbolic gesture of handing him his colonel's in-
signia. He also teaches him how to take orders and behave
like "a man": Maximo volunteers to spy and, captured and
tortured by the Japanese, he misleads them, forcing their
truck over a cliff. Thus, in Wayne's best manner, Maximo
prefers to die heroically, by tricking the enemy, than to reveal important military secrets.

In The Green Berets (1968), Wayne plays career officer Michael Kirby, commander of the Special U.S. Forces.
The film describes, among other things, the friendship between Hamchunk (Craig Jue), a Vietnamese orphan, and
Peterson (Jim Hutton), an American sergeant. Hamchunk
follows Peterson wherever he goes, finding comfort in sleeping alongside him. After Peterson's death in action, Kirby
tells the child, "Peterson was very brave, Are you going to
be?" He then puts Peterson's green beret on his head and
states, "You are what this is all about."

Kirby serves as an effective role model for everybody:
his soldiers, the Vietnamese kid, and even a pacifist reporter
(David Janssen), who is initially against the war. More than
anything else, the movie focuses on the transformation of a
dovish newspaperman--after he tastes "real action" with the
Green Berets. Indeed, Janssen's conversion to a hawk becomes complete when the encampment is under siege. Caught
gawking, a soldier tells him: "This is what it's all about;
are you just going to stand there and referee?" And as in
other war pictures, Wayne is the tough/sensitive leader, tolerant toward soldiers who repent their "sins." Here, he offers Janssen a job with the Green Berets, in case he is fired
by his newspaper, for the change in his political persuasion.

Another important element in the war movies is Wayne's rebellious or independent streak. His leaders are often impulsive, willing to disobey orders if they think their decision is right and an action is needed. They want to fight on the front, hating desk work. In this respect, Wayne's war hero stands in diametric opposition to William Whyte's "organization man," the conformist who goes by the book and adjusts himself to the organization's rule, doing all things "the company way."[5]

Wayne's construction engineer Wedge Donovan in The Fighting Seabees (1944) helps to organize the Fighting Seabees, special fighting units of civilian workers. He is told by Lieutenant Commander Bob Yarrow (Dennis O'Keefe) to ignore the Japanese snipers and to focus on construction. Compared with Yarrow, Donovan is hot-tempered and impatient with the enemy. He continues to obey orders until his friend is killed, then in defiance of the rules orders his men to fight back. But his stubbornness causes the death of many people, for which he is held responsible. Guilt-ridden, he redeems himself in a one-man action that costs him his life but saves the important oil tanks.

In Ford's They Were Expendable (1945), Wayne's Lieutenant Rusty Ryan insists that the P-T boats, equipped with guns and torpedo tubes, could slip into the Japanese harbors. His temperament stands in sharp opposition to Lieutenant John Brickley (Robert Montgomery), a calm, rational, and efficient commander. Ryan gets increasingly frustrated: the disbelief in the boats' potential and the lack of action bore him to death. Challenged by Brickley, "What are you aiming at, building a reputation or playing for the team?" Wayne replies, "For years, I've been taking your fatherly advice and it's never been very good. From now on, I'm a one-man band." He becomes even more frustrated upon learning that the boats are assigned to messenger duty, claiming he is "bored to death running messages." Later, when the boats are assigned to destroy a Japanese cruiser, he is eager to go out, but instead is rushed to the hospital for treatment of an infected arm. He arrives at the hospital screaming and when the nurse suggests, to calm him down, that they go dancing, he yells, "Listen, sister, I don't dance--and I can't take the time out now to learn. All I want is to get out of here."

After his boat has been sunk, Ryan is ordered to fly
back to Washington to organize new P-T Boat squadrons, but
he loathes leaving. He tries to get off the plane, offering
his place to another officer. When the latter asks him to call
his wife, Ryan explodes, "Phone her. I got business here
and you got business back in the States." All he wants is
to be at the battle zone. But once again, it is Brickley who
brings him into line: "Rusty, who're you working for?
Yourself?"

The source of conflict between Wayne and his wife in
In Harm's Way is his career: she wanted him to do something "useful," like working for the stock market. Wayne,
however, refuses, "I don't fit behind a desk. I'll dry."
But he is also reluctant to sit behind a military desk, and
suffers under the indecisive leadership of Admiral Broderick
(Dana Andrews). Leading the remnants of a Japanese attack,
he deliberately violates the orders, charting a straight course
for the enemy instead of the required zig-zag. As a result,
a torpedo splits his ship and he is injured. Brought before
a court, the punishment for his violation is desk work.
Frustrated, he watches forlornly as the American counter-
offensive is formulated without him. Later his case is reexamined by the higher command and, elevated to rear admiral, Wayne is placed in command of Operation Skyhook.
His ship is struck by the Japanese and he is injured again;
this time, his left leg is amputated. He is promised, however,
an artificial leg and the command of a new task force, to carry on the fight.

Wayne's War Movies in Perspective

Wayne was not the only star to appear in war movies,
but he was more closely associated with this genre than any
other actor. In the first place, he made more war pictures
than other actors of his generation. Compared with his 16
war films, Gary Cooper and Humphrey Bogart made each 15,
Robert Taylor and Errol Flynn each 12, James Cagney 9,
Henry Fonda and Jimmy Stewart each 7, Spencer Tracy 4,
and Clark Gable only 3. But the kind of war films Wayne
made was even more important than their numbers.

Bogart appeared in many war films, perhaps because
he, like Wayne, was too old to be drafted. Most of his war

films were produced by Warners during the war, between
1942 and 1945, fulfilling a similar function for his screen
image; like Wayne, he was at the height of his popularity
with such pictures as Casablanca and To Have and Have Not.
However, his films differ substantially from Wayne's. In a
typically Bogart war film, he wears civilian clothes, usually
a trenchcoat, and is placed in a foreign country. At times,
he is the only one or one of few Americans on the scene.
Across the Atlantic, for example, takes place in Panama, and
To Have and Have Not, on the island of Martinique. The titles of his films often reveal their locales: Action Across the
North Atlantic, Sahara, Casablanca, Passage to Marseilles.
Moreover, the typical Bogart war film is the international
espionage or intrigue story.

The kind of hero Bogart portrays in these films differs radically from Wayne's. He usually starts as the cynical, sophisticated, and uninvolved man who is reluctantly
drawn into the conflicts. His transformation is gradual,
though at the end he is fully committed to the cause. At
the start of Casablanca (1943), Bogart's Rick Blain, the
former soldier now a café owner, declares, "I stick my neck
out for nobody" and "I'm the only cause I'm interested in."
By the end, however, he gives up the woman he passionately loves (Ingrid Bergman) to help her husband (Paul Hen-
reid), an anti-Fascist leader, escape to freedom. Bogart's
cynicism derives from his disillusionment with the world's
apathy to the Civil War in Spain and to Ethiopia; he himself smuggled arms to Ethiopia and fought with the Loyalists
in Spain.

In Key Largo (1948), Bogart plays another disillusioned
war veteran, a disenchanted idealist tired of wars and kill-
ings. At the film's start, he refuses to kill Rocco the gangster (Edward G. Robinson) because "one Rocco more or less
isn't worth dying for." He tells a young war widow (Lauren
Bacall): "Me die to rid the world of Johnny Rocco? No
thanks." Nonetheless, when Rocco kills the deputy sheriff
and two Indians are wrongly accused and subsequently killed,
he cannot compromise anymore. He gets a gun from Rocco's
alcoholic moll (Claire Trevor) and devises a plot to kill Rocco
on his boat, endangering his own life.

A romantic affair is essential to the Bogart character
and central to his film narratives. Bogart's involvement with

Mary Astor (<u>Across the Pacific</u>), Ingrid Bergman (<u>Casablan-</u>
<u>ca</u>), Lauren Bacall (<u>To Have and Have Not</u>), and Katharine
Hepburn (<u>The African Queen</u>) defines his heroes as much as
the political issues; there is always a woman behind his heroics, which cannot be said about the Wayne war picture. If
the women and romantic interest were removed from Wayne's
films they would still be coherent and undamanged because
neither is of any importance. This, however, is not the case
with Bogart's films.

        James Cagney's image is most intimately connected with
the crime-gangster film, but he also appeared in a number of
war films, which were completely divergent from Wayne's.
In a typical Cagney war picture, he is cast as the rebellious
or selfish recruit who learns the hard way the importance of
military order and discipline, often from Pat O'Brien, his
frequent co-star. For example, in <u>Here Comes the Navy</u>
(1934), Cagney plays a hot-tempered, undisciplined sailor,
whose selfish individualism upsets the Navy tradition and
alienates his fellowmen. But at the end, after a court martial, he redeems himself with a heroic rescue, and his reputation is restored. In another picture, <u>Ceiling Zero</u> (1935),
Cagney, a devil-may-care pilot who enjoys his escapades,
irresponsibly causes the death of a fellow pilot. Flamboyant
and loose-fibered, his major "hobby" is women. But during
the course of the story, he reforms and, regretting his behavior, volunteers to test a newly invented deicer, an action
that costs him his life.

        <u>The Fighting 69th</u> (1940), produced by Hal Wallis as
Warners' contribution to the recruitment campaign, is probably Cagney's most characteristic and popular war movie, enabling him to display his specialty: explosive energy. Based
on an original screenplay, it is a fictionalized account of New
York's famed "Fighting Irish" regiment, which started during the Civil War and in 1917 was incorporated into the Army.
Cagney's Private Jerry Plunkette, a despicable tough Irishman from Brooklyn, sneers at the regiment's traditions and
jeers at its chaplain (Pat O'Brien). When his unit is sent
to the European front, he gets hysterical at the very first
sight of a dead body. Later, his cowardice and irresponsi-
bility, revealing to the enemy his unit's position, bring death
to many of his fellowmen. At the end, however, he dies
heroically, proving himself a worthy soldier--not before he
is taught basic values by the priest. The transformation of

the Cagney character is always from a cocky and obnoxious
recruit to a disciplined soldier. If Cagney had not been an
older (and bigger) star than Wayne at the time, one could
imagine Wayne's commanders making a man out of him: their
screen persona in their war films really complemented each
other.

        Gary Cooper made as many war movies as Wayne, though,
like Cagney, over half of them were produced in the 1930s
and thus dealt with World War I, lacking the immediacy of
the Wayne movies.   Cooper's war films were not as important
to his career as Wayne's and, more importantly, he usually
played romantic heroes, in love with Nancy Carroll (The
Shopworn Girl), Marlene Dietrich (Morocco), or Joan Crawford (Today We Live).   In Hemingway's A Farewell to Arms,
the first (1932) and better film version directed by Frank
Borzage, Cooper's Lieutenant Frederic Henry, an American
ambulance driver, falls in love with an English nurse (Helen
Hayes).   At the end of this extremely romantic film, Cooper
does not hesitate to desert the Army to look for her--an inconceivable act for the Wayne hero.

        The romantic interest features prominently in another
blockbuster war film, Sam Wood's For Whom the Bell Tolls
(1943), based on Hemingway's novel allegedly written with
Cooper in mind.   Here too, Cooper's Robert Jordan, a
courageous American teacher fighting with the guerrilla forces
in the Spanish Civil War, is in love with María (Ingrid Bergman), an orphan who had been raped by the Nationalist soldiers.   The movie does not neglect, of course, Hemingway's
notion of macho adventurism, conveying Jordan's single-
minded commitment to his task: blowing up a strategic bridge
in a mountain pass.   Yet the picture is so long (168 minutes),
diffuse, tedious in pace, with many close-ups, particularly
in Bergman's tearful farewell from Cooper at the end, that
all one remembers from this film is its romance.   Even its
production values, expensive technicolor, and some
good acting by the supporting players do not redeem its
solemnity.

        The movies Cooper made during and after the war were
mostly undistinguished, with one or two exceptions.   One of
these was Howard Hawks's Sergeant York (1941), probably
his best war picture and one of the most popular American
movies of all time.   Its wide appeal rested, of course, on its

timely release, but also on its perfect cast, including Walter
Brennan and Margaret Wycherly. Cooper is cast as Alvin
York, the pacifist Tennessee farmer who became the country's
greatest hero of World War I, after capturing and destroying
an entire German battalion single-handedly. As in the typical Bogart or Cagney war film, but unlike Wayne's, a transformation of character is at the center of the story. York
starts as a simple farmer who registers as a conscientious ob-
jector upon being drafted for service. And it takes a while
until he learns, and is completely convinced, of the necessity
of violence. The change in his persuasion occurs when he
is given a book on American history, which stresses the value
of freedom and the obligation to defend the rights of each
citizen--while evoking the name of Daniel Boone. Moreover,
York's anger and willingness to kill are caused by the death
of a close friend on the battlefront. What makes his heroics
coherent and amiable is that at the end of the war, after
showers of praise for his heroics, York returns to his former simple life on his Tennessee farm, where the movie begins. Sergeant York enjoyed tremendous popularity because,
among other things, it was one of the few biopictures to
have been made while their subject was still alive. It is
noteworthy that the real York consented to give Warners the
screen rights on one condition, that Cooper portray him,
which made it all the more credible and powerful.

        If one were to choose the most memorable war picture
of each of the great stars it would probably be Casablanca
for Humphrey Bogart and Sergeant York for Gary Cooper.
In Henry Fonda's case, it would undoubtedly be Mister Roberts, one of his most powerful roles and one with which he
will always be associated. Fonda first played Mister Roberts
on the Broadway stage for three years, winning acclaim and
awards, then recreated it with equal success on screen. The
story has had many incarnations, starting as a book by
Thomas Heggen, then a stage play by him and Joshua Logan,
and finally a screenplay by Logan and Frank Nugent. Mister
Roberts was nominated for the Best Picture Oscar and won
Jack Lemmon his first (supporting) Oscar as Ensign Pulver.
Fonda's performance was unaccountably ignored by the
Academy in a shameful oversight--but it is still vivid in the
public's memory.

        Fonda plays the first officer on the Reluctant, a cargo
ship miles away from the battle zone, whose route is described

by him as "from Tedium to Apathy and back again, with an
occasional side trip to Monotony." The war is close to an
end, and Roberts is anxious to get into combat before it is
too late. His numerous requests for transfer, however, are
all turned down by his tyrannical and mad captain (Cagney).
But with the assistance of the sympathetic crew, his wish is
finally fulfilled. Mister Roberts ends on a sad note when the
audience is informed that Roberts has been killed in action.

Mister Roberts provided Fonda the kind of distinctly
American role that he played to perfection. His contribution
to the war genre, other than this picture, which took place
rather late in his career (mainly in the 1960s), was undistinguished. He played, for example, several cameo roles,
such as an admiral in Otto Preminger's In Harm's Way, which
starred Wayne; a Navy captain in Robert Aldrich's cynical
adventure Too Late the Hero; and another bit part in the
blockbuster Midway, recreating the 1942 battle in the Pacific.

As for Errol Flynn's heroics, they used to make jokes
about his winning numerous battles so easily. As director
Edward Dmytryk observed: "I'm still proud that, at a time
when Errol Flynn--in Objective Burma and other pictures--
almost singlehandedly won battles in which they were not
only heavily outnumbered by the enemy, but somewhat handi-
capped by the presence of nonwhite allies, our film (Back to
Bataan) represented the Duke primarily in the role of adviser and contact man, while the Philippines themselves, led
by Anthony Quinn, did most of the fighting and occasional
dying."[6] Furthermore, despite his popularity as a star,
Flynn's war heroics lacked the strong impact that Wayne's
had, perhaps because he was not an American, an important
fact in patriotic times. Nor did Flynn portray Americans in
these movies: he was cast as an Australian in Desperate
Hours, Norwegian in Edge of Darkness, Canadian in Northern Pursuit, and French criminal in Uncertain Glory. American audiences found it difficult to identify with his foreign
heroes--despite their bravura.

Critical Acclaim and Commercial Popularity

Of Wayne's war movies, two have withstood the test of
time: The Long Voyage Home and Sands of Iwo Jima. Produced by Walter Wanger and directed by John Ford, The

Long Voyage Home (1940) was based on four one-act plays
by Eugene O'Neill ("Bound East for Cardiff," "In the Zone,"
"The Long Voyage Home," and "The Moon of Caribees").
Adapted to the screen by Dudley Nichols, the movie concerns the tough crew of Glencairn, the English tramp freighter dispatched from the West Indies to England with a cargo
of dynamite. What makes the film interesting is the psychological insights about the behavior of men under conditions
of pressure and isolation, similar in many respects to Ford's
earlier Men Without Women. Furthermore, because all three
creators, Wanger, Ford, and Nichols, were known for their
anti-Facist feelings, the picture was perceived as a war film
and tribute to Britain in its fight against Hitler. As Sinclair pointed out, "Ford was using Irish-American plays and
players to praise English patriotism."[7]

Wayne gave one of his best performances as Ole Olsen,
the naive, innocent Swedish sailor who dreams of returning
home to his farm. It was one of the first films that won him
really favorable reviews. Audiences too, liked his portrayal;
vacationing at Catalina Island, where the film was shot, he
was told by a stranger: "I was in the Merchant Marine when
I saw it, and you played that guy like you were one of us."[8]
The Long Voyage Home was highly praised by the critics.
Bosley Crowther wrote a rave review in the New York Times,
describing it as "a revelation of man's pathetic shortcomings"
and "one of the most honest pictures ever placed on the
screen." He particularly liked the "penetrating glimpse into
the hearts of little men," and thought that "because it shows
that out of human weakness there proceeds some nobility, it
is far more gratifying than the fanciest hero-worshipping
fare."[9] But despite the fact that it was one of the ten
nominees for the Best Picture Oscar of 1940 (the winner was
Hitchcock's Rebecca), The Long Voyage Home was not popular at the box office, perhaps because it was released in
October 1940, before the American involvement in the war.

The idea for Sands of Iwo Jima, Wayne's other notable
war film, was originated by producer Eddie Grainger, who
wanted to make a picture about the Marines' taking of Iwo
Jima. Harry Brown, a distinguished screenwriter (A Walk
in the Sun), wrote the scenario, but Herbert Yates, the head
of Republic, was reluctant at first to approve a big budget
for the movie. It was Jim Grainger, the producer's father
and head of sales at Republic, who persuaded Yates by

promising a good director (Allan Dwan) and a big star (John Wayne). Dwan did not ask for Wayne when he agreed to direct because he thought "there were three or four actors who could play it." However, when the producer mentioned Wayne's name, he got his blessing, "Go and get him--fight for him."[10] Dwan had previously asked a real soldier, General Arskine, to play the lead, believing "he was the perfect type for it," but the general said, "I'm not good enough to play a Sergeant again."[11] Nonetheless, three of the six marines who raised the flag on Mount Suribachi reenacted their real-life roles in the movie; the other three had died in the meantime.

At Dwan's request, General Arskine sent the toughest drill sergeant, "a big, husky guy--six foot eight--who could have lifted any two men in the company," to the set. At their first meeting, Dwan asked him "to make Marines out of these actors--full packs and rifles." "Give them the full routine including double time," he instructed, "I want them to get into physical shape." Dwan recalled that the sergeant "worked them for two solid hours until they fell on their faces. Then he let them sleep a little while and got them up and worked them some more. Well, after the third day, they were pleading for mercy, but they were Marines." In fact, "they hardened up" so much that "the Marines around didn't mind them anymore."[12]

Sands of Iwo Jima had a bigger budget ($1 million) than most Republic pictures; the average production at the time cost about $100,000. Due to its scope, the film could not have been made on a smaller budget, and it would have cost much more without the cooperation of the Marines. But the film made a huge profit; in its first two days of release in Los Angeles, it had an unprecedented attendance record of 20,000 people. Sands of Iwo Jima became one of the ten most popular films of 1950, grossing over $5 million in the United States and Canada alone, the equivalent of over $30 million at present.

Sands of Iwo Jima was not only Wayne's best war movie, but also a turning point in his career. It won him his first Academy Award nomination as Best Actor and also put him, for the first time, on the prestigious poll of the ten most popular stars in America. Wayne became "a big shot," according to Dwan, because the movie was such an unqualified

success and no actor "could have been better."[13] True,
Wayne was delighted to report that "the Marines and all the
American Armed Forces were quite proud of my portrayal of
Stryker."[14] At an American Legion Convention in Florida,
General Douglas MacArthur, whom he admired, told him:
"You represent the American serviceman better than the
American serviceman himself."[15]

     In addition to Sands of Iwo Jima, two other Wayne
pictures are on Variety's list of the top money-making war
movies. The Longest Day ranks eighth with $17.6 million,
and The Green Berets occupies the fifteenth place with $9.75
million. While The Longest Day featured many stars, with
Wayne just one of an illustrious cast, the success of The
Green Berets was totally attributable to his politics and
performance.

     Seen in perspective, the most popular war films are
indeed a mixed bag. Francis Ford Coppola's Apocalypse
Now (1979), a dark vision of the American involvement in
Vietnam with stunning cinematic effects, is the most commercial war picture, grossing $37.8 million in rentals. The
second place is occupied by Robert Altman's M.A.S.H.
(1970), a biting satire concerning life inside a Mobile Army
Surgical Hospital station during the Korean War, which
grossed $36.7 million. Michael Cimino's The Deer Hunter
(1978), describing the harrowing experiences of three young
Pennsylvania steelworkers in Vietnam, ranks third with $30.4
million. Franklin J. Schaffner's Patton (1970), the controversial portrait of the flamboyant World War II general, occupies the fourth place with $28.1 million. And Jack Smith's
Midway (1976), a patriotic reconstruction of the 1942 battle
on this Pacific island, ranks fifth with $22.3 million. With
the exception of Midway, an old-fashioned flagwaver which
cashed in on an all-star cast, the other movies are highly
distinguished. All four were nominated for the Best Picture
Oscar and two, Patton and The Deer Hunter, won. It is
noteworthy that all five pictures were made in the 1970s--if
the inflation factor were taken into account, Wayne's commercial successes would feature even more prominently.

     The Longest Day was Wayne's most commercial war film.
Based on a book by Cornelius Ryan and produced by Darryl
F. Zanuck, it was the collaborative effort of three directors
(Ken Annakin, Andrew Marton, and Bernhard Vicki), four

assistant directors, and no less than five screenwriters.
The Longest Day reconstructs the events leading to the
June 6, 1944 Normandy invasion of the Allied Forces.   It
has the dimensions of an epic picture, filmed in Cinemascope
and skillfully edited by Samuel E. Beetley.   Zanuck cast all
the cameo roles with big names; he wanted the audience "to
have a kick," so that "every time a door opened, it would
be a well-known personality."[16]

   The film enjoyed a great deal of publicity before it
was released and favorable critical reaction afterwards.
Crowther of the New York Times liked the picture for its
"huge documentary report, adorned and colored by personal details that are thrilling, amusing, ironic, sad."[17]
The film's mass appeal stemmed from an interesting and important theme, realistic action, and, of course, the fun of
spotting the large roster of Hollywood stars, including Henry
Fonda, Robert Mitchum, Robert Ryan, Rod Steiger, and John
Wayne, whose name appeared last on the credits to stress its
prominence.   Thus, The Longest Day became one of the most
popular films of 1962.   However, several critics thought that
the array of familiar stars actually weakened the film's authenticity.   "It's hard to tell about John Wayne and Robert
Mitchum," wrote the New York Post, "they stand out all
right, but whether they're too much themselves or make it
as what they're supposed to be who knows.   They certainly
still are Wayne and Mitchum, and no mere D-Day can hide
it."[18]

   Wayne had his share of bad and uninteresting flag-
wavers, such as Bernard Vorhaus's Three Faces West (1940),
concerning the fate of refugees escaping Nazi-dominanted
Austria.   Dr. Karl Braun (Charles Coburn) and his daughter
Leni (Sigrid Gurie) escape to the United States and settle
in Asheville Forks, a community in the dust bowl.   Wayne
portrays the farmers' dogged leader who is against deserting
the land after the government has condemned it as hopeless.
However, when his plea proves futile, he organizes the farmers' departure for better land in Oregon.   And he persuades
Leni, with whom he is romantically involved, and her father
to stay on despite the hardships.

   The film's worst element is its incredible subplot:
Leni's former lover turns out to be a Nazi who wishes to
take her back to the Reich to reap "the benefits and glory

of its conquests." Another problem is the incoherent combination of the two themes: the problem of the Midwest
dustbowl and the flight from Anschluss. Furthermore, Three
Faces West also suffered from comparisons with John Ford's
classic The Grapes of Wrath, starring Henry Fonda, which
deals with the same issue, though much more powerfully,
and released a few months earlier.

One of the interesting facts about Three Faces West
and other pictures of its kind is that even less discriminating audiences considered it to be too propagandistic. In
1940 the public reaction to the anti-Nazi movies was so mild
that many studios changed the original titles of their films
on this theme not to irritate the public. For example, The
Man I Married was initially titled I Married a Nazi, and the
original title of Three Faces West was The Refugee.[19]

Much worse than this picture was Reunion in France
(1942), a Joan Crawford vehicle. It was a shallow melodrama
with an unnecessarily complex plot about the courageous
French Resistance during the Occupation. Crawford plays
a French haute-couture model engaged to a seemingly pro-
Nazi industrial designer (Philip Dorn) who, in the course
of the movie, helps Wayne, a wounded RAF pilot, to escape
from a prison camp and reach London. In the movie's climax, Crawford realizes that Dorn's collaboration with the
Nazis is fake and that he is actually a French patriot. Despite its timeliness, neither movie nor stars were spared by
the critics. The New York Times wrote that "if Reunion in
France is the best tribute Hollywood can muster to the French
underground forces of liberation, then let us try another
time."[20] Time magazine described the film sarcastically as
"a Joan Crawford version of the fall of France,"[21] and the
New York Herald Tribune's reviewer complained that "a lot
of good players are wasted."[22] Other critics were amazed
by the "strange assortment" of accents, as the Post noted:
"Joan Crawford conversed in pure American when she is
supposed to be French,"[23] while other actors affected, un-
successfully, French and German accents.

Sea Chase (1955), a sea adventure, was another picture with a terrible screenplay and incredible casting. Wayne
plays Karl Ehrlich, a good German sea captain. Set in the
early days of the war, it was supposed to be a thriller, but
was actually a dreary picture. Karl Ehrlich has been relegated

to command a freighter following his opposition to Hitler's regime, but being a patriot, he wants to return home. Under the disguise of a Panamanian banana boat, the outlaw freighter slips out of Sidney, though there are many complications, including a suspected beautiful Nazi (Lana Turner) and a real Nazi. The freighter is also pursued by a British warship that penetrates the disguise and intercepts it. The film contains a strange, rather inconclusive, ending: the freighter sinks in the North Sea and all, but Wayne and Turner, die.

Panned by all critics, The Sea Chase was highly profitable at the box office, ranking as one of the ten blockbusters of 1955, with over $6 million in rentals. "The script writers have changed the book," Crowther complained, "so that it comes out partly as a conventional heroic and ideologically silly sea romance."[24] The best-selling novel by Andrew Geer was more straightforward, suspenseful, and exciting, but the movie it inspired, under John Farrow's boring direction, was a melodrama with a lot of talk but not enough action. Other reviewers criticized Hollywood's recent trend to elevate German officers to honorable heroes by casting them with major American stars, such as John Gavin in A Time to Love and a Time to Die, and Marlon Brando in The Young Lions.[25]

Wayne's war pictures enjoyed the support of the government and the Armed Forces. Considering this genre a vital morale booster, the administration often initiated or collaborated in the production of such endeavors. This cooperation between Hollywood and the administration became particularly intimate during World War II, when various agencies, such as the war and navy departments and the Office of War Information (OWI), gave the film industry technical advice, equipment, and armaments.

In 1944 Wayne was asked by the State Department to make a movie on the Philippine guerrilla forces--the result was Back to Bataan. This movie could not have been made without the assistance of the Army, the Navy, the Marine Corps, the Coast Guard, and the Philippine government, all of which were acknowledged in the credits. Rumor has it that there were clashes on the set between Colonel Clark, the film's adviser, and director Dmytryk, who allegedly ridiculed the former's patriotism and Catholic beliefs. Dmytryk

does not report any of these in his autobiography, though
he recalls one battle with the colonel. When the makeup and
prop men dirtied the Philippines' clothes, the colonel reportedly rejected this on the ground that they were "the world's
cleanest people."[26] Having served most of his career in the
Philippines and one of the few to have been evacuated before
the surrender to the Japanese, he was very loyal to their
country. According to Dmytryk, Colonel Clark had contempt
for General MacArthur--unlike Wayne who had unshakable
faith in him.

     Wayne's war films saluted various branches of the
Armed Forces. Flying Tigers, for instance, paid tribute to the American volunteer airmen who fought for China's
freedom. The Fighting Seabees saluted the construction en-
gineers of the Navy. The Hollywood war movies were so
propagandistic that many ended with explicit appeal to the
audience to enlist in the Armed Forces. In Pittsburgh
(1942), Wayne plays an ambitious coal miner who rises to
head a huge industrial enterprise, while unscrupulously abus-
ing his friends and associates. He redeems himself, however, during Pearl Harbor, when every American is needed
for the war effort. Pittsburgh starts as a rowdy comedy
but ends as a heavy-handed government propaganda movie,
stressing the nation's interest and the part played by the
coal industry in modern warfare--narrated by a voiceover
quite solemnly.

     What accounted most for the popularity of the war
movies was their timeliness and immediate relevance. Director Dmytryk recalled that the initial screenplay for Back
to Bataan showed "White Americans as responsible for all
the heroics," but with the help of adviser Ben Barzman,
the film became both more realistic and in tune with changing events. "While we were shooting," Dmytryk observed,
"the situation in the Pacific was changing from day to
day."[27] For example, General MacArthur's return to the
Philippines and the prisoners' release from the prison camp
of Cabantuan had to be incorporated into the scenario.

     By contrast, the most unfortunate thing about John
Ford's excellent They Were Expendable, was the date of its
release, December 1945. American audiences were saturated
with genre movies by that time. More importantly, once the
war was over, the public did not want to see a film dealing

with "the very early misadventures of the war four years ago,"
as Andrew Sarris wrote. "What could have seemed more perverse," Sarris comments in reference to the evacuation of
General MacArthur, "than Ford's celebration of gallant defeat in the aftermath of glorious victory."[28] It was somehow
anachronistic to see in late 1945 a film stressing the values
of self-service and devotion to duty. They Were Expendable
and other war films that followed, demonstrated that "once
the war was over, the war film tended to slide in social significance from the cause to a genre, from a statement of
principle to a set of platitudes."[29]

Wayne's influence on the war movie was described in
terms of the heroes he played, but his distinctive contribution to this genre is also reflected in the kinds of films he
did not make. For example, he did not appear in the espionage or international intrigue movies that were quite popular, such as Casablanca, Background to Danger, set in
Turkey; The Conspirator, set in Lisbon; or Confidential
Agent, set in the Spanish Civil War. Of greater importance
was Wayne's reluctance to make war films that depicted the
high price in human life during the war. A whole subgenre
is missing from Wayne's repertoire, that describing the dev-
astating effects--physical, emotional, and mental--on the
fighting soldiers and their adjustment problems to civilian
life. Wayne never played a struggling war veteran, one of
the most dominant characters in the American cinema. It is
interesting to mention that some of these films contain most
memorable performances and most powerful characterizations,
such as John Garfield's blinded soldier in Pride of the Marines, Harrold Russell's real-life portrayal of an amputated
soldier in The Best Years of Our Lives, Marlon Brando's
paraplegic in The Men, and Arthur Kennedy's blinded soldier in Bright Victory.

Wayne specialized in playing commanders, not the
rank-and-file fighters, which were effectively portrayed by
Robert Mitchum in William Wellman's The Story of G.I. Joe,
or Dana Andrews and Richard Conte in Lewis Milestone's
A Walk in the Sun, two of the best war dramas. However,
Wayne's commanders were ordinary, hard-working, upwardly-
mobile Americans, who became leaders for their strength and
commitment to the cause--not because of their backgrounds
or education. Wayne's most significant screen function, as
was mentioned, was to provide exemplary leadership and

unite a diversified group of soldiers--from all walks of life
and with different motives and fighting skills. His war films
stressed strong individual and charismatic leadership, but
they also emphasized collective values such as mutual responsibility, group discipline, and concerted action. They showed
that under conditions of pressure and crisis a genuine leader
can bring about the best in everybody, and what better conditions for that than actual war and fighting.

Nonetheless, because his war films were not made in a
social or political void, they suffer from the weaknesses of
the genre. Complicated issues were naively simplified in poor
screenplays that lacked realism or credibility. And while the
heroics of American fighters were glorified and exaggerated,
the portrayal of enemies, Germans as well as Japanese, was
stereotypical and one-dimensional. Furthermore, there was
little concern with cinematic aesthetics as such. Most pictures were social documents, emphasizing the contents of
their messages at the expense of their visual aspects. This
was the reason why Ford's They Were Expendable still stands
out: it was beautifully directed and photographed (by Joseph
H. August). James Agee first criticized the film, then in a
second review changed his mind and singled out its artistic
qualities. "Visually, and in detail, and in nearly everything
he does with people," he wrote, "I think it is John Ford's
finest movie." But he too conceded that the film is showing
"nothing much newer, with no particular depth of feeling,
much less idea."30

Another frequent charge against Wayne's war movies
is their blatant propaganda which, in retrospect, did not
differ from other pictures of the time. Historians see the
value of the war films in providing some information, albeit
distorted, about the issues, and in contributing to the morale of both the fighting men and the home front. "The
American war movie," Jones and McLure observed, "was
probably more important as a historical phenomenon than as
an artistic achievement." The genre's importance, according to them, was twofold: "to give unity of purpose for the
war itself and to give strength of purpose to the people of
the home front."31 However, as another historian observed,
the war movies "absorbed and diffused the experience of
war, but received little inspiration from it. Just as Hollywood had eluded many of the realities of Depression America,
so it refused to deal honestly with the realities of America
at war."32

Wayne did not mind that his films were accused of depicting false heroics and courage, thus contributing to a
myth which had no or little correspondence with the reality
of war. In November 1977 he hosted an ABC television special, "Oscar Presents the War Movie and John Wayne," which
included scenes from his World War II movies, from Sands of
Iwo Jima to The Longest Day; the Vietnam movie The Green
Berets was conspicuously missing. Praised for being "as
American as a Rocky Mountain," he described the war movies as "an indelible portrait of the best of what we were."[33]
The deference to Wayne in this show was seen as an indication that his hawkish politics during the Vietnam War (and
The Green Berets) were forgiven and forgotten. Actors
were praised for their service in the Armed Forces as well as
for their contribution to the government bond drives. Wayne
is reported to have been furious at the suggestion to include
Stanley Kramer's Home of the Brave, which deals with racial
prejudice and hatred in the army. Unconcerned with the picture's authenticity, he did not want the American public to
remember the fighting men in such a way. Where the image of
American soldiers was concerned, he chose myth--not reality.
He also ignored critics' claim that the program depicted the
war as a "glorious and glamorous adventure." One critic
specifically charged that the propaganda was presented "as
if it were historical truth, placing us in a past where everyone is June Allyson pure and John Wayne courageous." This
kind of "reactionary innocence" was found to be "insulting."[34]

Nonetheless, the myth of Wayne's courage and heroics
in the war movies seems to have had long-lasting effects. An
unusual act of heroism during the Vietnam War was, in some
circles, referred to as a "John Wayne act." Another report
noted that when an officer realized his unit was trapped in a
Vietcong ambush, he rallied his men yelling, "Don't worry,
it's only a John Wayne movie!"[35]

3. THE WESTERN HERO

Wayne played a variety of Western heroes in numerous films but, as in the war films, specific motifs reoccur. Three concepts describe his most durable roles: Wayne as an inner-directed hero, as a charismatic authority, and as a societal role model. Although these characteristics define Wayne's screen persona in general, they were most explicitly demonstrated in his Westerns, perhaps because they took place in a mythic and legendary past. By placing his heroes in nineteenth-century America, Wayne was able to draw a contrast between the values of the Old West and those of present-day America and to comment on the latter.

The Inner-Directed Hero

Wayne's heroes have a good deal of freedom from societal norms and constraints. They can be described as inner-directed, using David Riesman's typology of social characters.[1] The inner-directed person is endowed with moral strength and is motivated by a highly personal code of ethics--his conscience. There is a streak of rebelliousness and nonconformity in his nature, and he is willing to violate norms and to sacrifice himself to attain his goals. The inner-directed type prevails in societies characterized by social mobility, technological change, and constant expansion, all features of the American West in late nineteenth century. Such societies give a wider range of choice to their members, but also demand greater initiative from them. The inner-directed person differs from the tradition-directed, Riesman's second type of character--the conformist who uncritically accepts the tradition, religious or secular, of society, resisting any kind of change. But he is even more different from the other-directed, Riesman's third type, who is usually concerned with adjusting and adapting to the demands and

expectations of others. Unlike the inner-directed, whose
source of control is internal, that of the other-directed is
external: the family, peer group, work organization, and
community.

   Wayne's inner-directed heroes are devoted to duty and
committed to important missions. They are motivated by inner feelings, channeled toward the achievement of collective,
not personal, goals. His Westerners are collectively oriented,
serving a larger unit than themselves: the army, the cavalry, the community. In many films, Wayne portrays the fanatically obsessed hero, twisted by a sense of duty or revenge. His heroes believe that man's first commitment is to
his job (or duty), as defined by inner feelings, even if it
stands against the wish of family and friends. "Wayne had
his own mission," critic Molly Haskell observed, "his own
promises to keep--to a woman, to a battalion, to a dead
friend. A private sort of mission, one he wouldn't blab
about."[2] His protagonists believe in sacrificing themselves
to achieve their goals. The very essence of their conduct
is motivated by an inner code of ethics whose important
rules are: do not sneak, do not lie, do not dishonor, and
use force against force.

   His fanatic hero had numerous variations, but it first
took form in Stagecoach. The Ringo Kid is an honest and
good-humored youngster, wrongly condemned for a crime he
did not commit. He breaks out of jail in pursuit of the criminals (the Plummer brothers) who murdered his brother and
put him behind bars. Ringo stops the coach with a shot,
terrifying its passengers. However, he immediately establishes himself as a decent and likable guy, especially after
surrendering to the benevolent sheriff, until the coach gets
to Lordsburg. His intention to return to jail to serve his
term further establishes his credibility, though he intends
to do it only after his mission is accomplished. This mission
is sacred; no one can deter him from fulfilling it once his
mind is set. When Dallas (Claire Trevor), a prostitute he
meets on the coach, suggests he escape rather than avenge
his brother, he states unequivocally, "There are some things
a man just can't run away from."

   In Henry Hathaway's Shepherd of the Hills, based on
Harold Ben-Wright's 1907 best-selling novel, Wayne's Matt
Matthews is a hot-headed mountaineer obsessed with hatred

for his father, whom he has never seen. Believing that his
father has disgraced the family's name and caused his mother's early death, he is determined to seek revenge. At his
mother's grave, he reaffirms his commitment, "one of these
days I'll find him, him that never came back to you." Matt's
thirst for vengeance is an obstacle to marrying his girl (Betty Field), who will not confer her love so long as he is committed to his blood oath, but that does not halt him. At the
end, however, his father clears the way for his marriage,
after a shootout between them, in which Matt learns that his
father has always been a kind, though misunderstood, man.

In another Hathaway Western, The Sons of Katie Elder,
Wayne's John Elder is the eldest and toughest of four gun-
slinging brothers: a cardsharp and conman (Dean Martin),
a quiet one (Earl Holliman), and the youngest and hope of
the family (Michael Anderson, Jr.). They get together at
the funeral of their mother, a noble and brave woman who
died in poverty, and set out to investigate the death of their
father, which occurred on the night he supposedly gambled
away his ranch to the town's boss. The sheriff warns the
brothers to stay out of trouble, which of course does not
help. There are further complications in the narrative, including a vicious attempt to incriminate the brothers for the
sheriff's murder. In the process, two brothers are killed
and one is wounded. Wayne is now even more committed to
avenge the multiple deaths in his family, telling the deputy
sheriff in a characteristic manner: "This is something I
have to do for myself. " After killing the boss and clear-
ing the family's name, he fulfills another promise, sending
his younger brother to college.

The Wayne hero keeps his word and lives up to his
vows, regardless of their nature. His Robert Hightower in
Three Godfathers is the leader of an outlaw gang. In their
escape after robbing a bank, they meet a waif (Mildred Natwick) in the desert who, unaware that they are outcasts,
asks them to save her baby. "Yes, ma'am, I'll save him,"
Wayne promises the dying mother without any hesitation,
though he is embarrassed when she wants her baby to be
like "the fine man" he is. The story details their torturous
journey as they carry the baby to the town of New Jerusalem.
Wayne's two accomplices die on the way, but he continues
alone, despite harsh conditions, arriving in town on Christmas Eve. At first, he opposes the marshal's plan to adopt

John Wayne (right), Pedro Armendariz (left), and Harry
Carey, Jr. (far left) in John Ford's symbolic Western
Three Godfathers (MGM, 1948).

the baby, and it takes a lot of effort until he reluctantly
agrees to leave the baby with him--while he serves his term
in prison.

     The Western that best describes his fanatic devotion
to mission at all costs is The Searchers, in which Wayne's
Ethan Edwards is seeking his two nieces abducted during a
Comanche raid in which his brother's family is murdered.
Finding the mutilated bodies, he is guilt-ridden, feeling he
was not there when he was needed. He becomes obsessed
with recovering his two nieces and seeking revenge on the
Comanche. This fanatic search provides the only rationale
for his life and he is determined to succeed, "We'll fin'em
just as sure as the turning of the earth." The body of one
niece is found, but the search for the remaining niece, Debbie, continues for five years, with Wayne more concerned

with vengeance than with finding her. During the search, asked, "You wanna quit, Ethan?" he angrily replies, "That'll be the day!" and he repeats this phrase many times in the course of the film. In another scene, he gambles the life of fellow searcher Martin Pawley against his own marksmanship. When Martin asks, "What if you had missed?" "That never occurred to me," he replies. He is so sure of his abilities and the rightness of his mission that the idea of failure never occurs to him.

Wayne's Westerners are men of action, not words. The silence of the cowboy, as Mellen observed, was one of the main tenets of the frontier code, according to which cowboys did not talk much and did not ask unnecessary questions. The Westerner is judged by how silently he can endure the rigors of life and is expected to be silent, even secretive, about his past and present missions. Questioned about his actions, a typical response is that of Gary Cooper in The Virginian: "A man's got to do what a man's got to do." This is similar to Wayne's statement in Stagecoach: "There are some things a man just can't run away from," a recurrent motto in numerous Westerns.[3]

Action stands at the center of the Western film. Critic Michael Wood observed that a striking, though very American, feature of the Western is total separation of action from thought, to the point where the two cannot coexist.[4] Significantly, talk, explanations, and questions were considered effeminate behavior, whereas action and adventure were men's domain. In The Undefeated, for example, Wayne is a Civil War Union Cavalry veteran who makes his living rounding up wild horses. When a conference with Mexican bandits breaks down, Wayne shoots their leader without hesitation. "You went out there to talk. Why did you have to kill him?" asks a war widow. "Guess the conversation just kinda ... dried up, ma'am," he replies in a characteristic manner.[5]

Motion pictures as a medium lend themselves more to sweeping action than to intellectual and psychological debates. As Vincent Canby observed, "The screen is most hospitable to the activist hero, the man who never has to wrestle with his conscience and thus is free to act, to do, to move through hostile territory and deal immediately with problems as they arise." In Canby's view, "the politics--and the popularity-- of Wayne's films have less to do with labels of left and right

than with the concept of action and commitment."[6] This is
indeed the impression he made on the public's collective mind.
Joan Didion's clearest memories from the first Wayne Westerns
she saw was that he was the one to give orders, such as
"let's ride!" "saddle up!" or "forward ho!"[7] "Men of action
and strength" as Vito Russo noted, "were the embodiment of
our culture, and a vast mythology was created to keep the
dream in constant repair." The masculine character of the
earlier cinema reflected an America that "saw itself as a recently conquered wilderness," although there was no such
wilderness left in the twentieth century. Still, "the movies
endlessly recreated the struggles, the heroism and the romance of our pioneer spirit."[8]

Joan Mellen draws an interesting comparison between
Wayne and Sean Connery in his James Bond movies: "Where
Wayne is always flesh and blood, Connery is plastic, a bionic
man," and "where Wayne is meant to seem real, Bond is a
cardboard figure, an obvious fabrication." Wayne was always
the engineer of his actions, a free man who made his own decisions, set his own goals, and chose his own course. Bond,
by contrast, lacks any moral or spiritual sense of himself
and follows orders like a robot, mechanically fulfilling his
assignments. Wayne cares about what he is doing and how
he is doing things, Bond only about the end result of winning, regardless of his action's goal or means. Mellen believes that "it was his personal feeling that what he did was
valuable and freely chosen which made the John Wayne image
credible to many."[9]

Wayne's heroes are highly individualistic, often alienated from society and unable to conform to its norms. His
most powerful protagonists are autonomous, going out of
their way to maintain their sense of individualism. But
there is a price to be paid: his heroes never completely belong to society and its bonds of family and community. Indeed, they often have to sacrifice their personal lives to attain collective goals. Their solitariness usually derives from
their inability to compromise between the demands of their
careers and those of their families. The conflict between
single-minded devotion to a cause (or duty) and marital-
familial responsibilities is inherent to his screen heroes (see
chapter 6).

Wayne's most memorable anomic hero is Ethan Edwards

in The Searchers, described by Ford as "the tragedy of a
loner." It takes Ethan three years to come home, after
fighting on the losing side of the Civil War. He refuses to
attend the capitulation of the South, claiming, "I don't believe in surrender." We also learn that he continued to carry on the war on his own, taking the law into his own hands,
including a bank robbery. Ethan is in love with his brother's
wife, Martha, but unlike his brother, he is not the man to
settle down and raise a family. At his core, he is solitary,
antisocial, and withdrawn from any link to community life.
He respects family life but seems to be unable to take part
in it. His tragic fate is thus to wander, to live outside community. In many ways, Ethan embodies the most important
attributes of the Westerner: individualism, self-sufficiency,
strength, nonconformity, and loneliness. In this movie, his
solitariness is also stressed cinematically. At the film's start
he appears out of nowhere, from the desert, and, at the
end, after his mission is accomplished, he returns to the
desert. In the film's last shot, Wayne stands alone, sil-
houetted in the door's frame, while other people pass
around, ignoring his presence.

A Charismatic Leader

The authority of Wayne's Western heroes is charismatic,
to use Max Weber's typology of authority types.[10] Charismatic authority rests on the personal appeal of the leader
and his exceptional abilities, perceived by his followers as a
"gift of grace." The charismatic leader possesses extraordinary virtues, on the basis of which he demands and gets
personal devotion from his people. This kind of leader differs substantially from the legal-rational leader, Weber's
second type, whose authority is based on a system of explicit laws that define and limit his use of power.

The quintessential Wayne hero is charismatic because
he gains and maintains authority solely by proving his
strength in life. Wayne's strength in his films is moral,
physical, and emotional. In some Westerns (and war movies), his authority is a combination of the charismatic and
legal-rational, a mixture of types outlined by Weber. In
this case, the appeal rests on the leader's extraordinary and
charming personality, but he also occupies an official position
in the organization's hierarchy, be it the cavalry or the Navy.

Wayne's authority, however, is never traditional, Weber's
third type, for his power never rests on the sanctity of
tradition or on hereditary position. When Wayne occupies a
position, he has earned it through his outstanding qualities.
Furthermore, the Wayne hero is influential even when he
does not hold a formal job in the military or community
hierarchy.

     Charismatic and legal authority are explicitly contrasted
in Fort Apache, in which Wayne's Captain Kirby York is the
charismatic leader, whereas Henry Fonda's Colonel Owen
Thursday represents the legal-rational type. Fonda's ambitious and prestige-seeking officer from the East resents the
fact that he has been sent to Fort Apache, a remote post he
regards as a temporary appointment. Strict with his men,
he demands military discipline at all times. Thursday is arrogant and rank-conscious, unable to remember his officers'
names, for example. He criticizes the slack standards of
dress that York has introduced, despite the fact that they
are more comfortable (he himself looks ridiculous in his kepi),
and demands that his men always wear uniform. Serious and
humorless, Thursday treats his family the same way he treats
his soldiers. Strict with his daughter (Shirley Temple), he
forbids Lieutenant O'Rourke (John Agar) to court her because he did not ask for his permission, but also because he
is a sergeant's son--Thursday is extremely class-conscious.
He lives by the regulations of the book, which he applies
without examining their logic or practicality. In short, he
is arrogant, driven by ambitious power, and considers himself superior to his men.

     Representing charismatic authority, York is exactly
the opposite. He is passionate, warm, informal, and friendly with his soldiers. More flexible, he does not live by regulations, willing to bend or violate them if they are not applicable. Closer to the men than Thursday, he treats them
as equals, and it is clear that he is liked by them. York is
also gallant with women, including Philadelphia, Thursday's
daughter. In short, he lives by a personal code of ethics,
his integrity deriving from a strong sense of self, which
Thursday lacks.

     York and Thursday differ radically in their approach
to the Indian problem. Coming from the East, Thursday
holds rigid racial ideas, stemming in part from his ignorance

A contrast of leaderships: Henry Fonda (center), as the
legal-rational leader, and John Wayne (left), as the charismatic leader, in Fort Apache (RKO Radio, 1948).

of the West. He believes that humiliation and conquest are
necessary measures in dealing with the Indians. York, by
contrast, respects the Indians and understands them. His
knowledge of the problem is firsthand, based on his personal experience. York is motivated by ideological considerations, fighting the Indians from a sense of duty, whereas Thursday fights for selfish reasons: the gain of power
and prestige. And while York understands the value of
military discipline, he is also willing to violate it when he
thinks it necessary.

Thursday's ambitions cause him to underestimate the
Indians' strength and intelligence. First, he double crosses
the Apache, then betrays his word. York sympathizes with
the Indians' rebellion against their ill treatment because he
resents the crooked Indian Ring in Washington, described by
him as "the dirtiest, most corrupt political group in our history." He volunteers to go to Cochise, who hides in Mexico,
and persuades him to meet Thursday for peace talks. He is
therefore disgusted when he finds out that Thursday has

tricked Cochise. "Colonel Thursday, I gave my word to
Cochise," he protests angrily, "no man is going to make a
liar out of me, sir." This irritates Thursday, "Your word
to a breech-clouted savage! An illiterate, uncivilized murderer and treaty-breaker! There is no question of honor,
sir, between an American officer and Cochise." But York
insists, "There is to me, sir."

York claims that the Indians outnumber the cavalry,
but Thursday decides to lead his men against them. Earlier,
he issues a harsh ultimatum to Cochise, despite York's attempts at restraint. When York challenges Thursday's idea
of lining his troops up in columns of four (he thinks it is
suicidal), he is accused of cowardice, relieved of command,
and ordered to stay with the supply train. Thursday's contempt for the Indians' fighting skills leads him to charge his
men up a closed box canyon into an ambush, destroying his
command. It is York who rescues the besieged troops and
the wounded Thursday, though the latter insists on continuing to fight. Thursday wins some respect from York only
because he follows his convictions courageously up to the
bitter end--his death. Before he dies, though, he tells
York, "When you command this regiment--and you probably
will--command it!" At the end, York wears a scarf similar
to Thursday's, indicating the latter's influence on him.

The film's last scene, which takes place two years
later, conveys a meaningful message. York, now the post's
commander, sits behind a desk, above which there is a
painting of Thursday, and is talking to reporters. When
one reporter eulogizes Thursday as "the hero of every
schoolboy in America," and "a great man," York concurs,
"No man died more gallantly or won more honor for his regiment." York lies to reporters to maintain the legend of
the army and the myth of military authority. He disagrees,
however, with a reporter claiming that Thursday is remembered, but his men are not. "You are wrong," states York,
"they aren't forgotten ... they'll keep on living as long as
the regiment lives ... their faces may change, the names,
but they're here, the regular army." Moreover, "they're
better men than they used to be," because "Thursday did
that, he made it a command to be proud of." In this, he
confirms the sacredness and superiority of the military as
a whole over its individual members.

The narrative of She Wore a Yellow Ribbon takes place
after the massacre of General Custer at the Little Big Horn.
A narrator sets the movie's sentimental tone: "And wherever
the flag rises over some lonely army post there may be one
man--one captain--fated to wield the sword of destiny." This
man is Wayne's elderly Captain Nathan Brittles, who has spent
40 years in service and is about to retire to civilian life in a
few hours. The Indians begin a war and he wants to trail
them, but his major objects. Instead, he assigns Brittles to
escort his wife and daughter to a safer place, which the latter reluctantly accepts. At the station, Brittles is devastated
by the sight of mutilated bodies, all victims of the Indian
raid. "About time I did retire!" he tells himself. However,
realizing that he has only four hours of service, he decides
on a bold move against the Indians, outwitting them by stampeding their horses; humiliated and helpless, they sue for
peace. Having turned a failure into a successful mission--
the raid has no casualties--he is now ready to retire.

The picture's real hero, as in Fort Apache, is actually
not Captain Brittles but the collective he stands for--here,
the Second Cavalry Regiment. At the end of She Wore a
Yellow Ribbon, a somehow misleading title, the narrator
tells the audience: "So here they are. The dog-faced soldiers, the regulars, the fifty-cents-a-day professionals riding the outposts of a nation. From Fort Reno to Fort
Apache ... from Sheridan to Stockton ... they were all the
same. Men in dirty-short blue ... and only a cold page in
the history books to mark their passing ... but wherever
they rose and whatever they sought for, that place became
the United States."

Wayne's Lt. Colonel Kirby Yorke in Rio Grande is also
fully committed to fighting the Indians. At the film's start,
he returns from an abortive mission aimed at capturing Indians who have crossed over into Mexico. Fighting them has
almost become a lost cause because the American and Mexican
governments have agreed not to cross the Rio Grande under
the circumstances. The Apache, however, take advantage of
the situation, raiding the whites, then escape safely across
the border. This impasse irritates Yorke because the matter
is beyond his control--the border sanctuary set-up and the
shortage of troops impede his mission to make the place safe
for the settlers.

John Wayne (left) and Victor McLaglen in John Ford's <u>She</u>
<u>Wore a Yellow Ribbon</u> (RKO Radio, 1949), a great perform-
ance that failed to get recognition.

Following a further attack, General Sheridan gives
Yorke informal permission to cross the border and smoke
the Indians out of their hideouts, once and for all. A
breach of international law, Yorke puts his loyalty to Sheridan, his commander from the Civil War, over and above the
illegality of the mission. He accepts the plan wholeheartedly,
unable to conceal his frustration over the unchecked Indian
attacks. Yorke is even willing to risk court martial, though
Sheridan promises to handpick the court's members if it
comes to that. This streak of independence is integral to
the Wayne charismatic heroes, living by their personal code
of ethics rather than by a set of legal rules. The script
had initially called for a scene in which Yorke was punished
for his illegal action and was sent to London as a military
adviser. But director Ford thought it was both anticlimactic

and incongruent with the star's image, and the scene was
deleted.

   In The Searchers, Ethan Edwards's charismatic leadership is juxtaposed with two kinds of men. First, there is a
contrast between Ethan and his brother, the domestic man
who has no strength or authority. In effect, both his wife
and children rely more on Ethan's power than on his. The
second contrast is between Ethan's charisma and the authority of Reverend Captain Samuel Clayton (Ward Bond), which
is a mixture of two types: traditional (religious) and legal-
rational (military). Functioning as the community chaplain
as well as its military leader, Clayton is endowed with qualities that Edwards lacks--respect for tradition and law, religious duty, and the strong wish to stabilize the community's
life. Nonetheless, Clayton is not an effective leader when it
comes to protecting the community from the Indians. Significantly, Edwards's authority derives not from an official position he maintains, but from his charisma, based on his extraordinary moral and physical strength.

   The contrast between charismatic and legal authority
in The Man Who Shot Liberty Valance is even more interesting
because it parallels the difference between the values of the
West or Wilderness (Wayne) and the values of the East or
Civilization (James Stewart). Stewart's Ranse Stoddard embodies rational-legal authority, symbolically as well as practically. A decent lawyer from the East, he comes to practice law and bring order to the West. Wayne, by contrast,
is the uneducated leader who believes that "you make your
own justice here and enforce your law." He is the rugged
individual, using physical force, not laws, in fighting Liberty Valance, an outlaw, because it is the only efficient way.
It is Wayne who teaches Stewart how to shoot, and it is
Wayne who kills Valance (Lee Marvin), though lets everyone
believe it is Stewart. Later, when Stewart is accused of being a killer and walks out of the territorial convention, Wayne
explains that he fired his rifle from a shadow, to coincide
with Stewart's shot. He thus relieves Stewart of his guilty
conscience so that he can pursue his political career and
lead the territory to statehood. We also learn that Wayne
refused to accept nomination as a delegate to the convention
due to "personal plans" that are not specified.

   Stewart's gradual rise to power represents the coming

of law and order to the West, but it is also inversely related
to Wayne's deterioration, from a strong and necessary leader
to a doomed hero. Wayne's charismatic leadership and his
ideals of anarchic freedom cannot coexist with Stewart's legal
authority and ideals of order. In the transition from a dis-
organized to civilized community, Wayne is the instrument as
well as the victim, because there is no longer need for his
dogged individualism. Moreover, his ideals stand in the way,
impeding progress. James McBride has observed that Wayne
and Stewart represent two approaches to life as well as two
successive phases in American history. Wayne is the man
with the gun, the old-style frontier individualist. Stewart,
by contrast, is the man from the East, representing political
order of impersonal justice and bureaucratic authority.[11]
Stewart's rational authority inevitably supersedes Wayne's
charismatic leadership of the Old West. Wayne is therefore
the tragic hero, a man of the past, whereas Stewart is the
man of the future.

Sociological Father and Role Model

Wayne's relationship with the younger generation was
an extremely important element in his screen persona. In
most of his movies there are children, and the intergenera-
tional interaction has both real and symbolic meaning. One
of Wayne's most typical screen roles is that of the patriarch
involved in teaching his children (or his soldiers) to behave
courageously. His cinematic function was truly sociological,
having to initiate a group of youngsters into manhood through a
series of ceremonies and rites of passage. Wayne performs
this function in many films, but especially in his war movies
and Westerns. His paternalist treatment of the younger generation is based on the assumption that it is the elders' duty
to look after their children until they can assume mature responsibility and stand on their own.[12]

His Western heroes passed through three major phases
of the life cycle. In the first two decades of his career he
portrayed the rebellious and outspoken hero, the dashing romantic adventurer. In the second phase, from the late 1940s
to the late 1960s, his heroes graduated into mature and restrained fathers. Most of his pictures of this era (Red River,
Hondo, The Searchers) had a two-generational plot. In the
third and last phase Wayne portrayed aging gunslingers and

patriarchs (El Dorado, The War Wagon, Chisum). Some of
his movies (True Grit, Big Jake, The Cowboys) had a three-
generational story, with Wayne playing grandfathers.

Whiting, Kluckhohn, and Anthony have observed in
their anthropological study that modern society gives little
formal recognition to the physiological and social changes
that boys undergo at puberty. These changes from childhood to adulthood are often marked by a number of minor
events rather than a single dramatic ceremony. Thus,
neither physiologically nor socially is there a clear demarca-
tion between childhood and manhood in modern societies.
However, societies differ in the way they treat this transition. In some, it is gradual and smooth, whereas in others
the transition is marked by one dramatic event. In the
Thonga tribe in South Africa, for example, young boys must
go through an elaborate ceremony that includes six major
initiation rites: beatings, exposure to cold, thirst, eating
unsavory food, punishment, and threat of death. The re-
searchers also found that out of the 55 societies chosen for
the study, 18 have one or more of the following ceremonies:
painful hazing by adult males, genital operations, seclusion
from women, and tests of endurance and manliness. The remaining 37 societies either have no ceremonies at all or ceremonies different from those mentioned above.[13]

The problematic transition from childhood to adulthood
is at the center of many Western movies. Philip French describes the Western as a didactic, pedagogic form because it
assumes that "young people have a lot to learn from their
elders," and that "the process of learning is long and painful." The Westerner, according to French, "feels obliged to
pass on what he knows about life, which frequently comes
down to matters of handling guns, women, cattle and drink--
especially guns." In Shane, for example, Joey (Brandon De
Wilde) learns how to use a pistol from a mysterious outsider
(Alan Ladd), who tells him "some like to have two guns, but
one's all you need if you know how to use it," and "a gun
is as good or bad as the man using it."[14] And Steve
McQueen in the title role of Nevada Smith learns how to
shoot from a traveling salesman, but his education also includes learning to drink, play poker, and handle whores.
The socialization process is twofold, involving technical
skills as well as values, the most important of which are
"judgment, self-restraint, self-sufficiency, a code of conduct,
and morality which goes with the acquiring of character."[15]

Red River is probably the first and best illustration of
the essence of the socialization process--Wayne style. The
generational conflict in this film is between Wayne's Thomas
Dunson, the aging and single-minded cattle baron, and
Matthew Garth (Montgomery Clift), his surrogate son and
the only survivor of an Indian raid in which Dunson's woman
is murdered. Matt leaves to fight in the Civil War but returns to join the cattle drive that Dunson is taking to market in Missouri. Before hiring the men for the drive, Dunson spells out the dangers of the journey and states his
conditions, "Every man that signs on for this trip finishes
it--no one quits along the way." Later he shoots down three
quitters and, when three others disappear, he sends gunman Cherry Valance to bring them back, dead or alive. He
spurs the men, exhausting them so they will not have time to
consider quitting. When Valance returns with two of the
quitters, Dunson proposes to hang them up, as a public
lesson to the others. At this point Matt rebels against his
dictatorship and, supported by the others, takes over the
command. Dunson is determined to kill him for his betrayal.

Matt represents a different kind of leader: fair, considerate, and more egalitarian. Throughout the film, Dunson
criticizes Matt for being too soft; he even pokes fun at Matt
for not killing him after taking over the command. At the
film's climax, when the two meet, Valance, afraid that Matt
will not defend himself, shoots Dunson. Wounded, Dunson
moves toward Matt, who still refuses to draw. Dunson
shoots past his head and at his feet and when Matt continues
to stand still, he humiliates him: "You're soft! Won't anything make a man out of you?" He hits Matt three times and
knocks him to the ground, but suddenly Matt fights back
and they battle until Tess Millay (Joanne Dru), whom they
both love, fires a shot and shouts, "Anybody with half a
mind would know you two love each other!" Then she en-
courages them to go on fighting.

They reconcile and Dunson fulfills a promise he made
when Matt was a child, to share with him his brand, the
Red River D, when he earned it. Matt earns it through passing ritualistic ceremonies of manhood. Dunson accepts him as a
son, biologically as well as socially, only after he proves his
toughness and virility. Red River has been interpreted in
different ways, attesting to the film's richness in mood, tex-
ture, and meanings. There is no doubt, however, that the
contrast between Dunson and Matt, in terms of leadership

style and manhood, is at the core of the picture. Wayne
stands for the real frontiersman, the old-styled hero, tough
and indestructible, who acts alone and is responsible only to
himself. Matt, by contrast, represents a different brand of
leadership: he is sensitive, more egalitarian, and open-
minded. However, the film makes it clear that the ideal
consists of the combined styles of leadership. At the end,
Matt becomes as tough and competent (fast at the draw) as
Dunson, and there is good reason to believe that he will
follow in Wayne's footsteps. Dunson's capabilities as a role
model are emphasized throughout the story, especially the
idea that his socialization includes both the instruction of
skills and the transmission of a code of ethics befitting life
in the West. Matt would not have become the competent
leader he is, were it not for having to measure up to Dunson's stature.

The two-generational plot also prevails in She Wore
a Yellow Ribbon, but it differs from Red River in many
ways. For one, it is a more nostalgic Western, in which
Ford comments on the passing of heroes like Captain Brittles, an aging cavalry officer who has spent all his life
in the army. She Wore a Yellow Ribbon evokes and senti-
mentalizes the Old West; Red River looks ahead to the future
and is in favor of social change. Brittles does not trust
the younger generation and is reluctant to hand over the
command to Lieutenant Flint Cohill (John Agar) because
he thinks he lacks experience. Major Allshard (George
O'Brien) reminds Brittles that the youngsters have to learn
the hard way, just as he himself did. He also protests
that "everytime Cohill gave an order, men would turn
around and look at you, they'd wonder if he was doing the
right thing."

In this movie too, the younger generation adopts Brittles's way of life. Lieutenant Pennell (Harry Carey Jr.) decides to renounce an easy and comfortable life in the East in
favor of a military career--just like Brittles. Some of the
movie's most touching sequences describe the ritualistic ceremonies in which tradition is transmitted to the younger generation. On Wayne's last review of his troops, he gets a
present, a silver watch. He brings out his glasses and
sniffs back a tear as he reads the inscription, "Lest We
Forget!" with a slight choke in his voice. This is the only
informal interaction between Brittles and his men. It takes

Brittles a long time to soften: when he finally hands over
the command to Cohill, he calls him for the first time by his
Christian name.

   A more straightforward confrontation between the generations is presented in Rio Grande, with Wayne playing both
biological and sociological father. Putting duty before love,
during the Civil War, Lieutenant Colonel Kirby Yorke followed orders and set fire to his wife's plantation, for which
she has never forgiven him. A tough, disciplinarian commander, he does not glamorize the military way of life to his
recruits. On the contrary, in his first address, he makes
sure to spell out as realistically as possible the hardships of
such a life. He is genuinely disappointed that his son Jeff
(Claude Jarman Jr.) has failed at West Point Academy (a
reference to Wayne's own failure), and is ashamed that he
has to enlist in the army as a recruit. However, he tells
Jeff, who has been posted to serve under him, "Put out of
your mind any romantic ideas that it's a way of glory. It's
a life of suffering and hardship, an uncompromising devotion
to your oath and your duty." He also tells him that he can
expect no special favors, "on the official record you are my
son, on this post, you're just a trooper." And it is clear
that Yorke expects and will demand more of his son than of
the other recruits, because he is his son. Yorke does not
believe in failure and conveys this message authoritatively
to his son: "You've chosen my way of life. I hope you
have the guts to endure it." However, as in the war movies, his toughness is just a façade. He is the father who
watches through the hospital window how castor oil is admin-
istered to Jeff. And he is also the father who checks his
son's height against his own on the tent's sides, taking pride
in his growth.

   Yorke meets his wife, Kathleen (Maureen O'Hara), after fifteen years of separation, when she comes to the camp
to reclaim her son, announcing herself as "trooper Jeff
Yorke's mother." She wants to buy Jeff's release, but
Yorke refuses to sign the paper, claiming stubbornly, "Here
he'll stay and here he'll serve." Kathleen then talks to Jeff
against his father, "He's a lonely man ... a very lonely
man," but Jeff replies, "They say he's a great soldier."
"What makes soldiers great is hateful to me," she declares.
When Jeff refuses to leave the post, she is irritated, "You're
stubborn proud, Jeff, just like he is," but he contradicts

her, "Just like you, mother." Kathleen tries to persuade
Yorke but to no avail, "I could say yes very easily, but I
owe something to Jeff."

When the women and children have to be sent to a
safer area, however, Yorke relents and assigns Jeff to be
one of the escorts, which pleases her, "He'll hate you for
it, Kirby, but I'll love you for it." Jeff breaks through
the Indian camp and rides off to bring help, after the
women are attacked and some of the children abducted.
Tyree (Ben Johnson) then chooses Jeff as one of the two
men to creep into the camp and protect the children during
the raid. Later, when Yorke is wounded, Jeff pulls the
arrow out, a symbolic ritual, bringing the two men closer,
and also serving as a rite of passage, transforming Jeff into
a full-fledged man. By the end of the film, Yorke endorses
his son and admits he outdid him in his toughness. This
confirmation, both symbolic and pragmatic, is explicitly stated
by Yorke, "You did all right," and Kathleen, "Our boy did
well," indicating she both understands and accepts her husband and now son's way of life. It is the father's role to
put his son through the necessary male rituals by which he
will become a man, but the mother's confirmation of her son's
newly-gained status is also important.

Wayne's Hondo Lane in Hondo is an ex-gunfighter who
is now a dispatch rider for the U.S. Cavalry. Upon meeting
Angie Lowe (Geraldine Page) and her son, Johnny (Lee
Aaker), he learns that her husband has deserted them in
the wake of an Apache uprising. The movie's plot is similar to Shane, released a year earlier, in 1953, as both are
based on the premise that every child needs a sociological father to instruct him how to become a real man. Hondo helps
Mrs. Lowe restore the ranch and becomes a role model for her
son, teaching him, among many things, how to swim by
throwing him into the water. Moreover, Hondo starts as Johnny's sociological father and ends up as his legal parent, after killing his biological father, though he is unaware of his
identity at the time. And as in many Westerns, Hondo Lane
leaves with his new family to start a new life in California.

Wayne also functions as role model (Ethan Edwards) in
The Searchers, in which his obsessive search is conducted
with two men: Martin Pawley (Jeffrey Hunter) and Brad
Jorgensen (Harry Carey, Jr.). One of the film's more

John Wayne and Lee Aaker in John Farrow's <u>Hondo</u> (Warner, 1953), one of many roles he played opposite children.

interesting aspects is Edwards's relationship with Pawley, Jorgensen, and his brother's children. From the start, it is clear that Ethan is stronger and tougher than his brother Aaron, and is admired by his children. Facing an Indian raid, the son says, "I wish uncle Ethan were here, don't you ma'am?" They feel they can rely on Ethan's strength more than on their father's.

The search for the two nieces lasts five years, during which Ethan instructs Pawley, constantly putting his strength to test in a series of rituals. Pawley learns how to slaughter a buffalo, how to be more careful in bartering with the Indians, how to deal with ambushers--in short, how to survive. His earlier carelessness had resulted in acquiring an Indian wife, providing Ethan an opportunity to poke fun at him. When Ethan finds the mutilated bodies of his family, he absorbs the pain alone and quietly, with no outlet for his grief. Pawley, by contrast, is distraught even without seeing them. Later, when Ethan finds the body of his elder niece (Lucy), he

buries her in his army coat, keeping the whole incident to
himself--until Jorgensen asks him about it. In contrast to
Ethan, Jorgensen cannot face the truth and, losing self-
control, he charges into the Indian camp and loses his life.
As in Rio Grande, Ethan is wounded and asks Pawley to remove the poison from his wound. Removing bullets and ar-
rows has been a recurrent ritual in Westerns, with an explicit symbolic signification: it tests the hero's ability to
endure pain, but also strengthens the bond between the
wounded and the person removing the arrow. Significantly,
in Wayne's movies, this person is either his son or relative.

The climax of The Searchers is the confrontation between Ethan and Debbie (Natalie Wood), the only survivor of
the family. When Debbie tells him, "These [the Indians] are
my people," he draws his gun, determined to kill her, regarding miscegenation a cardinal sin. Obsessed with hatred
for the Indians, he has been living for one purpose--to kill
Debbie. After defeating the Indians, Ethan chases Debbie
and they come face to face. There is a suspenseful moment,
after which he says softly, "Let's go home, Debbie." He
leans down and picks her up in his arms. This scene is
considered to be one of the most touching and beautiful
in the American film. The reconciliation is the beginning of
a new relationship between uncle Ethan, now her sociolegal
parent, and Debbie, now his surrogate daughter. Critic
Molly Haskell has eloquently described the complex, contradictory emotions displayed in this scene: "Love dissolves
hatred, mercy dissolves authoritarianism, maternal and paternal instincts unite in a single, all-encompassing figure."[16]

Wayne functions as role model not only for children or
adolescents, but also for adult men who, for one reason or
another, have to be instructed with technical skills or have
to be restored to proper, i.e. manly, code of behavior. In
The Man Who Shot Liberty Valance, Jimmy Stewart's lawyer
is at first reluctant to use violent force in defeating Liberty
Valance. Gradually, however, he comes to accept Wayne's
code as the only appropriate behavior in the Wild West, that
is, that force should be used to meet force. But Stewart is
no good at shooting and Wayne has to instruct him, at the request of Hallie (the woman they both love). Wayne's sharp
lesson is done in semihumorous, semisarcastic manner, making a fool out of Stewart by puncturing paint tins used as
targets. Humiliated, Stewart angrily knocks Wayne to the

John Wayne and Natalie Wood in John Ford's epic Western
The Searchers (Warner, 1956), in one of the most famous
scenes in film history.

ground, demonstrating first steps in adjusting to the mores
of the West.

In two of Hawks's Westerns, Wayne's manhood is juxtaposed with other men's, and in both his is by far superior.
In Rio Bravo Wayne restores Dean Martin's drunken former
sheriff back to manhood. And he performs the same function for Robert Mitchum's drunken, self-pitying sheriff in
El Dorado. Moreover, one of his team members in El Dorado,
Mississippi (James Caan), is a tough man excelling in using
knives, but he cannot handle a pistol. Knives are useless
when fighting from distance, however, and Wayne has to
instruct him how to use a sawed-off, double-barrel shotgun.

In the last decade of his career, Wayne's function as a
role model was examined against very young children, who
could be his grandchildren, biologically as well as symbolically. Mattie Ross (Kim Darby) in True Grit is an adolescent

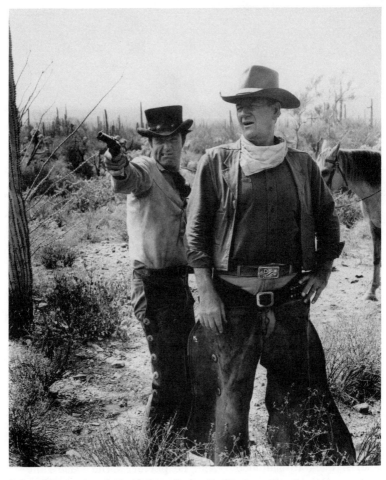

John Wayne teaches James Caan (left) how to shoot in
Howard Hawks's El Dorado (Paramount, 1967).

seeking to avenge her father's murder. Wayne is at first
amused by her proposition to hire him, but gets more interested when she mentions the remuneration. "I'm giving you
my children's rates," he comments when she tries to bargain
with him over the price--though he admires her guts. Leaving on his mission with a Texas Ranger (Glen Campbell), she
insists on joining them, and her stubborn determination
prompts Wayne to observe, "My God, she reminds me of me!"
They try to dissuade Mattie from tagging along, leaving her
behind, at a ferry crossing. But insistent, she swims across
the river on horseback, which gains her Wayne's respect.
True Grit, like so many pictures before, makes it clear that
Wayne expects Mattie to demonstrate that she too has true
grit and the courage to pursue a job against all odds.

Wayne has a better chance to pass down the violent
tradition of the West to his own family in Big Jake, a Western with a three-generational plot. Jake is joined by his
two sons (played by Patrick Wayne, his real son, and Chris
Mitchum, Robert Mitchum's son) in their search for the kidnappers of his grandson, Little Jake (played by Ethan,
Wayne's youngest son). Throughout the picture, contrasts
are drawn between Wayne and his sons. He uses a horse,
they a motorcycle, for example. And this comparison is always to his advantage (see chapter 13). In one sequence,
Wayne accuses his son of risking his grandson's life by acting foolishly and, to prevent it in the future, he punches
him twice! He also gets to teach his grandson a few useful
lessons in manly conduct. When Little Jake--Wayne is Big
Jake!--says he is scared, Wayne admits to also being frightened, but advises him, "Don't let them know." And at the
end, he hands him a gun but tells him, "Use it, when you
have to." Little Jake has an immediate opportunity to practice, firing a bullet from a derringer into the biggest member of the gang. The ritualistic ceremony of son helping
wounded father appears in this movie too, when Little Jake
helps put a tourniquet on Wayne's bleeding leg.

The passing of Western mores from the older to the
younger generation is at its most explicit in The Cowboys,
with Wayne playing an old rancher who needs help to bring
his cattle to market. As in Red River, Wayne's regular
hands have deserted him to make easy money in a gold strike
nearby, providing him an opportunity to recite his personal
philosophy: "In my day, a man stayed with you on a

handshake." He turns down the offer of the villain (Bruce
Dern), not because he is an ex-convict, but because he is a
liar. But, unable to find help, he is forced to hire 11
youngsters, ranging in age from 12 to 17. Suspicious of
their abilities, he is at first reluctant but, as in She Wore
a Yellow Ribbon, it takes an old friend to remind him, "How
old were you when you went on your first drive?" "What's
that got to do with it?" replies Wayne angrily. But his
friend insists, "How old, Will?" "Thirteen," Wayne snaps
back, but "I already had a beard."

During the cattle drive, the innocent and inexperienced
youngsters grow up under Wayne's tough guidance and demanding leadership. He instructs them how to use a gun,
how to drink, and even lets them see a brothel. In other
words, Wayne helps them mature into manhood through many
rites of passage. Wayne is a strict disciplinarian, but once
again his toughness is more of an exterior. He threatens a
lot, but in actuality, his worst deed is to push a dozing boy
off his horse. A benevolent father figure, he even gets to
perform some miracles, curing a stuttering boy by teaching
him how to curse, "You goddam, dirty sonnovabitch!" But
he warns, "I would not make a habit of calling me that,
son." Responsible for the boys, he commands his cook, after having been shot, to see them back home safely. "A
fellow always wants his children to be better than he was,"
he tells them, "You are." The boys' speech after his death
shows that they have been socialized effectively, internaliz-
ing his code of ethics. "It ain't how you're buried," one
says in Wayne's vein, "it's how you're remembered," placing
Wayne's tombstone where he died. And in avenging his
death, as if he were their real father, they also prove their
own true grit.

In his last picture, The Shootist, Wayne plays an aging gunfighter dying of cancer. At the center of the movie
is Wayne's relationship with a widowed landlady (Lauren
Bacall) and her son (Ron Howard). At first, Howard resents Wayne, but gradually he learns to respect him, ad-
miring him for being "the most celebrated" shootist in the
West. Howard, like other children in his films, learns how
to behave properly by observing and emulating Wayne's behavior. For example, spying on Wayne from the window, he
gets his first lesson, "If you want to see me, knock on the
door, like a man." Later, Wayne sums up his philosophy of

life to Howard, deeming it useful to the younger generation:
"I won't be wronged, I won't be insulted, I won't be laid a
hand on. I don't do these things to others, and I require
the same of them."

When Howard asks for a shooting lesson, Wayne agrees
but instructs him: "A man should know how to handle a gun
--with discretion." The film's assumption, as in Hondo, is
that every child, let alone an orphan, needs a sociological father to become a man. And, in similar manner to The Cowboys,
Howard adopts his master's style and philosophy. In the
last scene, he avenges Wayne's death in the saloon by using the latter's gun, then throwing it away.

4. WAYNE AND THE WESTERN MOVIE

Wayne's career was closely associated with the Western movie: he was described as the screen's greatest cowboy and the colossus of this art form. His very name became synonymous with the Western genre, and with good reason: he contributed to it, qualitatively and quantitatively, more than any other actor.

A Defining Genre

The identification between Wayne and the Western was so intimate that it looked as if he had been born in the Old West. "To many moviegoers," Gene Autry notes, "no Western or war picture is acceptable without John Wayne."[1] Of the two genres, however, the Western featured much more prominently in his career. Although Wayne starred in many non-Western pictures, it is the Western that justifies his claim to screen immortality. He gave the Western frontier an extended life, combining legend and myth. One critic described Wayne as a man who "knows the Western like a roadmap, because he's traveled the same route with the same cargo many times before."[2] And another critic sees Wayne's significance in being "the greatest figure of one of America's native forms." Wayne "had not created the Western with its clear-cut conflict between good and bad, right and wrong, but it was impossible to mention Westerns without thinking of the Duke."[3]

Director Raoul Walsh observed early in his career, "Anytime you put guys like Duke in civilian clothes, they're dog meat."[4] Many people had difficulties accepting him in a contemporary movie. "In a dark suit and ill-fitting soft collar," one reviewer noted, "John Wayne looks like a man who is lost without his horse and his spurs."[5] Critic Roderick

Mann claims that because most of his work was in costume
movies, he not only looked ill at ease and furtive in a lounge
suit, but acted "as though he were expecting at any moment
to be picked up by a suspicious shore patrol."[6] Wayne himself found it strange to wear anything but buckskins. Of
his experience of wearing a suit in Pittsburgh, cast as an
ambitious coal miner rising to the top, he said, "all the time
I was looking at the finished product, I kept telling myself,
'get behind a boulder, boy, and aim it at someone.'"[7] This
"uncomfortable" feeling prevailed in many other non-Western
films and was one of the major reasons for the failure of his
crime films, McQ and Brannigan, in the 1970s. Audiences
found it anachronistic to see him in urban settings, using a
car instead of a horse.

Wayne's association with the Western movie started as
a product of circumstances. In the 1930s, he was under
contract to the Poverty Row Companies, which produced for
the most part "B" Westerns. And in the 1940s, he worked
for Republic, which also excelled in making Western features
and serials. Nonetheless, once his intimate collaboration with
John Ford began, in the late 1940s, making Westerns ceased
to be a necessity and became a matter of personal choice.
Wayne used the Western as an ideological tool, through which
he expressed his value system and commented on contemporary life in America (see chapter 13).

To his credit, his commitment to Westerns continued
throughout his career, appearing in them consistently, even
when they were out of vogue in Hollywood and unpopular
with the American public. His Western pictures (83) amounted
to about half of his entire film output, overshadowing his contribution to other genres, including 26 action-adventures, 16
war movies, 11 sports films, and a few comedies and biopictures. He made Westerns in every decade of his career: 44
in the 1930s, 15 in the 1940s, 5 in the 1950s, 11 in the
1960s, and 8 in the 1970s. Paradoxically, he appeared in
the least number of Westerns in the 1950s, possibly the best
and most prolific decade for Westerns. The watershed year
in the genre's history is undoubtedly 1950, with no fewer
than 110 Westerns, featuring such classics as The Wagon-
master, Broken Arrow, The Gunfighter, and Winchester 73.
By contrast, most of Wayne's movies in the last decade of
his career were Westerns, a decade that saw this genre's
tremendous decline.

Wayne's influence on Westerns was greater than that
of his predecessors: "Bronco Billy" Anderson, William S.
Hart, and Tom Mix, all considered to be great Western ac-
tors. For one thing, Wayne's career spanned half a century,
compared with Anderson's 15-year career, Hart's 11, and
Mix's 26. The contribution of Wayne's contemporaries to the
Western genre was also pale. Against his 83 Westerns, Gary
Cooper made 40, Jimmy Stewart 19, Henry Fonda and Robert
Taylor each 16, Errol Flynn 8, Clark Gable 7, and Humphrey
Bogart and James Cagney 3 each. Even if Wayne is compared
with stars of the "B" Westerns, most notably Randolph Scott,
Gene Autry, and Roy Rogers, his Western oeuvre outnumbers
theirs in quality if not quantity. And none of the postwar
stars--William Holden, Kirk Douglas, Burt Lancaster, Robert
Mitchum--has left as strong a mark on the genre as Wayne.
He may have been one of the few stars to have been genuinely committed to Westerns ideologically, through the values
they embodied, and artistically, through their uniquely cinematic worth--not just as commercial vehicles.

Only three other actors of Wayne's generation and
stature have left their imprint on the Western genre: Gary
Cooper, Jimmy Stewart, and Henry Fonda. A comparison
among their Western output therefore highlights their distinctive contribution.

Cooper was one of the screen's great cowboys and,
next to Wayne, appeared in the largest number of "A" Westerns. There are many similarities between Wayne's and
Cooper's careers and their screen heroes. Though Cooper
was older than Wayne by six years, both started their careers in silent Westerns and were genuine creations of the
silver screen. Cooper, like Wayne, made Westerns quite
regularly, but especially in the first and last decade of his
career. In the 1920s Cooper made 15 Westerns and he returned to this genre with full energy in the 1950s with 13
pictures. In their Western portrayals, both were influenced
by William S. Hart's strong and silent cowboys, and their
similar acting style, straightforward naturalism, was most
appropriate for their characterizations. To many, Cooper
and Wayne looked perfectly natural in the Western prairie,
as if they had ridden horses all their lives. Indeed, the
subtle and sophisticated comedies that Cooper made for
Ernst Lubitsch (Design for Living, Bluebeard's Eighth Wife)
displayed his weaknesses as an actor, despite the original
idea of casting him against type.

The screen persona of the two stars was endowed with physical and moral strength, but there were important differences between their heroes. Cooper's Westerners were more laconic than Wayne's; Wayne talked a lot, particularly in the Howard Hawks Westerns. Cooper's silences, as one critic observed, were meaningful intervals in which he confronted his soul.[8] The quintessential Cooper hero is torn by an inner conflict: a struggle between his conscience or inner wholeness and his public responsibilities as a sheriff or marshal. In Cooper's most convincing roles, he undergoes a transformation from privacy, at times renunciation, to social obligations and commitment to action. In The Virginian, the third (1929) version of Owen Wister's popular book which established Cooper as a star, an innocent cowboy must choose between the Eastern values of his Pacifist girl and his own conscience, which tells him he must hang his best friend for cattle rustling.

Fred Zinnemann's controversial High Noon (1952), featuring Cooper's best performance for which he won his second Best Actor Oscar, presents a similar situation. Will Kane, an aging marshal, is about to leave town after marrying Amy (Grace Kelly), a pretty Quaker, when he learns that Frank Miller, whom he had sent to prison, has been released and plans to come back to Hadleyville with his gang to get even with him. Burdened with tremendous fear of fighting alone, after his plea for help is rejected by every member of the community, he must choose between running out of town and saving his neck, as his wife wishes, or face the four villains by himself. True to his nature, Kane meets the challenge single-handedly, winning his wife's understanding and ultimately her help.

Cooper's heroes think and debate with themselves before deciding to act, which makes them more interesting and more human than Wayne's characters. Cooper, like Wayne, is forceful, but he is more vulnerable, burdened, and less assured. In William Wyler's Friendly Persuasion (1956), based on Jessamyn West's stories and Cooper's most popular film of the 1950s, he is cast as Jess Bidwell, the head of a Quaker family in Southern Indiana at the start of the Civil War. Initially, he is opposed to the use of violence, denying approval of his son's wish to defend the community. But holding that, in the final account, every man should be guided by his own conscience, he lends sympathy to his son, especially after the latter is wounded in action. What makes Cooper's dilemmas

more dramatic is the fact that in both The Virginian and
High Noon he has to make crucial decisions on his wedding
day! Thus, whereas Cooper's Westerners ponder and tor-
ture their souls before choosing action, Wayne's heroes never
experience--at least never show--such inner turmoil. The
Wayne hero is unabashedly committed to action, at all times
and at all costs, which is why it is hard to imagine him
philosophizing about his lot, the way Cooper does in his
movies.

The heroes that Cooper and Wayne play are determined to see justice done, without any doubt as to which
side they are on. However, later in his career, Cooper was
willing to play more dubious characters: reformed bandits
(Man of the West) and even mercenaries (Vera Cruz). More
significantly, if the Wayne hero is often compared with younger characters, children, recruits, the quintessential Cooper
protagonist is often contrasted with his best friend or partner. In Robert Aldrich's popular Vera Cruz (1954), Cooper
and Burt Lancaster are American adventurers in Mexico during the 1866 Revolution. They decide to fight for whichever
side pays best--something Wayne would never do--but Cooper
is forced to kill his mate when the latter refuses to give the
gold back to the Mexican people, who Cooper believes rightfully own it. In Henry Hathaway's Garden of Evil (1954),
ex-sheriff Cooper and gambler Richard Widmark are on their
way to California's goldfields when a woman asks them to
help rescue her husband from a mine trap. Later, Cooper
finds out that his partner cheated him when they drew
cards to determine who would stay to cover their escape.
In a characteristic manner, he goes back through treacherous Indian territory at great risk to straighten out this
matter, only to find him dying. Family connections and
friendships are never an obstacle to serving justice, as he
demonstrates again in Man of the West, killing his own uncle, the head of his former gang.

In contrast to both Wayne and Cooper, Jimmy Stewart
appeared in Westerns rather late in his career. After a
small part in the musical Western Rose Marie, and a major
role in the Western comedy Destry Rides Again, Stewart
made no Westerns in the 1940s. However, in the 1950s he
made seven important Westerns, the best of which were directed by Anthony Mann. These Westerns opened up a new
career for him, changing his previous image from the innocent

idealistic hero in Frank Capra's <u>Mr. Smith Goes to Washington</u> and <u>It's a Wonderful Life</u> into a more complex and interesting persona.

In his most memorable Westerns, Stewart's heroes are cynical, at times even opportunistic. In Delmer Daves's <u>Broken Arrow</u> (1950), the film which changed the Indian image on the American screen, Stewart's cavalry scout is a self-appointed broker between the white men and the Apache. He manages to achieve a racial reconciliation and peace, but at a heavy price, losing his Indian wife. Stewart's protagonists are often obsessed with pursuing private quests of revenge. In Mann's <u>Winchester 73</u> he maintains his familiar mannerisms of drawling and fumbling his words, but his frontiersman is actually single-mindedly committed to avenging his father's death. In another notable Western, <u>The Man from Laramie</u> (1955), his wandering cowman seeks revenge on those who killed his brother. More significantly, unlike his comedies and biopictures, in which he is the epitome of the ideal husband-father, in his Westerns Stewart plays loners, usually men who lose their women in tragic circumstances.

Henry Fonda, the fourth major star after Wayne, Cooper, and Stewart, made his first Western at Twentieth Century-Fox, <u>Jesse James</u> (1939), a big, color movie which glamorizes the outlaw; Fonda was cast as Frank, the brother of Jesse (Tyrone Power). The two brothers are determined to avenge their mother's murder and to keep the family's land from a ruthless railroad baron. Despite the fact that Fonda had a secondary role, it was better written than the lead and, of course, better played; Power was badly miscast. <u>Jesse James</u> was so successful at the box office that Fox cast Fonda in a sequel, <u>The Return of Frank James</u>, under Fritz Lang's direction. Fonda's best Westerns in the 1940s were directed by John Ford, <u>My Darling Clementine</u>, a nostalgic evocation of Marshal Wyatt Earp's heroism, and <u>Fort Apache</u>, starring Wayne.

Another distinguished, though uncharacteristic, Western was William Wellman's <u>The Ox-Bow Incident</u> (1943), one of the few Westerns to have been nominated for the Best Picture Oscar. A grim, socially conscious film, based on a true story of a lynching in Nevada in 1885, it is an interesting study of mob behavior, in which Fonda plays a young cowboy unable to prevent the unjust lynching of three

innocent wanderers. He has one memorable sequence, similar
to his Tom Doad in The Grapes of Wrath, in which he reads
the mob a letter from one of the executed men to his wife,
after it is clear that an unforgivable error has been committed.

What distinguishes Fonda's Western roles, compared with
Wayne's, is their versatility, especially in the 1960s, when he
was often cast as a villain or hired gunman. This casting
against type, a deviation from established image, was exploited by Sergio Leone, the Italian director of "spaghetti"
Westerns, casting him as the hired killer of a ruthless baron
in his violent epic Once Upon a Time in the West (1968).
Fonda was reportedly given a choice of roles, but he opted
to play the vicious Frank who, among other things, orders
the slaughter of an innocent family and kills cold-bloodedly a
nine-year-old boy.

Of the four Western stars examined here, Fonda had
the widest range of roles, changing his image from one movie
to another. In Welcome to Hard Times (1967), based on E.L.
Doctorow's novel, Fonda's Will Blues is basically an antihero,
though he is the one to save the community when its cowardly citizens are willing to abandon it. And in his next Western, Firecreek (1968), he is cast again as the leader of a
gang terrorizing a town, a ruthless loner who cannot conform to order. This movie enjoyed great publicity because
it cast Fonda opposite Stewart for the first time in 20 years.
Stewart plays the good guy, the aging farmer and part-time
sheriff, highly consistent with his screen persona. And as
if playing a villain were not enough, at the end of Firecreek
Fonda is killed by a woman, something that would never have
happened in a Wayne Western.

The other stars of Wayne's generation did not make
Westerns because their studios lacked interest in the genre.
MGM, for example, was neither interested nor proficient in
producing Westerns, which meant that its three male stars,
Gable, Tracy, and Taylor, avoided the genre. Gable appeared in a bit part in the silent North Star, and as a villain in The Painted Desert, before becoming a movie star.
He made no Westerns in the best decade (the 1930s) of his
career, but in the 1950s, as an older and less popular actor, he returned to the genre. His most popular Western
was The Tall Men (1955), a routine vehicle directed by
Raoul Walsh and co-starring Jane Russell, featuring Gable

as an adventurous Texan heading for Montana's goldfields.
Significantly, most of Robert Taylor's Westerns were made
after his long-term contract with MGM had terminated. Taylor's earlier appearance in the title role of Billy the Kid
(1940) was used by MGM as an effective way to change his
image from a pretty-faced romantic star to a more virile and
tough one. And like Gable, Taylor made most of his Westerns in the 1950s, when he began to age and could no longer play convincingly leading men in romantic melodramas, his
earlier specialty.

Wayne made some action Westerns at Warners in the
1930s, such as Haunted Gold, but by and large, this studio
did not excel in producing them. Warners was at its best in
producing crime or biopictures. The image of James Cagney,
Warners' major star of the 1930s, was deeply rooted in the
urban crime drama. Indeed, his Westerns looked and sounded like gangster movies transplanted to a Western locale--so
firm was his persona. In The Oklahoma Kid (1939), one of
his few forays into the genre, Cagney plays a cowboy avenging
the unjust lynching of his father during the settlement of the
Cherokee Strip; Humphrey Bogart, still in his formative years,
is cast as a black-hatted villain. This piece of casting was
so incredible that Frank Nugent wrote in his review: "There
is something entirely disarming about the way he has tackled
horse opera, not pretending for a minute to be anything but
New York's Jimmy Cagney, all dressed up as a Robin Hood
of the old West."[9] Warners continued to use Bogart in unlikely roles, the most ridiculous of which was his sneering
Mexican bandit in Virginia City. But Bogart never felt comfortable in the Western prairie and, after establishing himself as a star in 1941, did not make another Western.

The only Warners' major actor to have appeared successfully in Westerns was Errol Flynn, though he too was
more credible in swashbuckling costume adventures, for
which his dashing style was perfect. Still, three of Flynn's
films are among the 50 most widely seen Westerns of all
time.[10] In Michael Curtiz's Santa Fe Trail (1940), advertised by the studio as "a thousand miles of danger with a
thousand thrills a mile," Flynn is cast as the real-life cavalry commander James Ewell Brown (Jeb) Stuart, who was
responsible for the capture of John Brown, the radical abo-
litionist, prior to the Civil War. A large-scale production
with some impressive action sequences, the film is far from

accurate in historical detail. Even more popular was Raoul
Walsh's They Died with Their Boots On (1942), Flynn's most
expensive Western, featuring an all-star cast. Focusing on
the life and death of General Custer at the Little Big Horn,
it not only fictionalizes history but is also inconsistent in
mood, attempting to be a romantic (the sequences with Olivia
de Havilland's Elizabeth Bacon Custer) and tragic epic at the
same time. In sheer size and scope, however, it was Warners'
biggest Western. Despite these successes, Flynn did not
leave his imprint on the genre and is still best remembered
for his handsome swashbuckling hero in such classics as
Captain Blood and The Adventures of Robin Hood.

The Western and the American Film Industry

The Western is considered the most uniquely American
film genre. The opening of the West in the nineteenth century has lent itself to filmmaking more than any other era in
American history. The American Revolution, by contrast,
an undoubtedly important historical event, never became a
popular subject for films. Perhaps, as one critic suggested,
it lacked individual heroism and was too remote in speech
patterns and costumes.[11] The Civil War was another heroic
event that has not inspired filmmakers, arguably because of
the controversy over slavery and the fact that it was a dis-
ruptive force in American history. The Civil War was mostly
used as a background or setting for Westerns, as in John
Ford's The Searchers or Horse Soldiers, both starring Wayne.

What is striking is that the opening of the frontier
lasted a shorter period of time, less than half a century,
than the 70-year history of the Western movie, from The
Great Train Robbery in 1903 to the mid-1970s. The Western has always been integral to the film industry, sort of
"bread and butter," with more Westerns produced than any
other genre. It is estimated that between 1910 and the late
1940s, about one-fourth of the 24,000 films made in the
United States were Westerns. In the 1950s the production of Westerns reached an unprecedented record: in
1950 alone, 110 of the 383 American-made movies (29 percent) were Westerns. Unlike other genres, until the late
1970s there has been no lengthy period in which no Westerns were made--despite fluctuations in popularity.

Wayne spent a lifetime defending Westerns as a uniquely American folklore, reminding that "more has been written
about the American cowboy and the frontier than any other
subject," because "the word West covers a wide area, historically and geographically."[12] Stories of the West were
first and foremost American, as "there isn't any kid who
hasn't said at some time, 'I wish I were Wild Bill Hicock.'"[13]
Wayne compared Westerns with "the same raw material Homer
used," dealing "in life and sudden death and primitive struggle, and with basic emotions, love, hate, anger."[14] The
strong appeal of Westerns, according to the star, derived
from their stress on healthy life: Westerners "hated healthily,
laughed healthily, and loved healthily."[15] Wayne believed
that the stories of the West were "the best vehicles for the
motion-picture medium," which for him was "a vehicle for
action," as "there is always high excitement in the movement
of a man on a horse."[16] He described the cowboy as "a
person who is always direct, no nuances," which fitted perfectly the image he wanted to project: "I am not a man of
words and nuances. I relish action, which is an essential
part of motion pictures."[17]

Wayne was deeply disturbed by "snobbish" critics,
such as Dwight MacDonald, who dismissed Westerns as an
"infantile" genre.[18] "Don't ever make the mistake of looking down your nose at Westerns," said Wayne, "They're
art--the good ones, I mean."[19] He believed that the position of the genre was secure: "We'll have Western pictures
as long as there is world," for "the Old West has a fascina-
tion that will never die out," with each generation discover-
ing it for itself.[20] The great significance of Westerns
stemmed from their themes: "pictures set against the ma-
jesty of nature, man against nature, and man against man."
In addition to embodying important values, Wayne believed
that they would "never go out of style because they're the
greatest entertainment in the world."[21] He vowed to "keep
making them until I stop acting," which he did; his very
last picture, The Shootist, was a Western.

Wayne felt the need to defend the genre because of
its low prestige among sophisticated critics. No other
genre has aroused such controversies about its worth,
cinematic and otherwise, than the Western. In the 1930s
many critics dismissed them as mindless, denigrating them

with such labels as "horse operas" and "sage brushers."
Others tended to lump all Westerns together, disregarding
their individual nuances and styles and failing to recognize
even the outstanding ones. This tendency, to treat all Westerns alike, has been a recurrent problem in film criticism,
especially in the 1940s and 1950s. Wayne's Westerns were no
exception; they too were victims of the critics' biases against
the genre as a whole.

The low regard for Westerns prevailed not only among
critics but also in the movie industry itself. For many years,
the industry had two popularity polls, one for the Top Ten
Western Stars and one for the Top Ten Box-Office Stars, as
if the two were different or separate categories. The Academy of Motion Picture Arts and Sciences has always served
as a barometer of dominant views and tastes within Hollywood. The consistent lack of appreciation for Westerns has
been reflected in their underrepresentation in the annual
contests for the Best Picture award. In the Academy's 58-
year history, only one Western (1.7 percent of all winners),
the epic Cimarron (1930-31) has won Best Picture and only
7 (2.4 percent) have been nominated: In Old Arizona,
Stagecoach, The Ox-Bow Incident, High Noon, Shane, How
the West Was Won, and Butch Cassidy and the Sundance
Kid.[22]

No filmmaker has ever won the Best Director Oscar
for a Western. John Ford, the master of Westerns, was
nominated five times for his directorial achievements, but
only once for a Western, Stagecoach. Significantly, Ford's
prestige in Hollywood and four Oscars were for other genres: The Informer, The Grapes of Wrath, How Green Was
My Valley, and The Quiet Man. "I don't think a lot about
honors," Ford is reported to have said disappointedly, "but
I think it is demeaning to the Westerns that I have received
honors for other films and none for my Westerns."[23] Howard
Hawks, another distinguished director who excelled in Westerns (Red River, Rio Bravo), was never nominated for an
Oscar, and his only directorial nomination was for a sentimental flagwaver, the war movie Sergeant York.

Very few players have won or have been nominated
for an Oscar award for a role in a Western. This paucity
of awards did not derive from lack of distinguished performances, but from the industry's underestimation of the

genre. Actors who excelled in Westerns, most notably Jimmy
Stewart, Henry Fonda, Kirk Douglas, and Burt Lancaster,
have never been nominated for a Western role. The Western
began to receive its long overdue recognition only when it
took itself less seriously. Thus, Lee Marvin won the 1965
Best Actor Award for a Western spoof, Cat Ballou, a self-
conscious parody in which he plays a dual role: a drunk,
has-been gunfighter and a deadly killer with a silver nose.
And Wayne won his 1969 Oscar for True Grit, in which he
poked fun at his own image as an old, fat, one-eyed,
whiskey-sodden marshal. The immensely popular success
of Mel Brooks's Blazing Saddles, a wild Western parody,
using every cliché of the genre, also attested to this trend.

But despite low status, Westerns have served important
functions in the film industry. For one thing, they supplied
effective training ground for many inexperienced directors
and actors. Almost every American director or actor has
made a Western at one time or another in his career. Every
decade saw the introduction of new filmmakers into the genre, which had the cumulative effect of enriching its content
and form. John Ford and James Cruze were at the front
rank of Western directors in the 1920s: Ford directed the
silent classic The Iron Horse (1924) and Cruze The Covered
Wagon (1926). Other notable directors, Victor Fleming, Allan
Dwan, William Wellman, and even William Wyler, served their
apprenticeships making Westerns. Showman Cecil B. DeMille
contributed to the genre in the 1930s with a series of epics,
such as The Plainsman (1936), starring Gary Cooper and
Jean Arthur, and Union Pacific (1939), with Barbara Stanwyck and Joel McCrea. Howard Hawks's first Western, Red
River, was so critically acclaimed that he continued making
them for the rest of his career. Other directors, by contrast, made a one-time foray into the genre, such as Fred
Zinnemann's High Noon (1952) and George Stevens's Shane
(1953), two all-time classics.

Actors have always held high regard for Westerns because they provided rich roles which, among other things,
did not require handsome looks. Playing cowboys was not
only a challenge, but an integral element of their role definition as American actors. "No actor I know would turn down
a good role in a Western," Kirk Douglas said, describing the
cowboy as "the cult idol around whom the whole form of worship revolves."[24] Burt Lancaster also believed that the

Western was probably the most fulfilling and cinematic of
experiences, because it required little verbalization and its
simple style provided opportunity for drawing modern parallels. Jimmy Stewart pointed to the genre's originality as the
basis of its long-enduring appeal, with Americans feeling
"this is ours."

What accounted for the continuous popularity of Westerns among mass audiences was their great adaptability.
Westerns have benefited from each technological innovation:
the advent of sound in the late 1920s, the use of color in
the 1940s, the various wide-screen processes in the 1950s.
The Western has been most flexible in terms of subject matter, theme, and form, ranging from musical Western, to serious psychological dramas, to comedies, to "darker" visions
of the West, using the stylistics of film noir. The Western
has become so varied in subject matter and style that it is
difficult to define its distinctive features. Every definition
of the genre subsequently appears to be confining, exclud-
ing many classic works. Critic Canby, attempting to resolve
these definitional problems, suggested that "if the film has
horses and it is set in the American West, usually between
1850 and 1913, then it's a Western, whether it was actually
shot in Spain (like some of Sergio Leone's nihilistic tales),
or whether it's funny, like Mel Brooks's Blazing Saddles."[25]

Ironically, the Western has been taken much more
seriously outside of the United States, especially in Europe,
where it is considered an exotic art form. In France, the
Western has been a most respected genre, with intellectual
critics regarding it as both an original and significant cinematic form. The distinguished French critic André Bazin
pointed out that "without the cinema, the conquest of the
West would have made of the 'Western stories' but one minor
literature," and that the cinema was "the only language capable ... of giving it the true aesthetic dimension."[26] Other
critics have treated the Western as national myth, comparable
to the Robin Hood legend in England, the Greek Odyssey,
and the Japanese Samurai. The noted German director Fritz
Lang believed that the Western is to America what the Wag-
nerian legends of the Niebelungen saga is to Germany.
Italian critic Castello observed that "the Western is a common patrimony because among all themes it is perhaps, in
its primitiveness, the most universal one," attesting to the
genre's twofold characteristics, at once uniquely American
and universal.[27]

Wayne's Westerns in Perspective

Wayne made at least nine Westerns that rank among
the best in the genre, of which four were directed by Ford
(Stagecoach, Fort Apache, She Wore a Yellow Ribbon, and
The Searchers) and two by Hawks (Red River and Rio Bravo).
His other distinguished Westerns were made by John Farrow
(Hondo), Henry Hathaway (True Grit), and Don Siegel (The
Shootist). To dismiss these Westerns is to dismiss the en-
tire genre, which some critics still do.

The diversity of Wayne's Westerns is quite striking,
including historical ones, such as Raoul Walsh's Dark Command, set in pre-Civil War Kansas and portraying the rise
to power of a Texan cowboy from a traveling companion of
a dentist to the community's marshal. Another historical
Western was Ford's The Horse Soldiers, set in 1863 during
the Civil War when the Union cavalry, led by Wayne, raided
the South. But he also made symbolic Westerns, such
as Ford's Three Godfathers, a Christian parable about the
sacrifice and redemption of three outlaws headed by Wayne.
Lady Takes a Chance was a naive Western comedy, at whose
center was the romance between Wayne's rodeo performer
and Jean Arthur's city girl. In the 1950s, in tune with the
current fashion, Wayne made a psychological Western, The
Searchers, which stressed character development rather
than action. In the 1960s he appeared in a number of
Western comedies, most notably Henry Hathaway's North to
Alaska and Andrew McLaglen's McLintock! In short, almost
every type of Western is represented in Wayne's versatile
gallery.

Equally important to the understanding of Wayne's
film oeuvre is the kinds of Westerns he avoided making and
his motives for not making them. Wayne's heroes tended to
be uncomplicated and antiintellectual, which meant that the
two trends of the postwar Westerns were missing from his
work. One trend was to depict the Westerner as more complicated, neurotic, and even disturbed character. For example, in Raoul Walsh's Pursued (1947), which used the
style of film noir, the protagonist (Robert Mitchum) is a
revenge-seeking cowboy who, as a child, had witnessed the
murder of his parents. Replete the Freudian psychology,
it is a glum picture about the tension between the cowboy
and his adoptive family--though all conflicts are resolved in
a happy ending. In Anthony Mann's The Furies (1950),

another psychologistic Western with heavy-handed Freudian
undercurrents, the narrative examines the neuroses of a
Southern family, particularly the relationship between a
patriarchal rancher (Walter Huston) and his tempestuous
daughter (Barbara Stanwyck), insanely jealous of her
father's new wife.

The other postwar trend was to stress the protagonists' sex appeal and to make Westerns more erotic. Howard
Hughes's The Outlaw, made in 1943 and released seven years
later because of a dispute with Hollywood's censorship, was
advertised as the film which brought sex to the West. It
shows more interest in Jane Russell's looks and bosom than
in the story of Billy the Kid and Doc Holliday. But despite
a shorter and more modest version than the one planned,
The Outlaw turned out to be a box-office bonanza. So was
King Vidor's Duel in the Sun (1946), possibly the most commercial Western ever made, exploiting the romances of a
half-breed girl (Jennifer Jones) with two brothers (Gregory
Peck and Joseph Cotten). The film is highly enjoyable as
camp, particularly its ridiculous final scene, a shoot-up between Peck and Jones, dying in each other's arms while kissing! Wayne objected to both the Freudian and overly erotic
Westerns and continued to play his simple, good-natured
heroes.

Wayne did not make many adult, psychological Westerns,
which enjoyed prestige and popularity in the 1950s, following
the success of Henry King's The Gunfighter and Fred Zinnemann's High Noon. This subgenre was concerned with the
psychology of the characters--their inner conflicts and moral
dilemmas. Wayne's motto, "I am not a man of words and
nuances," summed up his objection to this kind of Western.
He supported the Westerns shown on television for populariz-
ing the form, bringing them home and free to all, but had
serious reservations about their approach. For his taste,
they stressed too much "psychological insights," portraying
cowboys who were "introverted and over sensitive." "The
real cowboy," according to the star, "had fun and was lusty," but "didn't have mental problems." Wayne also charged
that television Westerns were "getting away from the simplicity and the fact that these men were fighting the elements of
nature and didn't have time for this couch-work."[28] In the
real West, men acted, for better and for worse, and did not
have time to ponder, debate, and subject their souls to

self-examination, as Gary Cooper does in High Noon, for
example.

The two new and most important directors of Westerns
in the 1950s were Anthony Mann and Bud Boetticher. Mann
directed eleven Westerns in this decade, most of which
starred Jimmy Stewart. His Westerns were psychological, violent, and marked by a visual style that was at once spectacular and austere. In The Naked Spur (1952), one of his
best Westerns, with an all-star cast (Stewart, Janet Leigh,
and Robert Ryan) and a taut screenplay (nominated for an
Oscar), all the characters are motivated by greed. Stewart
is cast as Howard Kemp, interested in capturing an escaped
killer (Ryan) for the money prize it offers, which he needs
to regain the land he had lost while fighting in the Civil
War. Despite excellent direction, photography, and performances, the film was too raw and brutal to the tastes of
many, including Wayne.

Boetticher, like Mann, was actually "discovered" by
the French critics before gaining prestige in the United
States. His most impressive Westerns, made in the late
1950s, were actually the creative efforts of a team, consisting of producer Harry Joe Brown, writer Burt Kennedy,
and star Randolph Scott. Despite the fact that some were
produced by Wayne's company, they differed from the latter's work. In a typical Boetticher Western (Seven Men
from Now, The Tall T), the hero is a loner, at odds with
society and bent on revenge, usually after his wife is killed.
His suspenseful Westerns can be read as allegorical dramas
in which the hero has to deal with treachery and moral
vacuum.

Following the traditions of both Mann and Boetticher,
Sam Peckinpah became the ultimate Western director in the
1960s, with two landmarks: Ride the High Country (1962)
and The Wild Bunch (1969). Peckinpah's premise was that
"the western is a universal frame within which it is possible
to comment on today."[29] His best work is endowed with a
strong personal vision of America, extremely graphic portrayal of violence, preoccupation with the omnipresence of
danger, and ambivalent morality. In Ride the High Country
--distinguished by Lucien Ballard's stunning cinematography
--two aging, retiring lawmen (Joel McCrea and Randolph
Scott) are transporting gold from a mining camp, in the

course of which a conflict arises when Scott attempts to
cheat his mate. The typical Peckinpah hero stands in sharp
contrast to Wayne's, being both more complex and uncertain
about his identity and moral position. The Wild Bunch, condemned by Wayne and many others for its "aesthetics of violence," particularly the use of slow motion and excessive
graphic details, is arguably the most important and controversial Western of the decade. And though insisting that it
is a simple story about what happens to killers interfering
in Mexico's internal politics, many critics still see it as a
cynical allegory about the American involvement in Vietnam.

The Peckinpah Westerns, with their strong emphasis
on violence and their moral ambiguity, coexisted with Wayne's
traditional, family-like films. But the popular television Westerns of the 1960s were also foreign to Wayne in their stress
on character analysis and extensive use of close-ups. Numerous offers to appear in Western television series were rejected by the star, who always favored the big screen.
Wayne did not like John Huston's The Misfits, based on a
screenplay by Arthur Miller for Marilyn Monroe, because its
hero, played by Clark Gable, is a lazy and idle cowboy making his living rounding up horses to be processed into tinned
cat food. The other protagonist, played by Montgomery Clift,
was even more deplorable to him because he is a drunk,
mother-fixated and defense-ridden neurotic. And the protagonist of Martin Ritt's excellent Hud (Paul Newman) was
criticized for being immoral: a young, opportunist rancher
who lacked any respect or feelings for his family. Once
again, the rationale for rejecting these movies was twofold.
First, the idea that the pioneers of the "real" West were
busy fighting the elements and thus could not afford to engage in psychological and pseudointellectual discussions.
And second, his firm belief in the Western myth and its
heroes--in diametric opposition to Peckinpah's attempts to
debunk and demythologize them.

The new trends in Westerns, set by Mann, Boetticher,
and Peckinpah, coexisted in the 1950s and 1960s with the
old and traditional school of Ford (Two Rode Together, The
Man Who Shot Liberty Valance) and Hathaway, who directed
two of Wayne's better Westerns, The Sons of Katie Elder
and True Grit. Hathaway's Westerns were relatively simple,
with straightforward narratives based on action and unclut-
tered by psychological nuances. These two veterans had

their own followers in the 1960s, Andrew V. McLaglen and
Burt Kennedy, who started their careers working for Wayne.
McLaglen's Westerns were traditional and mediocre in both
content and form, but achieved some popularity due to their
star presence: Wayne in McLintock!, Stewart in Shenondoah.
And Kennedy adopted Wayne's philosophy of Westerns, hold-
ing that "in movies, you're selling big open space and rit-
ual," and that "close-ups aren't what made the West."[30]
His Westerns tended to be good-humored (Support Your
Local Sheriff) and old-fashioned in their values (The War
Wagon and The Train Robbers, both starring Wayne).

Wayne did not embrace the tendency of many directors
to use the Western as a vehicle for propagating social protest and political ideas, such as the plight of the Indian.
From the late 1960s on, there seemed to be a complete re-
versal in the attitude on the American screen toward the
Indian, who in the past had been almost universally portrayed as a "red menace" to white civilization. Arthur Penn's
Little Big Man (1970), starring Dustin Hoffman as a veteran
of the Old West who grows up in his adoptive Cheyenne family and keeps shuttling between white and Indian cultures,
was one of the first and most notable of its kind. Among
other things, this film was the first to cast an Indian actor,
Chief Dan George, in a major role, as Old Lodge Skin, Hoffman's father. But there were many others, like Ralph Nelson's Soldier Blue (1970), based on the novel Arrow in the
Sun, in which a white girl (Candice Bergen) becomes critical of American culture after being abducted and living with
the Cheyenne.

The Indians, who for decades had been portrayed as
wild savages, were seen in the 1970s as innocent victims of
the white establishment, represented by corrupt military and
political leaders. Ford's last, and one of his lesser Westerns,
Cheyenne Autumn (1964), also showed a different attitude
toward the Indians, portraying sympathetically their heroic
fight to return to their old home after having been forced
by the white man to a new reservation.

Another trend of the 1970s Westerns was to glamorize
outlaws and idealize antiestablishment figures, which was in
tune with the tumultuous spirit of this decade. It started
with George Roy Hill's popular Butch Cassidy and the Sundance Kid (1971), a comic, loosely based treatment of the

two legendary outlaws starring Paul Newman and Robert Redford. The celebration of anarchy and cynic heroes also
marked Robert Altman's beautifully photographed McCabe and
Mrs. Miller (1971), depicting the relationship between a small-
time gambler (Warren Beatty) and a frizzy-haired, opium-
smoking whore (Julie Christie). The film is replete with
contemporary allusions, with the team of Beatty and Christie
running a successful brothel in a little mining town until
they are defeated by big business. As mentioned, Wayne
did not believe in antiheroes and thus very seldom portrayed
outlaws or anarchic figures.

      The consistency of Wayne's brand of Westerns is all
the more amazing, considering the dramatic changes in Western films and American society during his lifetime. He was
extremely aware of the fact that he was the last traditional
hero in Hollywood and that there would not be another actor
after him to embody with such commitment the virtues of the
classic Western hero. The recurrent making of Wayne's kind
of Western for half a century resulted in the creation of a
subgenre, "The John Wayne Western," which basically meant
reaffirmation of society's mainstream, traditional values of law
and order.

      Critics and audiences also became aware of the Wayne
formula, as the Variety critic wrote after McLintock: "Most
of all it is a John Wayne Western, and that is a category not
to be underestimated, since Wayne is about the last thriving
exponent of a great tradition." "The last active member of
a select fraternity of larger-than-life Western film heroes,"
Variety elaborated, Wayne is "the only one consistently at
large in this natural environment--the wide open spaces."[31]
Wayne himself was conscious of the label: "Rio Lobo certainly wasn't any different from most of my Westerns. Nor
was Chisum, the one before that."[32] He believed, however,
that "there still seems to be a very hearty public appetite
for this kind of film--what writers call a typical John Wayne
Western,"[33] but regretted that the label was used "disparagingly" by the critics. True, critics were getting tired of
his Westerns, which they complained were becoming a distinct genre. Society changed and the film industry changed,
Wayne's detractors claimed, but not his movies. In the
1970s Wayne began to lose his long-standing grip on audiences. The formula of his pictures became too predictable,
his rugged independence too simplistic, and the cumulative

result of all that was that his appeal became not only tire-
some but dated too.

Still, in addition to a lifetime commitment to the Western
genre, his contribution was undeniable in other respects as
well. Rejecting the old model of screen cowboy, he helped
to create a tougher, more complex Westerner. In Tom Mix's
silent Westerns, the hero was a white-suited nice guy who
was not allowed to smoke or drink. Wayne challenged that
and his cowboys were heavy drinkers and heavy smokers.
He was also one of the first screen cowboys to wear black
hats, a custom which was usually reserved for the villains.
Moreover, he is credited with having broken the taboo
against a Westerner using anything but fists in a fight, insisting on using the same devices (and objects) the villains
used to supplement fist fights.

Most important of all was his contribution to the im-
provement of stunt work and the perfection of fighting techniques, lending them greater realism and credibility. He
gave total credit for what he knew to Yakima Canutt, the
distinguished stuntman who had served as his role model for
horsemanship, stunt riding, etc. Wayne worked extensively
on the barroom brawl techniques with director Robert Bradbury, Canutt, and other stuntmen, techniques which were
later used in other Westerns or action pictures. Wayne and
Canutt developed what is known as the "near-missing swings,"
with the fist smacks dubbed on the soundtrack, but looking
real when photographed from the right angle. It actually
became a fight choreography, meticulously rehearsed and
photographed. Wayne held that screen fights should be
prepared blow by blow, like a balletic staging. "Screen
fight," he explained, "was the opposite of a real fight,"
because the camera has to see everything and you have to
reach way back and sock out." By contrast, "in real fight,
you hit short and close."

Wayne's Westerns are notable for their superior stunt
work by the greatest specialists. The stunts in Stagecoach,
by Canutt and Wayne, were described as having the beauty
of a ballet filled with danger. Wayne's technical prowess
made him one of the most sought-after action stars, and
stuntmen regarded him as one of the three top horsemen in
Hollywood; Randolph Scott and Joel McCrae were the other
two. Professional boxer Sugar Ray Robinson once claimed

that Wayne was one of the greatest punchers and brawlers
in films. Wayne's advice to younger actors who wanted to
become screen cowboys was: "Learn to fight. Learn to hit
and learn to roll with a punch. Learn to handle your body
easily and smoothly. You have to make it look good. Above
all, it has to be convincing."[34]

   The stunts in his non-Westerns were also excellent.
Seven Sinners, a romantic adventure, begins with a fight,
over which the credits are shown, and builds steadily to a
stunning climax, "the wildest, most uproarious, spine-tingling,
free-for-all [six-minute] brawl." Involving many sailors and
waterfront thugs, this barroom brawl has become one of the
greatest acrobatic stunt fights ever put on film. It utilized
the services of over 30 top stuntmen and acrobats, employing every type of breakaway furniture, with stuntmen being
hurled over balconies, through windows, into mirrors, down
stairs, against walls, and through doors. It took ten days
to shoot this brawl, at the end of which the bar set was reportedly completely destroyed.[35] Wayne did most of his
stunts throughout the whole fight.

   Wayne believed that reel fights ought to be "a big
show" and they were. The grand-scale climactic fight between him and Randolph Scott in The Spoilers was, as one
critic commented, "a minor masterpiece of stunt action."[36]
One of the classic brawls in film history, this fight has also
been the best scene in previous versions of The Spoilers
(Tom Santschi and William Farnus in 1913, Milton Sills and
Noah Beery in 1923; and Gary Cooper and William Boyd in
1930). But Wayne's topped the former versions and also the
fifth one (in 1956) on all counts--not just the fight. In his,
the fight starts in Marlene Dietrich's boudoir, cascading
through a balcony to the floor of the ginnery, out to the
street, and finally winding up in the wagon-churned mud of
the road. "The sluggish match," one reviewer observed,
was "something that could be staged profitably at Madison
Square Garden. It is that spectacular."[37]

   The fight between Wayne and Victor McLaglen over
Maureen O'Hara's dowry in The Quiet Man is one of its
highlights and one of the longest film brawls. What makes
it especially interesting is its humor and the way it is filmed,
in perspective, as seen through the eyes of the villagers.
North to Alaska, an otherwise old-fashioned romantic

adventure, contains a wonderful sequence of a mass brawl,
staged in silent comedy style. And one of the funniest
scenes in McLintock! is a fight that ends with Wayne,
O'Hara, and many extras in the mud.

Beyond their visual excitement and fun, the brawls
in Wayne's films also serve an ideological function, reflecting
Wayne's real-life attitude. In a typical Wayne fight, as Canby observed, all issues are reduced to a size resolvable by
man-to-man combat.[38] The fights in his films are slick, but
with bare hands. By comparison, the brawls in Anthony
Mann's Westerns are much more intense and brutally violent.
Wayne's heroes are willing to fight and are good at it, but
they do not go out of their way to engage in them. In a
characteristic Wayne sequence, the brawl starts either before his arrival or without his initial participation. His
heroes like to take their time, first watching and assessing
the situation, then deciding whether and at what point to
mix--which provides them more control over the action.

Wayne's Westerns were full of action but usually not
excessively violent. "Fights with too much violence are
dull," claimed Wayne, insisting that the straight-shooting,
two-fisted violence in his movies have been "sort of tongue-
in-cheek." He described the violence in his films as "lusty
and a little humorous," based on his belief that "humor nulli-
fies violence."[39] His conservative taste deplored the increasing latitude given to violence (and sex) in Hollywood. In
the 1960s, he launched a campaign against what he termed
"Hollywood's bloodstream polluted with perversion, and immoral and amoral nuances."[40] Most of his Westerns steered
clear of graphic violence--with a few exceptions. One such
was Rio Bravo, in which he hit his opponent Joe Burdette
with a rifle in his face, while assuring his mate, "aw, I'm
not gonna hurt him." Another exception was The Man Who
Shot Liberty Valance, in which he uncharacteristically kicks
Floyd in the face.

In the 1970s Wayne felt his movies should keep up
with changing norms of depicting violence on the American
screen. Arthur Penn's Bonnie and Clyde and Peckinpah's
The Wild Bunch, not to mention the "spaghetti" Westerns of
Sergio Leone, used new techniques to depict human slaughter
--slow motion and excessive blood. These and other movies
changed drastically the conventions of screen violence despite

protests, in and outside the industry. The violence in Rio
Lobo, for example, was both more graphic and brutal than
in the previous Hawks-Wayne Westerns. First, sheriff
Hendricks (Mike Henry) shoots himself accidentally in the
face, and Wayne's fight with one of Whitey's henchmen
(George Plimpton) is crueler than the usual, though far
from matching Peckinpah's standards.

The controversy over Wayne's Westerns increased after
the release of Big Jake and The Cowboys, both of which attested to the deterioration in the depiction of cinematic violence. The Cowboys was panned by some critics for its
graphic portrayal of violence aroused in the young cowboys
as they seek revenge.[41] And Pauline Kael dismissed the
movie on moral grounds, protesting Wayne's bad influence
on the youngsters and accusing him of turning them into
bloody avengers.[42] But the critics did not speak with one
voice and Sarris defended the star, noting that "he has
seldom played the classic role of the gunfighter in the
saloon shoot-out," nor "has he been noted for the phallic
frenzy of the fast draw." In his most murderous roles,
Sarris noted, Wayne used a rifle rather than a pistol. He
also claimed that when Paul Newman kicked an antagonist in
the groin in Butch Cassidy and the Sundance Kid or fired
on an enemy bearing a white truce flag in Hombre, the
critics were not shocked by his immoral and violent activities.[43]

Because The Cowboys was released after Stanley
Kubrick's A Clockwork Orange and Peckinpah's Straw Dogs,
some comparisons were inevitable. The Kubrick and Peckinpah movies were undoubtedly more graphic and brutal in
their violence than Wayne's pictures. Thus, Sarris pointed
out that it was one thing to favor Kubrick and Peckinpah on
aesthetic grounds--they were much better films--but another
to favor them on moral grounds. He addressed his comments
to Kael, who liked the Peckinpah movie, reminding her that
Wayne did not kill anybody in The Cowboys; he himself got
killed by a vicious villain. Sarris claimed that compared
with Warren Beatty (Bonnie and Clyde) and Dustin Hoffman
(Straw Dogs), Wayne (and Clint Eastwood in Dirty Harry)
"do not so much assert as confirm their virility by their
violent deeds." He also stated that in both Ford and Hawks's
Westerns, "violence serves as an impetus to social cohesion,"
an integrative force of a male group (in Hawks) or whole

community (in Ford) threatened by danger. What bothered
Sarris was not that the children in The Cowboys avenged
Wayne's death, but that their killing presumably left no mark
on them--or on the audience, for that matter--apparently due
to the movie's glossy and giddy treatment of violence. [44]

How did the American public respond to Wayne's Westerns and which ones enjoyed the widest appeal? He had no
reason to complain when it came to commercial appeal, for no
less than seven of his Westerns are among the top ten money-
makers of the years in which they were released: How the
West Was Won ranked second in 1962; Red River third in
1948; True Grit sixth in 1969; Rio Bravo ninth in 1959; The
Searchers, McLintock!, and Big Jake ranked tenth in 1956,
1963, and 1972 respectively.

Put in perspective (taking into account the inflation
factor), four of Wayne's Westerns are among the top 20
grossing Westerns of all time. How the West Was Won, the
first film to use Cinerama, was an epic but abortive attempt
to reconstruct the story of the West through interrelated
episodes of three generations. Using the talents of three
directors and an all-star cast, most in cameo roles, it occupies fifth position among the most commercial Westerns, grossing in rentals $12.2 million (equivalent to over $42 million at
present). Wayne is cast as General Sherman in the Civil
War episode, nostalgically directed by Ford. How the West
Was Won suffers from structural weaknesses: a contrived
plot and a diffuse screenplay based on numerous clichés.
But the public was intrigued by the stars and especially by
the novelty of Cinerama. It was unaccountably nominated
for eight Oscars, including Best Picture, winning three:
story and screenplay, editing, and sound.

Red River, the first Hawks-Wayne Western, ranks
ninth among the popular Westerns of all time, with $4.5
million in rentals (equivalent to over $30 million at present).
The two other Wayne films on this list are: True Grit,
which grossed in 1969 14.3 million (equivalent to $30 mil-
lion), and The Searchers, arguably Ford's most interesting
Western, grossing in 1956 $4.9 million (equivalent to over
$25 million at present).

None of the most commercially popular Westerns has
been a straightforward genre movie. The most widely-seen

Western of all time is King Vidor's <u>Duel in the Sun</u>, made by
producer David O. Selznick for his wife, Jennifer Jones, who,
with a tremendous publicity campaign, managed to win a Best
Actress nomination for an unimpressive performance. Its narrative is severely flawed, but with an all-star cast (Gregory
Peck, Joseph Cotten, and two great character actors, Lionel
Barrymore and Lillian Gish), a racial love theme, and most
important of all an emphasis on sex, it attracted large audiences. <u>Duel in the Sun</u> grossed $10 million in its initial re-
lease (equivalent to $70 million at present).

The second most popular Western is George Roy Hill's
<u>Butch Cassidy and the Sundance Kid</u>, nominated for Best Pic-
ture and six other Oscars, winning four: story and screenplay (William Goldman), cinematography (Conrad Hall), original music score (Burt Bacharach), and the highly melodic song
"Raindrops Keep Fallin' on My Head," which undoubtedly contributed to the film's appeal. Cashing in on Paul Newman's
popularity at its height, and making a household word of
Robert Redford, <u>Butch Cassidy and the Sundance Kid</u> is a
very untraditional Western, treating its two legendary outlaws in a comic, myth-like manner. The film had tremendous
appeal among young college audiences, and its casting of two
male stars as a sort of "romantic" team began a new trend in
Hollywood of celebrating male camaraderie and friendship,
with the sad result of almost no roles for female stars.

Mel Brooks's <u>Blazing Saddles</u> is the third most popular
Western, though some critics dismiss it as a nongenre film.
A zany comedy, it centers on the foiling of a crooked lawyer
by a black railroad worker and an alcoholic ex-gunfighter.
In its funniest sequence, the actors go to Grauman's Chinese
Theater in Hollywood to find out how the story ends. Cha-
otic and wild, it features Madeline Kahn in a hilarious performance as Lily von Shtupp, a conscious imitation of numerous cabaret singers played by Marlene Dietrich. <u>Blazing</u>
<u>Saddles</u> was the top money-maker of 1974, grossing in ren-
tals over $45 million.

In conclusion, because Wayne outlived his contemporaries, there is good reason to believe that no other actor
in American film will ever replace him in embodying the
myth of the Old West. At present, the only major star to
make Westerns, occasionally, is Clint Eastwood, but his
screen persona has not yet assumed Wayne's mythic quality.

Besides, Eastwood's Westerns, particularly those made after
his work with Sergio Leone and his television series Rawhide,
such as The Beguiled, High Plains Drifter, and most recently
Pale Rider, were not as popular with the public as his urban
crime pictures, beginning with Dirty Harry in 1971 and its
three sequels (Magnum Force, The Enforcer, and Sudden Impact). Audiences go to Eastwood's Westerns to see something
equivalent to "Dirty Harry in the Old West," not because
they are genuinely interested in his interpretation of the
West.

     One could make a good case, however, of the similarity
between Dirty Harry Callahan of the San Francisco Police
Force and the Westerners played by Wayne. This contemporary character is made of the same ingredients as Wayne's
screen creations: a man of action, obsessively committed to
a cause, an antisocial loner, and a hero who does not hesitate to choose illegitimate means if he thinks they will help
him battle the problem, usually crime. Eastwood's acting
style, not just his persona, is similar to Wayne and Cooper's,
though his range is considerably more limited than either.
Still one should credit Eastwood with creating a mythic folk
hero, who seems to respond, consciously or subconsciously,
to the right-wing fantasies of a large segment of the American public--a social and cinematic function fulfilled by
Wayne's Westerners for over three decades.

5. THE CREATION OF A POWERFUL
SCREEN IMAGE

Film is a collaborative art, the work of a creative team
of producer, screenwriter, director, actors, and technical crew.
However, not all team members are of equal power and importance. There have been different theories concerning the
question of which element is the most influential in shaping
the contents and form of motion pictures. According to the
auteur theory, which originated in France in the 1950s and
was propagated in the United States by Andrew Sarris, the
film's director is usually its auteur because the other production members are subsumed under his power and abide
by his notions. Thus, for the auteurists, the film oeuvre of
a particular director is both more important and revealing
than each of his individual films.[1] The auteurist critics
have been concerned with depicting thematic consistencies
and stylistic continuities in the works of major directors,
such as Hitchcock, Ford, and Hawks.

There have been different variants or emphases of
auteurism as an approach to film history. For example, in
contrast to those stressing the role of the director, others
have singled out the role of particular producers or screenwriters as auteurs.[2] The importance of players has been
underestimated by many auteurists, holding that their influence is usually limited because they are involved in just one
element of the filmmaking process--acting.[3] Some critics
claim that most stars have been studio creations, images
fabricated and manipulated by their studios' publicity machines, thus lacking control over their choice of screen
roles and, by implication, their careers. Richard Dyer's
(1982) work has been one of the few attempts to examine
the role of specific actors as auteurs, distinguishing among
those who controlled their images, those who contributed to
their images, those who were part of collective teams, and

those who had very little or no control over their careers.
However, even Dyer did not examine systematically how and
under what conditions stars have controlled or contributed
to their screen personae.

Some of the auteurists' notions can be extended and
applied to a small group of movie stars who were auteurs
because they--not their directors or producers--were the
primary source of influence over their screen images and
careers. Some of these stars became auteurs with the assistance of their studios (Clark Gable at MGM), others without any studio assistance (Cary Grant as a free-lance actor),
or even against their studios (Humphrey Bogart at Warners).
During the golden age of Hollywood, a small minority of
stars possessed, relatively speaking, more power than the
writers or producers of their pictures. At present, most of
the stars who are in control of their films, such as Clint
Eastwood, Jane Fonda, Goldie Hawn, and Barbra Streisand
have their own production companies to facilitate greater
control over their film products.

A defining characteristic of movie stardom is possessing a distinct screen image over a prolonged period of time
which, among other things, enables more intimate identification by mass audiences. A powerful screen persona is established when audiences bring to each new movie they see
memories of that star's previous movies, to the point where
each successive film supports the preceding one.[4] Many of
the great movie stars, Cagney, Gable, Crawford, Davis,
tended to play similar roles in similar narratives so that
they gradually developed consistent screen images. These
images were also powerful because they were based, to a
large extent, on their lives offscreen, with the cumulative
effect of audiences' inability to separate between their public and private personae.

The great movie stars function as cultural icons and
points of reference and stability in an otherwise changing
industry and society. As such, they stand in sharp opposition to players who display a wide range of abilities in diverse roles. The latter, the actors' actors, prefer to conceal, rather than reveal, their personalities by immersing
and submerging themselves as completely as possible in the
specific role they happen to be playing. Their screen assignments differ considerably from one film to another. Thus,

it is possible and makes sense to describe "a John Wayne movie" or "a Clark Gable movie," or to claim that Cary Grant tended "to play himself," but it is impossible to describe a "typical Laurence Olivier film" or to discern a consistent Robert Duvall, Dustin Hoffman, or Meryl Streep screen persona.

Wayne's career provides a unique case for examining the creation and maintenance of a powerful screen image for over half a century. Wayne has probably been the truest auteur of his films, as critic Andrew Sarris observed in 1971: "In this, the age of the director, there still are a few actors whose strong personalities can inform the mood, pacing, and structure of an entire film."[5] "Mr. Wayne's presence, physical as well as emotional," critic Vincent Canby concurred, "shaped his movies as much as the contributions of the writers, directors, producers, and cameramen."[6] Of all star-auteurs, Wayne was probably the only one to exercise such a degree of control over the construction and continuity of his image. A distinguishing feature of Wayne's work was his determination to carve his own career, which he did, from the 1940s on.

Wayne stands in sharp contrast to Gable or Taylor, who were the creations of MGM's publicity machine. Gable, for example, fully cooperated with his studio because he wanted to be a successful star and knew he could not achieve that without the studio's active sponsorship. He became a model of cooperation, never giving anybody trouble, always on time for photo sessions and always polite to the press. He accepted what the studio told him to do; his contract denied him choice of roles. "I just work here," he once said, "I try to work well and hard. It's my business to work, not to think."[7] Gable benefited from MGM's tight control because he was not a very good judge of his abilities--even when given the choice. He spent 23 of his 30-year career at MGM, which created a charming screen image for him and promoted his popularity through extensive exposure. Gable was even told how to lead his romantic life and spend his leisure time --and he listened. In 1955, however, he decided to become free lance, as was the fashion at the time, but none of the nine films he made until his death, with the exception of The Misfits, was superior in any way to his MGM formulaic movies. Gable realized that without the studio's machine, his career was not viable. Robert Taylor, another MGM product, also lacked control over his career. "I stayed with the studio for 24 years," he recalled, "did my work, took what they gave me to do." Much less ambitious and talented than either Gable or Wayne, Taylor summed up his career as "just a guy gifted with looks I had done nothing to earn, who fell into a career that I was never overly ambitious about."[8]

Bogart, by contrast, fought constantly with his employers at Warners for better scripts and better parts and, like Jimmy Cagney and Bette Davis, was suspended several times for refusing to abide by the studio's rule. In 1946, at the peak of his career as the screen's highest-paid actor, he signed a 15-year contract with Warners, which broke all precedents. Two years later, however, he formed his own company, Santana, releasing his movies through Columbia. But the six movies he produced, in four of which he starred, were for the most part undistinguished and unsuccessful at the box office. Bogart's experience as a free-lance actor and independent producer was unrewarding because he could not get the properties he wanted and also because he was not a very good judge of scripts suitable for him. His best work, in retrospect, was at Warners, despite the disagreements and suspensions.

Wayne's career resembled in some respects Cary Grant's, who started at Paramount in 1932, playing second fiddle to the studio's major star, Gary Cooper. But in 1937, after five years of routine pictures, except for the camp comedies opposite Mae West, he became Hollywood's first successful free-lance actor. Determined never again to sign exclusively with another studio, he became responsible for his own career, choosing most carefully screenplays and directors. Many of his films after 1937 were not only popular but classics of their kind, including The Awful Truth, Bringing Up Baby, and His Girl Friday. Wayne, like Grant, gave his best performances when he was on his own. Moreover, the distinctive screen image of both Grant and Wayne took shape after leaving their sponsors and home studios: Grant after Paramount, and Wayne after Republic.

Perhaps more than Grant, what made Wayne a unique actor-auteur was not only the coherence of his image, but also the fact that it completely blended with his personality offscreen --until the actor and the person became indistinguishable.

Wayne's work has gradually become a series of political statements and personal values, reiterated in film after film (see
chapter 13). His image was so consistent that audiences
knew what to expect of his pictures. Wayne "brings to each
new movie," claimed critic-director Peter Bogdanovich, "good
or bad, a resonance and a sense of the past--his own and
ours--that fills it with reverberations above and beyond his
own perhaps limited qualities," which "is the true measure of
what makes a great movie star."[9]

The Construction of an Image

The Wayne screen image did not emerge spontaneously;
it was built gradually and systematically. He himself admitted
it was a product of methodical creation: "When I started, I
knew I was no actor and I went to work on this Wayne thing.
It was as deliberate and studied a projection as you'll ever
see."[10] "I figured I needed a gimmick," he explained, "so
I dreamed up the drawl, the squint, and a way of moving
which meant to suggest that I wasn't looking for trouble,
but would just as soon throw a bottle at your head as not."
He took a risk, "it was a hit-or-miss project for a while,"
but gradually "it began to develop."[11]

Early in his career, he wanted to play a wide range of
roles, "a thief, a heavy, a clown," without limiting himself
to one type, thinking it was "terrible, playing the same kind
of guy all the time." But he got useful advice from Harry
Carey's wife. "Duke, take a look at Harry," she said.
"Would you want to see Harry any other way?" "You've
built a lot of friends who want to see you the way you are,"
she explained, "They pay money at the box office to prove
they like you that way. Don't try to change." Wayne
adopted her suggestion: "You have to become the image of
the character in the film. If you fool them or try to be
cute, you won't be the man they came to see." It was "a
fine advice at a time when I was just starting to get ahead,"
and it also convinced him, once and for all, to listen to his
own "gut feeling."[12]

The first step in constructing his image was getting a
screen name. His real name was Marion Michael Morrison
and in his early movies he was billed as Michael Burn or
Duke Morrison. Winfield Sheehan, then head of Fox, thought

that Morrison "sounds like a circuit preacher," and had "no
impact." Consequently, he and director Walsh started to
scribble names on paper. "My mind opened the history books
and real names of American pioneers," Walsh recalled. "From
them I got involved with the Revolution and came up with a
name I had always liked. When I told Sheehan, he looked up
and smirked as though he had thought of it. The name was
John Wayne."[13] Walsh believed it was the name of an American General of the Revolution, but according to other sources
it was taken from a Fox Western, in which the hero's name
was John Wayne.

Significantly, both Sheehan and Walsh considered Marion
Morrison to be a girl's name, thus far too effeminate for a
cowboy star. Defending his name, Wayne said, "taught me
to fight at an early age." In addition, what worked against
his real name was that "Duke Morrison didn't have enough
prestige" and "didn't sound American enough for them." By
contrast, the screen name chosen for him helped to particu-
larize his public image, suggesting both personality and national traits: it was genuinely American, masculine and easy
enough for audiences to remember." It was also one of the
few things Wayne "didn't have any say in," though he
thought "it was a great name," being "short and strong and
to the point."[14] Wayne continued to be sensitive to his
birth name throughout his career. At the suggestion of a
British reporter that Marion was a girl's name in England,
Wayne gave a sly look, grinned, and said slowly, in his
manner, "but in America it belongs to a man. It's a family name."[15]

Wayne's screen image, like that of other stars, took
form by trial and error, testing and retesting various ideas.
It is hard to believe today that Monogram attempted to make
a singing cowboy out of Wayne by creating the character of
"Singin' Sandy" Saunders. There were songs in some early
Westerns, but the novelty of Monogram was in creating a
distinct Western character who sang. Wayne was the first
singing cowboy in Riders of Destiny (1933), before Gene
Autry and Roy Rogers made successful careers out of this
concept. One major problem was that Wayne could not sing;
he had a limited baritone. At first, he just mouthed the
words while others, like Smith Bellow, sang. Another problem was Wayne's inability to play the guitar. Nevertheless,
he "sang" in The Man from Utah (1934) and in Westward Ho!

(1935); two songs were sung by a cowboy group and a third dubbed by Wayne. Wayne courts Sheila Manners, in the latter picture, while singing romantically "The Girl I Loved Long Ago."

But Wayne could not tolerate the idea of playing a character "who always sang when he got mad." He recalled in later years: "The fact that I couldn't sing--or play the guitar--became terribly embarrassing to me, especially on personal appearances. Every time I made a public appearance, the kids insisted that I sing 'Desert Song' or something." He finally went to the head of the studio and said, "Screw this, I can't handle it," and quit musical Westerns once and for all.[16]

Wayne was replaced as singing cowboy by Gene Autry, who first gained fame as a radio singer, then went on to become the most popular singing Western star. Autry writes humorously in his autobiography that two factors weighed against Wayne's rise as a singing cowboy, "other than the obvious one of finding a leading lady who wouldn't crack up."[17] First, his songs were dubbed by other singers and in those days the quality of lip synch was not very good. And second, the embarrassment he experienced in public tours, when his fans asked him to sing. But Wayne teased Autry about it: "I caught one of my old Singin' Sandy on TV, you know, it wasn't as bad as I thought." And, "If I'd kept on singing, and worked at it, you wouldn't have stood a chance," to which Autry replied, "It wasn't my singing that put me over, it was my acting."[18] The truth is that Wayne never liked the idea of musical Westerns; it somehow did not fit his image of the Old West. Thus, when asked to describe the difference between his Davy Crockett (in The Alamo) and the one played by Fess Parker, he was delighted to provide a quick answer, "I can't sing."[19]

The Distinctive Wayne Persona

The distinctive Wayne screen persona can be described in terms of specific basic elements, the most important of which were: a forceful screen presence, physical and moral strength, virility, honesty and sincerity, the portrayal of distinctly American heroes, and indestructibility. The Wayne screen hero was, as mentioned, inner-directed, charismatic, and independent. Wayne's characters were often lonely, in conflict with their marital and familial duties. But the single most important element of his persona was serving as a role model for soldiers, cowboys, and children--teaching them skills, a code of ethics, and a way of life.

Wayne's physical presence was probably his strongest asset and something he had always possessed--even before he developed as an actor. Louise Brooks, the beautiful silent star, recalled meeting Wayne on the set of an unmemorable Western, Overland Stage Raiders, one of her last screen appearances. On the first day of shooting, she observed two figures: "one was a cherub, five feet tall, carrying a bound script; the other a cowboy, six feet four inches tall, wearing a lovely smile. The cherub was director George Sherman; the star, Wayne." "Looking up at him," she thought, "this is no actor but the hero of all mythology, miraculously brought to life."[20]

Wayne was a giant of a man, rising to 6'4" and weighing well over 220 pounds at the peak of his career. He was so big, he tended to overshadow those around him. Everything he did on screen--talking, swearing, fighting-- was with full force and gusto. Wayne's bigness became central to his image in both real and symbolic ways. His pictures abounded with references to his size: he played the title roles in Big Jim McLain and Big Jake, for example. Even his enemies--real or fictional--were described as big, to stress his strength in conquering them. Wayne himself referred to his 1964 successful bout with cancer as "The Big C," thus coining one of his most quoted lines, "I licked the Big C." Audiences and critics also described him in terms of size or force. Numerous reviews of his pictures were entitled, "Wayne is bigger than the film," or "The Big Duke does it again." In addition to size, Wayne's physical presence was endowed with steely gray-blue eyes, a cold cynical look, and an ironic (lopsided) grin. His voice, incisive and curled at the edges, was particularly effective in expressing two somewhat contradictory feelings: contempt and emotion (in romantic scenes).[21]

One of his most distinctive trademarks was his walk, which he learned from Yakima Canutt. It was a slow, though sure, walk, sort of a shuffle with the cutting in of the hands across the body. Many actors tried to imitate it, but as Dean

Martin observed, "nobody walks like John Wayne."[22] "He's
so big, most people don't realize how graceful he is," said
Hawks. "He's as light on his foot as a dancer."[23] And
Edward Dmytryk, who directed him in Back to Bataan, reported that Wayne threw his huge body "like a lightweight
gymnast."[24] Katharine Hepburn described Wayne as a man
"with great legs and tight buttocks, a real great seat, and
small sensitive feet." "He carries his huge frame lightly,
like a feather," she remarked, and his walk was "very fine,
light."[25]

At the suggestion that his walk was sexy, Wayne sim-
mered, "God, I get hot when they say I wiggled my rear
and all that stuff." But when challenged by Playboy as to
whether sexuality was still part of his magnetism, he conceded, "Well, at one time in my career, I guess sexuality
was part of my appeal." As for later (1970s), "I'm 63 years
old now, how the hell do I know whether I still convey that."
"All that crap comes from the way I walk," Wayne once explained, "there's evidently a virility in it, otherwise why do
you keep mentioning it?" He denied, however, he was "conscious of my particular walk," though agreed that "I must
walk different from other people, but I haven't gone to any
school to learn how."[26]

Wayne's presence projected tremendous strength, physical as well as moral. President Reagan claimed that everything about Wayne, "his stature, his style, his convictions--
conveyed enduring strength."[27] And Katharine Hepburn recalled that during the shooting of Rooster Cogburn she
leaned against him as often as possible, even when the
script did not call for it, because "it was like leaning
against a strong tree."[28]

The names of screen characters sometimes suggest
personality traits. The names of Wayne's protagonists often
signified physical strength. For example, his hero's name
was Rocklin in Tall in the Saddle, Robert Marmaduke Hightower in Three Godfathers, Wilder in Blood Alley, Jack
Cutter in The Comancheros, and Captain Rockwell in In
Harm's Way. At times, his screen name implied more than
just physical force. In McLintock! his hero's name was
George Washington McLintock, and in both McLintock! and
Big Jake he played a respected citizen with towns named
after him.

His image glorified virility; fans admired him for being a man's man: "It is not enough for an actor to look the part and say his lines well," John Ford said of Wayne, "something else has to come across to audiences, something which no director can instill or create: the quality of being a real man."[29] Wayne himself believed that "I'm the stuff that men are made of." His roles varied, but their most common link was virility; whether he played a soldier or a cowboy, he was always the two-fisted, iron-willed man.

Honesty and sincerity were the key to his roles and the most consistent traits of his persona. In his early career, it was a youthful sincerity, playing likable heroes who were awkward but genuine. The tone of his voice and his open-mouthed grin indicated naiveté, with a manner that was gauche but charming. His heroes refused to lie. When they gave their word, even to Indians, it was as committing and abiding as law. They were genuinely committed to the truth, as he told Geraldine Page in Hondo: "Truth is a measure of a man." Ben Johnson, a colleague in several Westerns, described Wayne as real and profoundly honest. "If he tells you tomorrow's Christmas," Johnson said, "you can get your sock ready. He was that kind of person."[30]

Perhaps most important of all was Wayne's portrayal of genuinely American heroes. His entire work can be described as the glorification of the American hero and the perpetuation of American ideals. For many, he symbolized the essence of the American soul, described once by D.H. Lawrence as hard, isolate, stoic, and a killer. Wayne embodied the rugged virtues of America, both its toughness and ruggedness. Critic Joan Mellen regards Wayne as the symbol of the American frontier, being masculine, repressed, celibate, and brutalized.[31] In his best roles he epitomized the national virtues of rugged individualism and that pioneer heritage that right and justice must always triumph over evil.

Only a few movie stars have been described as great American heroes, most notably Gary Cooper, Henry Fonda, and James Stewart. Bob Hope and Bing Crosby have also been genuinely American figures but in different ways. As comedians or singers, they lacked definite screen personae that were associated with American values. Interestingly, none of the popular female stars, such as Joan Crawford, Bette Davis, or Doris Day, were regarded as distinctly

American heroines on the level that Wayne, Stewart, and
Cooper were. It seems that Americanism and patriotism have
been linked more intimately with male than female stars which,
if true, provides a revealing commentary on the differing attributes American culture has used in describing men and
women.

The social backgrounds of Wayne, Cooper, Fonda, and
Stewart were most appropriate to the legends they created.
They were all born and reared in small towns: Wayne in
Winterset, Iowa; Cooper in Helena, Montana; Fonda in Grand
Island, Nebraska; and Stewart in Indiana, Pennsylvania.
Small towns have been important in American culture, especially during the Depression, when these actors became
popular, because of the strong belief in the virtues of rural
life. At the center of the myth of small-town America, as
critic Kerbel pointed out, was the heroic, self-reliant farmer, the mainstay of America until industrialization--and to
a lesser degree afterwards. The farmer embodied the Puri-
tan ethos of honesty, hard work, and decent righteous living.[32] During the Depression, there was a short-lived return to the ideals of a simple rural life and the farmer became again a popular folk hero. This is probably the reason why Will Rogers was the most popular star from 1932 to
1935, when he died in an air crash: Roger symbolized the
"homespun philosopher" and "ambassador" of rural Americana
and common folk.

Fonda became the screen personification of the farmer-
pioneer with his screen debut, The Farmer Takes a Wife, in
1935, a romantic drama set in the 1920s, in which he plays
a farmer whose sole wish is to work the land and live peace-
fully with his wife. Later, Fonda played a fighting pioneer
in the pre-Independence era in Ford's Drums Along the Mohawk, and a farmer fighting social injustice in the powerful
film version of Steinbeck's The Grapes of Wrath, arguably
his strongest screen performance. Fonda continued to symbolize the ordinary American in Mister Roberts, and
fought for basic American ideals, such as trial by a fair,
democratic jury in Sidney Lumet's Twelve Angry Men.

If Fonda epitomized farmers, Stewart was best when
cast as a small-town lawyer, establishing himself as another
all-American hero in his pictures with Frank Capra, the director of "the American Dream." He usually played small-

town people who found pleasure and fulfillment in unglamor-
ous, ordinary existence. His Jefferson Smith in Capra's Mr.
Smith Goes to Washington is a naive Wisconsin senator committed to fighting graft and corruption. And his young
sheriff in Destry Rides Again, Thomas Jefferson Destry
(note the similarity in his protagonists' names), looks soft
and easy-going, but is actually hard as nails when he has
to fight. In Capra's ultimate American movie, It's a Wonderful Life, their first collaboration after a lengthy military
service, Stewart is cast as the simple but honest George
Bailey who, all his life, has been dreaming of breaking away
from his small town and doing "big things," only to realize
how meaningful that simple life is to him.

Capra also contributed to Cooper's image as spokesman
for ordinary people and ordinary life. In Mr. Deeds Goes to
Town, his Longfellow Deeds is a tuba-playing country boy
who finds himself fighting the big-city crooks and swindlers.
And in Meet John Doe, Cooper starts as a desperate ex-bush
league pitcher, but ends up fighting a Fascist publisher and
a corrupt political system.

Biographical pictures, in which Cooper and Stewart
played distinctly American, real-life heroes, also featured
prominently in their careers. No matter what figure they
portrayed, historical or contemporary, they always stood
for basic American values: simplicity, humility, honesty,
integrity, and courage. Of the many biographical roles
Cooper played, two stood out: Alvin York, the World War I
hero in Sergeant York, for which he won his first Oscar,
and Lou Gehrig, the admired baseball player, who died pre-
maturely, for which he received an Oscar nomination. And
Jimmy Stewart excelled in The Stratton Story, as the baseball hero who continued to play with an artificial leg, and in
The Glenn Miller Story, as America's most popular band
leader who died in an air crash in World War II; in both
movies he was cast opposite June Allyson, who played his
wife in idyllic marriages.

Compared with these two stars, Wayne played fewer
real-life heroes, and biopictures, as a genre, featured less
prominently in his oeuvre. Furthermore, these movies were
made rather late in his career and subsequently did not affect his image in the same way that they had affected Stewart's or Cooper's careers. For example, Wayne was cast as

Navy aviation commander Frank ("Spig") Wead, who became
a successful Hollywood screenwriter, following an injury, in
Ford's The Wings of Eagles. And his portrayal of Townsend
Harris, the first American ambassador to Japan, in John
Huston's The Barbarian and the Geisha, was even less successful (see chapter 8). Wayne took great pride, however,
in his characterization of Colonel Benjamin Vandervoort in
The Longest Day, and, of course, as Davy Crockett, Texas's
heroic fighter in The Alamo. Nonetheless, all things considered, Wayne built his reputation as a uniquely American hero
by playing mythic fictional Westerners, not real-life figures.

A Consistent Image

The extraordinary coherence of Wayne's screen image
over such a prolonged period of time is attributable to the
great control he exercised over his career. Wayne used
several means to obtain and maintain such control, the most
important and obvious of which was to produce his own movies. He preferred to be the producer of his pictures because
it provided him overall supervision that could not be achieved
otherwise. The first film in which he was both star and producer was Angel and the Badman (1947), a black and white
Western written and directed by James E. Grant. Its production values were high and Wayne's meticulous attention to
detail was noteworthy; another distinguished aspect was Archie Stout's cinematography. He went on to produce other
movies for Republic, such as The Fighting Kentuckian (1949),
one of his more obscure and forgettable Westerns, in which
he cast himself as a farmer fighting greedy land barons.

Working as a producer-star was such a gratifying experience that in 1952 he established the Wayne-Fellows Productions with Robert Fellows, a veteran producer. This
company was responsible for a series of films directed by
William Wellman and highly profitable at the box office. One
of the first was Island in the Sky (1953), a tale of survival
of a transport plane's crew, headed by Wayne, after a forced
landing. Another was the blockbuster The High and the
Mighty (1954), a forerunner of the "disaster" movies, which
became very popular in the 1970s. Similar in plot to that of
Airport (and its sequels), it is "grand hotel in the air,"
with a diverse group of passengers, each with a personal
problem, in the face of a crash landing. Both Island in the

Sky and The High and the Mighty were based on Ernest K.
Gann's books, and the latter was so popular with audiences that the Academy of Motion Pictures also gave it its
nod with four Oscar nominations, winning an award for
Dmitri Tiomkin's melodic music.

Because Wayne considered himself a valuable property,
he felt he should "protect that investment"[33] as much as possible and make movies that suited his political values. And
the best way to do it was to found his own production company, Batjac, and be its sole boss. Batjac was from the
beginning an intimate family operation, employing family members and close friends. His older brother, Robert Emmet
Morrison, served as production executive, and, in the 1960s,
Michael, his eldest son, took over the company's management.
Batjac produced Wayne's most personal and ambitious pictures,
three of which were highly propagandistic: The Alamo,
McLintock! and The Green Berets (see chapter 13). It is
unlikely that these movies would have been produced by
other studios, particularly The Green Berets, which was
highly controversial.

Wayne's repeated work with the same directors and
screenwriters also accounted for the amazing continuity in
his screen image. He worked, of course, with various writers, though only a few were important in establishing his
screen persona. Their screenplays were tailor-made to his
ideological specifications, but they were also written in terms
of what he could--and could not--do as an actor. The writers who wrote for him from the 1950s on, were so influenced
by his already established image that they did not dare deviate from the formula; they also knew that if they did, he
would ask for revisions.

James E. Grant, a popular pulp novelist and writer of
action pictures, was Wayne's favorite and most influential
screenwriter, contributing nine scenarios, beginning with
Angel and the Badman, which he also directed. Grant's
important scripts, in terms of image-making, were two war
movies, Sands of Iwo Jima and Flying Leathernecks;
two political vehicles, Big Jim McLain and The Alamo; and
two Westerns, Hondo and McLintock! Wayne relied heavily
on Grant's work and trusted him implicitly--until Circus
World, after which he was fired.

Allan Dwan recalled that when he directed Sands of Iwo Jima Wayne was so concerned that his role fit his image that he brought Grant to change some of the dialogue. The screenplay, written by Harry Brown, was "perfect for Wayne," according to Dwan, "except that he wants to say things in a certain way, and a writer sometimes writes a phrase a little differently." Wayne was "very simple and very plain," said the director, and "he seemed to think that Grant was the only man who could put the words the way he ought to say them."[34]

"We evolved a system," said Grant describing his contribution to the Wayne persona, "of making him a sort of bystander in situations, instead of actively taking part in them." Wayne typically played a man "who was not looking for trouble, but was relentless in tracking it when it affronted him." Grant thought it was an interesting device because of the contrast: "For an actor so consistently associated with action pictures and combats, Wayne did stand out as a passive figure."[35] True, Wayne thought of himself as a reactor: "I can react to a situation that has already been built up when I walk on. I do not like to have to explain that situation myself."[36]

Of his 18-year-collaboration with Wayne, Grant said: "Because he's built like an ox, lots of guys think Duke is a big, dumb lummox. He isn't." Apparently, the actor could "pick out the holes in them [scripts] faster than I can," Grant said. And contrary to his public image as "the big, calm rock of Gibraltar," he described the star as "eternally concerned with what he is doing in pictures and how he is going to come out."[37]

Another frequent contributor to Wayne's screenplays was Frank S. Nugent, former critic of the New York Times, who wrote some scenarios for Westerns directed by Ford, his father-in-law. Nugent wrote Fort Apache, Three Godfathers, She Wore a Yellow Ribbon (the last two with Lawrence Stallings), and The Searchers. But he also penned the idyllic romance The Quiet Man and the romantic adventure Donovan's Reef, the last in collboration with Grant. These two movies shared many thematic similarities, particularly in Wayne's sex image and attitude toward women (see chapter 6).

Leigh Brackett, a science-fiction and mystery writer,

wrote four of the five Hawks-Wayne movies: <u>Rio Bravo</u>
(with Hawks), <u>Hatari!</u>, <u>El Dorado</u>, and <u>Rio Lobo</u> (also with
Hawks). The fifth movie, <u>Red River</u>, was written by the
distinguished writer Borden Chase, who had written the
screenplay for Wayne's earlier war movie, <u>The Fighting Sea-
bees</u> (with Aeneas Mackenzie). Chase also wrote <u>Flame of
the Barbary Coast</u>, set in San Francisco during the 1906
earthquake, in which he named Wayne's character "the Duke."
Similar literary conventions were employed by Chase in constructing Wayne's character in these movies. In each, Wayne
plays a stubborn, individualistic man who alienates his friends
by his maverick conduct, until he learns the hard way that
he has erred and has to conform. Chase was highly aware
of the novelty in creating a new "character" role for the star,
but he was sure it would work, predicting after <u>Red River</u>
that Wayne would play variants of this role "for the next
twenty years," which he did.

Grant collaborated with Clair Huffaker on the scenario
of <u>The Comancheros</u>, which Wayne liked so much that he
asked the latter to adapt his book, <u>Badman</u>, to the screen,
resulting in <u>The War Wagon</u>, a routine Western opposite Kirk
Douglas. Huffaker's adaptation attested to great familiarity
with the ingredients of the star's typical hero, and Wayne
continued to employ him. His third and last screenplay for
the star was <u>The Hellfighters</u>, loosely based on the real-life
oil fighter Red Adaire. A contrived formula, it contained
all the familiar clichés, such as a loving wife who reluctantly
leaves him because she cannot handle the pressures of his
dangerous work; a daughter he has not seen for years; and,
of course, a happy reconciliation of all parties involved.

Perhaps the most effective means of maintaining tight
control over his career, however, was choosing screen roles
according to a set of strictly defined guidelines, and demanding revisions in those scripts that did not meet his specific
criteria. Wayne's choice of roles was extremely careful,
though not necessarily tasteful. He limited himself, for the
most part, to playing sympathetic heroes, based on his belief that "the whole world loves a hero." Extremely sensitive
to his public image, he held that "you tend to manage your
life and your thinking in a manner that is expected. I would
not want mine to be different."[38] As for guidelines in choosing roles, he said, "If I feel the character's interesting, I'll
do it," but he needed "to identify with something in the

character." Wayne favored "simple characters with simple
motives and emotions," because "nuance is out of my line."[39]
Always sticking to simple themes, he "stayed away from psy-
choanalyst's couch scenes," claiming that "couches are only
good for one thing." "I'm the big tough guy on the side of
right,"[40] as he once described his favorite role, but he was
also aware that the stories he liked were considered "corn"
by the highbrow critics.

Wayne's credo was "to give each character I play some
code of ethics"; even if they were brutal, they first had to
be "real men."[41] His characters could at times be cruel or
tough, but never mean or petty. This was also his philosophy of life, which motivated him to turn down any parts that
were "mean for no reason." "I killed men on the screen,"
he explained, "but it was always because they did not follow
the code."[42] Consequently, "if the script calls for something
I believe is foreign to the character's nature, I simply say,
'I'm too limited to put that across. I'm not that good an actor.'" Early in his career, he vowed "never to go low on
integrity," and never "to do anything that will humiliate a
man in the audience."[43] In retrospect, his films attest that
he lived up to his vow.

Wayne's choice of roles was also guided by his politics,
particularly his sincere concern with projecting a positive
image of America on the screen. He rejected, for example,
many offers to portray General George Armstrong Custer,
killed with his command in the 1876 battle at the Little Big
Horn. "Custer?" he is reported to have said, "that fool,
that jerk, that stupid idiot? I wouldn't be caught dead putting Custer's story on the screen!"[44] For the same reason,
he insisted on playing the good, anti-Nazi, German captain
in Sea Chase; he would never have considered playing a
Nazi, as Brando did in The Young Lions.

Wayne also turned down screenplays that were, in his
view, "dirty, mean or sleazy," including the tough San Francisco cop in Dirty Harry, played with tremendous success by
Clint Eastwood. Later, however, he regretted his decision.
"I wish I'd done that," he said, "it was a time when every
studio was doing dirty pictures. This one had been written
real dirty, so I said no. I should have realized it could
have been changed real easy." "I blew the first of the successful detective stories," said Wayne regretfully, "I could
have been good in it, too."[45]

His formula for good pictures was based on a combination of natural settings with courageous people. "Natural
settings alone," he explained, "won't turn the trick. You've
got to put characters who are interesting and believable."
Big Jim McLain, a terrible film, was used as an example of
his theory because it was filmed on location in Hawaii with
marvelous scenery and, he believed, an interesting story.
A good story for him was "any yarn that deals simply with
genuine and significant people," whatever that meant.
"Movies without great personal stories, don't mean anything,"
contended Wayne, films had to be about people and their in-
terrelations, stressing his preference of narratives about
"people who are less frightened and less inhibited."[46] And
because action was the key note for a good movie, he attributed the failure of many pictures to having "too much story."
For that reason, short stories "by their brevity can be
turned into the best pictures."[47]

Wayne's demand for revisions was based on strong instincts as to the elements that best suited him. He asked
Ford, for example, to make changes in They Were Expendable because he did not like the humiliation involved in the
evacuation scene from Bataan. Thus a new scene was added,
in which he shows his readiness to disboey orders by sneaking
off as a jungle guerrilla, until a superior officer orders him
back aboard.[48] By contrast, he liked the scene in which he
loathes leaving the battle front--"I got business here"--because
it was congruent with the independent and rebellious streak in
his screen persona.

Ford also changed the ending of She Wore a Yellow
Ribbon to a more optimistic one. Initially, Wayne was to
take his leave and be seen, at the film's end, riding off to
a new settlement. But Ford did not want to end the picture
on a sad note, with Wayne fading off, so he added a new
scene in which a dispatch rider is sent after Wayne, assigning him a new appointment as the chief of scouts with the
rank of lieutenant colonel.

A few changes were also introduced into Red River to
suit Wayne's public image. At first, Hawks wanted him to
play Thomas Dunson as a coward, which Wayne flatly rejected. Instead, he played him as a strong man who has
fears, reasoning, "as a man, you can be scared, but you
can't be a coward."[49] Because Wayne was only 41 when he
played the aging cattleman, Hawks asked veteran actor

Walter Brennan to teach the star how to walk like an old
man. Once again, Wayne objected, claiming that none of the
outdoorsmen he knew were tottery, stoop-shouldered, or
bow-legged.[50] The movie differs from the original story, on
which it is based, in other ways. In the book, Dunson competes with Matt Garth for the love of Tess Millay, but in the
movie, Tess is interested in Dunson just in order to protect
Matt, her true love. Moreover, contrary to the original, in
which Dunson is killed, Hawks decided to keep his character
alive; death was incongruent with Wayne's screen immortality.

Hawks's Rio Bravo originated in opposition to Zinnemann's earlier High Noon, which neither Wayne nor Hawks
liked, feeling that its spirit severely deviated from their
idea of the "real West." Hawks did not think "a good sheriff was going to go running around town like a chicken with
his head off asking for help." Instead, he claimed, "a good
sheriff would turn around and say, 'How good are you?
Are you good enough to take the best they've got?'"[51]
Wayne's objections to the film were even stronger than
Hawks's, describing its plot with great contempt: "In that
picture, four guys come in to gun down the sheriff. He
goes to the church and asks for help and the guys go, 'Oh
well. Oh, gee.' And the women stand up and say, 'You're
rats. You're rats. You're rats.' So Cooper goes out alone."
"It's the most un-American thing I've seen in my whole life,"
charged the actor, for the rugged men of the frontier, who
had battled the Indians as well as nature, would not be
afraid of four villains. Instead, they would have united, as
they had united "to make the land habitable." Wayne was
also humiliated by the movie's last scene, showing Cooper
"putting the United States marshal's badge under his foot
and stepping on it."[52] Walking away from his job, as Cooper
did, was inconceivable to Wayne's commitment to responsibility
and public office.

In Rio Bravo, Wayne's sheriff refuses all but selected
help, and he gets more assistance than he expects. Offered
help, he characteristically says, "If they are really good, I'll
take them. If not, I'll just take care of them." Another
major difference is that Cooper's marshal was scared and
faced a severe inner conflict before deciding to handle the
crisis by himself, whereas Wayne's sheriff is independent
and unwaveringly courageous. In contrast to Cooper, Wayne
plays a superior and self-assured sheriff, who could easily
inspire and rally the men around his leadership.

Wayne denounced another Western starring Cooper, They Came to Cordura, in which Cooper's Marshal Thomas Thorn is assigned, due to cowardice in battle, the degrading task of "awards officer" to the Mexican expedition of 1916. His task is to select five men as candidates for the Congressional Medal of Honor, because Washington needs heroes in a hurry for a World War I recruiting campaign. "How they got Gary Cooper to do that one," Wayne wondered, "to me, at least, it simply degrades the Medal of Honor." "The whole story makes a mockery of America's highest award for valor," Wayne elaborated, "the whole premise of the story was wrong, illogical," because "they don't pick the type of men the movie picked to win the award, and that can be proved by the very history of the award."[53]

By contrast, cast as Captain Rockwell in In Harm's Way, Wayne was in complete harmony with his favorite screen role. "In this picture," he described the role, "I must show that I care about other people. Otherwise, when they go off and get killed on my orders, people will hate me." He did not mind "audiences hating me," he said, as they "did perhaps in Red River, but they understood my point of view." In one crucial scene, Kirk Douglas, Wayne's brooding executive officer, rapes Jill Hayworth, the fiancée of Wayne's son. Later, she commits suicide and Douglas, to redeem himself, sacrifices his life in a risky mission. Wayne did not like the way the scene was written. "If I were playing this part," he said, "I would want the girl's boyfriend to return, face me, and kill me." Dying on screen did not bother him, he claimed, "if the confrontation is direct," based on his belief in "facing everything directly."[54]

His strict principles resulted in rejecting "sleazy" screenplays, like Dirty Harry, or "cleaning up" others. The Shootist's initial screenplay, by Miles Hood Swarthout and Scott Hale, was considered by him too graphic in its depiction of cancer and too heavy and downbeat in its ending. He suggested that it be less gloomy by adding a few light touches in the way his hero dealt with his fatal disease. In the original script Ron Howard was a punk who robbed Wayne after his death in the saloon. At Wayne's suggestion, Howard's character was made more positive, and, after avenging Wayne's death, he throws down his gun and runs out of the saloon.

In addition to the other strategies, what contributed to
the coherence of his image was a deliberate attempt, almost
from the very start, to blur the distinction between his real
name and those of his screen characters. Many of his films
used his name, John, or his nickname, Duke, to facilitate
audiences' identification with him--on screen and off. Wayne
was not the only Western star to use his name; Gene Autry
was quite frequently cast as himself in his films.

In most of his "B" Westerns of the 1930s, his hero's
name was John. His character was called John Drury in
Ride Him Cowboy, John Steele in The Big Stampede, John
Trent in The Telegraph Hill, John Bishop in Somewhere in
Sonora, John Holmes in The Man from Monterey, John Brant
in Sagebrush Trail, John Carruthers in Blue Steel, John
Weston in The Man from Utah, John Travers in The Star
Packer, John Robin in The Lawless Frontier, John Higgins
in Texas Terror, etc. In several pictures, his character's
name was Duke, as in Two Fisted Law. His hero's name was
Duke Slade in Adventure's End, Duke Hudkins in Lady Takes
a Chance, Duke Fergus in Flame of the Barbary Coast, and
Duke Gifford in Operation Pacific.

Another example of the continuity (or blur) between
his screen image and life offscreen was the borrowing of
family names, of his wives and children, for his protagonists.
Marlene Dietrich's heroine in Pittsburgh was named Josie,
the nickname of his second wife, and in The Comancheros,
Ina Balin's name, Pilar, was after Wayne's third wife. In
Donovan's Reef, Wayne's character was Michael Patrick Donovan, based on the names of his eldest (Michael) and second
(Patrick) sons. But the reverse also prevailed, with his
fictional heroes influencing his real life. Wayne liked so
much the character of Ethan Edwards in The Searchers that
he named his third and youngest son after him.

Wayne often used the same characters' names in different movies. He played Captain Kirby York in Fort Apache
and Lt. Colonel Kirby Yorke (with an e) in Rio Grande,
though it was not clear whether he portrayed the same hero.
Wayne also used the name Kirby in two war movies, Major
Dan Kirby in Flying Leathernecks, and Colonel Mike Kirby
in The Green Berets. In Hondo, Wayne's character was
Hondo Lane and Geraldine Page's Angie Lowe; twenty years
later, he used the same names in The Train Robbers: his

hero's name was Lane and Ann-Margret's widow was Mrs.
Lowe. Elsa Martinelli's photographer in Hatari! was named
Anna Maria, but her nickname was Dallas, after the heroine
of Stagecoach. And the villain in Ford's The Man Who Shot
Liberty Valance, Liberty Valance, bore resemblance to Cherry
Valance in Hawks's earlier Red River.

Departures from Image

Although Wayne's persona was remarkably consistent,
there were occasional departures from it, but these deviations
strengthened, rather than weakened, his established image
because they stressed the norm; they were equivalent to
casting against type, which is also based on audiences' familiarity with actors' typical roles. For example, Wayne usually portrayed indestructible heroes who triumphed against
all odds, so that the few movies in which his heroes are
killed neither changed his image nor altered audiences' expectations because they were regarded as the exception.
And audiences could expect that in the next picture Wayne
would again play his indefatigable and immortal heroes.

His non-American protagonists were definitely a departure from his established persona. Wayne's voice, Midwest-
ern accent, appearance, and character were so quintessen-
tially American that he was never really convincing in portraying foreigners. Sensitive to this aspect of his persona,
he rarely played non-American characters. Perhaps his only
successful attempt, Ole Olsen, the Swedish sailor in The
Long Voyage Home, was, curiously, his first. Coached by
Osa Massen, a Danish actress, he managed a rather credible
Swedish accent, though he once suggested to retitle the
movie as "Wayne's Long Struggle with a Swedish Accent."
"My natural accent is strictly Winterset, Iowa, where I was
born," he explained, "and it required a lot of persuasion to
make it turn Swedish for the role of Ole."[55]

Much more embarrassing was his portrayal of an anti-
Nazi German captain in the adventure Sea Chase. Most reviewers were harsh on the picture as well as on Wayne,
mainly because of its incredible casting. Critic Bosley
Crowther noted in the New York Times that Wayne played
the German captain "as though he were heading a herd of
cattle up the old Chisholm Trail,"[56] and another critic wrote

that this "fantastic bit of casting" was "like getting Lassie
to play a cow."[57] "Once you get used to All-American John
Wayne and sweater girl Lana Turner as Germans," one reviewer cynically commented, "the film is fairly acceptable."[58]

In Howard Hughes's The Conqueror, Wayne was cast
as Genghis Khan, the thirteenth-century Mongol emperor,
without much excitement--and out of obligation to his friend
Hughes, head of RKO, who had great hopes for this movie.
This time, both reviewers and audiences had difficulties dis-
associating Wayne from his American image, and it was a financial fiasco. The Conqueror was described by one critic
as an "Oriental Western" and Wayne's appearance as "a mite
startling at first," but "soon recognizable." "Once in the
saddle," he wrote, "he is the rough-riding John Wayne of
yore."[59] Similarly, the Time critic noted that the film suggested that "Mongolia is in the Western U.S.," and that the
part of "the Perfect warrior" was played by "Hollywood's
best-known cowboy, John Wayne."[60] Wayne himself attributed the film's failure to the fact that "people wouldn't accept me as Genghis Khan. I've been extolled as a rough
American personality, and they won't take anything else."[61]
But he also revealed that he interpreted the role of Genghis
Khan as a Westerner and that was the way he played him.

The Conqueror was named one of "The 50 Worst Films
of All Time," in a book edited by Medved and Dreyfuss.
One critic wrote in the Los Angeles Times, after watching
the movie in 1980, that it would definitely be on his list of
the 10, not 50, worst movies. "I can't think of a more improbable piece of casting," he continued, "unless Mickey
Rooney were to play Jesus in The King of Kings." Made as
a Western, The Conqueror looked "as if the wrong costumes
were delivered and they decided to shoot it anyway."[62]
Wayne was embarrassed at the least mention of this picture,
wishing to forget all about it. Fortunately for him, Hughes
was sentimental toward the movie, being his last at RKO,
and when the studio was sold, he bought back The Conqueror for a phenomenal amount of money and locked it in
a vault until his death; it was first shown on television in
1980.

Mickey Rooney never played Jesus, but Wayne was
cast in the improbable role of a Roman centurion, leading
Jesus to crucifixion in George Stevens's unsuccessful attempt

John Wayne in the title role of the historical adventure The Conqueror (RKO Radio, 1956), featuring the most embarrassing performance of his entire career.

at a biblical epic, <u>The Greatest Story Ever Told</u>, arguably
Wayne's worst appearance. Totally miscast, his only line,
"Truly, this man was a son of God," evoked laughter in the
audience and was sheer embarrassment. Wayne's performance,
however, was just one of many other "shattering and distasteful"[63] performances by many stars in cameo roles, including
Charlton Heston, Sidney Poitier, Carroll Baker, Shelley Win-
ters, and Telly Savalas.

Wayne's paucity of non-American roles was also charac-
teristic of the other Hollywood stars known as the great
American actors. Henry Fonda, for example, played only a
few foreigners in his lengthy career, and two of them before
his screen image took shape: a Canadian horse trainer in
<u>Wings of Morning</u>, and a peasant fighter in the Spanish Civil
War in <u>Blockade</u>. Later in his career, he was miscast as
Pierre in King Vidor's screen version of Tolstoy's <u>War and
Peace</u>.

Wayne's heroes fought against any imaginable types of
villains, from Indians, smugglers, and rustlers in his Westerns, to Nazis, Japanese, and Communists in his war and
political movies. But once in a while he allowed himself to
be cast as a villain, which was the second departure from
his image, though his villains usually repented in the course
of the narrative. He made sure that the few outlaws he
played were sympathetic or "likable," as he described his
roles in <u>Red River</u> or <u>True Grit</u>. Most of the villains in his
repertoire restored themselves to legitimacy and achieved
redemption either through self-sacrificial death or through
the love of an innocent girl. The normative range of his
roles was quite restrictive, being willing to deviate from
norms or violate the law only under specific conditions.
And when the screenplay did not "take care" of his villains'
redemption, he did not hesitate to demand revisions.

In <u>Angel and the Badman</u>, for example, Wayne's
wounded gunslinger is regenerated through the love of a
Quaker maid. Religious salvation is also the solution in
<u>Three Godfathers</u>, a symbolic Western based on Christian
mythology. At the film's start, Wayne is the leader of an
outlaw gang, which runs away after robbing a bank. But
he redeems himself after vowing to a dying waif in the
desert to bring her baby to safety in New Jerusalem, an
endeavor that costs the death of his two accomplices as
well as the sacrificial death of the baby's mother.

Pittsburgh is the tale of two coal miner friends (Wayne and Randolph Scott) who become wealthy magnates, but success affects them in different ways. Scott represents the conscientious altruist, viewing money chiefly as means to serve his employees, whereas Wayne is selfish, ruthlessly power driven, and abusive of friends and family. Early on, he tells his girl (Marlene Dietrich), "I know there ain't a thing in the world I can't do--once I set my mind to it," upon which he deserts her to marry into society. After success goes to his head, however, it turns against him: divorced by his wife, he is left with no friends. Realizing he has erred, he repents by starting all over again, at the bottom of the hierarchy of Scott's plant. And at the end, a higher and nobler cause, the nation's interest and the need of every citizen for the war effort, reunites him with Scott. Wayne's role in Pittsburgh has been compared with Thomas Dunson in Red River, because in both he starts as ruthlessly ambitious and inconsiderate, devoid of any humanity, but reforms in time to begin a new and better life.

The only picture in which Wayne plays a morally dubious character was Trouble Along the Way, cast as a cynical big-time football coach who was kicked out of the big league because he was unable to conform. Later, he is hired by the rector of a Catholic college, Father Burke (Charles Coburn), who wants to save the college from its financial difficulties by establishing an athletic program. Wayne uses unethical methods to put the college back on its feet, faking academic grades to get good players and even resorting to blackmail to get good playing dates. He refuses to admit to any shame, when reproached by the priest for his disreputable means. Throughout the film, he maintains a cynical view of the sports business, refusing to condemn corruption, so long as it is a useful means to win--which some interpreted as a realistic commentary on the corrupt practices of the American sports establishment.

The other stars of Wayne's generation also established reputations by playing sympathetic roles, to the point of being severely circumscribed by what the public was willing --and unwilling--to accept. Fonda played few villainous roles until the last decade of his career; his earlier portrayal of the outlaw Frank James, in two Westerns, was whitewashed and even glamorized. Fonda in fact was much more convincing as an innocent man accused of murder in Fritz Lang's You Only Live Once, and he gave a memorable

performance in Hitchcock's The Wrong Man as Manny Bales-
trero, the honest musician who was mistakenly identified as
a hold-up man. Like Wayne, his portrayal of villains or
criminals was an occasional departure, an exception. However, as critic French suggested, the casting of Fonda and
Wayne in villainous roles had different meanings: "When
Wayne is cast as a criminal, there is usually a suggestion
that something is wrong with the law in a local, easily resolved way; when Fonda is cast as an outlaw, the implication
is that there's something basically wrong with society." This
differential reading of Wayne's and Fonda's roles attests to
the immense power of their respective screen personae.

Wayne and Fonda were no exceptions. Most stars who
began their careers playing villains had to transform their
images before winning the public's acceptance and approval.
Clark Gable (The Painted Desert), Humphrey Bogart (all his
1930s movies), Alan Ladd (This Gun for Hire), Lee Marvin
and Charles Bronson (in most of their 1950s roles) were first
typecast as heavies, often gangsters. But once the studios
realized they had star potential, they stopped casting them
in such roles. Indeed, the public resented Bogart's return
to playing villains, as in John Huston's The Treasure of the
Sierra Madre, despite the film's high quality and Bogart's
distinguished performance. Some critics suspect that Bogart
failed to win an Oscar nomination, if not the award, because
he played a greedy and corrupt character; by 1949, Bogart's
heroic and romantic image had been firmly established, which
confined the range of his roles. Nor was Bogart's role as an
escaped convict shot down by the police, in his penultimate
picture, The Desperate Hours, welcomed by his ardent fans,
reminding them of an earlier, less popular, phase in his career when he specialized in such roles.

Vulnerability was the third major departure from
Wayne's established persona. As was mentioned, Hawks suggested that he play a character role in Red River before he
was old enough to do it, and it was also Hawks who convinced
Wayne that his increasing biological age should have some
bearing on his screen roles. This new trend, of making his
heroes less assured or more dependable, started with Rio
Bravo, which slightly altered his image, without diminishing
its power. Thus, Wayne's sheriff needs help in holding the
town, and a saloon girl protects him in crucial moments.
But it was El Dorado, dealing, among other things, with the

effects of age on man's capabilities, that marked a turning point. Here Wayne is a wandering gunslinger, not the sheriff, hired at first by ruthless barons to protect their interests against local settlers, though later he switches allegiance to help the sheriff (Robert Mitchum) fight a villainous cattle baron. Wayne is also less assured than in previous Hawks's Westerns. He is described as one of the three fastest shots --not the best--and he is no longer self-sufficient. During the course of the story he is accidentally shot twice--first by a woman, which almost paralyzes his right hand. The second time he is hit in the leg and must hobble around on a crutch. In short, Wayne is no longer in complete control, as he used to be. In El Dorado, he uses a trick to get the villain and, on another occasion, he is saved from death by a woman.

In most of his movies after El Dorado he is either wounded or shot--but not killed. Of his numerous pictures, Wayne died on the screen only eight times, and his death is usually heroic and/or sacrificial. In The Fighting Seabees, Wayne dies in a bold, one-man action, after realizing that his stubbornness has caused the deaths of many civilians. In Sands of Iwo Jima he is shot in the back by a Japanese sniper, after the battle is over but before the emotional flag-raising on Mount Suribachi. Wayne's death is disturbingly shocking precisely because it is unexpected; he is shot after telling his soldiers he has never felt so good. His death in this film had therefore a strong impact on audiences, stressing the high price in human life paid in war, despite glorious victory.

The conventions of the Western genre have been stricter than those of war films concerning death, their narratives typically ending with the triumphant survival of their cowboy heroes. Some Westerns changed the endings of their original stories to conform to audiences' expectations. A case in point is Columbia's The End of the Trail, which violated Zane Grey's story and kept its hero alive instead of going to the gallows. True to the narrative of classic Westerns, Wayne's cowboys almost always survive.

The Alamo, in which Wayne's Colonel Davy Crockett dies heroically for independent Texas, is one of the few exceptions. The picture depicts how at the end of the 13-day siege Crockett is run through by a lance. The

graphic details of Crockett's death upset many viewers.
One critic wrote that no additional impact was made
by emphasizing so violently--in close-ups--Crockett's
death, impaled with a lance in his chest.[64] Another critic
observed in a similar vein that "it is not how they died which
is important, but why."[65] Wayne's mother never saw the
second part of The Alamo because she reportedly could not
tolerate the idea of her son being killed on the screen.

Wayne's most irritating death was in The Cowboys, shot
down by a crazed killer (Bruce Dern). Director Rydell
feared that the star would not like the idea and even considered alternative endings to the story. He was therefore
pleasantly surprised when Wayne insisted on maintaining the
narrative intact, claiming such ending was both logical and
realistic. But critics and audiences were disturbed by his
death. Some disapproved of the way he was killed--shot in
the back--noting that Ford or Hawks would never have allowed such death in their films. They felt Wayne's image,
by now bigger than life, was damaged because he was not
given a chance to fight back. True, Wayne's immortality
was by now so firmly rooted that some critics thought he
was "unnecessarily killed," and others stressed the temerity
of Bruce Dern to murder him, thus desecrating an "American
institution." Dern recalled that before the death scene was
filmed, Wayne told him, "Dern, you're gonna be hated everywhere in the world for this one."[66] Moviegoers were so familiar with his screen persona that when one critic wrote in
the Los Angeles Times that The Cowboys marked Wayne's
first screen death, she reported to have received numerous
letters protesting the inaccuracy of her account.

In most movies, almost everything and anything possible was done to avoid Wayne's screen death, as the changes
introduced by Hawks in Red River's screenplay, to keep the
star's hero alive. At times, though, these attempts were
absurd. A case in point is In Harm's Way, in which Wayne
is injured multiple times. First, his ship is struck by the
Japanese and his arm is fractured; then, in another attack,
he loses a leg but is promised an artificial one so that he
can go on fighting. These predictable plot twists irritated
the critics, most of whom commented in their reviews on the
star's indestructibility. "You can't kill John Wayne," said
the New York Times, "that's the message--the only message--
that comes through loud and clear." "No matter how much

the enemy takes deadly aims at Mr. Wayne," this reviewer continued, "and no matter how rough his superiors in the U.S. Navy are on him, he comes through alive and a hero, minus one leg."[67] There was also a good deal of cynicism in Ivan Butler's comment that the picture says in 167 minutes what was scarcely worth saying in 80, "that John Wayne may lose an early battle, but is sure to win in the end."[68]

Happy endings, however, including triumphant survival against all odds, were integral to the image of most Hollywood stars during the golden age. The great male stars died before the cameras either before their public images took shape or very late in their careers when it no longer mattered. Take Clark Gable, for example, who died in only four of his 67 movies, with two of these screen deaths occurring during the first year of his career--a bootlegger gangster in Dance, Fools, Dance, and an underworld leader in A Free Soul. Gable also died romantically in Myrna Loy's arms in Parnell, another uncharacteristic movie that miscast him as a nineteenth-century Irish politician. His fourth reel death was in a war movie, Run Silent, Run Deep, one of his last pictures, in which he dies on duty, as a captain of a U.S. submarine during World War II.

When these deaths occur, as in Jimmy Stewart's pictures, they are most revealing in their insights about male heroism in the American cinema. In a typical Stewart movie, it is usually his girl or his wife who dies--not he. In three of his Westerns he loses his woman in tragic circumstances, as in Destry Rides Again, in which Marlene Dietrich's saloon owner is shot in the back while trying to save his life. Even more tragic is his wife's (Debra Paget) death in The Broken Arrow, paying a high price in the achievement of peace between whites and Indians. Stewart's frequent screen lady Margaret Sullavan often found her death in his arms, as in The Mortal Storm, an antiwar picture, in which both are shot as they cross the border to safety but she dies. Stewart's rare screen deaths are either heroic, as in the war drama Malaya, or accidental, as in the biopicture The Glenn Miller Story, dying in an air crash.

The only Hollywood star to have experienced multiple reel deaths were those specializing in the crime-gangster films, most notably James Cagney and Humphrey Bogart. Note that Bogart's heroes are shot in no less than one-third

(25 out of 75) of his pictures. Eighteen of these, however, are in movies prior to The Maltese Falcon (the movie which made him a star), when he played the heavies in films starring Cagney, Edward G. Robinson, or George Raft. Bogart once ironically observed that it was his screen deaths that kept his career alive, but he was wrong. It is doubtful that he would have become such a legendary figure had he continued to be killed in the last reel of his movies. After 1941, Bogart died in only seven of his movies--and in some, heroically. The movies that made him a big star and that the public associates most with his screen persona, such as Casablanca or To Have and Have Not, were those in which he survives. The lessons from Bogart's career, which Wayne exemplified in his, are that no actor in the American cinema has so far become a popular star if his roles were confined to playing heavies and destructible villains. Endurance in the audience's collective memories offscreen also requires the hero's immortality onscreen!

6. WAYNE'S SEX IMAGE: A TOUGH GENTLEMAN

Wayne's sex image, like other components of his screen image, underwent several changes during his career. Generally speaking, there have been three distinct phases in his sex persona: the naive gentleman, the estranged husband and alienated father, and the comfortable grandfather.

Phase One: The Naive Gentleman

During the first phase of his sex image, which lasted approximately until the late 1940s, Wayne portrayed the naive hero, innocent with women and awkward in romantic scenes. Stagecoach, a movie in which he was at his most sexually appealing, set the pattern for his screen sex persona for a decade. As the Ringo Kid, he meets Dallas (Claire Trevor), a prostitute with a golden heart who had been expelled from town by the "respectable" ladies. Wayne accepts Dallas for what she is, "I know all I need to know," and treats her as an equal. Furthermore, he requires that the others on the stagecoach also treat her as a lady, with the appropriate politeness and courtesy. When a vote is taken as to whether the journey should continue, he notes that Dallas had been overlooked. And later, he makes Hatfield offer her water, just as he had offered it to Mrs. Mallory. Unaware of issues of propriety, he invites her to join him and is amazed when Mrs. Mallory moves away and they are left to eat alone, "Looks like I've got the plague, don't it?"

Wayne's proposition to Dallas is very hesitant and awkward, telling her he has a ranch across the border and that "a man could live there ... and a woman.... Will you go?" He refuses to accept her advice and run away, arguing "there are some things a man can't run away from." And at the end, after avenging his family's murder, the two

131

John Wayne and Claire Trevor as the two outcasts in John Ford's masterpiece Stagecoach (United Artists, 1939).

leave for his ranch, with Doc Boone's blessing: "Well, they're safe from the blessing of civilization."

Naiveté and innocence are the two prevalent traits in his behavior with women. As the shy sailor in The Long Voyage Home, Ole Olsen is excited to see the native girls at a Caribbean stopping point, but it is clear that he has no knowledge of or experience with women. Ashore, upon meeting Freda (Mildred Natwick), a prostitute, he tries at first to get away, but being polite he accepts her invitation to join him for a drink. Nor does he suspect her intention to rob him. When he tells her of his past, she is addressed respectfully as Miss Freda.

In Sands of Iwo Jima, he buys a drink for another prostitute (Julie Bishop) in a Hawaii bar and she invites him to her home. Upon learning that she was deserted by her husband and works to support her baby, he softens and gives her some money--but refuses to stay. He even helps her to prepare the baby's food, which surprises her. "You know about babies?" she asks. "Yeah, I know about babies," he tenderly replies.

His awkwardness in romantic scenes must have been appealing to audiences. In The Fighting Seabees, as a civilian construction chief, he meets Constance (Susan Hayward), a news reporter. In an early conversation, she observes: "Watching a ship's wake always makes me think of things that time puts behind us for ever--hopes, dreams, illusions. What does it make you think about?" Wayne replies, "If they changed the pitch of that propeller, they'd get a couple of more knots out of this tub." Irritated she says, "I thought I'd caught you being human for once. Don't you have anything under that thick hide of yours but cylinders and carburetors?" Which amuses him, "A spark-plug maybe." This conversation was typical of Wayne's image as a man's man, with no time for nonsensical romanticism. Later, Hayward is wounded during a Japanese attack which he is responsible for, and he visits her at the hospital. When she tells him, "I love you," he is embarrassed, "What am I supposed to say?" Only when she faints and can't hear him, he screams "I love you."

He holds a similar kind of conversation with nurse Sandy Davyss (Donna Reed) in They Were Expendable. At the hospital, taking care of him, she suggests they go to dance one evening, but he gets impatient: "Listen, sister, I don't dance--and I can't take time out now to learn. All I want is to get out of here." But later, he calms down and he does go dancing with her.

Women never prevented the Wayne hero from accomplishing a task he was committed to. In Dark Command, Wayne's marshal is forced to arrest Mary McCloud's (Claire Trevor) kid brother and bring him to trial for murder. She is willing to give herself, if he releases her brother but he, of course, refuses. She marries a schoolteacher (Walter Pidgeon), not because she loves him, but because he is willing to defend her brother. At the end, however, Wayne proves her husband's corruption and asks her to start a new life with him in Texas.

In very few movies does his protagonist lose his head over a woman. One such exception was Seven Sinners, in

John Wayne and Marlene Dietrich in Tay Garnett's <u>Seven</u>
<u>Sinners</u> (Universal, 1940), a change of pace and costume
for Wayne and the first of their three popular films together.

which Wayne's naive Navy lieutenant falls passionately in
love with a saloon girl (Marlene Dietrich), willing to abandon his career for her. But she is forced, under pressure,
to slip out of his life. This was an uncharacteristic picture,
made as a Dietrich vehicle, long before his image had crys-
tallized.

A more typical film of that era was <u>Lady Takes a</u>
<u>Chance</u> (1943), with Wayne cast as Duke Hudkins, a simple,
easy-going rodeo rider who treasures his independence. He
gets involved with Mollie Truesdale (Jean Arthur), a bank
teller from New York, but makes sure to tell her he does
not believe in marriage. He is, in fact, contemptuous of his
married friends, describing them as pretending "they like it
because they're ashamed to admit they made a mistake." Refusing to settle down, he appears to care more about his
horse than about women. When his sneezing horse is rushed

off to a veterinarian, she observes: "Any fellow who can
love a horse can love a girl." That's how sophisticated the
script was! At the end, Hudkins claims Truesdale for himself--
though not before defeating three suitors--and takes her off
to a new life out West.

To describe Lady Takes a Chance as a naive movie is
an understatement; its outrageous scenario is replete with
awkward scenes. In one, Truesdale asks to touch Hudkins's
muscles to feel his strength. And in another, he tries to
kiss her, for which she orders him out. The film's publicity campaign is most revealing concerning the kinds of
audiences it wanted to attract. One advertisement stated:
"When a starry-eyed maid from Manhattan tames the wildest
'wolf' of the West--that's Fun!" It described the movie as
"a cross-country comedy of a girl with a two weeks' vaca-
tion and a life-time yen for the kind of kisses you dream of.
She gets 'em--but plenty! ... in a picture made for the big
money!"

Wayne displayed mistrust for women in most of his
1940s films. In Tall in the Saddle (1944), Wayne's Rocklin
is a cowboy arriving in Santa Inez to become a ranch foreman. Realizing his prospective employer has been murdered
and the ranch is now run by young Clara (Audrey Young)
and her aunt (Elisabeth Risdon), he declines to work for
women. "I never feel sorry for anything that happens to a
woman," he proudly declares. However, he helps Clara foil
the plot of her corrupt aunt to take the ranch from her.
Clara, a delicate woman from the East, is contrasted in the
film with Arly Harolday (Ella Raines), an independent and
aggressive woman. Arly, dressed in a Western costume,
fires a pistol and even flings a knife at Rocklin when she
is irritated. He, however, wards her off: "You might as
well know, no woman is going to get me hogtied and brand-
ed." In the film's happy ending Clara goes back to the
East--a safer place for women--but urges Rocklin to claim
Arly because she is his type of woman.

Wayne's philosophy toward women was expressed in
Without Reservations (1946), a cross-country romance similar to, but less witty and entertaining than, It Happened
One Night, both starring Claudette Colbert. Rusty Thomas,
a Marine flyer, meets Kit Madden (Colbert), a famous novelist who conceals her identity under the name of Kitty Klotch

after listening to his disparaging remarks about her book.
Colbert boards the train for Hollywood to assist in the filming of her book. Cary Grant promised to appear in the
lead, opposite Lana Turner, but after meeting Wayne, she
is convinced he is perfect for the part. Wayne does not
understand why Cary Grant accepted the part "because it
will make him look silly." "Why?" she insists, to which
Wayne explains, "Because Lana Turner keeps chasing him
for four hundred pages and he keeps saying no." Wayne
has read the book and thinks its hero is a jerk. Instead of
the values of cooperative society, which her book advocates,
Wayne lectures her on self-reliance. Colbert thinks Wayne
has "missed the point entirely," for the characters played by
Grant and Turner are "symbols," "he of the future, and she
of the past. The clash between them is purely ideological."
Wayne remains unconvinced. If he were to play it, he would
first treat Turner as a woman, then argue with her. For
him, worrying about women is "a mental fatigue."

     Furthermore, Wayne thinks the book's author knows
nothing about men and does not understand her place in a
man's world. He convinces her to revise the book, after
she realizes that her heroes are not interested in carving
out a new world, as she intended, but rather satisfied with
the old way. In the last scene, told of her idea to make an
actor out of him, he screams, "An Actor! You mean that
you've been lying to us? Then I almost fell for it. I was
beginning to believe you were on the level." "But I was,"
she says, though Wayne insists on getting his wings back.
"I don't want a woman who's trying to tell the world what to
do!" he tells her, "I don't even want a woman to tell me
what to do! I want a woman who needs me! A Miss Klotch
who's helpless and cute...."

     Without Reservations was a heavy-handed comedy, lack-
ing wit or charm. "The untiring monkeyshines of the three
unmistakably mature principals" (Don DeFore was the third),
the Time reviewer noted, "keeps reminding you that their
combined ages must total over a century."[1] Another critic
described the narrative as John Wayne "determined to make
an ardent girl of Colbert," and she "determined to make a
brainy actor of Wayne," but what Wayne tries to teach her
has "very little to do with the brain cells."[2] And another
critic wrote: "An exhaustive study of the inner development
--under the dizzying influence of propinquity to Mr. Wayne--

from a high-minded, deeply analytical, best-seller writer on world affairs, into a humble, love-sick maiden."[3]

Phase Two: The Estranged Husband and Alienated Father

The second phase in Wayne's sex image started in the late 1940s, with Fort Apache and Red River, and continued until the late 1960s. Wayne no longer played the chivalrous romantic cowboy, but mature men who were either estranged or divorced from their wives. This phase, which gave him the richest parts in his career, is best remembered as the "John Wayne movie" which contained, among other things, his most typical attitude toward women.

At the start of Red River, Wayne is seen as an ambitious young man, more interested in his cattle than in his woman, Fen. When he leaves to search for grazing land, he refuses to take her, claiming, "It's too much for a woman." "You'll need me," she tries to sway him from his decision, "You'll need what a woman can give you to do what you have to do." But he is determined, "I've made up my mind." "I'll send for you," he promises, "Will you come?" "Of course I'll come," she replies, "But you're wrong." He never gets a chance to send for her, for she is murdered by the Indians in a nasty raid, after which Wayne buries his mistake deep inside him.

In Fort Apache, Wayne's Captain York has no woman in his life and the film's romantic interest is provided by Fonda's daughter and two young officers. In another Ford Western, She Wore a Yellow Ribbon, Wayne's Captain Brittles is an aging widower whose wife has died nine years before. Sentimental, he visits her grave to water the flowers and to share with her the latest news. Wayne is the most alienated character in the picture--his only meaningful attachment is to his cavalry career.

Operation Pacific (1951), a typical movie of the 1950s concerning Wayne's relationship with women, casts Wayne as a submarine officer divorced from his wife, a Navy nurse (Patricia Neal), for 14 years, following the death of their son in infancy. It is clear, though, that he still loves her and wants to resume their relationship. He takes the blame for their split on himself: "We had something--I guess I

kicked it around." His ex-wife apparently did not mind his
absences from home, but she did mind that she could not
cry with him or comfort him when their son died: "You
went off into some corner alone, never realizing that by
comforting you I could have helped my own grief." She
also spurns him for his love with the Navy, "You don't
need anybody but yourself." But as in most of his films,
she is the one who has to compromise and accept him on
his own terms, as her superior at the hospital reminds her:
"You married him for what he is, and then tried to make
something else out of him, but you couldn't."

Sergeant Stryker's private life in Sands of Iwo Jima is
in ruins and he is tormented by past mistakes; his wife left
him five years earlier, taking their little son with her. In
Trouble Along the Way (1953), Wayne is a former football
coach whose marriage has broken up. He is engaged in a
battle with his ex-wife over the custody of their daughter,
the only thing he cares about. And in The High and the
Mighty (1954), Wayne plays a veteran flyer of a commercial
aircraft who cannot get over a plane crash in which he was
the only survivor--his wife and child were among the many
victims. Wayne's hostility toward the medical officer (William
Holden) in The Horse Soldiers (1959) derives, among other
things, from bitter memories of his wife's death. Two doctors operated on her for a suspected (but nonexistent) tumor, which cost her her life. Wayne is unable to forget the
harrowing experience of forcing a leather strap into her
mouth to stop her painful screams.

On screen, Wayne continued to treasure his stubborn
independence. For example, to Lana Turner's criticism of
his rigid toughness in Sea Chase, he replies: "I forgot to
mention why I never married, I like to run my own ship."
The priority of career commitments over family duties and
the apparent interference of women with men's work, were
two of the most recurrent themes in his movies. The romantic interest in Hondo is provided by Geraldine Page, an
abandoned wife and mother who runs a big ranch, and
Wayne, whose wife had died. In a typical conversation, she
tells Wayne, "everyone needs someone," to which he characteristically replies, "Most everyone ma'am. Too bad, isn't
it."

Maureen O'Hara was Wayne's most frequent screen lady.

They appeared in five films together, three of which were directed by Ford: Rio Grande, The Quiet Man, and The Wings of Eagles. The chemistry between them worked so well that they were paired in two other films, McLintock! and Big Jake. O'Hara was the kind of actress Ford liked, beautiful, sensuous, but also strong and fiery, thus able to stand up to Wayne's heroes. Ford described her as a "man's woman." There was a special rapport between them because they were similar: both could be earthy but also elegant and refined, when needed. At the center of each of their five films is a conflict between Wayne's commitment to his career and his marital or familial responsibilities. In most films, O'Hara has to accept her place in his world and put his interests before her own. But her heroines are not completely submissive and, despite conflict and resolution to his advantage, Wayne also has to accommodate.

Lieutenant Colonel Kirby Yorke in Rio Grande is a man who puts duty before love. During the Civil War, he followed orders to set his wife's plantation on fire, for which she has never forgiven him. After a separation of 15 years, they meet when she comes to his camp to reclaim their son Jeff, who becomes the battleground between them. She resents Wayne for his pride and stubbornness, though she possesses the same traits. Their conflict is summed up when she drinks to "my only rival--the U.S. Cavalry." At the end, however, she understands Wayne's commitment to his career and accepts their son's choice of a similar, military way of life.

In The Quiet Man, Wayne's ex-prizefighter returns to Ireland to settle down. The conflict between him and O'Hara is over her dowry, which she insists on recovering from her brother--but the whole issue seems unimportant to him. "In characteristic American fashion," critic Haskell has interpreted their conflict, "he feels his masculinity and ability to provide for her impugned, until she finally makes him understand that it is not the money, but what it stands for: the dowry and furniture are her identity, her independence." The furniture is part of her personality, "like a maiden name," and the money enables her not to be completely "absorbed" by him.[4] Indeed, when she finally recovers the money, she throws it into a furnace.

O'Hara resents the demands made on her husband,

John Wayne and Maureen O'Hara in John Ford's lyric tale
The Quiet Man (Republic, 1952), in one of the most romantic and erotic scenes in the actor's career.

Frank "Spig" Wead, in The Wings of Eagles. Unable to cope
with his frequent transfers, in line with his duty, she hopes
he will be thrown out of the Navy. But it does not happen
and they separate. Wayne becomes so estranged from his
two daughters that when he comes to visit them they do not
recognize him. A reconciliation between them is achieved,
but it is short-lived--she refuses to submerge herself into
his career. The motives for her behavior are not very clearly described, though there are suggestions that she might
have taken to drinking and neglected her children. Of all
their mutual films, in this one their relationship is the weakest because O'Hara's role is much less developed than Wayne's
--the focus of the narrative.

      In McLintock! O'Hara leaves Wayne, suspecting he has
been unfaithful to her. They meet when she comes to ask
him for a divorce and custody of their daughter, a college

student in the East. At the film's climax, he chases O'Hara
through town, then takes her over his knees and spanks
her. But instead of resisting, she throws herself into his
arms! In Big Jake, their last film together, O'Hara also
leaves Wayne, insisting she has no husband. She suspects,
as in McLintock! that he has shown too much interest in
other women. However, a reconciliation is managed when
she realizes he is the only man capable of getting back their
kidnapped grandson.

In all their films, Wayne displays great emotional attachment when he first sees O'Hara, always complimenting
her and behaving like a gentleman--in accordance with his
bourgeois ethics. In Rio Grande, he compliments her for
being "a fine figure of a woman," and it is clear that he is
still passionately in love with her. And in Big Jake, when
he meets her at the train station, he tells her, "You're as
young and as lovely as ever." He further demonstrates that
he remembers to the month and the day the length of their
separation!

Wayne's characteristic style of courtship and romance
was displayed in several action movies that also had light,
romantic touches. Apparently, it was Hawks, realizing that
Wayne's youthful appearance was declining, who suggested it
was no longer appropriate for him to chase young and attractive women. And congruent to his previous screen women,
Hawks made the saloon girl, Feathers (Angie Dickinson), in
Rio Bravo a stronger and more aggressive character than
women's conventional roles in Westerns. The director also
decided that the romance between them would be sort of a
battle of words, by innuendo and implication, rather than
explicit eroticism and carnality.

Feathers features more prominently in the narrative of
Rio Bravo than as just a romantic interest. A stubborn woman, she guards Wayne when he is sleeping, without his knowledge. She then helps him when he is caught unprepared by
some of Burdette's (the villain's) men. She is constantly on
alert, even when it seems she is relaxing or unaware of what
is going on. Her provocative manner makes her an ideal counterpart for Wayne's aging sheriff, who is shy in expressing
his emotions openly. It is Feathers who first kisses him,
then observes, after a second try, "I'm glad we tried it a
second time. It's better when two people do it." It takes

John Wayne and Angie Dickinson in a romantic battle of
words in Howard Hawks's Rio Bravo (Warner, 1959).

Wayne a while to admit he is glad she stays in town, and
her self-assurance--"I'm hard to get, John T. You're
gonna have to say you want me"--does not make it easier
for him. However, when she wears a sexy dress, ready to
go to the saloon, Wayne tells her, "You'd better not."
Asked for a reason, he replies, "You wear those things and
I'll arrest you." Delighted and crying, she turns back, "I
thought you were never going to say it." "Say what?"
asks Wayne. "That you love me," she replies. "I said I'd
arrest you," Wayne repeats, but to her, "It means the same
thing. You know that, you just won't say it."

Wayne's shyness in declaring love for his women was a
motif. In North to Alaska, he is literally forced into public
confession of his love for Capucine, this time on main street
of Nome, Alaska. His "mission" is to bring back his partner's French fiancée from Seattle. As usual, he mistrusts
women, having been almost trapped into marriage twice before. "The wonderful thing about Alaska," he tells his partner (Stewart Granger), "is that matrimony hasn't hit it up
here yet. Let's keep it a free country." Later, he declares
in similar vein, "Any woman who devotes herself to making
one man miserable instead of a lot of men happy, don't get
my vote." When he first meets Michelle (Capucine), he mistakes her for his partner's fiancée, who in the meantime has
married someone else. Falling in love with her, he tries
to call off the deal; he even becomes jealous. Capucine
is told by his partner: "I saw him once like this before,
when somebody had stolen his horse"--again the analogy
between women and horses. Wayne tries to prevent her
from leaving town, pursuing her on main street, while
a large crowd follows them. "You've got to stay, Angel," he says, "because you have to, that's why."
Unconvinced, he has to go one step further, "because I want
you to." But she is stubborn, "I don't understand. Come
on, tell me, Sam." The town's crowd also roars, "Come on,
Sam! Tell her!" Finally, he gives in and yells, "Because I
love you, that's why!"

In Hatari! Anna Maria, nicknamed Dallas (Elsa Martinelli), is a photographer who has inadvertently misled a
group of animal hunters about her gender; they expected a
male photographer. Dallas wants to gain acceptance on the
expedition, but Wayne believes that Africa is no place for
women and that she is not suited for what he considers to

be a man's work. "Why don't you find what kind of girl I
am before you make up your mind?" she suggests. Falling
in love with him, she wants to understand what he has
against women. "Oh, he thinks they're trouble," says his
close friend Pockets (Red Buttons), telling her of a woman
Wayne once brought out to the camp, who did not like it
and left. Pockets also provides an explanation for Wayne's
sexual code: "If he doesn't like you, he doesn't care and
he can be nice to you. But if he does like you, he doesn't
want to get in any deeper, so he acts mean." In short,
"the more he likes you, the meaner he acts." Dallas is not
discouraged by Wayne's indifference, however, and decides
to make a bold move. "Sean, how do you like to kiss?" she
asks, but he finds her question baffling and ends the conversation abruptly, "It's silly to stand around and talk about
it." Dallas decides to leave the camp; Wayne, as with
Feathers in Rio Bravo and Michelle in North to Alaska, cannot admit outright he loves her. But he goes out of his way
to make her stay, requesting the police's aid. One reviewer
succinctly summed up Wayne's pattern of courtship after seeing Hatari!: "Most of the male-female relationships occur in
that older, half-adolescent level which used to be good clean
fun in so many Hollywood outdoor pictures. The man's always very embarrassed and shy, despite his hairy-chested
virility, and the adoring girl has to encourage him."[5]

Phase Three: The Comfortable Grandfather

A further change in Wayne's attitude toward women
took place in the last decade of his career. His sex image
became softer and mellower, and his movies lacked or under-
played the romantic interest. In his most typical roles in
the 1970s, he played widowers and grandfathers, becoming
a sentimental, though respected, patriarch.

Rooster Cogburn in True Grit is a loner whose family
consists of a Chinese man and a cat. The film's most touching
scenes are those in which he tells Kim Darby, relating to
her as a granddaughter, about his past. We learn that
Wayne's wife left him with a note--"The love of decency
does not abide in you"--and that his son never liked him.
And Wayne's wife in The Undefeated left him to teach piano
in Philadelphia, reportedly because she did not take to his
going off hunting. The romantic interest in this film is

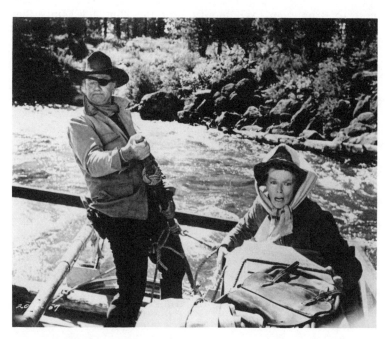

John Wayne and Katharine Hepburn in Rooster Cogburn
(Universal, 1975), a sequel to True Grit that borrowed
heavily from The African Queen.

between Wayne and a mature widow (Marian McCargo) whose
husband was killed by Wayne's troops in the Civil War.

Women play more important roles in Rio Lobo than in
previous Hawks-Wayne Westerns; for one thing, there are
three of them. Shasta Delaney (Jennifer O'Neill), a young
and beautiful woman, is attracted to Cordona (Jorge Rivero),
but likes Wayne's company; at night, she snuggles up against
him for security. Wayne suggests that she might do better
with Cordona, but she replies, "He's too young, but you're
older, more ... comfortable." At the end of the film, Cordona and Tuscarora (Chris Mitchum) go off with their girls
and Wayne, left alone, turns to Amelita (Sherry Lansing),
whose face had been disfigured by the villains. The film
implies that these companions settle for each other because
no one else will have them. Wayne has become a comfortable

old man, relinquishing his pursuit of young, attractive wom-
en. In Brannigan too, Deputy Jennifer Thatcher (Judy Gee-
son), Wayne's chauffeur, bestows a kiss on his cheek and an
affectionate hug, because he is "just so damn solid."

As a widower in The Train Robbers, he helps a young
and beautiful widow (Ann-Margret) to recover the gold her
husband stole. When she shows some interest in him, he
discourages her from any romantic notion or fantasy--"I've
got a saddle that's older than you are." Similarly, the relationship between Rooster Cogburn and Eula (Katharine
Hepburn) in Rooster Cogburn is based on mutual respect
and affection. However, there are hints, when they part,
that they will resume their friendship, which made Pauline
Kael note that they are "hardly at a time of life to postpone
romance." Or as John Simon put it, "When you are pushing
70 with John Wayne and Katharine Hepburn, you are not
playing Wyatt Earp and Calamity Jane any longer." Wayne
played a similar role in The Shootist: his gunfighter has
never been married and the relationship with his widowed
housekeeper (Lauren Bacall) is respectful, a friendly com-
panionship, but not a romantic affair.

The Ultimate Male

Wayne's movies were obsessed with defining the param-
eters of masculine behavior, repeatedly using two devices:
comparing him with women on the one hand, and with weak
men on the other. The pressures of being a real man, as
Vito Russo observed, were absolute and unyielding in the
American cinema, and the norms describing screen masculinity have not changed much over the years. Reel (and real)
men have been depicted as strong, silent, and ostentatiously
unemotional. They act quickly and never intellectualize--in
short, they do not behave as women. To be like a woman is
not only unvaluable, but also an insult, a stigma.[6] Wayne's
movies are replete with comparisons with weak and effeminate
men whose inferiority provided the yardstick for measuring
genuine virility.

Mention has been made of Wayne's cinematic function of
saving weakling youths and restoring their manhood. But to
promote the idea that he represented the ultimate male, many
of his films contrasted him with other mature men. In Red

River, his independent and unattached hero is juxtaposed
with Dan Latimer (Harry Carey, Jr.), the domesticated man
whose life is ruled by women. Dan's inferiority is further
accentuated by his stuttering, signifying his uncertain male
status.

For Wayne, real men never let their personal frustrations
--or emotions for that matter--interfere with their duties. In
Back to Bataan, he is contrasted with the leader of the Phil-
ippino guerrillas (Anthony Quinn), who moons over his sweetheart, believing she has been collaborating with the Japanese.
Quinn is so frustrated and embittered over his emotional life
that it affects his leadership. It is only after Wayne, dis-
obeying orders, tells him she is actually assisting the resistance movement, that Quinn pulls himself together and turns
out to be a courageous fighter. Wayne is not tough on Quinn,
even consoling him, "Sometimes, it's not easy to forget," but
it's clear that he is the role model for how men should behave, particularly in war times.

In Rio Bravo, the contrast is between Wayne's sheriff
and Dude (Dean Martin), a former deputy marshal, who has
become an alcoholic over the loss of his woman. Dude's
drunkenness, caused by an unhappy affair, is presented as
unmanly behavior. In the opening sequence, Wayne is astride
a horse, looking down disdainfully at the pathetic sight of
Dude, willing to do anything to get a drink. In a later
scene, Wayne has to roll a cigarette for him. But at the
end, he restores Dude to sobriety by providing a model for
self-respect and by getting him involved in a worthy action.
A similar comparison prevails in El Dorado between Wayne and
sheriff J.P. Harra (Robert Mitchum); the latter has become
a drunk after being jilted by a woman. Wayne feels
sorry for Mitchum, as he reloads his gun for him, and
his function is to restore him back to manhood. In
both pictures, Wayne serves as a symbol for weaker
males, demonstrating how real men should deal with their
emotional problems. And significantly, the weaker men are
played by actors possessing "macho" screen image in most of
their other films: Anthony Quinn, Kirk Douglas, Dean Martin, and Robert Mitchum.

Wayne's heroes are also hard-drinking, but their drinking is normatively prescribed and favorably depicted because
it is restrained, controlled, and does not interfere with their

John Wayne and Robert Mitchum engaged in a lesson in manhood in Howard Hawks's <u>El Dorado</u> (Paramount, 1967).

official duties. Drinking is integral to the Wayne screen
persona--and also one of his favorite leisure activities--but
it is never harmful. His heroes usually drink in solitude,
to overcome their despair. Thus, Wayne turns to drink in
Wake of the Red Witch, when he learns that another man is
going to marry his girl (Gail Russell). This is also one of
the few movies in which he allowed himself to be seen drunk
and violent with women; in one scene, he grips Russell's
hair for betraying him. In The Horse Soldiers, Wayne begins to drink after his wife's death on the operating table,
and in The Man Who Shot Liberty Valance, Wayne turns to
the bottle over his frustrated love for Vera Miles, who has
left him to become Jimmy Stewart's girl.

The Wayne heroes drink to console themselves, but
they do not let other people catch them drinking. In Three
Faces West, Wayne gets drunk after the Department of Agri-
culture informs him that the community of Ashville Forks,
located in a dust bowl, is doomed and its members have to
move to Oregon. In another war movie, Sands of Iwo Jima,
he drinks over his frustrations and strains as a commander,
but his drinking is not visible to his soldiers.

Wayne appeared with Kirk Douglas in three movies, in
each of which they represent completely different types of
men. In their first film together, In Harm's Way, Wayne's
ship commander is divorced and has not seen his son for 18
years, but he has buried his marital disappointments beneath
a cool and reserved exterior. By contrast, Douglas, his
brooding executive officer, has turned to alcoholism and self-
pity because he cannot accept his wife's promiscuity. Wayne
always acts honorably, whereas Douglas is impulsive, temper-
amental, and eventually self-destructive. Wayne is gentle
with women. Douglas, by contrast, is a selfish and lusty
womanizer. In the course of the film, he rapes Wayne's son's
girlfriend and, upon learning that she committed suicide,
volunteers for a deadly mission, unable to live with his
conscience.

The Man Who Shot Liberty Valance juxtaposes Wayne's
rugged Westerner and Jimmy Stewart's Eastern lawyer.
Wayne courts Hallie (Vera Miles) with old-fashioned gallantry,
bringing her cactus roses. Their courtship has been going
on for some time, and, though there is no talk of marriage,
Wayne builds an extension on his ranch for her. When he

John Wayne, Jimmy Stewart (center), and Lee Marvin (far
left) exemplifying three styles of manly conduct in John
Ford's nostalgic Western The Man Who Shot Liberty Valance
(Paramount, 1962).

brings Stewart to the restaurant where she works, however,
her affections focus on Stewart. Learning this, Wayne
starts to drink heavily; in one scene, his servant Pompey
has to take him home drunk. Furious and humiliated for being spurned, he sets fire to the room he was building for
her and neglects his appearance, appearing unshaven,
uncouth--his dignity hurt. The movie expresses nostalgia
for the disappearance of Wayne's type of man by making
Stewart look and behave effeminately. Stewart is more of a
domestic man, working in a woman's place, a restaurant,
where he wears an apron and serves food. Wayne drinks
whiskey; Stewart, coffee. Moreover, Stewart stutters and
is incapable of decisive action; he cannot even shoot, a skill
he has to acquire from Wayne.

Wayne's Sex Image in Perspective

The Western film has always been considered a masculine genre for the values it stood for: courage, strength,
endurance, risk, and action--all distinctly male values. Furthermore, the lack of strong parts for women in Wayne's
films has been characteristic of the genre in general. Wayne
himself admitted that "Westerns don't usually do much for
actresses." "I have to go clear back to 1944 and Tall in
the Saddle," he said, "to remember a good woman's part
[Ella Raines's] in a Western." He singled out The Train
Robbers as "one of the few films that offered a good part
for a woman" (Ann-Margret's widow).[7] The critics had good
reasons to complain about the paucity of women in Westerns,
with one describing Red River as a film that "keeps the appearance of women down to a bare minimum."[8] And another
critic asked the almost rhetorical question in his review of
The Comancheros: "Can't there be a reasonably plain but
sensible woman in a Western?"[9]

One of the genre's recurrent themes has been to describe its heroes as unburdened by family life and free from
domestic obligations. Cowboys preferred the company of
men, enjoying intimate relationships with their male buddies.
In many of Wayne's Westerns there are no women in his life
(due to separations, divorces, and other tragedies), and his
friendships are confined to male partners. Wayne's close
friend in Red River is Nadine Groot (Walter Brennan) and
his relationship with Matt (Clift) is intimate as well as complex. Asked about homosexual overtones in Red River, director Hawks said angrily that it was "a goddam silly statement to make."[10] In She Wore a Yellow Ribbon too, the only
person Wayne is close to is Sergeant Quincannon (Victor
McLaglen), who addresses him as "Captain darling." In
Rio Bravo, Wayne kisses his buddy (Walter Brennan) on the
top of his head, referring to him as "a treasure." Male
camaraderie also features prominently in Hawks's trilogy,
Rio Bravo, El Dorado, and Rio Lobo, though male bonds
have been a perennial theme in the American cinema, not
just in Westerns.

There has been a debate over the attributes and significance of the Hawksian heroine. Some critics stress that
Hawks's screen women have been more aggressive and independent than what was the norm for women in American film.

They claim that Feathers in <u>Rio Bravo</u> is not just a pretty
saloon girl, but a strong and intelligent woman who affects
Wayne's behavior as much, maybe more, than he does hers.
And photographer Dallas in <u>Hatari!</u> is doing a man's job in
a risky setting.[11]   But a counter, more conservative interpretation of these roles could be offered.   Feathers is still
earning her living as an entertainer, a traditional female
profession.   And Dallas displays a distinctly feminine behavior throughout <u>Hatari!</u> including infantile lines; her maternal instincts feature profusely in a silly scene with baby
elephants.   More significantly, the ambition of most women
in Hawks's films is to gain acceptance in a male's world,
and the most efficient way to accomplish integration and
thus prove their worth is by imitating the behavior of their
male counterparts.

Another convention of Westerns, reflected in Wayne's
films, has been the contrast between Western and Eastern
women, a comparison that goes beyond geographic distinc-
tions and includes psychological and cultural dimensions.
This comparison shows not only differing cultural orienta-
tions, but the superiority of Wayne's way of life.   In
<u>McLintock!</u> Maureen O'Hara wants to take her daughter back
East to become a society lady; she does not want her to be
"corrupted" by her father out in the West.   Wayne's romantic interest in <u>Donovan's Reef</u> is Amelia, a society belle from
Boston, looking for her father, who had neglected to come
home after the war.   And Wayne's devotion to his military
career in <u>In Harm's Way</u> has cost him a broken marriage.
His wife, a sophisticated lady from Boston, is accused of
corrupting their son, turning him into a weakling.   Soft
men in American films, not just in Westerns, have been regarded as products of overcaring, overprotective mothers--
usually from the East.

What made Wayne's sex image interesting is his pairing
with fiery and independent Southern belles.   His relationship
with his estranged wife in <u>Rio Grande</u> is similar to that with
Hannah Hunter (Constance Towers) in <u>The Horse Soldiers</u>.
In both movies, there is a strain on their relationships after
Wayne sets fire to their lands, of which they are tremen-
dously proud.   Both Southern ladies are strong-willed, demanding to be accepted as equals on their own terms.   And
in both, Wayne is a gallant gentleman in manners, but ruthless when his mission is threatened by their presence.

Caught spying in Horse Soldiers, Wayne demands that Hannah
be watched at all times, but he takes his hat off when he
sees her and even apologizes for the hardships she has to
endure. And he professes his love to her in a characteristically indirect manner: "It so happens that I'm in love with
you," taking her handkerchief as a souvenir.

The "taming of the shrew" is yet another narrative
convention in Wayne's attitude toward women. At first, he
is tough with his ladies, determined to break what he considers their independence--until they learn to accept their
place in his world. In The Quiet Man, he brings Maureen
O'Hara back to her brother as an unsuitable wife; the latter
refuses to give her her dowry. But at the end, he takes
her home--not before dragging her all over town kicking
and screaming. In McLintock! he repeats this treatment,
dragging O'Hara all over town, then spanking her. One
critic described this sequence and the whole film as "a
Western about Maureen O'Hara getting spanked by John
Wayne, a magnificent spectacle with the longest erotic
build-up,"[12] and another as "slapstick and burlesque comedy of a squabbling married couple."[13] And in Donovan's
Reef, Wayne spanks Elizabeth Allen and soaks her in public,
until she submits to his appeal.

In discussing Wayne's sex appeal and attitude toward
women, one cannot ignore the lack of sophistication of his
scripts, some of which made him say the most embarrassing
and ridiculous lines. One frequent and stilted cliché was to
compliment a woman when she was most irritated or upset.
It became one of his trademarks, expressed in half a dozen
variations. He tells Lana Turner in Sea Chase: "Did anyone tell you you're beautiful when you're angry?" and repeated almost the same line to Vera Miles in The Man Who
Shot Liberty Valance: "You look beautiful when you're
mad." And in his last film, The Shootist, he says to
Lauren Bacall: "You have a fine color when you're on the
scrap."

Wayne's worst dialogue with a woman is probably in
The Conqueror, costarring Susan Hayward as a Tartar
princess acquired by Wayne after slaying her husband.
Throughout the film he is tough on her, which she resents. Then in a supposedly lusty scene, he tells her
father, the ruler Kumlek: "While I live, while my blood

runs hot, your daughter is not safe in her tent!" And warned, "There is no limit to her perfidy," he responds, "She is a woman. Much woman. Should her perfidy be less than that of other women." Later, Hawyard tries to decapitate him with a sword while his back is turned, but he looks into her defiant face and delivers his favorite line, "You're beautiful in your wrath." He then carries her into the tent and tells her, "I shall keep you, Bortai, in response to my passion. Your hatred will kindle into love." But she is still defiant, "Before that day dawns, Mongol, the vultures will have feasted on your heart." To think that Susan Hayward agreed to appear in this film and recite these lines, when she was at the peak of her popularity, is still hard to believe. And as one critic observed, more than embarrassing, "the love scenes are laughable."[14]

Wayne's romantic-love scenes are, arguably, the poorest and weakest aspect of his work. His declaration of love to Geraldine Page in Hondo, as Arthur Knight observed, "with face as mobile as a granite builder," was "in simple Indian endearments that translate out into rather complicated and painful poetry."[15] In one scene, he states: "I'm part Indian and I can smell you when I'm down-wind of you ... I could find you in the dark, Mrs. Lowe." His romance with a war widow (Nancy Olson) in Big Jim McLain is so naive that one critic noted that it was surely "one of the healthiest, most wholesome love affairs ever represented on the screen."[16] And another critic wrote about Sea Chase: "Wayne is all that his following could ask when engaged in driving his ship and men, but as a he-man type, seems a little embarrassed in delivering some of the boy-girl talk."[17] Surprisingly, this naiveté continued to characterize his movies up to his last one, despite radical changes in the screen portrayal of gender, love, and sex.

A Gentle Wolf

A star's sex image is promoted, among other things, by the kinds of screen ladies he is paired with. For the most part, Wayne's leading ladies were not Hollywood's sex goddesses. Early on, a frequent lady was Claire Trevor, with whom he made three films, Stagecoach, Allegheny Uprising, and Dark Command. Many remember them as a team because of Stagecoach's importance to his sex appeal and

career. Wayne looked extremely good in the three movies
he made with Marlene Dietrich in her post-Josef Von Sternberg's era: Seven Sinners, The Spoilers, and Pittsburgh.
The contrast between her worldly, sophisticated women and
his shy, awkward men was particularly endearing because it
brought out the best of their respective screen personae.
By comparison, his movies with Susan Hayward, Reap the
Wild Wind and The Fighting Seabees, before either of them
was a star, did little to promote his sex image, and their
last film together, The Conqueror, was downright embarrassing.

The chemistry between Wayne and Maureen O'Hara
worked well from the start, on screen and off; they became
close friends. Wayne described her as his favorite screen
lady, "a big, lusty, wonderful gal," in short "my kind of
gal."[18] And she regarded him as "the softest, kindest,
warmest, most loyal human being I've ever known." Their
relationship was like "brother and sister," O'Hara said.
They were often mistaken as a romantic pair offscreen because of their five films together. O'Hara promoted his public image whenever she could: "Wayne is not interested in
anything less than 100 percent woman because he's 100 percent man." Or "Duke is what the world thinks the American
male is, and what a shame they're not." O'Hara said she
could not count "the number of places I've been where they've
asked me about Duke," and that "men want to know as much
about him as women."[19]

In the middle phase of his career he was cast against
young and attractive stars, most notably Angie Dickinson
(Rio Bravo), Capucine (North to Alaska), Elsa Martinelli
(Hatari!), Donna Reed (Trouble Along the Way), and Martha
Hyer (The Sons of Katie Elder). But in the last decade, he
was paired with stronger and older actresses, such as Patricia Neal (In Harm's Way), Colleen Dewhurst (The Cowboys,
McQ), Lauren Bacall (The Shootist), and Katharine Hepburn
(Rooster Cogburn). Wayne was much more powerful and convincing as an actor when playing against strong-willed and intelligent actresses. His casting against mature women prompted
critic Haskell to observe: "How many other maturing male stars
have allowed themselves to be paired with women who were
roughly their contemporaries, instead of dropping back one
generation, then another?"[20] Haskell's statement is not exactly accurate, for most of his costars, with the exception of Hepburn, were at least a generation his juniors. But she is

right about the appeal of these stars: none was the typical
Hollywood glamor queen.

Wayne was more aware of his progressing age and declining looks than other actors, as he said in 1957:   "My
problem is I'm not a handsome man like Cary Grant, who will
still be handsome at sixty five."   "I may be able to do a few
more man-woman things before it's too late, but then what?"
He was therefore determined not to play "silly old men chasing young girls, as some of the stars are doing."[21] And for
the most part, he did not.   In only a few movies he looked
ridiculous courting young women, as in Donovan's Reef, in
which his romantic interest was Elizabeth Allen, a former
fashion model half his age.   Wayne conceded that "Ford never
should have used me in that picture."   "He should have
picked some young guy," he explained, "it didn't require
much of him.   All he had to be was a good-looking young
guy, and I wasn't young enough."[22]

Another movie, exceptional in the incredible way it
treats Wayne's sex appeal was McQ, in which he is pursued
by women half his age.   Pauline Kael found it absurd that
"women are all hot for this sexpot," and that Colleen Dewhurst, playing a lonely waitress, had to apologize for being
fat and ugly before dragging him to bed.[23] But other critics thought that Wayne still possessed "a more extensive sexual range than younger, ostensibly hipper studs like Paul
Newman and Robert Redford."   Describing Wayne as "the
last movie star to make respect sexy," Jack Kroll claimed
there was "plenty of eroticism in the Duke, but it's a friendly eroticism that takes any woman on her own terms."[24]

Wayne was a true gentleman beneath the rough exterior
façade, and more accepting of his women than other stars.
A "tender Titan," Haskell wrote, "capable of two-fisted fury
but infinitely more capable of chivalry and fatherly wisdom."
"He was secure enough in his masculine identity to listen to
women," and "he could often respond to them with less van-
ity and more humanity than could a romantic lead."[25] True,
Wayne never had to display sexual prowess in the manner
that Clark Gable or Sean Connery did.   "Bond's crude sexual exhibitionism," critic Joan Mellen observed, "shows the
need endlessly to prove a capacity, the more secure Wayne
always took for granted."[26] Wayne's heroes acted effort-
lessly, "with neither self-doubt nor anxiety," and "because

his very reflexes guide him in how to be a man, he requires neither intellect nor the brutalization of women to prove himself."[27]

A consistent trait of Wayne's sex image was his tenderness with women. His gentle courtship had none of the compulsive womanizing of the male chauvinist. He was deeply emotional, which he expressed eloquently with his eyes and his voice. "If he thought he was better off on his own," Haskell noted, "it was not from the narcissism of the compulsive lover, but because he hadn't yet come to understand what he would come to understand: that men and women could be not only lovers but friends."[28] Still, his passion for women was restrained rather than carnal or lusty.

Wayne's gentleness stood in sharp opposition to Cagney's brashness or Gable's toughness with women. Gable's sex image, based on his handsome looks and erotic carnality, was almost diametrically opposed to Wayne's. Comparing the two, Hawks observed that "in a romantic scene, Clark Gable always forced the issue with a girl," whereas Wayne "is better when the girl is forcing the issue."[29] Gable always pursued women in his films, provoking their affection through aggression. Wayne's sexual authority was so secure, he did not have to. Women in Wayne's films were more sex-oriented than he was; they were the first to initiate romantic or sexual encounters. Furthermore, Gable's screen persona was defined by his relationships with women; he was always placed in an explicitly romantic or sexual context. Take the women out of Gable's movies and you are left with a void because they are the center of the narrative--which is not at all the case with Wayne.

Gable's most frequent screen ladies were Hollywood's glamor and sex goddesses, appearing in eight movies with Joan Crawford, seven with Myrna Loy (before she became the symbol of the American housewife), six with Jean Harlow, four with Lana Turner, and three with Ava Gardner. And his less successful performances were opposite gentle and more sophisticated stars, such as Helen Hayes and Greer Garson. Crawford, Harlow, and Gardner were his best female partners because they were similar to him in their screen image: lower-class, simple, sexy, earthy, and a bit vulgar.

The quintessential Gable hero was the aggressive male who manhandled his women to prove his superiority. He slapped Norma Shearer across the face in A Free Soul, and did the same to Barbara Stanwyck in Night Nurse and To Please a Lady. And Joan Crawford was roughed up in Dance, Fools, Dance and many other movies. Gable took no nonsense from women; he humiliated them by blowing smoke on their faces. He adored domineering women, as he characteristically told Norma Shearer in A Free Soul: "You make no bargains with anyone but me."

But Gable was much more constricted by his macho image than Wayne. As Rhett Butler in Gone with the Wind, he refused to cry, believing that crying was unmanly behavior that might tarnish his masculine image; director Victor Fleming had to plead with him until he agreed. Ironically, Gable was at first reluctant to play this role, though most people thought he was born for it.[30] Gable usually played the self-confident, flamboyant, unattainable male whom women adored because they thought they could not get--or hold--him. However, in the course of a typical Gable film, his character undergoes a transformation from the desirable, boyish bachelor to the domesticated husband who does not mind settling down--provided it is for and with the "right" woman. But until he finds the right girl, he flirts and has fun with many women. Usually there are two women, the bad (or good-bad) and the really good and innocent girl. In the popular Red Dust, Gable flirts with Mary Astor but sends her back to her husband, refusing to wreck her family life. At the film's climax, when she shoots him in anger, he tells her in his relaxed manner: "I'm not a one-woman man. I never have been and I never will. If you want to take your turn...." But in the final account, he is a one-woman man. Gable used his immense sex appeal to get higher-class women than himself, as was the case with Claudette Colbert in It Happened One Night.

But even Gable's image was mild compared to Cagney's, which was radically different from Wayne's. A short, rather grim-looking man, Cagney defied any romantic image. In his specialty genre, the crime-gangster movie, women did not feature prominently; they were cast as molls or mothers. When the Cagney hero meets an attractive woman, he eyes her from head to toe, measuring her as a sex object, with no time for flirtation. He knows what he is after and also

lets his women know; his playfulness is always intentional,
to get the woman.[31] Cagney's protagonists are extremely
brash with women, smashing a grapefruit on Mae Clark's
face in The Public Enemy, and roughing her up again in
The Lady Killer. His hero slaps Barbara Payton, as his
mistress in Tomorrow Goodbye, with a wet towel, and throws
Virginia Mayo around in White Heat as if she were a piece of
furniture. Unlike Gable, Cagney's men are not desirable to
women, hating and resenting his aggressive manner.

Humphrey Bogart, like Wayne, was at his best when
paired with strong actresses, such as Mary Astor (The Maltese Falcon), Ida Lupino (High Sierra), and Katharine Hepburn (The African Queen). And like Wayne, his typical hero
is basically an "old-fashioned" man, romantic beneath a tough
exterior, and monogamous, defining himself as a one-woman
man. Interestingly, the Bogart sex image became softer,
more romantic, and more glamorous as he became older. His
marriage to Lauren Bacall in 1945, who was a generation his
junior, rejuvenated his screen persona. Bacall was also his
most important screen lady, appearing in four of his best
known films, To Have and Have Not, The Big Sleep, Dark
Passage, and Key Largo.

Because Wayne was not as handsome as Cary Grant,
his sex image developed along different lines. Attractive,
suave, and sophisticated, Grant represented the most desirable male star in American film. His flirtatious manner is
different from Gable's; it is seductive but gentle. And unlike Wayne or Gable, his screen characters are typically middle or upper-middle class, which was reflected in the kinds
of women he was paired with: Katharine Hepburn (four movies, including Bringing Up Baby and The Philadelphia Story),
Irene Dunne (three, like The Awful Truth and My Favorite
Wife), Carole Lombard, and Myrna Loy. Grant, Wayne's
favorite star, retained his looks up to the end of his career
in 1966. Of the male stars of his generation, he was least
touched by age; some think he became more attractive with
the years. Which is why audiences did not notice that Grant
continued to flirt with beautiful women half his age: Grace
Kelly (To Catch a Thief), Sophia Loren (House Boat), Audrey
Hepburn (Charade), and Leslie Caron (Father Goose). He
could continue to play leading men for at least another decade, but he decided to retire early--at 62--because he did
not want to look ridiculous.

Wayne's sex persona, like other elements of his image, was more similar to Gary Cooper, Henry Fonda, and Jimmy Stewart, especially in their Frank Capra films. More than any other director, Capra is responsible for the creation of a distinctly American male image: the shy and naive simpleton, who was either a farmer or a small-town lawyer. Capra's heroes, Cooper in Mr. Deeds Goes to Town and Meet John Doe, and Stewart in Mr. Smith Goes to Washington and It's a Wonderful Life, are basically shy and have to be coached by women about love and sex. Cooper's casting opposite Marlene Dietrich (in two films) or Barbara Stanwyck (also two) was very effective because of their differences. The contrast between Cooper's shy professor and Stanwyck's burlesque queen stripper in Billy Wilder's Ball of Fire, or Marlene Dietrich's sophisticated jewel thief in Desire, is credible as well as charmingly poignant because they project an urbane and wordly image. Stanwyck was also Henry Fonda's favorite actress, appearing in three films with him. Fonda played the same kinds of roles that Cooper and Stewart did, as in The Lady Eve, in which his naiveté and clumsiness achieve perfect effects against Stanwyck's maturity; she flirts with Jack Carson, but when it comes to romantic commitment she chooses, of course, Fonda.

Cooper actually began his career as a romantic hero, often wounded or dying in a romantic context opposite Fay Wray (four movies) or Clara Bow (three). Once he started to work with Capra and Hawks, however, his image began to change into the tough, no-nonsense hero. And contrary to Grant, who aged well, and Wayne who ceased playing romantic roles at middle age, Cooper looked increasingly old and weary. In the 1950s he dyed his hair to achieve a youthful appearance, but to no avail, and his cosmetic surgery got embarrassing publicity. Aware or unaware of his age, Cooper made the mistake of continuing to appear in romantic leads opposite actresses younger than his daughter. He was much too old to play the American cowboy wooing and winning Audrey Hepburn in Love in the Afternoon, and looked terribly old in the love scene with model-turned-actress Suzy Parker in Ten North Frederick, two of his later films.

Two actresses were important in the formation of Jimmy Stewart's sex persona: Margaret Sullavan in the 1930s and June Allyson in the 1950s. Stewart costarred with Sullavan

in four romantic movies, such as The Shopworn Girl and
Mortal Storm, in both of which she dies in his arms. But
Allyson had more lasting importance on his image in their
three films, The Stratton Story, The Glenn Miller Story,
and Strategic Air Command. In these and other movies,
Stewart plays the wife-inspired husband and the ideal
father, monogamous and domestic. Unlike Gable, Stewart
does not flirt with married women, except in Vertigo, and
unlike Wayne, his heroes reconcile successfully a viable
professional career with a happy domestic life. Stewart
provided the model for the American male in the 1950s in
his dual roles as husband-father.

Wayne's sexuality is also monogamous; he neither betrays his screen wives nor flirts with married women. But
his domesticity tends to be more familial than marital, family and children are at the center of his pictures. "The
longer Wayne kept his promise, kept providing, stayed true,
kept being there despite cancer and illnesses and age itself,"
Michael Malone observed, "the more valued the strength of
his fidelity and the integrity of his identity came to be."[32]
Women's attraction to the values he stood for was so strong
that in the 1970s even the feminists came to admire him as a
protective paternal figure.

7. THE ACTOR

Throughout Wayne's career there have been controversies over his acting skills and abilities. Some critics consider him a screen personality, not an actor. However, even his detractors admit there was "something" special about his screen persona and acting style.

Acting Style

Wayne did not study in any drama school; he learned his skills in front of the camera. He belonged to the breed of self-made performers who started their careers at the bottom of the industry's hierarchy and were exclusively screen actors. "Wayne is a motion picture actor, first, last and always," film critic Charles Champlin observed, who "defined as powerfully as anyone else what that means."[1] And because his association with this medium was so intimate, it looked "as if he were born in Hollywood and belongs to the movies."[2]

When Wayne was under contract to Fox, his bosses thought he should learn some acting and assigned him a famous drama coach, a Shakespearean actor. This coach wanted to give him some classic stage training, or in Wayne's words, "he wanted me to act like some of those fancy leading men they had on Broadway."[3] He recalled that the coach had him "mincing on my toes, making sweep gestures with my right arm, rolling my r's like I was Edwin Booth playing Hamlet." He felt "ridiculous," and after a few weeks told his coach, "I don't think I'm getting anything of these lessons. I think I ought to stop them," to which the latter replied, "If you live to be a hundred years old, you will never become an actor."[4] Wayne also told his bosses that if they wanted him to act like that, "I didn't reckon I could

162

cut the mustard."[5] Fortunately for Wayne, Raoul Walsh happened to see one class and, after listening to his complaints, agreed that he should stop studying.

Walsh was impressed with Wayne's screen test for The Big Trail and thought that "for a college man, he read well enough, but he fell into the common trap of beginners. He overdramatized his lines." Walsh's first advice to Wayne was to play his part "with a cool hand, like I think you'd do on a football field." He also told him: "Speak softly, but with authority, and look whoever you're talking to right in the eyes."[6] Indeed, actors who have worked with him marveled at his ability to listen and his capacity of looking the other players in the scene straight in the eyes. Walsh recalled that from the day of the screen test, "I knew all he had to do was to be himself. His personality, looks, and natural mannerisms were made to order for motion pictures."[7]

One of Wayne's strengths was underacting. "He underacts," Walsh said, "and it's mighty effective. Not because he tries to underact--it's a hard thing to do, if you try-- but because he can't overact." During the shooting of The Big Trail, Wayne sometimes got discouraged: "I can't do the part that way," he said, "it's too hard. I'm not good enough for it." But Walsh learned to handle the problem by "letting him do the thing the way he feels he can, and he's fine."[8]

If there is any school to describe Wayne's acting, it is naturalism, as he explained: "I merely try to act naturally. If I start acting phony on the screen, you start looking at me instead of feeling with me."[9] But Wayne insisted, "You can't be natural; you have to act natural," because "if you're just natural you can drop a scene." His ideal was to act in such a way so that "the plumber sitting out there, and the lawyer next to him and the doctor don't see anything wrong."[10]

The closest thing Wayne came to having an acting coach was Paul Fix, a Hollywood character actor of the silent era, whom he had met in the 1930s under the suggestion of Loretta Young. Fix recalled that "Duke was bright enough but he didn't know how to prove it, what to do with his hands, and after three lines he was lost." Wayne and Fix worked out a set of signals: when Wayne was overdoing his "famed furrowing of his brow," for instance, Fix put his hands on his head. Fix was on the set with Wayne for years, but "nobody ever caught on."[11]

Wayne gave a lot of credit to Yakima Canutt, the distinguished rodeo rider and stunt man who taught him all his tricks, including how to fall off a horse without getting hurt. "I took his walk and the way he talked," Wayne said, "sorta low with quiet strength."[12] Wayne claimed that his furrowed brow, a distinctive mannerism, was a family trait because his brother also had it. But close friends have claimed that the waffled forehead, cocked eyebrows, and swivel-hipped walk were all creations modeled after Canutt's techniques.

Wayne also learned from Walsh and Ford to let the other actors in the scene guide his performance. He liked to think of himself as a reactor rather than actor: "I can react to a situation that has already been built up when I walk on. I do not like to explain that situation myself."[13] The difference between good and bad acting, he said, is "the difference between acting and reacting." "In a bad picture," he explained, "you see them acting all over the place. In a good picture, they react in a logical way to a situation they're in, so the audience can identify with them."[14] But Wayne insisted that reacting is a valid form of acting and also harder work than given credit to. Screen acting was to him "a matter of handling yourself," comparable to "sitting in a room with somebody." In film, "the audience is with you--not like the stage, where they're looking at you--so you've got to be careful to project the right illusion."[15]

Over the years, Wayne mastered the art of natural acting, which also characterized the style of Cooper, Gable, and Stewart. Ford described all of these performers as "great actors," because "they are the same off the screen as they are playing a part." As for Wayne's distinctive style, Ford said: "He's not something out of a book, governed by acting rules. He portrays John Wayne, a rugged American guy. He's not one of those method actors, like they send out here from drama schools in New York. He's real. He is perfectly natural."[16] Lee Strasberg, the late director of the Actors Studio and proponent of Method acting, also believed that "good acting exists when an actor thinks and reacts as much to imaginery situations as those in real life." "Gary Cooper, John Wayne, Spencer Tracy,"

Strasberg held, "try not to act but to be themselves, to respond or react. They refuse to do or say anything they
feel not to be consonant with their own characters."[17]

Katharine Hepburn described Wayne as an actor with
"an extraordinary gift. A unique naturalness, developed by
movie actors who just happened to become actors." These
actors possess "an unself-consciousness," and "a very subtle
capacity to think and caress the camera--the audience, with
no apparent effort." Wayne and other actors of his kind
"seem to develop a technique similar to that of well-trained
actors from the theater," arriving "at the same point from
an entirely different beginning." She described Wayne's
manner as "a total reality of performance," to the point
where "the acting does not appear acting," and becomes
"as powerful as his personality." Wayne was a "very, very
good actor," Hepburn said, "in the most highbrow sense of
the word," because "you don't catch him at that."[18]

"I read dramatic lines undramatically and react to situations normally," said Wayne of his distinctive techniques.
But he did not let critics underestimate it: "This is not as
simple as it sounds. I've spent a major portion of my life
trying to learn to do it well and I am not past learning
yet."[19] As for his tricks, he said he had only two. One
was "to stop in the middle of the sentence, so they'll keep
looking at me." The other was "not to stop at the end, so
they don't look away."[20]

Director Hawks felt that ironically "Wayne became a
much better actor since he suffered his bout with cancer."
"Because of the lung Wayne lost," he explained, "he reads
his lines differently. He pauses in the strangest places
simply because he hasn't got the breath he used to have."
This device was "terribly effective," because you keep your
eyes on him and wait for Wayne to finish because you don't
know what's coming next."[21] Wayne developed other devices
to express the unique qualities of his screen image--honesty
and sincerity. He had an interesting voice that stressed
every word in its own candid space. And he raised his eyebrows suddenly, so that his forehead crinkled with sincerity.

Wayne's acting style stood in sharp contrast to that of
the younger generation, particularly Method actors, such as
Marlon Brando, Montgomery Clift, and James Dean. He did

not like to be overly emotional or expressive in his acting
and preferred a minimum of dialogue--"one look that works
is better than twenty lines of dialogue."[22] He was also
against mannered acting, which he thought characterized
many stage actors from New York. "Let those actors who
picked their noses," he once said, "get all the dialogue,
just give me the closeup of reaction."[23] Wayne resented the
publicity and prestige that these actors received upon arrival
in Hollywood, based on the reputation of their stage work in
New York. And he was not the only one of his generation
to feel that way. Humphrey Bogart was even more vocal in
his criticism of the New York actors, particularly in 1951,
when his major competitor for the Best Actor Oscar was
Marlon Brando, for his stunning performance in A Streetcar
Named Desire; Bogart won (for The African Queen), though
many believed that it was Brando who deserved to win. The
Best Actor nominations that year marked a turning point in
the American cinema as far as acting styles were concerned.
Along with Brando, another distinguished actor and graduate
of the Actors Studio was singled out by the Academy: Montgomery Clift for A Place in the Sun.

    Bogart also shared Wayne's deep respect for acting,
but, unlike Wayne, he belonged to a breed of actors who
believed that acting was an acquired professional technique
and were therefore proud of their competence: "I don't approve of the John Waynes and Gary Coopers," claimed Bogart,
"saying, 'Shucks, I ain't no actor--I'm just a bridge builder
or a gas station attendant!' If they aren't actors, what the
hell are they getting paid for."[24]

    Wayne was usually much more relaxed in front of the
camera than most of his costars. Take Kirk Douglas, who
appeared in three movies with him and whose approach to
acting was highly emotional. Douglas's abundance of energy
and vitality somehow suited the kinds of roles he played--
manic, neurotic, and high-strung men: the unscrupulous
boxer in Champion, the selfish producer in The Bad and the
Beautiful. Compared with Wayne, who liked to ad lib sometimes, Douglas was a perfectionist who rehearsed every syl-
lable of the text. Douglas's acting was both combative and
impulsive; at times it looked as if he were going to explode
on the screen.[25]

    Despite these differences, Douglas admired Wayne's

way of reading lines, as he described after working with him
in In Harm's Way: "Wayne brings so much authority to a
role, he can pronounce literally any line in a script and get
away with it." Nonetheless, there was a line where Wayne
says "I need a fast ship because I want to be in harm's
way," that Douglas felt even Wayne could not get away with.
He recalled: "I thought, oh, shit, I've gotta hear him saying this line. But you know what? He said it, and he got
away with it." Which made him believe that Wayne was "the
perfect movie star."[26] Screenwriter Wendell Mayes also
praised Wayne's work in this movie: "John Wayne never
blows a line. He'll come in letter perfect. The other actors will blow lines but he will stand there patiently, wait
for them to get their lines, say his in his own way."[27]

Wayne's natural acting did not mean there was no work
involved or no preparation for the part. On the contrary,
every word he uttered, every move he made was studied and
planned meticulously. He rejected the critics' charge that he
"simply plays himself on the screen." For one thing, he
said, "it's quite obvious it can't be done." Moreover, "if
you are yourself, you'll be the dullest son of a bitch in the
world on screen." "You have to act yourself," he reasoned,
"you have to project something--a personality." The only
concession he made to the critics is that "perhaps I have
projected something closer to my personality than other actors have."[28] His favorite performers were therefore the
natural actors, Spencer Tracy and Gary Cooper, but he held
the highest regard for Cary Grant, whom he considered the
best actor in the business. The best film players, he claimed,
were not actors' actors, but the personality actors who "supposedly played themselves."[29]

But Wayne never liked to hear that his acting consisted
of just being himself. On the set of The Shootist, when
Elaine Newton, one of the sheriff's deputies, remarked how
natural he was, he jumped, "Natural, hell. Nobody's natural
in front of the camera. What she means is that I'm acting
natural." Natural acting, he repeated, was a "damn hard thing
to do, but when it works, it's just great."[30]

Wayne's response to situations on screen was what his
reaction would have been in real life, no matter what the
screenplay called for or the director required. He believed
that his success stemmed from "doing what comes naturally,

and, happily, people seem to like it."[31] "Wayne's total lack
of artificiality is the thing that puts him across," said Ward
Bond, who appeared in many of his movies, "everything he
does is strictly Wayne and nobody else."[32] The things
Wayne brought to the screen derived from his philosophy or
code of acting, described by him as "the code of manhood."
In any role, "I try to act as any man or woman would think
a real man ought to act in that situation."[33] Wayne's greatest reward was to hear people say "Old Duke there, he's
just like one of us."[34]

    He never thought of performing on stage, which he
felt was "completely out of me," and "a different racket al-
together." He thought stage work "may be good for new-
comers, but only because it gives them a certain confidence
and poise." But he also believed that "sometimes training
from stage coaching can be a handicap, not a help in motion
pictures."[35] His advice to younger people interested in a
screen career was therefore rather simple: "Go to school,
learn to handle liquor, mix with people, get into trouble,
work in lots of different jobs, and always remember reac-
tions to things and people. That's the best equipment in
front of the camera."[36]

Range

    Early on in his career, Wayne wanted to establish him-
self as a versatile actor, playing diverse roles, not just Westerners. "Not that I thought of becoming a song-and-dance-
man," he said, "but, like most young actors, I did want to
play a variety of roles."[37] Of his five-decade career, the
1940s were the most versatile years, providing the widest
range of roles. Along with cowboys and soldiers, he was
cast in sports pictures, comedies, and crime stories. That
he did not display great talent for comedy was evident in
Seven Sinners and Without Reservations; he lacked a sense
of timing in delivering his lines and seemed to be stiff. It
took another decade until he was comfortable in comedies.

    He was also unsuccessful in playing lawyers or other
contemporary roles. In A Man Betrayed (1941), Wayne plays
a backwood lawyer arriving in the big city to investigate a
friend's death, claimed to have been a suicide. In the process, he smashes the corrupt political underworld and, after

righting the wrongs, takes his girl, the city boss's daughter, to the peaceful life of a small town. Based on a Jack Motiff story, the screenplay was unoriginal and Wayne unconvincing as the small-town man fighting the big city graft ring, a role in which both Cooper and Stewart excelled.

In Lady from Louisiana (1941), based on the true tale of the rise and fall of lottery and racketeering in 1880s Louisiana, Wayne is cast as a young Northern attorney who comes, at the request of a crusading reformer, to eradicate the lottery controlled by the city boss. Once again, he is in love with a Southern belle (Ona Munson), the daughter of the lottery promoter. It was a modern crime yarn, dressed in period costumes, that did not work, primarily because of its casting. The New York Herald Tribune critic wrote: "John Wayne, an Iowan boy by birth, who speaks with the slow drawl of a Texan, is an extremely likable leading man, but he doesn't seem to fit the part of the upright young man from New England." "Not that Mr. Wayne can't throw a punch as well as any other rugged screen actor," he continued, "but his characteristic easy-going way of playing betrays the person he is supposed to be."[38]

After Red River, however, his attempts to expand his range declined and he was archetypically cast. He had found the kind of role he needed, and Borden Chase, the screenwriter of Red River, predicted that he could play such roles for the next 20 years. But this meant two things for his range as an actor. First, that his career became almost exclusively associated with the Western film. And second, that even within the Western genre, his roles became increasingly similar, to the point where critics and audiences could distinguish the John Wayne Western as an entity in its own right.

However, Wayne's occasional comedic Westerns provided an opportunity to demonstrate different kinds of skills. Hathaway's North to Alaska marked the beginning of a broader range, enabling him to demonstrate his newly acquired flair for comedy. The critics seemed to notice this new trend, as critic Eugene Archer wrote: "Knowing, no doubt, that Mr. Wayne's role as a big, brawling, hard-drinking American adventurer is as familiar to filmgoers as the Alaskan gold rush setting, director Henry Hathaway and scenarists have taken a refreshingly mocking attitude toward both."[39]

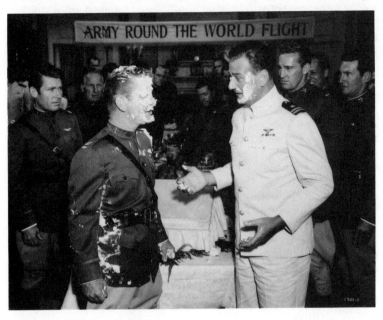

John Wayne and Kenneth Tobey following a slapstick brawl
in John Ford's The Wings of Eagles (MGM, 1957).

This mocking attitude, or self-parody, was further expanded
by Hathaway in True Grit, one of the funniest roles in
Wayne's career. But his sense of light comedy was also displayed in other Westerns, most notably McLintock! and The
Comancheros.

Wayne's last serious though abortive attempt to expand
his range was at the end of his career, when he tried to add
new roles to what was increasingly becoming too familiar a
gallery. He first appeared, as was the fashion in the 1970s,
as a cop-detective in urban crime stories, such as Brannigan
and McQ. This new addition was neither welcomed by critics
nor liked by his fans. "Surely Mr. Wayne should stick to
Westerns," a New York Times reviewer characteristically
wrote, "he's simply too slow [other critics thought too old]
to play any kind of policeman."40

In retrospect, it seems that Wayne's range as an actor

was much more limited than that of Bogart, Fonda, and Stewart, but no more limited than Gable's or Cooper's. However, a fairer judgment of his acting abilities is to examine whether he was competent in playing his specialized roles. Most critics would probably agree with Vincent Canby's assessment: "Mr. Wayne could never have played Lear, but Paul Scofield could never have played the Ringo Kid in Stagecoach or Rooster Cogburn in True Grit."[41] Charles Champlin concurs with Canby: "What he did as an actor within his range, which is to say in his own image, he did with confidence and excitement and authority," and "the roles he could not do, did not matter."[42] Sir Ralph Richardson, who was supposed to appear in Brannigan but withdrew from the project (the role was assigned to Richard Attenborough), thought Wayne could do even Shakespeare. "He is hypnotic," Richardson is reported to have said, "He conveys such a sense of mystery and that's invaluable in Shakespeare."[43]

One way to evaluate an actor's cinematic contribution is to examine his output in terms of movies that have withstood the test of time. Accordingly, Wayne gave at least ten marvelous performances in movies that have become classics of their kind. Allen Eyles has suggested that when the name of a screen role is as readily remembered as the actor who played it, it is a measure of the part's impact on audiences' collective memory.[44] There have been at least ten such roles in Wayne's career: Ringo Kid in Stagecoach, Ole Olsen in The Long Voyage Home, Thomas Dunson in Red River, Nathan Brittles in She Wore a Yellow Ribbon, Sergeant John M. Stryker in Sands of Iwo Jima, Sean Thornton in The Quiet Man, Ethan Edwards in The Searchers, John T. Chance in Rio Bravo, Rooster Cogburn in True Grit, and John B. Books in The Shootist. These performances are considered to be among the best portrayals in American film, not just in Wayne's oeuvre. Significantly, five of these roles were contained in John Ford's movies and two in Howard Hawks's.

These performances ensure Wayne a firm place among Hollywood's immortal stars. Some may consider this to be a modest contribution but, put in perspective, did Cooper, Gable, or Bogart give more than ten really good performances? One really has to stretch the imagination to compile a list of ten achievements by Gable. There is no doubt over four: It Happened One Night, The Mutiny on the

Bounty, Gone with the Wind, and his last film, The Misfits.
Gable was older than Wayne by a few years (born in 1901),
but began his career at approximately the same time. However, Gable became a star a few years after his debut, doing his best work during the first decade of his career, unlike Wayne. Gable appeared, of course, in many popular
movies, such as Red Dust, San Francisco, Boom Town, and
Mogambo, but it is doubtful that his work in these films
would be considered exceptional.

Even Cooper, who some considered an exception because he made better and more popular films than other
stars, did not give more than ten distinguished performances.
A list of Cooper's achievements would probably include,
chronologically, The Virginian, Morocco, A Farewell to Arms,
The Lives of a Bengal Lancer, Mr. Dees Goes to Town, The
Westerner, Meet John Doe, Sergeant York, The Pride of
the Yankees, High Noon, and Friendly Persuasion. Note
that like Gable, Cooper's best films were in the earlier part
of his career and that after 1942 he made very few good pictures, though he continued to be a box-office attraction.
Next to Wayne, Cooper is the actor who contributed most to
the Western genre, but of his best films only four were
Westerns.

Wayne's favorite films, those he considered "up to
standard," were usually those which got the critics' approval. Rooster Cogburn was his all-time favorite character, perhaps becuase of the recognition and the Oscar he received
for it. But asked whether True Grit was his best picture,
he said: "Two classic Westerns were better: Stagecoach
and Red River--and a third, The Searchers, which I thought
deserved more praise than it got, and The Quiet Man was
certainly one of the best."[45] Wayne also singled out The
Long Voyage Home, "the one that all the college cinematography students run to all the time." He named The Searchers as John Ford's best film, but said he enjoyed working
in two other Ford Westerns, She Wore a Yellow Ribbon and
The Horse Soldiers. "You like different pictures for different reasons," he said, so judging by the joy of making a
film, he had "the most fun making The Quiet Man."[46]

To his credit, he never denied making bad pictures,
"I've done a lot of things I'm not proud of and I've seen a
lot of pictures I wouldn't be proud to be in."[47] He refused

to name his worst pictures because "there's about 50 of them that are tied." "I can't remember the names of some of the leading ladies in those pictures," he added, "let alone the name of the pictures."[48]

Wayne had his share of bad pictures in every decade of his lengthy career. But in the late 1950s, more than in other decades, he struck "bad luck" and his career reached its lowest ebb. Between 1956 and 1958, he probably made his worst movies since the 1930s: Dick Powell's The Conqueror, Josef Von Sternberg's Jet Pilot, Henry Hathaway's Legend of the Lost, and John Huston's The Barbarian and the Geisha. These failures had an impact on his box-office popularity and 1958 was the only year between 1949 and 1974 in which he was not among the top ten money-making stars (see chapter 9). His worst picture in the 1960s was Hathaway's Circus World, and the two 1970s clinkers, McQ and Brannigan, accounted for his disappearance from the ten most popular stars in the United States. Fortunately, he improved his record with his last two pictures, Rooster Cogburn, which was a popular, though not artistic, success, and the critically acclaimed The Shootist.

What distinguished Wayne's career as an actor was not only its amazing durability and productivity, but also the fact that it had many sudden upheavals. Wayne probably made more bad pictures than other stars, but there seemed to be a recurrent pattern: a succession of bad movies was followed by an excellent performance, so that the bad pictures were soon forgotten. Wayne always emerged undamaged from his disastrous movies.

Wayne and the Film Critics

In the first decade of his career most of Wayne's films were not even reviewed, and the few that were, ignored his work. The Big Trail, for which he received favorable notices, stands as an exception: "Mr. Wayne acquits himself with no little distinction," wrote Hall in the New York Times, "his performance is pleasantly natural."[49] The reviews of other 1930s movies usually ignored his acting and focused on his appearance or technical abilities. Thus, the Herald Tribune wrote, for example, that The Lawless Nineties (1936) "gives Wayne a chance to demonstrate his prowess with his fists,

on a horse and with a lasso."[50] Another typical review was
Variety's of The Lonely Trail (1936): "Wayne is his usual
good-looking, erect-riding self but never impresses as being
convinced of his role."[51]

It is hard to blame the critics for overlooking his work,
because the pictures were not worth reviewing. He himself
did not regard his work as professional acting. "I never
learned [to act] and I never will, I just can't act," he told
a reporter on the set of The Shepherd of the Hills.[52] "I may
not be the world's greatest actor," he admitted, "but I know
what the public wants and I give it to them."[53] But the
truth is that it took him, not just the critics, a long time
until he began to take himself seriously. For two decades,
he looked down on himself, believing that he was limited as
an actor. "I'm not an actor," he told a reporter in 1956,
"and I don't pretend to be." His motto for over a generation was "All I can sell is honesty," acting was "something
I don't know much about...."[54]

However, much of Wayne's self-deprecation was cynical
and in response to the critics' charge that he could not act--
which actually infuriated him. "The French gave me the only
good notices I ever got in my life for my film The Alamo,"
he said in 1962, "Imagine! Thirty-four years making movies
and still they go on saying I can't act. Goddam! What in
hell do they think I've been doing up there on the screen
all this time?"[55] These statements about the critics were
actually incorrect; Wayne received fabulous reviews for his
good work from all critics, including those on the East Coast,
whom he resented, labeling them pseudointellectuals.

His first really good notices were for his ardent and
idealistic Ringo Kid in Stagecoach. It was "a movie of the
grand old school," Nugent wrote in the New York Times,
"they've all done nobly."[56] "I don't see how the acting
could have been much better," wrote Barnes in the Herald
Tribune, "John Wayne is fine as the outlaw."[57] And the
Daily News noted, "John Wayne is so good in the role of
the outlaw that one wonders why he had to wait all this
time since The Big Trail for another opportunity."[58] "First
honors go to the young John Wayne," wrote Cue, "a cowboy
actor who plays his first big-time role."[59] Stagecoach was
nominated for seven Oscar awards in 1939, including Best
Picture, but won only two: supporting actor (Thomas

Mitchell) and best music score (Richard Hageman and his collaborators). The big winner that year was Gone with the Wind, sweeping eight awards of its 11 nominations.

Thomas Dunson, the ruthless cattle baron in Red River, was Wayne's most memorable role since the Ringo Kid, enabling him to demonstrate real acting ability. Wayne said he was surprised that audiences of the time did not see the similarity between his part and Charles Laughton's Captain Bligh in Mutiny on the Bounty. True, even the critics did not notice, but they applauded his performance. Crowther wrote that Red River was "one of the best cowboy pictures ever made," and that Hawks has "several fine performances out of a solidly masculine cast, topped off by a withering job of acting ... done by Mr. Wayne." "This consistently able portrayer of two-fisted, two-gunned outdoor men," Crowther noted, "surpassed himself in this picture."[60] The Variety critic concurred: "John Wayne has his best assignment to date and he makes the most of it."[61]

In John Ford's She Wore a Yellow Ribbon Wayne departed again from his image playing another character role, the elderly Captain Nathan Brittles. British critic Allen Eyles claimed that Wayne's performance "withstands the closest scrutiny,"[62] and that in this film "performer and part have merged in the best tradition of great acting."[63] Crowther wrote that Wayne was "the absolute image and ideal of the legendary cavalryman,"[64] and Howard Barnes described his portrayal as a "tough, grizzled frontier strategist with a wry sense of humor."[65] The Variety critic defined the movie as "obviously Wayne's picture," and noted that despite the shock of seeing him as "a gray-thatched" captain, he makes his officer "an understanding two-fisted guy, without overdoing it."[66] However, the general critical reaction disappointed him because he thought he was trying something new. "I was a young man then," he recalled, "and I never got any credit for that performance, so I just went back to re-acting."[67]

Wayne's roles in the two other Westerns of Ford's cavalry trilogy, Fort Apache and Rio Grande, are also considered among his top achievements. One critic believes that Fort Apache "helped elevate him from a star into someone who possessed both a cinema magic and a true ability to emote on screen."[68] Crowther described Wayne as "powerful,

forthright, and exquisitely brave,"[69] and Barnes thought he
was "excellent as a captain who escapes the slaughter and
protects his superior's name for the sake of service."[70]
Wayne's distinguished performance as the duty-bound colonel
in Rio Grande also got him good notices. A "first rate portrayal," wrote the Herald Tribune, "Wayne has worked with
Ford so many times that it is a small wonder that he creates
a striking character."[71]

Wayne excelled in Ford's The Quiet Man, a romantic love
story, in which he was cast as an American ex-prizefighter
returning to his Irish homeland to settle down. This
role called for great restraint, but it still enabled him to display his masculine image. Most critics liked the film, which
was nominated for the 1952 Best Picture and six other Academy Awards, winning Ford his fourth directorial Oscar. Its
beautiful cinematography, by Winton C. Hoch, was also
honored with an Oscar. The reviews were ecstatic,
with the California press leading the band. The Los
Angeles Times wrote that Wayne "ably undertakes a role
which makes the best of his rugged physical qualities."[72]
And the Los Angeles Examiner described the film as both
"unusual and fascinating," and noted, "No surprise is John
Wayne's excellence.... As always under Ford's tutelage,
he's plain great. What is unexpected is the flair of comedy
he demonstrates here."[73]

Ford knew how to bring the best out of Wayne's acting
abilities, which he flaunted again in his portrayal of Ethan
Edwards, the fanatically obsessed hero torn by a sense of
revenge in The Searchers, considered by many critics to be
the finest performance of his career. The New York Times
described Wayne as "uncommonly commanding,"[74] and the
Herald Tribune as "a Western hero in the classic Western
mold," which meant that "he is not only tough, but inscruta-
ble."[75] Eyles believes that Wayne excelled because his role
went beyond his usual powerful screen presence, demanding
"a communication of interior feelings," that have been rarely
displayed before.[76] The Searchers was underestimated at its
initial release, but has since become a cult movie admired by
filmmakers and critics alike. This time, Wayne's performance
was universally praised; the Los Angeles Times published an
article entitled, "John Wayne Wins Eastern Critics," noting
that the "New York film critics are not among Wayne's most
avid fans, but they agree he gives an uncommonly commanding performance."[77]

Rio Bravo, in which Wayne played sheriff John T.
Chance, received extremely favorable reviews. A.H. Weiler
thought the film was "above the average Western," and that
Hawks was aided by the performance of Wayne "who after all
these years of riding the studios' ranges, is satisfyingly laconic and fast with a six-shooter and a rifle."[78] "Wayne
looks as always very comfortable in an old slouch hat,"[79]
wrote the Herald Tribune, and the Saturday Review noted
that Wayne was "as terse and competent as ever."[80] In this
film he appeared to be "more animated than usual, as if he
were actually enjoying himself,"[81] observed the Los Angeles
Times.

In the 1960s, however, the critics were getting tired
of Wayne's screen formula, too often contained in poorly
scripted, terribly directed movies. One reviewer noted after
The Horse Soldiers, one of Ford's lesser Westerns: "No matter what name he bears in the movie credits, he always remains the same big, rough and masculine master of men."[82]
And Circus World got deservedly nasty reviews, such as the
one in the Herald Tribune: "We can rely on Wayne to do
the right things and this level of plotting to lead to a cotton-
candy ending."[83] In many 1960s movies, Wayne's performance was just a repetition of well-worn mannerisms, to the
point where one critic complained, "it never Waynes but it
bores."[84]

Many critics complained that Davy Crockett in The
Alamo was "much less a convincing figure from history than
he is a recreation of Mr. Wayne," for he was still "the tall,
easy, leather-skinned outdoorsman who has taken adversi-
ties in stride," and "in pretty much the same sardonic way."[85]
And reviewing Hatari! , Variety wrote that "the veteran star
plays with his customary effortless (or so it seems) authority
a role with which he is identified; the good-natured and
hard-drinking, hot-tempered Irishman who thinks 'women
are trouble in a man's world.' "[86] Increasingly the reviews
got nastier and harsher, as the following New York Post
write-up attests: "There is no law preventing John Wayne,
rugged, longtime movie hero, who has made a pile of money
being that hero; there is no law saying he can't befoul his
own nest with slap-sticky, repetitious treatment of his own
material in a vein that verges on burlesque."[87]

Wayne received the harshest reviews of his career for
The Hellfighters, as the brave oil fire fighter. "The dialogue

and characters are the usual stock type," wrote the New
York Post, "and tough, dependable Wayne is his usual self,
coming in casual and salty to put out holocaust after holocaust."[88] The New York Times wrote in the same vein:
"After more than forty years of patriotic destruction of rene-
gade redskins and rustlers, Alamo-hating Mexicans, and vicious Vietcong for cameramen, our indestructible Duke again
has made actionful, if not stirringly meaningful, child's play
of exotic disasters."[89] Worse yet was the New York Daily
News review, entitled "Big John Does It Again," noting that
the movie had everything one expected in a Wayne film: "a
slug-out at a saloon (this one in Malaya); a few solid Wayne-
isms, such as 'it's worth getting all busted up for'; and the
old familiar faces of Bruce Cabot, Jay C. Flippen. In other
words, you have to like John Wayne to come out of this
movie smiling and happy."[90]

One problem in reviewing Wayne's films was the strong
opposition to his politics, explicitly stated in The Alamo, The
Green Berets, and other movies. At times his films were condemned for their conservative and anti-Communist politics
rather than their merit as films. Reviewers focused more on
Wayne as a public figure than as an actor, resulting in unfair judgments. Others failed to discriminate the good from
the bad work, as Kauffmann's review attests: "The Wayne
career of almost forty years, in which give or take the minor
characteristics here and there and changes of costume, the
star has altered only by very slowly growing older."[91]

Eric Bentley's critical article on Wayne's politics infuriated those who respected his work. Dismissing the idea that
"actors are of no political importance," Bentley held that
more important than "going into politics," is "what an actor
seems to the public to stand for."[92] And he found Wayne's
politics, on screen and off, repulsive and unacceptable, particularly The Green Berets, which was advertised, in his
view, "as a picture showing Americans happily blowing up,
no doubt yellow villagers."[93] In his response to Bentley's
article, critic Luhr noted that he is not dealing with films at
all, but with "a man as a popular symbol."[94] He resented
Bentley's "homogenization of virtually anything John Wayne
touches into anti-Communist propaganda," and protested
against other critics who "feel free to shuffle off whatever
film the man appears in, regardless of director or writer or
any other person involved, as 'another John Wayne movie.'"

Luhr felt that critics were irresponsible, lumping all of
Wayne's films into one category and then rejecting it. This
"clearly abandons any pretense at real criticism by introduc-
ing an assumptive catchphrase that enables a critic to ignore
the work at hand." On a superficial level, Wayne's movies
may have been alike, but on closer scrutiny there have been
many alterations and variations, some more significant than
others, of the so-called John Wayne movie.

Most critics realized that their reviews had no impact
on Wayne's standing at the box office, as one wrote after
Chisum: "By now, any judgment of John Wayne as an actor
seems as relevant as an aesthetic appraisal of Fort Sumter."[95]
Which is why Wayne ignored the critics, claiming cynically:
"Nobody seems to like my pictures but the people." "People
like my pictures," he reminded his harsh critics, "and that's
all that counts." "When people say 'a John Wayne picture
got bad reviews,'" he said half seriously, half humorously,
"I always wonder if they know it's a redundant sentence."[96]
He knew that most critics used the label "John Wayne movie"
disparagingly, but said it did not bother him because "if it
depended on the critics' judgment and recognition, I'd never
have gone into the motion picture business."[97] However, at
times, Wayne was profoundly disturbed by the unfavorable
reviews, as director Walsh recalled: "The poor fella, he
would tell me time and again, 'Jesus, I got terrible write-
ups from the critics in New York.'"[98]

The Oscar Award

Wayne's status as an actor changed somewhat after
winning the Academy Award for True Grit. He was nominated twice for an Oscar, though his first Best Actor nomination, for Sands of Iwo Jima, did not do much for his recognition as a performer. But 1949 was a year of strong
male performances, with Broderick Crawford winning for All
the King's Men--over stiff competition from Kirk Douglas in
Champion, Gregory Peck in Twelve O'Clock High, who won
the New York Film Critics award, and Richard Todd in The
Hasty Heart. Note that Wayne, Peck, and Todd were all
nominated for a role in a war movie.

In subsequent years, Wayne received many popularity
awards from the film industry but no critical acclaim as an

actor. He never had a picture in a major international film
festival, for example. In 1967, when the Cannes Festival
showed interest in The War Wagon, "the studio [Universal]
was chicken," according to him, and "there went my chance
for glory."[99]

In 1969, Wayne received his second Best Actor nomina-
tion. It was another year of intense competition, with the
other contenders being: Richard Burton in Anne of the
Thousand Days, Dustin Hoffman and John Voight, both for
Midnight Cowboy, and Peter O'Toole in Goodbye Mr. Chips.
Burton, Hoffman, and O'Toole have been nominated for an
Academy Award in the past. Earlier, Voight was cited Best
Actor by the New York Film Critics Circle and the National
Society of Film Critics, and O'Toole was singled out by the
National Board of Review.

Asked how he felt about the possibility of winning an
Oscar, Wayne's response was cynical: "You can't eat awards.
Nor, more to the point, drink them."[100] But friends detected
a good deal of frustration in his statement, "My pictures don't
call for the great dramatic range that wins Oscars."[101] In
1969, when rumors circulated about his chances of winning,
he became more cautious in his public utterances about the
prestigious award, for he did not want to alienate the film
colony; after all, it was his last chance to win.

Wayne was so moved when Barbra Streisand, the previous year's winner, announced him Best Actor that he had
tears in his eyes. In a brief, humorous acceptance speech,
he said: "I thought some day I might get some award for
lasting so long! But I never thought I would get this particular award.... I feel grateful, very humble." And he
concluded: "If I'd known what I know now, I'd put a patch
on my eye thirty-five years ago."[102]

Asked if "the Oscar meant a lot" to him, he replied:
"Sure it did--even if it took the industry forty years to get
around it." He thought his previous nomination was also
"worthy of the honor." "At 42, in She Wore a Yellow Ribbon, I played the same character that I played in True Grit
at 62," Wayne said, "but I really didn't need an Oscar. I'm
a box-office champion with a record they're going to have to
run to catch. And they won't."[103] However, he was deeply
appreciative of the award and said it was "a beautiful thing

John Wayne as Rooster Cogburn in Henry Hathaway's True
Grit (Paramount, 1969), his most popular Western which
earned him the Oscar award for Best Actor.

to have." "It's important to me," he explained, "it symbo-
lizes appreciation of yourself by your peers."[104] Wayne had
never realized the worldwide importance of the award. "What
opened my eyes to how much it means to people," he said,
"was the flood of wires, phone calls, and letters I've been
receiving from all over the world." He regarded them "as a
tribute to the industry itself, and to the Academy," which
fortified his belief in "the power of movies."[105]

Some critics felt that previous performances, in Red
River or The Searchers, were more deserving of the Oscar
than True Grit, and that it was unfortunate that neither had
been nominated. Others charged that the Oscar was awarded
as a sentimental recognition for his lengthy career and lifetime contribution to American films. But people within the
industry saw the Oscar as Hollywood's confession that it had
underrated Wayne as an actor for too long. Hawks, for one,
insisted that Wayne's Oscar had nothing to do with sympathy
or sentimentality, but with good acting. "All of a sudden,
they're saying he's a good actor," was the way director
McLaglen expressed his upset, "Well, he always was."[106]

Wayne's work in True Grit was almost unanimously acclaimed by the critics, even by his greatest detractors.
Richard Schickel reflected this change in the critics' opinion:
"Every bit as much as Bogart, Cooper, et al. he had created
a subtle heroic American archetype and had done so well
with a skill deserving of as much interest as has been lav-
ished on them posthumously." Schickel also noted that
"Wayne has done work that for years has represented a kind
of modest excellence in a very special line of endeavor--
movie-star acting." "You don't survive as long as he has,"
he reasoned, "without intelligence and a certain subtlety or
self-understanding."[107] Similarly, Andrew Sarris stressed
the fact that True Grit "has apparently accomplished the
difficult feat of making John Wayne a respectable culture
hero east of the Mississippi."[108] And Jay Cocks pointed
out that after this movie, Wayne was "at least taken seriously because he did not seem to be serious about himself."
"Since I had always taken Wayne seriously," he added, "I
wished the affectionate recognition had come sooner, and
for something, not better necessarily, but closer to him,
closer, anyway, to my idea of him and all he represented.
She Wore a Yellow Ribbon, say, or Red River. The Searchers would have been best of all. But I settled for True
Grit, and gladly."[109]

Wayne always enjoyed greater prestige as an actor among the auteur and younger critics--Andrew Sarris, Molly Haskell, and Peter Bogdanovich. Haskell, for example, held that Wayne has been "abused by the Eastern intelligentsia and more judged for his politics than his performances."[110] And Sarris made a similar observation addressed directly to Pauline Kael, apparently for her underestimation of his Westerns: "It is unfair to brand Wayne as a screen fascist," he wrote, "on the basis of his off-screen politics, when it is Peckinpah (whom Kael admires) who is the foremost fascist in this particular woodpile."[111] Sarris deplored "the unyielding resistance to the Wayne legend among New York sophisticates," and "the rabble-rousing temptation to dump on the Duke in this citadel of enlightenment." Furthermore, he suspected that there are reviewers "who have never seen more than a handful of the 40 or so Wayne projects that deserve preservation, over the 100 or so truly stereotyped time-killers on which he was employed."[112]

Rex Reed also changed his mind about Wayne's abilities, though after The Cowboys, not True Grit: "Wayne is proving to be a more intelligent actor than most of us ever credited him for being." Reed rated his performance in The Cowboys as "the best role of his career."[113] Archer Winsten, writing for the New York Post, also praised his work in this movie: "John Wayne, now in the autumn of his life when he should be tapering off to minor supporting character roles, again shows that he's like vintage wine, the older he gets the better." Winsten thought that "in this he resembles Errol Flynn, who went from a life as a swashbuckling non-actor to his best performance (The Sun Also Rises), just before the end." However, "Wayne looks as if he could go on getting better for another 20 years."[114] Reed pointed out that most aging actors drop out of their profession bitterly, accusing the industry for deserting them, when in actuality they can no longer bear to play in their proper age range. By contrast, "Wayne gets better in each role. He grows as an actor as the years gain on him.... He has learned the advantages of age."[115]

Some critics, like Pauline Kael, panned his movies consistently and indiscriminately. Kael never liked Wayne and, to her credit, never made a secret of it. But her reviews of his films were at times unnecessarily nasty. Of McQ, a bad picture by any criterion, Kael wrote: "What is one to make of the shamelessness of a big, old star? John Wayne

must be heading toward seventy, but he's trying to change
his image. In McQ he imitates his juniors; he lifts his name
from Steve McQueen and his tough-police officer character
from Clint Eastwood's Dirty Harry Callahan."[116] But Kael
did not mention the influence of Wayne on Eastwood and the
many ideas the latter lifted from the veteran actor, including
some elements of his screen image.

Worse yet was Kael's account of Rooster Cogburn, another lesser movie: "The two principal subjects of the
script's attempts at humor," she wrote, "are Wayne's gut
and Hepburn's age, which is to say that the film tries to
make jokes of what it can't hide." As for Wayne's work, she
noted: "We know what John Wayne is doing here; this role
is just a further step in the career of a movie star who was
never an actor. Once upon a time, he had a great, rugged,
photogenic body, and his transparency as an actor--his inability to convey any but the simplest emotions--gave him a
frank, American-hero manner." She also found his appearance to be like a "huge, puffy face as a Wallace Beery comic
mug."[117]

John Simon is another critic who never took Wayne's
acting seriously, describing him once as "a cross between a
face on Mount Rushmore and a head on Eastern Island atop
a doric column that moves with a swagger, talks in a mono-
tone to which a drawl adds a slight curlicue, and looks at
you with a lazy gaze that starts out downward but then
curves slowly upward." "The last century," Simon sarcastically wrote, "had its Iron Duke, Ellington; this century
has its granite Duke, Wayne. Every era gets the leader it
deserves: John Wayne is ours."[118] Of Rooster Cogburn,
which opened to mixed reviews, Simon wrote: "I have nothing against senescence or even senility on screen if the subject is treated with honesty,"[119] which he thought was missing. However, even Simon acknowledged Wayne's ability in
The Shootist, though he did not like the movie, particularly
its conventional script. "John Wayne gives a surprisingly
effective performance as Books, a role somewhat more demanding than Rooster Cogburn, his previous high," but he
concluded in his characteristically cynical style: "If at the
age of 69, after 47 years in the movies, Wayne can truly
have learned his trade, there is hope for every one of us,
no matter how slow a study."[120]

Wayne's Status as an Actor

There always have been and always will be critics who
like or dislike Wayne's work as an actor, depending on their
idiosyncratic tastes. Is it possible, however, to assess
Wayne's contribution to American film beyond the opinions of
individual critics?

If one takes the New York Times, one of the most es-
teemed and widely read newspapers, as an example, one
finds that contrary to Wayne's belief, most of its film critics
liked Westerns in general and his work in particular. In
1924, the Times began to compile its annual Ten Best lists
which, through 1968 were listed in order of preference, and
from 1969 on alphabetically. Surprisingly, this newspaper
has had only four major film critics in the last half century:
Frank S. Nugent (1936-40), Bosley Crowther (1940-67),
Renata Adler (1968), and Vincent Canby (1969-present).
Six of Wayne's movies have been on the Ten Best lists:
Stagecoach occupied the second place in 1939, The Long
Voyage Home, eighth in 1940; They Were Expendable, tenth
in 1945; The Quiet Man, seventh in 1952; The Longest Day
also seventh in 1962; and True Grit was on the list of 1969.

Crowther, one of the most durable reviewers and the
dean of the New York critics, included two Wayne movies,
Stagecoach and Red River, in his volume, Vintage Films:
50 Enduring Motion Pictures. Of Stagecoach he wrote: "It
was and remains a great film, possibly--all things considered
--the greatest all-around Western of all time."[121] The position of Stagecoach as a great Western and a classic film
seems to be secure. Orson Welles, who was greatly influenced by John Ford, cited it as one of the best films of all
time in the 1952 Cinémathèque Belgique survey.

For its July 1978 issue, the film magazine Take One
asked 20 leading film critics in the United States to choose
the ten best films of the decade (defined by the editors as
running from January 1, 1968, to December 31, 1977).
Three of the 20 critics singled out a John Wayne movie.
Vincent Canby and Michael Goodwin, associate editor of
Take One, chose True Grit, and Gene Moskowitz, the Variety reviewer in Paris, selected The Shootist.

Wayne's standing as a performer enjoys greater prestige

among the young generation of directors than among film
critics. Bodganovich, the critic-turned-filmmaker, named
four Wayne movies among his ten all-time favorites: <u>Red
River</u> ranked fourth, <u>She Wore a Yellow Ribbon</u> fifth, <u>The
Searchers</u> sixth, and <u>Rio Bravo</u> ninth; <u>Rio Bravo</u> featured,
in his view, "Wayne's most endearing performance." Bogdanovich noted that none of these pictures was recognized
at the time as more than "and John Wayne does his usual
job." Moreover, he felt that many of Wayne's roles were
unjustifiably panned by the critics and that the quality that
stars like him (and Jimmy Stewart) brought with them is
"unfortunately an achievement that normally goes unnoticed."
Unlike many of his colleagues at the time, Bogdanovich
thought that "John Wayne is at his best precisely when he
is being what we have to call John Wayne."[122]

Many critics see in Bogdanovich's best film to date,
<u>The Last Picture Show</u> (1971), an explicit tribute to the work
of Ford and Hawks. To begin with, the film is shot in black
and white, which fits its ambiance of despair and stagnation,
but was also influenced by Hawks's cinematography. And
for the last picture that the town's only theater shows, Bogdanovich chose <u>Red River</u>; we see on the screen the scene
in which Wayne calls the start of the cattle drive. Bogdanovich had a life dream to cast Wayne and Stewart in a Western, but it never materialized.

But if <u>Stagecoach</u> and <u>Red River</u> have attained classic
status as great Westerns, <u>The Searchers</u> has become a legendary cult movie, in and outside the United States. <u>The
Searchers</u> was underrated by critics when it was released,
enjoying only moderate success at the box office, barely
over $4 million in domestic rentals. But in the last decade
it has gained the respect of numerous critics and filmmakers.
A poll of 100 international critics found that 78 percent cited
the movie as one of their all-time favorites. Two of the
<u>Village Voice</u> reviewers cited <u>The Searchers</u> as one of their
ten favorite films. Sarris rated it fourth, preceded by
Welles's <u>The Magnificent Ambersons</u>, Murnau's <u>Sunrise</u>, and
Hitchcock's <u>Vertigo</u>. And Tom Allen placed the film at the
head of his list, followed by <u>Vertigo</u> and another Wayne film,
<u>Hatari!</u> Moreover, in the 1972 survey of <u>Sight and Sound</u>,
several Wayne movies were mentioned among the best films
of all time, but <u>The Searchers</u> was the most frequent choice.

Mention has been made of the popularity of Ford and Hawks's Westerns in France. Director Jean-Luc Godard, a leader of the French New Wave and one of the most experimental filmmakers, whose leftist politics were diametrically opposed to Wayne's wondered: "How can I hate McNamara and adore Sergeant La Terreur, hate John Wayne upholding Goldwater and love him tenderly when abruptly he takes Natalie Wood into his arms"[123] (in The Searchers). This scene is often mentioned as one of the most memorable and touching sequences in film history. Another noted French director, François Truffaut, liked The Searchers, but also admired Rio Lobo, which neither Hawks nor Wayne liked, as one of the ten movies in the 1970s he would like to see again, for its "magistral direction."[124]

The Searchers has inspired many directors and writers, including Martin Scorsese, George Lucas, and Steven Spielberg, all of whom acknowledge their great intellectual and cinematic debts to it. Paul Schrader, critic-turned-director-screenwriter, admitted that his scenario for Hardcore (1979) was virtually a reworking of The Searchers's plot. George C. Scott plays the Wayne role--a father obsessed with finding, then rescuing his teenage daughter from prostitution. The modern, urban scene of New York's pornographic world substitutes for the Comanche Indians. Spielberg also paid homage to Ford and Wayne in his blockbuster E.T.: The Extra-Terrestrial (1982). In a funny and moving scene, the creature from outer space is watching television and is aroused by the seduction scene between Wayne and Maureen O'Hara in The Quiet Man. Spielberg also offered Wayne a role in his war comedy, 1941, which fortunately he turned down.

If current interest in the work of Ford and Hawks continues, the status of Wayne as an auteur star-actor, will become even more firmly rooted.[125] It is impossible to examine Ford's or Hawks's oeuvres without acknowledging Wayne's contribution to their films. Some of their movies, Red River is a good example, were moderate achievements, critical and commercial, in their initial release, but they were somehow forgotten until the late 1960s, when a new generation of film students and directors reevaluated and reacclaimed their films, raising both auteurs to semicult status. This reexamination ensures a continuing interest in Wayne as well--both as an actor and a cultural icon.

8. THE ACTOR AND HIS COLLEAGUES

Wayne and His Fellow Actors

All the actors who worked with Wayne were impressed
with his thorough professionalism. Wayne was usually the
first on the set and the last to leave, and he did not disappear from the set when he was not needed. He was always
on time for his five a.m. makeup call, no matter how much
he had drunk or indulged the night before, and always in
command of his lines. His co-stars marveled at his ability
to memorize not only his lines, but almost everyone else's.
Unlike other stars, he never lost his excitement and passion
for making films--even after decades of working in the industry. He never came to regard moviemaking, as Gable did in
his last decade, as "a nine-to-five job," with his watch "the
equivalent of the factory whistle," leaving the set "the instant his wrist watch buzzed at five o'clock," as co-star
Sophia Loren once reported.[1]

As a consummate professional, Wayne worked under
the most demanding conditions. Filming Stagecoach and
other Westerns on location in the desert, for example, was
not an easy task; the days were extremely hot and the
nights extremely cold. But having started as a stuntman,
he was used to the most trying conditions and never complained. Producer Walter Wanger was reportedly horrified
when he visited the set of Stagecoach and saw Wayne climb-
ing from the interior of the coach to its roof--while in motion. Wanger was concerned that his star would hurt himself, but Wayne reminded him that after all he was still a
stuntman.

He preferred to do his own stunt work even when the
scene called for a dangerous or risky action. In one film
he had to run and leap astride a fast-galloping horse that

was careening precariously close to a cliff's edge. When he
finished, he exclaimed, "Let's see your Roy Rogers do that!"[2]
Indeed, Wayne became a star in an environment that despised
actors who did not take their own risks; doing one's stunts
was professional as well as "macho" behavior. Filming Legend
of the Lost, in the Sahara Desert, he demonstrated again his
work ethic--he was there to do a job and working conditions
did not matter at all.

Wayne continued to do his stunts even at an old age.
In The War Wagon, at 60, he mounted his horse on his own
steam, while co-star Kirk Douglas, ten years his junior, had
to leap aboard with the help of an unseen trampoline. Director Rydell was apparently shocked that in The Cowboys "he
did all of his own riding and fighting, and refused to use a
stand-in." Wayne was 65 years old and had only one lung.
"He will outlive us all," Rydell commented, "you'll have to
beat him to death with a stick."[3]

Extremely generous to his colleagues, he encouraged
younger talent, for which he had an instinctive eye. He
gave chances to inexperienced players and was ready to
gamble on them, probably because Ford had gambled on him.
Wayne launched the careers of several stuntmen, among them
James Arness, his previous double. He cast Arness in a major role in Big Jim McLain; later Arness proved his abilities
in the long-running Western series Gunsmoke, which had been
initially offered to Wayne. A number of popular singers
started their screen careers or got their break in a Wayne
movie, such as Ricky Nelson in Rio Bravo, Frankie Avalon
in The Alamo, and Fabian in North to Alaska. Avalon and
Fabian had made a few films but did not make any impression
until they were cast in good roles in Wayne's movies. Glen
Campbell was a top recording star with one bit role to his
credit, in The Cool Ones, before he got the second starring
role in True Grit. Campbell had grown up on Wayne's movies and realized a childhood dream to work with him. Similarly, Ann-Margret fulfilled a long-held ambition to perform
opposite the veteran star in The Train Robbers, though
judging by the outcome it was to neither's advantage.

The ingenue role in New Frontier (1939), a Republic
Western, was played by a young unknown actress, Phyllis
Isley, before she became a Hollywood star named Jennifer
Jones. Other actors who appeared in small roles in his films,

before becoming big names on their own, included James
Caan in El Dorado and Bruce Dern in The Cowboys. It is
hard to believe that such a gifted actor as Robert Duvall
played the unrewarding role of a villain in True Grit, but
such are the fickle realities of the movie industry.

Gracious and helpful to young players, he treated
them as equals rather than inexperienced novices. John
Agar, later Shirley Temple's husband, had to take harsh
treatment from Ford in his first film, Fort Apache, and he
took it badly, not knowing that this was Ford's way of getting a better performance. This reminded Wayne of his
treatment by Ford on the set of Stagecoach and, out of
sympathy, he felt the need to provide emotional support for
Agar, spending a good deal of time with him, reading over
the screenplay and giving him riding lessons.

Wayne gained unanimous respect from his co-workers
for his generosity. He believed that the anxiety of many
stars to appear constantly in the foreground spoiled many
good scenes: "The director should give the scene to whom
it belongs," he said, "even if it's an extra."[4] And he not
only meant it, but behaved accordingly. He was extremely
gracious to players of lesser stature, if he felt the scene
"belonged" to them.

Being the professional he was, Wayne moved three
times into the breach to replace actors who were cast in one
of his company's films. He substituted for Glenn Ford, who
withdrew at the last moment from Hondo, and took over the
lead in Blood Alley, when Robert Mitchum did not get along
with director William Wellman. Following some interest in
playing the lead in another Wellman movie, The High and
the Mighty, Spencer Tracy changed his mind and Wayne
took over, though he too had reservations about the screenplay and later about the picture itself.

Despite his reputation of being tough, the casts and
crews of his films never found him hard to work with.
Sophia Loren, who co-starred in one of his worst films,
Legend of the Lost, found him to be "exactly as advertised:
Big, authoritative, gruff but polite, and a pro through and
through." She recalled that Wayne "showed up right on the
minute, knew all his lines and moves, worked hard all day
long without letup." "There is no doubt," writes Loren,

"that he was in command, the captain on the bridge of the
ship." Wayne did not have to exert his authority overtly
"because everyone automatically deferred to him," even director Henry Hathaway. But he never abused his powerful
position, "he simply assumed his stance and kept it." Of
their working relationship, Loren recalled: "With me, he
was polite and pleasant, but distant," but that was his manner with all the others." Loren was impressed with the fact
that "everyone was in awe of him, scared of him somewhat,"
and that "a great concerted effort was made to anticipate his
needs," including "a special, king-sized bed,"[5] even though
he had not asked for it.

Patricia Neal, his co-star in Operation Pacific and In
Harm's Way, said she adored and held the highest regard
for him. And Colleen Dewhurst, who appeared in The Cowboys and McQ, reported of their first meeting: "I knew the
whole legend before I went out, plus the fact of his supposed
politics. The first morning that I was to meet him, I was a
nervous wreck. But he was the most gracious actor that I
ever worked with. He was very kind and very compassionate
to me--I guess he was a gentleman."[6]

"Before you meet him you think of possible friction,"
said black actor Roscoe Lee Browne after The Cowboys, "my
politics and his are miles apart, of course--but he's got a
rare joy-in-living attitude that makes you like him right off."
Browne came prepared to dislike him, but instead found "an
intelligent, courteous, and well-read man."[7] They spent
hours together, discussing among other things the poetry of
Shelley and Yeats. Genuine affection also prevailed in this
film between Wayne and the kids who played the cowboys.
Wayne insisted that they have free access to him at all times.
He talked to them man-to-man and they regarded him as a
buddy. The children were allegedly in awe of Wayne and
disciplined by his sheer presence.

Katharine Hepburn had always wanted to work with
Wayne in a Western and when she was given a chance in
Rooster Cogburn, she decided "to grab him before it was
too late--for him or for me."[8] She was right, the movie
was his penultimate. They got along fine. "We were very
candid with one another," she recalled, "we were also critical of one another. There was nothing phony about it. It
was totally honest."[9] Hepburn described Wayne as "tough

on the director who had not done his homework," and "very
impatient with anyone who was inefficient."[10] The whole experience was enjoyable because she found him to be "a funny
man, sharp, and delicious ... very bright, and very intelligent." Hepburn also believes that Wayne is "the most underrated actor in the business," and "underrated as an artist in
this country."[11] As for his side, before shooting began,
Wayne was concerned about working with Hepburn; after all,
she was a legend in her own time. But there was a good
deal of mutual respect. Wayne said he felt "great respect
for her talent," and that "she had the same for mine." It
was important to him "to let her know she wasn't fooling
around with some amateur."[12]

Hepburn was not the only big name to want to work
with him. Other big stars were glad to appear in his movies, even in small parts. Jimmy Stewart, who had costarred
with Wayne in The Man Who Shot Liberty Valance, accepted
a small part in The Shootist; the physician who informs
Wayne of his cancer. Lauren Bacall, who had appeared with
him 20 years earlier in Blood Alley, was delighted to be cast
as the housekeeper. Richard Boone shocked Wayne when he
agreed to appear in a bit part. "Dammit," was Wayne's reaction, "he's playing a part so small you wouldn't believe
it."[13] And Hugh O'Brian volunteered to work in The Shootist for practically nothing.

Actors who had never performed with Wayne were also
in awe of his professionalism. "When kids ask me what a
pro is," Steve McQueen is reported to have said, "I just
point to the Duke."[14] President Reagan said on numerous
occasions that he "always wanted to be in a film with him
and will always regret not having done so." Clint Eastwood,
considered to be Wayne's heir in terms of popularity and
screen image, has the highest regard for Wayne, but feels
that he was never given the true recognition he deserved.
Eastwood believes that "Duke was best in character parts,
in roles where he had to stretch as an actor," and that he
"should've evolved naturally into more character roles, like
his wonderful portrayal in True Grit." His favorite Wayne
movies, in addition to True Grit, are Red River, "one of the
all-time great Westerns," The Quiet Man, and The Searchers.[15]

Wayne served as a role model for several generations of
actors. "Duke Wayne cast a heroic shadow as a model for me

and so many others," Robert Stack said, "he was one of my
favorites--in and out of acting." Stack claims "it is a tribute to Duke's towering reputation that even those in our industry who disagreed with his politics acknowledge him as
one of the giants of film industry."[16] "He was bigger than
life but never abused it," said Jack Lemmon after Wayne's
death, "the loss to our profession and to each one of us in
it was enormous."[17]

Wayne and His Directors

The fact that Wayne is held in such high regard is attributable to his work with two directors: Ford and Hawks.
They were the only directors he trusted implicitly, but his
blind faith in them was justified by the films they made together. The collaboration between Wayne and Ford and
Hawks was mutually beneficial; their films benefited immensely from his presence and acting.

Ford and Hawks were older than Wayne by a decade;
Ford was born in 1895 and Hawks in 1896. Both started to
direct in the silent era and established themselves as filmmakers while Wayne was still making "B" Westerns. Their
close affinity derived in large measure from their similar
backgrounds and careers. All three were self-made men who
learned their crafts while working in various capacities in
the film industry. Both Ford and Hawks conceived of filmmaking as a job and regarded movies as entertainment for
the large public, not an art form. And despite differences
in thematic concerns, approach, and style, both made commercial pictures that aimed to appeal to the largest potential
audiences. Moreover, Ford, Hawks, and Wayne adhered to
Hollywood's "macho" culture, on screen and off. Wayne's
whole life style, not just his career, was influenced by his
two mentors.

Directed by Ford

Ford's career, like Wayne's, began as a stuntman,
then an actor in his brother Francis Ford's movies. In 1917,
when he was 22, Universal signed him to a directors' contract, initially making two-reel Westerns. Ford directed 28
features for Universal between 1917 and 1921, and his first,

Straight Shooting (1917), had five reels and was considered
a milestone at the time. In the 1920s, Ford directed some of
the best epic Westerns, The Iron Horse (1924) and Three
Bad Men (1926), but despite their popularity and success,
it took him another 13 years to return to this genre with
the classic Stagecoach.

Ford directed 18 pictures with Wayne, beginning with
Mother Machree in 1928 and ending with Donovan's Reef in
1963. Nine of these were Westerns: Stagecoach, Fort Apache,
Three Godfathers, She Wore a Yellow Ribbon, Rio Grande,
The Searchers, The Horse Soldiers, The Man Who Shot Liberty Valance, and an episode in How the West Was Won.
Other noteworthy Ford-Wayne collaborations included two war
movies, The Long Voyage Home and They Were Expendable,
and a romantic idyl, The Quiet Man.

Ford literally changed the course of Wayne's career:
starting as his prop man and stuntman, he gradually progressed until he became his major star, especially in Westerns. The relationship between Ford and Wayne was unique,
going beyond a director-actor collaboration. Ford molded
Wayne into a distinct screen personality in a manner that
sculptors work with clay. Ford also served as a father figure; Wayne's parents divorced when he was in high school
and Ford fulfilled parental functions at a time when Wayne
was confused about his career and lacked direction for the
future.

Their collaboration began in 1928, but it was Salute
(1929), in which Wayne had his first speaking role in a Ford
film, that marked the beginning of friendship. An incident
during the shooting accounted to a large extent for the mutual
respect they held for each other. Wayne enjoyed telling it in
great detail: "They'd always ask you how you crouched to
bust the line, and then they'd trip you. It was a corny
joke, but I always tried to be patient. Ford tried it and I
went flat on my face in the mud. I said, 'let's try it
again,' only this time I turned suddenly and let him have
my foot right where it would do the most good. This was
daring with an important director, but Ford loved it." After this picture, Ford and Wayne "learned to share all the
secrets of friendship."[18]

But it was another nine years before they worked

together again. It began when Ford asked Wayne to read
Ernest Haycox's short story, "Stage to Lordsburg." He
then asked him to suggest an actor for the lead. When
Wayne said there was only one actor who could play it,
Lloyd Nolan, Ford stormed, "Why, you stupid son of a bitch
... I want you to play it." The truth is that Wayne "was
hoping like hell that he wouldn't say Lloyd Nolan." Ford
was the only one who believed in Wayne, but "there was a
lot of resistance to my playing the part--and with good reasons. After all, a theater could get me in a Republic Western for five dollars. So why should they pay two hundred
dollars for me in Stagecoach?"[19]

Once Ford made up his mind, however, he was firm,
though it was not easy to convince producer Wanger, who
was enthusiastic about the project, but not about Wayne.
Wanger wanted Marlene Dietrich and Gary Cooper, who had
costarred successfully in Morocco and Desire, for the prostitute and outlaw roles, but Ford insisted that Wayne and
Claire Trevor play them. Ford was aware of the risk--Wayne
was by no means a "finished performer"--but "he was the
only person I could think of at the time who could personify
great strength and determination without talking much."[20]
Ford had had Wayne on his mind when he first read the
story and he convinced Wanger by saying, "We can get him
for peanuts."[21] Indeed, Wayne was paid only 6,000 dollars
for his entire work, much below the average at the time.

Ford took big risks casting Wayne as the Ringo Kid
because he was labeled a "B" Western actor. Wayne himself
had doubts as to whether he could play the role convincingly. But the timing of Ford's offer could not have been better, "just about the time I was ready to resign myself to being a run-of-the-mill actor for the rest of my life." "Everybody told Ford he was committing suicide," Wayne recalled,
"risking a third rate bum like me in a million dollar movie."[22]
Wayne was then "disgusted" with his bad pictures and "would
have gone back to being a prop man, if it hadn't been for
Jack Ford."[23]

The friendship with Ford did not spare him on the set
of Stagecoach. The veteran director was notorious for picking on inexperienced actors to provoke a good performance
out of them. And Wayne was no exception. "He dares you
to do," Wayne said, "to do it right--to do it good. You're

A gallery of types: John Carradine (far left), Chris Pin
Martin, Louise Platt, John Wayne, and Berton Churchill
(far right), Andy Devine (far left on stagecoach), George
Bancroft, Donald Meek, and Claire Trevor in Stagecoach
(United Artists, 1939), the film that made Wayne's career.

really sort of on trial all the time." Ford encouraged competitiveness and liked to play actors against each other.
"And you really don't know what he's going to think of it,"
elaborated Wayne, "Actually, you don't know what's going
to happen in the scene." The ambiance on the set was "ner-
vousness," and "tension every place, everybody's on edge."[24]
Ford was indeed merciless, criticizing his walk, delivery of
lines, expression, and practically everything he did. On the
first day of shooting, Ford yelled at Wayne: "Don't you know
how to walk? You're as clumsy as a hippo. And stop slur-
ring your dialogue and show some expression. You look like
a poached egg!"[25]

But under Ford's persistent attention, Wayne learned
how to act. It was not an easy task, partly because Wayne
had low regard for himself as an actor. He knew there was

something appealing about his screen presence, but he was
afraid to go beyond his limited experience. Ford's task was
to give him self-assurance, and he did. In a romantic scene
with Claire Trevor, Wayne had trouble showing his love for
her. Ford told him to raise his eyebrow and wrinkle his
forehead, a device that worked for he continued to use the
same expression for the rest of his career. More useful advice came when Ford told him, "Duke, you're going to get a
lot of scenes during your life. They're going to seem corny
to you. Play 'em. Play 'em to the hilt. If it's East Lynne,
play it. You'll get by with it, but if you start trying to
play it with your tongue in your cheek and getting cute,
you'll lose sight of yourself ... and the scene will be lost."[26]

Claire Trevor recalled that Ford was really tough on
Wayne, but he took it, and "he learned eight volumes about
acting in that picture."[27] As for Wayne, "the first two days,
I had to take the worst ragging in my career." Ford's technique worked; he kept Wayne on the edge by playing him
against the more experienced actors, Trevor, Thomas Mitchell,
Donald Meek, and George Bancroft. "I surrounded him with
superb actors," Ford said, "and some of the glitter rubbed
off on his shoulder."[28]

Despite their friendship, their relationship was always
that of master and apprentice. Gene Autry observed that
Wayne "could be tough and rowdy but in the presence of
Ford, whom he revered, he could be as obedient and innocent as an altar boy."[29] Wayne was actually afraid of Ford;
if the director thought he had had too many drinks he would
reproach him in public, "Act your age. You're not a prop
boy any more. Go to bed."[30] And Wayne would promptly
retire.

An incident that occurred when they worked on a television special was indicative of their special relationship.
The night before the telecast, Wayne was drinking and, uncharacteristically, arrived three hours late on the set. Ford
was furious at him for holding up the rehearsal, and Wayne
just kept ducking his head, scuffing his toe in the sand, and
saying, "I'm sorry, boss." Ford was determined to punish
him and subsequently demanded many rehearsals. "You'll not
get so much as a drop of water," he told Wayne, to which
the latter replied, "Yes, boss." At the same time, Ford told
Autry, who also appeared in the show, "Gene, about twenty

minutes before we get on the air I want you to give Duke a
good healthy slug of bourbon. And halfway through the
show give him another. But don't let him know that I
know."[31] Long after Wayne had established himself as a
star, Ford continued to treat him as a student, and he always took it as a scolded schoolboy, apologizing, "Sorry,
coach."

Wayne was on Ford's mind whenever he read new
scripts and indeed provided him with the richest parts of
his career. They had the most unusual contract, more of a
verbal agreement. Whenever Ford needed him, Wayne dropped
whatever he was doing and made himself available. "I've
never had a written contract with him," said Wayne, "but if
he wants me, I just ask, 'when, where, and what clothes do
you want me to wear?'" It was loyalty to "the man who gave
me my breaks," but Wayne also knew that the collaboration
would pay off: "any picture he puts me in will be a fine
picture, and probably a great picture."[32] He realized that
none of the "B" Western stars made it big and that without
Ford he would never have reached the heights of his profession. An offer from Ford, even for less money, had special
meaning and took priority over other commitments. He never
forgot he "owed" his career to Ford, as he said in 1946, "I'd
like to get up on housesteps and shout out what I owe to
that guy. I simply owe him every mouthful I eat, every dollar I've got and practically every bit of happiness I know,
that's all."[33]

Ford was the only director who Wayne never dared to
contradict, being literally terrified of him. Ford functioned
more than just as a director; he was Wayne's severest critic.
Wayne knew that "Stagecoach made me a star, and I'll be
grateful to him forever," but he had doubts whether Ford
"really had any kind of respect for me as an actor until I
made Red River. Even then I was not quite sure."[34] Ford
is reported to have said after this movie, "I never knew the
big fellow could act."[35] But he gradually changed his mind
until he was proud to proclaim in public that Wayne was "a
splendid actor who has had very little chance to act," and
that he was such "a good actor, he just does not know how
good."[36] Wayne recalled with immense pride how after She
Wore a Yellow Ribbon "Ford sent me a cake, with one candle,
that said, 'You're an actor now.'"[37] Ford's reaction was
particularly important because in this movie he departed
from his traditional hero image.

The association between Ford and Wayne was mutually fertile and was as long and productive as any between actor and director in American film. Wayne brought physical and moral strength to Ford's films and endowed them with qualities that were very different from Ford's movies with Henry Fonda, his other favorite star. The studios that released their films cashed in on their successful collaboration, as the advertisement campaign of Rio Grande, in its world premiere in Texas, illustrates: "Never in the history of motion picture industry, has a director-actor team given so many big money hits as John Ford and John Wayne."

Wayne's last films for Ford declined in quality and their collaboration weakened. The Wings of Eagles was a rather sentimental biopicture of Frank "Spig" Wead, and Ford's direction not very imaginative. The Man Who Shot Liberty Valance turned out to be a nostalgic Western in which Ford overindulged himself, shooting it on the studio lot. "The Old West," wrote the New York Times, "ravaged by repetition and television, has begun to show signs of age." Crowther thought that neither Wayne nor Stewart were "really convincing," because they "are obviously not the young men they are supposed to represent." The whole picture seemed "baleful evidence of creeping fatigue in Hollywood."[38] And their very last film, Donovan's Reef, an adventure comedy set in the South Pacific islands, was possibly their weakest together. Wayne's advancing age--he was too old for the part--and Ford's perfunctory direction seemed to dull the cutting edge of their collaboration. Ford's last movie was Seven Women in 1966; failing health, an eye ailment, and a broken hip hampered his activity in his final years.

Their friendship, and hero worship on Wayne's part, continued until Ford's death of cancer in 1973. Wayne kept a portrait of Ford that he admired in his California home. In 1978, five years after Ford's death, Wayne appeared at the front door of Old Prospector Trail in Palm Springs. "My name is John Wayne," he told a nurse, "I came to visit Mary Ford on her birthday." Wayne spent the entire day sitting by her bed and reminiscing nostalgically of their friendship and work. "I just came to reminisce," he later said, "We don't have many to reminisce with any more."[39]

John Wayne, in his first real character role, and Montgomery
Clift, in his very first screen role, in Howard Hawks's epic
Western Red River (United Artists, 1948), a film that juxta-
posed two styles of leadership and manhood.

Directed by Hawks

Howard Hawks was the second director who greatly
influenced Wayne's career. Wayne appeared in five films
directed by Hawks, four of which were Westerns: the classic epic Red River, and three that are considered a Western
trilogy because they share similar plots and themes: Rio
Bravo, El Dorado, and Rio Lobo. The fifth collaboration,
Hatari!, an adventure filmed in Africa, deals with an international team of animal hunters. What marked the collaboration with Hawks, as compared with Ford, is its greater mutual dependency, possibly because Wayne was becoming an established actor by the time Hawks cast him in Red River.

It was Hawks who approached Wayne with the idea of
Red River, his first foray into the Western genre. "You're

gonna be an old man pretty soon," he told Wayne, "and you
ought to get used to it." "You'd better start playing characters," Hawks advised, "instead of that junk you've been
playing."[40] Hawks was also the first director to give the
actor real freedom in interpreting his juicy role of Thomas
Dunson. Never beyond learning, Wayne was given useful
advice, "Do three scenes [memorable acting bits] in a picture and don't annoy the audience in the rest."[41] Hawks
believed that it was enough for performers to excel in a few
scenes, granted they did not irritate the audience in the
others.

Hawks thought <u>Red River</u> "made Wayne a good actor,
because he does not try hard to do things he's not capable
of doing." He was "a hell of a lot better than most people
think he is,"[42] said Hawks, and had "more power than any
other man on the screen." "The only problem with Wayne,"
the director felt, "is who do you get to play with him," because "if you get somebody who's not pretty strong, he
blows them right off the screen. He doesn't do it purposely
--that's just what happens."[43]

The famous brawl in <u>Red River</u> (United Artists, 1948).

Indeed, Wayne first had reservations about Montgomery Clift because he was a stage actor, with no screen experience, and a proponent of New York's Method acting, which Wayne and other Hollywood actors disliked. "Howard [you] think we can get anything going between that kid and myself?" he asked the director after his first meeting with Clift, to which Hawks said, "I think you can." After a few scenes, Wayne conceded, "You're right. He can hold his own, anyway, but I don't think we can make a fight." Hawks then told the star, "Duke, if you fall down and I kick you in the jaw, that could be quite a fight. Don't you think so?" Wayne reportedly said "Okay," and that was all there was to it. But it took several days to make Clift "tough enough to be pitted against Wayne because he didn't know how to punch or move when we rehearsed."[44] Clift himself was puzzled by the idea of fighting with Wayne, and he reportedly disliked the fight scene because it made the showdown with Wayne a farce.[45] But many critics singled out the casting of Clift opposite Wayne. "The greatest triumph," wrote one reviewer, "was creating the illusion of a hidden force of character capable of holding his own with Wayne, who is at least twice his size."[46]

Clift was apparently disturbed by Wayne's acting style. Wayne's technique was not to act for the camera, but to react to the situation called by the script as naturally as possible. Clift, by contrast, was used to stage work, to getting to know his fellow actors and relating to them emotionally. He complained to Hawks that Wayne did not look at him when they were in the same scene. But under Hawks's direction, they adapted to each other, with each playing off the other's differences, in appearance, voice, and manner, so that both ended up giving distinguished performances. Red River turned out to be an important experience for all participants, convincing Hawks to use Wayne in another Western, Rio Bravo, which also became a box-office hit.

Of their third film together, Hatari!, Wayne said, "I think it's a good story and Hawks and I have had great success together, so I have confidence in him."[47] Hawks described the special relationship he had with Wayne in the following way: "The last picture we made [Rio Lobo], I called him up and said, 'Duke, I've got a story.' He said, 'I can't make it for a year, I'm all tied up.' And I said, 'Well, that's all right, it'll take me a year to get it finished.'

He said, 'Good, I'll be ready.' And he came down on location and he said, 'What's this about?' And I told him the
story. He never even read it. He didn't know anything
about it."[48] Wayne confirmed this story: "I just ask the
director which hat he wants me to wear and which door I
come in."[49]

This implicit, almost blind, faith in Hawks had its
price: many critics felt Wayne's talent was misused in Rio
Lobo, their thinnest collaboration and a much weaker Western
than either Rio Bravo or El Dorado. Hawks himself attributed its failure to the casting, "I didn't like it. I didn't
think it was any good. I only made it because I had a damn
good story and the studio couldn't afford to put a man as
good as Wayne in it, so we ended up with the cast we had."[50]
Rio Lobo's cast, one of the worst in a Wayne movie, included
such unknown or inexperienced actors in leading parts as
Jorge Rivero, Jack Elam, and Chris Mitchum.

Hawks directed Westerns and action movies with other
actors, such as The Big Sky, starring Kirk Douglas, but
they were pale compared with those starring Wayne. "If
you try to make a Western with somebody besides Wayne,"
he observed, "you're not in the sphere of violence and action that you are when you've got Wayne."[51] Of the actor's
greatest assets, Hawks singled out his "force" and "power"
and the fact that "he thinks quickly and thinks right."[52]
Wayne was considered by far the best: "When you have
someone as good as Duke around, it becomes awfully easy to
do good scenes because he helps and inspires everyone
around him."[53] Curiously, Lee Marvin did not think so;
when he asked Hawks to direct him in Monte Walsh, he told
him he wanted it to be a Lee Marvin, not a John Wayne,
Western. Hawks is reported to have answered with a good
deal of sarcasm, that Marvin need have no worry about being as good as Wayne--and he did not direct the film![54]

The relationship with Hawks, like that with Ford, extended beyond making pictures. Hawks gave the actor, as
a token of appreciation for his work in Red River, a silver
belt buckle shaped into the design of the "Red River D."
And another pleasant surprise greeted Wayne when he returned to the set of Rio Lobo after winning his Oscar award.
Under Hawks's initiative, all actors and crew members wore
eye patches, a tribute to his one-eyed marshal in True Grit.

The Academy Award apparently confirmed what Hawks had known all along, "John Wayne has just come to be recognized for the good actor he is." "I've always thought he was a good actor," Hawks explained, "I always thought he could do things that other people can't do."[55]

Rio Lobo was Hawks's last picture. Although highly respected by French critics, he was underestimated in the United States until the late 1960s, when a new generation of critics reexamined his work. Hawks was awarded an Honorary Oscar in 1974 for his cumulative work of four decades, which was interpreted as a compensation for never winning a legitimate, competitive directorial Oscar. He was nominated for Best Director just once, in 1941, for the war biopicture Sergeant York, starring Gary Cooper. Hawks died at his home in 1977.

Other Directors

Until Red River, Wayne did not command much respect from Hollywood's directors. For instance, he was interested in playing Wild Bill Hickok in Cecil B. De Mille's The Plainsman (1937), but the part went to Gary Cooper. Rumor has it that De Mille's reponse to Wayne's request was, "you were in The Big Trail, weren't you? A lot of water has gone under the bridge since then." Wayne was apparently offended and remembered the incident. When De Mille offered him the lead in North West Mounted Police (1940), Wayne told an emissary, "just tell Mr. De Mille too much water has flowed under the bridge for me to want the role." The part was played by Robert Preston, but De Mille was provoked by Wayne's guts and two years later offered him a good part in Reap the Wild Wind, co-starring Ray Milland. This time Wayne accepted, but needled the director: "The only reason you called me here is to make Ray Milland look like a man."[56]

Wayne did not like De Mille's dictatorial manner, particularly his tendency to shout at actors. In theory, Wayne maintained that "there can only be one boss on the set and that's the director," and that the actor is "just paint, to be used by him."[57] In practice, however, he demanded civility if not professional respect from his directors, which is one reason why he did not enjoy working with Josef von Sternberg

in Jet Pilot. Sternberg reported in his autobiography that
Wayne was "scared stiff" of him.

Allan Dwan, who directed him in Sands of Iwo Jima,
recalled that Wayne was "very punctual," "always ready to
go," and that "never once in the five weeks we shot the
film did he show up late."[58] Dwan was particularly impressed with Wayne's preparation for the part of Sergeant
Stryker: "He went to the Marine Camp at Pendleton and
spoke with many marines," because "he wanted to know how
to be a Marine." The only "trouble" Wayne caused was his
late night drinking bouts with the other actors--Wayne could
carry liquor, he was "a Hollywood legend in that respect,"
but the others could not, and it affected their work. Wayne
never interfered with Dwan's direction. On the second day
of shooting, he told him, "You're my kind of director," shook
hands, "and that was the end--I don't think there was a bit
of friction."[59] Furthermore, when the actors were not doing
exactly what they were supposed to, Dwan recalled, "Wayne
said, 'God damn it! Will you bastards do what he tells you!'
And they did it then. I said 'Thanks.'"[60] Asked if Wayne
was truly one of a kind, Dwan did not hesitate to proclaim,
"He was the only kind."

One of the few exceptions to usually good working relationships with his directors was with Melville Shavelson,
co-writer and director of Trouble Along the Way. Wayne
disagreed with some aspects of the script and demanded
changes, which Shavelson apparently agreed to make. However, the director continued to pursue his ideas when working with the other actors. When Wayne came onto the set
unexpectedly and found out what was happening behind his
back, he exploded regarding it as a violation of trust.
Shavelson described Wayne as "one of the kindest and most
level-headed men," but "when crossed, and particularly
double-crossed, he can make an underground nuclear ex-
plosion seem like a baby's sigh."[61]

Another unpleasant incident occurred on the set of
The High and the Mighty, directed by William Wellman, whom
Wayne had met in 1933. Twenty years later, he made a deal
with him to direct for Batjac. "I started out like a race
horse," with Island in the Sky and The High and the Mighty,"
Wellman recalled, "and fell on my skinny butt with Blood Alley."[62] Wellman did not like Wayne's interference with his

work and once bawled him out on the set in front of the entire crew. Wellman resented the fact that Wayne "suddenly
wanted to become a director--he has that inclination." The
director recalled that "in front of the whole crew, which is
a big mistake, I chose him. I said, 'Look, you come back
here behind the camera and do my job, and you're going to
be just as ridiculous doing it as I would be going out there
with that screwy voice of yours and that fairy walk and being
Duke Wayne,' and it quieted him down. And I meant it.
And he behaved himself."[63] None of the pictures Wellman
directed with Wayne was good, however, though The High
and the Mighty was extremely popular at the box office.
Characteristically though, Wayne did not hold a grudge
against the filmmaker and asked him to direct other movies
for Batjac.

The most strained interaction Wayne ever had with a
director was with John Huston in The Barbarian and the
Geisha, one of his most embarrassing films. Despite good
intentions on Huston's part, Wayne was miscast as Townsend
Harris, America's first diplomatic representative to Japan.
Huston believed that "only one man is right for him and
that's John Wayne," his idea being that "his massive frame,
bluff innocence and rough edges would be an interesting
contrast to the small, highly cultivated Japanese; that the
physical comparison would help serve to emphasize their dis-
similar viewpoints and cultures." Wayne was the best choice,
Huston felt, "to symbolize the big, awkward United States"
of the past.[64]

Wayne was the kind of actor who needed to trust his
directors, but he lost his faith in Huston. And this time,
he was uncharacteristically vocal about his dissatisfaction,
complaining about the script and his role, which he thought
damaged his image. In one scene, Wayne was thrown to the
ground--with ease--by a tiny judo expert and was left sitting
there with a bewildered look. He feared that his fans would
not take it: "Huston made me walk through a series of Japanese pastels. Hell, my fans expect me to be tall in the saddle!"[65] Wayne told reporters that "the most successful films
I have made have been about people, not plots and backgrounds," and that he was "surprised at Huston's attack,
that all-out go for sheer beauty like a Japanese print." "I've
endured a lot of bad scripts and bad directors," he said, but
"the time comes when you gotta speak up."[66] He admitted

John Wayne, uncharacteristically cast as Townsend Harris,
the first American diplomat sent to Japan, in John Huston's
The Barbarian and the Geisha (Twentieth Century-Fox, 1958),
one of the star's few commercial failures.

that for a while I couldn't make up my mind whether to flat
quit and go home and let them sue me, or stay and give this
thing a whirl. Guess I'm in so deep now I can't back out--
but the Old Duke's not happy."[67] A consummate professional,
he felt the contract was binding, but he never worked with
Huston again.

Most of Wayne's fears were confirmed when the film was
released. Crowther represented many reviewers when he
wrote: "Wayne in the role of Harris appears a little bewildered and repressed, being much more accustomed to action."[68] Other critics were even harsher on the film and on
Wayne's performance. The Barbarian and the Geisha was
also a failure at the box office, grossing in rentals only $2.5
million; it cost over $4 million.

One of the major problems was the scenario, by Huston
(uncredited) and Charles Grayson, which was unfinished when
shooting began. "I found myself shooting in the daytime and
writing future scenes at night," Huston wrote in his memoirs.[69]
Later, Huston learned through a trade paper that Twentieth
Century-Fox had changed the film's title, The Townsend
Story, to The Barbarian and the Geisha, a title he never
liked. Nor did Wayne, fearing it was not sufficiently explained to the audience that the Japanese call foreigners
barbarians, not just his character. "It was a good picture
before it became a bad picture," Huston claimed, still believing he made "a sensitive, well-balanced work." He admits to making "pictures that were no good, for which I was
responsible, but this was not one of them." Huston suspected that Wayne took over after he left, because "he
pulled a lot of weight at Fox, so the studio went along with
his demands for changes." By the time, "the studio finished
hacking up the picture according to Wayne's instructions, it
was a complete mess," and by the time Huston saw it, "I was
aghast." The director considered taking legal steps to have
his name removed from the picture, but upon learning that
Buddy Adler, the producer, was terminally ill with a brain
tumor, bringing suit under such circumstances "was unthink-
able."[70]

Another unpleasant incident occurred with Frank Capra,
who started working on Circus World, but this time it was
James Edward Grant's rather than Wayne's fault. Wayne had
been needling Capra for years for using Cooper, Gable, and

Stewart, but never him. So the director "kept him in mind,"
because he thought that "in that big hunk of solid man,
there was the depth and the humanity of another Mr. Deeds,
a Mr. Smith, or John Doe." Capra apparently did not realize that "when you took on Duke, you took on a small empire," and that "part of that empire was a personal writer
by the name of James Edward Grant." Grant was, according to Capra, Wayne's "confidant, adviser, bosom playpal,
baby sitter, flatterer, string-puller, and a personal Iago to
incite mistrust between his meal ticket and film directors,
especially name directors." For obvious reasons, Grant preferred to work with television or young directors he "could
handle."[71]

When Capra asked Grant to write the script, he replied, "You're outta your mind.... No use writing anything
until Wayne gets here. Duke makes his own pictures, now.
So relax, fella. When he gets here, he and I will knock you
out a screenplay in a week." Capra was further disturbed
by Grant's attitude toward the screenplay: "All you gotta
have in a John Wayne picture is a hoity-toity dame with big
tits that Duke can throw over his knee and spank, and a
collection of jerks he can smash in the face every five minutes. In between, you fill in with gags, flags, and chases.
That's all you need. His fans eat it up!"[72]

However, when Wayne showed up, he did not like the
screenplay and demanded a new one written. Capra decided
to resign but, out of a sense of responsibility, recommended
veteran director Henry Hathaway, whom he described as
"one of our best 'get it done' directors who took no guff
from any actor," as his replacement. To Hathaway's query,
"Why in hell are you walking out on the Duke?" Capra replied, "Hank, I'm not walking, I'm running." After working
for six months, writing, casting, and auditioning circus
acts, Capra fled Madrid, where the film was shot, with "the
same relief one flees Siberia." He regretted the experience
because he felt he "could have cowed the big Duke into giving his best performance. I could have made a rousing hit
out of Circus."[73] Hathaway could not save the film either,
and Circus World turned out to be one of Wayne's clinkers.
Wayne felt that it was Grant's responsibility and, after two
decades of close collaboration and personal trust, decided to
fire him.

Wayne also worked successfully with directors whose politics stood in sharp contrast to his. Edward Dmytryk, one of "the Hollywood Ten" who were found guilty of contempt of Congress, wrote of directing him in Back to Bataan: "He was already beginning to consider himself some kind of political thinker, but we all make mistakes."[74] Rumor has it that Dmytryk clashed with Colonel Clark, the film's adviser, and poked fun at his religiosity and patriotism; though confronted by Wayne, he pretended it was a joke. Interestingly, Dmytryk does not even mention this in his memoirs. He does recall, however, that Wayne told him that "though our methods were different ... our political aims were really the same." The director also concedes that "due to the network set up by Hollywood Alliance for the Preservation of American Ideals, he knew things about me I had no idea he knew." But they got along fine during the filming and even attended a number of social events together.[75] Years later Wayne told Playboy that he knew Dmytryk was "Commie," when he used the word "masses," because "the word is not a part of Western terminology."[76]

Producer-director Otto Preminger also attempted to separate his politics from his work, holding that "there is no place in the casting of a film or a play for selecting a performer wholly on the basis of compatibility or friendship or shared political views." Preminger realized that "there is probably no star whose politics are more at variance with mine than John Wayne," but when he was looking for a "U.S. Navy Captain type," he "had no hesitations asking John Wayne to do it and he had none accepting it." However, on the first day of shooting, Preminger was given an article to read--which he did not. He told Wayne: "Look, John, anybody over 30 has made up his mind about politics. You know where you stand politically and I would never succeed in converting you. I would not even try. So you shouldn't try to convert me to your opinions. Let's agree not to talk politics and we'll get along very well." This conversation apparently helped, for they did not have problems working together. The shooting of In Harm's Way ended on a humorous note when Preminger presented each member of the cast with red flowers, which prompted Wayne to quip, "Now at last you are showing your true color."[77]

Wayne denied reports that he did not get along with Preminger, "He had my respect and I had his respect." The only thing he said about the director is that "he is terribly hard on the crew, and he's terribly hard on people he thinks are sloughing off." Wayne said he "came ready," and "was usually ahead of him on the set,"[78] which Preminger couldn't believe. True, Preminger regarded Wayne as "the ideal professional; always prompt, always prepared."[79]

Mervyn LeRoy first met Wayne when he directed "a frothy little comedy," Without Reservations, opposite Claudette Colbert. The film "began my friendship with Duke Wayne," writes LeRoy, "we became very close, and our friendship culminated in our association on The Green Berets."[80] When Warners asked the director to go to Georgia and help Wayne who was directing the film, his condition was that "Duke asks me first," which the latter did. "You're a pal--come on down," Wayne said. LeRoy had a free hand with the movie, even to close it down, which he never considered, "certainly not with such an important star and good friend as John Wayne." But he spent five and a half months, instead of a few weeks, on location, and though he was paid, he "wouldn't let them put my name on it, as I didn't think that would be fair to Duke."[81] LeRoy's decision not to get credit (Ray Kellogg received credit as co-director) was to his advantage; this propagandistic movie was unfavorably received by most critics.

Wayne's relationships with directors of the younger generation were of a different kind, and sometimes raised problems. He himself admitted having "interfered" with their work. He claimed credit for talking Andrew McLaglen, son of actor Victor McLaglen, out of television work and assigning him his first directorial task, McClintock! But he also felt the need "to say don't do that, do this," realizing that at times McLaglen resented his suggestions. However, those who knew Wayne claimed that his advice to directors stemmed from his passion for filmmaking rather than stubbornness or desire to have the last word. There were "just too many Svengalis in this business," was the actor's way of defending his interference. He worked with directors "who couldn't walk across the street without help,"[82] he said, ruining potentially good pictures.

Burt Kennedy was another young director ambivalent toward Wayne's directorial suggestions. Kennedy, first writing for Wayne then directing The War Wagon and The Train

Robbers, said the actor was "tough to work with and he'll
admit it," but "there's no doubt he knows what he's doing,"
for "he's doing it long enough."[83] Asked on the set of The
War Wagon, "How do you coach a legend?" Kennedy replied,
"Let John Wayne direct himself."[84] But this was precisely
the problem with many of his films; they looked as if they were
not directed or, at best, directed by him, though his directing abilities were much less impressive than his acting skills.

Mark Rydell thought Wayne was ideal for the lead in
The Cowboys, but was apprehensive because "Wayne represented ideas, opinions, political attitudes, quite different
from my own." Rydell came prepared "to fight with him, to
'handle' him," but found instead "one of the most incredible
professionals I have ever met." Wayne was "always ready,
always listens to reason," and Rydell was further surprised
that he "never changed a word of the picture to project his
own political philosophy as a right-wing conservative."
Wayne's famous Playboy interview, in which he expressed
his views about blacks and Indians, came out during the
shooting and Rydell told him, "We must never discuss anything because we're not even in the same world." However,
their political differences never interfered with the work and
as shooting progressed, Rydell admitted to have found himself "listening to him and learning."[85]

Rydell knew there are "very few stars of his magnitude," and realized that his magnetic personality and charm
must have been the reason "why for 41 years this man has
captured the world." "All you need," he observed, "is a
week with him to realize that his qualities are quite remarkable." Indeed, after a few days of shooting, "Duke had
everybody eating out of his hand," and everybody was impressed to find an "articulate, sensitive, and totally unself-
ish" person. Apparently, the kids in the film "crawled all
over him like a monkey bar in Central Park Zoo," and they
too were surprised that "the great dictator turned out to be
a lamb." Another unexpected realization was that Wayne was
"literate and well-read," and had a "sharp, Shavian wit with
an uncanny ability to make pungent observations." Wayne
did not intervene at all with Rydell's work as producer and
director. In fact, according to the director Wayne "was delighted to surrender all managerial rights and to be just an
actor in this film." "He was happy," said Rydell, "as a 20-
year-old and he called me 'Sir.' Me! He's been a star for

more years than I've been alive."[86] Wayne's success stemmed
from being "so secure as a man," which made Rydell realize
that "you don't have to worry about stepping on his toes.
His toes are invulnerable."[87]

Don Siegel, who directed Wayne's last picture, The
Shootist, was also pleased with his knowledge of filmmaking.
He could not "help feeling a bit in awe of him," realizing
that "for the first time in my life I'm conscious of working
with a legend."[88] But according to rumors, initially there
was friction between the two because, as one unit member
put it, "Duke is used to directing his films--even if there's
already a good director,"[89] which Siegel was.

In conclusion, two directors were responsible for
Wayne's best work: Ford and Hawks. However, it was
Ford who was instrumental in launching, then shaping
Wayne's career, challenging and stretching his acting abilities. In this respect too, Wayne's career stood out; there
have been few actors whose careers depended entirely on
one director.

Ford performed a similar function in Henry Fonda's
earlier career, casting him in seven pictures, most notably
Young Mr. Lincoln, Drums Along the Mohawk, The Grapes
of Wrath, and My Darling Clementine. However, because
Fonda was both a stage and screen actor and because his
career was not associated with one studio, he was more
flexible than Wayne in choosing film projects and directors.
Fonda would have become a great actor without Ford's help,
which is doubtful in Wayne's case. Moreover, Fonda might
have become the greatest screen actor, had he committed
himself to Hollywood; Fonda left Hollywood at the height of
his popularity and went back to the New York stage, not
making a movie for seven years. The collaboration between
Ford and Fonda ended abruptly and turbulently on the set
of Mister Roberts; their heated arguments resulted in a fist-
fight. Ford did not claim and did not get any credit for the
film; Mervyn LeRoy replaced him.

If Ford was the most important director in Wayne's and
Fonda's careers, no single director played such a pivotal
function in Jimmy Stewart's. Anthony Mann directed the
largest number of his films, nine, making Stewart the third
major Western star, next to Wayne and Cooper, in the 1950s.

Two of the nine movies were popular biopictures: The Glenn
Miller Story and Strategic Air Command, the life story of Lt.
Colonel Robert Holland. But early on in his career, Stewart
worked with Frank Capra, with their three films, You Can't
Take It with You, Mr. Smith Goes to Washington, and It's a
Wonderful Life, forever defining the Stewart screen persona.
Later in his career he worked with Alfred Hitchcock, who
used him to great effect in four movies, including Rear Win-
dow and Vertigo, which brought out aspects of his image
completely different from those in Capra's films. These
Hitchcock movies were such blockbusters that they contributed to Stewart's box-office popularity much more than his
Westerns for Mann.

Hitchcock's other favorite actor was Cary Grant, whom
he directed in two 1940s classic thrillers, Suspicion and Notorious, and brought out of semiretirement in the 1950s with
To Catch a Thief and North by Northwest, the latter featuring one of Grant's most memorable roles. Grant, like Stewart, did his best work in the late 1930s, and then in the
1950s. He was used most effectively by Hawks in a series
of zany comedies such as Bringing Up Baby, His Girl Friday,
and I Was a Male War Bride. Hawks excelled in two radically
different genres: Westerns and comedies. In each, he had
a favorite star: Grant in comedies and Wayne in Westerns.

9. THE MOVIE STAR

Wayne is considered the greatest star in film history.
His popularity lasted for decades and was worldwide, extending beyond the borders of the United States. But Wayne
was more than a star, he was a superstar, a select category
that includes Hollywood immortals on the order of Clark
Gable, Gary Cooper, Jimmy Stewart, and a few others. How
did he accomplish this amazing popularity?

Some actors achieve success in a single movie that
catapults them to stardom: Errol Flynn in Captain Blood,
Humphrey Bogart after The Maltese Falcon, and Alan Ladd
with This Gun for Hire. This was not the case with
Wayne. Though Stagecoach was a turning point in his career, it took another decade before he became a box-office
champion. Compared with Gable or Cooper, who became
stars during the first five years of their careers, Wayne's
rise to stardom took much longer--20 years after his debut
to be precise. In this respect, his career was similar to
Bogart's, who emerged as a full-fledged star a whole decade
after his first film. Wayne, like Bogart, achieved stardom
gradually, through careful training and a succession of bad
films. However, unlike Bogart whose stardom began to decline in the early 1950s, Wayne's popularity grew rather than
diminished as time went by.

Stardom is an elusive concept, difficult to measure in
a precise manner. There are, however, rough indicators of
stardom, such as the amount of money screen players make,
the popularity of their movies at the box office, billings,
and their standing within the film industry, which translates
into bargaining power in negotiations with producers and directors over film projects and choice of costars.

From Rags to Riches

Wayne's mobility on Hollywood's income ladder is one of
the most startling success stories. He eventually became the
highest-paid actor in the industry, but his beginnings were
far from auspicious. For his first movie, Brown of Harvard,
he was paid $7.50 a week, and as a prop man at Fox, $30.00
a week. In the 1930s, when Gable was paid $2,500 a week,
Cooper $5,000, and Fredric March $7,000, Wayne received
$6,000 for his entire work in Stagecoach.

Wayne's rise on the salary ladder was gradual. His
contract with Republic in the 1940s stipulated that he be
paid $10,000 per picture, much below the average. The
turning point was Angel and the Badman in 1947, which he
produced and starred in, for which he was paid $145,000.
And Red River, a year later, was the first movie for which
he was paid a salary ($150,000) plus a percentage of the
profits. For his work in Sands of Iwo Jima in 1949, Wayne
got $180,000 and 10 percent of the profits. In the same
year he signed a precedent-setting contract with Warners
that committed him to do one picture a year for seven years
for $175,000, 10 percent of the gross, and $50,000 for each
rerelease of a movie. He thus became the first actor to get
money when his movies were reissued.

With the establishment of Wayne-Fellows Productions in
1952, he was paid $175,000 per movie, but he was paid more
when he worked for other studios. His contract with Howard
Hughes's RKO for Flying Leathernecks, for example, paid
him $301,000, an all-time record in 1951 for a single role.
Hughes was willing to pay such a huge amount of money because he believed "Wayne's worth it," as "he's one of the
few sure-fire box-office things left in Hollywood."[1] His 1956
contract for Twentieth Century-Fox was even more lucrative:
a total of $2 million for three movies, making him the highest-
salaried screen actor in the world. He was able to command
such fees because there were few superstars around. He believed that the industry should develop new stars, but he
also understood Hollywood producers' fear to take risks on
young, untried actors at a time when television was such a
threat to the film industry.

In the late 1950s, Wayne was one of the few stars to
command over $700,000 for a film, which he received for The

Barbarian and the Geisha. By contrast, director John Huston
received for his work $300,000. And for The Horse Soldiers,
Wayne and costar William Holden were paid each $750,000 plus
a percentage of the profits; John Ford received only one-
third of that sum. Wayne continued to be one of the highest-
paid actors in the industry even in the last decade of his
career. For his work in Hellfighters he received $1 million
plus 10 percent of the gross, and for Rio Lobo he made close
to $2 million: a $1 million fee and one-third of the gross
profits.

Wayne did not get star billing after the success of
Stagecoach; this, too, was a slow process. He took second
billing to Claire Trevor in their other two films together.
Similarly, having failed to establish himself as an immediate
box-office draw, Wayne had to take second billing to Ray
Milland in Reap the Wild Wind. However, when the movie
was rereleased a decade later, Paramount redesigned the
film's poster and publicity campaign and gave Wayne and
Susan Hayward (who had played secondary roles in the
film) top billing as both had become great stars. By contrast, Ray Milland and Paulette Goddard, who had the major
roles, now received second billing because their popularity
had dwindled over the years. Milland, a great star in the
1940s and an Oscar winner, was forced to work for Republic a decade later, long after Wayne left this second-rate
studio; such are the fickle realities of the film industry.

Even in the 1940s, Wayne's name was not sufficiently
prominent to get star billing. Thus, Jean Arthur received
top billing in Lady Takes a Chance, and Claudette Colbert
in Without Reservations. And in the two films he made with
Randolph Scott, Pittsburgh and The Spoilers, Scott got star
billing. It is hard to believe today that in the 1940s Scott
carried more clout at the box office than Wayne.

From the late 1940s on, however, Wayne gained status
as a real star. He received top billing in Fort Apache, despite the fact that Henry Fonda played the lead. And in
The Man Who Shot Liberty Valance Wayne got costar billing,
though Jimmy Stewart's role was more central to the film.
It was a measure of his prestige that in The Longest Day,
in which he played a cameo role along with many other stars,
his name was considered such an important asset at the box
office that it was listed last in the credits; the other stars

were listed alphabetically. With a few exceptions of cameo
roles, Wayne always played leads, even in his sixties. Unlike other stars, who were forced to switch to character or
supporting roles in their old age, Wayne was the leading man
and sole star of his pictures up to the very end.

Box-Office Champion

Wayne's movies have grossed collectively more than any
star's, male or female, of his generation; the amount is roughly estimated at $700 million in the United States. Based on
annual film rentals, Variety named him the box-office champion of all time. Wayne has been the only movie star with
32 pictures on the Variety compilation of all-time money grossers. His earliest film on the list is Reap the Wild Wind in
1942, grossing $4 million, and his latest (and last) is The
Shootist, whose domestic rentals amounted to $6 million. On
Variety's compilation are two movies of the 1940s (Red River
is the other one), seven in the 1950s, sixteen in the 1960s,
and seven in the 1970s. Significantly, from 1967 to 1976,
only two of the sixteen films he made, The Train Robbers
and Brannigan, were not among Variety's all-time champions.
Wayne's movies have been consistently among the top grossing movies, regardless of their individual merit.

With the possible exception of The Big Trail, which
cost $2 million and was a financial fiasco, very few of his
movies failed at the box office. Even his "B" Westerns were
profitable. Westward Ho! for instance, cost $17,000 and
grossed over $500,000, a 30 to 1 payoff. Many films panned
by the critics proved to be popular smash hits. Sea Chase,
for example, received unanimously unfavorable reviews, but
grossed $6 million in the United States alone, an equivalent
of over $30 million at present. This was a fantastic figure
in the 1950s, when few movies grossed more than $4 million.

Wayne's box-office popularity becomes more dramatic
when compared with other stars of his generation. Contrasted with Wayne's thirty-two all-time grossers, Jimmy Stewart
and Cary Grant had each twelve, Henry Fonda nine, Spencer
Tracy eight, Clark Gable seven, Gary Cooper six, Humphrey
Bogart and James Cagney each three, Alan Ladd and Robert
Taylor each two, and Tyrone Power only one.

Beginning in 1932, the Quigley publications have asked movie exhibitors in the United States to name the top ten box-office stars of the year. These annual polls can be used as an approximate measure of popular taste over the last half century. Accordingly, Wayne has been the only star to appear 25 times on the top ten poll. His first appearance was in 1949 (ranking fourth), following Red River and Fort Apache. A year earlier, on the 1948 poll, Wayne occupied the thirty-third position. The last time he was among the top ten stars was in 1974, in the tenth position. With the exception of one year, 1958, the lowest ebb in his career, after such clinkers as The Conqueror, Jet Pilot, and Legend of the Lost, Wayne was on the poll for 25 consecutive years. Moreover, he occupied the top position, the most popular star in America, four times: in 1950, after the success of Sands of Iwo Jima; in 1951, after the war movies Operation Pacific and Flying Leathernecks; in 1954, following Hondo and The High and the Mighty; and in 1971, following his 1970 Oscar for True Grit and the moderate success of Rio Lobo.

In 1975 Wayne dropped out of favor with the American public, but his decline was gradual: he ranked fourth in 1972, ninth in 1973, and tenth in 1974. He continued to be popular, however, occupying the fifteenth position in 1975, and eleventh in 1976, due to the relative success of Rooster Cogburn and The Shootist. Film exhibitors ranked him as a popular star in 1977 (in 23rd position) and in 1978 (25th), despite the fact that he did not make any movie in these years!

Wayne was among the top ten seven years longer than Gary Cooper (18 years) and nine years longer than Clark Gable (16 years), the two previous champions. Cooper was popular in 1936-37, 1941, from 1943 to 1949, and from 1951 to 1957. He occupied the top position just once, in 1953, after his Oscar award for High Noon. Gable was on the poll from 1932 to 1943 (when he was drafted), from 1947 to 1949, and for the last time in 1955, but he was never at the top. Other performers of Wayne's generation were popular for a lesser number of years: Cary Grant for eleven years, Spencer Tracy and Jimmy Stewart each ten, Humphrey Bogart eight, James Cagney six, Robert Taylor and Tyrone Power each three, Alan Ladd two, and Errol Flynn one year only. Note that Henry Fonda, one of the most acclaimed actors in America, had never become a screen box-office champion.

The average durability of American players, measured by the number of years they were box-office champions, has been five for male and three for female stars. Of the current stars, only three have been on the poll for over a decade: Clint Eastwood 18 years, Paul Newman 13, and Burt Reynolds 12. Newman's last appearance on the list was in 1982 (The Verdict), which means that the only serious contenders to Wayne's crown as the world's box-office champions are Eastwood and Reynolds, assuming they continue to make popular films for another decade, which is doubtful in Reynolds's case.

It is amazing that Wayne continued to be a popular star long after his colleagues' popularity declined and long after many retired or died. Humphrey Bogart was the first of Hollywood's great stars to pass away, in 1957, at the peak of his career and at the young age of 58. Bogart was followed by Tyrone Power, who died in 1958, Errol Flynn in 1959, Clark Gable in 1960, Gary Cooper in 1961, Alan Ladd in 1964, Spencer Tracy in 1967, and Robert Taylor in 1969. Of the stars who began their careers in the 1930s, only three were making movies in the 1970s: Wayne, who died in 1979; Fonda, who died in 1982; and Jimmy Stewart, the only survivor of this breed. Cary Grant retired in 1962, and Cagney in 1961; the latter made a comeback in 1981 (Ragtime), but died in 1986, a year that also marked Grant's death.

Wayne's durability as a box-office champion spanned a generation, from 1949 to 1974, regardless of changes in the political, social, and cultural context of the times. One joke in the industry was that presidents and administrations have come and gone, but Wayne was still at the top. In the early 1950s Wayne was on the poll with Cooper, Gable, Tracy, and Stewart, and in the late 1950s with William Holden, Burt Lancaster, Glenn Ford, and Marlon Brando. Players appeared and disappeared from the poll quite rapidly, but he remained. In the early 1960s Wayne was a popular star along with Rock Hudson, Jack Lemmon, and Paul Newman, and later in the decade his star company included another set of actors--Sean Connery, Lee Marvin, and Steve McQueen. In the 1970s Wayne was joined by yet another generation of actors--Dustin Hoffman, Robert Redford, Clint Eastwood, and Charles Bronson.

That Wayne continued to be a viable star surviving the tumultuous decade of the 1960s is really striking. He made conservative movies and propagated conservative politics at a time when the entire society seemed to be moving to the Left. In 1969 Life magazine made a revealing comparison between the country's two greatest male stars, Wayne and Dustin Hoffman, as examples of the way American society seemed to be polarized. Wayne became an actor because of his looks, and his impressive height of 6'4" was an asset to his image; Hoffman became an actor despite his looks and his height of 5'6½". Wayne portrayed Westerners in outdoor action films; Hoffman symbolized young American city dwellers. Wayne played simple-minded heroes, optimistic about the future; Hoffman was typically cast as a liberal intellectual (The Graduate) who was pessimistic or at least critical of society. Wayne's heroes were larger than life, strong, decisive, moral, and always winners. Hoffman's, by contrast, were realistic, complicated, uncertain about their goals and identity, often alienated, and sometimes downright losers (Midnight Cowboy).

Wayne's and Hoffman's lifestyles and off-screen images were as opposite as their screen roles. Wayne was a traditionalist Republican, who knew who he was, what he thought, and where he was going. Hoffman's politics were democratic and he admitted to having doubts and questions about his life. Hoffman kept his perspective by regular visits to psychiatrists, something Wayne never did and, one suspects, did not approve of, being a self-made man and believing in self-help. Wayne's lifestyle was suburban-oriented, living in a big house in Newport Beach, California; Hoffman lived in an apartment at the heart of Greenwich Village in New York City.

Despite these differences, both Wayne and Hoffman were extremely popular, functioning as American folk heroes, not just movie stars. Each had a large following, split by generations, though many moviegoers, of differing ages and political persuasions, admired both. Hoffman was a top attraction from 1969 to 1972, and in 1980, after his Oscar award for Kramer vs. Kramer. In 1983, he emerged again as a viable star with the immense success of Tootsie. But despite being a much better and more versatile actor than Wayne, as well as the critics' darling, his name, unlike Wayne's, could not carry

a mediocre or even a good art film at the box office, as
Agatha or Straight Time demonstrated.

Wayne was popular outside the film world as well. A
public opinion poll found that more people recognized the
name and face of John Wayne than any other man in American history--with one exception, Abraham Lincoln.[2] His
face became not only familiar, but unique, as Dean Martin,
his costar in The Sons of Katie Elder, commented: "When
people see me, they sometimes say, 'Oh, there goes Perry
Como.' But there's only one John Wayne and nobody makes
any mistakes about that."[3]

Wayne's popularity was recognized and honored with
many awards, beginning with the 1950 Photoplay Gold Medal
for his performance in Sands of Iwo Jima, over tough competition from Broderick Crawford, Gregory Peck, Larry
Parks, and Spencer Tracy. An extensive poll of movie goers, conducted in 1951, found Wayne and Betty Hutton to
be America's most popular stars. And in 1952, Joan Crawford handed Wayne a plaque in honor of his "untiring efforts to bring credit to the motion picture industry," accorded by the Interstate Circuits of Theaters. In 1955 he
was voted "King of the Movies" by House Box-office magazine.

Wayne was even prouder of the awards honoring his
contribution to Western lore. In 1949 he became the first
winner of the Silver Spur award, sponsored by the Reno
Chamber of commerce and bestowed on people who have contributed to Western folklore through various media. He also
won the Gold Saddleman award of the Western Writers of
America, as "the man who has contributed most to the history and legend of the West." And in 1967, the National
Cowboy Hall of Fame used an armored stagecoach to notify
Wayne of his election to its board of trustees, representing
17 Western states.

Of greater significance was being chosen in 1962 as
"the Number One Action Star" by the film buyers of the motion picture industry. The Hollywood's Women Press Club
selected him as the most cooperative male star in 1965, be-
stowing on him their Golden Apple Award. In 1966 he received two important prizes: the Photoplay Gold Medal
award, for being the Champion Box-Office Star in film

history, and the Cecil B. De Mille Life Achievement Award, given by Hollywood's Foreign Press Association for lifetime contribution to film. In 1969 Wayne was voted "the Super-star of the Decade," and in 1970, he received the American Academy of Achievement's Annual Golden Plate award, for being "the movie star of the era." Former winners of this prestigious award include Bob Hope and Helen Keller. Wayne was also named "the Actor of the Year" for 1974 and 1975 in the annual People's Choice awards, based on a representative sample of 10,000 people from all over the country.

Wayne's Movie Audiences

The product of a small town, Winterset, Iowa, and growing up in Glendale, California, Wayne was more popular in rural America. Rural areas have always provided better markets for Westerns than urban centers. His widest appeal was probably in the Mid-West, due both to the nature of his movies and his conservative politics. Director Raoul Walsh's consolation, when Wayne was disturbed by the nasty write-ups for his movies in the East Coast, was: "Never mind New York. You're a big hit in Cincinnati."[4] An article in News Weekly, "John Wayne--Main Street's Hero," attempted to assess his appeal: "Wayne's drawing power is especially potent in small towns, where any of John Wayne's pictures, whether it is new or ten years old, will pack the house."[5]

Because the Western has always been a "masculine" genre, Wayne's ardent fans must have been men. A study conducted by the Motion Picture Research Bureau in 1942, based on 2,000 respondents in 45 cities, found that males liked Westerns better than females did.[6] Wayne himself said he played to men, attempting to make pictures that really appealed to male audiences. This was based on his belief that it was usually men who took women to the movies. Critics suggest that through Wayne's films his male fans have fulfilled their escapist fantasies about action, adventure, and heroism against all odds. As one writer put it: "Adventure film fans know they can expect at least one good fight, and lots of action in any of his films."[7]

Many, however, believed that he appealed to both genders because he played gentlemen on screen. Charles Skouras, the theater magnate, attributed Wayne's success

to the fact that he was one of the few movie stars liked by
men, women, and children: "Men regard him as a plain,
simple, hard-riding, two-fisted man of action," Skouras
elaborated, "women find him a shy, kindly protector with an
awkward tenderness and latent but super-charged sex potential." And children "admire the picturesque epic hero of the
Western plains, the Air Force, and the Submarine Service."[8]
Ford also held that "Duke stays at the top for the same reason Cooper, Gable, and Stewart stay up there. He's a clean-
cut, good-looking, virile, typically American type." Wayne
was a hero for all members of the family, or as Ford said,
"They all like him for a big brother, or a husband, or a
pal."[9]

Wayne was never as handsome as Cooper or Gable, and
lacked the explicit sex appeal of Cary Grant or Errol Flynn.
Still, he was admired by women who liked the idea that "he
doesn't look like an actor, he looks like a real man,"[10] as
one female fan said. During his divorce proceedings from his
second wife, his popularity among women increased. The
court was mobbed by female admirers, holding up signs that
stated, "John Wayne. You Can Clobber Me Any Time You
Want," referring to his wife's accusations that he had mistreated her.

Joan Didion recalled in her love letter to the star that
she had first seen a Wayne movie in 1943, when she was
eight years old. She still remembered how Wayne told the
heroine (Martha Scott) in War of the Wildcats that he would
build her a "house at the bend of the river where the cotton-
woods grow." "Deep in that part of my heart," Didion wrote,
"that is still the line I wait to hear." "When John Wayne
rode through my childhood, and perhaps through yours, he
determined forever the shape of certain of our dreams."[11]
For Didion, Wayne's appeal stemmed from the fact that in a
world characterized by doubts and ambiguities, "he suggested
another world, one which may or may not have existed ever,
but in any case existed no more: a place where a man could
move free, could make his own code and live by it." Furthermore, when Wayne spoke, "there was no mistaking his intentions; he had a sexual authority so strong, that even a child
could perceive it."[12]

Wayne has always had a special appeal among young
moviegoers, although is popularity went beyond age barriers.

A spokesman for Frontier Playhouse once observed that while
many parents may say they are watching Wayne's films to
keep their children company, they actually outnumber the
youngsters in the audience by 62 to 38 percent.[13] And in
response to a Playboy magazine query as to whether his
record rested on his appeal to adolescents, Wayne said:
"Let's say I hope that I appeal to the more carefree times in
a person's life rather than to his reasoning adulthood." He
also said he would like "to be an image that reminds someone
of joy rather than of the problems of the world." And to another query by Playboy, "Luckily, so far, it seems they kind
of consider me an older friend, somebody believable and down-
to-earth." Wayne attributed his popularity among youngsters
to having "played many parts in which I've rebelled against
something in society." "I was never much of a joiner," he
elaborated, "kids do join things, but they also like to consider themselves individuals capable of thinking for themselves. So do I."[14]

Wayne's movies had two generational plots, there were
always children in them, and his relationship to the younger
generation was central to his screen image, which also accounted for his popularity among adolescents. Furthermore,
in his last films there was an explicit attempt to cater to
youngsters, as True Grit, Big Jake, and of course The Cowboys attested. This commercial consideration had to do with
the fact that American moviegoers were getting younger and
younger; the most frequent moviegoers were well under 21.
To appeal to the largest potential audiences, The Cowboys
also had among its characters a Jewish cowboy and a black
cook. But the attempt to appeal to young audiences went
beyond commercial considerations. Wayne was influenced by
Western star Tom Mix who attempted "to keep my pictures in
such a vein that parents will not object to letting their children see me on the screen." This movie philosophy was
adopted by Wayne, whose idea of a good picture was one
which was designed for the entertainment of all the family.

Because his movies were uncomplicated, they provided
fantasy materials for adults too. Critic Kistler observed in
his obituary of Wayne that his films appealed to "every man
who wanted to be John Wayne when he was six and the world
was a simpler place, with only good guys and bad guys, and
when quick and uncompromising justice was dispensed by the
Big Man." As for mature audiences, Kistler believed that

Wayne appealed to "eveɪy man who, as an adult in a complicated, computerized world, has secretly yearned--if just
once--to sit tall in the saddle atop a prancing, foam-flicked
mount at the far side of a wide, fairytale expanse of Western
meadow to finally confront, outnumbered and alone, the men
of evil."[15]

    What set Wayne apart from other stars and made him a
cultural folk hero was the impact of his movies on the consciousness of his audiences. In his novel The Moviegoer,
Walker Percy observes that "other people treasure memorable
moments in their lives: the time one climbed the Parthenon
at sunrise, the summer night one met a lonely lady in Central Park," but what he remembered was "the time John
Wayne killed three men with a carbine, as he was falling to
the duststreet in Stagecoach."[16] What better proof of
Wayne's imprint on Percy's subjective imagination than this?
And because of the extraordinary dimensions of his stardom,
Wayne may have fulfilled the same fantasy for thousands of
youngsters, thus contributing to the formation of a collective consciousness.

    A more interesting revelation of Wayne's function in
American culture is found in Ron Kovic's book Born on the
Fourth of July, in which he shares with the readers the emotional experience of watching Sands of Iwo Jima on television: "We were glued to our seats," he recalled watching
Wayne's Sergeant Stryker charge up the hill and get killed
just before he reached the top. And when they showed the
men raising the flag on Iwo Jima with the Marines' hymn still
playing, he and his friend "cried in our seats."[17] From that
moment, every time he heard it, he would think of Wayne and
the flag. More emotionally disturbing is Kovic's account of
fighting in Vietnam, where he was wounded and paralyzed:
"Nobody ever told me I was going to come back from the
war without a penis," he wrote, "Oh God, Oh God, I want
it back! I gave it for the whole country.... I gave [it]
for John Wayne."[18] This is a "heavy burden to lay on a
movie star," critic Jack Kroll noted, but it also attests to
Wayne's great authority as "troop leader of the American
dream."[19]

    Wayne functioned as a role model, consciously and
subconsciously, for thousands of adolescents in America.
The fantasies he provided may have been escapist, but they

were also emotionally powerful, thus real. John Ritter, son
of Western star Tex Ritter and star of his own television
series Three's Company, grew up in an atmosphere surrounded by Western folklore. His childhood was probably typical
of many youngsters who grew up in rural America: "I grew
up on Westerns and just loved them," Ritter observed, "for
a long time, I didn't know they made other kinds of pictures." Ritter's favorite Western stars were, of course, his
father, followed by John Wayne, Roy Rogers, Rory Calhoun,
Tim Holt, and Hoot Gibson.[20]

    As for social class, it is plausible to assume that
Wayne's typical audiences came from white lower-middle or
lower classes. In his analysis of taste, Herbert Gans constructs a hierarchy that distinguishes among subcultures of
various classes in America. He uses variants of the Western
film to illustrate these taste differences. Westerns of lower-
middle subculture are typically concerned with conflicts between farmers and ranchers, whereas Westerns of lower culture deal with conflicts between cowboys and outlaws. In
this respect, Wayne made both lower-middle and lower culture Westerns. Gans also claims that sexual segregation,
differentiation between male and female roles in and outside
the family, and other working-class values have been reflected in the Hollywood action movie. The action film typically describes an individual hero's fight against crime and
other violations of the social order, and its issues are always
clearly defined.[21]

    The heroes of the two respective subcultures also dif-
fer. While the hero of the lower-middle subculture may have
doubts about the social usefulness of his function and about
the validity of his identity, the hero of the lower subculture
is devoid of these doubts. Other attributes of the lower subculture hero fit many of Wayne's movies: he is sure of his
masculinity, distrustful of governmental authority, works
either alone or with buddies of the same gender, is shy with
good women, and aggressive with bad ones.

    Perhaps most important of all is the classlessness of
the hero, despite the fact that the norms he espouses are
lower-class norms. In the typical Hollywood movie, heroes
are neither aware of their class nor is class a problem in
the narrative--the way it is, for example, in a typical British film. In Gans's view, Wayne, Gable, and Cooper were

all prototypes of the lower-class hero. The fact that none
of the young stars of today's action films has achieved their
predecessors' popularity is indicative, in his view, of low
culture's loss of dominance in America.[22]

Wayne's early "B" Westerns catered to white lower and
working classes, but gradually his popularity expanded to
the lower-middle and middle classes. He began his career in
low culture, but he managed to add new audience strata,
thus broadening his appeal as his career progressed. Gans
acknowledges that occasionally a cultural product or performer may appeal to several publics on the taste hierarchy, such
as Charlie Chaplin and Marilyn Monroe, whose appeal crosses
class lines. Wayne could easily be added to this group, particularly in his better Ford and Hawks Westerns. The multi-
cultural appeal of these performers is possible because their
movies' content and style is broad and varied enough to
cater to different publics, so that every public finds something in them. But Wayne also serves as an illustration to
Gans's claim that very seldom has a performer or a cultural
product been accepted by all subcultures or by all classes.[23]

Wayne's Popularity Outside of America

Wayne's popularity as a movie star was not confined to
the borders of the United States; he was popular all over
the world. In 1953, for example, Wayne and Susan Hayward
were voted the film world's favorite stars by movie fans in
54 countries, in a poll conducted by the Foreign Press Association. Fifteen years later he was cited again as the most
popular screen star on both sides of the Atlantic, followed
by Steve McQueen and Sean Connery.

Wayne was extremely popular in Europe, where audiences were not as exposed to Westerns as in America, regarding them as exotic and original art forms. British audiences, particularly in small towns, were among Wayne's
devoted fans. In 1952 he was voted the most popular Western star in England, followed by Alan Ladd, Randolph Scott,
Roy Rogers, and Jimmy Stewart.[24] Wayne received royalty
treatment in London when he arrived for the premiere of
The Conqueror, with his luggage cleared in double-quick
time. The customs head at the airport later declared:
"There's only one other person I would do that for, and

his name's Churchill."[25]   Nice company to be associated
with!

In France, Wayne also gained the esteem of film directors François Truffaut and Jean-Luc Godard, and critics,
most notably André Bazin, who elevated the Western into a
respectable art form. These filmmakers admired the work of
Ford and Hawks and praised Wayne's work in their pictures,
long before the movies or Wayne had gained the respect of
American critics. In 1950, for example, Wayne received
an award from the French cinema, as the most popular foreign
star there. And after his death, one of the major television
networks announced that his best pictures would be screened
in a tribute called "John Wayne, Duke of the Wide-Open
Spaces."

His popularity in Germany was unprecedented. German audiences were exposed to Wayne's films as early as
1930, with The Big Trail, the first sound Western to be
shown there. Contrary to Fox's fears that this movie would
lose the traditional foreign markets for Westerns and their
hesitations about dubbing it, The Big Trail proved a greater
success in Germany (and all over Europe) than in the United
States. The foreign version of this and other Westerns were
shot at the same time; the screenplay, sets, costumes were
alike, and the big action sequences were used in all versions.
German audiences did not see Wayne on the screen, except
in long shots--foreign actors were used in close-up. But
they all knew it was a John Wayne Western.

Wim Wenders, one of West Germany's leading directors,
described Wayne as an "original," and "the most popular
American actor ever to appear on the screen in Germany."
Wenders explained that "Cowboys are a little exotic in Germany," because the Western is seen "as an art form and a
myth." The Western is so far away from German culture
that "it becomes an even bigger myth." And "because there
are no horses or cowboys in Germany, John Wayne was our
link to the West." Wayne's popularity in Germany derived
from the fact that he displayed "a certain physical and mental strength, as well as stubbornness that the Germans liked
and needed." He himself decided to become a film director
out of admiration for the American cinema. As a boy, Wayne
was his hero, though "when I saw Wayne, he always spoke
German because his voice was always dubbed."[26]   Some of

Wayne's movies were more successful in Germany than in the
United States. The Alamo, for example, was cited by the
German Film Board as especially valuable, a category ac-
corded to pictures of exceptional merit.

Even the Soviets knew and were appreciative of Wayne's
Westerns. In the summer of 1973, at the Nixon-Brezhnev
summit meeting, the two leaders flew over the Grand Canyon
and Nixon asked the Soviet leader whether he had seen this
country. Brezhnev reportedly said he had seen it in a
Wayne movie. Then in a moment of humor, NBC television
cameras caught the two leaders grinning at each other and
making gestures of a typical Wayne gunfight.[27]

Japan also welcomed Wayne's movies, particularly after
Huston decided to shoot there The Barbarian and the Geisha.
Paradoxically, his war movies were extremely successful there
despite the fact that the Japanese played the villains and
their portrayal was one-dimensional. Wayne's pro-Vietnam
The Green Berets was panned by most Japanese critics, but
drew capacity crowds all over Japan. One film critic expressed his astonishment: "How on earth could the Japanese
stand to see, let alone enjoy, those scenes in which so many
Vietnamese people, who look very much like the Japanese,
are killed by the Green Berets?"[28] When Emperor Hirohito
of Japan visited the United States in 1975, one of the few
people he sought to meet was John Wayne. "As if he wished
to see the personification of the power and determination that
had defeated his country in World War II,"[29] wrote critic
Kroll. After Wayne's death, a leading Tokyo newspaper ran
the headline, "Mr. America Passes On," and other newspapers
referred to him as "The Pride of America."

Wayne's international popularity was summed up by
Miller in the Los Angeles Times, after returning from extensive traveling. In Australia, a farmer asked him when the
next John Wayne movie would come out, and in Burma, he
saw pictures of the star in restaurants and other public
places. A shop owner in Afghanistan said, in response to
the question of how life has changed under the new pro-
Soviet regime, that the John Wayne movies had gone. In
Eastern Turkey, upon telling a nomad that he was from America, the latter reached to his side in a mock draw and with
a big grin exclaimed: "John Wayne." And a South African
tourist in America asked Miller whether he knew Wayne had

died; he had heard the news from a Frenchman.[30] True,
Wayne was eulogized in the foreign press all over the world,
usually on the front page. The London Evening Standard,
for example, wrote in its editorial, "The Iron Duke--the Last
Hero of the Wild West," and the Lima (Peru) Noticias head-
lined, "Goodbye Cowboy."

Durability of Stardom

The ultimate test of movie stardom is durability at the
box office, which marked Wayne's career, though it is not
easy to explain. "Ask anybody to analyze the ubiquity and
professional longevity of such a fixture as Wayne," wrote
one critic in 1945, "and you'll precipitate about the same
mystification as if you asked a New Yorker to account for
the existence and persistence of Sixth Avenue or Chock Full
O'Nuts."[31] In 1953 another critic posed a similar question:
"It is still difficult to figure out why he is our leading male
box-office attraction. True, he never gets involved in any
cinematic situation beyond the comprehension of a toddler,
but the same could be said of a host of his colleagues."[32]

Some say that what explains his success is sheer luck,
along with some natural gift. He himself believed that a
star's popularity cannot last forever, and that his success
was just a big fluke. However, there must have been other
factors than luck to sustain his appeal, for there have been
many stars who had similar, even better, opportunities, but
they vanished rapidly from the public eye. For sure, it was
not just Wayne's looks that either got or kept him there.
And as for his talent, there were always doubts about it
and, in any case, it was not sufficient in itself to explain
such longevity. A combination of factors must have accounted
for his durability: luck, hard work, self-discipline, driving
ambition, some talent, and most important of all, a charming
image and personality.

Wayne worked during the height of the studio system,
which built and supported a star system through familiarity
and repeated exposure. Most stars of Hollywood's golden age
made at least four pictures a year, so that audiences could
count on seeing their stars on a regular basis. The studio
system had many advantages: it provided sponsorship,
tailored scripts to stars' specifications, employed its stars

continuously, and worked hard through its publicity machine
to sell an appealing screen persona to the public. Robert
Taylor, one of the best examples of studio-fabricated products, observed acutely: "I just wish the young guys today
had a studio [MGM] and boss [Louis B. Mayer] like I had in
those days; it made us stars. We were groomed carefully,
kept busy in picture after picture, thus getting exposure."[33]

Continuity of exposure was the name of the game. In
Wayne's 50-year career there was never a time in which he
was not either making or about to make a film. In the 1930s
he made 68 movies (at the average of seven a year!); in the
1940s, 32 movies (three a year); in the 1950s, 20 movies
(two a year); in the 1960s, 20 (two a year); and in the
first six years of the 1970s, 10 movies. At present, stars
are making at best one movie a year, because a lesser number of movies are being made. And with the demise of the
studio system, there is little chance that today's stars will
ever achieve the popularity of the older stars.

Wayne's continuous exposure was also sustained through
the rereleases of his old movies in theaters and their reissues
on television (chapter 10). In the 1950s, when Hollywood
experienced one of its severest crises due to competition from
television, many of Wayne's old movies were rereleased. In
1950 alone, no less than nine Wayne movies were shown in
Los Angeles first-run theaters. His business associates
worried that showing so many of them at once would burn up
his popularity, but quite the opposite happened: each rerelease made Wayne more popular. Many pictures, such as
The Long Voyage Home and Seven Sinners, were more profitable the second time around than in their initial release.
Wayne was proud to work in such volume and still be popular, "no actor can have that many pictures at one time and
not be finished."[34] The feeling among movie owners and
distributors was that "there's nothing about the movie depression a dozen of Wayne films couldn't cure."[35] Louis B.
Mayer is quoted to have said, "Wayne has an endless face--
he can go on forever."[36]

His continuous exposure for half a century made him
appeal to three generations of moviegoers: people of his
age, their children, and their grandchildren. He himself
joked about his durability: "I've been around movies long
enough for millions of people to have been born, have kids,

and die. But I'm still working."[37] "Maybe people have seen
me around so long," he once said, "they figure I'm one of
the family."[38] Joan Didion felt when she visited him on the
set that his face was in a certain way more familiar than her
husband's. Wayne was highly aware that the "secret" of his
success stemmed from the fact that "my buildup was done
through exposure." "By the time I went overseas to visit
our boys during World War II," he explained, "they had already seen my movies when they were back home. Now their
kids are grown up and their kids are seeing my pictures."[39]

Unlike most stars, Wayne became more popular as he
aged. But that his lengthy experience was an asset, rather
than a liability, was also related to the changing structure
of the movie industry: "The gamblers are all gone from the
motion picture business," he reasoned, "when they made it
strictly banking, they assured guys like Gable, Stewart,
and me a long career. They won't gamble on new people."[40]

Puzzled by his own success, Wayne rationalized in the
following way: "The type of pictures I've been in, so many
people can identify with, all over the world." "They can
immediately accept me into their social feelings," he continued, "'Old Duke, he was all right,' they might say, and I'm
not sure they'd say it to Laurence Olivier or about him,
wonderful as he is." He did not mind that "people say,
'John Wayne isn't an actor,'" in fact, he did not want "the
butcher or the baker or the candlestick maker to think I'm
an actor." Instead, he wanted them "to know I'm one of
them, and getting by."[41]

Audiences could identify with the characters he portrayed, but they also liked his personality off-screen and
the fact that he symbolized the American way of life (chapter 13). Wayne was aware that "I've been in more bad pictures than just anyone in the business," but "as long as
you project yourself, and you're not mean or petty, the
public will forgive you."[42] Which is why he never played
"mean or small characters," because "it's not my cup of
tea." He always tried "not to let the audience down about
the type of fellow they expect me to be." To surprise them,
yes, "but never fool them."[43] Wayne's philosophy of stardom was similar to Cary Grant's and based on the belief
that "the ones who have stayed the course are the ones who
behave most nearly like themselves." Grant held that "you

have to be true to what you are," because "the public has
an unfailing sense for spotting a fake."[44]

Believing that "everyone loves a hero," Wayne avoided
playing villains, or made sure that they redeemed themselves
in the course of the picture. He once attributed the continuity of his appeal to the fact that "people were getting fed
up with all those pictures about sick people and their minds,"[45]
referring to the Tennessee Williams protagonists whom he detested. "The people who come to see my pictures," he proudly proclaimed, "come to see John Wayne and that's all I try
to give them."[46] "I play the kind of person people want me
to be"; he described his ideal role as "a fellow with a code
of behavior."[47]

Herbert Yates, head of Republic, claimed that the two
qualities that made Wayne a big star were honesty and sincerity. "All I do is sell sincerity," Wayne confirmed, "and
I've been selling the hell out of that ever since I started."[48]
"When Duke is advertised in coming attractions," said Bo
Roos, Wayne's business manager, "movie goers know that
this picture is not going to be about racial minorities or the
decline of Civilization. A Wayne picture spells excitement,
action, and the triumph of virtue."[49] Other actors might
have been offended by Roos's comments, but not Wayne--he
wanted it that way. Robert Fellows, Wayne's partner, concurred: "Duke says he can't act. But whatever it is he
does, a lot of people will pay to see him do it."[50]

Wayne's name was solid enough at the box office to
carry a weak film and make it profitable. In most cases, it
did not matter much how good his films were; it was sufficient to advertise them as "A John Wayne movie." Audiences
in the past were less discriminating about pictures with their
favorite stars, whereas at present, most audiences seem to
judge every movie on its own merits. People do not go to
the movies any more; they go to see a movie, thus the film
experience has become a special event rather than routine,
as it used to be. Very few stars today, such as Barbra Streisand and Clint Eastwood, can command audiences regardless of
their movies' worth. By contrast, many people must have
gone to see Wayne's movies out of habit, sort of keeping in
touch with an older and favorite star. That Wayne succeeded in building a loyal following more than other stars is totally to his credit.

Despite his enormous popularity, Wayne remained modest throughout his career. From the beginning, he refused to cooperate with the publicity machine of his studios, especially when he thought the image sold to the public was too contrived. For the publicity tour of The Big Trail, Fox fabricated the idea that he was a former Texas ranger and an All-American football star. Wayne debunked this imagery and told reporters it was phony. To make Wayne's nickname, Duke, more appealing, the studio said it stemmed from a part he had played in a high-school play. This was consistently denied by the star, "I was not named after royalty. I was named for my dog." For the publicity tour of The Big Trail Fox dressed him in buckskins and gave him some props, but he quit in the middle of the tour because he felt ridiculous waving a hatchet on stage and aiming a muzzle-loading rifle. Fox also faked the idea that he knew how to ride a horse from his childhood--which many magazines "bought" at the time--but Wayne later said he had never been on a saddle before he went to Hollywood.

Wayne was uncooperative with the publicity department of Republic, which signed him to appear in Westward Ho! His answers to a standard publicity questionnaire were far from satisfactory for the studio's purposes. Allegedly, he listed his first job as picking apricots. When questioned about distinguished ancestors, Wayne supposedly claimed he never looked them up. His interviews with fan clubs were simple, laconic, and unserious. To the question, "What obstacles have you had to conquer to obtain your present success?" he answered, "Only about 150 leading men." And to another query, "What qualities do you like best in women?" he characteristically said: "Let's not get personal."[51] Throughout his career he refused to discuss his private life in public.

"Wayne is the only actor I've found in all my career," the head of Republic's publicity said in the 1940s, "who genuinely didn't give a hoot whether or not his name appeared in a paper."[52] This modesty puzzled his colleagues. Thus, when he produced his first movie, Angel and the Badman, his associates thought he deserved a little more formal respect and subsequently addressed him as "Mr. Wayne," but he ignored them--until they went back to using his nickname, Duke.

Unlike other stars, he neither collaborated with Hollywood's publicity machines nor was his ego inflated. Jimmy
Stewart described Wayne as "the biggest star in the world,"
who "retained the qualities of a small boy." "Duke never
changed," said Stewart, "as a man, he was exactly the boy
he started out [as]."[53] An associate of Wayne's also described him as a "little boy ... honest, foolish, mischie-
vous."[54] His increasing success never diminished his motto,
"I'm still a regular guy."[55] And once he became a star, he
objected to any phony image making, even if it were meant
to promote his career. Asked by British reporters to pose
with clenched fists, he jumped, "No, why try to build up
something that is not true."[56] Wayne could afford not to be
publicity-conscious, because he got tremendous publicity
whenever he wished and without working hard to get it.

His modesty was also reflected in his attitude toward
his fans. Mary St. John, his secretary in the 1950s, reported he received an average of 18,000 letters a month,
most requesting photographs. He derived great pleasure
from reading his fan mail and sometimes even answered it
himself. One letter he treasured was from a 94-year-old
woman who wrote she admired him because he reminded her
of her grandson. Never rude to his fans, he always remembered how much he depended on them, "Hell, I'd still be
pushing props at Fox, if it weren't for these people."[57]

On the premiere of Chisum, he found a message in his
hotel from a woman whose little girl was fatally ill in a local
hospital. She asked whether he could pay her a brief visit,
that it would mean so much to her. Sure enough, Wayne
visited her at the hospital, to everybody's utmost surprise.
He reportedly took great risks in signing autographs, touring a Marine encampment in Vietnam. Once he heard the
crack of a Vietcong sniper's rifle, but he ignored it and
continued to sign. A report later revealed that the bullets
actually tore up the turf within 17 yards from him.

Director Rydell was amazed at Wayne's patience when
"in the middle of meals, people would come up and ask for
his autograph or want him to go over and meet their friends
and relatives." He was "unfailingly courteous," and "re-
sisted no imposition on his life or privacy." Rydell said he
"never once knew him to turn anyone away."[58] And Katharine Hepburn described him as having "a most gentle and

respectful gratitude toward the people he feels have contributed very firmly to his success." He is "meticulous in
answering fan mail and really appreciates the praise heaped
on him." In this he reminded her of Bogart, because he
too "was simple in his enjoyment of his own success" and
possessed "this wonderful childlike open spirit" in appreci-
ating it.[59] Hepburn also was impressed with his being "so
successful, he couldn't have anything to do with it." "It's
Wayne's confidence in himself," in her view, "which gives
him enormous charisma," and "he's got charisma by the
buckets."[60] "When you buy a cotton shirt," she described
his heroic image, "you want to get a cotton shirt. Not ny-
lon ... just cotton, good simple, long-lasting cotton. No
aesthetics. That's what you get when you get John Wayne."
Most amazing of all was the fact that Wayne was "just exactly
what we've adored all these years. He is a hero. And he's
ours."[61]

Even reporters marveled at his respect for his movie
fans. Time critic Jay Cocks recalled that when he inter-
viewed the star at his Newport Beach house, kids kept buzz-
ing by the house in a motor boat calling him. Wayne walked
out on his patio, waved back, and talked to them--over the
distance and sound of the motor. Provoked by Cocks's question, whether, after so many years of that kind of attention
he did not get a little irritated, Wayne replied: "Why should
I? They expect it. They deserve it. It isn't much."[62]

10.   THE MASS MEDIA STAR

In the last decade of his life, Wayne was much more than a movie star, he was a folk hero. What contributed to his already immense popularity was his transformation into a cultural icon, using various mass media to promote his view of the American way of life. Wayne functioned as a mass media star through his frequent appearances on television, the screening of his movies on the small screen, his recordings, books, commercials, and advertisement campaigns. In the 1970s, the American market seemed to be saturated with Wayne appearances and products.

True Grit Offscreen: A Public Opinion Leader

Wayne proved the equation between his screen heroics and his true grit offscreen when he survived three major operations. The cohesion between Wayne the person and Wayne the movie star became complete in 1964, when he licked cancer. His endurance for another 15 years and his attitude toward cancer made him an influential public opinion leader.

During the shooting of In Harm's Way, Wayne developed a persistent cough that was first attributed to heavy smoking. He was a chain-smoker, using four to five packs of unfiltered cigarettes a day. The filming ended ten days ahead of schedule and Wayne went for a checkup, which showed a spot on his lung. The doctor was shocked to find out that the cancer had shown on his previous X rays too, but nobody had noticed it. Wayne checked into the Good Samaritan Hospital in Los Angeles on September 16, 1964. The severity of his illness was not initially revealed to the public--he was said to have respiratory problems, and when he was released from the hospital, on October 7, the Associated Press reported he had been treated for an old ankle injury.

Wayne shocked reporters in a press conference when he said that his cancerous left lung had been removed. He had wanted to reveal the truth from the start, but withheld it because "my advisers thought it would destroy my image." To the contrary, Wayne believed "there's a hell of lot of good image in John Wayne licking cancer."[1] His phrase, "I licked the Big C," became one of his most quoted lines. "I know how much solid hope my recovery could bring to many poor devils in the same fix," he said, "and if it encouraged people to get regular checkups, it would save lives. Image, hell."[2] Up until then, it was not in his nature to discuss his health or other personal matters in public. But he decided to use his experience as a public service. "I don't care if I never sell another ticket at the box office," he claimed, "I'd rather tell my story so that some poor soul some place can get a check-up with his doctor and be as lucky as I was."[3] Revealing the truth was the best thing he could have done to increase his popularity. He now became the star who had succeeded in vanquishing cancer, thus proving he was as indestructible in real life as he was in his movies.

Wayne had two operations: one for cancer, "as big as a baby's fist," and one for edema. "I wasn't uptight," he told Playboy, "when I was told about the cancer." But "when my family came in to see me and I saw the look on their faces, I figured, 'Well, Jeez, it must be just all through."[4] Finding out he had cancer was like "someone hit me across the gut with a ball bat," he said, "I stood shocked." And "naturally, I thought about the possibility of death." What bothered him most, was "the feeling of helplessness," for "I couldn't see myself lying in bed, not being able to help myself--no damn good to anybody. That, to me, was worse than the fear of dying."[5] He could not endure "to be a burden to my family," and have "my loved ones start to have sympathy for me rather than love."[6]

For the first time, he had prayed to God, "I thank the Man Upstairs for everything, he was looking after me." And he delighted in philosophizing, Wayne-style: "When the road looks rough ahead, remember the 'Man Upstairs,' and the word H-O-P-E. Hang onto both and tough it out."[7] "The fact that He's let me stick around a little longer--or She let me stick around a little longer," he said, "certainly goes great with me."[8] Wayne kept up his spirits "by thinking about God, and my family and my friends," and determined not "to end up my life by being sick. I want to go out on two feet--in action."9

    Religion did not play any role in his childhood, though. He described himself as a "Christian by heart," who lived by "Christian ethics," whatever that meant. But he always had "deep faith that there is a supreme being."10 However, like Cooper, Wayne chose to convert to Catholicism on his death-bed, taking place 27 hours before his death. His three wives had been Catholic and his children were brought up as Catholics, but it was his personal decision to convert.

    The public's response to Wayne's bout with cancer was overwhelming; letters estimated at over 50,000 came from all over the world. This volume surprised him too: "People have written to me from all over the world. Their letters are different, warm, personal, like letters from old friends." Consequently, he had never "felt so close to so many peo-ple"11 in his life. For example, Dan Gallery, brother of sports promoter Tom Gallery, wrote that his brother-in-law had cancer and asked Wayne to write to him, which he did. He received many similar requests: "People like to call me up and ask me to talk to their friends and relatives who've got cancer. They think I can give them a boost."12

    After his cancer operation, his doctors reported that they had received requests from many patients for the kind of operation John Wayne had. One medical report showed a sharp increase in checkups after Wayne's disclosure of the truth about his case. Wayne continued to perform this pub-lic function for the rest of his life. In 1975, for example, Carl Heart, a ten-year-old kid from Salinas, Kansas, had terminal leukemia and his greatest wish was to meet the star, after having seen so many of his pictures. A meeting be-tween the two was arranged in Wayne's house in California.

    What impressed the public most was Wayne's renewed energy and lust for life after his surgery. He became more appreciative of his life and was determined to prolong it as long as possible. "My idea of a good day," he said, "is to get up in the morning and still be there." "I say Hooray every time I wake up!"13 he admitted. At the same time he refused to believe that the best part of his life was over. When a television network wanted to do a special, a tribute to his life, his reaction was at once violent and cynical:

"What are they trying to do, bury me? Tell them to forget it. I've just got my second wind."[14] He responded similarly to people who referred to him as a legend of the past: "I figure legends are people who aren't around. Hell, I'm no legend. I'm here and I'm planning on staying around for a while longer."[15] But asked how he felt about being called a legend in his own time, he grinned, "I've been around for quite a while, enjoyed the fruits of Capitalism. I am part of the past, but I want to be a little part of the future too."[16]

Wayne became a role model and a public opinion leader in the true sense of these terms. He was aware that "the subject [cancer] makes a lot of people cringe. Don't drink out of the same glass as him--that sort of thing." In the numerous letters he wrote to cancer victims, however, his advice was "better to talk about it, bring it out in the open. And don't feel sorry for yourself!"[17] His major reward was: "If I can help some poor devil to take advantage of early checkups or at least give hope, then I am repaid enough."[18]

He also lectured and campaigned extensively for the American Cancer Society. The following is one of many ads that appeared under his name:

> My biggest fight wasn't in pictures, it happened in real life. I was just finishing my 99th ridin', jumpin', fightin' picture. Never felt better in my life. But my family nagged me into getting a medical checkup. And it turned out I had lung cancer. If I'd waited a few more weeks, I'd be kicking up daisies now.
> So, friend, I know what I'm talking about when I tell you, get a checkup. Talk someone you like into getting a checkup. Nag someone you love into getting a checkup.
> And when the lady from the American Cancer Society rings your doorbell, dig deep in your pocket. They're working to rid this world of cancer once and for all.
>
> American Cancer Society
> We want to wipe out cancer in your lifetime

"They are welcome to use my case," Wayne said in reference to these campaigns, "but I don't want to make a profession of this," because "before I know it, I'll be 'The Man Who Had Cancer.'"[19] He wanted to forget all about it, but the public would not let him. In 1973 he was named honorary chairman of the Western Institute for Cancer and Leukemia Research, and in 1977 served once more as the society's chairman of the fund-raising campaign. In 1978, a year before his death, another ad with his picture was used as part of a massive campaign. It read: "Maybe we'll cure cancer without your help, but don't bet your life on it!"

Wayne's everyday language increasingly sounded as if it were taken from his movies. In this respect too, there seemed to have been no distinction between his screen heroics and his life. He continued to refer to his bout with cancer as "I licked the Big C," and critics saw in this phrase a symbolic meaning, as if Wayne's enemies, in this case cancer, had to be big, like him, so that "Big John Wayne licked the Big C" acquired mythic dimensions.

Despite losing his left lung, his energy did not deteriorate, judging from the movies he continued to make. He put himself immediately back to work, appearing in The Sons of Katie Elder, a physically demanding action Western directed by Henry Hathaway. He enjoyed reminding those who were surprised to see him perform his stunt work, "I didn't get famous doing drawing-room comedies."[20] This picture would have been difficult for younger and healthier stars, let alone Wayne, who was 58 and had just lost a lung. "I went right back to work with the meanest man in the industry-- Hathaway," he said, who "never spared me one bit on that film," and "worked me like a goddamn dog." "And you know something?" he continued, "It was the best thing that ever happened to me. It meant I got no chance to walk around looking for sympathy."[21] Co-star Dean Martin was also impressed with Wayne's remarkable recovery. "Someone else would have laid around feeling sorry for himself for a year," he said, "but Duke, he just doesn't know how to be sick. He gets embarrassed about it. He's recuperating the hard way."[22] Hathaway, however, claimed that the cancer "knocked Duke on his keister to be sick," because "he suddenly found out he was vulnerable." "The humiliation is the hardest thing for him to recover from," Hathaway explained, "it's not his image that's been hurt, it's his pride."[23]

Wayne's immediate return to work encouraged many

people who had cancer. In some respects, his experience changed the public's perception of cancer, putting it in an entirely different perspective. Wayne's experience showed that cancer did not have to be the end; for him it was just an inconvenient interruption in his work schedule, not a permanent problem. Consequently, many people started to think of cancer as an illness one could live with--with certain, though not radical, modifications in their lifestyles.

Wayne and Television

Wayne's attitude toward television reflected the changing relationship between the big and the small screen over the years. Television and film have been natural enemies for years, and the competition between them much worse than that which prevailed between theater and film earlier in the century. Radio was never regarded as a threat by the movie industry. Rather, it was a legitimate medium, one in which many screen players had begun their careers and continued to appear on even after becoming movie stars. Television, by contrast, was regarded as a threat to the very existence of film and consequently there was a good deal of resentment and suspicion of the new and increasingly popular medium.

Hollywood's studios so feared the competition from television that in the 1940s and 1950s they prohibited their stars from appearing on the small screen. For example, Clark Gable's MGM contract in the 1940s stipulated specifically that he would appear in TV productions only if they became a substantial part of the business. Other stars too were allowed to appear on television under very specific limitations, one of which was to promote their movies. For better or for worse, this suspicion forced television to develop its own performers.

Most stars of Wayne's generation did not appear on television until the late 1950s, and even then only in a limited way. Gable launched his radio career in 1936, long after he became a movie star, but his lengthy screen career was marked by only two TV appearances, both in the late 1950s: the first when he presented an Academy Award at the annual Oscar ceremonies, and the second when he appeared on the Ed Sullivan Show. Humphrey Bogart also

avoided television, regarding it suspiciously as a threat to
his livelihood as a movie actor. He subsequently made only
one big TV appearance, recreating his previous stage and
film role as Duke Mantee in The Petrified Forest, telecast in
1955. Cooper also made his TV debut in the same year,
first as a guest on the Steve Allen Show, then on the Ed
Sullivan Show, promoting his film The Court Martial of Billy
Mitchell.

James Cagney's TV performances were also minimal,
though he too appeared numerous times on radio. Cagney
shocked the TV industry in 1969 when he refused a lucrative offer for a ten-second commercial; it was a matter of
principle to him, no matter how much money he was being
offered. Cary Grant first appeared on television in 1972,
when the Academy of Motion Pictures honored him with a
Special Oscar for life achievement.

Wayne avoided television for many years, preferring
to work exclusively in the film industry. "Television is not
my cup of tea," he used to say, "don't mention it. I don't
like it." The only programs he watched, he said, were
"sports events, documentaries, and travel films." "How can
you ask people to pay $1 or $1.50 to see you in a movie, if
they can see you for free on TV?" he reasoned. In 1955,
the ABC network approached him to star in "Gunsmoke," a
Western series, but he refused. "It's not that I look down
my nose at television," he explained, "but you have to admit movies are more important,"[24] which accurately reflected
Hollywood's view of television in the 1950s. He never regretted his decision, even after "Gunsmoke" expanded from
a half-hour black-and-white show into an hour in color,
running successfully for years.

Once again it was John Ford who convinced him to do
his first TV work. Wayne appeared in Ford's Rookies of the
Year, in 1955, as a sports writer. Ford also directed an
episode of the popular series "Wagon Train," starring Ward
Bond, on one condition, that Wayne be cast in a cameo as
General Sherman; significantly, Wayne asked to be billed as
Michael Morris. Wayne also appeared in the special The
Western, again directed by Ford and aired in June 1958 as
part of NBC's series "Wide, Wide World," starring Ward Bond,
Gabby Hayes, James Arness, and many others.

The turning point in the relationship between film and television occurred on September 23, 1961, when the first prime-time weekly film series, NBC's "Saturday Night at the Movies," made its debut with the comedy How to Marry a Millionaire, starring Marilyn Monroe. This choice was somehow ironic, as this 1953 movie had been shot in Cinemascope, to lure viewers from television back into the legitimate movie theaters. Gradually, however, the two once-bitter media became "willing and friendly collaborators," enjoying mutual dependency: the studios depended on television for profits from airing movies, especially those that did not do well at the box office, and television depended on movies for their ratings and audience shares.[25]

Movie attendance has declined dramatically in the last three decades, but ironically, more people are watching more movies today than ever before, though on television and on video cassettes--not in movie houses. As historian Garth Jowett observed, "Television had helped to destroy the old film industry, but it had also helped to create a new one."[26] Feature films still occupy a significant segment of what is shown on the small screen. And Hollywood studios are making tremendous profits from renting their movies. Some see symbolic meaning in the fact that Gone with the Wind (1939), one of the most popular films ever made, was the last holdout; NBC is reported to have paid $5 million to show it on its screen in 1976.

Television has increasingly become a profitable channel for old movies. But in addition to its market function, television and, in the 1980s, video cassette recorders, have come to perform a vital service in exposing young generations of viewers to Hollywood's past. The American cinema has created over its 80 years of existence a respectable body of work that is now shown on television and available on VCR, the most accessible channels for mass audiences. Television and the new industries help to preserve this rich cinematic tradition.

Wayne's initial animosity toward television, like that of other Hollywood stars, gradually subsided as he learned to live with it. He even learned to relax in front of the television cameras and enjoy his appearances. But in spite of becoming a popular TV figure, he always preferred to make

movies. There was a personal, nostalgic reason for this as
he explained in 1971: "This is not my racket. I prefer
movies. The boys at the box-office have been damned good
to me and I'll string with them as long as they want me."[27]

Wayne changed his mind about television when he realized how popular his old features were on the small screen,
playing to top ratings. His pictures have always been shown
on television, but after his death their volume increased immensely. In 1980, Variety compiled a list of the 200 most
popular movies in TV history. True Grit, which premiered
on ABC on Sunday, November 12, 1972, occupied the eighth
rank, with 38.9 of the ratings and 63 points of the audience
share.[28] True Grit was preceded by Gone with the Wind
(on two successive nights), Airport, Love Story, The Godfather: Part Two, Jaws, and The Poseidon Adventure, all
blockbuster movies that had been extremely successful at
their initial theatrical release.

In addition to True Grit, eight other Wayne movies
appeared on Variety's 200 most watched features: McLintock! ranked 56th, The War Wagon 78th, and The Green
Berets 97th, premiering in 1972, when the Vietnam War controversy was not yet over, with 28.9 of the ratings and 45
points of the audience share. In Harm's Way (part 2) occupied the 111th position, The Cowboys 133rd, The Sons of
Katie Elder 138th, McLintock! (repeat) 167th, and In Harm's
Way (part 1) 173rd.

Barry Diller, then ABC's head of feature movies, considered Wayne to be the only "authentic superstar in television," because he pulls audiences no matter what picture is
shown." Wayne's films on television are "pure gold," and
never out of style. According to Diller, the star's features
are guaranteed to have a minimum audience of 30 percent of
all viewers, and going up to 40 percent if the movie shown
is True Grit. Thus, ABC did not hesitate to purchase
Rooster Cogburn, by all counts a lesser picture than True
Grit, for $3 million; Wayne was reported to have received
$300,000 for his share.[29]

In Variety's poll of all theatrical features shown in the
1979-1980 season (from Steptember to August), the high ratings of Wayne's movies are amazing in light of the fact that
they were screened one year after his death. Five of Wayne's

pictures were found to be popular during that season: The High and the Mighty ranking 37th, Big Jake 72nd, The Shootist 109th, Rio Lobo 126th, and The Alamo 180th. Rio Lobo and The Alamo were more popular on television than in their initial release, which is true of many of his films.

Among the most watched television shows in the medium's history is the 1970 Academy Awards Show, honoring Wayne with his first Oscar award for his performance in True Grit. The high ratings of this particular Oscars show was attributed to the fact that Wayne was expected to win and many viewers wanted to watch this historic event.

Most of Wayne's appearances on television were in specials and variety shows, but he also appeared as a guest star in comedy series. He was, for example, in an episode of Lucille Ball's popular series "The Lucy Show" in November 1966. He even agreed to take part in "Laugh-In," in the bunny sketch, with Dan Rowan and Dick Martin in 1972. Wayne was dressed as a blue bunny, much to his friends' and the audience's surprise. He never would have allowed himself to appear in such nonsense in the 1950s, but in the 1970s he was willing to display some flair for camp and even poke fun at his own image.

A TV show with special meaning for Wayne was NBC's "Swing Out, Sweet Land," shown on November 29, 1970. One of the most expensive productions, costing about $2 million, it made Wayne the highest-salaried actor on television; he also owned the show after its first two runs. The other guest stars took lower salaries than usual because they wanted to work with him. "Swing Out, Sweet Land" was a musical comedy tribute to the United States covering three centuries (1600-1900) and consisting of vignettes from the annals of American history. As the narrator, Wayne walked through time meeting his guest stars, all playing historical figures along the way: Lorne Greene played George Washington; Rowan and Martin were the Wright Brothers; Bob Hope and Ann-Margret, entertainers at Valley Forge; Dan Blocker, an Indian selling Manhattan to Peter Minuit, played by Michael London; Dean Martin protrayed Eli Whitney; and Lucille Ball was the Statue of Liberty. The show reflected Wayne's politics, especially his patriotic flag waving. "Without preaching," he said, "we're trying to show this is a great country, and one to be proud of." The show did not

deny "there are problems, but we can deal with them together," and "fortunately, we've always been a people able
to laugh at ourselves." The show aimed "to spread a general feeling of good will and love."[30] He did it for his kids,
his motive being "to give them an idea about how their country developed, even if it's played for laughs."[31] "Swing
Out, Sweet Land" turned out to be one of the highest-rated
programs in the medium's history, watched by 76 million viewers. In 1972, the show was repeated and again attracted
many viewers.

A Genuine Media Star

In addition to his TV appearances, Wayne took part in
many advertising campaigns, further reflecting his change in
attitude toward the mass media. His most pervasive campaign,
for Great Western Savings and Loan Association, began on
December 1, 1977, with Wayne splashed in full-page newspaper advertisements, heard in radio spots and seen on television throughout California, saturating the media for two
months. During this period he appeared as commercial
spokesman on 26 TV stations, 18 major radio stations, and
24 newspapers in California (Great Western exists only in
this state). Wayne received more than $1 million for a three-
year campaign, whose purpose was to make him and Great
Western synonymous in the public's mind. Apparently, he
himself came up with the idea for the campaign. "People
don't want me telling them what percent the bank is paying," he said, feeling that he should rather talk about "lasting values," because "they're what matter."[32]

The first ad, which appeared in the Los Angeles Times
on December 1, 1977, as well as in other newspapers, stated:

> In the early days out West, a man took pride in the
> outfit he wore. Well, I've decided to throw in with
> an outfit that I can be proud of. The Big Western
> Savings, They've been around for years, survived
> a few national crises, helped Californians save money
> to build homes and take care of their families' needs.
> I like what they stand for.
>
> Great Western Savings

"He's Mr. America," James Montgomery, an executive
of Western Savings said, explaining the motives for using
Wayne. "We're in the happiness business, and we wanted
to capture his language and credibility as a man. We didn't
want him to say anything he wasn't comfortable with. We
wanted it to come from John Wayne's heart."[33] The whole
campaign capitalized on his intimate identification with the
great outdoors and the West.

Most of the ads were variations on the same theme, like
the one that appeared in the Los Angeles Times on October
5, 1978:

> The California Sequoias? Folks say they've been
> here a thousand years. Walk through them and it's
> like walking through a giant cathedral. It sure is
> a nice feeling to be around something that's going
> to last. That's how I feel about Great Western
> Savings. I've hung my money on a lot of things
> that were just passing through. But no more. To-
> day, I'm putting it with Great Western. They're
> still growing. Still helping people to build their
> homes and raise their families. And they're going
> to be around for a long time.

Wayne's endorsement of President Carter's Panama
Canal treaties, which gave the sovereignty of the Canal back
to Panama, upset many viewers and caused apprehension at
Great Western, which had invested a lot of money in him to
be its spokesman. After the first commercials aired, hate
mail was sent in protest, but very few actually threatened
to close their accounts. Fortunately, the overall impact of
the campaign was favorable and the Panama controversy was
soon forgotten. In fact, Wayne received the Los Angeles
Advertising Club award, a plaque in recognition of his
Great Western campaign. His contribution reportedly amounted to about $250 million in additional deposits. Great West-
ern continued the campaign after Wayne's death, but had to
introduce minor changes. The message was similar to Wayne's
campaign, but his part was now taken over by four Hollywood
celebrities: Ben Johnson, John Huston, Glenn Ford, and
Maureen O'Hara.

Wayne made other commercials. He was asked to be the

national spokesman for Datril pain relievers. Once again, the
emphasis was put on strength, a value intimately connected
with his image, as the following ad demonstrates: "I asked
the doctor about taking Datril 5000. He said, 'great.' Ask
your doctor. Extra-strength Datril 5000 is so strong."

His commercials and advertisements were so profitable
that he decided to try his luck in other media. In 1973 he
recorded an album of poetry, America, Why I Love Her,
which became one of RCA's big-sellers of the year, selling
initially around 100,000 copies. Backed by a chorus, Wayne
intoned lyrics written for the most part by John Mitchum,
Robert Mitchum's brother. This project originated when he
sat down with Mitchum and Billy Liebert and talked about
what he felt and liked about America. He also helped to
write one song, "Why Are You Marching Son?" about young
protestors. The collection also included "My Roots Are
Here" and "An American Boy Grows Here." "Face the Flag,"
the last song, stated: "If we want to keep these freedoms,
we may have to fight again, God forbid, but if we do, let's
fight to win. For the fate of the loser is futile.... No
Love.... No peace.... Just misery and despair." Wayne's
identification with these lines was complete--they appear over
and over in his movies.

The album won Wayne the George Washington Award
for expressing "proud and unabashed patriotism." The
Freedom Foundation has bestowed this award for "construc-
tive words and deeds which support America, suggest solutions to basic problems besetting the nation, contribute to
responsible citizenship and inspire love of country." He was
selected by a jury of 13 state supreme court justices and 29
representatives of national organizations. America, Why I
Love Her was described by the jury as a "sensitive reflection of a man in love with his country."[34] The album later
served as a basis for a Bicentennial book of the same title.
In April 1980, almost a year after Wayne's death, the album
was rereleased. RCA's executives felt there was enough demand for Wayne's patriotic reassurance--it was reissued during the hostage crisis in Iran, a time when political reassur-
ance and faith in America were much needed.

The success of the album and book whetted his appetite
for other projects. "There's so much Americana I'd like to
record," he observed, "I'd like to do my own Christmas

Special, using Williamsburg, Virginia." This project excited
him because "it's just so beautiful, so American primitive,"
for "when you go into the Governor's Palace, you think,
Thomas Jefferson once lived here! Patrick Henry once lived
here!" He was in awe of these historical figures "who had
major decisions to make and made them." "I'm getting tired
of TV specials," he noted, "but one that really talked about
Williamsburg and the elegance of the past would have meaning."[35]

With many patriotic movies and advertisements to his
credit, Wayne had gradually become the "ideal American citizen," with numerous awards and citations honoring his patriotism. In 1971 he was honored at the annual convention
of the fraternal order of Marines in San Antonio for his continuous efforts on behalf of the corps during World War II,
including recruitment drives and his two Marine films, Sands
of Iwo Jima and Flying Leathernecks. The citation read:
"Today, it is not the 'in' thing to be inspired by heroes or
to be overly impressed with our nation's past sacrifices and
trials. But all is not lost. We can still be aroused. We can
all, young and old, black and white, left and right, be
stirred from complacency and inspired to action by John
Wayne."

The Freedom Foundation awarded him its National Service Medal for his "consistent, unabashed loyalty to America
and its ideals," and for his many visits to GIs in combat
zones. He was also presented with the Outstanding American Award, given by the Los Angeles Philanthropical Foundation. And at the Veterans of Foreign Wars (VFW) meeting in
Texas, in August 1971, Wayne was awarded their American
Gold Medal award. Herbert R. Rainwater, the VFW commander, hailed Wayne as "more than an actor," as "a symbol of
courage in a world of anti-heroes." "More John Waynes are
needed," he said, the American youth should model itself
after him.[36] Bill Clement, governor of Texas, made Wayne
the Honorary Captain of the Texas Rangers, describing him
as an American original who could not be duplicated in this
or any other generation.

In the 1970s he was literally showered with awards.
In 1972 he received the American Patriot award at the forty-
fifth anniversary of the American Educational League. And
in 1978, the Los Angeles Area Council of Boy Scouts of

America honored him for his exemplification of the spirit of
America and for his living symbolism of all that is inherent
in the Scouts' principles.

Wayne's status as a media star was enhanced by the
large number of awards he received from organizations outside the film industry. In 1968 he was the recipient of an
honorary degree, Doctor of Fine Arts, for his distinguished
service in the film industry, from his old school, USC. The
Alumni Club of Notre Dame University bestowed on him the
Entertainer of the Year award in 1976. And in 1977 he received the Gold Medal award, given by the National Football
Hall of Fame, previously bestowed on former presidents
Eisenhower and Kennedy. In the same year he was the recipient of the Scopus award, bestowed by the American
Friends of The Hebrew University in Jerusalem for "high
standards of excellence" in one's chosen profession. He was
cited for his "involvement in a long series of humanitarian
endeavors with emphasis on youth and health." The creation of the John Wayne fellowship at The Hebrew University
was announced with the award. His humanitarian awards
included a citation from the American Human Association as
"the National Kindness Chairman" in recognition of his
career-long insistence that animals be treated humanely in
his pictures; apparently, there has never been misuse or
abuse of horses in any of his Westerns.

That he was much in demand as a media star became
clear in 1977, when he signed a most lucrative contract with
ABC that committed him to appear in six two-hour specials
over the ensuing two years. He was promised that each
program would be unique in concept and specifically tailored
to his talents and screen personality. Consistency, as was
shown, was Wayne's rule of thumb. However, because of
illness, he was unable to complete this project. He appeared
in the program celebrating the network's silver anniversary
in February 1978. In his second special, "Oscar's Best Actors," telecast in May 1978, he discussed his Oscar for True
Grit and the contribution of other stars. His last program
for ABC, "Star-Spangled Jubilee of Americana"--a tribute to
General Electric's one hundredth anniversary which he hosted,
was aired in September 1978.

In March 1978 he developed bronchial pneumonia and a
month later, after tests showed evidence of a heart murmur,

he underwent an open-heart surgery that replaced a defective mitral valve. In an interesting conversation, Wayne-style, he asked his doctor to open the window--they were on the eighth floor--and said to him, "Now, you're going to operate on me or I'm going to jump out of the window." He did not believe in postponing things, holding that "if something has to be done, do it and get it the hell over."[37] This was yet another phrase that could be taken from his movies; courage and direct confrontation were integral to his screen persona.

In January 1979 Wayne underwent another operation to remove his stomach, with surgeons fashioning a new stomach from parts of his intestines. This nine-hour operation followed tests showing an unusual low-grade malignant tumor in his stomach, discovered during a gall bladder operation.

During these operations, there was literally worldwide concern. Over 100,000 wires and telephone calls poured in, from crowned heads (Queen Elizabeth of England and Queen Juliana of the Netherlands) to heads of state to movie stars to ordinary people. "There were 100,000 people asking from the Man Upstairs to intercede with me," Wayne said in response to this volume of get-well messages, "I can't tell you how much that meant to me."[38] The outpouring of sympathy and affection for Wayne was interpreted in Europe as a reflection of America's longing for national heroes it no longer had. Indeed, 1979 was a low point in the country's politics, economics, and morale, and President Carter's popularity was declining rapidly.

At the hospital, Wayne again demonstrated his strength and endurance. "You can't keep a good old cowboy tied down for long,"[39] said a spokesman of the UCLA Medical Center. Wayne was reportedly walking around the hospital, chafing at his inactivity, and reassuring family and friends that he would soon get out. One of his last requests was that the Medical Center build a Cancer Research Center in his name. As soon as this was announced, hospital officials reported to have received numerous telephone calls from potential donors seeking information. And on the first day, without any previous publicity, a dozen checks arrived, averaging $100 each.

Wayne spent the last night before the operation with

his children and his secretary Pat Stacy. He could have one
drink only, so he ordered a big martini. Despite terrible
suffering, he refused to take pain killers because he wanted
to be alert, fearing that the drugs would knock him out.
This was also characteristic of his screen image; in The
Horse Soldiers, Wayne's Colonel Marlowe prefers to suffer
the pain of his wounds rather than take whiskey.

In recent years, there has been a suspicion that
Wayne and others had contracted cancer during the shooting
of The Conqueror in Saint George in the Utah desert. Many
of the 220 cast and crew members contracted various kinds
of cancer and died, including seven of the stars: director
Dick Powell (who died in 1963), Pedro Armendariz (1963),
Thomas Gomez (1971), Agnes Moorehead (1974), Susan Hayward (1975), producer Howard Hughes, and John Wayne
(both in 1979). Wayne's children, who had visited the set,
also contracted diseases; Michael developed a skin cancer
and Patrick was operated on for a breast tumor. There
was also a high proportion of cancer victims among the
small population of Saint George. There is still suspicion
that the cast members were exposed to highly radioactive
fallout from nuclear tests, conducted the year before at
Yucca Flat, Nevada. The government denied its reponsibility in a Congressional report. However, a Nuclear Defense Agency scientist is quoted to have said, "Please,
don't let us have killed John Wayne."[40]

The controversy over the government's reponsibility
subsided, though on March 8, 1981, KTVV aired in California the first segment of "The Great Hollywood Mysteries,"
which reexamined the issue. Entitled "Did America Kill John
Wayne?" it revealed that the movie was shot about 140 miles
from the atomic testing site, where the "Dirty Harry" bomb
went over the Nevada and Utah deserts. Rumor also has it
that Howard Hughes's repurchase of The Conqueror for a
huge amount of money, after selling RKO and its library,
had to do with his guilt over sending the cast and crew to
these radioactive places. The program reached no definite
conclusions; the questions are still open.

Many of the players who took part in the movie believed they had contracted cancer on the sets. Agnes Moorehead is quoted as saying: "A lot of people beside Duke got
cancer on that movie,"[41] before becoming a cancer victim

herself. And Mexican actor Pedro Armendariz, told by his
doctors that he had terminal cancer, decided to put a gun to
his head. "He had more guts than any of us,"[42] Wayne was
quoted as saying in private, though for obvious publicity
reasons he himself could not take his life--even if he had
wanted to. Michael Wayne believes that his father "stayed
alive on will power alone," and that characteristically he
"didn't cry over a lot of stuff that went by in the past,
things you can't do anything about." Michael had been advised to sue the government, but he refused--"this isn't going to bring him back."[43]

Wayne's last public appearance was appropriately at
the annual Oscar show, on April 9, 1979, three months after
his final cancer operation. He was there to present the most
prestigious award, Best Picture of the year. His appearance
at the end of the show was the emotional highlight of the
evening, receiving a lengthy standing ovation. "That's just
about the only medicine a fella ever really needs," was his
first comment, "believe me when I tell you, I'm mighty
pleased that I can amble down here tonight." This appearance was extremely important to him, undergoing a self-
imposed exercise regime so that he could stand firmly before hundreds of millions of TV viewers.

Thumbs in his pocket, Wayne said in his speech: "Oscar and I have something in common. Oscar first came to the
Hollywood scene in 1928. So did I. We're both a little
weather-beaten, but we're still here. And we plan to be
around a whole lot longer." Ironically, he presented the
Best Picture award to Michael Cimino's The Deer Hunter, a
powerful anti-Veitnam movie depicting the harrowing experiences of the war on three friends. It stood in sharp contrast to Wayne's earlier, patriotic The Green Berets. One
can only speculate what he felt at that moment, because he
did not say anything in public and did not show any resentment over the Academy's choice.

Wayne stole the show, but the climax of the evening,
which was "supposed to leave the audience with good feelings," as Vincent Canby observed, "apparently made many
people uncomfortable," because "it wasn't conventional television." The truth is that Wayne did not look good and the
public was shocked to see a really aged man, who had lost
over 40 pounds! "Perhaps, it's never a happy occasion,"

Canby commented "to see someone you care about in less than tip-top shape." Unlike the past, this time Wayne's appearance could no longer conceal the sad reality that "time moves on."44

11. AN AMERICAN LIFESTYLE

Wayne's lifestyle was intimately connected with his screen image. Unlike other stars who experienced tension between their public and private lives, in his case they supported and reinforced each other. Wayne's stature as an important star and national figure rested on the fact that he articulated and exemplified basic values in his lifestyle that were distinctly American. The most important of these values were the ethics of hard work and success, upward mobility, individual achievement, monetary success, ordinariness, and strong family life.

Ethics of Hard Work and Success

Work was Wayne's main interest; making movies was genuinely the core of his life. Work was more than a motivating force; he was compulsive and obsessive about it. He claimed there were two important things in his world, "the people I love, and the work I love."[1] Working hard brought real satisfaction. As he observed, "I am miserable when I am not working," and "the only reason I hate age is that I love this work so much."[2] Esperanza Baur, his second wife, described him as a person who is "always interested in his business." "He talks of it constantly," she said, "When he reads, it's scripts. Our dinner guests always talk business and he spends all his time working, discussing work, or planning work."[3]

He worked hard because he believed in the ethic of hard work; this was the force, he felt, that kept him alive-- and healthy. After 50 years in the film industry, he never tired of making movies. And unlike Gary Cooper and Clark Gable, who lost interest in their profession as they aged, Wayne never lost excitement for the prospect of making a

new movie. Jimmy Stewart once described him as having
"the enthusiasm for life that would make a high school football star envious."[4]

In the 1960s, many of his colleagues began to pass
away. "There aren't many of us left," he said, "so many of
my friends have died these years--Coop, Clark, Ward Bond.
But me, hell, I'll just go on doing what I do till they kick
me out."[5] At the reporters' suggestion that he should be
preparing for a peaceful retirement, after 35 years in movies, he said: "I'm 56 years old, for pete's sake. This is
an important time in my life. I've got to get in as much
work as I can, because how long can you hope to carry on
in this business?"[6] But he did carry on for another 15
years! "Every time I finish a picture," he once admitted,
"I go around saying I won't do another for a couple of
years. But two weeks later, I'm looking to see what's
around. I just gotta work, I love this goddamn business."[7]

In the early years he worked hard because he lacked
financial security. Coming from a relatively poor family, he
dreaded the idea of being broke; associates noticed that he
always carried large amounts of cash on him. And later he
continued to work hard to support a large family of seven
children. "It's not that I feel the need to establish myself,"
he explained, "but I do need the money."[8]

"I live well but I am not rich," was the way he described his social standing. "I oughta be rich," he felt,
"but I had bad business advice, and I lost a lot of dough."[9]
This was true, he was not nearly as wealthy as some of his
colleagues, say Bob Hope and Gene Autry, who were multi-
millionaires because they were shrewd businessmen--which he
was not. He lacked savvy as an investor, and several financial endeavors were badly managed. Among his unsuccessful operations, a $500,000 investment with Robert Arias
in a shrimp business in Panama proved unprofitable. He
later invested most of his personal capital in the production
of The Alamo, and lost his shirt.

In 1962 he was shocked when he suddenly realized
that after 35 years in the business he had to start out all
over again. He would just about break even, he said, if he
sold all his property which, to him, having worked hard for
so many years, meant being broke. Money-losing deals plus

three marriages and a free-spending lifestyle kept him working until he died; fortunately, he enjoyed it. In the 1970s,
however, his finances improved. His holdings included Batjac, his production company, a nice bayfront house in the
Bay Shore section of Orange County's Newport Beach, a cattle ranch in Arizona, and some other investments.

Retirement was never considered, not even after his
cancer operation. "Not me!" he said, "I want to go on acting just as long as people will have me, and then I want to
go into some other end of the business."[10] "Pictures have
been all my life!" he repeatedly said. He really believed
that "you die if you retire, if not physically, mentally." "A
hard day's work still appeals to me,"[11] continued to be his
favorite motto. When he was filming The Shootist, he
teased reporters: "Bull! It won't be my last film." "Unless I stop breathing, or people stop going to see my films,
I'll be making more of them."[12] Less than a year before he
died, he reiterated his gusto for life: "I couldn't retire.
That would kill me. What would I do? I'd go nuts." "Work
is the only thing I know," he used to say, "and as long as
I can keep my dignity, I'm going to go on making movies.
I like what I do. People who want to retire, don't."[13] Not
that he was unaware of his age. "I'm old, I guess. At
least I ain't new," he used to joke, "but I plan to just keep
making pictures. I'm having a helluvalot of fun."[14]

Wayne was immensely proud of being an American actor. "It gives me a genuine feeling of satisfaction to have a
part in the tremendous job this industry does in creating
entertainment, on a scale no other medium can ever attempt,"
he said on the opening night of Flying Leathernecks. "I
feel about motion pictures," he said, "something like the
Leathernecks do about the Marines. To the Marines the
greatest thing in the world is simply the fact of being a
member of the fightiest crew that ever bore arms. We can
use a lot of that spirit in our business." "We've got every
reason to be proud of motion pictures," Wayne elaborated,
"we should express that pride in giving our best in the way
of acting and technical performances and in conducting ourselves as self-respecting members of a highly respected industry."[15]

Conspicuous consumption and public display of wealth
are usually associated with movie stardom. Wayne's lifestyle,

however, was ordinary, modest, and far from glamorous.
Swimming pools, sumptuous clothing, and elegant parties
played no part in his life. There was nothing spectacular
about the way he lived. Unlike Gable or Cooper, he did
not care about fashion, and unlike Cary Grant, who dressed
so elegantly he wore his own suits in his movies, Wayne
cherished simplicity in every aspect of his life. Nor was he
the kind of star whose pictures appeared in fashion magazines; one could never suspect him of attempting to contend
for "the best-dressed man." On the contrary, he always
stressed that there was nothing glamorous about making movies, that it was in fact a hard job, requiring health, strength,
and self-discipline.

In his lifestyle, Wayne exemplified the most important
values of the American Dream: upward mobility, success,
and individual attainment. He was a self-made man, working
his way up to the top. He became an actor by accident and
luck played a crucial role in his career, but it was hard work,
driving ambition to succeed, and tremendous will power that
got him to the top. He believed that the most important
thing was to work steadily, which he did for half a century!
His career was a rags-to-riches story, starting at the bottom of the hierarchy as a prop man and progressing gradually, until he became the most popular star in film history.

Critic Joan Mellen claimed that the importance of the
Wayne phenomenon was that he was an ordinary American who
had risen to the top of the social ladder and by doing so had
become an emblem to the American democratic system. [16]
Wayne succeeded where most stars failed, in combining the
spectacular aspects of a career whose public image is glamour with the ordinary existence of the everyday man. The
durability of his appeal rested on a delicate balance between
two elements: star mystique or magic, necessary for becoming a celebrity, and the credibility of living an ordinary life.
His ordinariness, onscreen and off, turned out to be one of
his greatest assets.

The Family Man

Next to work, strong family life was the other defining
center of his existence. He was married three times and was
the father of seven children. At the time of his death, he

was the patriarch of a large family consisting of 21 grandchildren.

Wayne's first wife, Josephine Saenz, was the daughter
of a Panamanian consul in Los Angeles. They got married
on June 24, 1933, and had four children: Michael in 1934,
Toni in 1935, Patrick in 1938, and Melinda in 1940. But after a few years, their marriage was in trouble. Wayne practically lived for his work, which his wife found hard to accept. He was always surrounded by work associates and
friends from the film world, which did not interest her very
much. They also had differences of opinion about how their
children should be raised. Consequently, in 1943 they separated and a year later divorced.

Wayne met his second wife, Esperanza Baur Diaz, nicknamed Chata, in Mexico, while vacationing there. They were
married on January 17, 1946, in California. But unlike the
first, this marriage was rocky and quite volatile from the
very start. His wife was reportedly jealous of his devotion
to his work and to his four children; they had no children.
She also accused Wayne of having an affair with Gail Russell,
his leading lady in Angel and the Badman, which he denied.
The second marriage lasted seven years, coming to an end in
November 1953, when a superior justice granted them a divorce under a little-used provision of a California law, reserved for cases where neither party concedes the other's
charges. There were indeed charges and countercharges of
unfaithfulness, drunken violence, emotional cruelty, and
"clobbering." Wayne described his wife as a "drunken party-
goer who would fall down and then accuse him of pushing
her."[17] He deplored the publicity his divorce proceedings
received in the press, though they did not hurt his popularity.

He met his third wife, Pilar Weldy (born Palette) in
Lima, Peru, in 1953, while he was scouting locations for The
Alamo. It was part of a South American tour, a gift from
Howard Hughes, with whom he had a contract. Pilar was
younger than Wayne by 22 years and came from an upper-
class family; her father was a Peruvian politician. On November 1, 1954, the very day his divorce became final,
they got married. Unlike his previous wives, Pilar took an
active interest in his career. She herself was an actress,
with some stage experience, although she did not pursue her

own career. She bore Wayne three children: Aissa in 1956,
John Ethan in 1962, and Marisa Carmella in 1966; he was then
close to 60 years of age.

The third marriage lasted 17 years, but in November
1973 a trial separation was announced. Pilar complained
about Wayne's lengthy absences from home, even when he
was not working; he simply said they lost interest in each
other. In his last years, he lived with his secretary Pat
Stacy, but this romantic involvement did not get any publicity in the press.

The fact that all three of his wives were Latin American surprised Hollywood; this was the only "non-American"
aspect in his life. "I have never been conscious of going
for any particular type,"[18] Wayne said in response to a
challenge from the press, "it's just a happenstance. Whenever I've had free time, I've been in Latin America."[19]
Once he described his preference as "some men collect stamps;
I go for Latin Americans."[20] "I never found anyting wrong
with American women," he told one columnist, "all I ask is
that a girl be attractive and companionable."[21] But he made
a point to note that his wives have been as much American
as they have been Latin.

He was candid about his need for women's company,
but admitted they were a mystery to him. "I still don't understand women," he said, "I don't believe there's man alive
who does."[22] Asked what he looked for in women, he said,
"as long as they're feminine, I love them all--plump, skinny,
tall or short."[23] However, the quality most desirable in a
woman was being "simpática," which he defined as "being on
the same wave length."[24] Comparing American with Latin
American women, he observed: "Unfortunately, most women
dress for other women in America, whereas in Latin America,
they dress more for men." He also revealed his preference
for "understatement and simplicity in dress," but that didn't
mean "scarcity of clothing." He never cared for jewelry because "it's so easy to overdo and look flashy."[25]

In harmony with his screen image, he never chased
women. Grant, his favorite screenwriter, told Look: "Pushy
dames really scare him. Duke's really old-fashioned about
women; no off-color stories in their presence, for instance."
Grant also said that "there are a lot of disgruntled girls

around Hollywood who are sore at him for not succumbing to
their charms," and that "when his wife is not with him, he'll
stay up all night reading or arguing about movie making and
politics."[26]

Unlike other male stars, who were frequently romantically involved with their leading ladies, Wayne had a pretty
"decent" record, with one major exception--Marlene Dietrich.
Tay Garnett, the director of their first film together, Seven
Sinners, described how they met. "Marlene had the choice
of all her leading men. I decided not to mention Wayne to
her, but simply to place him in the Universal commissary
where she couldn't miss him. He stood between us and our
tables as we walked in for lunch, chatting with a couple of
actresses I had set up. She swept past him, then swiveled
on her knees and looked him up and down as though he were
a prime rib at Chasen's. As we sat down, she whispered
right in my ear, 'Daddy, buy me that!' I said, 'Honey, it's
settled. You got him.' Then at a pre-arranged signal,
Wayne came to the table. If you didn't know what was gonna
happen, you'd be as blind as a pit pony. Their relationship
got off like a fireworks display. They were crazy about each
other."[27]

Wayne and Dietrich starred in two other pictures,
Pittsburgh and The Spoilers. Dietrich went with him to
football games and prize fights, and they fished and hunted
together; she was his type of girl--a good sport, tough,
down-to-earth, and with a good sense of humor. Although
Wayne was then having problems with his first wife, and he
liked Dietrich, he was unwilling to give up his family life.
Their relationship lasted on-and-off for several years, then
faded away.

Basically, Wayne was a private man--a difficult task
when you are a movie star of his caliber. But he tried to
keep his sex life and marital problems away from the public
eye. He regretted that he and his second wife had to air
their dirty wash during their divorce proceedings. And he
refused to discuss his breakup from his third wife for the
same reason. He was least cooperative with reporters when
it concerned his sex life, summing once his leisure activities
as: "I drink as much as I ever did. I eat more than I
should. And my sex life is none of your goddamn business."[28]

The public was unaware that he was such a domestic man, gentle and sentimental with his wives and children, never forgetting a family birthday. It is hard to believe, but Wayne reportedly selected dresses for his wife. "He loves nothing more than to go shopping for his family,"[29] Pilar once confirmed. What he really liked to do when he was not working, he said, was to be with his children. He was therefore delighted when they told him they liked to have him around.

In 1969, he was the head of a family of seven children, ranging in age from 3 to 33, and 19 grandchildren. Appropriately, he was selected Father of the Year, which gave him an opportunity to express his family credo: "If I have anything in particular to pass on, it is let your children know you love them." He described himself as "a demonstrative man," "a baby picker, a hugger, and a kisser."[30] In fact, he liked large families and children so much that in 1970, during the shooting of Rio Lobo, he adopted 19 Mexican orphans in Cuernavaca.

Wayne had tremendous pride in his family, his greatest wish being that his children serve as role models for what "young America stands for." He was thus disappointed when his eldest son, Michael, decided not to go to the Military Academy at Annapolis, where his own application had been rejected. Wayne felt he could help Michael get admitted; by now he had the right connections. However, he did not interfere, respecting his decision to become a film producer.

Michael surprised reporters when he said Wayne's image as a family man was less known than his being a "hard-drinking, tough-talking man," and that his image as "rigid, set in his ways," was "only true with respect to himself and what he wants to do." With his family "he's been remarkably liberal," and has always "let us work things for ourselves."[31] However, his daughter Toni described him as an old-fashioned patriarch, "he has the master's voice and we all listen." He was conservative in the way he brought up his children. "He made me wipe off my lipstick when I was sixteen," said Toni, and "I didn't smoke in front of him until I was 21 and married."[32] He was intolerant of marijuana smoking and said he would be "terribly upset" if he found out his daughter used the drug. But if that happened, "I'd explain to her

that I know she loves me and her mother and that we'd
rather she didn't smoke that stuff." Patient explanation
was "the only way you can work on them," Wayne believed,
"it isn't going to do any good to beat the hell out of them."[33]

He conceded that the only difference between raising
his first set of children in the 1930s and his second in the
1960s was that "I spent more time with my present kids."
But his philosophy of life did not change over the years:
"I tried to get the same things across to them then as I do
now."[34] This philosophy was rather simple, consisting of
three basic rules he learned from his father: "First, always
keep you word. Second, a gentleman never insults anyone
intentionally. And third, don't look for trouble, but if you
get into a fight, make sure you win."[35] Wayne embodied
these rules in his movies as well as in his life. Only the
second of his father's guidelines changed in Wayne's personal credo. This became: "A gentleman never insults anyone unintentionally." "I try not to unintentionally hurt anybody's feelings," he explained, "but if I do hurt anybody's
feelings, I had all the intentions of hurting them." "I try
to live my life to the fullest, without hurting anybody else."[36]

And this was an important philosophy, he thought, to
pass on to his children and grandchildren. He told his kids
early on in their lives "to make themselves as attractive as
they can, physically and otherwise," and to "show respect
to other people, whether they're younger or older." He also
assured them that "I'll always help them if they get into
trouble, as long as they don't lie, but the minute they lie,
they lose my respect." Wayne's main hope was that "my
children will remember that I told them never to lie--to
other people or to themselves." He also hoped they would
say that "I was always a kind and fairly decent man."[37]
Which is why he treasured a framed poem, a love letter
from his daughter Aissa, wherein she thanked her parents
for what they have given her in decency and self-respect.

He was one of the great defenders of the American
nuclear family as a sacred institution. Irritated by the publicity accorded to Mia Farrow's giving birth out of wedlock,
he said: "Poor upbringing." Indeed, he always defended
the "morality" of the film colony, "How many actresses do
you know have illegitimate babies?" "There is no more
promiscuity in our business than there ever was," he

explained, "the only difference is that now when they have
an illegal baby, people say, 'Hearts-and-Flowers,' and 'how
wonderful!' instead of saying, 'Oh, the poor girl!'" He refused to believe that "just because one movie star has an
illegitimate baby," it meant this was "the normal procedure
in our society."[38]

Conservative Aesthetics

Conservatism and traditionalism marked every aspect
of his life, including his view of the film industry and the
function of motion pictures. He was eternally concerned
with the image of America and the film industry, in this
country and abroad. But, first and foremost, he stressed
the entertainment values of film. "I don't think the motion
picture business was intended to show the American Way of
Life," he said, "I think the motion picture business is a
business of entertainment." "My whole conception of our
business has been one of illusion," he explained, and "I
really try to stand by the theory of making motion pictures
on the assumption that people go in there to escape their
everyday problems."[39] Ironically, Wayne's movies, more
than any other star's, became increasingly propagandistic,
politically and socially, obsessively preoccupied with his
version of the American Way of Life.

He was proud of his profession and of serving and being regarded as spokesman, official and unofficial, of the industry. In the 1950s, when Hollywood conducted its big
"Movie-Time U.S.A." campaign against television, he served
as one of its major ambassadors, touring over 20 cities and
giving numerous personal appearances. Unlike his colleagues,
he was optimistic about the future of Hollywood, underesti-
mating the competition from television: "I don't think the
industry is going on the rocks," he said in 1958, regarding
the declining foreign market for American movies--not
television--as "our great danger today."[40]

Obsessed with projecting a positive image of both
Hollywood and America, he denounced every film that, he
felt, hurt the public's notion of the industry and the country. He thus deplored the new trend of antihero films, with
"psychotic weaklings as heroes," because they were "unfair
to the He-Man." "Ten or fifteen years ago, audiences went

to pictures to see men behaving like men," whereas at present, "there are too many neurotic types," which he attributed to "the Tennessee Williams effect on Broadway and in movies." Williams went "far afield to find American men who are
extreme cases," he reasoned, "these men aren't representative of the average man in the country, but they give the
impression that we are a nation of weaklings who can't keep
up the the pressures of modern living." He had no time for
"pseudo-intellectuals who belittle courage, honor, and decency," insisting that Americans "still handle their own problems today, but they are not being fairly represented."[41]

Wayne denounced the subject of homosexuality in Tennessee Williams's Suddenly Last Summer (1959)--which he had
not seen and had no intention of seeing--as "too disgusting
even for discussion." "It is too distasteful," he claimed, "to
be put on a screen designed to entertain a family, or any
member of a decent family."[42] He considered Easy Rider
(1969)--the youth-oriented, antiestablishment film, and Midnight Cowboy, which to his dismay won the Best Picture
Oscar--as "perverted" films. "Wouldn't you say," he told
Playboy, "that the wonderful love of these two men in Midnight Cowboy [played by Dustin Hoffman and Jon Voight], a
story about two fags, qualifies [as a perverse movie]?"[43]

He objected to any movie which, in his view, gave "the
world a false, nasty impression of us," and was not "doing
our people any good either." Robert Rossen's All the King's
Men, winner of the 1949 Best Picture Oscar, about the dangers of political demagoguery, he described as a film in which
"every character who had any responsibility at all was guilty
of some offense against society." The film deals with the
corruptive effects of political power and was based on the
career of Senator Huey "Kingfish" Long. "To make Huey
Long a wonderful, rough pirate was great," Wayne said,
"but, according to this picture, everybody was a shit except for this weakling intern doctor, who was trying to find
a place in the world." When Wayne received a copy of the
screenplay from his agent, Charlie Feldman, apparently being considered for the movie, he sent it back with a note,
"If you ever send me a script like this again, I'll fire you."[44]
Wayne also detested Stanley Kramer's On the Beach (1960),
concerning the threat of atomic war and the end of the world,
because it had a "defeatist story." "The growing attitude in
the Cold War, imposed on us by the Soviet Union," he

claimed, "is a disgrace and it is disgraceful that any Hollywood film would reflect such an attitude."[45]

One would not expect Wayne to like or praise Ernst Lubitsch's urbane, sophisticated comedies, but he did. "Lubitsch used to make pictures that were as risqué as any that are made today," he said, "but they didn't offend because they were subtle and skillful. They didn't hit you over the head like they do today."[46] He said that "movies used to be the cheapest and best entertainment for the masses," and were once made "for the whole family." At present, however, "with the kind of junk the studios are cranking out and the jacked-up prices they're charging, the average family is staying home and watching TV."[47] He also denounced the trend of many 1960s movies to take "all the illusion out of it and let the blood pour and show all the sweat and the flesh."[48]

In the 1970s he became concerned about undesirable changes in the structure of the film industry. He put the blame for the decline of movies on the breakdown of the studio system, the loss of leadership, and the manipulation of the industry by bankers and stock brokers whom he despised. "I'm glad I won't be around too much longer," he said in 1971, "to see what they do with it." "The men who control the big studios today are stock manipulators and bankers. They know nothing about our business. They're in for the buck." He missed the old-time moguls, Louis B. Mayer, Harry Cohn, Jack Warner, who may have been "strange," but "they functioned consistently through habit." The moguls took "an interest in the future of their business. They had integrity." By contrast, those who control the industry now reminded him of "high-class whores."[49]

As an example of the moguls's integrity and civil responsibility, Wayne cited the crime-gangster film. When they realized "that they've made a hero out of the goddamn gangster heavy in crime movies," he said, and "that they were doing a discredit to our country, they voluntarily took it upon themselves to stop making gangster pictures," out of responsibility to the public and "with no censorship from the outside." By contrast, today's executives "don't give a damn," for "in their efforts to grab the box office that these sex pictures are attracting, they're producing garbage."[50]

Wayne did not believe in the rating system, describing it as "ridiculous," because "everytime they rate a picture, they let a little more go." "There was no need for rated pictures," he explained, "when the major studios were in control." But being an optimist, he was "quite sure that within two or three years, Americans will be fed up with these perverted films," citing <u>Myra Breckinridge</u> (1970), which he described as a film about the deflation of the American male, as an example. He really wanted to believe that the conglomerates would reach "the point where the American public will say, 'The hell with this!'" At the same time, he realized that "once they do, we'll have censorship in every state, in every city, and there'll be no way you can make even a worthwhile picture for adults and have it acceptable for national release."[51]

He also deplored the use of profanity in film, believing that its proliferation derived from the filmmaker's idea of what adolescents liked to see. He rejected the notion that "foul language is a sign of machismo," and the feeling that "by using four-letter words they make somebody manly or sophisticated."[52] He was against "filthy minds, filthy words, and filthy thoughts in films," regarding movies as "a universal instrument at once entertaining people and encouraging them to work toward a better world, a freer world."[53] Wayne had strong ideas about preserving "morality standards" and making films with a positive point of view.

Wayne tried not to make films that exploited sex or violence, deploring the vulgarity and violence in <u>Rosemary's Baby</u>, which he saw and did not like, and <u>A Clockwork Orange</u> or <u>Last Tango in Paris</u>, which he had no desire to see. He thought <u>Deep Throat</u> was repulsive, "after all, it's pretty hard to take your daughter to see it."[54] And he refused to believe that <u>Love Story</u> "sold because the girl (Ali MacGraw) went around saying 'shit' all the way through it." Rather, "the American public wanted to see a little romantic story."[55] He took a strong stance against nudity: "No one in any of my pictures will ever be served drinks by a girl with no top to her dress."[56] It was not sex per se he was against. "Don't get me wrong. As far as a man and a woman are concerned, I'm awfully happy there's a thing called sex," he said, "It's an extra something God gave us, but no picture should feature the word in an unclear manner." He therefore

saw "no reason why it shouldn't be in pictures," but it had
to be "healthy, lusty sex."[57]

Leisure

In his leisure activities, essentially male pursuits, Wayne
was also influenced by the image of the Westerner. He con-
formed to the rigid Hollywood view of the "He-Man," demanding that male stars be shown in "virile" pursuits such as
hunting, fishing, sailing, etc., both on-screen and off.
These leisure activities, considered crucial for stars' popularity, were at times fabricated by the studios' publicity machines. Wayne loved the sea, and his yacht, the Wild Goose,
was his favorite family meeting place. In his later years, it
served as a substitute for horse riding, which he had to
give up on doctors' orders after the cancer. He also liked
fishing and hunting, particularly in Mexico, and skin and
water diving. A fanatic chess player, he always carried a
small chess set in his pocket. His favorite recreation between takes, when he was working, was playing poker.

One of Hollywood's legendary drinkers, drinking was
also integral to his screen image. He never made a secret
of his love for the bottle. "I love good whiskey," was the
first thing he mentioned when asked about his leisure time.
And challenged about his capacity, his typical response was,
"Well, I'm full grown, you know. I'm pretty big and got
enough fat on me, so I guess I can drink a fair amount."[58]
His capacity to drink amazed his colleagues, for after drinking all night, he was still the first to arrive on the set.
Henry Fonda described him as a man "who could outdrink
any man," and admitted that he "couldn't keep up with
him."[59] After the shooting of Fort Apache was completed,
Wayne and Fonda flew down to Mexico to join John Ford;
they spent their entire time going from one bar to another.
And director Dwan recalled that during Sands of Iwo Jima
Wayne liked to stay up at the bar quite late, "and he could
put away a lot, he had a terrific capacity." The trouble
was that none of the young members was used to it and they
were "a pathetic sight" the next morning.[60]

But Wayne never indulged while he was working. "You
can tell the guy who says so, I'll see him," he once said in

response to such an allegation. "If I have work to do, I
suffer," he explained, "but I don't drink."[61] "Anybody
who has worked that hard has earned a drink," was his
motto. His favorite drink was tequila "as fine a liquor as
there is in the world," and "better than any drink I ever
had in my life." "You hear about tequila," he said, "and
think about a cheap cactus drink, but this is something
extraordinary."[62] He believed that if he had the concession
for it, "I'd have made a fortune, not only from the amount I
drink myself, but from the people I've recommended it to."
"The guy that runs the company," he revealed, "sends me a
case now and then. He thinks I drink like other people.
But I buy five for every one he sends."[63]

   Another aspect of his life affected by his admiration
for the cowboy was his collection of Western art. His home
reflected this devotion to the Old West and its folklore, with
paintings by noted artists such as Frederick Remington and
Charles Russell. He also owned a large collection of period
guns and knives, and his Hopi Indian artifacts, particularly
the Indian Kachina dolls, were reportedly second only to
that of Senator Barry Goldwater. Wayne surrounded himself with tokens of the American frontier: printings and
rare books on cowboys and Indians. After his death, most
of his memorabilia was donated to the National Cowboy Hall
of Fame in Oklahoma.

The Eternal Comrade

   Most of Wayne's closest friends were people from the
film industry, which further integrated his work and leisure
into a unified entity governed by the same ethics. He preferred the efficiency of working with the same directors and
actors over and over; both time and trouble were saved by
customary cooperation. But it was also part of his idealistic
view of work as a social community marked by strong, long-
lasting bonds.

   Next to Ford, his closest friend was actor Ward Bond,
whom he had met when they played football at the University
of Southern California. When Wayne recruited players for
Ford's Words and Music, he naturally preferred to hire men
from his own Sigma Chi Fraternity. Bond was also inter-

ested in the project, but Wayne rejected him. "You're not
getting on this train, Bond," Wayne reportedly told him at
their first meeting in 1928, "You're too ugly to be in the
movie." "Screw you, Duke," said Bond, "not everybody on
this gravy train is going to be a sweetheart of Sigma Chi."[64]
That was the beginning of a lifelong friendship, which included making movies, playing poker, and drinking together.
While hunting, an activity they both liked, Wayne once accidentally shot Bond in the back, but both took the incident
lightly, with Wayne claiming, "this gun of mine sure throws
a good pattern."[65]

Wayne and Bond appeared in 19 movies together, most
of them directed by Ford; their last one was Rio Bravo.
For many years Bond was recognized by the public as "the
fellow who's always in those John Wayne movies," as one
critic put it, "a scenic attraction in Wayne's Westerns."[66]
But Bond became a star in his own right in the popular TV
series Wagon Train, in which he played Major Set Adams.
The last episode, directed by Ford and featuring Wayne as
General Sherman, was aired posthumously.

Bond also shared Wayne's political persuasions and
succeeded him as president of the Motion Picture Alliance
for the Preservation of American Ideals; Wayne believed that
Bond had lost many jobs in the 1950s because of his anti-
Communist activities. Bond suffered a heart attack in a
Dallas motel, on his way to join Ford for a visit on The
Alamo's set; Wayne made all the funeral arrangements. In
1961, a year after his death, Wayne went to Reno to accept
for Bond a posthumous Silver Spur Award, in honor of his
contributions to Western lore. He described Bond in one
brief sentence: "[One] hundred percent American."

Another unique and lengthy friendship was with Yakima
Canutt, the finest stuntman in Hollywood. Wayne remained
appreciative all his life for what he had learned from Canutt,
who doubled for him and was the second-unit director in
many movies (Dark Command, Angel and the Badman).
Wayne was instrumental in getting the Academy of Motion
Picture Arts and Sciences to award him a Special Oscar in
1966, for "creating the profession of stuntmen everywhere."
Moreover, he continued to employ Canutt (Rio Lobo) at old
age, when no other studio would use his services.

Wayne's work relationship with Victor McLaglen also spanned decades, appearing in five films together; the first, Hangman's House, as early as 1929, and the last, The Quiet Man, 23 years later. McLaglen's son, Andrew, started to work for Wayne as a unit director when he was sixteen and, later, it was the star who pushed Andrew's directorial career by giving him the opportunity to direct five of his pictures, including McLintock!, The Undefeated, and Cahill, U.S. Marshal. Harry Carey, one of Ford's favorite actors (Fort Apache was dedicated to his memory), appeared with Wayne in four movies; Red River was the last. After his death, Wayne employed his widow, Olive Carey, in three movies, and his son, Harry Carey, Jr., in nine.

Wayne proved to be a loyal friend to actors and directors who had been part of his earlier career, but later fell from favor in Hollywood. One example was George Sherman, who directed scores of low-budget Westerns in the 1930s, but in 1971 found himself unemployed; Wayne stepped in and asked him to direct Big Jake. Bruce Cabot, a star of many "B" pictures, returned to Hollywood in the 1960s after living in Europe for years. Wayne was the first to offer him work --Cabot appeared in ten of his movies.

Generosity to his colleagues was paramount; when they needed help, they turned to Wayne and he tried to come to their aid. John Agar made his debut in Fort Apache, but in later years his career was hampered by a bout with alcoholism. Wayne came to the rescue with parts in The Undefeated, Chisum, and Big Jake. Gail Russell, his leading lady in Wake of the Red Witch, whose career had also declined because of drinking problems, needed a job; Wayne offered her a role in Seven Men from Now, produced by his company.

Wayne's ideal of ambiance on a movie set was modeled after Ford, who had his stock of permanent actors and crew. Ford relied on family and friends in casting his pictures. The Quiet Man, for example, was a big family affair: Wayne's four children, Ford's brother and son, and Maureen O'Hara's two actor brothers from the Abbey Theatre, appeared in the film. And in The Searchers, Ford's stock company included Wayne, his son Patrick, Ward Bond, John Qualen, Harry Carey, Jr., his mother, Olive, Ken Curtis, and Hank Warden.

The screenplay was written by Frank Nugent, Ford's son-in-law.

Some of Wayne's best friends were stuntmen, and he launched the careers of several of them, like Cliff Lyons, who was employed as a second-unit director and exhibited his specialty of falling off a horse in The Comancheros. Richard Talmadge, endowed with extraordinary athletic ability, became a second-unit director responsible for choreographing the fist fights in North to Alaska. The fact that the same stuntmen continued to work for him was remarkable. Indeed, his loyalty to his crew was noteworthy. When filming The Quiet Man in Ireland, he was surprised to find that his longtime makeup man, Web Overlander, was not there. Upon inquiry, he was told by the producer that Overlander was not needed. "Well, then," he is reported to have said, "I've decided you don't need me either. When's the next plane home?"[67] Within less than a week, Overlander was back on the set. "They may be SOB's, but they are my SOB's,"[68] he said in reference to his crew, some of whom have been with him for decades.

Ralph Volkie was his trainer for decades, and Winton C. Hoch, winner of several Academy Awards for cinematography, worked on several of his movies, the last of which was The Green Berets. Indeed, 16 men of True Grit's crew had been with him for many years, and three of them were second-generation people; Wayne had worked with their parents before they had even been born. His preference to work with his old buddies was even more visible on the set of Big Jake, where 18 members of the staff had worked in over 100 of his movies.

But most of all, he enjoyed working with his own children, three of whom chose movies as a career. Michael became a producer and later head of production of Batjac, and Patrick and Ethan pursued acting careers. Patrick appeared in eight of his father's movies. All four of his children appeared in The Quiet Man, a film marking the only appearance of two of his daughters, Toni and Melinda. Wayne's second set of children also worked with him. Aissa made her film debut in The Alamo, and went on to appear in The Comancheros and Donovan's Reef. Ethan made his debut in Rio Lobo, a film in which Patrick Wayne and Chris Mitchum (Robert Mitchum's son) played Wayne's fictional offspring. In Big Jake, Ethan was cast as Wayne's fictional grandson.

McLintock! stood out as a real family experience, for
it was written by James E. Grant, directed by Andrew
McLaglen, and produced by Michael Wayne. Wayne's older
brother, Robert E. Morrison, served as production super-
visor, and two of his children, Patrick and Aissa, were cast
in small parts. Critics started to poke fun at this pattern,
as one wrote that McLintock! was a "family production," but
"what's good for the Wayne family is no bonanza for the
movie-goer in this simple-minded movie."[69]

Known for his professional integrity, if he had a contract, he honored it even if he was displeased with the director, which was clearly the case with John Huston's The
Barbarian and the Geisha. A strict code of professional
ethics characterized his career from the very beginning. In
1931, he signed a contract with Columbia Pictures, but was
suspended by Harry Cohn, the studio's head, for various
reasons, one of them being Cohn's alleged suspicion that
Wayne was having an affair with a starlet he himself was
interested in. Wayne never forgot this incident, and in
the future worked with many other studios--but never again
with Columbia.

He demonstrated his gentlemanly behavior, on- and
offscreen, while shooting Hondo in Mexico. His wife's law-
yers sent two private detectives to keep an eye on him,
suspecting him of adulterous behavior. Unable to speak
Spanish, the detectives accidentally wired the suite belonging to the governor, assuming it was Wayne's. Later, they
appealed to Wayne from prison for help, because they had
neither money nor connections. He reportedly not only paid
their fines and arranged for their release, but also paid for
their air fare back to the United States.

First Lady Nancy Reagan described Wayne as "the most
gentle and tender person I ever knew." She recalls that in
1960, when Reagan was president of the Screen Actors Guild,
he was involved in a labor dispute and accused of being responsible for the guild's strike. Until the strike settled,
Wayne called her every day. "I've been reading what these
damn columnists are saying about Ron," he said. "He can
take care of himself, but I've been worrying how all this is
affecting you." When a mass gathering was called to discuss
the settlement terms, Wayne left a party to escort her. Sitting next to him was "like being next to a force bigger than
life."[70]

President Reagan was also in awe of the actor's integrity, describing his handshake as an abiding contract. The president recalled that after Wayne sold his yacht, for an amount below the market price, he found out that its engines needed repair. He insisted on paying for the repair, because he had given his word to the buyer that it was in excellent shape.

12. THE POLITICAL FIGURE

John Wayne was not the only star to get involved in politics. What was distinctive about him, however, was that he succeeded more than other actors in integrating his politics into his professional career. His screen image as a Western hero blended almost completely with his conservative, right-wing politics. As Eric Bentley observed: "He even seeks, which is fairly unusual in Hollywood, to put his art at the service of his beliefs, and even in his less deliberately propagandistic efforts, he succeeds."[1]

Wayne's politics neither damaged his career nor affected his popularity, as might have been expected. He was the most popular star in the United States in 1950 and 1951, while he was president of the anti-Communist organization Motion Picture Alliance for the Preservation of American Ideals. He continued to be popular in 1969, after making the pro-Vietnam movie The Green Berets. In 1970, the Academy of Motion Pictures ignored his controversial politics and bestowed on him the most prestigious film award, the Oscar, for his performance in True Grit.

Wayne's political participation raised the controversial question of whether actors should get involved in politics. Most people would agree that actors, like other professionals, are entitled to express their political views in public. The dispute, however, is over their privileged position: they are constantly in the public eye and get tremendous media coverage for their lives on-screen and off. Consequently, players' views tend to get disproportionate attention and, by implication, importance. Wayne believed that the film industry was not and should not be an ivory tower, "an actor is part of a bigger world than Hollywood." "I have been in the public eye," he said, "and when people ask questions, I say what I think."[2]

His attitude toward politics was at best ambivalent,
considering it "a necessary evil." "I hate politics and most
politicians," he repeatedly declared, and "I am not a political
figure." At the same time, he conceded that "when things
get rough and people are saying things that aren't true, I
sometimes open my mouth and eventually get in trouble."[3]
"I get hooked into politics more than anybody,"[4] he admitted,
and one suspects that, despite many statements to the contrary, he enjoyed being a political personality. In congru-
ence with his screen image, he did not mask his beliefs or
mince words. When a principle was involved, he stated precisely what he thought, disregarding intellectual fashion in
society or the current vogue in Hollywood. Wayne said his
two worst faults were being "more highly emotional than I
appear" and, "given the choice, I find myself talking too
much."[5]

Unabashed Yankee-Doodle Patriot

It is hard to describe a coherent Wayne political philosophy, though there were some specific values that he fer-
vently supported. Critic Charles Champlin holds that Wayne's
politics were characterized by "a private code of beliefs in
such things as individual responsibility and honor, loyalty
to friends, a primer-straight patriotism, and adherence to
the American dream of enterprise, hard work, and reward."[6]
Wayne's brand of politics was personal; he was an advocate of
the rugged, romantic individualism of the nineteenth-century
frontiersmen, which he espoused emotionally rather than in-
tellectually. Like his Western heroes, he lived by a definite
code of ethics: "About the only thing you have to guide
you," he said, "is your conscience." One should not let
"social groups or petty ambitions or political parties or any
institution tempt you to sacrifice your moral standards," but
he conceded that "it takes a long time to develop a philosophy that enables you to do that." Integrity and self-respect
were his most cherished values, "If you lose your self-
respect, you've lost everything."[7]

Equally important was his unique brand of patriotism.
He described himself as "an old-fashioned, honest-to-goodness,
flag-waver patriot,"[8] which was in full harmony with his
Americanism, the most important attribute of his screen
image. In Eric Bentley's view, Wayne was "the most

important American of our time,"[9] and others also labeled
him as "unabashed Yankee-Doodle patriot." In a feature
article, Time magazine described him as "Hollywood's super-
American whose unswerving motto is 'Go West and Turn
Right.' "[10]

Over the years, his patriotism was panned for being
blind and unquestioning. It became an object of ridicule,
though even his detractors gave him credit for being honest
and consistent. "It annoys me," Wayne said in response to
these accusations, "because I have a normal love for my
country." His admiration for America, a country which "in
200 years has taken the wilderness and made it a farm that
feeds the world and a factory that defends the world,"[11]
was simplistic but profound. "This fabulous prosperity," he
held, "didn't happen in the United States because we have
no brains, no education, and no courage." He was sincere
when he declared, "We have a pretty wonderful country, and
I thank God he chose me to live here."[12] Wayne never lost
his unabashed patriotism, even in the late 1960s, when much
of the younger generation was full of criticism, even ashamed,
of being American.

Wayne liked to see "every man equal in front of the
law," but also "responsible to his country." "You see corruption and bribery, sure," he said, "That's why we have
laws."[13] He had a "very idealistic period," he said, when
he thought "everyone should have a good living," but was
disappointed to realize "everybody won't pay their dues."[14]
However, challenged about America's loss of dignity and
asked if he were gloomy about its future, his unequivocal
response was "absolutely not." "I think that the loud roar
of irresponsible liberalism," he said in 1971, "which in the
old days we called liberalism, is being quieted down by a
reasoning public." He always maintained his optimism about
the future of America: "As a country, our yesterdays tell
us that we have to win not only at war but at peace. So
far we haven't done that. Sadly, it looks [like] we'll have
another war to win peace." However, comparing the America
he grew up in and that of today, he believed that, "all in
all, it's practically the same."[15]

Wayne's politics underwent several transformations during the course of his life. He admitted to have been a socialist when he was a sophomore at U.S.C., but not when

he graduated. From the 1940s on, his politics were labeled
right-wing conservatism, but he continued to regard himself
a liberal, "because I listen to everybody's point of view and
try to reason it out in my mind, and then do what I think
is right."[16] But increasingly he found it difficult to define
his politics. "With today's semantics, I don't know what I
am," he said, "I used to believe I was a liberal, but I guess
definitions have changed." Regarding liberalism as "a way
of life," he suggested to "keep it out of politics."[17] For
him, liberalism meant that "a man ought to be allowed to get
up and express his opinion," but "very few of the so-called
liberals are open-minded." He therefore rejected the liberalism of those "who shout you down and won't let you speak."[18]
In the 1970s he gave up his fight to label his politics. "I'm
involved with what the semantics of today call conservatism
at a time when it's more fashionable to be a liberal. They
call me a reactionary. Well, maybe I am a goddamn reactionary."[19]

"He suffers from a point of view based entirely on his
experience," Katharine Hepburn remarked, describing the
origins of his politics. "He was surrounded in his early
years in motion pictures by people like himself. Self-made.
Hard working. Independent. The style of man who blazed
the trail across our country, who reached out into the unknown. People who were willing to live or die entirely on
their own independent judgment. 'Pull your own freight,'
this is their slogan."[20] Wayne's love for America was un-
critical because of his subjective experience. "The country
and its political system have been good to Wayne," observed
Vincent Canby, "It's no wonder that he cherished it in ways
that others, less fully blessed, find dumbfounding."[21]

Wayne's critics suggested that his reactionary views
derived from his Western movies, charging that his politics,
like his films, were oversimplified, rigid and disciplinary.
Furthermore, they claimed he reduced complex issues, such
as the Vietnam War, to simplistic denominators, viewing them
as a classic Western conflict between heroes and villains,
good and evil. And because he applied the simplistic solutions of his Westerns to contemporary problems, he was
viewed as a man of the past, unable to cope with problems
of modern society. In some ways, he approached political
problems like one of his Western heroes, favoring courage
and direct confrontation. For example, he claimed that "the

way to stop the war" was "to call Russia's Kosygin and say
that the next time a Russian-made gun is turned against us,
we'll drop a bomb right on him."[22] Wayne did not feel apologetic about his simplistic politics: "They tell me everything
isn't black and white. Well, I say, why the hell not?"[23]

Wayne's political character was rooted in the American
national grain. Richard Hofstadter defined the American
fundamentalist mind as one that "looks upon the world as an
arena for conflict between absolute good and absolute evil,
and accordingly it scorns compromise."[24] His politics were
contemptuous of complex or subtle issues, favoring plain,
straightforward talk, no compromises, and no tolerance for
ambiguity. Wayne was compared to General MacArthur, whom
he adored, because their political personalities were similar,
based on inner contradiction. They were proudly nationalis-
tic, tough with the Soviets, and obsessed with Communism as
an ideological threat, but they were also sincere, honest,
and highly emotional, not rational or intellectual, in their
politics.

Anti-Communist Obsession

In the 1930s Wayne was neither involved nor knew much
about politics. "When we first made movies together," Henry
Fonda recalled, "he couldn't even spell politics."[25] But
shortly after he was elected to the board of the Screen Actors Guild, in the 1940s, he began to be aware of the leftist
movement in the industry and of what he described as its
sneering attitude toward sacred American symbols, such as
the president and the flag. However, his real involvement
in political issues started during World War II, after being
rejected for enlistment into the Army. Enlistment was important to him; he even appealed to John Ford, then a lieutenant commander in the Navy, for help, but to no avail.
This rejection was a severe blow to his ego; most stars were
drafted, receiving tremendous publicity for it. Wayne's
patriotic feelings were thus compounded by guilt over portraying military heroes without participating in the actual
fighting. His subsequent obsession with making inspirational
war pictures stemmed from personal frustration at not having
fought in any American war.

His contribution to the war effort, like that of other

actors not drafted, was to make personal appearances in
military camps. In 1944 he went on a three-month USO mission, entertaining soldiers in the Pacific bases and battle
lines, from Brisbane Australia to the front on New Britain.
He visited wounded soldiers in hospitals during the day, and
at night appeared in shows. In a press conference he gave
after he returned, his message to the American public was
"Write Letters." "The boys are starved for news from home,"
he explained, and "the biggest day in their lives over there
is when the mailman hands them an envelope postmarked
[from] the United States." The soldiers "are not thinking
about any trouble at home because they are too busy fighting a war, but they do want to be sure they have something
to say when they get back."[26]

World War II created a strange situation because the
Soviet Union became, for the first time, a political ally of
the United States. Consequently, many Americans supported
its policies and were openly pro-Soviet. It did not last long,
however, and as soon as the war was over, the situation
changed dramatically. Wayne said he became politically conscious at the end of the war, when he realized the infiltration
of Communists into the film industry. In 1944 he decided to
join a group of actors, writers, and directors as a founding
member of the Motion Picture Alliance for the Preservation of
American Ideals (MPA). It was established with the explicit
goal of fighting the leftist movement in the movie colony.
Among its founders were Jim McGuiness, MGM's production
head (the organization started at an informal meeting in his
house); Roy Brewer, the theatrical union leader; directors
Leo McCarey and Sam Wood; actors Clark Gable, Robert Taylor, Ward Bond, and Adolphe Menjou; and screenwriters
Borden Chase and Morrie Riskind.

MPA's first president was Sam Wood, followed by Clark
Gable and Robert Taylor. Wayne became president in 1949,
serving three terms, until 1952, during the heyday of Senator Joseph McCarthy and the hearings of the House Un-
American Activities Committee (HUAAC). Some claim Wayne
was forced to join the MPA to please his more conservative
friends. Studio executives warned him that his affiliation
would ruin his career. "You're becoming a controversial
figure," they reportedly said, "it will kill you at the box
office. You will hit the skids." Ironically, a year after
being elected as president of MPA, Wayne became the top

box office attraction in the United States. Wayne said that those who warned him "must have meant it would ruin me with the Moscow fan clubs," because "when I became president of the Alliance, I was 32nd on the box office polls, but last year I'd skidded up near the top."[27] He remained at the top in 1950 and 1951, and in 1952 slipped to third place on the popularity polls.

The HUAAC had been in existence since the 1930s, when Martin Dies was its chairman. Dies was convinced that the Communist Party was responsible for the propaganda that he thought appeared in Fury (1936), a socially conscious film against lynching; Blockade (1938), about the Spanish Civil War; and Juarez (1939), dealing with the Mexican revolutionary leader, with allusions to the current political situation in Europe. He also published articles on the order of "The Reds in Hollywood," and "Is Communism Invading the Movies?" which contributed to the anti-Communist hysteria at the time. During the war, the HUAAC was inactive--for obvious reasons. But on September 25, 1947, it renewed its investigations into the extent of Communist infiltration in Hollywood.

The film industry was determined to demonstrate its political "cleanliness" even earlier.[28] The big studios regretted having produced such pro-Soviet movies as Warners' Mission to Moscow (1944), based on the career of U.S. ambassador Joseph E. Davies in Russia, or MGM's Song of Russia (also 1944), which described the Soviet war effort with utmost admiration. In 1948 Darryl Zanuck produced the prototypical anti-Communist picture The Iron Curtain, the story of a clerk in the Soviet Embassy in Canada who exposed a Soviet spy network. It did not matter that this and other movies, such as The Red Menace, The Red Danube, and The Woman on Pier Thirteen (originally titled I Married a Communist), were panned by the critics, failed at the box office, and were banned from release in some European countries.

The political hysteria in Hollywood reached unprecedented dimensions and has been well documented in several books. It got to the point where Lela Rogers, Ginger's mother and vice-president at RKO, was asked to examine all screenplays for questionable content; she was proud to declare that she found a line in Tender Comrade (1943) that

stated: "Share and share alike, that's the meaning of democracy." Dalton Trumbo, who wrote the screenplay, later became one of the Hollywood Ten. The "Friendly Witnesses" of
HUAAC included many Hollywood celebrities, such as Gary
Cooper, who reportedly condemned Communism because "it
was not on the level," whatever that meant. Or Adolphe
Menjou, whose credo was that Communism could be expressed
by players "by a look, by an inflection, by a change in the
voice."[29]

Ayn Rand's booklet "Screen Guide for Americans," published by the MPA and widely distributed throughout the studios, warned: "Don't Smear Industrialists," "Don't Smear
the Free Enterprise System," and "Don't Smear Success." It
also advised: "Don't ever use any lines about 'the common
man,' or 'the little people,'" because "it is not the American
idea to be either 'common' or 'little.'" Furthermore, she was
against telling people that "man is [a] helpless, twisted,
drooling, snivelling, neurotic weakling," and in favor of
showing the world, "an _American_ kind of man."[30]

In addition to the MPA, founded to combat what it believed to be the increasing domination of the film industry by
Communists, Hollywood established its own Fact Finding Committee on Un-American Activities under the leadership of
Jack B. Tenney. "Let no one say that a Communist can be
tolerated in American society and particularly in our industry," Wayne said in one of his most famous speeches as
president of MPA, "We don't want to associate with traitors."
He further hoped that "those who have changed their views
will cooperate to the fullest extent ... so that they can come
back to the fellowship of loyal Americans." "The bankers
and stock holders much recognize," he concluded, "that the
investments in the movie industry are imperiled as long as
we have these elements in our midst."[31]

There were rumors at the time that MPA gave the
HUAAC names of suspected Communists and that it was in-
directly connected with the imprisonment of the Hollywood
Ten. Wayne repeatedly denied these accusations, "I never
in my life did any such thing."[32] Moreover, he claimed that
it was the Communists who did the blacklisting, by forming
writers' cells so that those who did not belong to them could
not get writing jobs. He really believed that the Communists
aimed at taking control of the industry through violent strikes.

When Ronald Reagan was president of the Screen Actors Guild he was confronted with leftist attempts to take
over the union's leadership. He asked Wayne, then president of MPA, for help, and the latter attended a crucial
meeting. "I watched rather helplessly," Reagan recalled,
"as they filibustered, waiting for our majority to leave so
they could gain control." But then he heard a call for adjournment and "seized on this as a means to end the attempted
takeover." His opponents demanded to know who had called
for adjournment and Reagan realized there were only few willing to be publicly identified as opponents of the Communists.
"Why, I believe John Wayne made the motion," Reagan said,
shortly after which he heard the latter's strong and familiar
voice, "I sure as hell did!"[33] The meeting was over. "Standing up and declaring which side he was on," Morrie Riskind
later claimed, "was Wayne's biggest contribution to the fight
against Communism."[34]

The movie colony was sharply divided along political
lines. Many actors were appalled by the HUAAC hearings
and the MPA alike, for they were against any political interference with the film industry. In 1947, the Committee for
the First Amendment was organized by writer Philip Dunne
and supported by such liberal actors as Humphrey Bogart,
Judy Garland, Gene Kelly, Fredric March, John Garfield,
and directors John Huston and William Wyler. It did not
last long, though some of its members, most notably Bogart,
continued to fight against the HUAAC's infringing upon free
speech. But even Bogart found it difficult to express his
politics openly and maintain good standing in Hollywood as
well. When he became the target of criticism and was labeled
a Communist sympathizer, he moderated his statements and in
1948 even wrote an article entitled, "I'm No Communist." Bogart later admitted that the Washington Trip he had organized, with actors stopping en route from California to give
press conferences against HUAAC, had been a mistake.[35]

Wayne was quite active as president of MPA. He reportedly visited Clark Gable on the set of Key to the City
(1951) to warn him there was a Communist on the crew.[36]
And in 1951, when Cooper announced his plan to form a production company with Carl Foreman, Wayne was extremely
critical about it. Foreman was labeled an "Unfriendly Wit-
ness," because he refused to discuss his former affiliation
with the Communist Party. Cooper came under such severe

attack that he had to pull out; though in a statement to the
press he said he was still convinced of Foreman's loyalty,
Americanism, and ability as a picture maker. His statement
amounted to little more than lip service, as he did in fact
withdraw from the plan. Foreman understood Cooper's position and released him from his commitment to avoid damage
to his career. [37]

Wayne was vocal about his criticism of Foreman's screenplay for High Noon, which he described as "defeatist," and
"the most un-American thing I've ever seen in my whole
life." He was especially offended by Cooper putting his U.S.
marshal badge under his foot and stepping on it at the end
of the film. Wayne said he never regretted "having helped
run Foreman out of this country." When asked, "what gave
you the right?" he did not hesitate to reply, "I thought he'd
hurt Gary Cooper's reputation a great deal,"[38] ignoring the
fact that Cooper had won his second Oscar for this movie,
which also rejuvenated his declining career. Foreman was
forced into self-exile in England, working there "underground," using various pseudonyms. He received no credit
for his screenplay for The Bridge on the River Kwai (1957),
which won Best Picture and Best Screenplay, honoring the
book's author, who had had nothing to do with the script.

Another figure regarded unfavorably by Wayne was
writer-director Robert Rossen, whose film All the King's Men
(1949) dealt with political corruption. Wayne described him
as doing "things that were detrimental to our way of life."[39]
Rossen was identified as Communist by several witnesses and
was subsequently blacklisted by the industry. But after two
years of inactivity he requested a second hearing, at which
he admitted to membership in the Communist Party. His
name was restored to respectability and he was able to work
again, directing with great success The Hustler (1961), but
he never returned to Hollywood.

Wayne actually belonged to the more "liberal" element
of the MPA. When Larry Parks, for example, admitted he
had been a member of the Communist Party, Wayne said,
"Too bad," but he showed respect for Parks's repentance:
"It takes courage to admit you're wrong."[40] Unlike his
more chauvinistic colleagues, he expressed hope that Parks's
career would not be hurt. Screenwriter John Lee Mahin
also recalled that Wayne was one of the first to publicly

battle for those who broke from the Communist Party. But
other members, like Hedda Hopper, who served as one of his
vice-presidents at the MPA, could not forgive Parks and
could not understand Wayne forgiving him: "Duke is a little
dumb about these things," she said, publicly chastising Wayne.
"The life of one American soldier," Hopper is reported to have
said, "is worth all the careers in Hollywood. We must be
careful lest we give sympathy to those who do not deserve
it--and Parks certainly does not."[41] Hopper "gave me fifteen minutes of the roughest go," Wayne recalled, " 'Our
boys are dying in Korea and the whole bit.' Real enough.
And I had to take it."[42]

Wayne believed that some of MPA's active members later
paid with their own careers for their involvement. Adolphe
Menjou was out of work for three years and worked only
sporadically afterward. Ward Bond made few movies, mostly
directed by Ford, until his comeback in the TV series Wagon
Train. And Morrie Riskind, a successful writer and winner
of both the Pulitzer prize and Oscar award, also found himself out of work. Wayne's and Ford's careers remained unaf-
fected, probably because they were then too popular and too
established.

Long after MPA disbanded, Wayne continued to express
his anti-Communist ideas. He considered Senator McCarthy
to be one of America's "most misunderstood heroes," "the
awakening of America," who rang "the bell to get up." "I
admired the work he did," he said in 1960, "whether he went
overboard or not, he was of value to my country."[43] McCarthy was a close friend, respected for "the courage to take
on everyone," but "like most of our so-called conservative
leaders, did not have the backing of the Eastern establishment press, which ultimately ruined him." He did believe
that McCarthy was "murdered by the leftists," and regretted
that "now his name is a bad word."[44]

Even in the 1960s, Wayne was boastful about MPA's
achievements. "Five years ago, Communism seemed to be almost a fad in Hollywood," he said, but "I think we've driven
most of them underground now." But he was still concerned
that "many of the leaders in this country don't seem to worry
about what's going on."[45] In 1960, when Frank Sinatra hired
screenwriter Albert Maltz, one of the Hollywood Ten, to do a
script, he came under severe attack and, under pressure, had

to fire him. Wayne did not approve of Sinatra's hiring, but
asked for a response, he snapped, "I don't think my opinion
is too important."[46] There were also rumors, denied by
Wayne, that when the two met at a Hollywood nightclub they
had an argument. Nonetheless, as time went by, both forgot the whole thing, which was typical of Wayne; he always
knew how to maintain old friendships despite political differences.

Wayne and Vietnam

Unlike World War II which functioned as a unifying
and integrating force in American society, the Vietnam War
was rather divisive. Once again, Wayne found himself in
the midst of a heated political controversy. It started in
June 1966, when he visited Vietnam to cheer American troops
on the front and wounded soldiers in hospitals. The mission
of the tour was twofold: it was a goodwill trip, and at the
same time provided him the opportunity to gather first-hand
material for a film. It is unclear whether the idea to make a
film on Vietnam originated before or during the trip. Before
he left for the three-week tour, sponsored by the Department
of Defense, Wayne said he was "going around the hinterlands
to give the boys something to break the monotony." "I can't
sing or dance," he said, but "I can sure shake a lot of
hands." And he felt a sense of urgency, "I just couldn't
feel right until I had gone over there."[47]

Wayne received VIP treatment, but insisted on visiting
the soldiers on the battle front. One report mentioned that
a Vietcong sniper's bullet hit the ground about 50 feet from
him, and another told how his helicopter landed in the midst
of the action. Both reports enhanced his courageous image
and popularity among the Marines, and he was delighted when
they called him Sergeant Stryker, his character's name in Sands
of Iwo Jima. Upon return, he rushed to tell the press he
"never heard complaints from privates up to Generals."[48]

What really got him into trouble was his hawkish, some
say imperialist, view of Vietnam. "I get mad these days,"
he said, "when I see our boys there getting killed and
maimed and people back home aren't behind them." "However the world views us," he continued, "we are reaching
the point where further appeasement might well mean disaster."

He could not accept his opponents' argument that "we are
miles from home and on foreign territory," because "we were
on foreign territory too when we joined Britain to push back
Hitler and crush the evil of Nazism." "If we had not done
that," he argued, "where would these liberals be today?"[49]
To make his point, he drew an analogy between World War II
and Vietnam: "We fought in Germany because of what they
were doing to the Jews and to freedom, and as far as I'm
concerned the Communists are the enemy, not the Russian or
Chinese People." And he continued: "Does anyone believe
after the Stalin purges, the labor camps, the repression of
free expression, opinion, and artistry, the jailing of brilliant
writers, that Communism--either Russian or Chinese--with its
enslavement and stifling of liberty and individual freedom, is
any less an evil?"[50]

He firmly believed that the United States "had the
right to be in Vietnam," but he also praised the South Vietnamese's effort to "come up with a form of constitutional
government during a war, when they were hard pressed and
were the underdogs." "It took the colonies of America 11
years," he noted, "after our little set-to with England before we could come up with anything all 13 colonies would
sign." America, he held, should serve as an example to
small nations: "We've been telling the people of oppressed
nations, 'Stand up for your rights and we'll back you up.'
We've been saying this for years, and now, suddenly, it's a
terrible thing that we are keeping our word to the Vietnamese."[51]

Wayne's right-wing view of Vietnam, rooted in his old
hatred of Communism, made him many enemies in Hollywood,
of which he was well aware. "I'm unpopular in the industry," he said, "because my political philosophy is different
from the prevailing attitude." But he decided not to reply
to his colleagues in Hollywood because "political street-
fighting is unprofessional."[52] Indeed, even his politics
were conducted according to a gentlemanly code of behavior.
For instance, he did not approve of using the platform of
the Oscar ceremonies for promoting personal politics, de-
nouncing Marlon Brando's rejection of his 1972 Best Actor
award (for The Godfather). Brando protested against the
treatment of Indians, on- and offscreen, sending an Apache
activist to accept the award in his name and deliver a de-
cidedly political message. Committed to direct confrontation,

Wayne said, "It was sad that Brando did what he did. If he had something to say, he should have appeared that night and stated his views, instead of taking some little unknown girl and dressing her up in an Indian outfit." Wayne felt that Brando "was trying to avoid the issue that was really on his mind, which was the provocative story of <u>Last Tango in Paris</u>,"[53] a sensational sex drama between a desperate middle-aged man and a young French girl that included sexually explosive dialogue and graphically depicted sex.

White Supremacy

Wayne was accused of being racist because of his belief in white supremacy in America. And his intimate association with the Western film, which has traditionally ignored or, at best, underrepresented all ethnic minorities, was used by his critics as further proof of his racism. Most of all he was attacked by American Indians and blacks.

Leaders of the American-Indian community rejected his rationale for white hegemony: "When we came to America, there were a few thousand Indians over millions of miles, and I don't feel we did wrong in taking this great country away from these people, taking their happy hunting grounds away." "There were great numbers of people who needed new land," he explained, "and the Indians were selfishly trying to keep it for themselves." He not only believed that the whites were "progressive," but that they were also doing "something that was good for everyone." It therefore astonished him that the Indians indignantly protested his views of the necessity of eliminating what he considered handouts to the Indians. Later, by way of apology, he explained that the writer of <u>Playboy</u> and he "were kidding around about the Indians in Alcatraz," and that he had said not too seriously that "he hoped they'd taken care of their wampum, so maybe they could buy Alcatraz like we bought Manhattan."[54]

"I can't imagine any Indian," Wayne said in his defense, "not realizing that over the past forty years I've done more to give them human dignity and a fine image on the screen than anyone else who has ever worked in pictures."[55] "Indians were part of our history," he elaborated, "I have never shown the Indians on the screen as anything but courageous and with great human dignity."[56] To substantiate his point, he used some of his Westerns as examples, particularly the Indians in Fort Apache and Hondo.

The fact remains that the Indians have been mistreated in American film for generations. Most Westerns did not deal with white racist policies, the violations of treaties with the Indians, their confinement on reservations, their exploitation by white agents, and the disintegration of their whole culture. New trends toward more equitable treatment of the Indians did not begin until the early 1950s, echoed again in the late 1960s (see chapter 4). Broken Arrow (1950) is considered a turning point, because the narrative depicts the "Indian problem" from their point of view; Jimmy Stewart plays an army scout who brings about peace between the white man and the Apache. But despite the fact that Cochise was established as a hero, he was played by a white actor (Jeff Chandler), as was the trend in the 1950s.

In retrospect, Wayne's Westerns were no different from other mainstream Westerns. In Fort Apache, for example, one of the major conflicts between Wayne and Fonda concerns their approach to the Indian problem. Unlike Fonda's racist hatred and commitment to their extermination, Wayne sympathizes with their plight, describing the Indian Ring in Washington as "the dirtiest, most corrupt political group in our history." In She Wore a Yellow Ribbon, Wayne defeats the Indians by guile, stampeding their horses, rather than by violent conquest. And in Rio Grande, he is contrasted with the white villainous trader, who objects to peace because he knows it means an end to his illicit traffic.

Critic Jon Tuska regards Hondo as Wayne's closest personal statement of his view of the Indians.[57] To begin with, Hondo was married to an Indian woman who died. The movie also depicts favorably Vittorio, the Indian chief, justifying his anger, following the treaty violations by the whites. "There's no word in the Apache language for lie," Wayne says, "an' we lied to 'em." Finally, the film comments on the sad passing of Indian culture: Hondo regards the end of the Apache as "an end of a way of life, and a good one." Tuska also views McLintock! as a sequel to Hondo, because both were written by James E. Grant and both show the Indians' loss of their dignity, culture, and homeland.

By contrast, The Searchers was probably Ford-Wayne's strongest case in defending the purity of the white race. Alexander Walker sees in it a more extreme example of inbred hatred of non-Americans than in any of Wayne's earlier Westerns, which he explains as a product of the McCarthy era, when the film was made.[58] In this narrative, Wayne cannot accept Debbie's choice to live with the Indians because he considers it "unclean" and "morally degraded;" as if saying, women must keep "pure" because the continuity of the white race depends on them. Furthermore, he continuously taunts Martin, his companion, for being partly Cherokee, thus impure. Still, with all the criticism, Wayne's character is in fact closer to the Indians than any other white character in the film, understanding their ways and even speaking their language. The other white characters are described as bigoted, ineffectual, and treacherous.

From the late 1960s on, in tune with the times, Wayne's Westerns had their share of token Indian characters. In The War Wagon, an Indian (Howard Keel) is one of his allies in his vengeance plan, and in The Undefeated, his adopted son (Roman Gabriel) is a Cheyenne Indian. In the narrative of Big Jake, an old Indian friend helps him to find his kidnapped grandson, and in Cahill, U.S. Marshal, he has an Indian sidekick (Neville Brand).

Even more controversial were Wayne's views of the blacks' position in America, which irritated and upset the black community. Ebony magazine accused him of making films whose explicit message was that nonwhite people were the villains--which he denied. But he did not feel apologetic about his attitude: "I don't feel guilty about the fact that five or ten generations ago these people were slaves." "I'm not condoning slavery," he explained, "It's just a fact of life, like the kid who gets infantile paralysis and has to wear braces, so he can't play football with the rest of us."[59]

As for his policy toward employing black actors in his movies, Wayne said, "I've directed two pictures and I gave the blacks their proper position. I had a black slave in The Alamo, and I had a correct number of blacks in The Green Berets." He said he was guided by clear criteria: "If it's supposed to be a black character, naturally I use a black actor. But I don't go so far as hunting for positions for them."[60] He noted that in The Man Who Shot Liberty

Valance (1962), his faithful employee was black (Woody
Strode), which was actually a letdown for this actor, because Strode had played the leading role in Ford's Sergeant
Routledge, concerning the trial of a black soldier accused of
rape and murder. And in The Cowboys, Roscoe Lee Browne
had a relatively large role, cast as Wayne's cook.

The underrepresentation of blacks in Westerns was
striking considering the fact that about one-fourth of the
working cowboys in the nineteenth century were black.[61]
Blacks had played bigger roles in the 1930s and 1940s in
films specifically designed for black audiences. The Western, in fact, incorporated black characters into its narratives much later than the serious-problem films dealing with
blacks, such as Pinky, Lost Boundaries, and Home of the
Brave, all in the late 1940s. It took another decade before
Westerns began to deal with black characters or black issues
and, when that happened, it was a result of the realization
that there was a profitable black market and a number of
talented black actors (Sidney Poitier, Sammy Davis, Ossie
Davis, and Harry Belafonte).

Wayne held that the Hollywood studios of the 1970s
"are carrying their tokenism a little too far." And while he
believed that "there should be the same percentage of the
colored race in films as in society," he also realized that "it
can't always be that way," because "more than likely, ten
percent haven't trained themselves for that type of work."
"It's just as hard for a white man to get a card in the Hollywood craft unions," he said, which meant that it would take
a long time until blacks would be integrated into the film industry. He believed in gradual integration: "We can't all of
a sudden get down on our knees and turn everything over
to the leadership of blacks." At the same time, he considered their "resentment along with their dissent," to be
"rightfully so."[62]

What irritated blacks most was his belief in "white
supremacy until the blacks are educated to a point of responsibility. I don't believe in giving authority and positions of leadership and judgment to irresponsible people."
Challenged as to whether he was equipped to judge "which
blacks are irresponsible and which of their leaders inexperienced," he replied: "It's not my judgment. The academic
community has developed certain tests that determine whether

the blacks are sufficiently equipped scholastically." Thus,
he did not approve of blacks who tried "to force the issue
and enter college when they haven't passed the tests and
don't have the requisite background," fearing that by doing
so, "the academic society is brought down to the lowest common denominator." He refused to believe that "blacks have
been forbidden their right to go to school," because "they
were allowed in public schools wherever I've been." Moreover, he claimed there was a reverse discrimination in America: "I think any black who competes with a white today
gets a better break than a white man." But he never lost
his optimism about the tremendous opportunities in America:
"I wish they'd tell me where in the world they have it better than right here in America."[63]

Wayne and Presidential Elections

In the 1950s, Wayne became one of Hollywood's outfront
Republican actors and, along with Bob Hope, Lucille Ball,
Bing Crosby, Robert Taylor, and Jimmy Stewart, supported
Dwight D. Eisenhower in 1952 and in 1956. During the Cold
War, he felt that both parties were too soft with the Soviets
and too remiss in not selling American supremacy to the
world. "Why don't both our presidential candidates," asked
Wayne in 1960, "emphasize that this is the greatest nation in
the history of the world?" He was displeased with "the gentle treatment" of Khrushchev at the United Nations: "I want
to go on record saying I'm proud the President of the United
States is a gentleman, but I wouldn't care if he walked up
and punched Khrushchev in the nose. I'd applaud and hol-
ler, 'Attaboy Ike.'" "I want no one running our country,"
he stated, "who doesn't have the brains, strength, and pure
guts to face any other country that wants to take its best
shot at us."[64]

Wayne backed Richard M. Nixon in 1960, 1968, and
1972, and Senator Barry Goldwater in 1964. He never served
as delegate to a convention, preferring to rally and donate
contributions to his favorite candidates. Rumor has it that
George Wallace considered Wayne as a vice-presidential candidate, which the actor denied. "Mr. Wallace has some good
ideas," he said, "but I'm certainly not a backer of his."[65]
He also denied the rumor that he had given three weekly
checks, each for 10,000 dollars, to Wallace's campaign,

inscribing on the back of the last one, "Sock it to 'em, George."[66]

In 1968, Wayne feared The Green Berets "will help re-elect President Lyndon B. Johnson because it shows the war in Vietnam is necessary," and he was relieved when Johnson decided not to run for a second term. Wayne's speech at the 1968 Republican National Convention in Florida, which received wide TV and press coverage, gave him a unique opportunity to express his patriotic views. He recounted an earlier conversation with Dean Martin, who had asked him what were his hopes and dreams for his young daughter: "I told him I wanted her to be as grateful as I am. Grateful for every day of my life that I wake up in the United States of America." He said he would teach his daughter the Lord's Prayer and some of the Psalms, "I don't care if she memorizes the Gettysburg Address, but I hope she understands it."[67]

After winning the 1970 Oscar award, President Nixon told him on the telephone, "I'm proud of you, on-screen and off." He also received a congratulatory wire from former president Johnson; both Nixon and Johnson watched the Oscar show on television. Despite his partisan politics and consistent support of the Republican platform, he won the respect of Johnson and other Democratic leaders. Johnson called him on his sixty-fifth birthday to express his personal wishes. Challenged about his friendly connection with the Democrats, he said: "I was raised Republican, but when a good Jeffersonian Democrat does a good job, I'll say so."[68]

Wayne had a special relationship with President Nixon, whom he respected, particularly in his handling of the Vietnam War. "The only way to get 52,000 men home," he said, "was to make the decision to mine Haiphong Harbor," and Nixon "had the courage to make the decision." "When the other side started using prisoners of war as pawns," elaborated Wayne, "he had to make the awesome decision to bomb Hanoi, which he did, and then he brought the prisoners of war home."[69]

During the Watergate crisis, Wayne felt the press was hostile to Nixon and was "out to get him just because a bunch of jerk underlings acted stupidly." He believed that "the President is too great a man to be mixed up in anything

like Watergate," and reminded the public of his achievements
in foreign policy and his record in "China, inflation, and
Vietnam, a war he did not start."[70] He was therefore
shocked by the results of the scandal and Nixon's resignation. He credited reporters Bob Woodward and Carl Bern-
stein of the Washington Post for their investigation--he read
and enjoyed their first book, All the President's Men. But
he did not approve of their second, The Final Days: "They
made their points and got their fame and money, but it
wasn't enough and they went on to that dirty, vulturish
book, that so far as I'm concerned broke the heart of that
lovely lady, Pat Nixon."[71]

   Regarding Watergate as "a sad and tragic accident in
history," he stated firmly: "They're wrong, dead wrong
those men at Watergate. Men abused power, but the system
still works. Men abused money, but the system still works.
Men lied and perjured themselves, but the system still
works." He strongly believed in the American political system and was convinced that "when they're writing the history of this period, Watergate will be no more than a footnote."[72]

   Wayne was the chairman of an exclusive organization,
the Golden Circle Club, whose aim was to raise money to
elect Republican candidates to the Senate and the Assembly.
Members joined this club by invitation only, at fees ranging
from $1,000 to $5,000. He was also on the board of a group
that launched a campaign to ensure Spiro T. Agnew was on
the GOP ticket. Agnew's resignation, following the scandal
over his tax evasions, was yet another political blow. He
refused to comment on the incident, confirming that he endorsed Agnew's attitudes, but "I knew nothing of his private affairs," and "was sadly disappointed to discover his
feet of clay."[73]

   Wayne supported Ronald Reagan, his close friend,
throughout his political career, first as president of the
Screen Actors Guild (from 1947 to 1952 and in 1959-60),
then as governor of California (in 1966 and 1970), and finally as a presidential candidate in the 1976 Republican
nominations. He was reportedly furious at those poking fun
at the idea of having an actor for governor and later president. "Jimmy Stewart was a Colonel and he led 150 airplanes
across Berlin," he noted. "What is all this crap about Reagan

being an actor?"[74]   Once, on their way to Reagan's second
inauguration as governor, Stewart and Wayne encountered a
crowd of demonstrators waving the Vietcong flag. Stewart
had just lost a son in Vietnam. Wayne excused himself for
a moment and walked into a crowd; within seconds, the demonstration retreated.[75] He backed Reagan as the Republican
candidate in 1976, because he was "the last voice in the wilderness," as the nation drifted, in his view, toward "democratic despotism." He was an advocate of Reagan's policy of
"less regulation, less taxation," which he viewed as part and
parcel of Republican federalism.[76] When Reagan lost the
party's nomination, he rallied behind Gerald Ford. One suspects that, had he lived, Wayne would have been proud of
Reagan's regal style of presidency in the 1980s.

But despite partisan politics, he maintained good rapport with the Democrats. He accepted an invitation to the
preinaugural gala for president-elect Jimmy Carter in January 1977, shocking many of his fans. "I'm told it is a non-
political affair," he explained, "and the proceeds will be
used to cover the inaugural activities ... and will relieve
tha tax payers of that burden." He appreciated the invitation because after all, "he is my President too, and he
asked me."[77] Unlike the past, he now considered himself
"a member of the opposition, the loyal opposition," with "accent on loyal ... I would not have it any other way!"[78] He
said he occasionally wrote Carter a note about foreign policy
or other matters. President Carter proclaimed that Wayne
was one of his most favorite movie actors, and considered
him "a national asset." In May 1979 Carter visited him at
the hospital and told him he had the "love and affection and
best wishes, not only of all the people of our nation who admire him so much, but of millions of people around the
world."[79]

There has been no other actor who has won the consistent praise of six presidents: Eisenhower, Johnson,
Nixon, Ford, Carter, and Reagan. "Wayne was true grit
on and off the screen," said Nixon. "The screen roles he
played and the life he lived will inspire Americans of generations to come." Wayne was described by him as "a definite part of the education, or should we say the condition-
ing, of most Americans."[80] Former president Ford said that,
like so many other good Americans, Wayne "never lost that
sense that there is some higher good." "No one can discharge

his duties or obligations as a good citizen who isn't involved in causes," Ford continued, "even though they are somewhat controversial."[81] And former president Carter eulogized him as "a symbol of many of the most basic qualities that made America great." "In an age of few heroes," Carter elaborated, "he was the genuine article." "Wayne's ruggedness, tough independence, sense of personal conviction and courage --on and off the screen--reflected the best of our national character."[82]

The Mellowing of a Hawk

In the 1970s, Wayne showed little concern that the world around him had changed and that his ideas had become obsolete. Yet it is precisely this old-fashionedness that made people of all political persuasions accept him as an American institution. He became a legend in his own time, a term he said he disliked, but one suspects really enjoyed. He continued to advocate his old American ideals, but curiously, they increased rather than diminished his popularity. Wayne's fans and detractors agreed on one thing--what he said "is not nearly as important as the fact that he says it."[83]

After winning the Oscar award, his political views mellowed, even his lifelong hatred of Communism. "Communism is quite obviously still a threat," he proclaimed in 1974, "yet, they are human beings, with a right to their point of view." This statement is very different from his view of Communism a decade or two earlier. Not that he endorsed it as a legitimate ideology, "you certainly don't want your children to share their points of view." But his major concern now was to see that the Communists "don't disrupt what we've proven for 200 years to be a pretty workable system, in which human beings can get along and thrive."[84]

He also started to meet more frequently with the press, though he preferred to talk about his work rather than his politics, which was another significant change from the past. True, he muted many of his views, and observers noted that those he did express had become more moderate--just like his screen image. He deliberately avoided political arguments in talk shows and was reluctant to discuss controversial issues. In the past, he was pushed, he said, to make extreme statements that seemed bland orally, but outrageous when printed. There have been too many inaccurate and nasty remarks about his politics, which now he was determined to avoid. In fact, he became so sensitive to his public image that he demanded approval of every word written about him before granting an interview.

All of a sudden, his critics became aware that he was more intelligent, literate, and witty than he had ever been given credit for. People began to realize that his personality was more complex and volatile, that his views were more subtle than previously assumed. His basic views had not changed much; what changed was his style, the way he said things rather than what he said. His interviews became more cautious and his wording more self-conscious. He also became more tolerant of opposing views, determined to get involved only "when I think things need saying."[85]

This change of style had immediate results on his standing with the American public. He began to win the respect of people who used to despise him. Terry Robbins, a Chicago coordinator for the radical SDS, described Wayne as "terrific and total." "He's tough, down to earth, and he says and acts what he believes," Robbins said, "He's completely straight and really groovy." Abbie Hoffman, leader of the Yippie movement, admired Wayne's "wholeness, his style." Even those who continued to disagree with him on political grounds, found it impossible not to like him. "There are some people with whom I wouldn't agree politically," said singer Joan Baez, but "they haven't made themselves that offensive to me, like John Wayne."[86] She never forgot his appearance in Laugh-In, in which he held up a red-white-and-blue daisy and solemnly recited, "The sky is blue, the grass is green, get off your butt and be a Marine." This reflected, in her view, two important qualities he possessed: self-parody and naiveté.

Wayne said that one of the ways he changed was that he only spoke his mind when he had "something worth saying." Asked for his opinion of Jane Fonda, he replied, "I think she's a little mixed up in her thinking," and Fonda, in her reaction to his comment said, "I don't know the man, but I think he's got guts."[87] Wayne ignored his political differences with Jane Fonda and showed up at a party celebrating her Oscar award. Joan Baez, Jane Fonda, and others stood at the opposite pole of the political spectrum; they were to the Left what Wayne was to the Right, but they came to live with each other's views.

In the last decade of his life, his politics, unlike his screen image, defied easy labeling because it was inconsistent. "Nobody knows what my politics are," he said in 1976, "they think they do, but they don't." He even seemed to take the press less seriously: "The Eastern writers would always come out and ask me about my politics and I'd tell them, but I could see that they weren't the right answers. It wouldn't be what they'd expected, so they'd go off and write what I didn't say." At present, though, "when they ask me I tell them, 'Is this what you want me to say?' and I tell them what they expect to hear and they go away satisfied."[88]

One of the referendum issues on the California ballot in the 1972 elections was a proposition that would have rigidly codified public obscenity laws, encouraging arrests of pornography peddlers. Wayne, and nearly two-thirds of California's voters, found the proposition repressive and untenable. This "liberal" attitude astonished his friends, especially when in his radio commercials he told voters: "You don't get rid of a bad situation with a badly written law, or cut off a foot to cure a sore toe."[89]

Even more astonishing was his support of the Panama Canal treaties, which outraged many of his conservative fans. He became the target of hate mail, he said, accusing him of "falling off my horse too many times." However, he stood firm and justified his support: "I've recently studied the Treaties, and I supported them on the basis of my belief that America always looks to the future and that our people have demonstrated qualities of justice and reason for 200 years." He noted that when Eisenhower appeared to have given the sovereignty of the canal away, by allowing the Panamanian flag to fly there, "neither Congress, the press, nor the conservatives uttered any kind of cry."[90]

Wayne's support of political issues, if they were on the "right side," were sought by the administration. Lobbying for the legislation needed to implement the Panama treaties was one of his last public acts. In a mailgram to Thomas O'Neill, the House speaker, Wayne wrote: "We made a commitment to Panama and we must live up to it.... Is it too much to ask for a friendly nation which has sided with us in every international emergency since its existence?" He also sent a telegram to General Omar Torrijos, Panama's leader, offering "best wishes for a good relationship between our countries." He said he had sent the message as a matter of "polite protocol," after having had business and personal ties in Panama for almost 40 years.

The best indication of his mellowing was his attitude toward the younger generation, "the future of America." Unlike the past, he now said he did not blame the kids for their restlessness and that "ideally, they're right, of course, in demonstrating for what they believe." But he still wished "they knew more about Communism than just its theories. I wish they knew its reality." He could not tolerate seeing some of them carrying the Vietcong flag in demonstrations. "Many people seem to stupidly think," he warned, "that by just doing anything, Communism will go away. It won't. And then we'll have another Dark Age."[91]

He always felt it was "much easier for me to start a conversation with a younger person than the other way round."[92] And he did; the kids who appeared in The Cowboys were all over him all the time. He did not think there was a great difference between yesterday's and today's kids: "I think it's more a matter of our social and political leaders changing their attitudes rather than the kids changing theirs." However, he thought "there's not enough 'Don't do that! and don't touch!'" As his movies stated, he believed that human behavior "requires a certain amount of restraint from the responsible people in the country to keep the young generation on the straight-and-narrow."[93] "Kids today are thrown in contact with temptations to new experiences that my generation wasn't," because "communication is so much better." However, "it hasn't seemed to affect the younger generation as the blue noses would expect." "The only generation gap," he said humorously, was "soap and water ... Goddamn, if they'd just wash a little more."[94]

He became increasingly aware of his functions as a public figure, functions that went beyond being a movie star. He lectured against the use of drugs to youngsters on several occasions. In 1972 he went with Bob Hope to his former school, the University of Southern California, to talk to

students. He insisted on writing his own speech, about the
radical movements on campus, the university as a learning
place, and the importance of tradition. He told the students
they should have respect for the faculty and for the institution, that violence and vandalism are never justified, and
that they do not have the right to control their schools because they are owned by the taxpayers of California. He
later reconstructed this experience: "When I stood up to
speak, Bob Hope went over to the other side of the stage.
He thought I was going to get everything in the place thrown
at me. And so did I."[95] At first, there was booing and
hissing, but once again his honesty and straightforwardness
proved winning and by the end of his speech the students
gave him a standing ovation.

Wayne complained that the younger generation "doesn't
seem to have any respect for authority anymore." "These
student dissenters," he said, "act like children who have to
get their own way about everything." "Under the guise of
doing good, these kids are causing a hell of a lot damage,"
and "they're starting something they're not going to be able
to finish." He also denounced the youngsters' challenge of
"every law in the U.S. and the rules of decent personal conduct, which we have established through generations and
generations of human relationships." "It's sad that each
time they do something provocatively, they get so much newspaper and TV space," because "it's only one or two percent
of the kids who are involved in things like taking over college offices." "All the publicity draws other kids to them,
the hero-worshippers," instead of being classed "as they
should be, as an unwelcome part of our social life." He
was even more upset with the faculty: "They get away with
it because maybe 10 percent of the teaching community is
behind them, urging them on."[96] He could not conceal his
bias against intellectuals and academics, also expressed in
his movies. "It takes fifteen years of kissing somebody's
backside for a professor to get a chair somewhere and then
he is a big shot in a little world, passing his point of view
to a lot of impressionable kids." He considered the academic
world an ivory tower, with its inhabitants possessing "a completely theoretical point of view of how it [the world] should
be run and what we should do for our fellow men."[97] Once,
in a moment of anger, he claimed that "the disorders in the
schools are caused by immature professors who have encouraged activists."[98]

The Harvard Lampoon Club invited Wayne in January 1974 to premiere his film McQ in Cambridge, challenging him to debate its liberal students. The club's editors sent him a cynical invitation: "We've heard you're supposed to be some kind of legend, everybody talks about your he-man prowess, your pistol-packing, rifle-toting, frontier-taming, cattle-demeaning talents, your unsurpassed greatness in the guts department." "You think you're tough," wrote James M. Downey in the invitation, "We're not so tough. We dare you to have it out, head on, with the young whelps here who would call the supposedly unbeatable John Wayne, the biggest fraud in history." Wayne liked the "guts" of the challenge, but replied, "Sorry to note in your challenge that there is weakness in your breedings, but there is a ray of hope in the fact that you are conscious of it."[99] Provoked by their suggestion that "I didn't have the courage to go," he decided to attend.

He was not in the greatest company; the previous visitor of the Lampoon Club was Linda Lovelace, the star of the pornographic movie Deep Throat. But amused by the mock of it, he showed up with an iron horse and soldier sidekicks, provided by the Army Reserves, much to the dissatisfaction of the Pentagon. He arrived in a tanklike personnel carrier, stood in the hatch carrying an unloaded and inoperative gun. Some Lampoon members dressed as cowboys, firing toy guns, while others threw snowballs at him. But he took the whole thing humorously and throughout the ceremony waved and signed autographs.

Wayne first met with the club's editors, then faced a mass meeting of students, who fired questions fast, but he answered all of them. The following is a sample of the exchange:

Q: Do you look at yourself as the fulfillment of the American Dream?

A: I don't look at myself more than I have to.

Q: Is the session being taped?

A: Well, if it is I hope the guy taping is is a Democrat, because if he's Republican you would lose it.

Q: Would Nixon portray John Wayne in the filmed biography of Wayne's career?

A: Well, Richard's good enough actor to do it, I suppose.

Q: What's your opinion of the women's liberation
     movement?

A: I think women have a right to work anywhere
     they want to ... as long as they have dinner
     when we want it.

Once again, he proved he could handle any crowd and any
query. Extremely relaxed, he seemed to have great fun
communicating with the students. As time went by their
initial hostility subsided and he won the students over. In
the midst of the debate, a female student shouted, "I don't
care what they say, you're still a man!"[100]

13. THE PROPAGANDIST

The integration between Wayne's screen image and his
real life was so remarkable that it is unlikely that there will
ever be such a special linking of a private man with his
screen image. As Vincent Canby stated, "in no other actor
of recent decades, has the confusion between the private
person and the public personality been so complete."[1] Wayne
succeeded in convincing his audiences that his screen image
and personal life were inseparable, to the point where it was
impossible to determine whether he had gradually become his
film heroes or whether he transformed his roles into personal
statements of his politics. Underlying this process was a
very conscious use of the screen as an ideological weapon,
promoting two different types of propaganda, political and
sociological.[2]

Political propaganda usually involves techniques of influence used by a political group (government, party) to affect the public's political behavior. The themes and objec-
tives of this propaganda are limited to the political arena,
and it is most effective in the short run, when its aims are
specifically defined. Political propaganda is therefore most
effective during election campaigns or duing national crises,
such as wars or revolutions. Sociological propaganda, by contrast, is much more comprehensive because it aims at affecting the entire lifestyle, not just political opinions. This
propaganda provides the means by which society seeks to
integrate and unify its members according to a desirable
pattern. Advertising in America, for example, aims at economic ends in the short run, but its long-run purpose is to
spread a certain lifestyle, what some critics have labeled the
American way of life. It is much more difficult to grasp sociological propaganda because it is diffuse, spontaneous, and based
on a general atmosphere that influences without having the
appearance of propaganda. Its goal is to make each individual

305

participate actively in society through adaptation to a specific way of life. Sociological propaganda can express itself
in many forms, education and schooling, technology, advertising and consumerism and, of course, popular culture, television, and movies. The 1934 Production Code of the Motion Picture Association has been analyzed as a form of sociological propaganda because it was specifically designed to promote "the proper conception of society," "the proper standards of life," and "to avoid any ridicule of the law (natural
and human) or sympathy for those who violate the law."[3]

Wayne's films were replete with sociological propaganda,
intentionally as well as unintentionally, consciously and subconsciously. Some ideas recurred in his movies because he
took them for granted as basic tenets of American life. But
the propaganda in his films gradually became more calculated
and deliberate. The American way of life functioned for
Wayne both as an ideology and a criterion of value: everything that expressed or reinforced it was good, and everything that criticized or disturbed it was bad. And once this
way of life was used as the criterion or measure, other
judgments necessarily followed, such as the idea that anything un-American is evil and must be conquered, be it
Communists in his political movies, Japanese and Nazis in
his war movies, outlaws in his Westerns, and weak or corrupt men in his other pictures.

Wayne was a true prophet of the American way of life,
committed to it as a unifying force and instrument of assimi-
lating the diverse elements of American society: ethnic minorities, religious groups, and even political parties. His
aim was to achieve psychological unity and sociological stan-
dardization, based on the lifestyle of white, middle-class,
capitalist America. In this respect he succeeded more as an
agitator than politican, to follow philosopher Jacques Ellul's
terms. The agitator stirs public opinion by appealing to
principles and values but, unlike the politician, does not engage directly in political action nor propose specific reforms.
Wayne was against any un-American or foreign element, be
it socialist, Communist, or internationalist. More specifically, he was against the values of the New Deal, favoring instead
laissez-faire liberalism, in politics as well as economics.

Wayne's movies aimed at reaching adolescents at their
most impressionable age, with no strong identities formed

and not yet integrated into society. His propaganda worked most effectively on this age group because they took it at face value, without much questioning. Like other agitators, Wayne's forms of propaganda were diffuse and pervasive, aiming at the promulgation of general ideas rather than specific doctrines or actions. His was a propaganda of integration, of conformity, based on the idea that every American should share the same beliefs--and prejudices too.[4] He worked by himself, outside the ranks of any political party or group, using his immense power as a movie star, though his sympathies were clearly with the Republican Party.

Wayne's movies functioned as both political and sociological propaganda. Sociological propaganda acts slowly, gently, by gradual integration, and it is most effective in relatively stable eras. It is less adequate in times of crisis, where a more specific and more political propaganda is needed. In political crises, the ideological weakness calls for a stronger need to redefine the prevailing dominant culture, to make it at once more explicit and more conscious. Sociological propaganda is therefore more efficient in preparing the background for a more direct political propaganda.

A continuous interplay between these two kinds of propaganda permeated Wayne's work. His political movies were made during times of national crisis: the inspirational war movies during World War II, the anti-Communist films during the McCarthy era, and the pro-Vietnam movie at the height of this conflict. Sociological propaganda, by contrast, appeared in most of his movies, particularly in the last two decades of his career, when he assumed tremendous power, on-screen and off.

Political Propaganda

Wayne's main objective in making movies was entertainment for the entire family but, as he said during his work on The Alamo, "if at the same time, I can strike a blow for liberty, then I'll stick one in."[5] Along with his flag-waving war movies, Wayne made other political features that were blatant in their anti-Communist propaganda.

The first and possibly most notable of these was Big Jim McLain, a Wayne-Fellows production released through

Warners in 1952. Perfunctorily directed by Edward Ludwig,
its screenplay was written by Richard English, James E.
Grant, and Eric Taylor. Wayne plays a special agent for
the House Un-American Activities Committee who, along with
a fellow investigator (James Arness) sets out to investigate
the activities of a worldwide Communist ring in Hawaii. The
Communists' assignment is to halt vital shipping to Korea
through a work stoppage engineered by a labor leader, and
an epidemic is also planned by a Communist bacteriologist.

Wayne's character, Jim McLain, had the same initials
of Senator Joseph McCarthy, which was seen as more than
coincidence. Wayne made the picture while he served as
president of the Motion Picture Alliance. It is doubtful that
other actors, less popular than he, would have agreed to
play such a role. It is one of his most propagandistic films,
enhancing his image as right-winger and anti-Communist
much more than his political statements offscreen. He himself believed that Big Jim McLain helped the election of Senator McCarthy for a second term in 1952.

The screenplay was crude and blatant in its ideological
propaganda. The Communists are depicted in the film as a
bunch of pseudointellectuals and ruthless gangsters engaged
in criminal activities, in which immoral party leaders callous-
ly sacrifice their fellow members. Big Jim McLain also uncritically praised the activities of HUAAC, without questioning its power to jail people for contempt of court, or its
damaging effects on the careers of many artists it summoned.
And it clearly reflects Wayne's disgust with the way members
of the Communist Party took refuge behind the Fifth Amendment. The movie ends with a question: What can be done
with unpatriotic traitors who hide behind the very Constitu-
tion they aim to destroy? Furthermore, it implies that the
investigations are futile so long as the Communists can use
the protection of the Fifth Amendment. Still, at the end of
the picture, Wayne decides not to quit his work as investigator, despite serious doubts, because it is not in the
American--or Wayne's--way to quit a patriotic mission.

Most critics' reaction to the film was harsh, with
Crowther finding it hard to tell whether it is "supposed to
be taken seriously as a documentation," of the work of the
HUAAC, "or whether it is merely intended to arouse and
entertain." In his "direct, uncomplicated raid," on the

Communists, Crowther wrote, Wayne demonstrated that "the best medicine for a cowardly Communist is a sock in the nose," based on his character's attitude that "it is painful to think too deeply, and the fist is mightier than the brain." And he concluded: "The over-all mixing of cheap fiction with a contemporary crisis in American life is irresponsible and unforgivable."[6] Guernsey of the Herald Tribune was even harsher, depicting Big Jim McLain as "part travelogue, part documentary-type melodrama, and part love story," but being "pedestrian in all of these phases." "A minor thriller," he summed up the end result, "padded out with some rather poor commercials for our most excellent product of American democracy."[7]

The movie received, comparatively speaking, better notices in California than in New York. "Commendable as it is in purpose, and presenting as it does a new slant on the Red Menace," wrote the Los Angeles Times, "this feature is unfortunately too sketchy in its dealing with its plot."[8] "For all its authentic backgrounds, timeliness of its topic, and the extremely good work from the actors involved," noted the Hollywood Citizen News, "Big Jim McLain is not much more than standard melodrama."[9] The Los Angeles Examiner thought that Wayne brings to his role "an added potency, a sort of 'I mean every word of this' quality, which comes through like a beacon light."[10] But most praising of all was the Hollywood Reporter, stating that "the testimony of its success is the thoughtful anger it arouses in audiences," and that it is "a successful motion picture from any angle."[11] The movie was much more commercially successful than most anti-Communist films of the 1950s, grossing close to $3 million in the United States.

Variety praised Big Jim McLain's "timely subject" and "excellent dialogue,"[12] which was ludicrous, because this was its major shortcoming; it was vulgar and simplistic. To appeal to mass audiences, the producers conceived it as "a gangster-action film," but by equating Communism with terrorism, it "could have only reinforced the feelings of the very simple-minded,"[13] as critic Eyles wrote. The film's overall assessment was succinctly described by Alexander Walker: "As film-making, it was unconvincing; as propaganda, it was hysterical. By implication, it gave its nod of approval to informers and offered its pardon to Communists who confessed their errors."[14]

Another propagandistic film was <u>Blood Alley</u>, based on A.S. Fleischman's novel, produced by Batjac, and directed by William Wellman. Supposedly an adventure film, it is replete with anti-Communist slogans, depicting the escape of the Chiku Shan village in Red China to freedom in Hong Kong. Wayne plays a courageous merchant marine captain rescued from a Red jail by the villagers who need his knowledge of currents and ports to guide them in their escape. He is intrigued by the idea of "a whole village scratched off the Red map and put down in Hong Kong." Wayne's condescending, paternalistic attitudes are demonstrated throughout the movie. For example, he is extremely considerate with a pro-Communist family that had poisoned the food on the ship. "Your China is misguided," he tells them, but he also gives them opportunity to continue to Hong Kong, which all but one take. At the end, Wayne guides the villagers through the 300-mile blood alley and is praised for accomplishing his mission.

<u>Blood Alley</u> was not received favorably by the critics, though some thought it was rather "a good comic-strip adventure and incidentally far more effective anti-Communist propaganda than <u>Big Jim McLain</u>."[15] The movie was also better received than Wayne's preceding vehicle, <u>Sea Chase</u>, another sea adventure, which was nonetheless bonanza at the box office. And once again, the West Coast reception of <u>Blood Alley</u> was more favorable than its Eastern counterpart. Critic Philip Schewer described it as "a good movie of the old epic school,"[16] though it was less successful at the box office than either <u>Big Jim McLain</u> or <u>Sea Chase</u>, grossing $2 million in domestic rentals.

RKO's <u>Jet Pilot</u> was even more embarrassing than <u>Blood Alley</u>, but no less propagandistic than <u>Big Jim McLain</u>. Initiated by Howard Hughes, it was produced and written by Jules Furthman and directed by Josef von Sternberg; it was his first color film and his only comedy. Sternberg had no control over the casting and was forced to start shooting before the script had been completed. He was told by Hughes and Furthman that they did not want an erotic movie, of the kind he made so well with Marlene Dietrich, but a "strict" reading of the scenario, with priority to the aerial sequences.[17] <u>Jet Pilot</u>'s budget was exceptionally big, close to $2 million, because it had to be reshot and reedited several times, though each time it worsened. Shooting began in 1950 and was completed in seven weeks, but then it was reprocessed for the wide screen. Later, Hughes rehired a second team to update the air footage, and the actors were brought back for extra work. It was finally released in September 1957, seven years after its preparation had begun.

One would expect a reasonably good film after so much work and money, but it was a clinker or, as Sternberg described it, "a lamentable failure," due to the fact that he accepted "a cart-before-the-horse assignment."[18] Ironically, Sternberg's previous achievements were forgotten, for he was asked to take a test to demonstrate his directorial abilities. Sternberg's direction was not great, though he had no say over the casting or the screenplay. Indeed, the major problem was the script, because it was not only crudely replete with stereotypical characters, but downright silly. Janet Leigh played a Soviet flyer who lands at an American air base, claiming to have escaped from the Soviet Union. Wayne's Colonel Shannon is assigned by Washington to get information from her on the Soviet Air Force. When Washington realizes she is not going to reveal any secrets, they decide to jail her, but Wayne marries her, unaware that she is a spy. When he finds out, they escape to the Soviet Union to avoid jail. But back in Siberia, she begins to see her home in a negative light. Soon she is full of criticism of the Soviet system, which motivates them to escape to America with secret information and a Soviet jet. They wind up in Palm Springs eating oversized steaks!

The propagandistic elements in Jet Pilot were beyond belief, even in the context of the 1950s. Every idea was made literal, in case audiences might miss its "significance." For example, Anna realizes that the Soviet system does not work when the door knobs come off in her hand, or when suddenly there is no light. Just about everything is inferior to the luxurious, good life she experienced in America. The symbols of American affluence are elegant nightgowns and lingerie or a big steak. Newsweek described the film as Janet Leigh falls in love with John Wayne and Capitalism.[19] For her investigation, Leigh is taken, of all places, to Palm Springs. "There is a kind of 'Rovers Boys' approach to serious problems," the Hollywood Reporter observed, "a frolicsome attitude about deadly situations, such as the Russian treatment of opposition from its own citizens and others, that is in questionable taste."[20]

John Wayne, as an American colonel, and Janet Leigh, as a Russian pilot, in Josef von Sternberg's Jet Pilot (RKO Radio, 1957), a film that took seven years to release and one of the most naively propagandistic features, using elegant lingerie as a symbol of American affluence.

The dialogue of Jet Pilot is outrageous, particularly the romantic love scenes. In one Leigh tells Wayne: "One minute I want to kill you, the next minute, I want to kiss you and kiss you." Leigh, for whom the movie was made, looks and sounds ridiculous, maintaining her American appearance, without even attempting a Russian accent; her command of English is perfect! The "corny approach to sex," noted one critic, is "a dog-eared copy of Film Fun magazine, one of the early cheesecake books,"[21] and another described it as "a make-believe juvenile fantasy."[22] In another scene, Leigh submits to Wayne's search by removing one garment after another, while jets overhead function as a substitute to the audiences' whistling.

Most critics could not take this trifle seriously.

Crowther wrote that the film was so "silly" that "we blush
to tell you what is its story." And as for the performers,
they play their "quaint roles like a couple of fumbling kids."[23]
The seven years that elapsed between its production and release showed how dated the material was, though it is doubtful that audiences in 1950 would have digested its ideas.
Curiously, screenwriter Furthman believed that the movie's
release was delayed because "we kid the Russian situation,
and the tone was not quite the right tone to use during the
Korean war."[24]

Jet Pilot enjoyed less than moderate success and, after
its short initial run, Hughes withdrew it from the market for
over two decades. In 1979, Universal City Studios acquired
from Summa Corps eight movies produced by Hughes for $1.5
million, including Jet Pilot and The Conqueror. Neither was
ever licensed on television and, for twenty years they were
seen by Hughes alone. Premiering on television in October
1981, Jet Pilot proved that the only way to enjoy it was as
high camp.

Remember the Alamo

The Alamo reflected Wayne's personal politics more
than any other movie, working on it intermittently for 14
years. It began with some research in Texas in 1946, then
with the support of Herbert J. Yates, Wayne scouted locations in Panama in 1949. Because the picture had been a
dream of Wayne's for years, he was extremely disappointed
when Yates changed his mind and withdrew his support.
But he was so committed to the idea that he decided to produce and direct the movie by himself. There have been
other movies on the subject, such as D.W. Griffith's Martyrs
of the Alamo, which he did not direct, the first historical
Western to deal with the topic. Or Republic's Man of Conquest in 1939, an interesting account of the life of hero Sam
Houston. Nonetheless, the story was never approached with
the dedication and attempted scope and grandeur of Wayne.

Wayne was initially going to play a small part in order
to devote his entire time and energies to the film's production. United Artists, however, agreed to back the project
only if he starred in it; they felt, with good reason, that it
was too much of a risk without him. The Alamo became

Wayne's most ambitious project, involving himself in every minor aspect of the production. Wayne believed that it was "the big American story that I don't think anyone could do better than I." "It's the first time in my life," he proudly stated, "that I've been able to express what I feel about people."[25] He said he gambled "all my money and my soul," and hoped it would pay off, "and I don't mean just in money."[26] He hoped that "something more than profits will result from The Alamo," that "the battle fought there will remind people today that the price of liberty and freedom is not cheap." Making the picture, he said, "has given me the privilege of feeling useful in this world. If there is anything better than that, I don't know what it is." There was a tremendous sense of pride in playing "a part in bringing this picture to the world."[27]

Wayne wrote his own publicity for the movie: "We wanted to recreate a moment in history which will show to this living generation of Americans what their country really stands for, and to put in front of their eyes the bloody truth of what some of their forebears went through to win what they had to have or die--liberty and freedom."[28] He intended it to be at once a message film, "it's America, a segment of history," and "entertainment." The motive behind making it was his lack of patience with "those pseudo-sophisticates, the people who belittle honor, courage, cleanliness." These are "perilous times," he felt, "when the eyes of the world are on us," and "we must sell America to countries threatened with Communist domination."[29] His greatest wish was that the cry, "Remember the Alamo," would "put new heart and new faith into all the world's free people," that the movie would "shake hell out of the world."[30]

The picture was supposed to demonstrate the value that "in order to live decently, one must be prepared to die decently." The Alamo's appeal was aimed at "all who have an interest in a thing called freedom," because "I think we've all been going soft, taking freedom for granted." He viewed Texas's struggle for independence, not only as "one of the most heroic moments in American history," but also as a "metaphor of America." He wanted the film to "show the world the sort of spirit and indomitable will for freedom that I think still dominates the thinking of Americans, despite this contaminated celluloid, which is the exception, not the rule, of Hollywood."[31]

John Wayne (right), Laurence Harvey (center), and Richard
Widmark in The Alamo (United Artists, 1960), the most ambitious and greatest disappointment in Wayne's professional
career.

Wayne portrayed David Crockett, the former member
of the House of Representatives from Tennessee, who turned
up at the Alamo with 23 patriots and died for the idea of a
free Texas. Earlier, he considered playing Sam Houston
(played by Richard Boone), and later, regretted not playing
Colonel Travis (played by Laurence Harvey), who commanded
a Texas force completely destroyed by Santa Anna's Mexican
army. At the time, however, Wayne's identification with
David Crockett was complete. Asked if there were any particular historical figure he might have liked to be, his immediate response was David Crockett. There is an abundance of value statements in The Alamo about patriotism,
democracy, the sacredness of life and death, and even religion. Following the death of one of his men, Wayne addresses a long entreaty to God, whom he calls "Sir." In
another scene, he expresses his personal view: "Republic--

I like the sound of the word. It's one of those words that
makes me tight in the throat."

 The Alamo's release was neatly timed for the presidential election year, opening in California in July 1960 and in
New York in October, a few weeks prior to the elections.
Most reviews were at best lukewarm, though the critics did
not speak with one voice. "How this complete rearrangement
of frontier iconography is likely to hit that generation of
youngsters," wrote Crowther, "is a speculation that scares
us. Is the whole warp and weft of their belief in American
history likely to be shredded?" "For all its bigness--and
big and long it certainly is!" Crowther noted, "it is but another beleaguered blockhouse Western."[32] The battle and
action scenes were praised by the New York Herald Tribune
for their "energy" and "visual excitement," but its critic
found Wayne to lack "John Ford's agility and pointedness as
a director." He also criticized the dialogue, which tended
"to orate, to spell out in paragraphs certain sentiments of
patriotism and religion that one feels would have been better
seen than heard."[33] The screenplay came under the severest attack for its homespun quality, which some, like the
Newsweek reviewer, found "silly and banal." "The history
book was a great deal better," he wrote, finding the film
"meandering and talking too much."[34] The New York Post
reviewer also focused on the script, which "sinks almost to
the juvenile levels at its worst and rises only to heavy educational speeches at best."[35]

 The reaction to the movie on the West Coast was once
again better than its Eastern counterpart. "Wayne realized
his dream of many years," wrote the Los Angeles Times, and
"if he failed, he still would have deserved an A for effort."
Although "it may not be the last word on the subject--it will
stand, particularly in its several battle sequences, as the
definitive one for a long time to come."[36] "The Alamo is a
well-timed new movie spectacular, wrote the Los Angeles Mirror in an overall praising review, arriving during a period
"when a wary America is in the mood for a rousing patriotic
shot in the arm." This critic liked the film's boost, "with a
Fourth of July cannon-cracker which is likely to move many
viewers emotionally."[37] Because Wayne said that he made it
as a message film, comparisons with his other political films
were inevitable. One critic felt that The Alamo's message
"exemplified that it was better to be dead than Mexican,

similar in many ways to the message of <u>Big Jim McLain</u> that
it was better to be dead than 'Red.'"[38]

The film's advertisement campaign was not only extensive, but also overly propagandistic. One ad compared the
Alamo's fighters with contemporary politicians: "There were
no ghostwriters at the Alamo, only men." The movie campaigned with the highest promotional drive, managing to receive seven Academy Award nominations, including Best Picture. One full-page ad read: "What will Oscar say this
year to the world?" with a small picture of the battered for-
tress below. Wayne was reported to have spent a huge
amount of money on advertisement, and his publicist, Russell Bidwell, was accused of "buying nominations" and later
Academy votes. A whole controversy followed concerning
the ethics of advertising movies and individual performers.
One critic resented the fact that "Oscar voters are being
appealed to on a patriotic basis," and the notion that "one's
proud sense of Americanism may be suspected if one does
not vote for <u>The Alamo</u>."[39] At Wayne's request, Bidwell
replied to this accusation, claiming that "this is a gratui-
tous and erroneous conclusion."[40]

At the annual Oscar show, <u>The Alamo</u> turned out to be
a big loser, demonstrating not only that it was a mediocre
picture, but that its ad campaign might have been effective
in the nomination but not in the winning process. It was
up against Billy Wilder's <u>The Apartment</u>, which won Best
Picture; <u>Elmer Gantry</u>, <u>Sons and Lovers</u>, and <u>The Sundown-
ers</u>. <u>The Alamo</u> won only one technical award: best sound
to Gordon E. Sawyer and Fred Hynes. The audience's response also disappointed Wayne's hopes for a blockbuster.
Highly priced, it cost over $12 million, with immense pre-
production costs: it took almost two years to build the
replica of the Alamo in Bracketsville, Texas, and location
shooting lasted over four months. The movie grossed a little over $7 million in domestic rentals, though it was much
more successful abroad. Wayne denied reports that the film
was a fiasco, but admitted that he did not make any money
on it because he made a bad deal. He later sold his percentage to United Artists, which made some profits on subsequent rereleases, including television. <u>The Alamo</u> coin-
cided with the beginning of the Kennedy administration and
a new era in American politics. By 1960, relations between
the United States and the Soviet Union had improved, after

a decade of Cold War. Wayne himself claimed that such a
time was hardly propitious to remember the Alamo.

However, there were minor rewards he treasured, such
as a viewer's letter to the Los Angeles Times: "We were so
moved by its message," wrote Dr. Sven Wahlroos, "that we
feel we must write and urge all patriotic citizens to see this
magnificent film." "It has been at least 20 years," he continued, "since movies were made as a tribute to gallantry,
chivalry, and patriotism. We had lost hope of ever seeing
such a movie from Hollywood again." And he concluded:
"My wife is a refugee from Hungary. She saw in the Alamo
the siege of Budapest in 1944 and 1956. I am from Finland.
I saw in this film a tribute to Finnish valor and to the fight
for freedom of all people everywhere."[41] This is precisely
the kind of impact Wayne was hoping The Alamo would have
on its viewers.

Wayne regarded the film as the realization of his personal and political ambitions and continued to defend its message for the rest of his life. Once, on Irv Kupcinet's talk
show in Chicago, he clashed with Herman Finer, a University
of Chicago professor. "We were talking about the picture
and the definition of a hero," he recalled, "and this professor started right out twisting words in my mouth and said
that all the good traditions were just legends." According
to the star, Finer also said he was afraid to let his wife and
daughters go out on the streets of Chicago. Wayne restrained
himself while the show was on the air, but later attacked the
professor: "The people who developed Chicago didn't know
whether they were going to be alive the next day, or whether
their kids would be chopped by the Indians, or whether they
could raise enough food to develop this place for you. And
you are whining, sitting in your easy chair over at the university and teaching kids this philosophy?"[42]

Wayne felt that if The Alamo were rereleased in 1963,
during the crisis between the Soviet Union and the United
States, it "would have done better," because "America's mind
is more intelligent now."[43] The film has been shown with
great success on television, usually on the Fourth of July.
And many people have changed their minds about it as time
has passed. Critic Canby was one of them, holding that although The Alamo's "drama is primitive, the characterizations
far from subtle and the politics questionable, the film has a

visual sweep that lends grandeur to its concept of history."
"What's important is not what he was saying," Canby noted,
"but how he was saying it. The Duke has style."[44] In
1978, Wayne felt the mood of the country had changed and
that the movie could be rereleased because "even the liberals
aren't so blatantly against me anymore that they wouldn't
recognize there was something to that picture besides my
terrible conservative attitude."[45]

The Green Berets

Upon returning from his 1966 visit to Vietnam, Wayne
decided to make a movie on the Green Berets. He wrote to
President Johnson that "it was extremely important that not
only the people of the U.S., but those all over the world
should know why it was necessary for us to be there." Apparently, his view of the conflict was much harsher than the
administration's, for the first draft of the script was rejected
as too strongly anti-Communist. Michael Wayne, the film's
producer, did not tell his father about it because "I was
actually afraid that he would say, 'You dumb son of bitch!'"
Jack Valenti, then the president's communications assistant,
reportedly told Johnson: "Wayne's politics [are] wrong, but
in so far as Vietnam is concerned, his views are right. If
he made the picture he would be saying the things we want
said."[46] Consequently, Batjac received the administration's
blessing and support.

James Lee Barret's screenplay was based on the best-
selling novel by Robin Moore, who attributed the book's success to the American people's need for a hero image at times
that lacked such heroes. The book also inspired a song,
"The Ballad of the Green Berets," whose sales topped 3 million copies in a few weeks. Many changes, Moore claimed,
were imposed on the screenplay by the Department of Defense in order to keep up an unpopular war.

The movie aroused political controversies even before
it went into production. Wayne denounced warnings that he
would "lose his shirt at the box-office," because "people
don't want to be reminded that our boys are dying in Vietnam."[47] He reportedly turned down other screenplays about
World War II (Dirty Dozen) in order to realize his ambition.
Most Hollywood studios, however, steered clear of the project.

John Wayne was the producer, director, and star of The
Green Berets (Warner-Seven Arts, 1968), the first major
Hollywood film about the Vietnam War.

United Artists, for example, showed some interest in The
Green Berets, but later backed out. Wayne decided to produce it himself and release it through Warner-Seven Arts.

Wayne's motive was to glorify the American soldiers as
the finest fighting men "without going into why we are there,
or if they should be there." He felt "compulsion," he said,
to do the movie because he was "so proud of our men, particularly of the Special Forces," and he was determined to
show "what a magnificent job this still little-known branch of
service is doing." "I wasn't trying to send a message out
to anybody," he reasoned, "or debating whether it is right
or wrong for the United States to be in this war."[48] He
was accused, however, by liberal groups of glorifying an
unpopular war, which irritated him: "What war was ever
popular for God's sake? Those men don't want to be in
Vietnam anymore than anyone else." "Once you go over
there," he said, "you won't be middle-of-the-road."[49]

But even Wayne set his film cautiously in 1963, when the war was less controversial and the issues clearer. At that time, the official role of the U.S. force was limited to "advise" the South Vietnamese Army. The narrative starts with the Green Berets' training at the John F. Kennedy School for Special Warfare in North Carolina. Wayne's Colonel Michael Kirby, a dedicated career officer, is contrasted in the movie with a pacifist war correspondent (David Janssen), who has doubts about the American involvement in Vietnam. But at the end of the film, the correspondent changes his mind about the war and pitches in with the fighting men, committed as they are to its noble cause.

The screenplay of The Green Berets was simple-minded and modeled on Wayne's Western formula. The outpost, for instance, was named Dodge City, after a popular Western starring Errol Flynn. And Wayne delivers such lines as "Out here, due process is a bullet," in a vein similar to that in many of his Westerns. He plays his role as yet another cavalry officer, this time fighting the North Vietnamese (not the Indians), but the morality is basically the same. Even his motives for making the picture seemed to be taken from one of his Westerns. "This is the right course" for the United States because "we gave our word," a phrase taken from Fort Apache, in which Wayne's hero gives his word to the Indians, which is binding. Wayne was eternally concerned with the image of the United States abroad: "For a number of years we established a pretty good picture of America throughout the world with these pictures, but they don't think of that nowadays."[50]

Most critics panned The Green Berets as film and as politics. One critic wrote that "people who are against the Vietnamese war will consider this picture vicious propaganda," whereas "people who are for it have a choice; they can consider the picture a rousing war tale in the John Wayne muscular tradition, or a solid blow for our side."[51] "Wayne's war could not be simpler," stated the Newsweek critic, "Wayne has over the long years of vocational superheroism and avocational superpatriotism, preserved his innocence intact."[52] Schickel of Life magazine also found the film to be "stupid ideologically speaking--as you were afraid it would be--and far worse as an action film than you suspected it could be." The war fought in The Green Berets,

Schickel continued, "bears no resemblance whatever to the
reality of Vietnam," because Wayne's "reference point is not
life but movie tradition, as he is still fighting the same battle he waged 20 or 30 years ago."[53]

Other critics were even harsher, as Korda's review in
Glamour magazine attests: "There is no room, even in a free
society, for the kind of obscenity that this film represents,
and I do not know how it would be possible to produce a
more revolting motion picture, short of giving Martin Bor-
mann several million dollars to make a technicolor movie showing that Auschwitz was a wonderful place to live." Korda
thought the film was "immoral, in the deepest sense," and
"simple-minded in praise of killing, brutality and American
superiority over Asians."[54] But "worst" of all was Renata
Adler's report in the New York Times: "The Green Berets
is a film so unspeakable, so stupid, so rotten and false in
every detail that it passes through being fun, through being funny, through being camp, through being everything."
"Vile and insane," the movie had the effect of saying that
"the left-wing extremist's nightmare of what we already are,
has become the right wing extremist's ideal of what we ought
to be."[55]

Unlike the past, this time, the reaction of West Coast
critics was only slightly milder. Kevin Thomas wrote in the
Los Angeles Times that The Green Berets is just another
John Wayne movie and that "it's a sincere but dismayingly
clumsy patriotic gesture." He also pointed out weaknesses
that other critics ignored because they were too preoccupied
with its ideology. The major problem was "the very lack of
confidence Wayne himself inspires," being 61 and thus too
old for the part. Thomas found one of the film's most disturbing and curiously touching aspects to be "the betrayal
of a great star's image of mythic strength by the passing of
time." For example, when Wayne comforts a little Vietnamese
boy, "we're not at all assured the way we used to be back
when Wayne was fighting World War II at the Saturday mati-
née."[56]

The Green Berets stirred controversies among audiences too. In some theaters in New York, protestors waved
the Vietcong flag in front of the screen, and in London, the
movie was picketed by some pacifist groups. In Germany, a
local antiwar group, the German Peace Association, protested

to the Ministry of Interior Affairs demanding that all Wayne
movies be forbidden on the grounds that the movie "honors
the Vietnam war with massive falsification and unmistakably
incites racial hatred and murder."[57] In Stuttgart, a major
newspaper compared it with Goebbels's propaganda movie
made during the Third Reich. The movie was also put
out after a short run in Munich and Frankfurt, because
it generated strong anti-American feelings.

Wayne anticipated harsh reviews by the critics: "The
liberal elements will find some way to get at me the way they
did with The Alamo, when they quoted me as saying, 'anyone
who didn't go to see the picture was unpatriotic.'" And:
"If they could get at me with The Alamo, they'll sure as hell
find a way to do it with Green Berets."[58] "That little clique
back there in the East," he said in response to the nasty reviews and anti-American demonstrations, "has taken great
personal satisfaction reviewing my politics instead of my pictures. But one day, those doctrinaire liberals will wake up
to find the pendulum has swung the other way."[59] The movie
was panned by most critics, but the reviews did not bother
him, claiming they were written for "the psychic income of
the writers," who "get a heck of a kick seeing their words
in print." He accused the "so-called intellectual groups," of
not being "in touch with the American people."[60]

In spite of "Fulbright's blatting and Eugene McCarthy
and McGovern and Kennedy," he said, "the American people
do not feel that way." "Instead of taking a census," he
suggested the liberals should "count the tickets that were
sold to that picture."[61] "Hell, why should I be mad," he
explained, "the critics overkilled me, the picture, and the
war. As a result, so many people went to see it that I had
a check for eight million dollars from the distributors in
three months. That's the cost of the picture."[62] The Green
Berets was an expensive movie to make, and Batjac was expected to just break even. However, it grossed close to $9
million in rentals, ranking tenth among the year's most popular films. The movie has grossed $2 million more since then
and over $10 million abroad. Andy Stapp, then editor of
Bond, a radical antiwar newspaper for servicemen, said:
"Packed theaters mean there's enough of a pro-fascist men-
tality"[63] in the United States. That The Green Berets was
so profitable is still an enigma, and that it is shown on television to good ratings is even a greater mystery. The

movie ranks second only to True Grit of all Wayne's money-
making films.

The Green Berets stirred another controversy: the
administration's support of the film.   The Department of Defense had supported many of Wayne's war movies, but for
this one he received extensive equipment, technical advisers,
and military personnel.   The dispute started when Benjamin
S. Rosenthal, the Democratic Congressman from New York,
accused Wayne and the Army of conspiracy, charging that
the movie became "a useful and skilled service employed by
the Pentagon to present a view of the war which was dis-
puted in 1967 and is largely repudiated today."   In a press
conference in Washington, D.C., Rosenthal released a General Accounting Office (GAO) report showing that Batjac had
been charged just $18,623 for Army assistance.   It did not
pay for the loan of weapons, use of combat equipment, aircraft, and troop costs, and was charged only for the use of
three buildings and expendable supplies, such as ammunition. [64]

In response to the article "John Wayne-Superhawk,"
published in the New York Times, Mr. and Mrs. Levine from
Hamden, Connecticut sent a letter of protest to the Times on
January 14, 1968:   "Whatever its political stance," they
wrote, "John Wayne's picture is a purely private, profit-
making enterprise, freely competing with other private, profit-
making enterprises.   He is not making a Government-sponsored
propaganda film, nor is his a governmental agency or a non-
profit corporation."   They therefore demanded to know, "by
what right does the military make available tax funds to re-
duce a filmmaker's costs to help insure this private profit?"
And "how does progressive-conservative, anti-Communist and
pro-free-capitalism John Wayne justify his acceptance of government subsidy, a subsidy which may possibly represent an
illegal abuse of tax monies?" [65]

"There was not anything given to us that would be
competing with commercial enterprises," said Michael Wayne,
because "they will only give you equipment that you can't
get other places."   He explained that the government "will
give cooperation to the producers of a film that is in the
best interests of the United States."   The Green Berets met
"the qualifications of a government picture," and was "in the
national interest," because "it shows our fighting men in the

best possible light." Wayne was furious at Congressman
Rosenthal, calling him "a publicity seeker" and stressing
that they received "good treatment within the letter of the
law." In a statement to the Times, he repeated that the
Pentagon had been "more than careful" in billing Batjac, and
that the 18,623 dollars was not a token payment, but represented only a small part of the total $1 million used, includ-
ing $171,000 they spent on the base, building a camp the
Army later used, and $305,000 they paid for extras for 70
days of shooting.[66] Interestingly, the support of the Defense Department was omitted from the credits, though individual officers were thanked, which was interpreted as the
Pentagon's reluctance to become explicitly involved in the
movie and, by implication, the controversy of the war.

Both The Alamo and The Green Berets were Wayne's
labor of conviction and as such called for comparison. Both
were considered highly propagandistic, but while the former
received lukewarm or mixed reviews, The Green Berets was
panned by most critics. Nonetheless, The Alamo failed at
the box office, whereas the Vietnam film was commercially
successful, proving again that critics had no impact on
Wayne's standing at the box office. And there is no doubt
that The Alamo was a better picture.

In retrospect, some critics and historians have changed
their minds about the movie. British critic Ivan Butler
claimed that the movie's unpleasantness was equaled by the
repulsiveness of the demonstrators, jeering delightedly whenever an American soldier was killed on the screen. "Viewed
away from partisan passion," he wrote, "the film appears no
more and no less nauseating than the great majority of propagandistic war pictures," consisting of the same ingredients:
action, loaded dialogues, and contrived sentimental situations.
Because of the climate of its time, Butler thought that The
Green Berets was a "more courageous production than similar
epics issued, when all opposition is silenced or all public
opinion in favor. "At the very least, one can have little
doubt as to its maker's sincerity."[67] Critic Molly Haskell
concurred: "As a film, The Green Berets wasn't all that
bad, and it surely deserves some sort of prize for going so
strenuously against intellectual fashion."[68] The shy quiet-
ness of Hollywood during the Vietnam conflict indicated that
most filmmakers wanted to steer clear of these troubled waters.
Wayne had at least the courage to make a pro-Vietnam movie

at the height of the controversy, when Hollywood's radical
and liberal elements did not make any anti-Vietnam War movies.

Prior to The Green Berets, there had only been a few
movies on Vietnam, such as Marshall Thompson's A Yank in
Vietnam (1964). This was a routine action film of some authenticity, about a small American unit helping the South Vietnamese. There was also Loin du Viet-Nam (Far from Vietnam,
1967), a French collaborative attempt of Jean-Luc Godard,
Alain Resnais, Agnes Varda, and others, depicting this
conflict-ridden area. John Ford directed a documentary,
Vietnam! Vietnam!, but this was three years after Wayne's film.

The Vietnam War had little immediate impact on literature and the arts. Unlike World War II, which saw the production of hundreds of war movies during the war itself, the
Vietnam conflict remained an unpopular and untouched subject in film for many years. For instance, Gregory Peck
produced but did not star in The Trial of the Catonsville
Nine (1972), a modest and mediocre film about the trial of
Father Daniel Berrigan, his priest brother, and seven other
men charged with breaking into a draft center and burning
Army files as protest against the war. Peck took the film
from one studio to another, until Paramount finally distributed it--without much advertising. The movie failed to find
bookings and was removed from the screen in the few big
cities in which it was shown.[69] It took about a decade until major American directors started to deal with the Vietnam
War. Most of these films were anti-Vietnam, in one way or
another, such as Michael Cimino's The Deer Hunter and Hal
Ashby's Coming Home, both of 1978, and Francis Ford Coppola's Apocalypse Now of 1979. No one could have predicted
that in a few years the political mood of the country would
change, resulting in a cycle of action films attempting to revise the Vietnam War and the Vietnam war movie, such as
First Blood and its sequel, Rambo, both starring Sylvester
Stallone.

Sociological Propaganda and Self-Advertisement

The propaganda in McLintock! a Western comedy, was
not limited to politics. Rather, its messages were social and
most pervasive, embracing all aspects of life. This movie

was significant because it marked the beginning of Wayne's
attempt to impose his general views, not just politics, on his
pictures. Most of his work after <u>McLintock!</u> thus expressed
his opinions about education, family, economics, and friendship.

Based on James E. Grant's screenplay, the film's hero
is George Washington McLintock, a self-made cattle baron,
banker, and leading citizen who rules a town named after
him. McLintock is ageless and commands respect and authority because, as somebody says, "he earned it." Significantly, the sign on the railroad depot reads: "McLintock.
Six Thousand Feet Above Sea Level." He plans to leave his
property to the nation, to become a national park. The
movie is all about respect for authority, with McLintock demanding it from the town's youngsters: "Mostly men my age
call me Mac or McLintock. Youngsters call me Mr. McLintock."

The movie expressed Wayne's conservative politics and
laissez-faire economics, defending the possession of wealth as
long as it is in the hands of "responsible citizens." The actor's belief in hard work, fair play, and competitiveness is
also expressed. When a young man tells McLintock, "of
course, I should have been grateful, you gave me a job," he
snaps at him, "Gave? Boy, that's all wrong. I don't give
jobs. I hire men. You intend to deliver me a fair day's
work every day, don't you? And for that, I'll pay you a
fair day's wage." He also makes sure that the norms of
their contractual agreement are clear: "You're not giving
me anything and I'm not giving you anything. We both
hold up our heads."

McLintock is in favor of statehood as a means of dis-
posing of the political appointees who run the town ineffi-
ciently, reflecting Wayne's alleged contempt for politics and
politicians. The governor's name, Guthert H. Humphrey,
was interpreted as a less-than-subtle reference to the late
Minnesota senator Hubert H. Humphrey, whose democratic
politics stood in sharp opposition to Wayne's. In his first
encounter with his estranged wife, McLintock tells her that
he has seen a photograph of her dancing with the governor.
Her description of the governor as a gentleman irritates him:
"You have to be first a man, then a gentleman. The Governor misses on both counts."

McLintock! also reflects the actor's view of government.
When one of the settlers tells him "the Government gives us
each a hundred and sixty acres," Wayne replies, "No government gave anybody anything." "Governments are in the business of taking away from people," he explains, "not giving."
This laissez-faire philosophy was also expressed by him off
screen. "I don't want any handouts from a benevolent government," he said in an interview, "I think government is
naturally the enemy of the individual, but it's a necessary
evil like, say, motion-picture agents are." His political credo
was: "I do not want the government to take away my human
dignity and insure me anything more than a normal security."[70]

Of greater significance is McLintock's suspicion of
higher education and academics. He describes the political
appointees as "running the country according to what they
learned in some college, where cows are something people
milk, and Indians are statues in front of cigar stores." In
another scene, McLintock is labeled a reactionary by the
college-educated son of a politician. Moreover, he is engaged in a conflict with his estranged wife over the custody
of their 17-year-old daughter, who is attending college in
the East. This provides an opportunity for the juxtaposi-
tion of Eastern and Western ways of life, a recurrent issue
in many of his Westerns. His daughter is courted by two
rivals, Wayne's cowhand and a Harvard University student,
but she chooses, of course, the cowhand and thus reaffirms
her father's way of life.

The point of departure of El Dorado, a major social
statement that followed McLintock! by four years, was Harry
Brown's The Stars in Their Course, but Hawks and screenwriter Leigh Brackett borrowed substantially from Rio Bravo
in plot and characterization. The movie was yet another
variation of Hawks's two favorite themes, professional competence and male camaraderie. And because the director was
aware that Wayne was older and unable to play the kind of
hero he was in Rio Bravo, the new movie examined the impact of age and how the characters deal with declining abilities.

On the surface, the narrative concerns a drunken
sheriff (Robert Mitchum) helped by a gunfighter (Wayne) in
his fight against a greedy landlord (Edward Asner). Wayne

and Mitchum are old friends who have not seen each other
for a long time. Throughout the film, they test each other's
abilities. "I just wanted to see if you've slowed down,"
Wayne tells Mitchum in a crucial scene, to which the latter
replies, "Not that much." El Dorado was preoccupied with
the issues of awareness and fear of one's declining strength.
For example, the doctor refuses to take the bullet out of
Wayne, because "I'm not good enough." And James Caan re-
lies on a knife, because he is not good enough with a gun;
he learns to use it from Wayne, who is good enough to teach
him. Wayne also takes him to a gunsmith who is good enough
to know what weapon Caan should use to make up for his
limitations. And later, Caan defends his (dead) friend, accused of cheating at cards, claiming "he was good, he didn't
have to cheat."

Another Hawksian motif, also reflecting Wayne's credo,
was courtesy and respect, even between enemies. Wayne
and the hired gunslinger, McLeod, respect each other
because they know they are both good. Wayne is intrigued
by "a little question unanswered between us," that is, who
is better with the gun. Later, Wayne shoots down McLeod
several times, with the dying McLeod protesting, "You didn't
give me any chance at all, did you?" To which Wayne replies, "No, I didn't. You were too good to give a chance
to."

Most critics singled out the film's autobiographical
themes, though not necessarily as being its assets. "Humor
and affirmation on the brink of despair are the poetic ingredients of the Hawksian Western," wrote eloquently Andrew
Sarris. "And now memory. Especially memory. Only those
who see some point in remembering movies will find El Dorado
truly unforgettable." Sarris liked the film's message, that
life is hard on heroes, but they must go on in good humor,
even if they have to walk on crutches to gunfights.[71] Time
magazine also praised Wayne and Mitchum who "with crutches
as swagger sticks, they limp triumphantly past the camera--
two old pros demonstrating that they are better on one good
leg a piece than most of the younger stars are on two."[72]
However, critic French found it repetitious that about every
five minutes someone says, "Because I'm not good enough,"
and did not like the film because it was "inordinately slow,"
and "so talkative."[73] Similarly, Pauline Kael thought that
Wayne and Mitchum parodied themselves, looking, just as the

film itself, exhausted, like a late episode of a TV series.[74]
Nor did critics like the idea that except for the opening
scene, the movie was shot on the studio lot.

Of Wayne's last and most obvious sociological movies,
True Grit was artistically the most distinguished, marking the
best collaborative effort of three Hollywood veterans: producer
Hal Wallis, director Henry Hathaway, and Wayne. Considered
one of the most popular Westerns ever made, it proved that
there was still appeal in the old conventional and formulaic
Western. Wayne had read Charles Portis's novel at the gal-
leys phase and liked it so much he bid $300,000 for the screen
rights, but Wallis outdid him, buying them for Paramount reportedly for $500,000. Wallis, however, approached the star
with a tempting deal he could not resist--an excellent part
and a salary of $1 million plus 35 percent of the gross profits.

There were rumors at the time that Portis modeled the
character of Rooster Cogburn after Wayne. "The author
claims he didn't have me in mind," Wayne told reporters,
"but everyone who read the book mentions me."[75] In True
Grit, Wayne is his own age, early sixties, and constructs his
role as a composite of many previous roles, particularly
Thomas Dunson from Red River and Nathan Brittles from She
Wore a Yellow Ribbon. It was a perfect type-casting, as he
described: "Rooster was a mean old bastard, a one-eyed,
whiskey-soaked, sloppy son-of-a-bitch, just like me." "Of
course, it could have been Lee Marvin," he said in reference
to the latter's success in the spoof Cat Ballou, "but he might
have made it too theatrical. I can get away with a little
theatricality because I seldom use it."[76] Marshal Rooster
Cogburn provided one of his richest roles and also enabled
him to poke fun at his own image.

The movie includes many memorable scenes that were
both humorous and self-referential. Cogburn, like Wayne,
was indifferent about his appearance; he did not try to conceal his age and did not care about the impression he made
on others. His most touching sequences are with Kim Darby,
especially when he tells her how, as a young man, he had
single-handedly charged a whole gang of outlaws. In another, he tells her of his past, his broken marriage and his
son who did not like him. In the climax of the picture,
Wayne confronts the four outlaws, calling out, "I mean to
kill you or see you hanged at Judge Parker's convenience.

Which will it be?" Sneering at him, "Bold talk for a one-
eyed fat man." He cries, "Fill your hand, you son-of-a-
bitch!" putting the horse's reins in his teeth, a rifle in one
hand, a pistol in the other, firing with both guns. "The
climactic gunfight in which Wayne flips his weapons ostentatiously," observed Sarris, "is more moving to a spectator
who knows Wayne's total career, than to one who does not."
"Wayne has never been ostentatious in his past," he explained,
"It is only now that he is so near the end that he will give
the dudes one last show with the broad, vulgar gestures of
machism alien to the true spirit of the actor and the genre."[77]

The last scene at the grave was not in the book, but
screenwriter Marguerite Roberts wanted to end the movie on
a sentimental note. Recovering, Mattie expresses her gratitude by offering Wayne a place in her family graveyard,
when the time comes "to meet eternity." Wayne declares
characteristically that he will put off the day as long as possible. He invites Mattie "to come and see the fat old man
sometimes," then jumps his horse over a four-foot fence and
rides off into the winter sunset. Frozen on screen, this last
image was so fine that many wished it would become Wayne's
cinematic epitaph.

True Grit was also viewed as a political film, reflecting
the actor's conservative views. The movie makes a clear
statement in favor of tougher laws and tougher handling of
criminals. Cogburn has no scruples confiscating whiskey
from his captives, which we see early in the film. Criticized
in court for shooting without any apparent hesitation, he
says in defense, "You can't serve papers on a rat," which
was interpreted as a statement of Wayne's right-wing politics.
Cogburn is described as a person "simply trying to make
life habitable for the most people in his territory," another
expression of Wayne's self-appointed role offscreen. "He
feels the same way about life that I do," Wayne described
the character he played, "he doesn't believe in pampering
wrongdoers, which certainly fits into the category of my
thinking. He doesn't believe in accommodation. Neither do
I."[78] Critic Kauffmann wrote: "Readers may remember it
as a book about a girl, but it's a film about John Wayne."[79]

One of the most interesting interpretations of True
Grit was provided by Vincent Canby, comparing it with The
Green Berets.[80] In the war film, Wayne befriended an

orphaned Vietnamese boy; in the Western, an orphaned girl.
However, the imperialist tone of the Vietnam film is not as
disturbing in the Western because "we accept Rooster Cogburn in the old West, but we don't want him dictating foreign policy in this day and age." On the more positive side,
Canby thought that Cogburn was "practically a perfect representation of the resourceful, commonsensical, essentially
good, self-contained, rugged individualist who--we like to
think--settled the country." Canby saw in him "the untamed
WASP, the one who refused to stay in Boston and aspire to
the brotherhood of the Brahmins," thus an ideal role for
Wayne, with which he could identify.

In Chisum, an old-fashioned Western about the 1878
Lincoln County cattle war, Wayne plays the historical figure
of John Simpson Chisum, the powerful cattle baron of New
Mexico, fighting against a corrupt businessman and saved by
Billy the Kid and Pat Garrett. The movie shares similar concerns with McLintock!, particularly the contrast between competitive and monopoly capitalism. There was a complete identification between actor and role, with Chisum being "fat,
wealthy, tough, trusting, stubborn, generous, and sentimental."[81] Regarded as a political allegory, Chisum was set
in 1878 but expressed some of Wayne's current values. The
attitude toward Indians, for example, was in tune with the
times, depicting them as decent human beings. In one
scene, Wayne threatens to kill an army sergeant if he continues to mistreat Chief White Buffalo, who is held captive.
This and other contemporary issues prompted one critic to
observe: "Could it be that the voice of the Old West has
become the Voice of Middle America," and that "it's all a bit
like white suburbia with cattle, instead of cadillacs?"[82]

Chisum was self-conscious and in awe of Wayne, especially in the opening and closing scenes, which were similar: Wayne is sitting heroically astride a horse on a hill.
It looked as if he were "preparing himself for the immortality of something like, say, a commemorative postage stamp."[83]
One critic compared him to "a stone face on Mount Rushmore."[84] And the title song stated autobiographically and
rhetorically, "Chisum, Chisum, can you still keep going on?"
Which prompted the London Observer to note: "Chisum
clearly sets out to demonstrate that he can and will [go on];
that he is still the virility symbol in that American dream of
open spaces, clenched fists and high corn."[85]

Jacob McCandles, the hero of <u>Big Jake</u>, was yet another respected citizen who, like George Washington Mc-Lintock, had a town named after him. His single-minded mission is to avenge a mass raid on his property and the kidnapping of his grandson, Little Jake. At first, his estranged wife asks the Texas Rangers to get the kidnappers, only to realize that Wayne is the <u>only</u> man capable of doing the job. <u>Big Jake</u> is abundant with expressions of Wayne's personal value system. First, there is a contrast between old-traditional and modern-progressive values. Wayne's horse, for example, outlasts the motor bike of his son. The narrative occurs in 1909, making comparisons between life in the East and in the West. Even at the turn of the century, life in the West was wilder, more dangerous, and more demanding. The movie describes Wayne as a man of the past, who people do not recognize anymore--a reference to his declining popularity in the 1970s. At least four times during the picture, he is told, "I thought you was dead," to which he typically replies, "Not hardly," or "that will be the day" --the latter phrase taken from <u>The Searchers</u>. Wayne had no intention of quitting, as Big Jake or as an actor.

The film is based on a three-generational plot, enabling Wayne to pass down the tradition of the West to his sons and grandsons. For instance, he cannot stand his son calling him "daddy," telling him firmly, "You can call me father, Jack, or son-of-a-bitch," but advises him not to use the latter too frequently; the same idea reappeared in <u>The Cowboys</u>. Later, finding his son lying on the ground, looking dead, he punches him twice: once for "scaring the hell out of me" and taking ten years off his life, which he cannot afford--another reference to his old age--and the second, for risking the life of his grandson by acting foolishly.

<u>Big Jake</u> reflected Wayne's concern with age, depicting him as less self-assured than in the past. And at the end, after finding his grandson, he gives him a useful lesson in manhood. He hands him a gun, but advises to use it only when he has to. He also tells him never to show other people that he is scared--it is a sign of weakness. The film also abounds in references to Wayne's previous work. The search for the kidnapped grandson is similar, but not as powerful as in <u>The Searchers</u>. Wayne is also less self-reliant, needing a dog for self-protection, similar to <u>Hondo</u>. And pulling out his glasses to read the ransom note

reminded many of a better scene in <u>She Wore a Yellow Ribbon</u>,
in which he used glasses to read the inscription on the watch
he got from his subordinates.

   <u>The Cowboys</u> was even more self-referential and self-
congratulatory than <u>Chisum</u>. "In this one," Wayne said
about his role, "I play a 60-year-old rancher with eleven
kids under my wing and I try to get all through a cattle
drive."[86] Aware of his repetitive screen roles as a paternal
figure, he said the movie was based on a formula that worked
in <u>Goodbye Mr. Chips</u> and <u>Sands of Iwo Jima</u>. In all three
films, an adult takes a group of youngsters and initiates
them into manhood by instructing them the "right" skills
and values. Wayne did not hesitate to appear in <u>The Cow-
boys</u>, despite the fact that "no actor in his right mind,
would try to match the antics of eleven kids on screen,"
but for him it became "the greatest experience of my life."[87]
Director Mark Rydell was also aware of his image as authoritative father: "It's about an old rancher in his declining
years in his last cattle drive, and the boys bursting into
young men before his eyes--the whole contrast of fathers
and sons and 'the king is dead, long live the king.'" What
attracted Wayne to the role, Rydell said, was "the sense of
passing on the mantle to a younger generation. I think he's
about ready."[88]

   Many articles on the actor's paternalism, on- and offscreen, were written during the shooting of <u>The Cowboys</u>.
One feature in <u>Seventeen</u> entitled, "Do You Think of the
Duke as Big Daddy?"[89] stated that Wayne had become a
universal father figure in American culture. And Canby
described him as "an almost perfect father figure,"[90] whose
fictional sons died because they went wrong. But most reviews were harsh about the film's philosophy. One critic
wrote that Wayne's testament to the younger generation was
"be like me, and you can't go wrong," and that "the West
is safe" because "we have with us a new generation of
Waynes."[91] Other critics opposed <u>The Cowboys</u>' message
that kids are old enough to kill, but not old enough to be
initiated into sex. They called attention to the idea that
"to kill, in cold anger, is not only justifiable in itself, but
somehow the key to manhood,"[92] as one critic noted. Most
damning was Pauline Kael's review: "The movie is about
how these schoolboys become men through learning the old-
fashioned virtues of killing." She denounced the presentation

of Wayne as "an idealized Western father figure," summing up
his philosophy as "there are good men and there are bad
men; there are no crossovers or nothing in between. People don't get a second chance around him; to err once is to
be doomed."[93]

Wayne's last picture, The Shootist, was a most appropriate end to an illustrious career, playing an aging cowboy
who is dying of cancer. He seemed to be the natural choice
for the part, though it had been first offered to Paul Newman, who reportedly pulled out for personal reasons, and to
George C. Scott, who demanded too many changes in the
script. In retrospect, producer Mike Frankovich was delighted with the casting, because "nobody could have been
better for the part than Duke. He's perfect."[94] There
were many advantages in casting Wayne as John Bernard
Books, for director Don Siegel wanted to show the progres-
sion of the gunfighter from his early glorious days to his
tragic death, and what better than using old clips from
Wayne's own Westerns, Stagecoach, Red River, and Hondo.
In this way, the movie became a self-conscious invocation of
the Wayne screen legend and a tribute to his career. It
looked as if the film were designed as an epitaph, though
Wayne had the intention at the time to make more movies.

There were many parallels between the narrative and
Wayne's life. John Bernard Books is dying of cancer, a
theme that was unpalatable and unmentionable to many actors, but not to Wayne: "Hell, no. It means nothing to
me," he told an interviewer, "I'm a member of the club,
after all."[95] However, he did not want to make cancer the
film's major concern and, under his request, it was mentioned just twice. Moreover, the conversation between
Wayne and the physician (Jimmy Stewart), confirming his
fear of having cancer, was in harmony with his image.
Stewart tells him the grim truth about cancer, even hint-
ing about suicide as a way of avoiding pain. Upset, Wayne
protests, "You told me I was strong as an ox," to which
Stewart replies, "even oxen die."

In many ways, The Shootist was Wayne's most self-
righteous and self-aggrandizing movie, described in it as
"the most celebrated shootist," and one who never killed a
man "who didn't deserve it." As in Big Jake, he is concerned with increasing age and the coming of modernization

to the West--the movie takes place in Carson City in 1901.
Wayne is a man of the past, not in tune with his times.
When he first rides into town and obstructs the traffic, he
is told, not too gracefully, "Get out of the way, old man!"
He is also greeted as, "Hey, Methuselah!" We learn that
Queen Victoria is dead; she, like Wayne, is a symbol of the
past. Wayne likes the queen because she had dignity, "she's
the kind of gal I'd like to meet." Moreover, when Serepta
(Sheree North), a woman of his past, comes to visit and suggests they get married so she can gain some money from
writing a book about him after his death, he tells her, "I
won't be remembered for a pack of lies." But being a true
gentleman, he gives her money for her travel and sends her
back.

He even gets an opportunity to sum up his life as
"All in all, I've had a helluva good life," which he states
with utmost offscreen conviction. The closing scene is also
most congruent with his way of thinking and public persona:
he dies on his birthday, wearing his best clothes, and he
dies with his boots on, at the saloon, after a shootout.

The movie was acclaimed by most critics, even those
who used to pan his work. The reviewers approached it as
an autobiographical statement, as Janet Maslin wrote in Newsweek: "The Shootist never jeopardizes its hard-boiled integrity by making apologies for either Books or Wayne; it unabashedly advocates the manly art of self-defense, the occasional necessity for vigilante justice,"[96] and other things
that Wayne stood for. The movie is "the compleat John
Wayne reader," wrote Combs in the London Times, "it
proves to be not so much indulging as measuring these
[Western] myths."[97] "The whole is such a self-conscious
theatrical artifice," this critic wrote, "that it acquires the
dry, self-reflecting quality of inconceivable myth." For
Frank Rich, the principal virtue of the movie is allowing
"Wayne's distinctive star qualities to emerge in all their
splendor," making him "by turns, heroic, sardonic, chivalrous, mean, romantic, tough, frightened, fatherly and ever
so tentatively sentimental."[98] Most critics regarded The
Shootist as a well-designed swan song, self-conscious and
reverential.

John Wayne and Lauren Bacall in The Shootist (Paramount, 1976), a mythic Western and most appropriate swan song to an illustrious career.

NOTES

The notes indicate the authors of books and years of publication. For complete information on these sources, see "Bibliography." Complete information is given for newspapers, magazine articles, and other periodicals.

Chapter 1

1. Goldstein (1979), p. 12.
2. Time, March 3, 1952.
3. Ford (1979), p. 41.
4. Ibid.
5. Ibid.
6. Time, March 3, 1952.
7. Ford (1979), p. 48.
8. Hedda Hopper, Chicago Sunday Tribune, February 13, 1949.
9. Hopper, Los Angeles Times, May 11, 1947.
10. Time, March 3, 1952.
11. Louella Parsons, Los Angeles Herald Examiner, September 8, 1946.
12. The Hollywood Reporter, April 30, 1954.
13. Time, March 3, 1952.
14. Walsh (1974), p. 238.
15. Ibid., p. 239.
16. Los Angeles Times, February 2, 1958.
17. Time, March 3, 1952.
18. Mordaunt Hall, New York Times, October 25, 1930.
19. Louella Parsons, Los Angeles Herald Examiner, September 8, 1946.
20. McCarthy and Flynn (1975), p. 365.
21. Ibid.
22. Louella Parsons, Los Angeles Herald Examiner, September 8, 1946.

23. Variety, October 28, 1936.
24. New York World Telegram, August 2, 1937.
25. Variety, November 10, 1937.
26. Los Angeles Times, February 2, 1958.
27. Louella Parsons, Los Angeles Herald Examiner, September 8, 1946.
28. Hedda Hopper, Los Angeles Times, May 11, 1947.
29. Action, September-October 1971.
30. Los Angeles Herald Examiner, November 28, 1954.
31. Ibid.
32. Action, September-October 1971.
33. Kate Cameron, New York Daily News, March 3, 1939.
34. Tuska in Nachbar (1974), p. 39.
35. Schickel (1972), p. 235.
36. Everson (1969), p. 241.
37. Roderick Mann, Los Angeles Times, March 7, 1976.
38. Nora Sayre, New York Times, February 7, 1974.
39. Judith Crist, New York, February 2, 1974.
40. Goldstein (1979), p. 120.

Chapter 2

1. Current Biography (James Stewart), April 1941.
2. In this book, the commercial appeal of films is measured by their domestic rentals, that is, the amount of money paid to film distributors for exhibiting films in the United States and Canada. The figures are taken from Variety and do not include film rentals in foreign film markets. Variety's figures are the most accurate indicators of films' commercial success and the only measures that permit historical comparison. If the inflation factor is taken into account, Sergeant York's $6 million in domestic rentals are equivalent to over $30 million at present.
3. Jowett (1976), p. 316. The production of war films reached an all-time high in 1943, when 133 war films, or 33 percent of the total film output, were released.
4. Gussow (1971), p. 226.
5. For a discussion of "the ideology of organization man," see Whyte (1956), pp. 3-59.
6. Dmytryk (1978), p. 66.
7. Sinclair (1979), p. 102.
8. Saturday Evening Post, July 9, 1949.
9. Bosley Crowther, New York Times, October 9, 1940.

10. Bogdanovich (1971), p. 144.
11. Ibid., p. 147.
12. Ibid., pp. 145-46.
13. Ibid., p. 144.
14. Playboy, May 1971.
15. Ibid.
16. Gussow (1971), p. 226.
17. Bosley Crowther, New York Times, October 5, 1962.
18. Archer Winston, New York Post, October 5, 1962.
19. Shindler (1979), pp. 19-21.
20. Theodore Strauss, New York Times, March 5, 1943.
21. Time, January 4, 1943.
22. Joseph Pihodna, New York Herald Tribune, March 5, 1943.
23. Irene Thirer, New York Post, March 5, 1943.
24. Bosley Crowther, New York Times, June 11, 1955.
25. Jeavons (1974), p. 178.
26. Dmytryk (1978), p. 66.
27. Ibid., p. 63.
28. Sarris (1975), p. 110.
29. Ibid., p. 112.
30. James Agee, The Nation, January 5, 1946.
31. Jones and McLure (1973), p. 15.
32. Charles Alexander, quoted in ibid., p. 16.
33. James Wolcott, Village Voice, December 12, 1977.
34. Ibid.
35. John Reddy, Reader's Digest, September 1970.

Chapter 3

1. The following discussion draws on Riesman's (1950) typology of social characters.
2. Haskell in Peary (1978), p. 506.
3. Mellen (1977), pp. 13, 135-36.
4. Wood (1975), p. 68.
5. Ibid., p. 67.
6. New York Times, June 3, 1979.
7. Didion (1979), p. 30.
8. Russo (1981), pp. 5-6.
9. Mellen (1977), p. 262.
10. In his pioneering work, Weber (1918) distinguished among three types of authority. See Gerth and Mills (1946).

11. McBride and Wilmington (1974), pp. 174-89.
12. French (1977), pp. 70-75.
13. Whiting, Kluckhon, and Anthony in Maccoby, Newcomb, and Hartley (1958), pp. 359-70.
14. French (1977), p. 70.
15. Ibid., p. 73.
16. Haskell in Peary (1978), p. 507.

Chapter 4

1. Autry (1978), p. 185.
2. Richard Goldstein, Los Angeles Times, February 5, 1967.
3. Richard Shepard, New York Times, June 13, 1979.
4. Dean Jennings, Saturday Evening Post, October 27, 1962.
5. Michael Wall, Sunday Express, November 2, 1962.
6. Roderick Mann, Los Angeles Times, March 7, 1976.
7. Dorothy Manners, Los Angeles Herald Examiner, November 12, 1961.
8. For a discussion of Gary Cooper's screen persona, see Malone (1979), pp. 118-20; Mellen (1977), pp. 34-35.
9. Frank Nugent, New York Times, March 11, 1939.
10. The list of the top 50 money-making Westerns is taken from Pirie (1981), p. 208.
11. Barbour (1981), p. 13.
12. Hollywood Diary, August 1, 1961.
13. Newsweek, January 3, 1965.
14. Los Angeles Times, January 18, 1965.
15. Newsweek, January 3, 1965.
16. Hollywood Diary, August 1, 1961.
17. Ibid.
18. Dwight MacDonald, The Miscellany (1929), quoted in French (1977), p. 6.
19. Steven Zmijensky, Liberty, September 1974.
20. Hollywood Citizen-News, January 1, 1963.
21. Dorothy Manners, Los Angeles Herald Examiner, November 12, 1961.
22. See Levy (1987) on the Western film and the Oscar Award.
23. Libby (1980), p. 176.
24. Thomas (1972), p. 225.
25. Vincent Canby, New York Times, September 12, 1982.
26. André Bazin quoted in Fenin and Everson (1962), p. 8.
27. Fenin and Everson (1973), p. 16.

28. Hollywood Diary, August 1, 1961.
29. Tuska in Nachbar (1974), p. 38.
30. Toeplitz (1974), p. 138.
31. Variety, November 13, 1963.
32. Playboy, May 1971.
33. Richard Goldstein, Los Angeles Times, February 5, 1967.
34. Ricci, Zmijewsky, and Zmijewsky (1970), p. 26.
35. Bart Andrews, "Falling for Stars," September-October
    1965, Seven Sinners file, Library of the Academy of
    Motion Picture Arts and Sciences.
36. Everson (1969), p. 184.
37. Variety, April 15, 1942.
38. New York Times, June 3, 1979.
39. Los Angeles Times, January 25, 1970; Tomkies (1971),
    p. 125.
40. Hollywood Reporter, January 11, 1960.
41. Ann Guarino, New York Daily News, January 14, 1972.
42. Pauline Kael, The New Yorker, January 22, 1972.
43. Sarris (1979), pp. 119-20.
44. Ibid., pp. 121-24; quote on p. 123.

Chapter 5

1. For earlier formulations of the auteur approach, see
   Sarris (1968).
2. Richard Corliss (1974) has stressed the role of powerful screenwriters as auteurs, and Richard Dyer
   (1982) of producers.
3. One of the few scholars to examine systematically actors
   as auteurs has been Patrick McGilligan in a book
   about James Cagney, appropriately titled Cagney:
   The Actor as Auteur (1975).
4. See discussion of this issue in Levy's "The Democratic
   Elite: America's Movie Stars" (1987), and in Weis's
   collection of papers on movie stars (1981).
5. Michael Kerber, Village Voice, July 1, 1971.
6. New York Times, June 3, 1979.
7. Tornabene (1976), pp. 134-35.
8. Quirk (1975), p. 11.
9. Bogdanovich (1973), p. 14.
10. Richard Shepard, New York Times, June 13, 1979.
11. John Wayne file, Academy of Motion Picture Arts and
    Sciences Library, 1962.
12. Seventeen, October 1971.

13. Walsh (1974), p. 241.
14. Los Angeles Times, February 12, 1975.
15. Michael Wall, Sunday Express, November 2, 1962.
16. Playboy, May 1971.
17. Autry (1978), p. 35.
18. Ibid., p. 36.
19. Erskine Johnson, Los Angeles Mirror, October 25, 1960.
20. Kroll in Weis (1981), p. 376.
21. Walker (1970), p. 315.
22. Newsweek, March 1, 1965.
23. Eyles (1976), p. 18.
24. Dmytryk (1978), p. 67.
25. New York Times, March 11, 1979.
26. Playboy, May 1971.
27. Ronald Reagan, Reader's Digest, October 1979.
28. Los Angeles Times, March 11, 1979.
29. Photoplay, March 1951.
30. Kroll in Weis (1981), p. 381.
31. Mellen (1977).
32. Kerbel (1975), p. 10.
33. Time, March 3, 1952.
34. Bogdanovich (1971), p. 147.
35. Los Angeles Times, March 4, 1951.
36. Michael Wall, Sunday Express, 1962.
37. Los Angeles Times, 1951.
38. Goldstein (1979), p. 120.
39. Look, August 1953.
40. John Reddy, Reader's Digest, September 1970.
41. Daily Mirror, February 21, 1963.
42. Life, July 11, 1969.
43. Tomkies (1971), p. 122.
44. Stack (1980), p. 4.
45. Roderick Mann, Los Angeles Times, March 7, 1976.
46. Seventeen, October 1971.
47. Hedda Hopper, Los Angeles Times, May 11, 1947.
48. Walker (1970), p. 319.
49. Roderick Mann, Los Angeles Times, August 6, 1978.
50. Meyer (1979), p. 168.
51. McBride (1972), pp. 15-16.
52. Playboy, May 1971.
53. The Hollywood Reporter, January 11, 1960.
54. Tomkies (1971), p. 124.
55. Saturday Evening Post, July 9, 1949.
56. New York Times, June 11, 1956.
57. William K. Zinsser, New York Herald Tribune, June 11,
    1955.

58. Sea Chase File, Library of Academy of Motion Picture
        Arts and Sciences.
59. A.H. Weiler, New York Times, March 31, 1956.
60. Time, August 9, 1956.
61. Jack Smith, Los Angeles Times, May 1960.
62. Ibid., September 15, 1980.
63. Bosley Crowther, New York Times, Feburary 16, 1965.
64. Dick Williams, Los Angeles Mirror, October 27, 1960.
65. James Powers quoted in ibid.
66. Current Biography, October 1978.
67. Bosley Crowther, New York Times, April 7, 1965.
68. Butler (1973), p. 103.

Chapter 6

1.   Time, June 3, 1946.
2.   Ruth Waterbury, Los Angeles Herald Examiner, June 14,
        1946.
3.   Cecelia Ager, PM Reviews, June 9, 1946.
4.   Haskell (1974), p. 269.
5.   Archer Winsten, New York Post, July 12, 1962.
6.   Russo (1981), pp. 5-6.
7.   Good Housekeeping, February 1973.
8.   Otio Guernsey Jr., New York Herald Tribune, October
        1, 1948.
9.   New York Herald Tribune, November 2, 1961.
10. Joseph McBride and Gerald Peary, Film Comment,
        September-October 1982.
11. For a detailed discussion of the "Hawksian woman," see
        Stuart Byron in Nobile (1973), pp. 266-67.
12. London Observer, January 26, 1964.
13. Cue, November 13, 1963.
14. Edwin Schallert, Los Angeles Times, February 23, 1956.
15. Arthur Knight, Saturday Review, December 5, 1953.
16. Newsweek, November 3, 1952.
17. Variety, May 18, 1955.
18. Good Housekeeping, February 1973.
19. Boswell and David (1979), p. 84.
20. Haskell in Peary (1978), p. 507.
21. Look, August 2, 1960.
22. Eyles (1976), p. 66.
23. Pauline Kael, New Yorker, February 11, 1974.
24. Kroll in Weis (1981), p. 380.
25. Haskell in Peary (1978), p. 506.
26. Mellen (1977), p. 264.

27. Ibid., p. 149.
28. Haskell in Peary (1978), p. 506.
29. Morgenstern and Kanfer (1970), p. 249.
30. Walker (1970), pp. 309-10.
31. Jacobs (1968), p. 533.
32. Malone (1979), p. 127.

Chapter 7

1. Los Angeles Times, June 12, 1979.
2. Sidney Skolsky, Hollywood Citizen News, May 8, 1970.
3. Bryan Buckingham, News of the World, January 26, 1964.
4. Maurice Zolotow, Los Angeles Herald Examiner, November 21, 1954.
5. Bryan Buckingham, News of the World, January 26, 1964.
6. Walsh (1974), p. 240.
7. Los Angeles Herald Examiner, October 19, 1960.
8. Los Angeles Times, February 2, 1958.
9. Look, August 1953.
10. Los Angeles Times, February 2, 1958.
11. Gene Vier, Los Angeles Times, February 2, 1981.
12. Roderick Mann, Los Angeles Times, March 7, 1976.
13. Michael Wall, Sunday Express, November 2, 1962.
14. New York Times, November 7, 1948.
15. Ricci, Zmijewsky, and Zmijewsky (1970), p. 26.
16. Los Angeles Herald Examiner, October 19, 1960.
17. Boseworth (1979), p. 135.
18. TV Guide, September 17, 1977.
19. Los Angeles Times, February 2, 1958.
20. Variety, January 29, 1976.
21. Hollywood Citizen News, April 28, 1970.
22. Tomkies (1971), p. 122.
23. Bacon, p. 181.
24. Time, June 7, 1954.
25. Meisel in Peary (1979), pp. 403-4.
26. Ebert in Weis (1981), p. 201.
27. Eyles (1979), p. 15.
28. Variety, January 29, 1976.
29. Hollywood Citizen News, February 26, 1953.
30. Roderick Mann, Los Angeles Times, March 7, 1976.
31. Los Angeles Times, February 21, 1958.
32. Ibid., March 4, 1951.

33. Goldstein (1979), p. 113.
34. Roderick Mann, Los Angeles Times, March 7, 1976.
35. Hedda Hopper, Los Angeles Times, February 13, 1949.
36. Ibid.
37. Guy Flatley, Cosmopolitan, March 17, 1974.
38. New York Herald Tribune, May 15, 1941.
39. Eugene Archer, New York Times, November 11, 1960.
40. Nora Sayre, New York Times, February 7, 1974.
41. Vicent Canby, New York Times, January 13, 1969.
42. Los Angeles Times, June 13, 1979.
43. Beaver, p. 274.
44. Eyles (1976), p. 104.
45. Playboy, May, 1971.
46. Jon Tuska, Views and Reviews 5 (September 1973):
    9-17.
47. Variety, September 25, 1978.
48. Playboy, May 1971.
49. Mordaunt Hall, New York Times, October 25, 1930.
50. New York Herald Tribune, June 29, 1936.
51. Variety, October 28, 1936.
52. Donald Hough, Los Angeles Times, June 29, 1941.
53. Bryn Buckingham, News of the World, January 26,
    1964.
54. Cue, March 24, 1956.
55. Sunday Express, November 2, 1962.
56. Frank Nugent, New York Times, March 3, 1939.
57. Howard Barnes, New York Herald Tribune, March 3,
    1939.
58. Kate Cameron, New York Daily News, March 3, 1939.
59. Cue, March 4, 1939.
60. Bosley Crowther, New York Times, October 1, 1948.
61. Variety, July 14, 1948.
62. Eyles (1976), p. 115.
63. Ibid., p. 118.
64. Bosley Crowther, New York Times, November 18, 1949.
65. Howard Barnes, New York Herald Tribune, November
    18, 1949.
66. Variety, July 27, 1949.
67. James Bacon, Los Angeles Herald Examiner, May 19, 1969.
68. Meyer (1979), p. 183.
69. Bosley Crowther, New York Times, June 25, 1948.
70. Howard Barnes, New York Herald Tribune, June 25,
    1948.
71. Ibid., November 20, 1950.
72. Los Angeles Times, October 3, 1952.

73. Los Angeles Herald Examiner, October 3, 1952.
74. Bosley Crowther, New York Times, May 31, 1956.
75. William Zinsser, New York Herald Tribune, May 31, 1956.
76. Eyles (1976), p. 152.
77. Los Angeles Times, June 11, 1956.
78. A.H. Weiler, New York Times, March 19, 1959.
79. New York Herald Tribune, March 19, 1959.
80. Saturday Review, March 14, 1959.
81. Los Angeles Times, March 19, 1959.
82. Ken Johnson, Toronto Globe and Mail, June 27, 1959.
83. New York Herald Tribune, June 26, 1964.
84. Richard Shepard, New York Times, June 13, 1979.
85. Bosley Crowther, New York Times, October 27, 1960.
86. Variety, May 23, 1962.
87. Archer Winsten, New York Post, November 16, 1963.
88. Frances Hovidge, New York Post, February 6, 1969.
89. A.H. Weiler, New York Times, February 6, 1969.
90. Kathleen Carroll, New York Daily News, February 6, 1969.
91. Stanley Kauffmann, New Republic.
92. Bentley (1960), p. 310.
93. Ibid., p. 309.
94. Luhr and Lehman (1977), p. 24.
95. Alex Keneas, Newsweek, August 17, 1970.
96. Los Angeles Times, January 25, 1970.
97. Playboy, May 1971.
98. Jack Kroll in Weis (1981), p. 376.
99. Los Angeles Times, January 25, 1970.
100. Tomkies (1971), p. 118.
101. Cue, March 24, 1956.
102. Wayne's Oscar acceptance speech, Academy Awards ceremony, April 7, 1970.
103. Playboy, May 1971.
104. Maurice Zolotow, Los Angeles Herald Examiner, November 21, 1954.
105. Hollywood Reporter, May 13, 1970.
106. Morgenstern and Kanfer (1970), p. 254.
107. Schickel (1972), pp. 235-36.
108. Andrew Sarris, Village Voice, August 21, 1969.
109. Cocks in Nobile (1973), p. 34.
110. Molly Haskell, New York.
111. Sarris (1979), p. 119.
112. Ibid.
113. Rex Reed, New York Daily News, January 14, 1972.

114. Archer Winsten, New York Post, January 14, 1972.
115. Reed, New York Daily News, January 14, 1972.
116. Pauline Kael, New Yorker, February 11, 1974.
117. Ibid., November 3, 1975.
118. Kroll in Weis (1981), p. 376.
119. John Simon, New York, November 10, 1975.
120. Ibid., August 23, 1976.
121. Crowther (1977), p. 44.
122. Bogdanovich (1973), p. 114.
123. Kroll in Weis (1981), p. 375.
124. Steinberg (1980), p. 168.
125. In the last 15 years, there has been a proliferation of scholarly books on both Ford and Hawks. Interestingly, most of the literature on Ford was written in the late 1960s and 1970s, whereas the books on Hawks are for the most part product of the 1980s. Close to ten books, examining Ford's life and work, have been published. Remember Robin Wood's 1967 essay entitled "Who the Hell Is Howard Hawks?" followed by his 1968 volume on the director? Well, at least three books have attempted to answer these questions in the last two years. And surely more are yet to come. See "Bibliography."

Chapter 8

1. Hotchner (1979), p. 141.
2. Cosmopolitan, November 1954.
3. Eyles (1979), p. 14.
4. Hedda Hopper, Los Angeles Times, May 11, 1947.
5. Hotchner (1979), p. 113.
6. New York Times, June 13, 1979.
7. Eyles (1976), p. 14.
8. Time, November 18, 1974.
9. Los Angeles Times, January 24, 1974.
10. TV Guide, September 17, 1977.
11. Los Angeles Times, January 24, 1974.
12. Bacon.
13. Roderick Mann, Los Angeles Times, March 7, 1976.
14. Morgenstern and Kanfer (1970), p. 249.
15. Essoe (1981), pp. 170-72.
16. Stack (1980), pp. 3-4.
17. New York Post, June 13, 1979.
18. Hedda Hopper, Chicago Sunday Tribune, February 13, 1949.

19. Action, September-October 1971, p. 24.
20. Photoplay, March 1951.
21. Action, September-October 1971, p. 10.
22. Maurice Zolotow, Los Angeles Examiner, November 28, 1954.
23. Louella Parsons, Los Angeles Herald Examiner, September 8, 1946.
24. Sinclair (1979), p. 84.
25. Los Angeles Herald Examiner, November 28, 1954.
26. Kroll in Weis (1981), p. 381.
27. Action, September-October 1971, p. 25.
28. Ibid., p. 10.
29. Autry (1978), p. 186.
30. Saturday Evening Post, December 23, 1950.
31. Autry (1978), p. 186.
32. Saturday Evening Post, December 23, 1950.
33. Louella Parsons, Los Angeles Examiner, September 8, 1946.
34. Look, August 2, 1960.
35. Goldstein (1979), p. 48.
36. Morgenstern and Kanfer (1970), p. 249.
37. Kroll in Weis (1981), p. 381.
38. Bosley Crowther, New York Times, May 24, 1962.
39. Sinclair (1979), p. vii.
40. Tuska in Nachbar (1974), p. 39.
41. Current Biography, John Wayne, July 1972.
42. Mast (1982), p. 297.
43. Michael Goodwin and Naomi Wise, Take One 3, July-August 1971, p. 21.
44. Schickel (1977), p. 120.
45. Bosworth (1979), p. 125.
46. Kyle Crichton, Collier, October 9, 1948.
47. Hedda Hopper, Los Angeles Times, October 23, 1960.
48. Sight and Sound, Spring 1971.
49. Sidney Skolsky, Hollywood Citizen News, May 8, 1970.
50. Mast (1982), p. 347.
51. Schickel (1977), p. 120.
52. Eyles (1976), p. 18.
53. Bogdanovich (1973), p. 115.
54. Mast (1982), pp. 15, 364.
55. Goldstein (1979), p. 112.
56. Higham (1973), p. 263.
57. Tomkies (1971), p. 122.
58. Ed Levitt, New York Herald Tribune, May 12, 1969.
59. Bogdanovich (1971), pp. 144-45.
60. Ibid., p. 147.

61. Shavelson (1971).
62. Wellman (1974), p. 96.
63. Schickel (1977), p. 200.
64. Huston (1980), p. 265.
65. Eyles (1976), p. 18.
66. Los Angeles Times, February 5, 1967.
67. Eyles (1976), p. 18.
68. Bosley Crowther, New York Times, October 3, 1958.
69. Huston (1980), p. 265.
70. Ibid., pp. 266-67.
71. Capra (1971), p. 489.
72. Ibid., pp. 489-90.
73. Ibid., p. 490.
74. Dmytryk (1978), pp. 67-68.
75. Ibid.
76. Playboy, May 1971.
77. Preminger (1977), pp. 192-93.
78. Bishop (1979), p. 164.
79. Preminger (1977), p. 193.
80. LeRoy (1974), p. 164.
81. Ibid., p. 218.
82. Roderick Mann, Los Angeles Times, March 7, 1976.
83. Eyles (1976), p. 85.
84. Richard Goldstein, Los Angeles Times, February 5, 1967.
85. Eyles (1976), p. 14.
86. Ibid.
87. David Castell, Films Illustrated, May 1972.
88. Variety, January 29, 1976.
89. Roderick Mann, Los Angeles Times, March 7, 1976.

Chapter 9

1. Hedda Hopper, Los Angeles Times, May 25, 1958.
2. Beaver, p. 275.
3. Newsweek, March 1, 1965.
4. Kroll in Weis (1981), p. 377.
5. News Weekly, December 19, 1949.
6. Fenin and Everson (1973).
7. News Weekly, December 19, 1949.
8. Pagan Magazine.
9. Vinant X. Flaherty, Los Angeles Herald Examiner,
      October 19, 1960.
10. News Weekly, December 19, 1949.
11. Didion (1979), p. 30.

12. Ibid., pp. 30-31.
13. Saturday Evening Post, December 23, 1950.
14. Playboy, May 1971.
15. Robert Kistler, Los Angeles Times, June 12, 1979.
16. Kroll in Weis, (1981), p. 375.
17. Kovic (1976).
18. Ibid.
19. Kroll in Weis (1981), p. 378.
20. Essoe (1981), p. 176.
21. Gans (1974), pp. 84-93.
22. Ibid., pp. 90-91.
23. Ibid., pp. 110-11.
24. Essoe (1981), p. 176.
25. Daily Mail (London), January 2, 1956.
26. Ed Levitt, New York Herald Tribune, June 12, 1979.
27. Nachbar (1974), p. 3.
28. Los Angeles Herald Examiner, August 9, 1968.
29. Kroll in Weis (1981), p. 377.
30. Charles Miller, Los Angeles Times, June 23, 1979.
31. Gladwin Hall, New York Times, November 7, 1945.
32. New Yorker, December 19, 1953.
33. Quirk (1975), p. 11.
34. Los Angeles Times, March 4, 1951.
35. Hedda Hopper, Los Angeles Times, May 25, 1958.
36. Look, August 11, 1953.
37. Look, August 2, 1960.
38. Vinant X. Flaherty, Los Angeles Herald Examiner,
    October 19, 1960.
39. Southland Sunday, March 17, 1974.
40. Jack Smith, Los Angeles Times, May 29, 1960.
41. Charles Champlin, Los Angeles Times, November 26, 1976.
42. Los Angeles Times, February 5, 1967.
43. Seventeen, October 1971.
44. Guthrie (1977), p. 189.
45. Hollywood Citizen News, May 20, 1960.
46. Sidney Skolsky, Hollywood Citizen News, May 8, 1970.
47. Daily Mirror (London), February 21, 1963.
48. Time, March 3, 1952.
49. Pagan Magazine.
50. Cue, March 24, 1956.
51. Time, March 3, 1952.
52. Hedda Hopper, Los Angeles Times, May 11, 1947.
53. Goldstein (1979), p. 7.
54. Los Angeles Times, February 5, 1967.

55. Sound and Stage, December 1964.
56. Daily Mail (London), February 21, 1963.
57. Los Angeles Daily News, February 16, 1953.
58. Eyles (1976), p. 14.
59. TV Guide, September 17, 1977.
60. People, November 18, 1974.
61. TV Guide, September 17, 1977.
62. Nobile (1973), p. 35.

Chapter 10

1. James Bacon, Los Angeles Herald Examiner, December
   30, 1964.
2. Hedda Hopper, Los Angeles Times, March 2, 1965.
3. Ibid.
4. Playboy, May 1971.
5. James Bacon, Los Angeles Herald Examiner, March 14,
   1965.
6. Life, May 7, 1965.
7. John Wilch, Blackhawk Film Digest, August-September,
   1979.
8. "Barbara Walters Special," ABC-TV, March 13, 1979.
9. James Bacon, Los Angeles Herald Examiner, March 14,
   1965.
10. "Barbara Walters Special," ABC-TV, March 13, 1979.
11. Hedda Hopper, Los Angeles Times, March 2, 1965.
12. Variety, January 29, 1976.
13. Jane Aidmore, Sunday Woman, March 4, 1979.
14. Hedda Hopper, Los Angeles Times, March 2, 1965.
15. Los Angeles Times, January 25, 1970.
16. "Barbara Walters Special," ABC-TV, March 13, 1979.
17. Roderick Mann, Los Angeles Times, March 7, 1976.
18. Los Angeles Times, June 12, 1979.
19. Hedda Hopper, Los Angeles Times, March 2, 1965.
20. James Bacon, Los Angeles Herald Examiner, December
    30, 1964.
21. Roderick Mann, Los Angeles Times, March 7, 1976.
22. Newsweek, March 1, 1965.
23. Ibid.
24. Essoe (1981), p. 222.
25. Jowett (1976).
26. Ibid., p. 434.
27. Los Angeles Times, March 18, 1971.
28. Variety, September 17, 1980.
29. Maurice Zolotow, TV Guide, November 4, 1972.

30. Morton Moss, Los Angeles Herald Examiner, November 1970.
31. Joseph Finnigan, TV Guide, November 28-December 4, 1970.
32. Los Angeles Times, December, 3, 1971.
33. Saturday Review, May 13, 1978.
34. Los Angeles Times, February 19, 1974.
35. Jane Aidmore, Sunday Woman, March 4, 1979.
36. Hollywood Citizen News, August 17, 1971.
37. Sunday Woman, March 4, 1979.
38. Goldstein (1979), p. 126.
39. Los Angeles Times, January 24, 1979.
40. Essoe (1981), p. 118.
41. Los Angeles Herald Examiner, March 6, 1981.
42. Ibid.
43. Essoe (1981), p. 120.
44. Vincent Canby, New York Times, April 15, 1979.

Chapter 11

1. Time, March 3, 1952.
2. Hedda Hopper, Los Angeles Times, February 13, 1949.
3. Life, July 11, 1969.
4. Time, March 3, 1952.
5. Goldstein (1979), p. 7.
6. Barry Norman, London Daily Mail, December 21, 1963.
7. Roderick Mann, Los Angeles Times, August 6, 1978.
8. Norman, London Daily Mail, December 21, 1963.
9. Ibid.
10. Los Angeles Times, January 18, 1965.
11. Los Angeles Herald Examiner, February 19, 1974.
12. Goldstein (1979), p. 120.
13. Roderick Mann, Los Angeles Times, August 6, 1978.
14. Reader's Digest, September 1970.
15. Hollywood Citizen News, October 5, 1951.
16. Mellen (1977), p. 149.
17. Evening Standard (London), October 25, 1953.
18. Jack Hamilton, Look, July 1969.
19. Morgenstern and Kanfer (1970), p. 255.
20. Time, November 15, 1954.
21. Hedda Hopper, Los Angeles Times, May 25, 1958.
22. Los Angeles Times, October 21, 1970.
23. Arlene Dahl, Hollywood Citizen News, November 2, 1961.
24. Evening Standard (London), October 20, 1953.

25. Arlene Dahl, Hollywood Citizen News, November 2, 1961.
26. Look, August 2, 1960.
27. Higham (1977), p. 197.
28. Playboy, May 1971.
29. Tomkies (1971), p. 68.
30. Los Angeles Herald Examiner, June 15, 1969.
31. Good Housekeeping, February 1973.
32. Jack Hamilton, Look, July 1969.
33. Ingénue, January 1972.
34. Good Housekeeping, February 1973.
35. Playboy, May 1971.
36. Goldstein (1979), p. 120.
37. Good Housekeeping, February 1973.
38. Ingénue, January 1972.
39. Will Tusher, Hollywood Reporter, February 5, 1975.
40. Hedda Hopper, Los Angeles Times, May 25, 1958.
41. Hollywood Citizen News, May 20, 1960.
42. Hollywood Reporter, January 11, 1960.
43. Playboy, May 1971.
44. Ibid.
45. Hollywood Reporter, January 11, 1960.
46. Los Angeles Herald Examiner, May 13, 1979.
47. Joan Haber, Los Angeles Times, June 21, 1970.
48. Hollywood Reporter, January 11, 1960.
49. Joan Haber, Los Angeles Times, June 21, 1970.
50. Playboy, May 1971.
51. Joan Haber, Los Angeles Times, June 21, 1970.
52. Will Tusher, Hollywood Reporter, February 5, 1975.
53. Hollywood Reporter, January 11, 1960.
54. Los Angeles Herald Examiner, May 13, 1979.
55. Will Tusher, Hollywood Reporter, February 5, 1975.
56. Tomkies (1971), p. 125.
57. Louella Parsons, Los Angeles Herald Examiner, October
        23, 1960.
58. Hollywood Reporter, 1970.
59. Fonda (1981), p. 177.
60. Bogdanovich (1971), p. 145.
61. Look, July 1969.
62. Playboy, May 1971.
63. Roderick Mann, Los Angeles Times, March 7, 1976.
64. Ford (1979), p. 48.
65. Essoe (1981), p. 81.
66. New Yorker, December 19, 1953.
67. Goldstein (1979), p. 33.
68. Los Angeles Times, April 13, 1969.

69. Judith Crist, New York Herald Tribune, November 14, 1963.
70. Ronald Reagan, Reader's Digest, October 1979.

Chapter 12

1. Bentley (1972), p. 310.
2. Maurice Zolotow, Los Angeles Herald Examiner, November 28, 1954.
3. Scott Eyman, Focus on Film, Spring 1975.
4. Good Housekeeping, February 1973.
5. Los Angeles Herald Examiner, February 19, 1974.
6. Los Angeles Times, November 26, 1976.
7. Seventeen, October 1971.
8. Barbour (1974), p. 15.
9. Bentley (1972), p. 308.
10. Time, March 3, 1952.
11. Los Angeles Herald Examiner, February 19, 1974.
12. Barbour (1974), p. 15.
13. Newsweek, March 19, 1973.
14. Seventeen, October 1971.
15. Playboy, May 1971.
16. Good Housekeeping, February 1973.
17. Hollywood Citizen News, May 8, 1970.
18. Morton Moss, Los Angeles Herald Examiner, November 1970.
19. Daily Mail (London), December 21, 1963.
20. Reader's Digest, September 17, 1977.
21. New York Times, June 3, 1979.
22. John Reddy, Reader's Digest, September 1970.
23. Morgenstern and Kanfer (1970), p. 254.
24. Hofstadter (1962).
25. Fonda (1981), p. 177.
26. New York Herald Tribune, March 22, 1944.
27. Saturday Evening Post, December 23, 1950.
28. For an insightful discussion of this era in Hollywood, see Sayre (1982), Shindler (1979).
29. Shindler (1979), p. 109.
30. Quoted in Sayre (1982), p. 50.
31. March 22, 1951. Quoted in Bentley (1972), p. 308.
32. Southland Sunday, March 17, 1974.
33. Ronald Reagan, Reader's Digest, October 1979.
34. Los Angeles Herald Examiner, July 21, 1972.
35. On Bogart's politics, see Benchley (1975) and Eyles (1975).

36. Tornabene (1976), p. 330.
37. Kaminsky (1975), p. 175.
38. Playboy, May 1971.
39. Ibid.
40. Goldstein (1979), p. 96.
41. Navasky, pp. 371-72.
42. Time, March 3, 1952.
43. Walker (1970), p. 320.
44. Michael Wall, Sunday Express, November 2, 1962.
45. Los Angeles Mirror, May 5, 1961.
46. Dean Jennings, Saturday Evening Post, October 27, 1962.
47. Los Angeles Times, July 6, 1966.
48. Ibid.
49. Tomkies (1971), p. 131.
50. Ibid., p. 132.
51. Ibid.
52. Life, January 28, 1972.
53. Southland Sunday, March 17, 1974.
54. Playboy, May 1971.
55. Ibid.
56. James Bacon, Los Angeles Herald Examiner, June 25, 1973.
57. Jon Tuska, Views and Reviews, September 1973.
58. Walker (1970), p. 319.
59. Playboy, May 1971.
60. Ibid.
61. French (1977), p. 94.
62. Playboy, May 1971.
63. Ibid.
64. Hedda Hopper, Los Angeles Times, October 21, 1960.
65. Tomkies (1971), p. 130.
66. Dorothy Manners, Los Angeles Herald Examiner, August 5, 1968.
67. Tomkies (1971), p. 130.
68. James Bacon, Los Angeles Herald Examiner, July 21, 1972.
69. Guy Flatley, Cosmopolitan, March 17, 1974.
70. James Bacon, Los Angeles Herald Examiner, June 25, 1973.
71. Los Angeles Times, November 26, 1976.
72. Guy Flatley, Cosmopolitan, March 17, 1974.
73. Ibid.
74. Morgenstern and Kanfer (1970), p. 288.
75. Los Angeles Times, January 5, 1971.

76. Ibid., March 7, 1976.
77. Variety, December 31, 1976.
78. Eyles (1976), p. 263.
79. Los Angeles Times, May 6, 1979.
80. Bentley (1972), p. 311.
81. Variety, September 25, 1978.
82. New York Times, June 13, 1979.
83. Rob Bryant, Orange County magazine, December 1976.
84. Southland Sunday, March 17, 1974.
85. Hollywood Citizen-News, August 17, 1971.
86. Morgenstern and Kanfer (1970), p. 250.
87. "Barbara Walters Special," ABC-TV, March 13, 1979.
88. Charles Champlin, Los Angeles Times, November 26,
     1976.
89. Los Angeles Herald Examiner, May 13, 1973.
90. Ibid., October 26, 1977.
91. Tomkies (1972), p. 133.
92. Seventeen, October 1971.
93. Ingénue, January 1972.
94. Good Housekeeping, January 1973.
95. Reader's Digest, September 17, 1977.
96. Ingénue, January 1972.
97. Good Housekeeping, February 1973.
98. Life, January 28, 1972.
99. Barbour (1974), p. 127.
100. Newsweek, January 28, 1974.

Chapter 13

1. New York Times, June 3, 1979.
2. The distinction between political and social propaganda
    and the following discussion of these concepts is
    based on Ellul (1973).
3. Ibid., p. 67.
4. Ibid., pp. 70-78.
5. Kanfer (1971), p. 254.
6. New York Times, September 18, 1952.
7. New York Herald Tribune, September 15, 1952.
8. Edwin Schallert, Los Angeles Times, August 30, 1952.
9. Margaret Harford, Hollywood Citizen News, August 30,
    1952.
10. Kay Practor, Los Angeles Herald Examiner, August 30,
    1952.
11. Hollywood Reporter, August 25, 1952.

12. Variety, August 27, 1952.
13. Eyles (1976), p. 135.
14. Walker (1970), p. 320.
15. Eyles (1976), p. 149.
16. Los Angeles Times, September 29, 1955.
17. Sternberg (1965), p. 114.
18. Ibid., p. 281.
19. Newsweek, September 23, 1957.
20. James Powers, Hollywood Reporter, September 19, 1957.
21. Dick Williams, Mirror News, September 26, 1957.
22. Los Angeles Times, September 26, 1957.
23. New York Times, October 5, 1957.
24. Newsweek, September 23, 1957.
25. Goldstein (1979), p. 80.
26. Michael Wall, October 27, 1960.
27. Sound and Stage, 1960.
28. Michael Wall, October 27, 1960.
29. Louella Parsons, Los Angeles Herald Examiner, October
      23, 1960.
30. Michael Wall, October 27, 1960.
31. Hollywood Reporter, January 11, 1960.
32. New York Times, October 27, 1960.
33. Paul V. Beckley, New York Herald Tribune, October 27,
      1960.
34. Newsweek, October 31, 1960.
35. Archer Winsten, New York Post, October 27, 1960.
36. Philip Schewer, Los Angeles Times, October 27, 1960.
37. Dick Williams, Los Angeles Daily Mirror, October 27,
      1960.
38. French (1977), p. 31.
39. Philip Schewer, Los Angeles Times, March 6, 1961.
40. Daily Variety, March 21, 1961.
41. Los Angeles Times, March 8, 1961.
42. Dean Jennings, Saturday Evening Post, October 27,
      1962.
43. Walker (1970), p. 321.
44. New York Times, June 3, 1979.
45. Roderick Mann, Los Angeles Times, August 6, 1978.
46. Kroll in Weis (1981), p. 377.
47. Glenn Hawkins, Los Angeles Herald Examiner, Novem-
      ber 12, 1967.
48. Los Angeles Times, January 28, 1968.
49. Tomkies (1971), p. 112.
50. John Reddy, Reader's Digest, September 1970.
51. Archer Winsten, New York Post, June 20, 1968.

52. Joseph Morgenstern, Newsweek, July 1, 1968.
53. Richard Schickel, Life, July 19, 1968.
54. Michael Korda, Glamour, October 1968.
55. New York Times, June 20, 1968.
56. Los Angeles Times, July 3, 1968.
57. Variety, September 25, 1968.
58. Goldstein (1979), p. 102.
59. Chicago Sun-Times.
60. Felix Kessler, Wall Street Journal, July 3, 1968.
61. Morgenstern and Kanfer (1970), p. 256.
62. Los Angeles Times, January 20, 1970.
63. Variety, June 21, 1968.
64. Ibid., July 2, 1969.
65. New York Times, January 14, 1968.
66. Los Angeles Times, June 27, 1968.
67. Butler (1974), p. 133.
68. Molly Haskell, New York.
69. Freedland (1980), pp. 212-3.
70. Dean Jennings, Saturday Evening Post, October 27, 1962.
71. Village Voice, July 27, 1967.
72. Time, July 28, 1967.
73. Philip French, Observer (London), July 23, 1967.
74. Kael (1968), pp. 42-46.
75. Hollywood Citizen News, May 21, 1969.
76. Wayne Warga, Los Angeles Times, April 13, 1969.
77. Village Voice, August 21, 1969.
78. Life, January 28, 1972.
79. Stanley Kauffmann, New Republic, July 26, 1969.
80. New York Times, June 3, 1979.
81. Richard Corliss, Village Voice, July 30, 1970.
82. Stanley Price, Observer (London), July 30, 1970.
83. Richard Cohen, Women's Wear Daily, July 30, 1970.
84. Archer Winsten, New York Post, July 30, 1970.
85. Observer (London), July 30, 1970.
86. Steve Ditlea, Show, March 1972.
87. Ibid.
88. Edwin Miller, Seventeen, September 1971.
89. Ibid.
90. New York Times, January 14, 1972.
91. Kevin Saviola, Women's Wear Daily, January 14, 1972.
92. George Melly, London Observer, March 26, 1972.
93. New Yorker, January 22, 1972.
94. Roderick Mann, Los Angeles Times, March 7, 1976.
95. Ibid.

96. _Newsweek_, August 16, 1976.
97. _Times_ (London), October 8, 1976.
98. _New York Post_, August 12, 1976.

BIBLIOGRAPHY

Autry, Gene. Back in the Saddle Again. Garden City,
N.Y.: Doubleday, 1978.

Barbour, Alan G. John Wayne. New York: Pyramid, 1974.

Baxter, John. The Cinema of Josef von Sternberg. New
York: A.S. Barnes, 1971.

Bazin, André. What Is Cinema. Volume Two. Berkeley:
University of California Press, 1971.

Benchley, Nathaniel. Humphrey Bogart. Boston: Little,
Brown, 1975.

Bentley, Eric. Theatre of War. New York: Viking, 1972.

Bishop, George. John Wayne. Thornwood, N.Y.: Caroline
House, 1979.

Bogdanovich, Peter. Allan Dwan: The Last Pioneer. New
York: Praeger, 1971.

_____. Pieces of Time. New York: Arbor, 1973.

Bosworth, Patricia. Montgomery Clift. New York: Bantam,
1979.

Brooks, Louise. Lulu in Hollywood. New York: Knopf,
1982.

Butler, Ivan. The War Film. New York: A.S. Barnes,
1974.

Capra, Frank. The Name Above the Title. New York:
Macmillan, 1971.

Carpozi, George. The John Wayne Story. New Rochelle,
N.Y.: Arlington, 1972.

Corliss, Richard. Talking Pictures: Screenwriters in American Cinema. Woodstock, N.Y.: Overlook Press, 1974.

Crowther, Bosley. Vintage Films. New York: Putnam's,
1977.

Didion, Joan. Slouching Towards Bethlehem. New York:
Touchstone, 1979.

Dmytryk, Edward. It's a Hell of a Life but Not a Bad Living.
New York: Times Books, 1978.

Dyer, Richard. Stars. London: British Film Institute,
1982.

Ellul, Jacques. Propaganda: The Formation of Men's Attitudes. New York: Vintage, 1973.

Essoe, Gabe. The Book of Movie Lists. Westport, Conn.:
Arlington, 1981.

_____. The Films of Clark Gable. Secaucus, N.J.:
Citadel, 1970.

Everson, William K. A Pictorial History of the Western Film.
Secaucus, N.J.: Citadel, 1969.

Eyles, Allen. The Western: An Illustrated Guide. New
York: A.S. Barnes, 1975.

_____. Bogart. New York: Doubleday, 1975.

_____. John Wayne and the Movies. New York: Barnes,
1976.

Fenin, George, and William Everson. The Western. New
York: Bonanza Books, 1973.

Fonda, Henry. My Life. New York: New American Library, 1981.

Ford, Dan. The Life of John Ford. Englewood Cliffs, N.J.:
Prentice-Hall, 1979.

Freedland, Michael. Gregory Peck. New York: William
    Morrow, 1980.

French, Brandon. On the Verge of Revolt. New York:
    Ungar, 1978.

French, Philip. Westerns: Aspects of a Movie Genre.
    New York: Oxford University Press, 1977.

Gallagher, Tag. John Ford. Berkeley, Calif.: University
    of California Press, 1986.

Gans, Herbert. Popular Culture and High Culture. New
    York: Basic Books, 1975.

Gerth, H., and C. Wright Mills (eds.). From Max Weber:
    Essays in Sociology. New York: Oxford University Press,
    1946.

Goldstein, Norm. John Wayne: A Tribute. New York:
    Holt, Rinehart and Winston, 1979.

Gussow, Mel. Don't Say Yes Until I Finish Talking. New
    York: Doubleday, 1971.

Guthrie, Lee. The Life and Loves of Cary Grant. New
    York: Drake, 1977.

Haskell, Molly. From Reverence to Rape. New York: Holt,
    Rinehart and Winston, 1974.

Higham, Charles. Cecil B. De Mille. New York: Scribner's,
    1973.

_____. Marlene: The Life of Marlene Dietrich. New
    York: Norton, 1977.

Hotchner, A.E. Sophia: Living and Loving. New York:
    Morrow, 1979.

Huston, John. An Open Book. New York: Knopf, 1980.

Jacobs, Lewis. The Rise of the American Film. New York:
    Teachers College Press, 1968.

Jarvie, I.C. Movies and Society. New York: Basic Books, 1970.

_____. Movies as Social Criticism. Metuchen, N.J.:
   Scarecrow Press, 1978.

Jeavons, Clyde. A Pictorial History of War Films. Secaucus,
   N.J.: Citadel Press, 1974.

Jones, Ken D., and Arthur F. McClure. Hollywood at War.
   New York: Castle, 1973.

Jowett, Garth. Film: The Democratic Art. Boston: Little,
   Brown, 1976.

Kael, Pauline. Kiss Kiss, Bang Bang. New York: Bantam, 1968.

_____. The State of the Art. New York: Dutton, 1985.

Kaminsky, Stuart. John Huston. Boston: Houghton Mifflin, 1978.

Kerbel, Michael. Henry Fonda. New York: Pyramid, 1975.

Kovic, Ron. Born on the Fourth of July. New York: McGraw
   Hill, 1976.

LeRoy, Mervyn. Mervyn LeRoy: Take One. New York:
   Hawthorn Books, 1974.

Levy, Emanuel. And the Winner Is: The History and Politics of the Oscar Awards. New York: Ungar, 1987.

Libby, Bill. They Didn't Win the Oscars. Westport, Conn.:
   Arlington Books, 1980.

Luhr, William, and Peter Lehman. Authorship and Narrative
   in the Cinema. New York: Putnam's, 1977.

McBride, Joseph, and Michael Wilmington. John Ford.
   London: Secker and Warburg, 1974.

McCarthy, Todd, and Charles Flynn. Kings of the B's.
   New York: Dutton, 1975.

Maccoby, Eleanor E.; Theodore M. Newcomb; and Eugene L.
   Hartley. Readings in Social Psychology. New York:
   Holt, Rinehart and Winston, 1958.

McGilligan, Patrick. Cagney: The Actor as Auteur. New York: Da Capo Press, 1979.

Malone, Michael. Heroes of Eros: Male Sexuality in the Movies. New York: Dutton, 1979.

Mast, Gerald. Howard Hawks, Story Teller. New York: Oxford University Press, 1982.

Mellen, Joan. Women and Their Sexuality in the New Film. New York: Horizon, 1973.

_____. Big Bad Wolves: Masculinity in the American Film. New York: Pantheon, 1977.

Meyer, William R. The Making of the Great Westerns. New Rochelle, N.Y.: Arlington, 1979.

Morgenstern, Joseph, and Stefan Kanfer (eds.). Film 1969-1970: Anthology of the National Society of Film Critics. New York: Simon and Schuster, 1970.

Nachbar, Jack (ed.). Focus on the Western. Englewood Cliffs, N.J.: Prentice-Hall, 1974.

Nobile, Philip. Favorite Movies: Critics' Choice. New York: Macmillan, 1972.

Peary, Danny. Close-Ups: The Movie Star Book. New York: Workman Publishing, 1978.

Pirie, David (ed.). Anatomy of the Movies. New York: Macmillan, 1981.

Preminger, Otto. Preminger: An Autobiography. New York: Doubleday, 1977.

Quirk, Lawrence J. The Films of Robert Taylor. Secaucus, N.J.: Citadel, 1975.

Ricci, Mark; Boris Zmijewsky; and Steven Zmijewsky. The Films of John Wayne. Secaucus, N.J.: Citadel, 1970.

Riesman, David, with Nathan Glazer and Reuel Denny. The Lonely Crowd. New Haven, Conn.: Yale University Press, 1950.

Russo, Vitto. The Celluloid Closet: Homosexuality in the Movies. New York: Harper and Row, 1981.

Sarris, Andrew. The American Cinema: Directors and Directions. New York: Dutton, 1968.

_____. Confessions of a Cultist. New York: Simon and Schuster, 1970.

_____. The John Ford Movie Mystery. Bloomington: Indiana University Press, 1975.

_____. Politics and Cinema. New York: Columbia University Press, 1979.

Sayre, Nora. Running Time: Films of the Cold War. New York: Dial Press, 1982.

Schickel, Richard. Second Sight: Notes on Some Movies. New York: Simon and Schuster, 1972.

_____. The Men Who Made the Movies. London: Elm Tree Books, 1977.

Shavelson, Melville. How to Make a Jewish Movie. Englewood Cliffs, N.J.: Prentice-Hall, 1971.

Shindler, Colin. Hollywood Goes to War: Films and American Society, 1939-1952. London: Routledge and Kegan Paul, 1979.

Sinclair, Andrew. John Ford. New York: Dial Press, 1979.

Stack, Robert. Straight Shooting. New York: Macmillan, 1980.

Steinberg, Cobbett. Reel Facts. New York: Facts on File, 1980.

_____. TV Facts. New York: Facts on File, 1980.

Sternberg, Josef von. Fun in a Chinese Laundry. New York: Macmillan, 1965.

Thomas, Tony. The Films of Kirk Douglas. Secaucus, N.J.: Citadel, 1972.

Toeplitz, Jerzy. Hollywood and After. Chicago: Henry
    Regnery, 1974.

Tomkies, Mike. Duke: The Story of John Wayne. Chicago:
    Henry Regnery, 1971.

Tornabene, Lyn. Long Live the King: The Bibliography of
    Clark Gable. New York: Simon and Schuster, 1976.

Walker, Alexander. Stardom: The Hollywood Phenomenon.
    New York: Stein and Day, 1970.

Walsh, Raoul. Each Man in His Time. New York: Farrar,
    Straus and Giroux, 1974.

Weber, Max. The Theory of Social and Economic Organiza-
    tions. New York: Free Press, 1950.

Weinberg, Herman G. Josef von Sternberg: A Critical
    Study. New York: Dutton, 1966.

Weis, Elizabeth (ed.). The Movie Star. New York: Viking,
    1981.

Wellman, William. A Short Time for Insanity: An Autobiog-
    raphy. New York: Hawthorn, 1974.

Whyte, William F. The Organization Man. New York:
    Simon and Schuster, 1956.

Wood, Michael. America in the Movies. New York: Basic
    Books, 1975.

INDEX